ALSO BY ELLEN HAWKES

FEMINISM ON TRIAL: THE GINNY FOAT CASE

THE SHADOW OF THE MOTH:
A NOVEL OF ESPIONAGE WITH VIRGINIA WOOLF
(WITH PETER MANSO)

BLOOD *and* WINE

THE UNAUTHORIZED STORY
OF THE GALLO WINE EMPIRE

ELLEN HAWKES

SIMON & SCHUSTER

NEW YORK LONDON TORONTO SYDNEY TOKYO SINGAPORE

SIMON & SCHUSTER
SIMON & SCHUSTER BUILDING
ROCKEFELLER CENTER
1230 AVENUE OF THE AMERICAS
NEW YORK, NEW YORK 10020

DESIGNED BY KAROLINA HARRIS
PICTURE SECTION DESIGNED BY BARBARA BACHMAN
MANUFACTURED IN THE UNITED STATES OF AMERICA

1 3 5 7 9 10 8 6 4 2

LIBRARY OF CONGRESS CATALOGING-IN-PUBLICATION DATA
HAWKES, ELLEN
BLOOD AND WINE : THE UNAUTHORIZED STORY OF THE GALLO WINE EMPIRE /
ELLEN HAWKES.
P. CM.
INCLUDES INDEX
1. GALLO FAMILY 2. VINTNERS—CALIFORNIA—BIOGRAPHY. 3. WINE AND WINE
MAKING—CALIFORNIA—HISTORY. I. TITLE.
TP547.G35H39 1993
338.7'663'209794—dc20   92-46789 CIP
ISBN 0-671-64986-8

To my mother, Anita,

and to Peter

CONTENTS

AUTHOR'S NOTE   11

PROLOGUE   13

PART ONE: THE FAMILY   21

PART TWO: THE WINERY   109

PART THREE: THE FEUD   293

EPILOGUE   392

ACKNOWLEDGMENTS   397

NOTES   400

INDEX   455

THE SECRET OF GREAT FORTUNES
WITH NO APPARENT SOURCE IS A
FORGOTTEN CRIME, FORGOTTEN
BECAUSE IT WAS PROPERLY
CARRIED OUT.

—HONORÉ DE BALZAC, *PÈRE GORIOT*

AUTHOR'S NOTE

The following narrative of the Gallo family history, the development of the winery, and the brothers' conflict is based on court documents and official records, as well as my research, interviews, and recollections and family anecdotes provided by a variety of sources, as cited in the book's endnotes.

Joseph Gallo, Ernest and Julio's younger brother, and his family were interviewed extensively for this project. I tried to confirm their statements with other sources but in some instances their accounts were the only ones available to me. Neither Ernest nor Julio has cooperated with this book, although Ernest did offer some comments to me during the 1988 court proceedings but then withdrew from a proposed post-trial interview. (He is said to be cooperating with an authorized book.) In writing this book, I have as much as possible included Ernest and Julio's available testimony when they contradicted their brother Joe, as well as others' statements or official records and reports. Because the brothers' recollections about certain events were sometimes at odds, I have had to draw my own conclusions based on documents, other sources, or ultimately my assessment of the continuity of evidence or credibility of the testimony.

I have presented some scenes through quoted dialogue reconstructed by at least one party to the conversation either in depositions or in interviews or both (but whenever possible I have also tried to indicate when two recollections of the same exchange differed substantially). Dialogue reconstructed from summaries or paraphrases from reports or third-party recollections in testimony or interviews is set off in italics and cited as such in the endnotes. My intention was to recreate the past in a dramatic form while shaping a narrative that reflects various versions of events and conveys, whenever appropriate, different points of view. But ultimately, the book had to be based on my own interpretation of Gallo history as it unfolded in my research.

A 1988 court decision granted a summary judgment to Ernest and Julio because of one key aspect of law: Finding no evidence of "extrinsic fraud" in a 1941 probate hearing, the judge ruled that the issue of Joe's inheritance could not be reopened in the 1988 case. As a result, evidence, documents, and testimony dealing with the early family history were not presented to a jury nor did the judge's ruling address all aspects of this background. I have included such material from this part of the 1988 lawsuit; I have also contributed information that was not before the court but that I discovered in my research and interviews. By giving readers access to this part of the story, I hope to allow them to reach their own understanding of the Gallo brothers' family feud.

PROLOGUE

On a foggy morning in November 1988, Ernest Gallo paced the hallways of the federal courthouse in Fresno, California. The lawsuit for trademark infringement that he and his brother Julio had brought against their younger brother Joseph was in recess, and now the reclusive chairman of the world's largest winery was stalking reporters, surprising them with his sudden eagerness to speak to the press.

Rarely accessible to the media, Ernest and Julio Gallo have long attracted attention because people want to know the secrets of their success. Building their empire, the California wine barons not only revolutionized the wine industry and altered public taste and drinking habits; they also created and continue to run one of the major privately owned manufacturing companies in the country. Through their efforts during the last fifty years, they have changed both the making and selling of wine and the methods of marketing consumer products in general. Their accomplishments and influence have been largely attributed to Ernest's entrepreneurial and financial genius. Indeed, few leaders of American business have achieved his dominance over one industry as well as amassing such extensive personal and political power.

Short and wiry, Ernest was then four months away from his eightieth birthday, although he had long ago banned celebration of the date as if denial ensured immortality. He showed his age only in the thinning gray hair swept back from his pale, lined face and in the two hearing aids and heavy-framed, thick glasses he wore. Otherwise, he was forceful and energetic despite a slight disjointedness to his determined gait and staccato bursts of speech. Long ago he had adopted his father's habit of clasping his hands behind his back and thrusting his head forward. As he moved aggressively down the corridor, he backed me toward the wall, leaving only an uncomfortable few inches between us.

"Now do you see why I can't have *my* name on that cheese?" he demanded.

Ernest routinely spoke in rhetorical questions, especially when he was in a confrontational mood. From an early age he had developed an argumentative style, so much so that his father had nicknamed him *l'avvocato*, Italian for "the lawyer." His relentless and aggressive drive to conquer lay behind the E. & J. Gallo Winery's dominance of the wine industry. Some employees called him a combination of Machiavelli and Napoleon; others referred to him as "the Godfather."

In the last few years he had become obsessed with the family name, firm in his belief that Gallo was synonymous with wine, much as "Kleenex" had become the household word for facial tissue. He had filed this lawsuit to prevent the use of the name as a trademark by his brother Joe's cheese company, and this morning his hired cheese expert was alleging that the cheese in question was of such "poor quality" and "such a potential health hazard" that Ernest and Julio couldn't risk confusion between their winery and the cheese company.

"Do you realize how many tests that cheese failed?" Ernest continued. "You wouldn't let your name be put on such terrible stuff, would you?"

"I want to listen to the other cheese expert, the one for the defense," I replied. "I hear he's going to testify that your expert made mistakes in his calculations."

"Why does that matter? He still found problems. How can I let people think my winery makes the cheese when it's so bad?"

"If it's that bad, why has it always passed federal and state inspections?" I countered. "Why is it still on the grocery shelves?"

"I thought you people in the media were supposed to be smart," Ernest sneered. "Does the government have to tell you not to eat *garbage?*"

He glared, then turned and stomped away in search of his next target.

Those of us who were lobbied that morning were struck by the

man's vehemence and growling hostility. After all, it was "Joseph
Gallo Cheese" that he was calling "garbage." But no fraternal love
restrained Ernest or tempered his language as he proceeded down the
hallway to repeat to another reporter his charge that his brother's
cheese would make people sick. Not only did he want to prevent Joe
from using his own name on his cheese label; he also seemed willing
to smear his reputation as a dairyman and cheesemaker.

Inside the courtroom, Joseph Gallo, Jr., sat with his lawyers at the
defense table waiting for the trial to resume. Ten years younger than
Ernest, nine younger than Julio, he had been raised by them from
the age of thirteen. His resemblance to his brothers was obvious,
although he was slightly taller than both, sturdier and more physically
fit from spending most of his time outdoors raising cattle and growing
grapes on his ranches. He was also hard of hearing, but refused to
wear a hearing aid, which sometimes gave him a distracted air. Most
of all, though, he appeared stunned and pained, his green-brown eyes
sad behind his horn-rimmed glasses, his face pale and drawn as if he
were in mourning.

He now looked straight ahead, his back to the courtroom door as
Ernest returned and took his usual seat in the observers' pews. His
brother always sat directly behind him instead of at the plaintiff's
table, but Joe never turned in his chair to catch a glimpse of him.
Indeed, the bad blood between the two could be measured by Joe's
almost physical aversion to Ernest during the trial. During court re-
cesses, Joe often waited until Ernest had left before he departed; he
was careful to walk to the opposite end of the hallway and to avoid
taking the same elevator; or, as he had this morning, he simply remained at the defense table, loath to witness the corridor campaign
against him and his cheese.

He seemed to have less enmity toward Julio, however. Only on the
opening day of the case had the other Gallo brother made an appearance in the courtroom. Surrounded by several winery lawyers, he had
been escorted to a seat in the public section. His shoulders were
hunched, his hands trembling as he sat in silence. Unlike Ernest,
whose dark eyes were small, his right eye often squinting, Julio's
brown eyes were larger and more expressive, and a few times during
the first session he seemed in tears. He also wore two hearing aids,
but he appeared lost in his own thoughts rather than listening to the
proceedings.

From the first he had begged Ernest not to pursue the case, to try to settle the conflict out of court. That it had come to this seemed to overwhelm him, reviving as it had his feelings of grief over events that he had long ago tried to repress.

During the midmorning recess that first day, Joe had ignored the legal bodyguards and approached Julio.

"How are you feeling?" he asked, shaking his hand. "You okay?"

Joe knew how upsetting his brother found the lawsuit, how he had resisted giving his deposition on medical grounds. Despite his lawyers' doubts about Julio's actual condition, Joe was genuinely concerned about his brother's health.

"Fine, fine . . . ," Julio replied. His voice trailed off, and he abruptly turned away, glancing in Ernest's direction as if afraid to be caught talking to Joe.

At noon Julio had left, not to return until he made an unexpected appearance at the end of the trial. His absence underscored what Joe had long believed—that the fight was with Ernest and Ernest's side of the family; that Julio had been forced to join the legal dispute, unable or unwilling to break with his older brother. Despite the public image of Ernest and Julio as equals, Ernest was the patriarch of both the winery and the family. Once again, Joe felt, Ernest had gotten his way. Intent as he was on victory, Ernest seemed oblivious to Julio's anxieties and unconcerned that the litigation had caused a bitter family feud.

The irony was that Ernest had always insisted, "Family comes first." Suspicious almost to the point of paranoia, he believed that he could trust only family members. The winery was strictly family-owned and family-run. Yet Ernest's commitment to family was obliterated by his zeal to control the Gallo name.

Mike Gallo, Joe's thirty-eight-year-old son and partner in his cheese, dairy, and ranch operations, had been shocked when the conflict escalated into a full-scale court battle. But hearing Ernest's comments in the hallway this morning, he reassessed his uncle's insistence on family loyalty.

"Ernest always told us, 'Blood is thicker than water,' " he recalled. "But what he really believes is that wine is thicker than blood."

On one level Ernest and Julio's lawsuit, filed in 1986, was simply a matter of trademark law: Did the two older brothers have an exclusive claim to the name Gallo, or did Joe have the right to put his name on his cheese? But the legal conflict unleashed long-simmering resentments and jealousies; it reopened old wounds and brought to light the tragedies and mysteries at the heart of the Gallo saga that had been shrouded in secrecy for over half a century.

Ernest and Julio considered themselves self-made men, and the Gallo legend had replaced long-hidden family history. According to their version, repeated to their brother Joe as well as to the public, they were two virtually penniless young men who had established the E. & J. Gallo Winery in 1933, just after their parents' death and in anticipation of the repeal of Prohibition. They cast themselves in a Horatio Alger, rags-to-riches, American dream: They were, they said, the sons of Italian immigrants who, with nothing but $5,900 to their name and only a small knowledge of winemaking gleaned from a library pamphlet, had started their winery and through hard work and determination built it into the wine company that outsold its next two competitors combined.

The winery's headquarters is a grand neoclassical structure on a four-hundred-acre site in the California Central Valley town of Modesto. Referred to as "Parthenon West" or "Temple on the Tuolumne" (the name of the county's river) by local residents, the building features high columns and a two-story, glass-enclosed atrium, courtyard fountains, and reflecting pools filled with tropical fish (nicknamed "Ernest's piranha tanks" by employees). The surrounding grounds are formally landscaped, and peacocks stroll across the well-trimmed lawns. On one side of the temple are the less ornate, one-story buildings that house the winery's chemical laboratories, grower relations department, and in-house printing division. On the other side is the glass plant that makes all of the winery's bottles. The rear acreage is filled with row upon row of huge steel storage tanks, all painted white, which give the facility the look of an oil refinery.

No sign announces that this is the E. & J. Gallo Winery—as Ernest likes to quip, "I've never gotten lost." The brothers neither expect nor encourage visitors, and security guards and surveillance cameras make sure no outsiders intrude. But here Gallo stores, blends, bottles, and ships its products, although wine is actually made only at the brothers' other wineries in Livingston and Fresno to the south and at the new Sonoma winery, Julio's project for producing "upscale" varietals, wines made predominantly from one variety of grape, such as Cabernet Sauvignon or Chardonnay.

It is estimated that Ernest and Julio themselves or in the name of family members and corporate titles own over seventeen thousand acres of land in California; they own outright (as well as in the name of offspring or company executives) wine distributorships, trucking lines, and aluminum cap and glass manufacturers, all vertically integrated into the winery's massive production, sales, and distributing operations. In 1992 the Gallo Winery's total sales reportedly exceeded $849 million. Its brands have included fortified wines such as sherry, port, white port, Tokay, and muscatel as well as Thunderbird and Night Train Express, known as America's favorite "street wines," those preferred by "winos"; table wines, from generic and jug wines, like the Carlo Rossi line or William Wycliff wine sold only in bulk to restaurants, to so-called "premium wines" like Hearty Burgundy, Chablis Blanc, Pink Chablis and "upscale," cork-finished varietals; Bartles & Jaymes, the number-one-selling wine cooler, and fruit-flavored wines such as Ripple, Spanada, and Boone's Farm; André, Eden Roc, and Tott's "champagnes," other sparkling wines, vermouths, and E & J Brandy. In 1992 the Gallo Winery produced and shipped an estimated 67 million cases of wine and wine-based products, representing 48 percent of that year's California wine grape harvest.

Fortune magazine calculated that one out of every four bottles of wine sold in the United States is made by Gallo. *Forbes* magazine roughly estimated that the jointly owned winery is worth "at least $600 million," although the two brothers are rumored to have larger individual fortunes, especially Ernest, who has an extensive personal stock portfolio.

Their brother Joe, however, shares neither the winery's extraordinary success nor his brothers' celebrity and personal fortune. So far removed is he from their limelight that one newspaper dubbed him "the unknown Gallo brother."

He lives a half hour south of Modesto in Livingston, one of the many small agricultural towns that dot the Central Valley along Route 99 between Modesto and Fresno. As a teenager he had worked for the winery, and in 1946, after serving in the army, he returned to manage Ernest and Julio's vineyards in Livingston. He bought his own vineyards adjacent to his brothers' property and built his home there, and during the ensuing years he accumulated over three thousand acres of vineyards and expanded his own cattle and dairy businesses. In 1967 he left his brothers' employ to concentrate on his ranching and dairy enterprises. By 1984 the Joseph Gallo Cattle Company and Joseph Gallo Vineyards owned nearly twenty-five thousand acres of farmland, orchards, grazing land, livestock ranches, and vineyards.

Although he is virtually anonymous to the public, with that much acreage and over twenty thousand head of dairy cattle, Joe is well-known in agricultural circles as one of California's leading grape growers, cattle ranchers, and dairy farmers and is considered as shrewd and determined a businessman as his more famous brothers. In 1979 he established the Joseph Gallo Cottonwood Dairy in Atwater, twenty minutes south of Livingston, and then, in September 1982, he designed and built the Joseph Gallo Cheese Company next to the dairy. In March 1983 the plant went into full production of cheese from Grade A milk, principally supplied by his own dairies. At first the cheese was sold only in bulk to grocery stores, but a year later Joe and his son Mike began to market consumer-size packages under the label "Joseph Gallo Cheese."

In 1987 Joe and Mike renovated a turn-of-the-century farmhouse to serve as their cheese company's headquarters. A far cry from Ernest and Julio's temple, it is a modest but attractive example of old California rural architecture. Wide-porched and white-clapboard, the building includes two offices upstairs on either side of the oaken central staircase where Joe and Mike plan their company's marketing programs. Although their cheese is distributed mainly in California and other western states, in 1992 bulk and retail sales of Joseph Gallo's cheese—cheddar, Monterey Jack, Swiss, and mozzarella—totaled over $35 million.

It was the Joseph Gallo Cheese label that in 1986 had provoked Ernest's wrath. Joe usually obeyed his brothers, often acceding to their wishes. They had become surrogate parents after the violent deaths of his mother and father in 1933, and even as an adult he tended to believe that Ernest knew best. But in this instance, he had refused to submit to Ernest's demand to remove his name from the label. Nevertheless, he had tried to work out a compromise until he came to believe that his brother wanted nothing less than complete control of his name and his company. Joe was perplexed. Why was his own brother trying to take away the name given to him by their father, Joseph, Sr.? Why was he obsessed with having the exclusive use of the family name even to the point of being willing to sue his own brother and destroy his cheese business?

It was only after his lawyers began to prepare his defense that Joe came to believe that the dispute went far deeper than trademark law. He had known very little about the family history. At thirteen, after his parents had died in an alleged murder-suicide, the past had become taboo and a family-induced amnesia had set in. He had accepted Ernest and Julio's self-creation story and all his life had remained in awe of his brothers' talents and accomplishments. But when his lawyers began to investigate the winery's trademark infringement claim, they unearthed evidence from the past that shed a different light on the official Gallo legend. Instead of the Horatio Alger parable that Ernest and Julio had so often repeated, the attorneys discovered a story that seemed more like the biblical tale of "Joseph and his brothers."

In their investigation they found documents that suggested a different version of Gallo history—that the winery had originated not with the two older brothers but with their father, and that at thirteen Joe should have inherited an equal interest in both the family business and the family trade name. On the basis of his lawyers' conclusion that he had been denied his inheritance, Joe filed a countersuit against Ernest and Julio for a one-third share of the winery, worth at least $200 million by the lawyers' valuation.

Joe himself felt a profound sense of betrayal by the two people he had trusted most throughout his life. But like the biblical Joseph, he finally broke his brothers' bonds; fighting for his name and his birthright, he was no longer intimidated or controlled by them. Whatever the eventual outcome of the lawsuits, he would recover the past that had been denied him for so many years; he would at last be free of their dominance.

"History doesn't do a thing for me," Ernest once announced. History seems to matter to him only when he can make it do *something* for him and the winery. Over the years, he and Julio developed a siege mentality—the Gallos against the world—and secrecy about their past became as much their signature as their names on their wine labels. Since they sued their brother in court, the story behind the Gallo legend could at last be revealed. And, to paraphrase a recent winery advertising slogan, it would change the way the public, and Joe, thought about Gallo, and his brothers, forever.

PART ONE
THE FAMILY

CHAPTER ONE

Like so many other first-generation Italian-Americans, Ernest, Julio, and Joseph Gallo, Jr., trace their roots to their ancestors' youthful visions of a better life across the ocean. At the turn of the century their father, Giuseppe, and their uncle Michelo were teenage boys who had heard tales of California's sun-drenched orchards and gold-studded rivers and dreamed of some day reaching their El Dorado where fortune smiled and nectar flowed.

Giuseppe, born July 15, 1882, and Michelo, born February 25, 1885, were the middle sons in a family of six boys and one girl. They grew up in Fossano, a village in Piedmont, the agricultural region in northwest Italy known for its vineyards and wine. Their father was a wholesale butcher and horse trader in the town's livestock market, and their mother ran a boardinghouse or *pensione* where she cooked meals for the residents and served the family's homemade wine. Neither business was large or particularly successful, and their father, a stern, humorless man with an imposing handlebar mustache and an equally dominant personality, expected his sons to begin working at an early age. His eldest son helped in the livestock market, but the other sons had to scramble for employment outside the family business. The next oldest sons shipped out to Venezuela to find work, first in the wheat fields, then in canneries.

Shorter and slighter than their three older brothers, neither Giuseppe nor Michelo was enamored of manual labor. They hoped that they might escape hardscrabble field work by emigrating. At seventeen and the younger of the two, Michelo was more gregarious and ambitious, and lured as so many immigrants were by tales of overnight success, he set his sights on America. Although a few Gallo cousins had already settled in Philadelphia, Michelo sailed to California to seek his fortune. Upon his arrival, he dug ditches until he found work as a bartender in the Italian neighborhood in Oakland, the city across the bay from San Francisco.

Giuseppe first traveled to Venezuela, then to Philadelphia, staying with his cousins who ran pensiones and saloons. Unable to find employment in the city, he moved to the coal region to work in the mines and finally saved enough money for a train ticket to Oakland.

He moved into a pensione near Michelo's bar, but when no local saloon needed another bartender, he resigned himself to digging ditches for the municipal sewer system. The ditchdiggers were paid according to the length of the trench they completed each day; Giuseppe always placed himself at the head of the crew, then dug straight along without squaring off the corners, leaving that to the men behind him and thus receiving credit for digging a longer ditch.

But the real expert at working the angles was Michelo—or Mike, as he was now calling himself. Having heard that more money was to be made in the Sierra Nevada foothills east of Sacramento where gold was still being mined, he set out for Amador County. He took a job in a mine near Plymouth but spent most of his time in neighboring Jackson, the county seat, which had become a kind of "Barbary Coast" with its saloons, gambling parlors, and houses of ill-repute. It was a rough and ready town, much like the Old West with the heady excitement of the Gold Rush still in the air. It catered both to the many miners in the area and to businessmen and politicians who came down from Sacramento for a weekend of pleasure.

Never one to miss a trick, Mike devised a scheme to make quick money. He met a woman with whom he lived for several months, and together they ran a badger game—she enticed men into her hotel room, Mike arrived on the scene to shake them down. But one night they chose the wrong victim, a local businessman who was not afraid to go to the police. Mike hightailed it back to Oakland, but with the man's thousand-dollar payoff in his pocket.

Mike now had the stake with which he and Giuseppe would begin their first business venture in America. In their Oakland neighborhood and in San Francisco's North Beach, the pensiones that catered to Italians usually had small saloons where locals gathered at night to drink the red wine so reminiscent of home—what many called "dago red." The wine was served from five-gallon kegs that stood on the bar. On the side of each barrel was stenciled the name of the company supplying the wine. The customers, including neighbors who brought containers to be filled, ordered their wine by name, choosing from among the several brands that in those days included Italian Swiss Colony and Lackman and Jacovi. The names, the brothers learned, did not always refer to a winery but to the company that bought wine in bulk from winemakers, then barreled it and sold it to pensiones. It was a rudimentary form of distribution that met the needs of Italian communities where wine was considered an essential part of everyday life.

Growing up in the Piedmont region of Italy and watching their parents press local grapes into wine, Giuseppe and Mike knew something about vineyards and winemaking. The wine business seemed a natural opportunity for them. With his charm and already-established contacts among saloon and pensione owners, Mike would become the salesman, making his pitch and taking orders. Giuseppe would go on the road, visiting small wineries in the Central Valley where Italian winemakers were looking for distributors to whom they could sell their bulk wine.

The brothers needed little to begin with: They bought a second-hand truck for Giuseppe to drive from winery to winery; they stocked a supply of barrels on which they stenciled "GALLO" in red; they rented a small office in Oakland and put up a sign reading "THE GALLO WINE COMPANY." By the end of 1906 they had founded a wine company in the Gallo name.

The maternal side of the Gallo family was also steeped in the wine tradition. Battista Bianco was a third-generation vineyard worker and winemaker in Alessandria, an agricultural town in Asti, the fertile grape and wine region north of Genoa and west of Bologna. He had married Virginia Campadelli, a woman five years older than he, and they had four children: Tillie, born in 1885, Walter, born in 1887, Assunta, born in 1889, and the youngest, Celistina, born in 1891. Through friends and relatives, Battista learned that land for vineyards was available at low prices in California, and since he had always wanted to run his own winery, he announced his plan to his family. He would use his savings to head for California and establish himself in winemaking. Then he would send for Virginia. The children would stay behind with their grandparents until there was enough money for them to come.

In the spring of 1893 he sailed steerage to America, carrying with him cuttings from Asti vineyards. He landed at Ellis Island in New York harbor, then took the train cross-country to Hanford, a railroad town south of Fresno surrounded by wheat fields and vineyards, where Bianco cousins had already settled. Working in a local flour mill and living in a pensione in the Italian neighborhood along West Fourth Street, he saved enough money to send for Virginia. She had not been idle, however, having vowed to the children that she would never leave any of them behind. She had taken in laundry and sewing and done housework and cooked for wealthy families so that she could surprise Battista by sailing with all four children in tow, as well as returning the money he'd sent for her passage.

Soon Battista was able to buy a house at the corner of West Fourth and Redington streets, directly across from the boardinghouse where they had been staying. It was a pleasant white frame building with a wide front porch, but the house's main appeal for Battista was a full-length basement and a long backyard leading to a large shed. Here he opened his winery, installing a grape press in the outbuilding and storing barrels of wine in the cellar. He used grapes bought from other growers as well as those from the eighteen-acre vineyard he had purchased outside of town and replanted with his vine cuttings from Asti. By 1901 the Bianco Winery was in full operation, producing bulk wine and selling it through distributors to North Beach saloons, pensiones, and restaurants as well as shipping it by tank car to Little Italy in New York.

Virginia added to the family income by working at the Hanford Steam Laundry. The four children were enrolled in the town's elementary school but were also expected to help around the house and in the family business. If there were any complaints, Battista told them, "We must work, work, work, and save, save, save." Walter helped his father in the vineyard, and when each daughter finished eighth grade, she joined her mother at the laundry.

The family was respected and popular in the community. Battista's discipline was softened by his sense of humor and enjoyment of friends. Virginia was an accomplished cook and often invited friends to share her favorite Bolognese specialties. Her other passion was opera, and she taught her daughters arias, which they often sang for guests. The Bianco house became a gathering place on Sundays after Mass, with families from the neighborhood and outlying farms, as well as sheepherders and vineyard workers, stopping in for their week's supply of wine.

By 1906, the Bianco roots were well-established; the winery was running well, and Battista bought several houses along West Fourth Street as well as an apartment building in San Francisco. Virginia managed these investments, renting them to other Italian families, while Battista and Walter cultivated the grapes and made and sold the wine. Assunta, who now called herself Susie, and Celestina, now known as Celia, continued to work at the laundry. They were considered lovely young women, their dark hair swept back and coiled on top of their heads, their eyes dark and lively. Of the two, Celia was the taller and more outspoken and flirtatious. Susie was shy but had a gentle voice and spontaneous laugh.

Both attracted their share of male admirers, and on Sundays they entertained them on the front porch. Sometimes their mother and they sang; sometimes Tillie played the mandolin, since she'd taken lessons—although her sisters considered her the only Bianco with a tin ear. Above all, they hoped that their father would not arrive on the porch to embarrass them with some outrageous joke, or worse, with a stern interrogation about a young man's intentions.

Which was what worried Battista when in 1907 Giuseppe Gallo, who now called himself Joe, began to make regular stops at the winery. He had bought wine once from Battista, but having met Susie on that occasion, he began to visit often, more to see her than to replenish his wine supply. Mike accompanied him once, and meeting Celia, he became as infatuated with her as his brother was with Susie. Battista knew that his daughters were pretty and charming, Susie with her quiet warmth, Celia with her teasing laughter, yet he was cynical enough to suspect the motives of these two city slickers who arrived to court his daughters in dark three-piece suits, starched white shirts, and black fedoras. Having dealt with them in business, he felt they could be wily and ruthless, and a few times when Joe hadn't won an argument about price, he had flared, betraying a temper.

Unlike the Biancos, the Gallo brothers seemed to have no roots or family connections. Neighbors and friends gossiped: Weren't these fellows a little flashy? Wasn't it too convenient that men who ran a wine company should be so interested in the daughters of a winery owner? Didn't they talk too much about making a fortune, and didn't

Mike brag a lot about the important people he knew in San Francisco who would help him with his next business investment? Battista was a plain and honest man, even a puritan, and he wasn't convinced that he could trust these young men either in business or as husbands for his daughters.

Yet they persisted in their courtship. One summer evening Battista went out of his way to embarrass them. Joe and Susie and Celia and Mike were sitting on the front porch, chaperoned by Virginia and suffering another mandolin concert by Tillie. Battista stomped out onto the porch. The mandolin music died away as everyone turned to him and saw that his fly was open. He pointed at his gaping trousers and shouted in a loud voice, his Piedmontese echoing up and down the block, "I need a button right here." Later the sisters would tell this story and laugh, but at that moment they blushed with humiliation. They realized that their father was playing the crude *paesan* to try to frighten away the city boys.

But Joe was not dissuaded, especially when a new business scheme made him more anxious to marry. Through Mike's previous connections in Jackson, the brothers bought the Central Hotel. Joe was to run the boardinghouse and saloon, and he proposed to Susie, asking her to join him in his new home and hotel venture. She accepted, despite her parents' disapproval. So opposed were they that when she told them about her fiance's hotel and asked for financial help, Battista refused to provide a dowry. Instead he and Tillie together loaned the couple $1,000. Still suspicious of Joe, Battista required him to sign a note in which he agreed to repay the loan within two years with 10 percent interest charged semiannually. It was hardly the blessing that one would hope from prospective in-laws. Instead of having a church wedding, Joe and Susie eloped, and they were married by a judge in the Hanford town hall on March 18, 1908, with Celia as their only family witness. Whether the clerk was unfamiliar with Italian names or Joe misspelled his own name, their marriage license read "Galli" instead of Gallo, and the announcement in the *Hanford Weekly Sentinel* repeated the mistake, at the same time conveying Virginia and Battista's disapproval by noting their absence from the civil ceremony.

If they had seen how Joe treated their daughter during the next year, their anxieties would have been confirmed. The Central Hotel had twenty-five rooms upstairs that Susie alone cleaned every day; she cooked for the residents on the old stove in the kitchen while Joe tended bar. They lived at the nearby Union House, a family pensione, but rarely finished working at their own hotel until midnight, Joe usually staying later to drink and socialize in the saloon. Frustrated by the hotel's poor profits, Joe then began to drink too much and rage at Susie. *You God damned bitch! You God damned whore!* he shouted. Then he beat her with his fists until her arms and breasts were black and blue.

Even after Susie became pregnant, Joe was unable to control his temper, and every two or three weeks he would slap her around and call her names. Celia came to Jackson several times during the fall of 1908, her visits decorously noted in the social column of the *Amador Dispatch*. Perhaps Susie had asked her to stay, perhaps she offered comfort and safety because Joe was on his best behavior in her presence. It was even possible that she came to Jackson to see Mike, who sometimes drove into town for the weekend, although his business affairs usually kept him well-occupied in San Francisco and Oakland.

Mike had taken on another partner, Fred Bertola, and added an Oakland saloon to the wine operation, now called Gallo and Company. Unlike Joe, Mike had the sleek look of success, wearing made-to-order suits and shirts, flashing a gold watch fob and a diamond pinkie ring, and driving the latest-model car. Celia was taken by his sophisticated city ways and his prosperity and chose to ignore her father's continued disapproval.

On March 18, 1909, a year from the day of her wedding, Susie gave birth to a son. They called him Ernest, although in his early years he was known as "Nino" in the family. Ernest was a frail, sickly child, and his parents' circumstances went from bad to worse. Within a few months, Susie was pregnant again. The Central Hotel was losing money every week, and Joe had to hire more help since Susie was unable to work full time. It was soon obvious that they would have to give up this venture, and Joe was forced to make other plans.

One possibility suggested itself when the Biancos announced that Battista was going to take an extended trip to Italy. In previous years he had suffered from severe bouts of pneumonia, and his doctor recommended a vacation from the damp fog of Central Valley winters. Mollified by the birth of their first grandson, concerned for their daughter's welfare, they asked Susie and Joe to return to Hanford where Joe could help Walter in the winery. Virginia was especially anxious to have Susie home, because on August 17, Celia had married Mike (in a church wedding but without her father's presence) and had departed for her new home in Oakland. Joe agreed to the plan and in late August ran an advertisement in the *Amador Dispatch*:

FOR SALE—CENTRAL HOTEL, JACKSON, doing good business and making money, will be sold at a bargain; reason for selling, proprietor going to Fresno to take charge of business of father-in-law, who will shortly go to Italy. For particulars inquire of G. Gallo on the premises.

This was an exaggeration on two counts: Battista and Walter would have been surprised to hear that Joe was to "take charge" of their winery, and the hotel was not making a profit. But Joe knew a good sales pitch, and soon he persuaded Pietro Genolio and his wife, recent arrivals from Italy who were staying at the hotel, to buy the business. Whatever doubts the man had, his wife was convinced by Joe's story that he was only selling the hotel so that he could run his father-in-law's winery. She trusted him as a fellow Italian, and she pleaded with her husband to take the risk. Finally he agreed, paying $2,000 in cash, and the following morning, August 31, 1909, Joe registered the sale with the County Recorder.

A week later, Genolio came to regret the purchase, after learning of the hotel's losses and realizing that he had been gulled into a disastrous investment. A front-page headline and story in the *Amador Dispatch* recounted the unfortunate consequence:

DESPONDENT, HE TRIES RAZOR ROUTE

*Too Much Liquor and Bad Investment
of Money the Cause*

Crazed and despondent as the result of overindulgence in alcoholic stimulant, caused by what he deemed an unwise investment of his money in the purchase of the Central Hotel, Peter Genolio, about noon Wednesday, attempted to end it all by slashing his throat with a razor. Just prior to committing the rash act, Genolio had quarreled with his wife, blaming her with inducing him to buy the business. He had been drinking heavily and, telling her he would settle the matter went to his room. His absence was noted soon, however, and he was found on the floor in a pool of blood, a three-inch gash in his throat and a bloody razor at his side. Doctors Gall and Sprague were called and soon had the wound sewed and dressed, and the man has now an even break for life. The razor cut into the windpipe but did not completely sever it. Fortunately the carotid artery and jugular vein were not cut, but some of the smaller branches of these were severed. At no time was Genolio unconscious and no anaesthetic was administered during the operation of closing the wound. Mr. Genolio now regrets his rash act and says he did not realize what he was doing. He purchased the hotel business from G. Gallo some days ago.

Genolio was stuck with the hotel, and Joe was long gone, already settled with Susie and Nino in one of the Biancos' houses on West Fourth Street. But Joe wasn't happy in Hanford either. He learned more about running a winery, but he disliked taking orders from his in-laws. He still bought bulk wine from the Biancos and other wineries that he distributed through Mike and Gallo and Company. He also purchased land outside town where he intended to plant a vineyard once he had saved enough money for the vines. But Battista put an end to Joe's plan when he returned from Italy and demanded repayment of the outstanding loan. After Joe's repeated refusals, Battista lost patience and sued him for the $1,000, the interest owed, and attorney fees.

The Biancos' earlier disapproval of Joe worsened when the court ordered him to pay. Joe began to beat Susie again. By January of 1910, the beatings had become so frequent that she was often black and blue. One day the young girl who helped around the house walked into the kitchen as Joe threw Susie to the floor and kicked her, all the while ranting that he would kill her. When he stopped, Susie escaped to the bedroom, but a few hours later when she dared to come out, he struck and threatened her again, so frightening her that she grabbed Ernest from his crib and fled to the sanctuary of her parents' home. Banished by the Biancos, Joe departed for Oakland.

Susie hired a lawyer and filed for divorce on January 27, 1910. In her petition to the court, she alleged that her husband treated her "in a cruel and inhuman manner" and showed her "constant inattention and neglect." She cited "mental and physical cruelty" by Joe, recounting numerous incidents of calling her "vile and oppribrious [sic] epithets" accompanied by beatings "with his fists or club or anything his hand could get hold of." She claimed that these beatings had begun only two months after their wedding, continued at intervals for two years, and culminated in the even more vicious attacks of the previous month. She concluded that she now was "in fear of her life."

However real her fears, a month later she succumbed to Joe's pleading and joined him in Oakland where he had established the Joe

Gallo Saloon on Broadway in the Italian community. But she left Ernest behind with her parents, planning to bring him to Oakland after the birth of the second child. Julio Robert was born on March 21, 1910. (Presumably Joe and Susie were trying to give the Italian name "Giulio" an English spelling, but strangers sometimes think that "Julio" is a Spanish name and pronounce it "Hulio.")

Like Ernest, Julio had dark brown eyes, although his complexion was fairer and his hair a lighter brown. He was also frail, and when Susie was unable to breast-feed him, he developed an allergy to cow's milk. He grew thinner and weaker until the doctor prescribed a gruel of rice and water, after which he began to gain weight. Still concerned about Ernest's health, Susie then decided to leave him with his grandparents, since he appeared to benefit from the country air, although he would always be small for his age. Meanwhile Joe's saloon and wine company were prosperous enough for him to buy the hotel next door. Convinced that their marriage was now on an even keel, Susie petitioned the Kings County Superior Court to dismiss her divorce action on October 15, 1912.

But almost immediately Joe's mood turned ugly again. Whether he was worried about money or whether he was drinking too much during the long, late hours tending bar, he again became abusive. Whatever the cause, Susie had seen it all too often, and after yet another beating, she fled with Julio to her parents and Ernest in Hanford and filed a second divorce petition.

Their parents' separation as well as the two divorce filings became the first of Ernest and Julio's family secrets. In later descriptions of their childhood, they would refer to spending several years at their maternal grandfather's winery in Hanford. When asked to explain why they were there, they would insist that "the father's business," his frequent sales trips to distribute wine, required it. Perhaps that was what their mother told them, although it would seem likely that even as children they must have questioned their father's continued absence. They must have perceived their mother's sadness, the difficulty of her situation, and seeds of hostility toward their father were undoubtedly planted. As much as they tried to hide the facts of their childhood, their early anger at his desertion would often simmer in their recollections years later. Julio's resentment, for example, was expressed by the aloof referral to "*the* father," not "my father." Ernest and Julio would try to explain the fact of their parents' separation, but they couldn't hide their feelings.

. . .

At the time of Joe and Susie's second separation, the Gallo name became headline news, thanks to what Mike often called his "investment schemes." He and Celia had twin sons, Mario and Edward, born the same year as Julio (Edward died later in childhood of pneumonia), and they moved into an expensive, grandly furnished home. They dressed in fashionable clothes, and Mike especially enjoyed the high life of San Francisco, making the rounds of the popular nightclubs of the city's famed Barbary Coast. Celia sometimes accompanied him, meeting Mike's friends—his business associates, he called them—as they came by their table.

One night when they were having dinner at Caesar's Grill, he introduced her to Frank Esola, a police detective on the bunko squad, he said. Several weeks later they were dining at the Jupiter Cafe, when Mike saw Esola and waved to him. The detective turned his back and walked away.

"He's mad at me," Mike told Celia. "He thinks I'm not paying him enough."

He went on to explain that in his business he had to pay bribes to the police for protection, that this was how things worked in the city. Cops like Esola were friends who drank and played poker with Mike and his business partners because they were also involved in their "investment schemes."

What these investment schemes actually were became clear only on December 20, 1912. Mike and his "partners" convinced Charles Folda, a visitor from Modesto staying at the Palace Hotel, to invest $900 in a land venture. Mike dressed as a priest and spoke Italian to convince Folda that the investment was legitimate, a favor for a countryman. As instructed, Folda brought cash in a satchel to a meeting in front of the hotel. While Mike distracted him, his partners switched an identical-looking empty bag for the one with the cash, then headed down the street. But before they could make their escape, two detectives swooped down and arrested them all for grand larceny.

Unable to bribe these cops—unlike Esola, they were not on the take—Mike began to sing. He cooperated with both the grand jury and the police commission, testifying against Esola and several other bunko squad detectives whom he and his partners had been paying off. But his expectation of probation in return for his testimony was thwarted when Police Captain John Mooney convinced the judge

that Mike deserved the severest punishment. He was, Mooney asserted, the leader of an "Italian bunko ring" of nearly forty people,
had been arrested many times but had bribed his way out of prosecution, and had cheated his victims out of more than $300,000. The
judge was convinced and sentenced Mike to five years in San Quentin. Esola accosted both Celia and Mike before he was driven away to
prison, promising them money and early parole as long as Mike "kept
his mouth shut."

Neither money nor parole was forthcoming, and Mike became the
prosecution's star witness at Detective Esola's trial in June 1913.
Dressed in a well-tailored brown suit with a jaunty red carnation
in his lapel, Mike looked more the successful businessman than a
San Quentin inmate. During direct examination, he was calm and
unflappable, even bemused as he testified that Esola had received
half the take of every bunko scheme he and his partners had ever
pulled. Esola's attorney cross-examined him, enumerating nearly fifty
scams, including ones in Los Angeles, in which Mike had adopted
different roles, told various stories, and convinced his marks, usually recent Italian immigrants, to hand over money. Mike listened
and answered, often with a grin on his face as if he were enjoying
the account of his exploits and the heated exchanges among the
attorneys.

Only once did he become flustered. Mike had testified that he had
"turned bunko man" merely three years before. Esola's attorney confronted him with a police report from Amador County: Hadn't he
extorted $1,000 from a local businessman at the point of a gun?

"That was just an accident," Mike insisted. "I caught him in a room
with a woman everybody called my wife. He gave me $1,000."

"You got $1,000, didn't you, because you had worked what is com-
monly known as the 'badger game' on him?" the attorney pressed.

"No. He offered me $1,000."

"But you took it?"

"Yes, of course, I took it."

Whatever her reaction to this incident and a "woman everybody
called my wife," or the revelations about Mike's bunko schemes—
which must have accounted for much of their prosperous lifestyle—
Celia kept them to herself. She stood by her man and testified on his
behalf. Dressed in a fashionable fawn-colored suit, a high-necked
white lace blouse, and a wide-brimmed white and black hat with an
egret plume, she sat poised and alert on the witness stand, her chin

held high. She related her conversations with Esola in which he had promised parole and money in exchange for Mike's silence.

Esola's attorney tried to rattle her.

"How long were you aware of your husband's illegal activities?" he asked.

"For quite a while," she replied.

"But you testified before that you'd been aware that he was involved in bunko games only two and a half months before his arrest," he argued.

"At the time I made that statement, I believed it to be correct," she said. "I have learned differently since then."

What or when she had learned about her husband's activities, she did not elaborate. A reporter at the scene commented that she was "more imperturbable and possessed of more poise than Gallo himself" and by the end of her testimony concluded, "The woman is, from a lawyer's standpoint, a good witness. She refused to allow herself to become excited or confused, never tried to explain her answers or qualify them, and replied categorically and briefly to the questions." Her testimony, coupled with her husband's, convinced the jury to find Esola guilty, and he, too, was sentenced to five years, his term to be served in Folsom Prison. Mike was returned to San Quentin, the only reward for his testimony an agreement by the DA not to prosecute him for the other bunko schemes that had come to light during Esola's trial.

Mike had shown little remorse during his testimony and had even laughed when the defense attorney had railed at him, calling him a "professional liar" with "a talent for making up stories on the spur of the moment as necessity required." Mike's response was to counterattack: "I'm laughing at you because the bunko man gets his money from his victims the same as a lawyer does from his." At a subsequent sentencing hearing, he had insisted that his testimony was the "absolute truth," even though he conceded, "My business is that of a professional liar."

Mike's testimony led to the indictment of forty other bunko men in his organization. By bringing down fifteen San Francisco cops who had taken his bribes, he became the center of a major scandal, and the story, along with his and Celia's photographs, ran on the front page of both city newspapers for a week. Mike himself seemed to regret only that he had been caught, and his five years in prison would do nothing to cramp his style or mute his flamboyant schemes for wealth and success. As early as 1913 he had brought the Gallo name into the public eye and given it notoriety if not prominence.

Ernest and Julio were proud to accept their maternal grandfather's winemaking as part of their heritage. In interviews, they would brag about their grandfather Bianco and his winery as if to establish themselves as a generations-old wine family in the European tradition. They recalled watching their grandfather and their uncle Walter tend their vineyards, crush their grapes, and sell their wine.

While staying with their grandparents, Ernest and Julio were called "the boys." Walter had married, and he and his wife Lydia had a three-year-old daughter, Stella, who trailed after her cousins, delighted to have new playmates. She took to Ernest immediately, regarding him as the leader of their little band, especially when he stood up to their grandfather. Stella had always been slightly afraid of Battista, who could be stern but also liked to play tricks on her. For example, he had a favorite white mint he bought at the Italian grocery store down the street. One day he called Stella to his side, a wide grin on his face.

"Stella, here's a quarter," he said in Italian. "If you go and get me my candy, I'll show you five cents when you come back."

Stella ran down the street, bought the candy, and hurried home to her grandfather. She handed him the bag and his change, then waited for her reward. He held up a nickel in front of her face.

"There, I've shown you five cents," he said, roaring with laughter and pocketing the coin.

When Ernest came to live with them the second time, Battista pulled the same trick on him. Stella was surprised to see Ernest grin, almost as if he enjoyed the joke. Later she asked why he hadn't been upset.

"What makes you think he fooled me?" he replied, already responding to a question with a question, a habit that would become a favorite weapon in his verbal arsenal. "The joke's on him," he explained. "I took candy out of the bag before I brought it home."

"Even when he was a little boy, nobody could put anything over on Ernest," Stella said, recalling the incident and Ernest's extended stay with her family.

When in later years others tried to draw the conclusion that Ernest and Julio (as well as their father) had learned about the winery business during their stay with the Biancos, Ernest and Julio resisted the suggestion. Despite documents that confirmed that Joe, Sr., had stayed in Hanford for at least a few months and had intended to work in the Bianco winery, Ernest and Julio would deny that their father had lived in Hanford or that he or they could have learned anything about winemaking from the Biancos. They would declare that the Bianco winery was so small as to be insignificant, that it was so much like "home winemaking" that "being around it" had taught them nothing.

Public records, however, contradicted their statements about the Bianco winery's small size and rudimentary operation. It had produced enough wine to come under attack in 1913 when the local temperance movement had declared Hanford a "no license territory." In 1911, well before national prohibition went into effect, the California legislature passed the "Wiley Local Option Law," which allowed individual townships to ban the manufacture and sale of "intoxicating liquor" within their boundaries. In 1912, Hanford declared itself dry; Walter and Battista Bianco continued to make wine, however, having discovered that the Wiley law exempted wineries already in existence as long as they sold only two gallons of wine to each customer. In 1913, though, the Hanford sheriff visited the winery and arrested Walter for selling him a two-gallon container of wine.

Walter fought the arrest in court on the basis of the law's exemption. The sheriff, however, convinced the judge that the exemption did not apply, since the Bianco winery was no small operation. Walter had been happy to answer the sheriff's questions about winemaking and give him a tour of the premises. The sheriff told the court that he had seen at least eight floor-to-ceiling vats as well as numerous smaller barrels stored in both the full-length cellar and what he called a "warehouse" in the backyard. "Probably the quantities run up in the thousands," he said, a figure that Walter did not dispute. Despite Walter's argument that he was selling wine legally, both in the specified two-gallon containers and shipping it in bulk outside Hanford's dry territory, the judge fined him $500 and ordered him to cease his local sales.

Thus the court apparently concluded that the Bianco winery was neither as small nor as insignificant as Ernest would later declare. But as a result of the court order, its sales and wine production decreased dramatically. Also, Battista's lung condition had worsened; Walter was running the winery alone and suspected that business was likely to dwindle as more and more "dry" restrictions were enforced. Bulk wine sales outside the city limits barely supported the family, and the future began to look especially bleak for Susie. Her solution was to yield to Joe's pleas for reconciliation.

Joe had been doing well in Oakland and had added a retail liquor business to his wine company, saloon, and hotel. (The telephone classified listings of liquor and wine merchants showed a rapid turnover each year, but his was one of the few names that appeared consistently from 1914 to 1918.) As if to confirm his mended ways and good intentions, he transferred the ownership of his saloon and hotel to Susie's name. Convinced that he meant to do well for her and the children, she returned with them to Oakland. Ernest and Julio were enrolled in public school, and their home life took on a regular routine. With no major financial worries, Joe controlled his temper and even treated them to family excursions, like a visit to the 1915 International Exposition in San Francisco, where Ernest and Julio were photographed in proper dress suits, their dark brown eyes staring somberly into the camera.

When Battista died on January 17, 1916, he left at least nine thousand gallons of red wine still in stock, which along with the Hanford and San Francisco properties, were the principal assets of his estate. Susie and her sisters and brother ceded their shares of the estate back to their mother, but the financial difficulties were so extreme that Virginia and Walter were forced to sell the Hanford house and winery. (Walter and Lydia resettled on a prune ranch in the Santa Clara Valley, while Virginia stayed with Tillie and her husband in one of the Biancos' San Francisco apartments until she later moved to a home in Oakland near Mike and Celia.)

Joe's prosperity was threatened by the nation's growing Prohibition campaign. "Dry" lobbyists convinced Congress that wartime emergency measures required strict controls on the use of foodstuffs to manufacture liquor, and on December 18, 1917, both houses passed the proposed constitutional amendment to ban the manufacture and sales of all intoxicating beverages, including wine and beer. The liquor industry was confident that the proposed amendment would never be ratified by the required thirty-six states within the six-year deadline. Instead, the legislatures acted within thirteen months. California had rejected Prohibition three times in popular votes, but in the election of November 1918, temperance candidates gained control of the state legislature. California's ratification was one of the last required, and three days after the new legislature's approval in early 1919, the Eighteenth Amendment became national law, to go into effect on January 20, 1920.

There had been much talk in the California wine industry of what to do when Prohibition would so drastically affect the state's numerous wineries and wine distributing companies. Some wineries would be licensed to make and sell sacramental and medicinal wine; others would have to shut down until the law could be changed; still others would simply go out of business. But already people in the industry discussed two other solutions: Some winemakers and distributors were ready to retreat underground, producing and selling wine illegally or in excess of the amount permitted for medical or religious purposes. Others proposed shipping wine grapes rather than turning them into wine. Under Prohibition law, private individuals would be allowed to make two hundred gallons of wine at home for personal consumption. The wine industry predicted a rapidly expanded market for wine grapes, particularly in eastern cities with large European immigrant populations. And if, as rumored, many of these "home winemakers" would be making more than the two-hundred-gallon allotment, the demand for California wine grapes would become even greater. Once Prohibition was inevitable, it was a logical transition for anyone in the wine business to become a grape grower and shipper.

Joe Gallo was not unique when in 1918 he closed his liquor and wine business, then sold the saloon and hotel in order to buy vineyard property. It was what many people in the wine industry, including winery owners, would do—simply change the form in which they sold their product from wine to wine grapes. Although Ernest would later insist that Prohibition put his father out of the wine business, raising and selling wine grapes was considered the legal form of the banned wine business. Joe did make a mistake, though, by buying a vineyard in Antioch, a farming community at the western edge of the Sacramento River delta, a swampy region more suited to raising vegetables than grapes.

If anything seemed to harden Ernest and Julio's hearts against their father it was their few years at the Antioch ranch. They remembered those years as a nightmare: In the first place, they would say, their father was so inexperienced that he had bought land that was penetrated with clay from river backwash. The original vineyard on the ranch was planted to Thompson seedless, a hardy grape used more for raisins than for wine. Joe was foolish enough to think that he could raise Zinfandels and Alicante Bouschet, the favored grapes among Italian winemakers but unsuited to the poor soil. Then, his sons recalled, he was misguided enough to buy four large workhorses in San Francisco instead of closer to home. A bargain, he said, except that he was faced with the logistics and expense of bringing them across the bay on the ferry. Also, he had no idea what other crops to grow on his land. He tried garlic—that was a failure—then potatoes, another failure. Having learned that sheep did well in the area, he bought a flock, forgetting that the sheep would invade the vineyards and strip the vines of their leaves and ripening grapes.

In retrospect, their father seemed ignorant and stubborn to the sons; worse, he was a tyrant who forced them to work long hours in the vineyards, before and after school, from before sunrise to long into the night. They were the ones who did the cultivating: The ground was so swampy, the plow wouldn't cut through it. When the plow didn't move, the horses rebelled and stopped pulling, and then Julio had to push the soil over by hand to convince their father that they were finishing each row. It was Ernest and Julio, too, who did the pruning and irrigating, cultivating and tying up vines, as well as picking and packing the grapes in the fall harvest. And when they had completed all these jobs, they were expected to remove nails from old boards and hammer them together into lug boxes for shipping the grapes. Their father, they said, rarely did anything but give orders; they remembered him pacing back and forth on top of the water tower that overlooked the vineyards. From there he could supervise his sons, making sure that they did their chores. And if he was dissatisfied, he whipped them with a leather harness strap, the buckle leaving bruises and cuts on their backs.

In later years Julio would recall how hard "the father" had been on them—the relentless toil, the beatings that scarred his childhood memories. One day after school, for example, his father ordered him to clear the sheep out of the vineyards. He ran up and down the long rows chasing the animals, but then, sitting down to catch his breath, he was so tired that he fell asleep. Awakened by his father's angry shouts, he trotted back to the house. There Joe stood, lashing the leather strap at his side. Julio submitted in silence, the strap raising long red welts, and he always remembered the beating as one of the worst he had ever received, and completely undeserved.

Visiting with her parents and new baby brother Aloysius or "Ali,"

Stella Bianco was appalled by the work that her cousins were now forced to do. She got up with them before dawn when they went out to the barn to harness the horses for plowing. They were so short that they had to stand on two fruit boxes just to lift the harnesses around the animals' necks. Ernest looked very small, she thought, sitting way up on top of the plow, and Julio, leading the horses up and down the vineyard rows, trudged forward as if he had the weight of the world on his shoulders. These two little boys are doing a man's job, she thought to herself. It was work, work, work, before school, after school, even after supper when it was already dark; they didn't dare stop to play with her, she realized, because they were afraid of being punished.

In his adult years Ernest often bragged that he was driving mules and horses and plowing before he was ten, the accomplishment a symbol of how he had learned to work hard at a very young age. This recollection with a moral, a parable of his drive and ambition, masked his anger at what Julio would openly refer to as their father's cruelty. Whatever resentment the two sons had felt during their father's earlier absence must have grown to bitterness in the swampy vineyard of Antioch. The badges of courage and endurance that Ernest awarded himself from these years would hide antagonism toward a father whom he regarded as a domineering and punishing patriarch. But he also seemed to learn another lesson from the emotional toll of these years: Become as stern, unyielding, and controlling as your antagonist; never reveal a weakness, never expose your vulnerability.

Then, as if to stoke the fires of their resentment, a brother was born on September 11, 1919, and honored with his father's name: Joseph, Jr. During her pregnancy, Susie had hoped for a girl, but when a son was born, he seemed to become his parents' favorite child, or so Ernest and Julio seemed to believe. The baby was tended and cared for while his older brothers were treated like slave labor. The sibling jealousy would deepen in subsequent years when the family's money worries abated and "Pete" or "Petey," as Joe, Jr., was nicknamed, could be permitted the childhood denied his older brothers.

After three years Joe decided to give up the Antioch farm as a lost cause. Once again it was his brother Mike, now released from San Quentin, who offered new possibilities. With his nose for the quick buck and lucrative schemes, he knew how to turn a profit from Prohibition, and he enlisted Joe's help. Mike had closed his Oakland saloon, but his San Pablo Bottling Shop provided a cover for bootlegging. Oakland was still his headquarters, and with his newfound source of income, he built a large stately home on Grosvenor Place for Celia, the surviving twin, Mario, and their infant daughter, Gloria. But he also owned a small cattle ranch and farmhouse in Livermore, the vineyard-rich community to the east of Oakland where local brandy distillers and winemakers supplied him with brandy and wine that he distributed to customers throughout the Bay Area.

He also owned his own stills, and in 1921 he offered Joe the use of the Livermore house in exchange for "caretaking" the ranch and his business interests. Meanwhile Joe could look for better vineyards in the Central Valley. The suggestion wasn't a simple act of charity. Mike's operation was large enough to require his brother's assistance. Mike had installed a brandy still in the barn on the ranch—in California grape brandy (or grappa) stills were as much a part of bootlegging as whiskey stills and bathtub gin in other parts of the country. Joe could supervise the still as well as deliver to Mike's local customers.

Whether or not Susie knew and endorsed Joe and Mike's plans, she was glad to leave Antioch. If Joe didn't have to worry about money and a failing farm, perhaps he would treat her and the boys more kindly. It was with relief that Ernest and Julio helped load the family's belongings into the small pickup truck on moving day that fall. Their father tied a mattress over the boxes and suitcases, and they climbed on top of the mattress and clutched at the tie ropes so that they wouldn't fall off during the journey to their new home. Two-year-old Pete sat in the front seat between his mother and father. On her lap Susie held the serving dish that her mother had given her, cradling it as if it were as fragile as her hopes for a happier future.

Ernest and Julio soon found that their work days in Livermore would be just as long, only their chores would be different. Instead of working in a vineyard before and after school, they were expected to tend the large metal contraption in the barn that Joe called a "still." They would load either barley mash or grape pomace into the large kettle-like container, add sugar, and then keep the kerosene burner underneath the pot going at a low flame. When liquid dripped from the tubing, they were to fill gallon containers from the siphon, capping each when it was full and moving an empty one into position. Joe would deliver the containers of brandy to Mike's Livermore customers, and sometimes the boys would be needed to help with this as well.

Ernest and Julio must have been aware that their father and uncle were engaged in an illegal activity. Whenever their father asked them to accompany him on his route, they were frightened by the atmosphere of secrecy and danger. One evening his father dropped Julio off on the side of a country road with a gallon of brandy to await a customer. The man failed to arrive, and Julio hid behind a bush, trembling every time a car approached, sure it was the sheriff come to arrest him. Finally his father returned and picked him up, and although Julio couldn't voice his fright or refuse to make deliveries, he never forgot how terrifying he found the experience.

Mike's operation distributed brandy and wine to the establishments that had replaced the saloons in Livermore and went by the names of "soft-drink parlors" or cigar and tobacco shops. Many of the owners were Italians, and they had come to depend on Mike both as a reliable supplier and as a "fixer" with enough clout among cops and politicians to keep them out of trouble.

The son of a "soft-drink parlor" owner was always impressed when Mike came calling to take an order or make deliveries. "He drove a fancy car, I think it was a Chrysler," he recalled, "and he was very slick looking, with expensive suits and a black fedora, like pictures of gangsters in Chicago. He smiled a lot and told stories, but all of us kids knew he was someone you didn't mess around with—we were told that he carried a gun. He was one of the first bootleggers to build up such a big business in the area, and we heard that he had a lot of friends in high places as well as tough guys on his payroll. Everybody knew that he had done five years in San Quentin, and so to us in the East Bay, Mike Gallo was as notorious and powerful as Al Capone in Chicago. One day my father and I were walking down the street in Oakland. I saw Mike Gallo drive into the intersection where a cop was directing traffic. Mike was turning left but he stopped in the middle of the intersection and reached out the car window to shake the cop's hand. That's when my father explained that Mike was giving him more than a handshake, that he paid off the police to stay in business."

By 1921, California was already called "the wettest state in the country" and a "bootlegger's paradise." Because of its length of seacoast and the Mexican border, smuggling was especially easy. And in rural areas like Livermore, bootlegging went relatively undetected since the few federal agents assigned to California tended to concentrate on the larger cities. Many grape growers supplied the local wineries, such as the Raboli Brothers, Concannon, Garatti Brothers,

Wente Brothers, and Cresta Blanca, with grapes to make sacramental and medicinal wine. But the growers' annual tonnage usually exceeded the wineries' needs, and they also sold to individuals, nominally for home winemaking, but often for more commercial purposes —supplying individual wine and brandy makers in the area. The local police generally chose to ignore the small winemakers and sellers, and the few incidents of arrest were handled quickly, if not by the municipal court and a justice of the peace, then by the city council, and usually resulted in a fine (sometimes as little as $50, sometimes as much as $500), a one- or two-day jail sentence, if any, and perhaps the suspension of a "soft-drink parlor" permit for a few months.

No one worried much, and among the bootleggers and distributors there was a kind of camaraderie. Everyone knew everyone else and spoke openly about their occupation. Bootlegging of wine and brandy was so widespread that it was hardly considered scandalous or sinful, and it wasn't so much malicious gossip as admiration for their success that led people to talk about Mike Gallo and his brother Joe. "Oh yeah, Mike and Joe Gallo, they had a big operation." "Sure, he and my dad always talked about how the bootlegging was going." "Oh, of course, Mike and Joe sold their stuff down at the Rock House Deli, the Hub, Damas Place, to almost all of the fifteen or twenty speaks here and even the ones out in 'Old Mexico,' that end of town where so much cactus grew." "My father got his liquor from Mike and Joe Gallo. I guess just about everybody did."

While most of Joe's friends and associates were Italians, he also became acquainted with Albert Wagner, a German immigrant who was considered an expert in cognac and winemaking. "My father and Ernest and Julio's father got to know each other when they were both bootleggers in Livermore," Rudy Wagner recalled. "We had a chicken ranch, and Joe would often stop by and have a glass of wine with my father. Perhaps my father was supplying Joe with wine and brandy to sell, I'm not sure, but I know they stayed friendly throughout the years of Prohibition. After Repeal it was logical for ex-bootleggers to go into the wine business legally, and Ernest and Julio must have remembered that my father was an expert, because they asked him to work for their winery. He refused—'Why spoil an old family friendship?' he said. Joe was his friend, not Ernest, and from what he had heard about the son, he figured he would be a difficult boss. He took a job at a southern California winery instead. Ernest and Julio were embarrassed by what their father was doing during those years, but I wasn't. It was through my father that I learned the trade. My father and their father both had reputations for making and selling good stuff, so Ernest and Julio must have learned something from Joe, too, no matter what they said later."

By 1922 federal agents were descending on Livermore and its surrounding farms, having heard that it was a "hotbed" of still operators, winemakers, and illegal sellers. Most violators, however, were charged under Livermore's local dry ordinance, not under the national Volstead Act, and paid fines of $250 or $500 in the local court rather than having to stand trial in San Francisco federal court. "Round up the usual suspects," was the motto whenever agents or the sheriff decided to get tough on Livermore bootleggers in periodic raids. But the arrests and minimal fines rarely put anyone out of business; nor did they severely diminish the high profits of bootlegging, especially from wine, as evidenced in the appraised $18,000 inventory from a 1922 hotel raid in the Livermore area: 5 fifty-gallon barrels of wine, 12 cases of champagne, 15 cases of sauterne, 28 gallons of whiskey, and 240 one-gallon bottles and 600 quart bottles of wine. The hotel owner paid a $500 fine, and two months later, he was arrested again for an equally extensive stock of wine replenished by the many local winemakers.

In general, bootlegging in California had its own flavor because of the plenitude of grapes and the popular feeling that Prohibition against wine was not only ridiculous but hurt one of the state's most important industries. The illegal wine and brandy business in California didn't have the criminal taint associated with Chicago and Al Capone, although some of his gang would try to make inroads with grape growers and winemakers toward the end of Prohibition. With lax law enforcement and raw materials so available—both grapes and grain—bootlegging was lucrative and fairly safe, and Mike Gallo's marketing skills and talent for having the right friends in the right places reaped rich rewards with little effort and less risk.

Mike did, however, have a brush with the law in 1922. The incident reported in the *San Francisco Bulletin* and then picked up by the *Livermore Herald* the following day was more a matter of local amusement than of concern:

Arrested on Liquor Charge—

Thursday's *San Francisco Bulletin* said: "Mike Bianco, Livermore rancher," was arrested on Steiner Street early today by Policeman Edward

A. Mitchell while transporting 10 kegs of liquor in an automobile. He was charged with violation of the State Prohibition Enforcement Act.

What had once been described as Mike's bunko talents served him well again; as a "first offender," he was simply fined, the cops unaware that Mike Bianco was in fact Mike Gallo, an ex-con, parolee, and the man already identified in federal investigations as a "notorious East Bay bootlegger." But Mike's friends in Livermore caught on when they read the item. He had often bragged about his in-laws, the Biancos, and their winery, and they knew that he owned a small cattle ranch outside town where his brother was living, running a brandy still and making deliveries in town. Even the newspaper editor seemed to be in on the joke when he put quotation marks around Mike's name and occupation.

Despite their reputation, Mike and Joe's Livermore operation remained undisturbed. Joe had now saved enough money to buy a new Hudson, and when his schedule of deliveries permitted, he drove across the mountains to the Central Valley to look at vineyards for sale. With the family's increased income, there was less anxiety at home, and Susie was able to buy finer material and sew the boys better shirts and trousers. They went to school every day, their father sometimes driving them into town, and the new family car prompted admiration from their classmates.

Ernest took to his studies much more seriously than Julio, and he was especially good in arithmetic. But he was also impatient; if his classmates talked too loudly when he was listening to the teacher, he took it upon himself to shut them up, usually boxing their ears. He seemed to keep to himself and he had a kind of defensive rigidity as he walked, much like his father, with his hands clasped behind his back, his head bowed and tilted to the side.

Julio was softer, seemingly more relaxed, and popular among his classmates. While Ernest's slight build and lack of coordination made him the "last kid" chosen for the schoolyard teams, Julio was always among the first, his larger size and batting talent making him a star of the baseball games. But neither boy ever had much time to play. After school they were expected home immediately—they had to relieve their father, sometimes their mother, supervising the still, and there were always the farm chores to be done as well.

Young boys want something more from their parents than a strict regimented upbringing. Their mother sometimes tempered Joe's sternness with hugs and laughter and singing. But to Ernest and Julio their father still seemed strict and aloof, his cold insistence on duty and obedience rarely relieved by the warmth or affection that he sometimes showed little Pete. Ernest rose to the paternal expectations by drawing into himself and becoming a "manly" little boy, unspontaneous and dignified. As one classmate put it, he was "eleven going on fifty." But Julio, despite his sturdiness and devil-may-care attitude, was more sensitive, and his father's abrupt commands still brought tears to his eyes.

In the summer, when they had no school, their orders were even more strict, every hour of the day assigned to work. Ernest loaded up the car and accompanied his father on his deliveries. Julio was expected to watch the still, siphoning the brandy into one container after another. On the morning of July 5, 1922, Joe and Ernest drove off on a round of deliveries, and Julio was left in the barn to replenish the brandy supply. By noon he had filled several containers, and with everything running smoothly, he stopped for lunch.

He was sitting at the kitchen table, talking to his mother and playing with Pete, when they heard a car coming up the driveway. Julio thought it must be his father, home early. Then he stiffened with alarm.

A second car arrived, screeching to a stop; doors slammed; a deep voice shouted, *Scatter.*

He and his mother ran to the window. They saw men in dark suits storming the barn with axes raised. The wooden door splintered with a crash, and a few minutes later they pulled the still into the yard and chopped it to pieces. Then they began to load the canisters of brandy into the trunks of the cars, while the commanding officer marched up to the house.

Susie swept Pete into her arms, and Julio hurried behind as she went to answer the loud knocks at the door.

The man flashed his identification, announcing that he was a federal marshal and demanding to know who owned the still.

Susie shook her head. *It's rented, I don't know who,* she stammered in broken English.

Where was her husband? Who owned the house? Who was making the brandy? he hammered away.

Susie said she didn't know where her husband was—out on business, and, no, she had never been told who rented the barn and she'd never, ever known about the still.

Finally the agent gave up and ordered his men to search the property for the woman's husband. For two hours they clambered up and down the slope behind the house. They found nothing, but their commander kept sending them back through tangled underbrush, certain that the still's owner could be flushed out of hiding if they waited long enough.

Joe and Ernest had been driving toward the farm on the road from Livermore at the very moment the agents had arrived. They had just approached the turn for the driveway when Joe spotted the cars and the men swinging axes at the barn door.

It's a raid! he exclaimed, suddenly accelerating and speeding past the driveway.

Hushing Ernest's anxiety, he drove back to town, taking a roundabout route on dusty farm roads so as to avoid the marshals. In town he stopped at the department store where he bought a tie and shirt and changed out of his farm clothes so that he would look like a respectable businessman if the agents found him. Then he and Ernest drove up and down Livermore streets, hoping that when darkness fell the agents would leave.

But the marshals were still searching when they arrived home. Ernest stood stalwart and solemn at his father's side while Joe responded in short, quick answers to the commander's interrogation. Feigning innocence and disbelief, he played the rustic paesan who could barely understand English, much less the questions about the barn and this thing called a "still."

Believing that the threat of prison might force some answers, the marshal arrested Joe and shoved him into the backseat of his car. At the jail he was allowed his one phone call. He dialed the person he knew could help: his brother Mike. The next morning, July 6, he was arraigned in municipal court where he was charged with violating the local Prohibition law. True to his word, however, Mike arrived to "fix" everything up, and Joe was released. Although his name stayed in the court records, the case was never brought to trial, and on December 29, 1925, the indictment against him was officially dismissed.

The incident became part of Gallo family lore, as Joe, Jr., would later recall. Both his aunt Celia and uncle Mike liked to tell of Mike's influence with the police, how he'd taken care of things when Joe had gotten into trouble in Livermore. In retrospect, however, Ernest and Julio seemed to find their father's arrest and their uncle's reputation as a "kingpin bootlegger" too embarrassing, and the story became another Gallo secret.

With the ranch a likely target for future raids, it was time to leave the Livermore operation behind. Joe soon found a twenty-acre vineyard and an old farmhouse to buy in Escalon, an hour east of Livermore in San Joaquin County. Susie may have felt that the arrest had taught Joe a lesson, but his new property put him right in the heart of Central Valley wine grape country.

CHAPTER TWO

Once an inland sea, the four-hundred-mile-long Central Valley is California's richest agricultural region. Its basin stretches fifty miles across between the camelback ridges of the coast ranges on the west and the towering peaks of the Sierra Nevada on the east. It is divided in half, the upper region known as the Sacramento Valley, the lower as the San Joaquin Valley. Because of its fertile land, warm weather, and extensive irrigation, grapes grown in the San Joaquin Valley today account for 70 percent of the state's annual wine production. And most of these vineyards were planted during Prohibition when wine grapes were in such high demand.

Joe Gallo's newly acquired twenty-acre property was just one of the thousands of vineyards gridding the landscape around Escalon in the early 1920s. He had become familiar with the small agricultural town when he had traveled the San Joaquin Valley to buy bulk wine for his pre-Prohibition wine company. The ban on wine hadn't diminished the local industry; because of the market for wine grapes, the number of vineyards had increased to 23,686 acres by 1924. According to the *Escalon Tribune*, that same year the area's growers shipped an estimated 12,398 railroad cars or $13 million worth of wine grapes to eastern markets. But these vineyards also supplied grapes to the numerous winemakers in the area, either to already established wineries that produced legal sacramental and medicinal wine and sometimes sold in illegal quantities, or to individuals who were bootlegging wine as well as grappa. Escalon then was an ideal location for the new

Gallo enterprise, even though the vineyard on the north side of town wasn't level and as a result was difficult to plow and irrigate.

It did, however, have a particular selling point: Half of it was planted to Alicante Bouschet, the grape variety favored for shipping to eastern markets. Its thick skin made it less perishable, and home winemakers valued its deep red pigment and its strong flavor, which produced a robust, heavy wine similar to the wines of "the old country." It was the grape of preference for bootleggers of wine as well, because it could go through several pressings to produce a larger volume of wine. While a ton of other grapes yielded an average of 150 to 160 gallons from one pressing, bootleggers could produce 600 to 700 gallons of "wine" from one ton of Alicante by re-pressing the grape several times. Each pressing yielded a pigmented liquid (though hardly real wine) to which sugar and water were then added. Although Joe's vineyard produced only 2.5 tons of grapes per acre (the best vineyards then yielded 3.0 to 3.5 tons), he was aware that the price for Alicantes was soaring in the eastern markets.

The rest of his twenty acres was planted to Carignane, a hybrid varietal developed from the Carnelian grape to produce high yields in the Central Valley climate (though its wine tended to be heavy and coarse) and Petite Bouschet, a grape used by winemakers to add color and sweetness. Despite his uneven soil, Joe did particularly well with his Petite Bouschet, and in 1924 he won second prize for this grape at the San Joaquin County Fair.

In a few short months, he was able to buy another twenty-acre vineyard in Keyes, a grape-growing region outside Modesto, the larger San Joaquin Valley town eleven miles south of Escalon. This property had better soil and was planted to Zinfandel, another favorite among Italian immigrants, since it resembled (and was probably related to) a variety common in vineyards of southeastern Italy where it was called Primitivo di Gioia. Although the Zinfandel was more perishable in shipment, it was also favored by both home winemakers and bootleggers because it produced wine high in alcohol content.

The Keyes vineyard yielded 3.0 to 3.5 tons of grapes per acre. Ernest and Julio worked both vineyards, and with no labor costs, Joe was soon making a profit. While he was by no means one of the larger property owners, he became part of an informal circle of Italian winemakers and grape growers in the Escalon area to whom Ernest and Julio could later turn for advice.

Angelo Petri, for example, was a Tuscan emigrant who, like Joe, had started in the pensione and saloon business; after going into the cigar-making business he then acquired a small winery at Alba Station near Escalon in 1886 to supply wine to his San Francisco hotels. In 1916, he increased his vineyard holdings and enlarged his winery operation so that he became one of the major producers and shippers of bulk wine, not only throughout California but also to Chicago and New York. During Prohibition, his winery operation officially closed, but he and his son Louis stayed in the business by buying up more vineyards and shipping grapes. Using the Cella Brothers (owners of the huge Roma Winery) as their agents, they supplied grapes to boot- leg wineries in eastern cities. Joe Gallo knew him from Escalon, and later, after Repeal, Ernest allegedly approached his father's grape- growing colleague, who by then sat on the board of the Bank of America, to request his support for a loan application. When Petri refused, the Gallo and Petri wineries became archrivals.

Another Escalon acquaintance of Joe's whom Ernest later found useful was Dante Forresti. An Asti native, he too had been in the hotel business in San Francisco before purchasing the large Stockton Vineyards in Escalon, where he hired Louis Sciaroni, a Swiss vintner, to build and run a small winery. (In 1913 Sciaroni built his own Escalon winery with his nephew Charles Cadlolo; Cadlolo bought a vineyard as well, a property situated across the road from the Gallo ranch.) During Prohibition, it was common knowledge that Forresti continued to make and distribute wine. Considered a local character, he openly bragged about the federal agents he wined and dined and paid off while he continued in the wine business. He frequented The Valley Inn, the local bar and pool hall, and loved to tell his Prohibi- tion war stories, how he pulled off one deal or another or outfoxed another sheriff or an agent, or put something over on the Prohibition Office.

The Valley Inn, which had been bought by Cadlolo when he closed his and his uncle's winery in 1919, served as an informal Italian club, and Joe, like many of the grape growers and winemakers, would drop by for a glass of near beer (some said glasses of wine were served in the back room), a game of gin rummy, and an evening of gossip. He and his friends were often entertained by Forresti's tales of his latest exploits. If anyone knew the ropes of the wine business, it was For- resti, a fact that Ernest remembered to his advantage after Repeal.

Although Ernest and Julio later denied it, it would seem that Joe established a grounding in wine for his sons not only through his informal circle of friends and his grape growing, but also by making wine and wine brandy. He may have been secretive about it in deference to Susie's concern; perhaps he himself had been frightened by his arrest. But Escalon was as open as Livermore, and residents didn't think of winemaking as a shameful enterprise. Most Italians made wine at home anyway, but people knew which individuals made more than their two-hundred-gallon allotment and sold the excess; they also were aware of those who made enough wine to supply "distributors," bootleggers like Mike who bought both wine and brandy, then distributed it to their customers.

According to Sal Curzi, who grew up in Escalon, Joe soon had a reputation for producing good reliable wine, and townspeople regularly called at the Gallo ranch to replenish their supply. There was also common gossip that Joe supplied both wine and grape brandy to a bootlegger as well, and those who were more in the know mentioned his brother's extensive bootleg ring. Years later, when one of Julio's classmates was asked if Joe Gallo was a grape grower, he exclaimed, "Hell, no, he was a bootlegger! He made wine and brandy. How else could he afford his fancy cars that he drove Ernest and Julio to school in."

While Julio and Ernest later denied that their father continued in the illegal operation, Joe, Jr., recalled differently. He was old enough to notice that his father often loaded the car with containers and drove away for the day. Sometimes his father even asked him to come along when he made his deliveries. Joe, Jr., remembered one trip in particular, not because it was unusual to deliver a canister of brandy to the Lodi area north of Escalon, but because that day his father ran over a sheep and they brought it home for dinner.

Deliveries in Lodi were frequent enough to attract attention. Neighbors near a large wooden warehouse and railroad loading dock just outside Lodi had noticed gatherings of men in the area and the constant traffic of cars and pickups. They complained to the police, and deputies conducted an investigation, gathering enough evidence for the San Joaquin County district attorney to file a criminal case in superior court. On December 17, 1923, he lodged the complaint against P. Triolo, W. J. Armanino, Vincente and Samuele Giovannoni, Bud Thompson, and last but not least J. Gallo, alleging that "on December 7, J. Gallo, Bud Thompson, John Doe, and Peter Poe (true names unknown) sold, kept and bartered certain intoxicating liquor, to-wit: whiskey, jackass brandy, or by whatsoever name called." Triolo, Armanino, and the Giovannoni brothers were named as the owners of the property, who, the citation alleged, were aware of the bootlegging of these tenants and, in fact, were part of the operation.

The accused were issued summonses by a sheriff's deputy; whether fines were paid and by whom was not recorded, but the case never came to trial. Lodi was another agricultural region where bootlegging had become a lucrative business. Mike Gallo had already expanded his operations to this location, and it was rumored that the men named in the 1923 indictment were all part of the same organization with Mike Gallo at its head, a loosely structured network that used numerous suppliers of wine and widespread distribution points throughout the Bay Area and the northern Central Valley.

It would be several years before the stories of Mike Gallo's far-flung activities were verified by the authorities. But even by 1923, it was obvious to Mike's family, friends, and business acquaintances that he had become a wealthy man. Unlike Joe, Mike enjoyed conspicuous displays of wealth, from his expensive home and its elegant furnishings to his clothes—monogrammed silk shirts and tailor-made suits as well as his gold watch fob and his diamond-studded initials that dangled from it. With his continuing success and high profits, he couldn't resist taking his family on a visit to Fossano to see his parents. His return to his native Piedmont village was much in the style of "the conquering hero." Not only did the family sail first class, Mike also had his latest-model Chrysler shipped to Italy so that he could drive into town as if he were leading a ticker-tape parade. After their tour, they came home with expensive gifts and tales of their enthusiastic welcome. On their next visit to Joe and Susie, Celia presented her sister with a handmade lace tablecloth, an heirloom that Susie promised to Pete on his wedding day but that Ernest eventually kept in his own family.

Joe, however, indulged in no outward shows of wealth except his automobiles. Instead he invested his money in more land and properties, including a hotel in Manteca, a town to the west of Escalon. But the family's higher income didn't lighten the burdens imposed on Ernest and Julio.

Joe's strictness was legend among Ernest and Julio's classmates. "Julio was my friend then," recalled Joe Sciaroni, another Escalon student, "and he had to work harder for his father than any of the other farm kids who helped out at home. He could never stay after school for games, and none of us ever went to visit him out on their ranch. Julio said they weren't allowed to have friends over, and everyone talked about what a terrible temper his father had, how he was always yelling at his wife and sons."

Julio had one moment of rebellion in the fall of 1924 when he stayed after school to play in the annual baseball game between his eighth-grade class and the seventh grade. He hit two home runs, the second in the bottom of the ninth to win the game, and his triumph was noted in the local newspaper. If Joe was proud, he didn't let on but shouted at Julio for being late. And when Joe was angry, his voice was so loud that the Cadlolos across the road could hear him berating his sons at all hours.

Joe seemed to be a different man toward his youngest son, Pete, imposing none of the discipline to which Ernest and Julio had been subjected. While Ernest was withdrawn and Julio seemed fearful around Joe, Pete was a smiling, rambunctious little boy. He adored his older brothers and trailed after them to help them with their chores. He did not think of Joe as an angry, forbidding presence but as a fond and generous father, who, for example, gave him a shiny new bicycle on his fifth birthday in September 1924.

In his own way, Joe was as much an entrepreneur as Mike, and he watched for new opportunities. In January 1924, he had purchased four commercial and residential properties in downtown Modesto, after having been advised that the town to the south was growing rapidly and that real estate was a good investment. He then made plans to expand his business by becoming a grape shipper as well as a grape grower, prompted by the success of Giuseppe Franzia, a large grape grower and shipper in nearby Ripon.

An emigrant from Genoa, Franzia had bought eighty acres of vineyards and started a small winery in 1906. He and his wife had five sons and two daughters, and when Prohibition closed his winery, Franzia and his sons turned to grape growing and shipping. His shipping business was one of the most successful in the area, with many growers consigning their grapes to him to sell in the eastern market. Every fall he accompanied the railroad cars loaded with grapes to Chicago, and since grape prices remained high and he had a good reputation among the Chicago grape dealers, he was turning a large profit from growing and shipping.

His example wasn't lost on Joe, who soon made plans to become a shipper himself, at the same time deciding to invest in more and better vineyards. He sold both the Escalon property and the Manteca hotel but held on to the productive Keyes vineyard. He then bought land just west of the town of Modesto. The property, purchased from Claude Maze, would become the enduring home base of the Gallo family—first forty acres on the north side of Route 4 (later called Maze Road), then another thirty contiguous acres.

Modesto was a logical location for Joe's proposed shipping business since it was a major stop on the Santa Fe line. Joe rented a shed next to the tracks from which to load the grapes into freight cars and then persuaded a number of local growers to consign their harvests to him. The new Gallo business was ready to begin full operation in the autumn of 1925.

Joe also had enough money to build a new home. The family lived in town in one of Joe's rental properties for a year while the Gallo residence was designed and constructed. (It remains standing to the present day and is referred to in the family as "the home ranch" or "over to home," although it now is officially Ernest's property, where a winery employee usually lives.)

It was set on the edge of the original forty-acre vineyard, fronting the road, and its white stucco walls, wide front porch with arched columns, and red tile roof gave it a sun-drenched Mediterranean appearance. It had three bedrooms and one bath, a living room and dining room, and a kitchen that opened in the rear onto an enclosed sun porch that was the family's favorite gathering place, even where they ate their meals instead of in the dining room. To the right of the house a gravel driveway led to the garage and barn. Its total construction cost was $8,000, no small sum in 1925, but for the first time Joe seemed willing to spare no expense, even allowing Susie to consult her sister Tillie, a professional decorator in San Francisco, and choose new furnishings.

Like his brother Mike, he now seemed ready to enjoy the fruits of his labor, his new residence and property announcing to the community that he was a prosperous rancher and successful businessman. The new home struck neighbors as expensive and impressive. Indeed, the Gallos had come quite far from the pensiones and run-down farmhouses they had lived in before; in Modesto they had finally achieved the outward signs of financial comfort and respectability.

As Joe, Jr., later recalled, his father again installed a brandy still in the basement, where he also stored his wine press and barrels (Ernest and Julio later denied the existence of the brandy still and insisted that the barrels and press were only for home winemaking). But even this equipment was not unusual in the grape-rich Modesto surroundings, and since Joe's reputation—along with that of his brother Mike —had preceded him, he was welcomed by other grape growers and local winemakers. He joined the Modesto Italian-American Club and the Old Fishermen's Club and made the acquaintance of local businessmen and farmers, particularly his fellow Italians. He counted among his good friends the sheriff of Stanislaus County, who lived in Modesto and who, according to several grape growers, made a point of knowing the local brandy- and winemakers.

The family also joined St. Stanislaus Catholic Church although they had never been regular churchgoers except on religious holidays. But this was another step toward becoming respectable and well-regarded. In Modesto, however, they encountered a more rigid social structure than they had found in the rural community of Escalon. Modesto was now the Stanislaus County seat and largest city, and prejudice and class resentment were deeply entrenched.

Founded as a railroad town in 1870, Modesto formerly had a reputation for lawlessness, gambling, prostitution, and vigilantism against "the foreign elements," notably Chinese and Italians, who were held responsible for the town's sins. At the turn of the century and with the introduction of irrigation, the town entered a period of growth and civic prosperity. Farmers moved to the area and bought land where they cultivated grapes, olives, apricots, plums, prunes, almonds, and walnuts. Real estate agents passed out free railroad tickets to easterners and midwesterners, their slogan "To Modesto from Anywhere" enticing prospective investors. Those who came to buy land and build houses filled the ranks of the middle class and upper middle class. They looked upon themselves as the true settlers of Modesto and the backbone of the community, since it was with their arrival that municipal services, schools, and churches were established. Predominantly white, Protestant, and of either English or German descent, they were boosters of respectability and civic pride, and in 1912 they constructed an "Ornamental and Electric Arch" in the center of town to announce Modesto's new motto:

WATER   WEALTH   CONTENTMENT   HEALTH

As much as the slogan heralded the rewards of living in Modesto, the town's conservatism fostered the rigid hierarchy into which the Gallos moved in 1925. The families that had developed the town in the early 1900s considered themselves to be of a kind of *Mayflower* lineage in the Central Valley and regarded recent arrivals, especially immigrants, as outsiders at the bottom of the social ladder. If one's neighbors were Italian, even if one dealt with them in business, they bore the added stigma of rumored bootlegging. Al Capone's notoriety tainted all Italians, and the extensive bootlegging networks in San Francisco and the Central Valley made every Italian suspect. In Joe Gallo's case, the rumors about his illegal activities coupled with his brother's prison record and East Bay bootlegging put him and his family beyond the pale.

Ernest and Julio may have felt the corrosive effects of these attitudes for many years, which may have led to their later secrecy about their family background, as well as to the yearning for respectability that would provide a central theme in their winery's advertising. As teenagers they might have hoped that others would "change the way they thought about Gallo," but the repeated gossip as well as their father's strictness kept them fairly isolated from their Modesto high school classmates. In Ernest's case especially, the feeling of being from the wrong side of the tracks seemed to linger throughout his life, an angry I'll-show-them attitude fueling his ambition.

Ernest also adopted a defiant response to his father now that he was taking courses in agriculture at Modesto High School. Having become interested in the economics of farming, he joined the Agricultural Club and began to announce to his father how he could improve their vineyards with new methods and equipment. Rather than silently following Joe's orders, Ernest became argumentative, openly questioning what he regarded as his father's old-fashioned and stubborn ways. Joe considered such discussions to be signs of rebellion; Ernest's insolence was not to be tolerated. He might be older and better educated, but he still was a son who should know his place. Any time Ernest raised objections, Joe shouted him down. But now Ernest wasn't afraid to answer back when he was unable to suppress his anger and resentment. For the most part, though, he and Julio followed their father's orders and continued working from dawn until well past dusk to prepare for Joe's first shipment of grapes in the fall of 1925.

Joe's shipping business required Ernest and Julio to add another job to their long list of duties. Not only did they hammer together the several thousand Sanger lugs in which to ship the grapes, they also had to stencil a label on the sides of the boxes.

By the time Joe started his business, shippers were advised that labels on their boxes were selling points in the eastern market. Buyers who became familiar with the grapes of a certain shipper would rely on his grapes' quality and sugar content, and they would come to trust the shipper's identification much as consumers recognize a brand name. Other buyers would hear that a shipper had a good reputation and would seek out his label in the grape market. In fact, the California State Department of Agriculture was urging grape shippers to choose a name—preferably the shipper's own name—and label their boxes accordingly. A representative of the State Department of Agriculture made speeches throughout the state and sent articles to rural newspapers and farm journals, stressing the importance of keeping uniform quality of grapes under "private labels," since "certain brands are established on the market as satisfactory, and buyers place their valuation on carload lots by the boxes on display."

Joe's decision to use his own name as a brand label not only was officially encouraged but also suited him well. He liked the fact that "Gallo," the Italian word for "rooster," suggested pride and strength. He had, after all, put his own name on the barrels of wine he had sold before Prohibition.

Joe had a local woodworker cut a stencil; Ernest and Julio were instructed to lay the stencil over the end boards of the grape boxes and paint over it with red paint. When the stencil was removed, each box was labeled in bright red letters:

JOE GALLO

To the side of the name was the outline of a rooster.

The family name—a brand label first on wine, then on grapes— would become another part of the Gallo history and the three sons' legacy. But over the years its significance was either honored or exploited, denied or denigrated as required by circumstance.

Joe accompanied his first eighteen freight cars of wine grapes east that fall and encountered a strange, new world. The Chicago grape market was as much a part of the wine industry during Prohibition as California wineries were before and after the "dry" years. Despite Ernest's subsequent disparagement of his father's knowledge as well as the size of his business, Joe learned the ropes of this phase of the business and sold the freight cars as they were packed and sent almost daily from Modesto by Ernest and Julio—close to two hundred cars altogether.

Although there were three other grape markets in the city, Joe chose to sell at the Santa Fe yards at Twenty-first and Archer streets on the South Side. This was the rail terminus favored by independent shippers who sold to the market's grape dealers. Grape dealers were the middlemen of the system, the "distributors" who bought "wholesale" from the shippers, then retailed the grapes in their market sheds at the side of the yard to their customers, either to predominantly Italian home winemakers who bought a hundred or so boxes for their annual supply, or to "speculators," the polite term for bootleggers who were producing wine in basement wineries throughout the city and who required many carloads.

Upon arrival in Chicago, Joe's cars were shunted onto spur tracks that lined the yard. Like the other shippers, he opened the side doors of his cars so that the stacks of grape boxes with their labels were visible. The dealers walked up and down the lines, greeting shippers they knew from previous years, then climbed onto the car roofs to look through the top crawlspace, even pulling out grapes to inspect them and sample them. Testing for sugar content was done simply by taste, and the dealers were expert at deciding which grapes would make good wine. But they also knew that their customers depended on certain shippers for quality and for variety, and they tended to look for the same labels year after year.

Joe was pacing up and down in front of his cars when suddenly a young boy jumped in front of him.

"Excuse me, mister," he said. "Are you a shipper?"

"Yes, from Modesto," Joe replied. "I'm Joe Gallo." He gestured behind him to the label on the grape lugs.

"Have you sold these cars already, or do you still have some left?"

"No, they're all for sale," Joe replied, launching his sales pitch. "Alicantes, Zinfandels. Take a look. Pick out any box you want. They're all the best quality."

The boy had noticed that Joe spoke broken English, and he now addressed him in Italian, telling him that he was Paul Alleruzzo. He worked for his father, he explained, who owned Santa Fe Grape Distributors—he gestured to a market shed at the side of the tracks— and might be interested in these grapes. Then he scrambled up on top of the car, pulled out one lug and tasted a handful of the dark purple grapes. The teenage boy had been trained by his father, Paul, Sr., from an early age to find grapes with a good sugar level and consistent color and ripeness. He now called across to the Santa Fe shed, and his father arrived to make the first purchase of Joe Gallo grapes.

During the year Alleruzzo ran a small vegetable and fruit store in Chicago's Italian neighborhood. But in 1924, he had added grape distributing to his business. Because he was so well known in the community, a large number of customers came down to the Santa Fe yards to buy their annual supply from him. He demanded high quality in the grapes he distributed, he cared about wine (he, too, made his legal two hundred gallons each year), and he took the time to get to know the grape shippers with whom he dealt at the yards.

At the height of the grape season he sold as many as twenty-five carloads of grapes a day. Each car held about 1,000 boxes; customers who made the legal limit of 200 gallons of wine for their family usually bought from 50 to 100 boxes, figuring that about 24 boxes made a barrel (or 50 gallons) of wine. Of course, some of his customers were making more than a few 50-gallon barrels. Although no one admitted to bootlegging, these customers were regarded as the "big winemakers." Alleruzzo knew that almost every house in the Italian neighborhood had barrels full of wine, but he was also aware that some of these home winemakers were supplying wine to "distributors." It was not something that people discussed openly, since most wine distributors in Chicago were under the control of Al Capone. But Alleruzzo was far enough removed not to have to worry about them. The large number of customers he had were all experienced winemakers. They returned to him every year, and during the 1920s he usually made a profit of about $100 per carload of grapes.

His profit depended on finding the best wine grapes in the market, and Alleruzzo had an intuition that Joe was a good prospect. This new man from California was similar to the grape shippers whom he liked to deal with: Unlike larger produce brokers who shipped a variety of crops throughout the year, these men specialized in grapes; they were not shipping agents who represented smaller growers in California but had no real connection to the growing of grapes. Dealers like Alleruzzo had eliminated the need for such brokers and agents by establishing connections directly with individuals like Joe Gallo, men from California who grew grapes as well as shipped them, who knew about winemaking and the variety and quality of grapes that would satisfy his customers. Most of these fellows were Italian, and Alleruzzo often developed friendships with them. He felt he could count on them and their grapes—so much so that he telephoned them in California several times in the course of a year, asking about their families and inquiring about the year's prospective harvest.

When his father completed his first deal with Joe, Paul Alleruzzo carried several sample lugs of Gallo grapes over to the Santa Fe Distributors' shed. He set them next to the other sample lugs, each labeled with the shipper's name. Most of them were Italians from the Central Valley: Franzia from Ripon, Turano from Visalia, Panteleo from Fresno, Ursini from Modesto, and DeLuca from Lodi. In fact, Lodi was known as "the Zinfandel capital" of California, and the grower and shipper from whom Alleruzzo bought the most grapes was Cesare Mondavi. The Gallo and Mondavi labels thus appeared side by side on grape boxes as early as the 1920s, long before their labels became competitors in the wine market.

The Mondavi and Gallo family histories were quite similar. In contrast to Ernest and Julio, however, Cesare Mondavi's sons, Peter and Robert, remained proud of their past and what they had inherited from their father (although the two brothers eventually had a falling out and now own separate wineries). Cesare Mondavi emigrated from Sassafarento on the Adriatic coast of Italy, but he first settled in a mining town in the Iron Mountain range of Minnesota. There he and his wife, Rosa, ran a pensione for Italians who had come to work in the mines—providing a home away from home for "her boys," as Rosa often called them, even while she also raised their four children, Mary, Helen, Robert, and Peter. Like other owners of pensiones, Cesare sold wine from barrels on the bar in the downstairs saloon. He made the wine every year from grapes shipped from California, and like Joe Gallo, he, too, placed his name, Mondavi, on the side of his barrels. (In Minnesota, the name was pronounced Mon-day-vi, not with the broad "ah," "Mon-dah-vi," that was used later.)

Mondavi then added a grocery store to his business where he sold bulk wine as well. With Prohibition, he had to stop selling wine in his store, but because he was knowledgeable about wine grapes and had established contacts with California growers and vintners, the local Italian-American Club sent him to California to place its orders for the next year's harvest. Visiting throughout Napa, Sonoma, and the Central Valley, he fell in love with the land, and realizing, like so many others, that grape growing and shipping would be a profitable business, he bought vineyards in Lodi in 1922. He moved his family West and that fall shipped carloads of wine grapes to Chicago as well as to the Iron Range and to New York.

The Lodi vineyard was the original site of the Mondavi family business, just as Modesto was the Gallos'. And like Ernest and Julio, Cesare's two sons, Peter and Robert, helped their father in the vineyards and with the shipping business. They, too, hammered together the grape lugs and applied the Mondavi label to their sides, a label that by 1925 had a sound reputation among customers in the grape markets. Like Joe and the other shippers, Cesare accompanied his carloads east every fall and became acquainted with grape-dealers like Alleruzzo, establishing social as well as business connections. Although Cesare was quiet, sometimes even as taciturn as Joe Gallo, he befriended many growers, shippers, and grape dealers, who came to trust him for his honesty and fairness.

"My father told my brother and me over and over that this was the basis for success," Robert Mondavi recalled. "All the people he bought from and sold to in the grape business regarded him as a trusted friend. And in fact those friendships would become the foundation for his later wine business. He relied on them after Repeal when he transformed his grape-shipping business into a winery, and many of the dealers who had bought and distributed his grapes then bought and distributed his wine. Their faith in his grapes was transferred to his wine."

Ernest would later deny any similar connection between his father's grape-shipping business and Gallo wine. But after Repeal Ernest and Julio would find Joe's circle of associates useful. During this first shipping season, Joe met Charlie Barbera, another grape dealer who bought Gallo grapes and who, following Repeal, became the first wine distributor to buy Gallo wine. Barbera introduced Joe to Tony Paterno, who owned a popular Italian grocery and then began to buy Gallo grapes in addition to Mondavi grapes to sell in his store. (Paterno also made the hard-crust pies topped with tomato sauce, cheese, and slices of salami or pepperoni that he remembered from his childhood in Naples and was celebrated as the man who brought pizza to Chicago.) After Repeal, Barbera and Paterno became partners in the Pacific Wine Company, which bought and bottled bulk wine, including Gallo's.

Another respected grape dealer who became a longtime friend of Joe Gallo and his family was Jacob "Jake" Matkovich, who had come from Yugoslavia in the 1880s. He owned a grocery store on Wentworth Avenue in what would later become Chicago's China-town, and every autumn he went down to the grape market to stock up on grapes for his customers, fellow Yugoslavs who, like so many Italians, made wine every year. He also ran a small bank out of his grocery, and many shippers left their day's proceeds with him for safekeeping. His three sons helped in the grocery as well as in the grape business, but his son Guy was also working his way through law school.

"Old man Matkovich" and son Guy befriended Joe, and knowing the grape market and the city so well, they were able to give him useful hints about the business. Always deposit the checks for the day's sales immediately, they advised, or they'll probably bounce, or an unscrupulous customer might stop payment. They also warned him about the hoodlums who hung around the grape market waiting to rob the shippers of their cash. Run as fast as possible, either to the bank to deposit the money or back to your hotel, they said. And then, too, they told him to be careful when he was asked to make a delivery of grapes to a known syndicate bootlegger.

The grape market had a number of "toughs" who made their presence felt—either Al Capone's boys or members of the Genna gang, previously Capone's rivals but now his allies. Both groups were supplying grapes to an extensive network of tenement winemakers throughout Chicago (having distributed thousands of empty barrels to be filled by these "home winemakers," Sam Genna was called "the Wine King of Little Italy"). Instead of going through market dealers, these men bought grapes directly from shippers since they required such huge quantities. Al Capone's henchmen always placed large orders of grapes, and the grape shippers could hardly refuse when they were strong-armed into charging lower prices and were told to deliver them either to houses in town or to Capone's headquarters out in Cicero after dark.

" 'COD,' they'd tell the grape shipper," Alleruzzo recalled. " 'You get your money when we see the grapes.' "

Upon delivery of the grapes, a packet of money was handed over. All too often, the shippers were stopped on their way home and the payment repossessed. As a result, shippers and dealers alike began to carry weapons in the mid-twenties, and they often took circuitous routes back to their hotels. They drove through back streets with their headlights darkened; if they were on foot, they either had to outrun their pursuers or brandish a gun.

Sometimes they were asked to deliver the grapes directly to Al Capone's in-town headquarters at the Lexington Hotel on South Michigan Avenue. Every autumn Capone liked to dispense wine grapes to families in the Italian community, like a politician handing out gifts at Christmas; but instead of bottles of wine or liquor, Capone had lugs of grapes delivered, knowing how much local families appreciated having extra grapes for their annual winemaking. In turn they would give Capone bottles of their homemade wine to sample. Capone also liked to brag that he made his own wine, although it was suspected that he simply had various minions perform the task. Whatever the source, Capone always had a large supply of wine on hand, usually keeping it in barrels in the basement of the Lexington Hotel or at his base in Cicero. Whenever he entertained, he served the finest liquor smuggled in from Canada, but he always forced his dinner guests to drink what became known as "Capone's dago red" while he extolled the virtues of his homemade wine.

Since the supply of wine grapes was essential to its bootlegging, the syndicate had already muscled into the other grape markets at the Northwestern yards and the Rock Island yards. Grape shippers and dealers began to complain that the fix was in with auctioneers at those two yards. When a shipment of grapes wasn't sold within a few days, the shippers would then have to put them up for auction. But if an auctioneer had become part of the syndicate, he demanded bribes from the shippers to do well by them. Or if a gang member wanted grapes at a lower price, the auctioneer let him have them, cheating the shipper in the bargain. Capone and Genna gang agents were also trying to extort tribute or protection money from shippers—sometimes as high as $50 per car. They had already gotten away with this at the other two yards, and the police had done little about it. The independent shippers and dealers at the Santa Fe yards had so far been able to resist, but the mobsters hovering around Twenty-first and Archer streets were a threatening presence.

Though pleased with the profit he made his first season, Joe did not particularly enjoy his six-week sojourn in Chicago. The dangerous aspects of grape shipping frightened him; he hated running away from muggers; he was lonely staying in an ugly room at the State Street Hotel, one of the rundown establishments near the yards. (He paid seven dollars a week in advance, and if residents weren't prompt with their money, the manager tossed their belongings into the street.) He was tired of the sandwiches he bought from vendors for his meals (except when the Matkoviches invited him home for dinner). Even in his business dealings he had problems. He was impatient with haggling over prices. As part of the bargaining, grape dealers argued about his grapes' quality, and he sometimes lost his temper. He did not take criticism well, even when it was just part of the market ritual. He was not a good bargainer, some dealers said, because he either gave in to a lower price too quickly or became irate and walked away in a huff, losing the sale completely.

In later years, Ernest would say that Joe had so often exploded in rage and refused to have further commerce with dealers at whom he was angry that he lost all his best customers. He also bragged that he had been sent to Chicago in 1926 because his father "couldn't do business with anyone back there."

According to Paul Alleruzzo, however, many of the dealers remained on friendly enough terms with Joe that Ernest could rely on their goodwill for many years to come. He also recalled that the "Joe Gallo" label had significance in the market and that the Gallo shipping business was "medium to large" and competitive with that of Cesare Mondavi, who was already established in the grape market. "They were all big shippers of wine grapes," explained Alleruzzo. "The Gallos, the Mondavis, the Franzias . . . and our customers looked for the label. Joe Gallo's had a good reputation—people would see his name and the rooster, and his grapes were in big demand."

The next grape season, Joe had Ernest skip the first six weeks of the school year to accompany him to Chicago so that he could train him to take his place in the grape market in the following years. Ernest plunged into selling with enthusiasm and met the dealers whom his father had come to know—the Alleruzzos, Barbera, Paterno, and the Matkoviches. He seemed to enjoy the wheeling-dealing of the grape market much more than Joe, intent as he was on driving a hard bargain and proving his mettle.

"I remember that first year I met Ernie," said Paul Alleruzzo. "He was like a smaller version of his father. They both wore black fedora hats, and they walked almost exactly alike, their hands behind their backs, their shoulders hunched forward. His father was training him, but Ernie was already a shrewder businessman and a harder bargainer. We continued to buy Gallo grapes; the label was the same, and we knew that Joe would be managing the growing and shipping in California. So the grapes would still have his reputation for good quality. We just had to work harder to get the price we wanted. To this day Ernie never forgets the time that I forced him to take a dollar instead of a dollar ten per box in a car of overripe grapes. I proved that I could be as stubborn as he was, but he just hated to lose, I could see that."

Jake Matkovich also continued to buy Gallo grapes, and during the grape season he invited father and son to family dinners. Guy, the Matkoviches' son, and Ernest became friends as well, perhaps sensing in each other similar drive and ambition. The Matkoviches warned Ernest, as they had Joe, about the mob's attempt to infiltrate the grape market. Not only were the Capone and Genna bootleggers to be avoided, but Ernest should be on the lookout for syndicate men who would first contract for carloads of grapes, then try to extort protection money.

One morning Paul Alleruzzo saw two men approach Ernest. Alleruzzo recognized them as Capone's henchmen, but they told Ernest that they were dealers at the Northwestern yards. They had come to the Santa Fe yards, they explained, because they needed more grapes than were available in their market, and they wanted to buy all the Gallo cars that had arrived that day.

We can put you on a regular contract with us, Alleruzzo heard them say. *That way you'll have a guaranteed sale and a guaranteed price.*

Suddenly Jake Matkovich stormed into their midst. The Yugoslav had also seen these men accost Ernest.

You men clear out, Jake shouted. *We've told you we don't want you here. Don't come pushing our people around, or we'll call the police.*

A number of other grape dealers and shippers began to shout and threaten, and the two men flung themselves into their car and sped away.

Don't ever do any business with them, Jake now instructed Ernest. *Those guys are part of Capone's gang that's taken over the Northwestern and Rock Island yards. You sell them one box of grapes, you're under their thumb. Just stay away from them, and if they give you any more trouble, tell me or my son.*

While Ernest had his own suspicions about the strangers, he may also have dealt with Al Capone. One of his favorite stories in later years was about the delivery of grapes he made to "Scarface" himself at the Lexington Hotel. There was a kind of romance to seeing the infamous Chicago gangster and receiving money from him, money that Ernest recalled wrapping in a newspaper to fool any hoodlums as he hurried back to his room.

When Ernest returned to Modesto High in November of 1926 to

complete his senior year, his classmates remarked upon his new "city slicker" ways; they thought that the dark suit and black fedora that he now wore even gave him the appearance of the Chicago mobsters that he talked about seeing during his trip. He seemed even more aloof than before and approached his schoolwork as preparation for what he called "running the family business." He was elected to the HiY Club, a school honor and service organization whose members were chosen on "the basis of merit" and "good character." He served as secretary-treasurer of the Agricultural Club, and at its annual parent-student banquet, he gave a speech discussing "the agricultural outlook" of 1927. And in June of 1927, he graduated with honors, having received all A's and B's despite his extended absence the previous fall.

When Ernest reminisced as an adult about his Chicago experiences, he attributed his success in his first year to his marketing brilliance, ignoring the fact that his father's reputation as well as his business contacts had contributed to their profits. In his recollections, Ernest seemed to consider his aggressiveness as the mainstay of the Gallo business, his achievement in the grape market an early confirmation of his drive, ambition, and intelligence.

Even that first season in Chicago, however, grape dealers wondered just how far Joe Gallo's son would go to make a sale. One day Paul Alleruzzo saw him interrupt a fellow shipper when he was bargaining with a dealer over a car of his Zinfandels.

Hold on, mister, Ernest called out to the customer. *Try my grapes first. Taste how much sweeter they are.*

The customer wandered over to Ernest's car.

Now look at this box—the grapes are all perfect, Ernest said as he dumped the lug upside down and spread the grapes on the pavement. *Taste this one, and this one, and even this one, and it's from the bottom of the box.*

The other shipper had been watching this demonstration from his car, and now Ernest hailed him.

Come on, mister, empty one of your boxes, he challenged the older shipper.

The man could hardly refuse. Some shippers were known to "face" their boxes, putting moldy or overripe grapes at the bottom, then adding a layer of their better grapes. Upon inspection, the buyer would see only the good grapes and thus be cheated out of full value. This shipper did not have the reputation of "facing"; nevertheless, he had been challenged to prove that his boxes were of consistent quality. He brought a lug of his grapes over to Ernest and the buyer, then turned them out on the pavement.

Ah, ha! exclaimed Ernest, pointing to a few overripe grapes. *See, these are already getting soft.*

Only two or three, he objected. *The rest are fine.*

But the dealer contracted for a carload of Gallo grapes. Disappointed, the shipper walked away, shaking his head at Ernest's showmanship. It was not surprising to find a few overripe grapes in any box that had been "field" packed—that is, picked and directly loaded into boxes in the vineyards. Some larger shippers had warehouses to which growers delivered their grapes for sorting before being packed. But he knew that Joe Gallo, like himself, field-packed without sorting. Then how could Ernest be so sure that a box of Gallo grapes would have no overripe or moldy grapes? he wondered. When the story of this incident made the rounds of dealers and shippers, some claimed that Ernest must have repacked one box of "perfect" grapes that he could use in his demonstration.

After watching Ernest complete this sale, Paul Alleruzzo approached him.

"You always have a sales pitch, don't you, Ernie?" he teased.

"Isn't that what I'm here to do?" said Ernest defiantly.

When Ernest recounted stories about his early years as a shipper, he told them as parables of his marketing talents. One of his favorite anecdotes, later recited to his employees as well as to his sons, was of how he handled a customer who complained that some of the grapes in a Gallo carload were too ripe and were starting to rot. According to Ernest's son Joe, the dealer had demanded a refund for his purchase.

Okay, I'll give you some money back, Ernest said, *but only as long as you buy another carload.*

The customer agreed, Ernest would recall by way of reciting the moral that became another one of his favorite mottoes: "That's when I learned to turn a disadvantage into an advantage."

In the fall of 1927, in an effort to expand his market, Joe sent Julio to New Jersey to oversee the sale of Gallo grapes at the Kearny auction yards. While Ernest seemed to thrive on his new responsibility (this year Joe stayed in Modesto), Julio loathed his new assignment. He first went to Chicago with Ernest, then proceeded to the auction yards alone. As new shipments of Gallo cars came into Chicago, Ernest sent those grapes that remained unsold to Julio in New Jersey to be auctioned. Ernest enjoyed the high-pitched, competitive, and sometimes rough world of the grape market, but Julio found his first outing a trial by fire. Yet he was lucky enough to meet an older man who took him under his wing.

Jack Riorda was a fellow Californian who before Prohibition had been a winemaker for Italian Swiss Colony and now was the company's grape shipper. He knew many of the grape growers and shippers in California, including Cesare Mondavi and Joe Gallo, and he befriended Julio, introducing him to the ways of the auction yards and later taking him around to the homes of his winemaker customers in Hoboken. Italian Swiss Colony had added a winemaking advice service to their grape-selling venture. Riorda, as their representative, called on his grape customers and helped them with their winemaking.

To keep their bulk wine from going bad during the year, Riorda furnished his customers with packets of metabisulfite, the chemical wineries used to stabilize the fermentation process. He was also an expert blender of grape varieties, and Julio now learned about more sophisticated techniques of making the best-tasting wine by combining the flavors of different grapes. Riorda became a kind of mentor for Julio, who consulted the older man in future years as well. Just as Ernest would later depend on his father's acquaintances in the grape market for wine distribution, so Julio would rely on Riorda's advice, both about winemaking and about the wine industry in general.

In the fall of 1927, Riorda was already optimistic that the California wine and grape lobby would soon convince the government to exempt wine from Prohibition laws. He forecast the next step for grape growers and shippers—instead of sending grapes to the eastern market, they would be able to press them and ship the juice in tank cars. Shippers would no longer have to worry about grape perishability, and if the juice arrived in an already fermenting state, so much the better for their winemaking customers. Riorda was not alone in this prognostication; the grape and wine industry saw it as the coming trend.

Whatever Ernest and Julio had learned from their experiences in the eastern markets did not affect the way their father treated them when they returned home. While they had successfully assumed adult responsibilities and faced difficult situations alone in big cities, Joe still expected them to follow his orders and work the vineyards when they weren't in school. Julio was completing his senior year (and having a difficult time catching up in his chemistry class); Ernest was enrolled in agriculture courses at Modesto Junior College. It was less expensive for him to stay home, go to the local junior college, and also work for his father. Whether or not this was Joe's decision alone, Ernest later blamed his father for his lack of formal education —although he also liked people to know that he was essentially self-taught in a wide variety of subjects, particularly politics and economics. Eventually, though, he left school, claiming that the long hours required by his father interfered with his studies. In later years he seemed to hide his defensiveness about his lack of formal education by the often repeated sarcastic remark, "Just think what I could have done if I'd gotten a college degree."

Joe, Jr., was now old enough to be assigned chores as well. He hoed weeds in the vineyards, helped with irrigating and pruning, and every day drove the car to a nearby dairy to pick up the family's milk supply. Like most farm boys, he learned to drive at an early age, sitting on a stack of magazines so that he could see over the steering wheel. One day when he was nine, he was asked to take his mother to a doctor's appointment. A local cop stopped him downtown, but when Susie explained that she couldn't drive and needed to go to the doctor, the officer sent them on their way.

At the time, he was fun-loving and outgoing, so much so that sometimes he was kept after school for talking in class. In contrast to his brothers' hostile memories of Joe, Sr., he remembered seeking out his father to explain why he was late getting home.

"The teacher said, 'Joe, you have to stay,' " he told him.

"So she said, 'You have to stay,' did she?" his father repeated with a laugh, as if his son's minor mischief reminded him of himself as a boy. His father almost seemed to enjoy these stories, and Pete had no fear of either a beating or cross words from him.

His favorite chore was keeping the rabbits out of the vineyards. His father had given him two greyhounds, King and Queenie, to help him with his hunting. He went out with his shotgun and dogs in the early morning for an hour or so and usually brought back two or three rabbits he had shot for his mother to make into stew.

In their later recollections, Ernest and Julio seemed to condemn him for his love of hunting, as if this were a sign of indulgence rather than a chore his father had given him. More, they seemed to resent that he hadn't been asked to undertake the arduous work that they had been forced to do "before the age of ten." If, as Ernest and Julio later insisted, Joe, Jr., had an easier time of it, it was probably due less to favoritism than to the family's improved financial situation. Whereas the older boys had plowed at an early age, their father now hired ranch hands to take care of the livestock and help with the heavy fieldwork. Thus, instead of leading workhorses through the vineyards, Pete was given a pony to play with.

When the family drove to the State Fair in Sacramento to pick up Pete's present, Joe attached a carrier to the trunk of the Hudson. But the pony kicked through its slats. Joe's solution was to remove the rear seat and shove the pony into the car next to Ernest and Julio. Sitting on the floor of the car, they had to endure the pony's kicks all the way home.

The pony became a menace, at least to Pete. Whenever Pete tried to ride it, the pony bit and kicked him. Joe asked him why he never played with his pet, and Pete complained, "He's just a mean little devil." Joe eventually traded him to another farmer for a load of horse manure with no recriminations or arguments.

Pete grew up regarding his two older brothers as his heroes. He loved to go out with them into the vineyards; when they returned from the eastern grape markets they brought him presents and told him stories. They played with him and thought up interesting things to do. He grew up thinking that he wanted to be as smart and strong as they seemed to him.

He was aware of tension between his father and Ernest, although he didn't know why they seemed unable to get along. He thought of his father as obliging and loving. He was too young to perceive the reasons for their arguments or understand that Ernest wanted a stake in the family business, especially now that Prohibition laws applied to wine were about to change.

Mike Gallo had heard the forecasts of change in the wine industry, and in the spring of 1928 he decided to buy into an already existing winery. A winery would allow him to expand his bootlegging operation with more storage facilities, and when wine became legal again he would have a large supply on hand to market. Learning that the owners of the Woodbridge Winery had decided to sell, Mike moved quickly.

The Woodbridge Winery had been founded in 1904 when twenty-five Lodi area grape growers incorporated themselves as the Woodbridge Vineyard Association and built a facility on a ten-acre site along the Woodbridge Road to produce bulk wine from their annual tonnage. They also installed a distillery where they produced grape brandy, which they sold, along with their wine, to bottlers and distributors in San Francisco. During Prohibition, the Woodbridge Winery was officially closed, although its members were allowed to make wine in order to "salvage" any grapes that they had been unable to sell in the grape market. The Prohibition Office issued a permit, licensing the winery to store the "salvage" wine on the premises or sell some portion of it for "sacramental or other nonbeverage purposes." Because the acidity of wine stored in wooden barrels tended to rise after a few years, the winery was also permitted to buy fresh wine and brandy from other licensed wineries to blend with its reserves of wine and to fortify its sherry.

Despite these permits and legal exceptions, the winery was losing money. In 1928 its directors proposed to sell, and Mike asked an Oakland real estate agent to approach J. H. Thompson, president of the Woodbridge Vineyard Association, with an offer for both "the premises and the wine stored therein." As of January 1, 1928, the winery's assets included the physical plant and ten acres of land as well as 706,356 gallons of wine and 84,217 gallons of grape brandy and sherry. Mike's offer of $60,000 for the winery and its holdings was accepted.

Mike did not buy the winery alone. Celia invested—or thought she did—with money she had inherited from her mother. Several years earlier, Virginia Bianco had bought and moved to a bungalow on Scott Street in Oakland where she lived until her death in 1927, when she bequeathed the property to Celia along with thirty-seven shares of capital stock of BancItaly Corporation. Celia signed these stocks over to Mike for him to sell and to invest the proceeds in Woodbridge Winery shares. He did so, but put only one share in her name, the rest in his name. He sold shares to his real estate agent as well as to his lawyer, who negotiated the transactions for him. Mike then brought in John Severino (police records indicated that his real name was Cherino and Severino was one of his several aliases) to manage the Woodbridge Winery. (Severino had been an employee in his "San Pablo Malt and Bottling Company" and also ran a still for Mike on the premises of his late mother-in-law's Scott Street residence in Oakland.)

Finally, Mike approached yet another individual and offered him a one-third interest in the winery. Perhaps he wanted to reduce his own investment; perhaps he needed to bring someone into the venture whose name wouldn't set off alarms with the Prohibition Office. Perhaps he had gone looking for someone who had dealt with winery permits and knew how to handle federal supervision as well as the strictly regulated procedures of acquiring new wine for blending. Whatever his motives, Mike now found the perfect partner—Samuele Sebastiani, the Sonoma vintner and founder of the Sebastiani Winery.

Born in 1874 in Farneta, Tuscany, Samuele Sebastiani was taught to make wine by monks in a local monastery. Arriving in San Francisco in 1897, he moved to Sonoma to work in the rock quarries, then held a job at the Riboni family's Burgess Winery until it burned down in 1903. A year later he arranged to buy the Milani Winery from a distant relative, the contract a verbal one, sealed with a handshake, and the purchase paid for by the proceeds from his first year's sales. He sold wine door to door in the town of Sonoma, then later shipped bulk wine in fifty-gallon barrels throughout California and to eastern cities. In the same manner as Cesare Mondavi and Joe Gallo, he stenciled "Sebastiani" on the side of the barrels, and soon the name was well known in the wine business. By 1913, the winery had a capacity of three hundred thousand gallons, and Sebastiani was a wealthy, prominent, and ambitious wine producer.

Sebastiani always considered the winery a family business, and his two sons, Lorenzo, born in 1907, and August, born in 1913, were trained in winemaking from an early age. They grew up helping their father in both the winery and his vineyards with the expectation that they would carry on his tradition, much as European family wineries passed from one generation to the next. (This was not uncommon among Italian winemakers in California; in that respect Ernest and Julio would be the exception, inasmuch as they would make such a point of disavowing any tradition or legacy inherited from their father.)

Prohibition, however, disrupted Sebastiani's plans. Although his winery was also officially closed, it was bonded to manufacture and sell medicinal and sacramental wine. (The family joke was that many people must have become either sick or religious, given the amount of wine Sebastiani sold during these years.) Through these sales as well as by running a cannery and shipping some of his grapes to market, he was able to keep his winery going.

Optimistic that Prohibition against wine would soon end, he accepted Mike Gallo's 1928 offer to become a one-third partner in the Woodbridge Winery. (In 1930, when he acquired the Woodbridge Winery in his own name, Sebastiani would explain to his family that he had long thought it advisable to have a foothold in the Lodi region where grapes were less expensive and where, in the future, he could enter the sweet dessert wine, sherry, and grape-brandy markets. Nevertheless, according to both Sylvia Sebastiani and her son Don, the family was never aware that Sebastiani had already expanded to Lodi in 1928, nor had they ever heard about the Gallo-Sebastiani partnership.)

With Sebastiani's decision to join Mike Gallo in the Woodbridge Winery venture, they both acquired a large supply of wine and brandy in storage and sacramental, medicinal, and blending permits already granted and renewed every year.

On February 24, 1928, he and Mike Gallo recorded their partnership in the winery, the equity divided one-third to Samuele, two-thirds to Mike. On April 12, 1928, the new stockholders in the Woodbridge Vineyard Association met at the winery and elected their board of directors: Samuele Sebastiani, Michael Gallo, Mrs. Celia Gallo, and John Severino. Samuele was elected president. On April 17, they sent a letter to the Prohibition Administration in San Francisco advising them of the change in ownership and the new officers.

Thus, the Sebastiani and Gallo families were linked in a winery partnership several years before they became competitors in the wine industry. Mike had given the Gallos a foot in the door of a winery, years ahead of Ernest and Julio's proclaimed vision and independent achievement.

Although Joe was neither a board member nor a shareholder in the Woodbridge enterprise, on Sunday, April 8, less than two weeks after the winery purchase, Mike and Celia gave an elaborate Easter dinner honoring "Mr. and Mrs. Joseph Gallo." Mike was known to extol the benefits of having a brother who was a grape grower and shipper, and perhaps Joe planned to use the Woodbridge facility for crushing and storing grapes in greater volume. The Gallos traditionally gathered for Easter, but this occasion seemed to have had such significance that the invitation and menu (the Cresta Blanca, Chianti, and Angelica wines provided from Mike's plentiful stock were noted along with the dinner's eight courses) would remain among the family's mementos for the next sixty years.

Following this dinner, Joe's name began to appear routinely in the lists of California winemakers and grape growers and shippers who attended meetings to plan their lobbying campaign for a wine exemption. And Joe sometimes invited Ernest to join him on these occasions.

Ernest recalled such meetings, again using the incident to make a point about his own business acumen. "I watched these men who were leaders in the industry, the well-known California vintners," he later told one of his sales managers. "They would sit through the meal with full glasses of fine wine in front of them but never drank more than a sip. Most of them were Italians, Yugoslavs, men from backgrounds where the family always drank their own homemade wine. It became obvious to me that none of them really liked the fancy stuff they were served. What they preferred was something that tasted more like their homemade wine. And that's when I realized that for a winery to be really successful, it had to make the kind of wine that people wanted to drink, not the high-style, expensive stuff."

Ernest would later assert that his father had nothing to do with Mike Gallo's ventures; however, according to Joe, Jr.'s recollections, Mike was visiting Modesto often that spring, coming alone to discuss business. Julio himself confirmed Mike's presence when he later recalled that his uncle had been responsible for one of his long-remembered youthful triumphs.

Even during his senior year, Joe had continued to forbid Julio to join the track team even though he was one of the fastest and strongest runners at the high school. But when one of the other runners was injured, the coach asked Julio to try to convince his father to let him substitute. Mike was visiting the evening that Julio approached his father to ask for permission. At first Joe refused, lecturing him that there was too much work to be done. But Mike finally convinced him that the boy should have some fun. Joe finally relented but made Julio promise to be home by seven in the evening.

Entered in the 100- and 220-yard dashes and the half-mile relay, Julio ran as if he hadn't a care in the world. His legs were so strong from his fieldwork that he won blue ribbons in his first two events, and his relay team came in third. But it was almost seven-thirty before he arrived home. He rushed up the back steps and into the sun porch, already hearing his father's angry voice.

Sorry I'm late, Julio said, his voice pleading as he rushed into the room. *But look—I won!*

He held his hands up in front of him, each one clasping a blue ribbon, and walked toward his father.

Joe put down the strap he still kept to punish his sons and examined the ribbons. Julio's victory seemed to cheer him, and that night Julio avoided a beating. As a result of his track victories, he was awarded a letter at the end of his senior year, and he always remembered his uncle's presence and intervention with gratitude.

Nearly ten years old, Pete was aware of his uncle's discussions with his father that spring and summer of 1928. "I was only a kid," he said, "but I remember that Uncle Mike was quite a character. He had fancy clothes and he talked about shows he went to or baseball games with the mayor. He was always a lot of fun, but he also came to talk to my father about business. My father enjoyed having him around and listening to him, but he always said that Mike took too many risks, that his life was too up-and-down for him. I think we must have been making more money that year—and maybe it had something to do with Uncle Mike—because my father bought a new car, this time a Packard, which was bigger and fancier than the Hudsons we'd had before. Still, my father said he didn't want the dangerous life that Mike led."

Although Joe was removed from the action that his brother Mike seemed to enjoy, the Woodbridge Winery enterprise would have consequences for the Modesto Gallos; indeed, in the following year, Mike's circumstances would change, and it seemed that Joe would have to adjust accordingly. His impulsive decision coincided with—and appeared to be prompted by—Mike's difficulties. Despite what Ernest and Julio would later claim, the evidence suggested that their father might have been making plans for the future of the Gallo family business.

CHAPTER THREE

Mike's troubles began almost immediately after his purchase of the Woodbridge Winery. Neither he nor Sebastiani spent much time at the winery themselves. Mike left the day-to-day operation to Severino, and Samuele sent his twenty-one-year-old son Lorenzo, as well as his Sonoma winemaker, Enrico Castagnasso, to help supervise. By late May, Samuele and Mike had already received permission from the Prohibition administrator to purchase one tank car of 6,500 gallons of wine from the Louis Martini Winery and sixty barrels totaling 3,120 gallons of wine from the California Wine Association in San Francisco, both "for blending purposes only." But the delivery of the wine prompted a flurry of other activity on the premises.

Mike's delivery trucks arrived at all hours of the day and night; stenciled labels on barrels were sanded off the sides of barrels before they were loaded into the trucks; the distillery was once again running full time. With so much traffic and lights burning well past midnight, the winery began to attract attention in the community. Lorenzo Sebastiani had reassured the winery's neighbors that he was only blending sacramental and medicinal wine and fortifying the sherry in stock with new brandy—all perfectly legal, he said, but suspicions were still aroused.

Whether anyone reported such suspicions or whether Prohibition agents were already investigating Mike's activities, he and his employees began to have problems. One night he was delivering a load of wine to the port in Richmond, from where it was to be shipped to southern California. He was driving on small rural roads from Lodi, running without headlights, when he realized that a car was coming up fast behind him. He was sure that it was either a federal agent or a county sheriff. He punched the accelerator and hit speeds well over eighty miles per hour as he careened down the road, then across a field to a deserted barn where he hid the truck and waited. Two hours later he felt sure he had outrun the marshal this time, and he proceeded to Richmond with the barrels of wine.

John Severino, along with Pete DeRosi and Joe Silva, two other employees of Mike, weren't so lucky. On May 22, 1928, they were carrying a supply of wine from Woodbridge to Mike's East Bay depots when they were stopped by a traffic cop near Martinez in Contra Costa County. The officer arrested the men and confiscated eight fifty-gallon barrels of wine, all with faint remnants of stencil labels belonging to the California Wine Association. The truck showed no registration, but the officer discovered that it was listed in Alameda County criminal files because in 1927 it had been impounded in Oakland as evidence in an unsuccessful investigation of Mike Gallo's bootlegging.

Mike didn't hide his connection to this load of illegal wine. The next morning he arrived at the sheriff's office, asking, *Where are my men?* Then he confronted the arresting officer and demanded half his wine back.

Look, here, he said when the cop refused. *You may not realize who I am, but I intend to run liquor through Contra Costa County. I suggest you get together with me. I'll make it worth your while. I have all the other counties fixed, so you'd better play ball here.*

The Martinez policeman's response was to indict Mike along with his employees. All pleaded not guilty, and Mike posted $1,000 bail for each of them. But even this incident didn't particularly alarm Mike— as usual, his attorney began filing motions to challenge the search and seizure and quash the evidence.

However, the arrest seemed to attract further attention from the Prohibition Office. Another one of Mike's employees was arrested with a truckload of wine in San Francisco. Then, on June 21, 1928, federal agents raided a home on Scott Street in Oakland. John Severino opened the door to them, and in the basement they found a small still, nineteen fifty-gallon barrels containing sherry, muscatel, Cabernet, and Angelica wine as well as hundreds of cases of champagne, Cresta Blanca, Chianti, burgundy, and port. No wonder Mike had been so unstinting with wine at his Easter dinner party. This home was only a few blocks away from his own, and although its deed was registered to Virginia Bianco, the agents soon discovered that Mrs. Bianco was deceased and that her son-in-law was none other than Mike Gallo.

Again Mike was indicted, this time in federal court. But his lawyer convinced the judge that the raid had been illegal, since the agent had no warrant to search a "private dwelling." The judge dismissed the case, infuriating agents who were by now out for Mike's scalp. Setting other legal wheels in motion, they presented their evidence of Mike's activities to a federal grand jury, at the same time informing the *San Francisco Chronicle* of their probe:

ILLEGAL WINE GANG HUNTED

Federal investigation of the activities of Mike Gallo, alleged Oakland rum runner, has been launched here, it was learned today.

Ramifications of what is asserted to be a conspiracy to divert "blending" wine from a winery near Lodi to illegal channels, flooding not only Oakland but San Francisco with the product, has been brought to the attention of the Federal Grand Jury.

Federal Officers several weeks ago seized a truck alleged to belong to the Lodi winery with an illegal load.

One of the associates of Gallo, whose identity is unknown, was recently caught in San Francisco in a wine deal, and it is alleged that he is an agent of Gallo on the peninsula side of the bay.

On October 9, 1928, the grand jury was convinced that the agents' evidence at least proved there was illegal activity at the Woodbridge Winery, and it brought indictments against Mike Gallo, John Severino, Joe Silva, Pete Ozella, Enrico Castagnasso, and, last but not least, Samuele Sebastiani. They were charged with "prohibited and unlawful acts of possessing wine and of transporting it from a winery known as Bonded Winery No. 60, located at Woodbridge, in San Joaquin County, California, to divers places unknown."

All defendants pleaded not guilty and posted bail of $2,500 each. Subpoenas and petitions went flying; both the California Wine Association and the Louis Martini Winery were asked to provide records of their shipments of wine to the Woodbridge Winery. Telephone records and utility bills were subpoenaed. Prohibition agents continued to investigate, linking Mike to the ownership of various trucks cited in other bootlegging cases throughout the East Bay.

On October 20, 1928, Samuele Sebastiani's attorney petitioned the court to separate his case from those of the other defendants, arguing that he could not be charged on the basis of the testimony he had given before the grand jury in response to a subpoena the previous September. As the court case dragged on into 1929, Samuele also agreed to give evidence against Mike Gallo. He insisted that although he had known Mike for a year before they had gone into partnership, he was unaware that he was a "kingpin bootlegger." In April 1929, the indictments against both Sebastiani and his winemaker Castagnasso were dropped on the condition that they testify for the prosecution at the trial of "Gallo et al.," scheduled to begin August 29, 1929. Sebastiani's reputation as a respectable vintner and prominent citizen stood him in good stead. Although he was president of the winery and his son Lorenzo actually lived on its premises, they managed to keep their hands clean. Mike was left twisting in the wind; his years of disregard for the law and boastful tales of his exploits would now come back to haunt him.

The extent, if any, of Joe's involvement in the Woodbridge Winery scheme remained unclear and a matter for later speculation. He continued to grow and ship grapes, with Ernest and Julio handling the autumn shipment to Chicago and New Jersey once again. Whether Joe received more profits from wine grape sales or whether he earned more money through Mike's venture was never determined. Nevertheless, in 1928 Joe could afford $25,000 to buy 160 acres across Maze Road from the home ranch, and he and Susie also purchased 2,653 shares of Transamerica Corporation stock.

Ernest now began to argue even more forcefully that he should be made a partner in his father's business, and his insistence only heightened the tension between them. Joe was so irritated by his son's legalisms and "know-it-all" attitude that Joe, Jr., recalled hearing his father refer to Ernest behind his back as *l'avvocato*, Italian for "the lawyer." Even at the height of Joe's prosperity, he was not about to let his son have an equal role. Julio had graduated from high school and now worked for his father full time as well; both sons received $30 a month in wages. Joe only shouted at them when they voiced any complaints, and in the fall of 1929, he again sent them east on their annual shipping assignments.

Then two disasters struck. First Mike announced that he had been forced to sell his shares in the Woodbridge Winery to Sebastiani for

$40,000, $10,000 of which would be in a promissory note. (In 1930, the winery would be renamed Sebastiani Winery, the previous Gallo connection obliterated.) The judge had suppressed much of the evidence against Mike in his October 1929 hearing and in March 1930, the attorney general in the Northern District of California, reasoning that the suppression of evidence substantially weakened his case, dismissed the charges against Mike, Severino, DeRosi, and the others. Nevertheless, Mike had already sold his share of the winery to Sebastiani, and thus, in October 1929, Mike no longer had large winemaking and storage facilities at his disposal.

To make matters worse, the stock market crash on "Black Thursday," October 24, 1929, not only deflated the value of Joe and Susie's Transamerica stock, it also sent wine grape prices plummeting. Ernest and Julio both reported rock-bottom prices and few sales in the east. "Don't ship any more grapes," they advised their father. "There isn't a hope in hell of selling any more carloads. We'd have to give them away."

Joe was frantic. Tons of wine grapes remained on his vines ready to be picked. Carloads of grapes consigned by other growers stood at his shed awaiting shipment. He had to find a quick solution. Perhaps he came up with the idea on his own, perhaps Mike had suggested a new venture, as Ernest would later suspect.

Early one morning in late October, Joe, Jr., was awakened by the sound of grinding motor gears just beyond his bedroom window. He looked out and saw his father seated atop a tractor fitted with a front scoop. A rectangle was marked with stakes, and Joe was cutting into the soil, bringing up great mounds of earth and depositing it to one side. The hole was already three feet deep and getting larger and deeper by the minute.

The son dressed quickly and ran into the kitchen.

"What's Father doing out there?" he asked his mother. "Why is he digging such a big trench."

"It's for underground tanks," Susie explained. "Your father and Mike need it for the business."

Within the week Joe had framed the underground structure and poured the cement walls. The in-ground tank was divided into five chambers—three of them with about an eight-thousand-gallon capacity each, the other two with about a four-thousand-gallon capacity each. Immediately Joe began to crush grapes directly into the tanks.

It was a primitive process, but for several years winemakers had been installing underground tanks in which to hide their stores of wine. While many wineries had gone out of business during Prohibition, hundreds of small, clandestine wine operations actually came into existence at the same time, their only necessary equipment a wine press and underground tanks from which bootleg wine was siphoned into barrels and distributed. Winemaking had gone underground, and while the technology of cement tanks would be perfected later, even in their rudimentary form they became a crucial part of the bulk-wine business well before Repeal. In fact, recognizing an innovation in wine production and storage methods, even those winemakers who were not bootlegging began to install underground tanks in order to stockpile a supply of wine in anticipation of its predicted legalization.

"Underground tanks became essential during Prohibition," Robert Mondavi confirmed. "My father told me that hundreds of wineries went into business during those years, largely because of the use of those tanks. After all, over three hundred thousand acres of vineyards were planted during Prohibition, and not all of those millions and millions of tons of wine grapes were shipped to the grape markets. Especially after the stock market crash and grape prices fell so drastically, growers had to crush them into juice and store it just to save their harvest. So if you had an underground tank, you were in the winery business for all intents and purposes."

At the time, Pete had thought no more about his father's construction of the underground tanks. It was only as an adult that he would remember them already filled with wine in the summer of 1933. If his father had built them to store wine, then he had in effect started a winery in the fall of 1929. He was not alone in his recollection: Other Modesto residents, such as Anthony Ciccarelli, remembered talk about "underground tanks that Joe built out at his ranch." These people were not surprised when the existence of the wine tanks came to light many years later.

Ernest and Julio would later give their recollections of their father's activity in 1929. They explained that they had been in Chicago and New Jersey when their mother, in a panic, informed them that Joe was building tanks because, as Ernest claimed, "he had some understanding with Uncle Mike that they were going to make alcohol for whiskey." They had rushed home to put a stop to it, they said. Reminded that Joe had crushed grapes into the tank, Ernest insisted that his father was making pomace, a mash of grapes only a few feet in depth in the tank, from which to distill grape brandy. Nevertheless, he could not explain why thirty-two thousand gallons of tank capacity would have been necessary if Joe were simply planning to produce a small amount of pomace for brandy. Ernest declared that he had convinced his father to close up the tanks—that the "illegal" endeavor was too risky and upset their mother too much.

But if Joe were proposing to crush juice and store it for wine, not brandy, his endeavor would not have been illegal. The Prohibition Administration had just exempted grape juice from its regulations, a fact which no grape grower and grape shipper would have ignored in 1929.

This important change in the law had come about in great part through the efforts of the California Vineyardists Association, which had been organized in 1926 to promote the merchandising of grapes. Headed by Donald Conn, a railroad-traffic specialist from the Midwest, the CVA had recruited nearly ten thousand vineyardists for membership during its first three years. Conn lobbied the government to legalize the manufacture and marketing of grape juice and concentrate, and he finally convinced Herbert Hoover that the exemption would stabilize the grape market and relieve the grape surplus problem. Hoover and the Justice Department agreed that the manufacture and sale of juice to be used in home winemaking was not a violation of the Volstead Act. Having won this concession, Conn, in January 1929, formed Fruit Industries, which was composed of a number of existing and recognized California wineries, and it began to produce juice from grapes it contracted to buy from the members of the California Vineyardists Association.

Then in the summer of 1929, Conn won legal sanction from the Prohibition director for Fruit Industries' sale of concentrates. On August 6, 1929, the commissioner of Prohibition in Washington, D.C., sent a letter to his administrators and special agents throughout the country, advising them that the portion of the Volstead Act referring to fruit juices was to be disregarded and that "the shipment of juice grapes, grape juice and concentrates by carload lots, or otherwise, for resale . . . is entirely within the law." As a result, the Prohibition Office later eliminated the two-hundred-gallon limit on home wine-making, since the regulation of juice storage no longer applied.

The news of this change was announced in newspapers and farm journals throughout the state and was heralded as a last-minute reprieve for the California wine and grape industry. Since no limits on the amount of wine kept in storage would be imposed, vintners and grape growers alike could make and store wine in anticipation of Repeal. As Joe and Mike—and Ernest and Julio as well—must have realized, crushing grapes into juice for wine was the only way to salvage that year's harvest, and the tanks were a sanctioned method by which to store it.

If Susie had been upset during this time, as Ernest later recalled, it may have had less to do with anxiety about the underground tanks than with antipathy toward Mike and his treatment of Celia. For well over a year Celia and Mike had been fighting, and Susie took her sister's side, Joe his brother's. Celia had often complained about her husband's arrests and court battles, his late hours and womanizing, but his behavior in February 1929 had been especially cruel.

"He walked right in and said, 'There's another woman taking your place,' " Celia declared in her divorce petition. "Then he dared me, 'What are you going to do about it?' I told him I would divorce him, but that he wasn't going to get away with hiding his money."

Mike moved into a downtown Oakland hotel, and on April 6, 1929, Celia filed for divorce, charging adultery and mental and physical cruelty by enumerating incidents of name calling, face slapping, and associating with other women. She also cited his "late and unusual hours," but whether this was because of his "other women" or his bootlegging, Celia didn't elaborate. Still, the tacit threat to reveal the nature of his business loomed over the divorce action.

The community property that Celia listed indicated just how wealthy Mike was (indeed, bootlegging was one of the few businesses not dramatically affected in the early Depression years): household furniture worth $4,000; two Chrysler automobiles, also valued at $4,000; a promissory note of $10,000 from Sam Sebastiani (for the Gallo shares in the Woodbridge Winery); a promissory note for $24,000 from "a man named White."

The family home in Oakland was also included, but Celia went on to allege that Mike had concealed additional real property and deposited over $12,000 in bank accounts under various aliases. She also said that he had threatened to hide even further assets, and the judge issued a restraining order until a thorough financial investigation could be completed.

Mike suddenly had second thoughts about the impending divorce;

doubtless, he had no desire to divulge any details of his financial affairs, especially since he was still under federal indictment at the time. He begged Celia to reconcile, and a few days later she agreed, allowing him to move back into the family home. Within two weeks, however, Mike and his son Mario, who was now a partner in his business and another man-about-town, were again staying out all night. Mike said it was his work that kept him away, but Celia didn't believe him. Mike might have to make deliveries, but many of them were to speakeasies where he would meet his favorite and flaunted showgirls.

One day Celia answered the phone, and a Western Union operator announced that there was a telegram for Mike Gallo. She said that her husband wasn't home but that she would take the message. The phrases read aloud to her meant little, except that they involved a sum of money and an address.

When Mike came home, she said, she repeated the message, then asked what it meant.

"God damn it, woman!" he shouted. "You're just trying to find out where I have my money. You'll never find it, I tell you, never."

Celia was convinced that Mike had come back to her only to avoid the court's investigation of his business and income. Indeed, her feeling that it all came down to money was soon confirmed. At the same time that Mike and Joe were constructing underground tanks in October 1929, Mike told her he wanted her to borrow money from the bank for him. When she refused to sign the promissory note, he stormed out of the house, returning for dinner but still angry and sullen.

He smoldered in silence at the table; suddenly he slammed his fist down and broke his plate. More dishes went flying as he shattered them against the dining-room walls, and Celia cowered in the corner until Mike cursed her and stalked out of the house again.

A month later he came into the kitchen and tried to cajole her into signing the note. Once again she refused, and she later related his threat to the court.

"You bitch," he cried, picking up a knife from the counter. "I'll murder you as sure as you walk the streets."

That was enough for Celia, and on January 8, 1930, she refiled for divorce. She had been able to discover more of his assets, and this time her list of community property was more extensive, including Mike's San Pablo Bottle, Malt, and Supply Company, valued at over

$10,000; three trucks (the same trucks that federal agents had impounded during bootlegging arrests and were still trying to prove belonged to Mike); and three "touring cars" (the trucks and the cars together worth $6,500). She also raised her estimate of Mike's hidden money and stocks from $12,000 to over $50,000, adding that her husband owed her approximately $10,000 from 1928, when she had given him the thirty-seven shares of her BancItaly Corporation stock to sell and invest in the Woodbridge Winery. Mike, she had discovered, had put only one winery share in her name, and now she wanted the value of her original BancItaly bonds as well as half the money owed to him by Sebastiani.

Once again she asked for alimony and child support, this time for Gloria only, since Mario, although still under twenty-one, had married five days earlier, on January 2, 1930. The young couple was living over one of Mike's speakeasies (after 1933 it was called a "nightclub") where Mario also worked. (This marriage lasted until October 1933, when Mario's' wife Adelaide also filed for divorce, charging him with physical abuse—slaps and punches to the face and body—and mental cruelty.)

Mike countersued, disputing Celia's financial estimates and alleging that she had herself hidden money and stocks from the list of community property. He also accused her of pulling a gun on him in April 1929. When he had told her he was leaving her, he said, she had picked up a gun and shouted, "I'll kill you first, you son of a bitch." Only by promising not to leave her had Mike been able to stop her from pulling the trigger, he claimed. Where Celia had gotten the gun, Mike didn't say, although he had been seen carrying a gun while making his deliveries, and a pistol would be confiscated and identified as his in a subsequent arrest.

When Mike failed to appear in court on his cross-complaint, the judge ignored his countersuit. Celia was granted the divorce, awarded approximately $25,000 in cash as well as property, and assigned custody of Gloria, for whom Mike was ordered to pay $50 a month. Mike and Celia's divorce was newsworthy enough to merit a story in the *San Francisco Chronicle* on January 22, 1930. Mike was identified as a "wealthy Oakland merchant," and the item stated that the court settlement left him "the business of the San Pablo Bottle, Malt and Supply Company and other holdings."

"There were a lot of people who breathed a sigh of relief when they read that," recalled the son of a Livermore customer. "My father said that a number of people were afraid that the divorce would pull the whole operation down around Mike's ears. When he said he was fighting the divorce, they thought she'd blow the whistle. Better that he stayed out of a court battle, gave her the money and kept the business."

Rather than remain in the family home, Celia moved to an expensive apartment in San Francisco. It had a doorman and gilt-edged mirrors in the lobby and an elevator, and she hired Breuner's furniture store to decorate it. Obviously, Mike had been right to assume that Celia had saved extra money from the marriage: As everyone in the family agreed, she had always been as shrewd in money matters as her husband. After the divorce, she seemed to flourish, still giving festive dinner parties for family and friends in her new home. She and Gloria continued to visit Susie and Joe in Modesto, but the subject of Mike and his latest exploits was avoided.

Whatever the tension between the Gallo brothers and Bianco sisters, Joe and Ernest's continued hostility provoked even more conflicts. Their discussions often turned into angry debates, then shouting matches. Joe was impatient when any statement of his was analyzed, refuted, or held up to ridicule. Julio didn't argue as Ernest did, but he also considered his father unfair and stubbornly resistant to any of his sons' good advice. Years later both sons remembered the same occasion that for them marked the height of their father's incompetence and stubbornness.

In the winter of 1929 Joe ordered them to prepare his recently purchased 160-acre vineyard for replanting. This time Joe at least admitted that a horse-drawn plow was inadequate to the job and decided to rent a large tractor and scraper. But he also had a plan to save money: Ernest, Julio, and Joe, Jr., would do everything that had to be completed before the ground could be scraped—clearing weeds, removing stumps, pulling roots.

Then I'll rent the equipment and you'll run it twenty-four hours a day. We'll save on the length of the rental, he said.

But we shouldn't be scraping at all in the winter time, Ernest argued. *The soil is too wet, and you'll ruin it by doing this now.*

Joe overrode Ernest's objections and stomped back across the road and into the house.

Ernest, Julio, and Pete prepared the acreage as their father had ordered. When the land was ready to be scraped, Joe rented the machinery for the weekend. Ernest and Julio fired up the tractor and began their marathon—twenty-four hours around the clock, running the tractor and scraper.

Just as Ernest had predicted, it began to rain in the middle of the night. The boys went to the house and tried to convince their father that they should stop. They might be saving money, but they would ruin the soil—ultimately they would lower the yield of the vineyard —if they continued in the wet. Joe refused to listen and sent them back to work.

They finished the scraping in two days, and Joe returned the rented equipment, pleased at how much money he'd saved. That spring the boys planted and grafted Zinfandel and Carignane vines. It would be three years at least before the vineyard came to full yield. But even in its first growth, the vines looked stunted; the wet soil had been too compacted by scraping in the rain. In later years Julio would often remark, "That vineyard was always poor because the father killed the soil. It took years to subsoil and try to recover the land."

Ernest continued to irritate Joe by persisting in his demand to be made a partner as well as to make plans for starting a winery. Sometimes Joe said he would think about it; more often than not, he shouted his refusal, and father and son would be at it again.

Ernest had stepped up his campaign in 1930, because he was aware that everyone else in the industry said that wine production would soon be a most profitable business, and other families were already preparing for this eventuality. Ernest had met Giuseppe Franzia and his sons through Joe and saw them every season in Chicago. He now heard that they were already planning to resume their Ripon winery after Repeal, with the sons given full partnerships in the enterprise.

He would have hoped for the same from his father, but when Joe continued to refuse him, he turned his attention to one of the Franzias' two daughters, nineteen-year-old Amelia, whom he had once met two years before. She was short and stocky with light brown hair and blue eyes, and while she couldn't be called pretty, she was good-natured and loyal, a down-to-earth, old-fashioned daughter. Ernest now asked her father if he might take her to the movies.

"Only if you take Ann with you," was the reply. Ann was two years younger than her sister but came along as the official chaperon on Ernest and Amelia's first date.

The Franzias seemed wary of Ernest's interest in Amelia, but Ernest continued to pursue her, at the same time arguing his case even more stridently with his father. If he were going to propose marriage, he needed to know whether he could expect a raise in salary and whether Joe was going to develop a family winery in which he would be made a partner. From one day to the next, Joe changed his mind; either he postponed the decision or erupted in a temper tantrum at his son's repeated questions. Ernest was frustrated: his father seemed to undermine his every attempt to shape his future.

One morning Ernest and Julio had it out with their father. They were ready to present him with an ultimatum; either they would be given a raise and equity in the business or they would find jobs elsewhere.

Joe had been in the vineyard behind the house, firing his shotgun at rabbits to keep them out of the vines. When he returned, he found his sons waiting for him at the rear door.

At the same time, Pete Cisi, a friend of the family who sometimes did odd jobs for Joe, had just driven up in his old Dodge touring car. "Cheesey," as he was nicknamed, started to get out of the car, and, as he later recalled to Rudy Wagner, he realized that Ernest and Julio were in the midst of an argument with their father. Their voices were raised. Ernest's hands chopped at the air.

A *partnership or not?* Ernest demanded loudly. *Otherwise, I quit!*

That's right, Julio said more quietly. *We need an answer.*

Joe's face flushed red. *You'll work for me if I say so. Don't you threaten me, Ernest.*

Joe, please! Susie called, her husband's shouts bringing her from the kitchen.

Shut up, Joe screamed. *Not another word or I'll kill you.*

He lowered the shotgun and walked toward her. She edged toward the vineyard, but Joe kept advancing.

Run, Mama, run! Ernest and Julio cried.

Susie turned and fled into the rows of vines. Joe ran after her, waving the shotgun. Ernest and Julio sped after their father, shouting, *Don't shoot our mama! Don't shoot our mama!*

Cheesey rushed after them to the side of the vineyard. He could see the top of Susie's head as she ducked in and out of the vines. Joe was gaining on her with the boys in pursuit.

Suddenly Joe wheeled in his tracks and aimed his gun at them, shouting that he would shoot them too. Ernest and Julio turned and dashed back down the row and out of the vineyard and into the house. A few minutes later Joe walked out of the vineyard, panting. He stopped when he saw his old friend, then without a word, he proceeded to the back steps, leaned the gun against the side of the house and sat down, burying his face in his hands.

Cheesey went to his side to calm him but Joe wouldn't look up. Soon Susie came out of the vineyard and approached Joe tentatively. He shook his head, as if in disbelief at his own behavior, and she went inside.

A minute later she ran out of the house. *The boys are gone! The boys are gone!* she exclaimed.

Ernest and Julio were already en route to the bus station in Modesto, after hitching a ride into town. They took the first bus out of Modesto, heading south.

They were worried about their mother, but they could do nothing as long as she tolerated their father's behavior. They decided to strike out on their own, and since vegetables were coming into season in southern California, they thought they could get work there, perhaps even find farming prospects for themselves. They traveled all day and night, and the next morning arrived in El Centro, the hub of vegetable farming in California's great Imperial Valley just across the border from Mexicali, Mexico.

Upon their arrival they went to a hotel, a pink stucco building at the center of town. At the desk they asked the owner how much a room cost.

"A dollar a night," the man said.

"Can't you make it fifty cents a night?" asked Ernest.

The man looked them up and down. "You guys must be really hard up."

"We sure are."

Fully aware of how poor people were these days, particularly in a farming community like his own, the man relented and agreed to the reduced rate.

In later years Ernest tried to locate the hotel owner, so grateful was he for the man's generosity. He asked one of his distributors in the Imperial Valley to search for him, explaining the man's good deed by reminiscing about why he and his brother had spent the spring of 1930 in southern California.

"That's when the troubles started," Ernest said, referring in his customary way to the problems with his father as "the troubles" and to his father as "the father," as if to deny any emotional involvement.

"The father chased us around the vineyards with a shotgun," he explained. "Julio and I started running and we didn't stop until we got to El Centro. That's why we spent two months sitting on our asses in that hotel."

While in El Centro, Ernest and Julio called their aunt Celia in San Francisco every week since they did not want to risk speaking to their father. Celia relayed their messages to Susie, then reported back to them.

Your mother's pleading with you to come home, Celia told them. *She misses you so much.*

At first Ernest dug in his heels. He replied that they missed their mother, but they couldn't tolerate their father's temper and unfair treatment.

Later Celia announced that their father was now begging them to come home, too, that he promised things would change.

Ernest and Julio were still unconvinced, but they were not finding work because the Depression had hurt so many farmers in the area. They were running out of money, and finally they decided to leave. Not yet ready to return home, they took the bus to San Francisco and stayed with their aunt Tillie while they continued to talk to their mother by phone. One day Susie came to the city to plead with them. Once again she insisted that Joe had promised to change, in fact had changed. She was in tears as she repeated how much she needed her boys, how much their father needed them, how much their little brother missed them. Since their mother was so convinced that things would be different, they finally agreed to return.

Before they went near the ranch, however, they stopped at their brother's school to talk to him during his lunch hour.

"How are your mother and father getting along?" Ernest asked him.

"Fine," said Joe, Jr., with a shrug.

He was overjoyed to see them. He had been mystified and saddened when they had left, and since he had been at school, he hadn't understood what had caused their sudden departure. He had no idea why Ernest and Julio were questioning him or why they seemed so worried. He'd witnessed no arguments between his parents. He was only aware that his mother missed Ernest and Julio, as did he. If their coming home depended on it, he could honestly say that things were peaceful at home.

"They're getting along fine," he said again when Ernest repeated the question.

"Is your father taking care of your mother?" Ernest asked again.

"Sure," Pete repeated. "No problem at all."

Ernest and Julio were convinced, and Pete was relieved when they appeared at the dinner table that night. The family returned to its usual routine. Ernest and Julio worked for their father throughout that summer and into the fall, having been reassured that their father would do right by them.

Joe's mood was brighter, too, since the 1930 grape harvest was a good one. He had a larger supply of grapes from his own vineyards, including two new ones that he had acquired, one in Stockton and one in Ripon. He had gained possession of these properties when the owners, each elderly Italian widows, had taken crop mortgages with him and then failed to repay him. Joe had won the lawsuits brought by their children, who charged that their mothers were incompetent and had been coerced into signing such agreements. But when the grape-growing community heard about them, they muttered about Joe's questionable business dealings.

Joe and Ernest had joined Donald Conn's California Vineyardists Association and were appointed official shipping agents for the organization in the autumn of 1930. After the disastrous 1929 grape market, Conn had offered CVA members a guaranteed price for their grapes as long as they paid a "stabilization fee" of $1.50 per ton. As CVA agents, Joe and Ernest were expected to collect these fees from growers whose grapes they shipped, then send the money to the CVA offices. A lawsuit filed by the CVA the following year, however, alleged that the Gallos had withheld a full accounting of fees collected on the tonnage consigned to them.

Joe initially objected to the complaint, declaring that he had paid $277.36, but then had Edward Taylor file an accounting, which indicated that $775.70 was still due for stabilization fees collected. However, in the accounting was an explanation for the deficit payment: One part of the shipment "brought red ink with no funds in hand from which to deduct any fees." Although Joe may have thought that if the grapes arrived as liquid, he was excused from paying fees on these cars, he finally had to settle the suit with a check of $775 to the CVA.

"Red ink" usually described grapes that arrived at market so overripe that they were in liquid form and unsellable. But was it possible that the grapes had been turned into "juice" or "concentrate" and shipped in that form to the eastern market—a method of shipment and sale that was neither an unusual or illegal practice that year?

California growers had begun to ship and sell the legal juice as "grape concentrate" in enough volume to attract the attention of the crime syndicate. Alarmed that he would lose control of the wine business in Chicago, Capone reportedly threatened to kill several California shippers if they shipped juice or concentrate without making a deal with him first. When Donald Conn's Fruit Industries began to produce and sell concentrate, Capone tried to coerce him into surrendering a percentage of the sales, then allegedly sent him death threats. Conn announced that Fruit Industries would not be frightened into making deals with "racketeers," and news stories about these threats prompted even greater demand for Fruit Industries' product, known as Vine Glo and sold in eight varieties (Port, Virginia Dare, Muscatel, Tokay, Sauterne, Riesling, Claret, and Burgundy).

In September 1930, the Justice Department suggested to J. Edgar Hoover that it might be advisable to offer Donald Conn protection, and the next month Hoover assigned Chicago agents to interview grape dealers and shippers. At first the agents simply compiled a list of the major shippers who, they were told, had been contacted by Capone's henchmen, Tony Romano and Manny Schraiberg.

These two were exacting "tributes" of $50 per car in the yards. Joe Fusco, who had been the head of Capone's beer operation, now supervised wine as well and was allegedly trying to extort levies on any grape concentrate or juice sold in the Chicago area.

Appearing on the list of shippers to be interviewed by the FBI was Joe Gallo. The FBI wanted to talk to him because he was known as one of the larger shippers at the Santa Fe yards. Whether he and his agent, Ernest, had also attracted the syndicate's attention because they were shipping and selling concentrate wasn't determined. Unable to locate Joe Gallo (since he no longer came to Chicago), the FBI agents seemed unaware that Ernest had taken his father's place and did not interview him.

But Ernest must have been worried about something—like other grape dealers and shippers, he decided to protect himself. Perhaps he was alarmed by the growing violence at the yards; perhaps he himself had been threatened by the syndicate, either because he refused to pay protection money for his grapes or because he, too, was selling juice or concentrate. Whatever the reason, it was during this 1930 season in Chicago that he bought a gun—a .32-caliber Smith & Wesson revolver.

He told Paul Alleruzzo at the time and subsequently confirmed that he had purchased a gun in Chicago. But what eventually became of this weapon, he could not recall when asked about it in later years.

Ernest would also deny that he and his father had been producing and selling "juice" as early as 1930. However, in intervening years and among winery associates, he would sometimes refer to his Prohibition activities. According to one of his marketing executives, when the winery ran afoul of federal shipping or distributing regulations, Ernest would quip with a knowing wink, "Label it juice or jelly or concentrate like we did in the old days."

After wine tastings when he was at his most expansive, Ernest especially enjoyed reminiscing with Charlie Rossi. (Connected to the Franzias through his first wife, Charlie was later dubbed "Carlo Rossi" for the brand label on one of Gallo Winery's lower-tier wines.) Rossi had also begun his career in the wine business, becoming a grape shipper during Prohibition as well, and he liked to tell winery associates how he had first met Ernest. He had heard that the Italian-American Club in Virginia, Minnesota, needed an extra supply of grapes. Usually the club bought from Mondavi, but Rossi traveled by bus in freezing weather to reach Virginia first and make the sale. "But Ernest had heard the same thing," Rossi would explain. "When I got to the club, I saw this short little guy leaving. He introduced himself and said he'd just signed up the grape order. I don't know how he did it, but he beat me there and scooped my sale. That's when I realized that Ernest would go far."

During Ernest and Rossi's reminiscences, employees became convinced that before Repeal both of them had been involved in shipping wine under "juice" labels. At other times, though, Ernest said that his father had made and sold wine but denied any implication of bootlegging by telling two of his executives, for example, that his father had been licensed to make sacramental and medicinal wine. No license for Joe, Sr., was filed in the Prohibition Office records, however, and in later years Ernest would contradict such informal remarks with his statements that his father never sold wine or shipped juice during Prohibition.

Mike would also suggest that he and Joe, Sr., were making, selling, and shipping "juice" during the years just before Repeal. When Mike was in his eighties, he liked to brag about his nephews' success by recalling his and his brother's early wine operation.

"We never thought when we started that it would become anything like this phenomenal company," Mike told a Gallo regional sales manager who delivered a monthly supply of Gallo cream sherry and Paisano wine to his rusted house trailer in Henderson, Nevada. "Back then when we were selling bulk wine and grapes, it was just a smart way for Joe and me to make money. We made good money, too, from all that juice, but it was nothing like the boys' big company."

Julio was not sent to New Jersey in the fall of either 1930 or 1931, which would also have been logical if Joe had already moved into the "juice" business. In previous years any unsold carloads of grapes were "salvaged" by Ernest's rerouting them from Chicago to Julio at the auction yards. If Joe were already salvaging excess grapes in California by crushing them into "juice" and either storing it in the underground tanks, distributing it through Mike, or shipping it East for sale, then Julio's assignment in New Jersey would no longer have been necessary.

In 1930 Ernest also let grape dealers know he intended to go into the wine business after Repeal. He was sufficiently confident of his future to announce that he was planning to marry the following year.

"Who's the lucky girl?" asked Paul Alleruzzo.

"Amelia Franzia," he replied.

"Giuseppe Franzia's daughter? Well, you son-of-a-gun," Alleruzzo said, knowing that the Franzias were wealthy and sure to reopen their winery after Repeal. "You'll be fixed for life, Ernie. I guess if your father won't start that winery, your father-in-law will."

He didn't add what he was thinking—that Ernest was about the shrewdest businessman he knew, even when it came to marriage.

Ernest and Amelia began to make plans. They would live with Ernest's parents until Joe could help Ernest build a new home across the road. Amelia was already a good cook, but Susie began to teach her how to make her son's favorite recipes. Ernest and Amelia were married on August 23, 1931, and Susie took a photograph of her three sons posed in front of the Gallo front porch. Ernest and Julio wore new three-piece black suits and white hats that they had bought at Roos-Atkins in San Francisco. Little Joe stood between them, dressed identically. (He had insisted on this, but was upset that his outfit had come from the Emporium; he wanted to be like his brothers down to the last detail.) After the ceremony and a small reception at the Gallos' home, Ernest and Amelia boarded the train for Chicago; they would combine their honeymoon with Ernest's annual duties in the grape market.

When they returned home in December, they found Joe in another dark mood. That October a Kansas City federal judge had ruled that anyone selling grape juice and concentrate "containing more than one-half of one percent alcohol was guilty of violating the Volstead Act." Conn and Fruit Industries set out to overturn the decision, but in the meantime "juice," concentrate, and other wine-related products were again illegal. Prohibition agents then stepped up their arrests in a last-ditch effort to crack down on bootleggers.

Mike Gallo was one of their obvious targets. In April 1930 agents had raided one of his distilleries on a ranch outside of Stockton, noting in their report that he was head of the operation: "He has the general reputation of being very wealthy, having made all his money from the illicit liquor business. His automobiles and his home are registered under other names, but he is co-proprietor and manager of the San Pablo Bottle, Malt and Supply House and the Blue Label Malt Shop . . . and is reputed to own several wineries."

On August 14, 1931, Mike was arrested in Albany, near Oakland, driving a truck carrying six hundred gallons of wine. At the time, Mike identified himself as "George Bruno" and offered the cop $1,000 to let him off. The cop refused and later traced the truck and "Bruno's" fingerprints to Mike Gallo. When two of Mike's trucks carrying nine hundred gallons of wine were seized and his employees were arrested on November 13, 1931, Mike arrived at the El Cerrito police station and was overheard asking his driver, "Why didn't you pay the officers with that $300 you had?" The arresting officers soon discovered that the truck involved in this incident was the same truck in which "George Bruno" had been arrested and matched Bruno's fingerprints with those of Mike. The Justice Department then joined the investigation and cited their interest in Mike Gallo's son and brother as well.

Mike was again arrested, at his home, on December 18, 1931, and hundreds of printed wine labels were found there. Agents then raided another one of his depots, arresting his employees and confiscating a large cache of assorted wines, labels, bottling equipment, and capping machines. Mistakenly assuming that he would be treated lightly,

Mike pled guilty and posted $2,500 bail, but with his plea, federal agents broadened their investigation. Indeed, the *San Francisco Chronicle* ran a story the next day in which federal officials announced that "they had captured one of the 'big shots' in an East Bay wholesale liquor business and head of a Coast chain of malt shops." Ten days later another story appeared recounting a second indictment against Mike in Los Angeles where one of his trucks had been seized while making a delivery of three hundred gallons of wine and brandy. At the delivery site, officers found Mike's Chrysler as well as a suitcase with "MG" monogrammed in gold and a loaded .45 Colt revolver, which Mike later confirmed was his. The truck's driver was allowed to plead guilty to the reduced charge of "transporting liquor" in exchange for testimony about Mike's "state-wide operation."

On January 29, 1932, another one of Mike's liquor depots was raided. Earl Warren, then the Alameda County district attorney, first came to political prominence by announcing that he would clean out "the bootleggers and gangsters" from his county. He, too, had become interested in Mike Gallo's activities, and accompanied by deputy sheriffs as well as federal marshals, he raided the premises on Twenty-third Street in Oakland, the alleged "operation base" and "wine warehouse" of "Gallo's coast-wide liquor ring." According to a news story in the *Oakland Tribune*, Mike was at the location and was again arrested. Among the evidence confiscated were eleven fifty-gallon barrels of wine. Warren was exultant, announcing that "this was only another . . . step in uncovering and halting the extensive activities of the wine baron Mike Gallo."

Coincident with Mike's problems with the law and the continuing Justice Department investigation, Joe seemed increasingly worried, according to Ernest and Julio's later recollections. But whatever the source of Joe's anxiety, he didn't explain to his family at the time; he retreated into a shell during the first months of 1932 and was unwilling to make plans. He changed his mind about the two projects that he and Ernest had previously discussed. Not only did he refuse to proceed with the building of a home for Ernest and Amelia, but also, according to Ernest, he seemed reluctant to make plans for starting a winery after Repeal. According to Ernest's recollections, whenever he urged his father to proceed, Joe turned noncommittal and indecisive.

By the winter of 1932 the California wine industry was certain that Prohibition would be voted out in the next election. But Joe refused to give a definite answer, Ernest would later declare. Over the next weeks, Ernest and Joe fumed at each other. Joe, Jr., sensed the tension in the family and was perplexed. As usual, no one explained, and he knew better than to ask. Then one day he returned from school and found his mother and father gone. They were away on a trip, his brothers told him, but offered no reason for their sudden departure.

A numbing silence descended. The parents' disappearance was treated as a secret, not to be discussed, and even as an adult, Joe, Jr., was mystified by their sudden flight. There was an emptiness at the heart of the family, an inexplicable blank in the story. Years later, he remembered that spring and the following year as a bewildering miasma of unexplained events that he never understood.

On March 4, 1932, Joe and Susie returned home. But the mystery of their absence only deepened when Joe explained that the day before he had bought vineyards in Fresno, sixty-five miles south of Modesto. The property was called Fruitvale Ranch, and the next day Joe and Susie packed up a few boxes and suitcases as well as two cot mattresses from the shed and moved to their new home. Pete, they said, would remain with Ernest and Amelia and Julio until his school term was finished.

It was all straightforward yet still puzzling. Their move was kept a secret from the rest of the family as well as from Modesto neighbors and acquaintances. The Fresno ranch house had neither telephone nor electricity. Once they had left, they dropped out of sight and out of contact, almost as if they were going underground. Pete accepted the situation at the time, but wondered if it had something to do with Ernest. "Maybe Father made an agreement with Ernest when he came back from El Centro," he thought. "Perhaps Father said if they didn't get along again, he and Mother would leave the next time."

From an adult perspective, however, the explanation hardly seemed adequate. Why would a man who so insisted upon being the head of the family relinquish his home to his son? If they weren't getting along, why wouldn't the son leave? Why would a mother who had decorated the home with such loving attention agree to the move? Why would they live in a house with no telephone, virtually out of touch with family and friends?

When the school term was over, Joe arrived as promised to take Pete and his dog, Pooch, to the Fresno ranch. Joe loaded up the back of one of the Modesto pickups with a few more boxes and a cot. Then he piled magazines on the front seat and told his son that he would be driving the truck to Fresno. While Pete often took the pickup around the vineyards or to the neighbors' ranches or even into town, he was surprised that his father was asking him to drive all that distance. And he wondered why Ernest and Julio weren't taking the truck down for their father.

If Pete had been bewildered by his parents' move six weeks earlier, he was even more shocked when he saw their Fresno home. It was old and dilapidated, the front porch sagging badly, the steps falling into the front yard. To one side was a tank house, and across the yard from the house were two ramshackle cottages for farmhands. To the rear were two barns and a hog pen and several hundred yards away were two small warehouses. All of the outbuildings were in disrepair, their wood rotting and paint peeling.

Inside the main house the walls were dark and badly stained. There were only a few sticks of furniture, rickety kitchen chairs, a scarred wooden table, and rusted iron camp beds. Pete couldn't imagine his mother living like this—it was in such stark contrast to their comfortable Modesto home. But he said nothing when his mother greeted him with a warm hug, not even when she lit a candle because of the lack of electricity. He made no comment either when he noticed that suitcases and cartons in the house remained unpacked. Was his mother so unhappy here that she was refusing to settle in? Or were his parents leaving things packed up so they could leave quickly? Neither his mother nor father offered an explanation.

As the summer weeks went by, Pete pushed aside his questions, even when he noticed that Ernest never seemed to visit and Julio came only a few times. His parents had begun to relax; they often took him to the movies in Fresno, buying a bag of dried shrimp at the Italian market to eat during the film, then stopping for an ice cream on the way back. Despite the rundown house, their family life seemed normal to Pete, and in contrast to Ernest and Julio's recollections, he did not consider his father depressed or worried during these months. They met a few of their neighbors, including Peter Brengetto, a dairy farmer who lived a few miles down Whites Bridge Road. The Brengettos were also Piedmontese, and the families began to exchange visits. There were family dinners, and sometimes Peter Brengetto dropped by for a glass of wine and a neighborly chat with Joe, usually bringing his son Gino along.

Ernest and Julio were left in charge of the Modesto vineyards and shipping business. In September of 1932, Ernest first went to New

York to sell melons that his father shipped to him, then returned to Chicago. Having disliked the rough and tumble world of the grape market during her honeymoon, Amelia didn't accompany him this time but stayed with her family in Escalon while he was away.

Julio was alone at the Maze Road house. While he was usually busy with the grape harvest, one evening he ventured to a dance in town. There he recognized a young blond woman who gave him shy glances from across the room. He remembered her face from high school, and mustering his courage, he introduced himself and asked her to dance. She accepted and introduced herself as Aileen Lowe. (Julio has always pronounced her name A-leen, with a long "a," while she calls herself I-leen, as does the rest of the family.)

Even before Julio had introduced himself, she knew who he was. During her sophomore year she had always taken the same route between classrooms just to catch a glimpse of the handsome senior with the chiseled jaw and intense dark eyes who seemed to watch her as she walked by. Through friends she had learned that this was Julio Gallo, but since her parents hadn't allowed her to go out on dates when she was in high school, nothing had come of this mild flirtation. Now nineteen, she was working in a Modesto department store (her godmother had encouraged her to go to college, but her family couldn't afford it during the Depression). She was still living at home, and although her parents were rather strict and tended to be overprotective, they now allowed her to go to town dances with her girlfriend.

Born April 29, 1913, in Manteca, Aileen was the daughter of Nilus and Anna Lowe, who had moved to downtown Modesto when she was seven. Her father was a mining engineer who also sold insurance, and her mother took care of the house and the two children, Aileen and her younger brother. She thought of herself as a city girl, and in high school she knew few of her classmates, who, like Julio, lived out in the country. But once she and Julio began to dance and he told her about the vineyards and the grape harvest, she was fascinated. She knew virtually nothing about grapes, much less about wine, since her family never served it at home. But as he talked, she sensed a maturity and strength well beyond his years, and she gladly accepted his invitation to the movies the following weekend.

Her parents were also impressed with Julio's quiet manners when he arrived to pick her up. But driving away from the house, he asked if she would mind if they skipped the movies. He had to stop by the shipping shed to pack a carload of grapes.

Aileen was raised to believe that a woman should defer to a man, and she readily agreed. Besides, as she would later reminisce, she was just happy to be with him.

At Zim's Station, where the trains stood for loading, Aileen watched Julio lift box after box into the freight car. "How strong he is," she thought to herself, the image of him on their first date already engraved in her memory.

They continued to see each other throughout the winter months. While her parents, especially her father, had taken a liking to Julio, she had not met his parents. The family situation seemed unusual, but Julio did not explain why his parents were living in Fresno or why he saw them only when he was delivering farm equipment needed by his father. Julio had, in fact, confided in his mother about Aileen but never brought her along on these trips. He did invite her to the Maze Road house for the family's traditional Christmas *bagna cauda*, and she then met Ernest and Amelia. Aileen enjoyed the Italian ritual: dipping pieces of crusty bread into a pan of warm garlicky oil, then drinking red wine between dippings. But why the parents weren't present, she still had to wonder; neither brother mentioned their absence, and she felt too shy to question Julio further.

That spring she and Julio became engaged. Whether because of her parents' financial problems, or because of the situation with Julio's parents, they decided to elope to Reno when Julio's work schedule permitted it.

That was easier said than done, since Julio was working overtime in the vineyards, pruning, tying up vines, plowing, and irrigating. After Hoover's defeat in the November 1932 election, Congress had passed the Twenty-first Amendment, which repealed Prohibition. After speedy state ratification, Roosevelt had set December 5, 1933, as the official date of Repeal. California wine-grape growers were in a flurry of activity, preparing for the large 1933 crop that would be needed now that winemakers were taking the necessary steps either to establish new wineries or to refurbish their operations to go into business immediately after Repeal.

What Ernest was doing at the time was hidden from his family as well as from history. Ernest later claimed that he had gone down to Fresno several times to talk to his father about "starting a winery." His father, Ernest recalled, had remained indecisive and moody and ultimately declared that he wanted no part of a winery. Ernest also said that when he asked his father to sell him his grapes, to be paid for by shares of later wine sales, his father refused because he needed immediate cash. (Neither Julio nor Joe, Jr., however, remembered either Ernest's visits or discussions about a winery.)

Despite Joe's alleged indecision, he already had the basic equipment for a winery: underground tanks and a ready supply of grapes— even, according to Joe, Jr.'s recollections, possibly a store of juice in the tanks. If Joe did not crush his grapes that fall in anticipation of starting a winery, his only option was to ship them to eastern markets. But Ernest now played his trump card: he announced that he would not go to Chicago on his usual assignment for his father. Perhaps this forced Joe to take action himself.

In the spring of 1933, Joe discussed his problems with his neighbor Peter Brengetto and proposed a solution. He wanted Peter to buy part of the Fresno acreage.

I need to get cash out of this land, Joe told him over their ritual glasses of wine. *I need it to save my business up in Modesto. I have to make sure I have enough money to protect my operation up there.*

Brengetto wasn't sure what Joe meant by his talk of "protecting" or "saving" his business in Modesto. He told his son Gino that he thought Joe was worried about "his winery" in Modesto. But as much as he would like to help his friend, he couldn't afford to buy any more acreage.

After Brengetto said he couldn't purchase the property, Joe became even more worried. He often had stomach pains and gasped for breath, and he withdrew into long, angry silences.

One day in mid-May, Julio paid his parents a visit. It was late in the morning and Pete was at school when Julio drove up to the ranch and helped Aileen down from the cab of the truck. On May 5, 1933, they had been married and now Julio wanted to surprise Joe and Susie with the news.

Susie came rushing out onto the porch and, guessing who Aileen must be, she gave her a welcoming hug. According to Aileen, Joe had been sitting in a rocking chair on the porch, his head down, his arms clenching his stomach. Now he stood up slowly and came forward to shake Aileen's hand. Still, he barely said a word during lunch. Although Susie tried to cover these awkward silences, Aileen couldn't help but notice that something seemed very wrong: her father-in-law's mood, the barren and dark house, the boxes and suitcases that stood unpacked in various rooms. On the drive back to Modesto, she ventured only one comment. "I liked your mother very much," she told Julio, "but I thought your father was very quiet."

"Yes, he can sit through an entire meal without saying a word," Julio replied. Beyond that he didn't explain, and Aileen didn't ask, as mystified as she was by the living arrangement.

Aileen was not alone in sensing a mystery at the heart of the Gallo family. Max Kane, the ranch hand whom Joe had hired the previous year, was also perplexed. An Austrian immigrant who had shortened his original name, Kapustiak, Max lived in one of the Fresno ranch cottages. At thirty-one he liked the security of working for one boss, especially when there were so many transient farmhands looking for jobs in the Central Valley. Joe treated him well, and he felt loyal to the family.

From the beginning of his stay, Max had realized that the Fresno ranch was unproductive. The vineyards were old—except for a few acres planted to muscat grapes, all the vines were Thompson seedless grapes that were dried for raisins. Joe had hoped to replant with wine grapes but the land was so overgrown with Johnson grass that it would be hard to clear it all and regraft within a year. Max had to wonder why his boss had chosen this property and moved from his Modesto home, but Max was in no position to ask. Here at least he had food to eat and a roof over his head. His cottage was across the yard from the main house, and he took his meals with the Gallos—six o'clock breakfast, then dinner at noon, and supper after his fieldwork was done. At breakfast Joe would usually go over what Max was to do that day, and if the job required more help he asked Max to hire extra men.

But during the previous months, Max had noticed changes in his boss. Because Joe and Susie usually spoke Italian to each other, Max didn't always understand what they were saying. Although they had usually seemed to get along, he now noticed Joe's silence at meals and his pacing up and down in front of the house, muttering.

There was also the strange incident that spring when Joe had overturned the car into a nearby irrigation canal. He had pulled Susie out of the car and carried her to the bank. Max had then helped tow the car out of the water, but then wondered how and why it had happened. Again, he didn't dare ask, and the Gallo blanket of secrecy descended on this occasion as well.

Joe was still trying to raise capital. He couldn't ask Mike for a loan since Mike had only recently been released from prison and federal agents had closed down his businesses. (Although his lawyers had gotten several indictments dismissed, he had been sentenced to three months in the county jail in Redwood City. On November 4, 1932, his sentence was reduced to thirty days when he declared that the woman with whom he had been living and whom he identified in his court petition as his wife, Irene, "had suffered a nervous breakdown." Joe went to Celia instead. Remembering the problems when Joe had borrowed money from her family before, she loaned him only $4,000. Joe then decided to remortgage his property. On June 5, 1933, he took out two loans on his vineyard holdings: one for $16,000 from the Federal Land Bank, the other for $15,000 from the Bank of America.

Ernest was proceeding on his own as well. On June 14, 1933, he filed an application with the Prohibition Office in San Francisco to open a bonded wine storeroom. He proposed to rent a warehouse in San Francisco to which he would then ship wine in bulk for storage and sales. He told neither Julio nor anyone else in the family about the application. Like his father's remortgaging, the application never saw the light of day until many years later. Father and son were both adept at Machiavellian maneuvers, it seemed. But after all, the father had schooled the boy; perhaps each was taking such steps to gain power over the other, or perhaps each was simply forging ahead with his plans in his own hardheaded manner. Whatever the motive, it was anyone's guess how these strategies would play themselves out when father and son seemed on a collision course.

Ernest received a setback on June 20, 1933. The Prohibition Office in San Francisco informed him that his application to open a bonded store room had been denied. He was advised that in order to receive approval he had to own a bonded winery. And according to the Prohibition Office's regulations, he would have to own vineyards before he could be bonded as a winery. Ernest, of course, had no vineyards to his name—only Joe had these. He was stymied; only with his father's agreement—and his grapes—could Ernest hope to establish a winery. Yet his father had been unwilling to proceed with him.

On the same day that Ernest's application was rejected, Julio and Aileen drove to Fresno to pick up Joe, Jr., and bring him back to Modesto to spend part of his summer vacation with his older brothers. Why Julio went on that particular date, and apparently unannounced, would never be explained. In the light of subsequent events the question would haunt the family for years: "Why that day?" And when they were later asked to recall what had happened, Joe, Jr., and

Julio and Aileen would have dramatically different versions of this visit.

According to Julio and Aileen, when they drove up to the house, they saw neither Joe nor Susie. Julio unloaded the irrigation equipment he had brought for his father, then they went looking for his parents. They said that they found Joe behind the barn, pacing up and down, wringing his hands behind his back and muttering.

"Where's Mother?" Julio asked.

Joe pointed to the nearby field. Susie stood on top of a haystack, pitching hay into a wagon below.

Julio swore under his breath, then ran to the wagon.

"Here, Mother, I'll do that." He climbed up and took the pitchfork from her. "You and Aileen go make lunch and get Pete ready to leave."

Aileen recalled walking back to the house with Susie. She heard Julio berating Joe as he pitched the hay. Susie spoke over the angry words, cheerfully listing what she had in the larder for lunch.

"Why were you pitching hay?" Aileen interrupted, Julio's anger giving her courage.

"It had to be done," Susie said, shrugging, then glanced at her anxiously.

Aileen said that she hadn't felt confident enough to question her further. As much as Julio was upset by his father's treatment of his mother, it wasn't her place to force a discussion.

Inside, Aileen and Susie prepared the meal, and when Pete came in from the vineyards, they helped him pack his suitcase.

As Julio remembered it, he and his father came in from outside, and Joe washed up at the sink. But instead of joining the others at the table, Joe stalked out to the front porch. There he sat, bent over in his chair, his head in his hands. Julio went outside and spoke to him in a low voice, finally convincing him to come in and eat. Again he said nothing during the meal except for a few mumbled words when Julio attempted to draw him out. His face was pale and pinched, but whether he was physically ill or sick with worry, Julio said he did not know.

As an adult, Joe, Jr., would remember that when Julio and Aileen had first arrived, Julio had told him to take the pickup and drive Aileen and Susie around "to see the ranch." His mother had not been pitching hay, he said, and he and his parents had all three come out of the house to the yard to greet Julio and Aileen upon their arrival.

His brother's command had been abrupt, Joe, Jr., recalled, and he had been under the impression that Julio wanted to be left alone with their father. As he got into the truck, he said, he saw Julio and his father sit down on a bench under a tree and begin to talk.

As instructed, Pete drove his mother and Aileen around for about forty minutes. When they returned to the yard, he saw that Julio and his father were having a heated conversation, what in retrospect he thought was an argument. But once he and his mother and Aileen got down from the truck, Julio told him to go get his bag, because they were leaving immediately.

Joe, Jr., remembered getting his suitcase and calling Pooch, who was coming with him to Modesto. But he insisted that Julio and Aileen did not stay for lunch and, therefore, his father couldn't have behaved at the table as Julio would later describe. He said that his father had not been angry or depressed before Julio's arrival, and at the time he thought that whatever Julio had told his father must have upset him, that there must have been some sort of conflict between the two. What Julio had said, he had no idea, but it seemed to him that it was the reason his brother had him drive his mother and Aileen around and then wanted to leave as quickly as possible. Indeed, his father suddenly seemed troubled by whatever had been discussed and was sitting in silence on the front porch when Joe, Jr., came out with his suitcase.

Both Julio and Joe, Jr., later agreed, however, that as they were departing, Susie hugged her youngest boy, then grasped Julio by the shoulders and gazed into his eyes.

"I don't care what happens to me," she said in a quavering voice. "All I want is for you boys to work together and get along."

She stopped suddenly as Joe roused himself and came down the steps to Pete's side. He squeezed his shoulder.

"Be good, and mind your brothers," he said in Italian. Then without a word to the others, he turned and went inside the house.

According to Max Kane, the following morning, June 21, began as usual. He ate breakfast with Joe and Susie at six-thirty, and then he and Frank Madrigal, a temporary fieldhand, drove the horse and wagon into town to pick up a load of hay. They returned at ten and pitched the load into the barn. They left to pick up a second load without seeing either Joe or Susie.

At noon they came back to the ranch for their midday meal. Max pulled the wagon up to the barn. Out of the corner of his eye he caught a glimpse of bright blue printed cloth on the ground near the hog pen. He looked again. What he first thought was a rag he now recognized as the edge of Susie Gallo's dress.

He jumped from the wagon, handing the reins to Frank, and ran across to the hog pen.

Susie lay facedown in a pool of blood. There was a wound at the back of her head. Her straw sun hat had fallen nearby, a bullet hole through its blood-soaked brim.

Max dashed across the yard, shouting for Joe. Hearing no reply, he jumped into the farm truck and sped to the nearest gas station. He telephoned the sheriff's office and then returned to the ranch.

Two sheriff's deputies arrived at the ranch fifteen minutes later. They examined Susie's body and then went into the house to look for Joe.

They found him in the dining room. He was sprawled on his back beneath the mirror on the side wall, a bullet hole through his right temple. His blood-spattered black fedora lay on the floor near his feet. A yard away from the curled fingers of his right hand was a .32-caliber Smith & Wesson revolver.

PART TWO
THE WINERY

CHAPTER FOUR

Ernest learned of his parents' deaths in a telephone call to the Maze Road house. Who had made the call and at what time would later become a matter of dispute. He claimed, however, that a *Modesto Bee* reporter had informed him of the "murder-suicide." He then told Aileen and Julio the tragic news and departed for Fresno.

Julio was grief-stricken, and for years would feel that he should have done something to prevent the tragedy.

Ernest had already left for Fresno when twelve-year-old Joe, Jr., came in from hunting rabbits. Julio and Aileen then sat him down and explained that his mother and father had died in a terrible accident.

"Don't worry, it will be all right," Julio comforted him. "We'll take care of you. You'll live here with us, just like before."

The boy seemed stunned, barely able to fathom what his brother was saying, but he clung to his brother's reassurance that he would always have a home with them.

In Fresno, Ernest identified his parents' bodies and answered the coroner's questions at a brief "inquiry" convened that afternoon.

Deputy Coroner William Creager began by asking about the murder of Ernest's mother.

"Do you know of any motive for it, or your father's suicide?" he asked.

"Possibly financial reverses," said Ernest.

"You are satisfied in your own mind that it is a plain case of murder and suicide?"

"Yes."

"Had they had family troubles, or anything like that, that you know of?"

"No," was all Ernest had to say, and he was dismissed from the stand.

Max Kane was then called to explain how he had discovered the body of Susie Gallo. After describing his actions of the morning, he was asked whether anything in his employer's behavior would lead him to believe that Joe Gallo would commit suicide.

"I can't say," replied Kane. "He was sick for the last 4 or 5 days. He hardly talked and he kept to himself. Usually he comes out there and works with the men but lately, for the last week, he kept himself in the house or around the yard, but he never mixed up with the men."

"So far as you know he and Mrs. Gallo got along all right?"

"No doubt," said Kane. "I noticed—all the time they talked their own language which I don't understand but as far as I could see they got along as well as the average."

Kane confirmed that a crew of five men had been cutting weeds in a ditch about six hundred yards away from the ranch and that one of them might have heard the shots or noticed something. But none of these men was identified or called during the inquiry. The coroner then asked if Kane was also satisfied that it was a murder-suicide.

"Yes, it looks that way," Kane said. "He was a man very nervous. He gets so sick he would have to hold himself for a while." He clutched his chest. "He would get out of breath."

Creager interrupted Kane's testimony and turned to Ernest. "Did you know he had this gun?"

"Yes."

"A new gun?"

"About a year old," Ernest replied. (According to the sheriff's report, Ernest had already told the investigating officers that his father had bought the gun two years before in Modesto.)

Finally Frank Madrigal, the other hired hand, was called to confirm that he had been with Max Kane when he found Susie Gallo's body. But Madrigal claimed that he couldn't understand English, and he was excused from testifying.

With no further hesitation, the deputy coroner returned his verdict: murder-suicide.

The *Fresno Bee* ran a front-page story that evening. "FRESNO FARMER AND WIFE VICTIMS OF MURDER AND SUICIDE," the banner headline read. Two days later, the *San Francisco Chroni-*

cle also reported the deaths: "Although no note was found, officers were satisfied that Gallo, who had been despondent lately, suddenly decided to take his own life and that of his wife. . . . Ernest Gallo, a son, who resides in Modesto, said his father had been bothered lately by financial conditions and was given to brooding. Max Kane and Frank Madrigal, workmen at the ranch, said Gallo had been in poor health and that he was morose."

During the Depression, suicides prompted by financial failures were common enough among farmers in Fresno County that the coroner saw no reason to investigate the Gallos' deaths any further. Yet the brief inquiry that established ill-health and money worries as Joe's motive left several questions unanswered. The medical examiner, for example, reported only the gunshot wound as the cause of Joe's death, but failed to indicate whether he had searched for or discovered symptoms of disease. According to Joe, Jr.'s recollection, Ernest hadn't seen their father in months; nevertheless, the coroner accepted Ernest's explanation of poor health and "financial reverses" as possible motives for suicide. The sheriff's report, however, indicated that Joe had averaged $500 a month in his Fresno Bank of America account for some time, and that the combined balances of husband and wife totaled more than $3,000, a sum that was well above what was considered "financial ruin" in the 1930s. (The investigating deputies also had no way of knowing that the Gallos had other bank accounts in Modesto.)

Despite the coroner's verdict, the sheriff's report raised doubts as well, especially since there was no suicide note. One of the investigating deputies, Wallace Moore, continued to wonder about the case, remarking on its inconsistencies often enough that even after his death colleagues remembered his doubts. He had trained himself as the department's fingerprint expert and asked why the print on the grip of the gun was only a portion of a palm, too smudged to be identified, while Joe Gallo's fingerprints were found on its barrel. Why, he wondered, had Joe not fallen with the gun in his hand? If he had dropped or flung the gun with the shot's impact, why were his right index and middle fingers curled as if they still grasped the gun?

The deputy also wondered about the bottle of wine on the kitchen table. He identified Joe's fingerprints on it but found no glasses with fingerprints nearby. Had Joe poured a drink for himself and a guest in the Italian tradition? Had the glasses been washed and put away to conceal any sign of a visitor?

The deputy was equally perplexed by the payment of property taxes to the tax collector found in the mailbox. Susie Gallo had signed the check for $60 due for the next quarter, but the deputy imagined that she would have done so only on her husband's orders. Why would a man so financially strapped pay his taxes in advance and just hours before his suicide?

Nevertheless, the investigation of the Gallos' deaths was officially closed. Years later, such questions would be revived but would remain unanswered. None of the brothers could resolve the mystery of their father's purchase of a Smith & Wesson revolver a year or two before. Joe, Jr., remembered seeing a revolver in his father's bedroom in Modesto, but he didn't know when or why he had bought it or whether he had taken it to Fresno.

Ernest's own recollection would be slightly refreshed by reading the sheriff's report over fifty years later, but he himself could not remember telling the deputies that his father had bought a handgun a year or two before his death. While he could not confirm the make and caliber of his father's gun, he added that he thought his own standard Smith & Wesson had been a better model than his father's revolver. He was also sure that his father had not asked to borrow his Smith & Wesson, but neither he nor his brothers could recall what had become of Ernest's weapon.

None of the brothers knew why Julio hadn't gone to Fresno to testify at the inquest. If, as Joe, Jr., and Julio recalled, Ernest hadn't come to the ranch for months, he was hardly the one to describe his father's mood before the deaths. Nor could any of the brothers later explain why Julio and Aileen had arrived to pick up Joe, Jr., on the day before the shooting. No date had actually been set, and Joe, Jr., had not been told that they were coming on that particular date. More, his adult memory of the visit was still at odds with Julio's description. Years later, he still had the impression that Julio had wanted a private and urgent conversation with his father; he did not think that his father had been depressed, as Julio recalled, but he had seemed upset by his talk with his son. Over fifty years later, Julio was still so distraught about the parents' deaths that he could supply few answers to the renewed questions surrounding his trip to Fresno that day.

Joe, Jr., would also come to realize that his memories of the morning of his parents' deaths were in direct conflict with those of his brothers. Ernest recalled hearing about the shootings from a *Modesto Bee* reporter after the deputies' investigation. But Joe, Jr., remembered getting up early in the morning, about seven, to take his dog out to hunt rabbits, then returning home about nine. It was then that Julio and Aileen told him about the terrible event, he said. He claimed that Ernest—and he thought Amelia—had already left for Fresno, having received a phone call, which, he remembered being told, was from Max Kane. But according to the sheriff's report, the deputies hadn't been summoned to the ranch until 12:25. Joe, Jr., had no idea what accounted for the time discrepancy unless Max had discovered the bodies early in the morning, telephoned Ernest, then waited for his arrival at the ranch before the sheriff was called. (The medical examiner had not estimated a time of death.)

Further, Joe was later mystified when he learned of Max Kane's testimony that he had made two trips for hay that morning before discovering Susie's body. His father, Joe insisted, had raised his own hay and there would have been no reason for Max to drive the wagon into town. (Julio, he pointed out, had suggested that there was an ample supply of hay at the barn when he had recalled his mother pitching hay the day before. Although Joe disputed that his mother was loading hay the morning of Julio's visit, he noted that Julio must have remembered that there was a large haystack near the barn.) Thinking about the events as an adult, comparing his own memories and the official reports, Joe began to wonder if the story of the trips into town was a way to explain what seemed to be a delay between what he recalled as an early morning phone call to Ernest and Max's noon notification of the sheriff's office. And if his father had been so hard up for money, he questioned why Ernest had then given Max the family's Packard, as he was told and as Max would later confirm.

Adding to the puzzle was the account of Peter Brengetto, the Gallos' neighbor and friend. He had neither been interviewed by the sheriff's deputies nor asked to appear at the coroner's inquest, even though, according to his son Gino, he had found the bodies, reported the deaths to the sheriff and remembered the scene vividly for years to come. The Gallos had been expected for dinner at the Brengetto home the evening before. Worried because they had failed to show up, Brengetto drove to their ranch just before noon the following day. He told his son that he had discovered the two ranch dogs shot, Susie dead near the hog pen, and Joe inside the house with a bullet wound in his temple. He returned home immediately to telephone the sheriff. Hearing nothing from the deputies and reading the newspaper account the next day, he reasoned that Max Kane must have found the bodies and called the sheriff within minutes of his own report. But the shooting of the dogs bothered him, his son recalled, and he would always wonder if someone had killed them to silence their warning barks. (The sheriff's report mentioned no dogs.)

The deaths provoked a good deal of talk at the time. Because of Mike Gallo's reputation, there was speculation among Italians in both Fresno and Modesto that Joe and Susie had been in hiding because of threats by the "big-city mob." Had Joe given information to federal agents during their investigation, had he supplied names of his brothers' business associates who had mob ties? For two years rumors had circulated about several unexplained deaths in the Central Valley of men who were known to make deliveries for syndicate bootlegging operations based in San Francisco. Because of the loose ends in the Gallo case, similar stories spread that this was a double homicide by "hit men."

Brengetto also told his son that he had been surprised by Ernest's reported explanation that financial difficulty was his father's motive for the murder-suicide. Joe had previously told Brengetto that he wanted to liquidate some of his acreage, not because he was destitute but because he had to "protect his Modesto business," which Brengetto assumed was the winery that Joe often mentioned. In early June, however, Joe had informed Brengetto that he had solved his problem by remortgaging the Fresno ranch. Could he have been destitute if banks were willing to loan him money?

(In fact, Joe's two loans, one from the Bank of America, the other from the Federal Land Bank, totaled $31,000. Nevertheless, the proceeds from these two loans weren't recorded in his bank account or reported in his probated estate, and in later recollections, neither Ernest nor Julio could explain what happened to this money.)

But these questions surfaced only many years after the tragedy and prompted hazy and contradictory memories. At the time, there was no further discussion among family members and friends. In fact, none of the Biancos even knew that Susie and Joe had moved to Fresno. Susie's brother Walter, living on his prune ranch in Santa Clara Valley, was devastated when a telegram arrived with the news of his sister's death. Why hadn't they been told that Susie and Joe were living in Fresno? he remarked to his daughter Stella. Why was there so much secrecy? How had Joe suddenly fallen into such desperate straits?

Even at the funeral in Modesto no one could or would offer an explanation either for the move to Fresno or the deaths. Celia, too, was upset and mystified, and although she had loaned Joe $4,000 in the previous few months, she could hardly believe that financial ruin had motivated him to take Susie's and his own life. Recently released from jail, Mike also attended the funeral. He might have had some clue as to why Joe had gone into hiding on a rundown ranch in Fresno, but whether his brother's actions and anxiety had been connected to the bootlegging investigations and his arrests, he didn't say.

Joe and Susie were buried in the St. Stanislaus cemetery. Many friends and neighbors attended the service and there was much whispering among them. With no explanations for the deaths, mourners spoke of "warding off the evil eye." The Gallo sons couldn't or wouldn't talk about the family violence. Julio was too traumatized, Joe, Jr., too sad and confused, and Ernest had imposed a code of silence.

From that day forward the family referred to the event as "the troubles" or "the accident." The mystery of how and why Joe and Susie had died was buried with them. The events of June 21, 1933, were veiled in secrecy, the violent tragedy too upsetting for the family to discuss among themselves, much less reveal to others. For Julio it may have been a relief to suppress these memories, but throughout his life he remained so grief-stricken that he could barely think about his parents' deaths, much less discuss what had happened.

As a boy, Joe, Jr., was too stunned to question his brothers. As a man, he remembered little except his sense of loss and unexpressed sadness. When he was forced to summon his own memories of the event, he was shocked to discover that his recollections were at odds with those of his brothers. "It was made clear that this subject was not open for discussion," Joe later recalled. "I never knew why my parents moved to Fresno. I never understood what might have caused their deaths, although I don't remember my father being ill or financially ruined, as Ernest and Julio say he was. But after my parents' deaths, we weren't supposed to talk about it so I was left in the dark."

"It was a big, big secret in the family, even many years later," Mike Gallo, Joe's son, commented. "I didn't even know how my grandparents actually died until I was a teenager. I think I had been told something about pneumonia or dying in a flu epidemic. Then a high school classmate said, 'Did you know your grandfather shot your grandmother and then killed himself?' I guess his parents or grandparents remembered the story. It was a shock to me, but when I asked my father, he could tell me very little about it. It was as if he'd made himself block out the memory. It was something that was not referred to by either my father or my uncles."

Joe, Jr., wasn't allowed to mourn, and his dependency on Ernest and Julio took root, as if he were frightened that he might lose them too. More, his father's last words to him in Italian, "Be good and mind your brothers," became a deeply ingrained commandment. Julio would have difficulty coping with his sorrow. Ernest, however, seemed content to put the past behind him and move on to the future, creating and recreating himself and the Gallo legend.

While his two brothers mourned, Ernest maneuvered. *L'avvocato*, his father's derisive nickname for him, was never more fitting.

On March 1, 1928, Susie had written a short will as well as her limited English allowed: "I being of sound mind & body This is my last will & testament I leave all my real & personal property stocks and everything I possess to my three sons Ernest Gallo 19 years Julio Gallo 18 years Joe Gallo, Jr. 8 To be divided in equal parts as soon as each one becomes 21 years of age Will leave The Bank of Italy as executor."

Strangely enough, Joe did not leave a will, even though he had consulted Edward Taylor, Sr., a Modesto attorney, on legal and business matters for many years. Ernest now asked Taylor to represent him in the probate of both his mother's and father's estates. On July 10, the probate court appointed Ernest the administrator of his father's estate, and on July 19, the Bank of America (formerly the Bank of Italy) appointed Taylor executor of Susie's estate. (Although Joe had died intestate, the three sons were still the legal heirs to his estate as well.)

No longer hampered by his father's indecision or his reluctance to make him a partner in the family business, Ernest swung into action. The Bureau of Alcohol had rejected his application to open a bonded winery only the day before his parents' deaths because he didn't own vineyards. Ernest then telephoned Dante Forresti, his father's old acquaintance—and fellow winemaker—in Escalon. If anyone knew how to deal with the Prohibition Office, Forresti did, and he gave Ernest the name of John Walsh, a Washington, D.C., lawyer adept at cutting through the red tape of licensing laws. Ernest worked fast, and within the week he had contacted Walsh. He now announced himself as a vineyard owner—even though it was the father's estate (each son to inherit one-third) that actually owned the vineyards.

If Walsh was aware of the actual owner of the vineyards, he nevertheless ignored the existence of the estate on July 3 when he wrote a letter to William Woods, the San Francisco supervisor of the Bureau of Industrial Alcohol:

Dear Sir:

Mr. Ernest Gallo, Maze Road, Route D, Box 1525, Modesto, California, has sent to me your letter to him of the 20th of June last.

Mr. Gallo informs me that he has under cultivation about five hundred acres of wine grapes. He intends to operate a wine press and bonded warehouse or a storeroom in connection therewith, but under present conditions he can have his grapes pressed far cheaper than to equip a winery.

I have advised him that upon proper showing a permit will be granted to him to have his grapes manufactured into wine and sold for medicinal purposes, and a permit for the storage thereof.

Will you please send him blank applications in conformity with the desires herein expressed?

Reassured that Ernest owned the requisite vineyards, the bureau sent him application forms, advising him that if he was going to manufacture and store wine, he had to furnish plans for the proposed bonded premises. Now Ernest put on another hat: As the executor of his father's estate, he petitioned the probate court on August 17, 1933, for an "Order Authorizing Continuing Business." He advised the court that he would have to decide what to do with the estate's wine grapes "for the purpose of realizing the greatest return for and on behalf of the said estate." He listed various options—selling the grapes, delivering them to markets in either California or the East, or crushing them and holding the juice "under proper governmental authority." He did not add that he was simultaneously establishing a winery "under proper governmental authority" where he intended to crush the grapes from the vineyards that he had represented as his own to the Bureau of Alcohol.

Granted permission to continue his father's business on August 28, 1933, Ernest now included Julio in his plans. Although Julio had previously planned to go into cattle ranching, he agreed to join his brother in the winery venture. Neither asked Joe, Jr., to become a partner, even though his share of the vineyards and his father's estate were being used to fulfill the Bureau of Alcohol's requirements for founding a winery. Instead, Ernest and Julio formed a partnership and called their enterprise the E. & J. Gallo Winery—as if it were separate and unrelated to continuing their father's business and using his vineyards to gain governmental approval. Further, they had stationery printed on which their names appeared with two designations—"Winery" and "Grape Growers and Shippers." But E. & J. Gallo alone did not own a growing and shipping company—that was part of their father's estate and the continuing business. Nevertheless, the stationery served the purpose of confirming Ernest's representations to the Bureau of Alcohol.

Ernest and Julio first considered building the winery on the Maze Road property where their father's underground tanks would provide ready-made storage. But realizing that they would not be able to construct a building and receive approval in time for the autumn harvest, Ernest consulted the Modesto and Empire Traction Company from which his father had rented his grape-shipping shed. The company's owner, who had had a long and satisfactory relationship with Joe, Sr., offered to rent his sons a warehouse at 11th and D streets in downtown Modesto. Thus, on August 14, Ernest could apply to the Bureau of Alcohol in the name of his new business— E. & J. Gallo—for permission to "manufacture, possess and sell wines and to buy from other Bonded Wineries wine for blendings" in a winery with a "50,000 gallon capacity."

At the same time he enclosed a letter in his and Julio's names, which again announced themselves as "grape growers with over 400 acres of grapes" and urged speedy approval of their application: "We feel that in order to insure ourselves that our crop will not again be another total loss we must acquire a small winery to crush at least a part of our crop."

But in fact Joe, Sr., had already taken the first steps toward establishing a small winery himself: building underground tanks, establishing the Gallo trade name in a wine business that dated to before Prohibition and in a wine-grape-shipping business during the next decade, and a month before his death remortgaging his property for $31,000, which, according to his neighbor's recollection, was to "protect his winery in Modesto."

Yet as executor of his father's estate, Ernest did not list either his father's wine-grape business or his trade name as assets in the probate accounting. He also omitted from the record the grape-crushing equipment as well as the underground tanks; the probate accounting also did not disclose the $31,000 that had somehow disappeared. (Years later Julio confirmed that he must have had a key to Joe, Sr.'s safe-deposit box. However, neither he nor Ernest could recall what had been in the box at the time, whether their father had routinely kept cash in it, or what had become of the money raised from the mortgages.)

If Joe, Sr., had lived, he would have almost certainly fulfilled the requirements to establish a winery after Repeal. Indeed, it would have been the natural extension and continuation of his business, a logical step that many wine-grape shippers, including Cesare Mondavi, took that summer and fall. As his son Robert recalled, "Going into the winery business was a natural transition or evolution of the grape-shipping business. It was what many shippers were preparing to do once Repeal was announced."

In later years Ernest would repeatedly insist that he and Julio alone started the winery with no knowledge of winemaking except for a pamphlet from the public library, no experience in the wine business, and only $5,900.23 between them. But according to their official bonding applications from 1933, Ernest and Julio could only have received approval for their winery on the basis of the estate's vineyards and assets and by continuing the family business of grape growing under their own names.

If Julio knew little of these legal maneuvers, Joe, Jr., was completely ignorant of how Ernest was using his share of the estate to establish a winery and a partnership that did not include him. At thirteen, he was simply glad to have a home and two brothers who had promised to take care of him. What they did in the vineyards or downtown in the warehouse was part of the adult world about which he wouldn't think to ask, much less doubt his brothers' decisions.

Just how far Ernest revised history became clear with the winery's next legal hurdle. On August 21, 1933, Leonard Rhodes, an inspector from the Bureau of Alcohol, visited the warehouse at 11th and D to interview Ernest. (Julio was not present, but Ernest said that he could speak for both of them.) Rhodes had become concerned with what he had turned up in his "personnel investigation." Not surprisingly, the Gallo name had set off alarms in the government agency. That Mike Gallo was "known to this office," as Rhodes put it in his investigation report, was an understatement. Prohibition agents had pursued him as a "kingpin bootlegger," and the bureau would refuse to bond a winery if its owners had anything to do with a notorious bootlegger.

Are you and your brother the only parties who have an interest in this winery? the inspector reported asking Ernest.

Of course, said Ernest. *Just me and my brother.*

What about this fellow named Mike Gallo?

I don't know him, Ernest replied.

He's not a relative?

No, no relative of ours.

So he wouldn't have any part in the management of your winery? Rhodes persisted.

No, none at all, said Ernest.

Rhodes noted his emphatic denial and asked if Ernest was willing to sign an affidavit to this effect.

Ernest complied immediately, confirming in writing that he neither knew nor was related to Mike Gallo.

Whether Rhodes suspected that Ernest was lying or whether he was conducting a routine investigation, he proceeded to interview people in town about Ernest and Julio and the Gallo family. After confirming Ernest and Julio's financial stability with J. M. Williams, the manager of the Modesto branch of the Bank of America, the inspector asked if Mr. Williams had ever heard of Mike Gallo. The bank manager replied that he understood that Mike Gallo was an uncle.

This prompted Rhodes to question H. B. Wright, the undersheriff of Stanislaus County. Wright had been a good friend of Joe, Sr., and he stated, according to Rhodes, that the Gallo brothers "were personally known to him and that they were law abiding, hard working citizens, never having been involved in any violations of the law." He added that he was aware that the brothers had an uncle named Mike Gallo who "had a rather poor reputation," but he knew of no connection other than the familial one.

Rhodes's final step confirmed what he had already been told. Visiting the Shannon Funeral Chapel, he consulted the records for Joe and Susie Gallo's funeral. Mike Gallo had indeed attended the service and had identified himself as the decedent's brother.

Rhodes then interviewed Ed Taylor, "attorney for the estate of Joe Gallo," who stated that the three Gallo brothers were the sole heirs of their father, although there were other relatives. Rhodes indicated that he was pursuing the investigation because Ernest had "emphatically denied [a] relationship with Mike Gallo who is known to this bureau." Taylor showed him a will that he alleged he had prepared for Joe Gallo, Sr., two years before but that was unsigned. Taylor pointed out that the will disinherited all relatives other than the three sons. Mike Gallo, however, wasn't specifically named, and Rhodes now sought the reason for Ernest's "disclaiming knowledge of, or relationship to Mike Gallo."

Ernest and Julio were summoned, and when they arrived Rhodes informed them of the "apparent publicly known relationship" between them and Mike Gallo.

Once more Ernest did the talking. *Mike Gallo was an uncle*, he announced, *but in the last two years he has become an unknown stranger. Our father disinherited him, disowned him, and because of that we felt he had been removed from us as a relative or someone known to us.*

Rhodes indicated that he had taken note of "the purported will." But why it had suddenly come to light, why Joe, Sr., would have found it necessary to "disinherit" all other relatives, including a brother who wasn't likely to inherit anyway, and why this will had neither been signed nor officially filed, no one explained, either then or later. At the time, Ernest and Julio apparently did not mention to the investigator that, for all their emphatic "removal" of Mike Gallo from their family, Mike had stayed at the Fresno ranch for a few weeks after Joe and Susie's death; that their uncle still came to see them in Modesto; that Julio and Aileen had recently visited Mike and the woman with whom he was living in a San Francisco apartment.

After listening to Ernest's explanation, Rhodes asked, *Do you wish to retract this affidavit you signed?*

Not at all, he replied. *Consider it a stipulation that Mike Gallo will have no part in the management of our winery.*

In his report Rhodes concluded that "the apparent feeling of resentment on the part of the applicant appears to be a family affair with no direct bearing on applicant's dealings with this bureau, and further investigation was deemed inadvisable."

Ironically, the inspector's financial investigation of Ernest and Julio also contradicted the later official Gallo story of the two penniless brothers. Rhodes's report to his bureau assured his superiors that the proposed winery would be financially sound. Again, it was the parents' estate that convinced the government agent. During the initial interview, Ernest had explained that he was not actually the owner of his vineyards but the administrator of his father's estate, which comprised "several vineyards totaling in excess of 400 acres of which in excess of 240 acres of wine grapes make up the home ranch located about three miles from Modesto" as well as "in excess of 200 acres of grapes (wine and table) near Fresno." Since attorney Taylor had also confirmed that Ernest, Julio, and a third brother, Joseph, Jr., were "the sole heirs to the estate," Rhodes concluded that the vineyard holdings and the sons' inheritance satisfied him that "they are financially able to promote the enterprise for which application has been made."

Furthermore, the Modesto bank manager had attested to their financial well-being by citing the estates of both Joe and Susie. As Rhodes added in his report, the manager had reassured him that there was "considerable vineyard in addition to property" and that "in addition to a third brother they were sole heirs . . . and were financially able to promote the enterprise." Despite these statements acknowledging him as one of the sole heirs, Joe, Jr., continued to be excluded from both his brothers' partnership and the winery enterprise. And he was certainly unaware that Ernest and Julio's winery was approved on the basis of the shared inheritance of "considerable vineyards in addition to property."

After Rhodes filed his report, the Bureau of Alcohol agreed to bond the E. & J. Gallo Winery on August 30, 1933. The parents' estate had played a crucial role in winning and hastening official approval. It was another fact that Ernest would later disavow, repeatedly insisting that he and Julio had accomplished this feat with only $5,900.23 to their names.

Because the parents' estates were still in probate the brothers were forced to ask for loans from relatives. First Aunt Celia turned them down—much to Ernest's annoyance she was already clamoring for repayment of her $4,000 loan, even filing a claim against the estate. Finally Teresa Franzia, Ernest's mother-in-law, agreed to put up the $5,000 fee required by the Bureau of Alcohol for the bond (based on Ernest's application for a fifty-thousand-gallon capacity winery).

The remaining $900.23 of the famous Gallo start-up figure allegedly represented Julio's own savings. According to Ernest, the winery was equipped with redwood tanks on extended credit—the construction of tanks with a total one-hundred-thousand-gallon capacity (not the fifty thousand for which the winery was licensed) to be paid for in 90 and 180 days. For about $2,000, Ernest and Julio also purchased a motor-driven press and crusher, again delaying payment until after their first sales.

Soon after this came another financial transaction, suggesting that the brothers' assets exceeded their later $5,900 figure. Their father's estate included a lien on a twenty-acre vineyard in Ripon. When the owner had died, $4,195 was still due on the $11,000 promissory note to Joe, Sr., and the property was to have been auctioned on June 24, 1933. At Ernest's request, the sale was postponed for a month, and on July 21, 1933, the vineyard was sold to the highest bidder: one Julio Gallo for $4,195. In Ernest's first estate accounting, he listed a net receipt of $3,198.48 for this debt, but the property itself did not go "through the estate," as Ernest's accountant later confirmed, but was put into the Gallo Bros. Ranches partnership in Julio's name. It was an irregularity in accounting that neither Ernest nor Julio could explain in later years. Julio, however, would say that he doubted he actually had the money to buy this property, but neither he nor Ernest could explain how they accomplished this purchase if they had no funds available beyond the $5,900.23 total.

As the winery went into full production that autumn, Ernest and Julio also depended on their father's previous business contacts. Their first employees at the winery were men their father had originally hired or knew from earlier years. Max Kane became a jack-of-all-trades around the winery. Pete Cisi and Jack Jenkins, both originally hired by Joe, Sr., were given jobs by Ernest. He also sought out Albert Wagner, his father's bootlegging colleague in Livermore, but Wagner refused the job offer. Then Ernest and Julio hired Joe Sciaroni, a school classmate but also the son of the Escalon butcher who was known to be a bootlegger. The son had become an experienced winemaker, having helped his father and worked for other bootleggers during Prohibition. But Sciaroni quit after a few days, finding the hours demanded by Ernest too arduous and the commute from his home in Escalon too difficult.

In addition, Ernest employed several day laborers to help in the construction of the winery and the winemaking, storing, and shipping. Yet all these salaries, including Ernest and Julio's wages of $60 each per month, were debited not to the winery but to Joe, Sr.'s estate account. Even conceding that the brothers, as well as their employees, did some work on the home ranch or in the estate's vineyards, most of their hours were spent at the winery—those long, long hours that Ernest and Julio always cited as the key to their success. (As Joe, Jr., later recalled, he often did "chores" for them down at the winery as well, and his "salary" was listed as "allowance" and also paid by the estate, according to the probate accounting.) Further expenses of gas and oil and machinery and truck repairs were charged to Joe, Sr.'s estate account, with no indication of whether these supplies and equipment were winery-related.

Meanwhile the winery was turning out an extraordinary amount of wine. In October 1933, Ernest received permission from the Bureau of Alcohol to make an additional 130,000 gallons. Where had all the wine come from? In the first place, Ernest had convinced many of Joe, Sr.'s extensive contacts with grape growers to consign their grapes to the winery rather than to ship them. His argument was logical—with the grape market still depressed, with Repeal official in December, growers stood to make more profit from the sale of wine than from grapes. He offered them $30 a ton, calculating that a ton of grapes produced about 150 gallons of wine and that wine would sell for about fifty cents a gallon. Many of their father's previous shipping clients agreed, and Ernest and Julio had a good supply of grapes.

They also crushed grapes from their father's vineyards. Nominally the estate was selling grapes to the winery, but in this instance, too, the bookkeeping was rather confusing. The estate's first accounts showed $3,525.72 due from the winery for "sale of wine" (although the winery accounts listed $12,094 owed to the estate). If the estate accounting was accurate, then either Ernest paid the estate far less for its grapes than he paid other growers, he underreported the total tons of grapes produced by the estate's vineyards or the yield of the estate's vineyards was far below a usual harvest. What should have been closer to 500 tons of grapes harvested from at least 240 acres of grapes was assigned a value equal to about 118 tons of grapes. Even if the winery's account was more accurate, the $12,094.40 was not entered on the estate books. In any case, Ernest and Julio would later concede that it was unlikely that either amount was actually paid into the estate account that first year; hence they were informally using estate funds as a bank from which to borrow.

If, as Joe, Jr., later claimed, the underground tanks already contained wine upon his return from Fresno to Modesto in June 1933, it was also possible that Ernest and Julio were including that wine in their production totals. Indeed, Ed Taylor wrote the Alcohol Tax

Unit in June 1934 to inquire about regulations covering the sale of "wine made by a deceased grape grower" or the "administrator of a deceased grower." He was informed that a deceased grower's wine was taxed at the same rate, ten cents on the gallon. At any rate, despite Ernest's later denials, Taylor's inquiry suggested concern about a supply of wine on hand from Joe, Sr., "a deceased grower," or a plan to produce wine by the estate's administrator.

Ernest and Julio used their father's underground storage tanks during their first two years of operation without the required inspection and approval of the Bureau of Alcohol. When he finally made a formal application for their use, Ernest told the district supervisor that the tanks were like those of Italian Swiss Colony and had been built when he and Julio had planned to start a winery at the Maze Road house. Later he would concede that he had already been using the tanks but hadn't wanted the government agency to know that his father had constructed the tanks during Prohibition for illegal purposes.

But the thirty-two-thousand-gallon capacity tanks hadn't been illegal when Joe, Sr., had built them. Joe, Jr., would later come to believe that Ernest was concealing a different fact—that the tanks were part of his father's estate and had been constructed for storing wine. Instead of listing them as an estate asset, Ernest and Julio had taken possession of them and, as they admitted, had never paid the estate for the continued use of them by the E. & J. Gallo Winery.

The Bureau of Alcohol, however, refused to give approval, finding the tanks too primitive for a bonded winery. (Since there were openings only at the top of the tank instead of the required outlet at the bottom, the quantity of wine could not be monitored for government taxation purposes.) As a result, the tanks had to be provided with new coverings and gauges. Despite Ernest's later assertion that his father had never made or stored wine in these tanks, Joe, Jr., recalled that not only had he seen wine in them when he returned from Fresno, but also, after the Bureau of Alcohol's refusal to approve them, he was assigned the task of pumping the stored wine into a tank truck. The wine was delivered to the winery, where, Joe said, he then helped pump it into barrels for shipment to Los Angeles. Once the home ranch underground tanks met the bureau's requirements, wine was pumped back in, and Ernest and Julio again used their father's tanks for storage until 1942 with no fees ever paid to the estate.

Ernest and Julio's goal was quantity rather than quality, and their winemaking that first year was as basic as the technique used by their father and his colleagues. Julio would later ask for advice from oenologists at the University of California, but that fall he concentrated on mass production, not on blending or aging. Their bulk wine suited the market after Repeal. In the early 1930s wine was a commodity, not a brand product. Wine consumers were relatively unsophisticated and preferred wine that tasted like what they had made themselves during Prohibition.

Assured of a vast supply of wine, Ernest now set out to line up sales in anticipation of the official date of Repeal. Most wineries were shipping wine in bulk to distributors, who then bottled the wine under their own labels to prepare for the first sales that December. Here, too, Ernest benefited from the associations that his father had made in the grape-shipping business.

Charlie Barbera and Tony Paterno, two of the Chicago dealers to whom Joe, Sr., had sold grapes, had gone into partnership and founded the Pacific Wine Company. Barbera sent letters to California wineries announcing that he was buying wine in bulk, and in early December 1933 he contacted Ernest as well. Ernest immediately flew to Chicago. It was a daring and unorthodox move for those days, but it put him in Barbera's office with samples of wine the very next day, and just as he had reached Minnesota before Charlie Rossi, he was well ahead of the competition.

Barbera welcomed "Ernie," and since he'd been happy with Gallo grapes, he now placed the first order for Gallo wine, five thousand gallons at fifty cents a gallon, accompanied by a check. It was the beginning of a long association and friendship, with Barbera becoming one of the first and main distributors of Gallo's bulk wine in the Midwest. In subsequent years Barbera teased Ernest and Julio that their first shipment of wine had been their best, since it had tasted most like homemade wine. He sometimes joked that they must have watered their later wines. In fact, the brothers had only upgraded their production facility, adding a filter system that removed the "homemade" flavor that Barbera had liked in their first year's wine.

Ernest headed to the East Coast, where he found distributors in New York and New Jersey. He made contact with grape dealers who were familiar with Gallo grapes and were looking to buy bulk wine. To find even more potential sales, he asked glass manufacturers for the names of companies that were ordering supplies of wine bottles, a sure sign that they were going into the wine-distribution business.

Then he traveled South, taking orders from distributors and bottlers in Florida and Texas. Returning to southern California, he convinced several bottling companies as well as a barrel house in Los Angeles to order a supply of Gallo wine. (Customers bought on the premises, with wine siphoned directly from barrels into the customers' containers.)

As of Repeal that December, Ernest and Julio began to ship their wine, usually in fifty-gallon barrels on which "Gallo" was stenciled. They later explained that they had chosen the name to honor the family and the tradition their father had established in both his pre-Prohibition wine business and in his grape-shipping company.

In later years Ernest bragged that through his and Julio's hard work they earned a profit of $34,000 during the winery's first year. (How he had arrived at this figure was never clear, since it did not appear in any of the financial records later produced by the winery.) The volume of wine sold was astonishing if the brothers had started with virtually nothing—no wine and a meager $5,900.23—as they insisted. Using Ernest's $34,000 figure, the profit would have represented a return of 650 percent on their initial investment. An extraordinary success, a real rags-to-riches story, all attributable to the two Gallo brothers' genius. The genius and the hard work were undeniable; yet when documents concerning the winery's initial year of operation came to light in the 1988 case, Joe and his attorneys would wonder if Ernest and Julio had begun with more than what they had publicly proclaimed.

In the first place, Ernest and Julio had relied on their parents' combined estates to convince the BATF to approve their winery application—not only the vineyards but the financial stability acquired in their inheritance were mentioned as significant in the bureau's report. In the probate court records, the combined estates were valued at $127,144 gross and $83,269 net (the approximate equivalent of $800,000 today). The estate's real property was appraised at $61,849.80, and each brother was to inherit one-third of all properties. Joe, Jr.'s accounting expert would later conclude from these records that the estate was in a far better capital situation than Ernest and Julio themselves. He contended that it had more "liquid capital" ($11,000 was his figure) than Ernest and Julio and "the ability to convert fixed assets to current assets by sale and by refinancing."

Ernest, in fact, took some of these steps. In October 1933, with permission of the probate court, he sold the Fresno ranch for $34,000, receiving a note for $24,000 along with a 1934 crop mortgage for $10,000. Ernest then acquired Federal Farm loans on the Maze Road property for $30,000; he had told the court then that refinancing was necessary to pay the debts of the estate. Ernest also received permission from the court to sell some of the Transamerica stock (2,652 shares) in the estate, but then in the closing of the estate, he advised the court that it had been unnecessary to sell after all; yet in 1936 (after the probating of the parents' estate), Ernest sold the shares for $33,077.95, and Joe's one-third share (totaling more than $11,000) was "loaned" to the winery without either receiving court permission or advising Joe.

Joe and his attorneys would later question why, as administrator, Ernest hadn't established the winery in the estate's name. In fact, they argued, that would have been Ernest's fiduciary responsibility. Ernest and his attorneys, however, saw it simply as his choice to start his own winery in 1933.

During his deposition for the 1988 case, Ernest was asked: "Did you give any consideration to having the estate apply for a permit to crush and store wine?"

"No, I did not," he replied, adding, "[It] never crossed my mind."

Nor did it occur to him that the estate could generate at least the same working capital of $6,000 with which he and Julio allegedly began their winery.

"I didn't think about it," he responded when confronted with this possibility, "because I wasn't going to put the estate in the wine business. . . . I was already going into the wine business for myself."

Even though Ernest, his attorneys, and his accounting expert would later explain that there had been an "open book" accounting between the estate and the winery, he regarded the winery as a distinct entity established and owned by himself and Julio. Once the probate court approved the estate's final accounting, Joe, Sr.'s continued business was effectively transformed into a winery separate from the estate. Joe, Jr., was then excluded from the partnership and the business established by his two brothers. Although Ernest and Julio had been able to use the estate as the basis for founding the winery and, according to Joe's attorneys, as a bank from which the winery could "borrow" both funds and grapes, Joe did not receive the same benefit from the legacy as his brothers.

In later years, Ernest came to believe so strongly that only he and Julio had created the winery that he seemed to forget his younger brother's very existence. In another court case, when he was questioned about his father's estate and the prior and continuous use of the Gallo name, he announced without hesitation, "My brother and I inherited our father's property and business."

After their parents' deaths, Ernest and Julio became Joe, Jr.'s guardians, although it wasn't until February 1934 that they actually filed "Letters of Guardianship" with the probate court. Then they let the matter slide for another year, perhaps feeling that there was no pressing need to make official their care of their younger brother. But when Joe, Sr.'s estate was finally probated, Joe, Jr.'s share of the inheritance had to be transferred into a guardianship estate. In April 1935, Ernest and Julio completed the guardianship procedure by having their mothers-in-law underwrite the required $2,000 bond. They now had the legal standing to supervise Joe, Jr.'s inheritance. But they failed to file both the requisite first accounting of the guardianship estate and subsequent yearly reports, and for some reason the court ignored the omission. (The court had already approved Ernest's application to waive official court notices sent to Joe, Jr., since he was a minor and living in the same home. Thus, Joe would have had no independent notification of the judicial procedures, even if at thirteen he would have understood the transactions that his older brothers were carrying out.)

More than likely, Julio was unaware of these legal requirements, but Ernest's lawyer, Ed Taylor, would certainly have known that a yearly accounting was an established practice for guardians. Why these reports were not filed, Ernest himself could not later explain, even though he continued to keep an "open account" between Joe, Jr.'s guardianship estate and the winery, just as he had with their father's estate.

In later years Joe would say that he had no memory or knowledge of Ernest's legal actions on his behalf. The February 1934 petition to the court to have his brothers named as his guardians did show his signature. "But Ernest would often just hand me a piece of paper and tell me to sign it," he recalled. "I always did—no questions asked—and especially at that age I wouldn't have wondered what I was signing."

In September 1933, he had entered his freshman year of high school. He was now called Joe (except by his brothers and their wives, who continued to call him Pete), and his classmates thought he was shy and somber. But they had heard about the family tragedy and could understand why he didn't smile very often. He had a passive, watchful quality about him, too, as if he were used to observing others' moods and taking care to do what was expected of him. He was learning that this was how to get along in the new household with two new sets of parents. Julio and Aileen could be warm and affectionate, but Amelia seemed more distant and demanding and Ernest was the disciplinarian, much as his father had been. Small wonder that Joe grew up obeying his oldest brother with no questions asked—that was what was expected. In later years, no one recalled "good times" or feelings of happiness; it was all work, work, work.

Joe would later remark, "I don't understand my brothers' resentment about my father's treatment of them. They raised me just the same way, and I still looked up to them and did everything they told me to do."

The Gallo household was run in a regimented fashion. Amelia and Aileen alternated cooking duties; one week, one of them cooked, the next week, the other. Amelia was the better cook, having learned Italian specialties from her mother, but she was willing to teach Aileen so that the "boys" would have their favorite dishes. The week that one wife was preparing the meals, the other wife took care of the dishes. Amelia became Ernest's unofficial secretary (she was paid no salary), and while she was at the winery office, Aileen cleaned house, did the laundry and ironed, tended to the kitchen garden, and canned vegetables and fruit.

Joe's days were routine as well. He did his chores in the morning, went to school and then came home to more chores. He fed the hogs and chickens, weeded the garden, and picked up milk from a neighboring dairy every day. He helped in the vineyards, and on weekends and during the summer Ernest sent him to the winery to do odd jobs. In the mornings and evenings he sometimes took his dog into the vineyards to hunt rabbits with his shotgun, a necessary chore, which he regarded as more fun than work. And there was always the hammering together of lug boxes to prepare for grape picking in the fall.

Ernest now laid out a plan of study for his younger brother. While Joe wanted to study agriculture in high school, as most of his friends would be doing (and as Julio had done before him), Ernest directed him to enroll in college preparatory math, chemistry, and physics courses so that he could be accepted by the University of California at Davis. In previous years Joe had received A's and B's; after his parents' deaths, his grades began to suffer as a result of his grief, his lack of interest in the new subjects, and the long hours he spent on his chores and work in the vineyards.

"From what Joe told me about this time," Joe's wife Patricia Gallo later said, "his world was turned upside down. He was distressed that Ernest forced him into those courses. He missed his parents, he was separated from his old friends and playmates, and I think he must have been a sad, lonely boy. He talked about these days as a kind of haze, and although his heart wasn't in his new studies, he took his father's last words seriously. He would always mind his brothers, even down to the school courses that Ernest chose."

Like Julio, Joe was athletic and was thrilled when he made the basketball team. But Joe recalled that Ernest put a stop to it after he brought home a report card with all C's. "These grades aren't acceptable," Ernest lectured. "You must be better than average." Ernest banned basketball practice after school, but the coach was impressed enough with Joe's talent that he allowed him to play in scheduled games without attending practice sessions. He was on the team for all four high school years, but Joe could not remember his brothers' coming to watch him play.

While Ernest later denied telling Joe what courses to take or forbidding him basketball practice, according to Patricia Gallo, Joe simply talked about these two demands imposed by Ernest as "givens" of his teenage years. "It wasn't as if he later complained about it," added Patricia. "I think he just felt that it was the way things had to be. But I have the impression that he was basically a young boy, deprived of his parents and any answers to his questions about their deaths, plus no one to talk to since he'd also been cut off from his boyhood friends. He was shoved into a strange scholastic environment and had very little encouragement or time to adjust to all that had happened."

As a teenager Joe was also asked to put in more time in the vineyards and at the winery. In his sophomore year he was responsible for spraying the vines with sulfur from three to seven in the morning. The following two years he was heading the crews of workers to tie up vines and pick the autumn harvest. And when Ernest and Julio bought the Hall Ranch vineyard in 1937, Joe was assigned to graft and prune those vines as well.

The Gallo household was joyless. Without their mother's warmth (and despite Aileen's attempts to inject some lightness of mood), Ernest and Julio lived as if under siege. They worked over sixteen hours a day in the winery or the vineyards, then came in dirty and weary for dinner. Aileen and Amelia served them their meals, and if silence didn't descend over the table, Ernest would quiz Joe about his studies. As part of the traditional pattern, after dinner Ernest and Julio were left alone to discuss business matters. Even though Amelia sometimes worked at the winery, even though she and Aileen sometimes signed winery documents, they would later say that they had no idea or understanding of business matters. All they knew, they insisted, was that their husbands worked day in and day out to make the winery a success.

Joe found some emotional respite in his friendship with Nilus Lowe, Aileen's father. He had retired and spent a good part of the day at the Maze Road home, sometimes even turning up for breakfast. Lowe shared Joe's interest in livestock and cattle ranching, and he also enjoyed fishing and hunting. He and Joe often sat in their favorite spot under the trees behind the sun porch and talked. Perhaps Lowe sensed Joe's emotional needs; perhaps he could give the teenager the warmth and affection that Joe so missed in his older brothers. Lowe also took Joe on a week-long fishing and hunting trip every year. Later Ernest cited these vacations as "proof" of his younger brother's unwillingness to work hard.

By and large, though, Joe conformed to his brothers' expectations. For example, Ernest disapproved of one of Joe's high school girl friends because she was Portuguese and therefore, in his opinion, socially unacceptable. He told his brother to stop seeing her, and Joe obeyed, afraid to risk his brother's displeasure.

Aileen and Julio's first son, Robert Julio, born on August 18, 1934, seemed to add warmth and affection to an otherwise sad and silent household. But for the most part, Ernest still set the tone; although Julio was nominally an equal partner, he also seemed to accept his older brother's control of the family as well as the winery.

Ernest's vision was to build Gallo into the largest winery, first in the state, then in the country. In later years, the brothers would attribute their achievement to their famous division of labor—Julio making the wine, Ernest selling it. But Ernest's "genius" in marketing and sales was said to be the driving force behind the Gallo success story. The founding of the winery itself, however, suggested another talent: his ability to shape circumstances to his benefit. He had derived the necessary results from both the probate court and the Bureau of Alcohol; he controlled the means by which to establish the winery and sustain it through its first months of extraordinary production (nearly 180,000 gallons during the autumn of 1933). Thus, the pattern was established from the beginning. During the next decades of the winery's rapid expansion and development, the ends would always seem to justify the means as Ernest worked toward his goal of becoming number one. This should have been no surprise: As Ernest liked to quip to his employees, "Does the leopard change his spots?"

By 1935 the E. & J. Gallo Winery was producing 350,000 gallons of wine annually. Ernest was often on the road, sometimes for as long as five months at a time, to find new distributors and buyers. When he returned to the winery, he would once again take control, often berating Julio and employees for problems or lapses in his absence. Ernest expected them all to work back-breaking hours to increase wine production and support his plans to expand the company.

His first idea was to join forces with another winery, and he proposed a merger with his Franzia brothers-in-law. After consulting their father, Giuseppe, they turned Ernest down. Through Amelia, Ernest heard that her father had sneered, "We don't need all his junk." Whether Franzia was referring to Gallo wine or the rundown warehouse in which it was made, he never specified. But Ernest stored the remark away, nursing his resentment. In a pattern repeated whenever he felt rejected or snubbed, he set out to "show them." As Amelia often remarked to winery employees over the years, "Ernest married me for my family's winery. When he couldn't get that, he put them out of business."

Ernest then decided to build a larger winery facility with up-to-date equipment and technologically sophisticated and efficient production methods. He would turn winemaking into an assembly-line process. After acquiring a forty-acre grain field adjacent to the Santa Fe railroad line on one side and Fairbanks Avenue on the other, Ernest and Julio undertook the construction of a half-million-dollar plant. Most of the cost went into massive concrete storage tanks (following Italian Swiss Colony's design, they were larger and cheaper to build than redwood cooperage) and elaborate equipment rather than into the winery's office buildings, which were modest one-story concrete and wooden structures.

Completed in 1936, the new winery had a capacity of 1.5 million gallons of wine; conveyor belts led to two rotary centrifugal crushers capable of processing sixty tons of grapes an hour; refrigerating coils cooled the wine to seventeen degrees; wine was pumped through an elaborate filtration system and a network of pipes into the huge storage tanks. After consulting experts in the oenology department at both UC Berkeley and Davis, Ernest and Julio spared no expense to bring technology and mass production to winemaking. It was their first step toward making the Gallo Winery the huge and efficient operation that it is today. "All the biggest" was Ernest's motto long before "All the Best."

Although Ernest and Julio plowed most of their profits into their new facility, they still needed money wherever they could find it. Following the probate court's final distribution of Joe Sr.'s estate on April 29, 1935, Ernest continued an "open book" system of accounting between the winery and what on January 2, 1936, he designated as the "Gallo Brothers General Ledger," in which he included Joe, Jr.'s guardianship estate. On April 20, 1936, Ernest applied to the bank in his and Julio's names and as guardians of Joe for permission to sell the 2,653 shares of Transamerica stock that the three had inherited from their father. Given permission to proceed, Ernest then entered the $33,077.95 earned from the stock in the winery's account. It wasn't until 1941 that he advised the court that his younger brother's share had been "loaned" to the winery.

No one, however, would dispute that Ernest and Julio achieved success through hard work. Ernest was also a notorious penny-pincher, and he expected his employees to put in the same long hours that he and Julio did. Because jobs were hard to come by, most of the employees tolerated the sixteen-hour days and small and often late paychecks. Sometimes Julio rebelled, especially when Ernest returned from one of his selling trips and found fault with his management of the winery. Employees heard the brothers shouting at each other in Ernest's office. *Make your own goddamned wine,* was often Julio's exit line when he stalked out of the winery, furious that Ernest had once again called his competence or diligence into question.

Ernest drove himself even more mercilessly, and during the winter of 1936 his exhaustion took its toll. He was hospitalized for six months, and according to a winery employee, Rudy Wagner, "No one was supposed to know that he was in a hospital up in Ross, I think, somewhere near Oakland or Livermore." Julio was left to run the winery, and soon he was overwhelmed by having to handle both his and Ernest's jobs, supervising the final construction of the new winery facility, taking care of the vineyards, purchasing grapes from growers, and taking sales trips in Ernest's place. He later regretted how little time he had to give to his family, especially after Aileen had given birth to their second child, a daughter, Susann Aileen, on May 28, 1936.

But most upsetting to Julio were the financial and legal problems with which he now had to deal, especially those that had arisen because of Ernest's activities. Before Julio could remain ignorant or oblivious; now that he had to face them head on and without Ernest's bravado or talent for talking his way out of tricky situations, his nerves were beginning to fray.

Twice that spring an agent from the Alcohol Tax Unit arrived at the winery, demanding to speak to Ernest. He was told that Ernest was unavailable, the first time that he was home ill, the second time away on a business trip. The agent was not to be deflected. In an investigation of another winemaker accused of coloring his wine with coal tar dyes, the agent had discovered that the San Francisco chemical company that had supplied the dyes had also shipped two orders, fifty pounds each, during a three-month period to Ernest Gallo of the E. & J. Gallo Winery in Modesto. With the records in hand, the agent returned to the winery a third time. Told that Ernest was again not on the premises, the agent demanded to speak to Julio.

According to the inspector's report, Julio explained that since he ran the ranch and the vineyards, he knew little about the winery, which was managed by Ernest.

But are you aware that your brother ordered coal tar dyes last year for the winery? the inspector asked.

Julio paused, then conceded that he was aware that Ernest had purchased some the year before and experimented with its use.

Experimented? the agent asked, tacitly remarking on the number of pounds ordered in a three-month period for only what Julio was calling an experiment.

My brother travels a lot in the East, Julio explained. *Some winemakers back there told him that adding dye to wine was a common practice.*

Who were these winemakers? the inspector demanded. The adding of dye to wine was prohibited by the Bureau of Alcohol, Tobacco and Firearms (BATF). Any winemaker admitting to the use of dyes would be warned or fined and even stood to lose his winery's license.

My brother didn't mention any names, Julio replied.

Did your brother then start using the dye in your wine?

No, he didn't. He found that the dye settled to the bottom of the bottles and left a purple stain on the glass. So he decided not to use it at all.

The inspector must have had his doubts. If the experiment had been unsuccessful, why had Ernest placed the second order? And what did it matter whether the dye stained bottles if the winery shipped its wine in bulk and in barrels? He left with a stern warning, then filed his report with the bureau.

After Ernest was released from the hospital, he and Amelia rented a two-bedroom house in Modesto. He returned to manage the winery, already pursuing his ideas for expansion. Not only did he increase the storage tank capacity to 2 million gallons, he added a distillery adjacent to the fermenting rooms. Gallo now would have grape brandy to market as well as to use in fortifying dessert wines and sherries.

Distilling had to be carefully monitored and gauged since Bureau of Alcohol regulations were even more stringent for the production and sales of brandy. Ernest now assigned his employee Rudy Wagner to supervise the new distillery room, because he knew that Rudy had learned the art of distilling from his father, Albert Wagner, the Livermore cognac maker and friend of Joe, Sr.

In 1938 Joe went to work for the winery full time. He had graduated from high school in June of 1937, and even though he had failed to raise his grades and gain admission to UC Davis, Ernest presented him with a car. (For years Joe would mention the gift as proof of his brother's generosity, although his attorney, John Whiting, would later claim that Ernest had deducted the cost of the automobile from the guardianship estate account.) Joe had then enrolled at Modesto Junior College. Ernest again urged him to get high grades in chemistry and physics so that he could transfer to Davis for his junior year. The science courses required long hours in the laboratory, which Joe sometimes had to miss because of his job in the winery. When his grades failed to improve, Ernest scolded him and, as Joe recalled, he finally ordered him to give up school and come to work in the winery full time.

It wasn't a question of giving Joe a partnership in the company, however. Ernest assigned him to the crushing and fermenting rooms as well as to the distillery. Although he did menial jobs, working the same long hours as others, employees wondered what the third Gallo brother's role actually was. They saw Ernest berate him angrily, and they noticed that Joe never talked back.

"He'd just hang his head and scuff his feet," said Rudy Wagner. "Ernest was about the meanest SOB I've ever worked for. He was hard on all of us, but I had learned to shout back at him, especially when he was wrong about something. But Ernest was even meaner to Joe, and he just stood there and took it. So we all wondered why Joe wasn't a partner and our boss like his brothers, and why he was always catching hell from Ernest."

Curious to know what the story was, Rudy asked Max Kane, who also worked in the distillery room and had known the family for years.

"He's a silent partner," Max explained to Rudy. Apparently not understanding what the term meant, he added that Joe would become a full partner once he was of age. "It's because he's under twenty-one that he isn't called a partner and doesn't give orders."

Max's explanation only made Rudy more curious.

After witnessing another angry scolding from Ernest, Rudy went to Joe's side. "I don't understand, Joe. How come you put up with that kind of treatment?" he asked.

"Because he's my brother," Joe said with a shrug.

Ernest depended on his younger brother's unquestioning loyalty, especially in 1939 when Ernest once again ran afoul of the Alcohol Tax Unit's regulations.

One run of brandy was light in flavor and pale in color, which was not an uncommon occurrence. The BATF allowed a distiller to rectify such problems by adding caramel at the time of the brandy's production. But once the brandy had been barreled, gauged, and BATF-inspected and bonded for shipment, nothing could be added. Ernest had received a complaint from one of his New York distributors that the sample of the brandy he had ordered was "undesirable because of color." Rather than lose the customer or distill a new supply, a plan was devised.

Just before noon on May 15, Charles Herd, the "storekeeper-gauger" from the Alcohol Tax Unit in San Francisco, arrived at the winery for the last regauging of the Gallo brandy before shipment. As usual, he first checked in with Rudy Wagner at the distillery, and Rudy accompanied him to the warehouse where the fifty-gallon barrels of brandy were stored. Herd regauged the barrels' contents and applied the tax stamps.

This warehouse is about to be locked and placed under seal, he called out. *All employees must now leave.*

Rudy and another warehouseman exited with Herd, who padlocked the door, then searched in his pocket for the official seal that would show that the lock hadn't been tampered with.

Damn, I left the seals at the hotel, he muttered to Rudy. *I'll have to come back.*

Herd drove off, and Wagner returned to the distillery. Twenty minutes later he saw the agent drive through the main gate and head down the lane to the brandy warehouse at the rear of the property. Then he spotted Ernest running out of his office. He jumped in his car and, according to Wagner, drove after Herd, all the while honking his horn.

When Herd arrived at the warehouse, Ernest was right behind him. The gauger heard voices and banging coming from within, and he flung the door open.

Max looked up in surprise, holding a five-gallon can of caramel, and Joe slipped toward the rear of the building. They had hidden in the warehouse when it was locked. Assuming that the inspector had sealed the building, they had begun knocking out the bungs from the barrels.

Herd ordered them out of the warehouse. Max tried to remove the can of caramel, but Herd stopped him.

Can't you forget it? Ernest now requested.

Better not talk to me, Herd replied. *I may have to use anything you say as evidence against you. These premises are now under detention.*

Herd announced that he was driving to the home of John Scott, the storekeeper-gauger for the Alcohol Tax Unit, to discuss the incident with him. Ernest followed him in his own car and accompanied him to the door. After explaining to Scott what he had discovered at the winery, Herd suggested that Scott return to the winery with him.

Ride with me, Mr. Scott, Ernest urged.

Scott agreed, and on the drive back to the winery, Ernest tried to convince him to advise Herd that it wasn't necessary to report the incident to the chief inspector.

You would not lose anything by taking a lenient view of the matter, Ernest added.

Scott, however, intended to pursue the investigation and simply informed Herd of Ernest's remarks in the car.

When they arrived at the warehouse, Scott went inside and noted the five-gallon can of caramel, a funnel, basins covered with caramel, several brandy barrels "already tampered with" and a rope that apparently Max and Joe had planned to use to climb out a warehouse window. Concluding that there seemed to have been an "illegal entry" into a sealed warehouse and "illegal rectification of brandy," Scott announced that until there was a further investigation by special agents, the warehouse would remain locked.

But can't you omit telling them about the can of caramel found in the warehouse? Ernest pleaded.

Scott once again refused, and he and Herd left to inform their superiors of the incident.

Joe later recalled that after Scott and Herd's departure, Ernest stalked back to his office. Joe followed and found his brother sitting at his desk, his head in his hands, his shoulders heaving. When Ernest looked up, Joe remembered that he was surprised to see tears running down his cheeks.

Oh, God, what are we going to do? he sobbed to Joe. *We'll be ruined if they charge us.*

Joe had never seen his brother so distraught.

I'll tell them it was my idea, that you didn't have a thing to do with it, Joe said after a moment, desperate to find a solution to his brother's problem.

Joe recalled that Ernest leaped at the suggestion: *You could say you did this without my permission or knowledge,* Ernest replied. *You could tell them that I put you in charge of the brandy and that you did it on your own.*

Joe was nodding, eager to help, whatever the consequences might be for himself.

No, Ernest interrupted himself. *You're underage. They wouldn't like that either.*

What about Max? You could say he was the boss here—

That's it! Ernest exclaimed, according to Joe, and then called Max into the office.

Max had been loyal to Ernest ever since the Gallo parents' deaths, and he agreed to Ernest's suggestion. By the time the special investigators arrived from San Francisco, Joe recalled, he and Max and Ernest had all agreed on their story. The investigators collected the evidence from the warehouse, including fingerprints on the can and basins of caramel; they recorded that the bungs of sixteen barrels had been removed, which, according to their later report, represented "an anticipated shipment" of brandy. Then they interviewed Ernest.

I told Max to go through the proper channels to get permission to color some of the brandy, he responded to the investigators' questions. *I assumed that this had been done, and I went ahead and bought the caramel. But I was not responsible for my brother and Max's being in the warehouse.*

But the agents noted that the purchase was not within the legal time limit, having already checked the winery's purchase orders. And because of Ernest's position of authority, they were not convinced that Max and Joe had done this on their own.

The agent sent Ernest out of the office. He then called Max and Joe in. He asked Max what his official position was at the winery. Max announced that he was the bonded representative of the Haslett Warehouse Company. (One of the ways the winery expanded its storage capacity at a lower cost was to have warehouse companies construct the buildings, then lease the premises. Max received a salary from the warehouse company, but the winery reimbursed Haslett, the check receipts so noted in the winery records.)

I'm sort of a foreman for the E. & J. Gallo Winery, Max added when the investigators indicated that they knew of the reimbursement.

Max then admitted that he had deliberately hidden in the warehouse with the caramel and remained there after gauger Herd told everyone to leave and announced that the premises were under seal. He also declared that he had asked Joe Gallo to assist him.

But I did it all on my own, he declared, insisting to the investigators that he had, as the report described his statement, "committed this unauthorized act on his own initiative."

Joe supported Max's statement. *I helped Max do this because he is the boss*, he explained. *All of us who work at the winery consider him the boss.*

Max and Joe's replies did not persuade the agents. They called Ernest back in.

Isn't it true that you and your brother own and run this winery?
Ernest said this was so.

And when your brother isn't present, you are in charge?
Completely, Ernest agreed.

And the brandy in that warehouse was made by the winery and was being prepared for shipment to a customer in New York? they asked.

Ernest admitted this as well. Then, since the investigators had already found the customer's order in the correspondence file, as well as his complaint that the samples he'd received were undesirable because of their color, Ernest also had to concede that it was necessary to improve the brandy's color with an injection of caramel.

But, as the agents pointed out in their report, the caramel had been purchased ten days after the date when the winery was legally permitted to add coloring.

Then the agents pressed their final questions: Wasn't it to Ernest that the customer had complained about the brandy's flavor and color? Wasn't it Ernest himself who had ordered the caramel after the legal time limit? Despite Max's employment by the Haslett Warehouse Company and its payment of his salary, didn't the winery reimburse Haslett $200 a month for Max's salary?

Ernest had to admit that this was the case and that, as the report indicated, Max "worked under his direction" (the investigators later confirmed the arrangement with Haslett's assistant general manager).

The San Francisco investigators ended the interview and later concluded in their report that the evidence suggested that Ernest had ordered Joe and Max to hide in the warehouse and add the illegal coloring. Besides Ernest's reputation for keeping watch over every detail of his company, the investigators also remarked upon his rushing after Herd, which suggested that he must have known Max and Joe were in the warehouse; Ernest's knowledge of the illegal activities was even more confirmed by Wagner's later recollection that he had also honked his car horn, as if to warn Max and Joe of Herd's return.

Ernest later had only a vague recollection that "something happened about coloring the brandy" but that it was "no big deal" and not illegal; nevertheless, in 1939, he, Max and Joe were charged in federal court with violating internal revenue liquor laws. All three pleaded nolo contendere; the court fined Ernest $5,000 and ordered him to fire Max but took no action against Joe (noting that he had no assets of his own).

Ernest paid the fine, but rather than firing Max, he put him on a six-week paid leave-of-absence.

"Ernest just told him to disappear for a while," said Rudy Wagner, "and then he returned when the inspectors weren't keeping such a close watch. Max had the kind of loyalty Ernest demanded, and eventually he was set up on a ranch. Ernest and Julio had owned it, but I don't know whether they gave it to him or sold it to him at a low price. But we all felt that because Max would do or say whatever Ernest wanted, Ernest fixed him up for life."

Joe, however, wasn't so richly rewarded. Perhaps his role was already well-defined, both as a tacit understanding within the family and as an emotional imperative in his own mind. As the BATF report indicated, he had "no financial assets," and he was neither promoted

at the winery, nor did Ernest or Julio suggest that he become a partner in the company, not then and not when he turned twenty-one
two years later.

In later years the federal charge against Joe was rumored to be the
reason he had never been made a partner. Winery employees repeated an incorrect version of the brandy incident, alleging that the
court had held Joe responsible for the violation and prohibited him
from ever participating in the winery's ownership. The story was resurrected during the 1988 lawsuit as well. When he heard this story,
Joe could only laugh at the irony; his willingness to take all of the
blame for the illegal activities had become another reason for his
exclusion from his brothers' partnership.

CHAPTER FIVE

With the addition of the distillery in 1937, the Gallo Winery was producing a full array of both table and sweet fortified wines: burgundy, claret, barbarone, Tokay, muscatel, Sauterne and Rhine as well as sherry, port, Angelica, and white port. But these wines were still sold in bulk to bottlers, who distributed the wine under their own labels.

One of Ernest's talents was his quick study of the market, and he realized that the coming trend was winery-bottled and labeled brand products. Large companies like Italian Swiss Colony, Cresta Blanca, Guild, Roma, and Petri were already selling under their own names. In 1937 Ernest, too, set out to develop and promote a Gallo label.

He first considered calling his wine "Modesto," but the similarity to "modest" hardly fit his personality. He then returned to the Gallo name along with the logo of a rooster, a label much like the one his father had used on both his wine and his grapes. But when he asked his New Orleans and Miami distributors to bottle and sell his wine under this label, he was disappointed by their resistance and lack of enthusiasm.

The cost of building the new winery prevented Ernest from financing an extensive advertising campaign for the proposed Gallo brand, and since neither distributor was willing to promote his brand over its other wines, Ernest's project met with little success during its first two years.

This resistance helped Ernest to realize that he needed to own or at least control distributorships. An opportunity presented itself when he learned that Franek, his New Orleans distributor, was in financial difficulty. Ernest bought the company in June 1939 and reorganized it as the first Gallo-controlled distributorship.

Laws regulating direct winery ownership of distributorships varied from state to state, and Gallo now instituted its vertical organization. The New Orleans company was established as a separate corporation with E. R. Anderson, who worked for the winery in its Los Angeles distributorship, installed as president. Ernest and Julio owned stock and were named directors. The winery then licensed the distributorship to use the name Gallo Wine Company of Louisiana as it made the transition from bottling and selling its previous brands of Cream of California and Great Valley to marketing Gallo-labeled wines.

In the following year, when Distillers Outlet, his Los Angeles distributor, also suffered financial setbacks, Ernest bought half the company from its owner, Sam Watt. Ernest and Julio became partners in the firm and licensed it to call itself Gallo Wine Company. Watt was appointed president and general manager, Ernest secretary, and Ed Taylor, the winery's lawyer, was added to the board of directors.

With this acquisition, Ernest set out to learn how to market, merchandise, build, and sell a brand. During the winter of 1940–41, he spent most of his time in Los Angeles, driving down from Modesto and making what would become his routine inspections of liquor stores. He interviewed owners and managers, clerks and customers. It was this informal version of a consumer survey that would eventually form the basis for the Gallo marketing method, one of the most structured and intensive sales programs that the wine industry had ever seen. But as yet Ernest had neither the money nor the army of salesmen to put his ideas into full operation. Instead, he was foot soldier and general, and he worked with Watt to devise a Gallo label that he thought would best sell the product.

If any wine was the flagship of the Gallo Winery, it was white port. At the time most wine drinkers still preferred dessert to table wines because of their sweet taste and high alcohol content. Usually made from Thompson seedless, Malaga, muscat, and sometimes French Colombard grapes, white port was relatively inexpensive to produce, and fortified by brandy to 20 percent alcohol, it had the kick customers wanted. Sitting at the Watts' dining room table, Ernest and Sam and his wife designed the Gallo White Port label. Once again he adopted his father's rooster logo, this one appearing at the top of the label with Gallo spelled out below. At Mrs. Watt's suggestion, he added the homey touch of a "recipe" for "White Port Sherbet" on the label's left side.

On the right side, Ernest included the message, "This wine is made from grapes raised in California produced solely by vines grown from imported cuttings. . . . Which grapes are selected by myself for their high quality, color, sweetness and soundness. The entire operation is under my personal supervision. None is genuine without my signature." Beneath the print appeared a facsimile handwritten "Ernest Gallo."

Leaving aside the exaggeration (Thompson seedless were not considered high-quality wine grapes), the self-promotion conspicuously omitted Julio's name. Although the label still referred to wine made by the E. & J. Gallo Winery in Modesto, Julio's role of selecting grapes and making wine seemed to have been subsumed by Ernest. What had become of Julio? Had Ernest maneuvered him into a secondary position?

In fact, Ernest's announcement had obliquely revealed another Gallo secret rooted in the family tragedy.

While Ernest spent much of his time in Los Angeles over the winter and spring of 1940–41, Julio once again had to shoulder most of the work of managing the winery and the vineyards. He rarely saw his children, now three in number, the youngest of whom, Phillip, had been born on February 5, 1939. Even more frustrating were Ernest's continued complaints upon his return from Los Angeles or another sales trip. Julio was overworked and on edge; he had insomnia, he lost his appetite. He could barely speak to Ernest for five minutes without becoming upset and angry.

According to Rudy Wagner, he and other winery employees noticed that Julio sometimes disappeared for several days at a time. When Ernest was away, Julio frequently dropped in at the distillery to check an evening's run of brandy, and he became friendly enough with Wagner to complain openly about Ernest, how he drove everyone too hard and always found fault. Wagner recalled one such exchange:

"I suppose you've noticed that I sometimes go away," Julio remarked one evening.

Wagner nodded, aware of the dark circles under his boss's eyes and the tremor in his hands.

"Sometimes the strain just gets too much for me and I have to get out of here," Julio continued. "So I go off by myself to San Francisco and take a room in a nice hotel. It's the only way I can try to relax."

"I'm sure it's good for you to unwind, especially after all the hours you have to put in here," said Wagner.

"Not just the long hours but the way Ernest is. It gets so I just can't listen to him anymore. All his talk about what has to be done and has to be done his way."

Julio seemed about to say more, but he stopped himself and hurried off to check the distillery proof gauges. He was worried about something, Wagner was certain.

Ernest and Amelia now had children—their first son, David Ernest, had been born on June 12, 1939, and Joseph Ernest or "Joey" on March 12, 1941. To accommodate their larger family, Ernest had cleared a site on the Gallo property across Maze Road from the family's original ranch and built a new home. It was a $14,000 modern structure featuring a fieldstone exterior and floor-to-ceiling windows overlooking the vineyards. With more room, Ernest invited his brother Joe to live with them. However, Joe, who had turned twenty-one on September 11, 1940, chose to remain with Aileen and Julio in the old family home.

Julio had begun to confide in Joe that he was upset by Ernest's constant criticism, the arduous demands on his time, and the business discussions Ernest insisted on having during their routine lunch meetings. In the spring of 1941 Julio seemed to become even more depressed, according to Wagner. His eyes filled with tears, and he referred to his parents' deaths, which Wagner had heard stories about from fellow winery employee Pete Cisi. But why Julio's grief had been resurrected at this particular time, no one seemed to know.

Winery employees now were worried by their employer's nervousness; indeed, they thought he seemed on the verge of a "collapse," said Wagner, and then in April 1941, he noticed that Julio hadn't appeared at the winery for several weeks. The official explanation was that he was away on a trip, but when his absence continued throughout the summer, there was talk at the winery that Julio had gone away to a hospital.

Thus, when Ernest was promoting his "personal supervision" of Gallo wine, Julio was absent from both the winery and Ernest's activities that spring and summer. In April and May, however, the board of directors of the Los Angeles Gallo Wine Company met twice. In the minutes for both meetings, prepared by Ed Taylor and Ernest,

Julio was listed as present and his signature appeared on the report. But, as he would later confirm, it was physically impossible for him to have attended either of these meetings since he was "still in the hospital." Whether Ernest had signed for him or had visited him in the hospital and asked him to sign the papers, Julio could not recall. But in either case, a record was created that indicated Julio's participation in business decisions, and Ed Taylor signed the minutes of the meeting.

During that same June, Ernest was involved in another legal procedure. Once Joe had turned twenty-one on September 11, 1940, Ernest and Julio were expected to give a final accounting and close his guardianship estate in probate court. Nothing had been done about it for nine months. But on June 14, 1941, at Ed Taylor's request, the winery's accountant, I. W. Fiscalini, sent a "rough draft" of an accounting of the guardianship estate to him.

Taylor then copied Fiscalini's rough draft as the "first and final account" to be filed with the court. It began by listing Joe's inheritance from his father that had been placed in trust. Yet there were several discrepancies between Joe, Jr.'s guardianship estate and what had been listed in Joe, Sr.'s probated estate. For example, the seventy-acre Maze Road home ranch was valued at $12,000 in the guardianship estate rather than the $16,000 valuation that appeared in the final accounting of Joe, Sr.'s estate. The twenty-acre Keyes vineyard was halved in appraised value in Joe, Jr.'s estate. The guardianship accounting indicated the sale of the parents' Transamerica stocks but reported that Joe, Jr.'s one-third share of the proceeds had been "loaned" to the winery, and that with interest on the loan, he was due $14,812.83 from the E. & J. Gallo Winery.

Since Joe, Sr.'s continuing business, tanks, and trade name had not been listed in the probating of his estate, Joe's one-third share in these assets did not appear in the guardianship accounting. But what was surprising—and would remain mystifying—was an item listed under the category of "an undivided one third interest in and to the following assets." On the second line appeared "E. & J. Gallo Winery," and across from this entry the sum of $16,492.26 was designated. What this amount represented and how it had been computed wasn't specified, and although it was ambiguous, it appeared to be a separate figure from the amount due Joe from the sale of his stock.

While almost a year had passed since Joe had turned twenty-one, the guardianship estate was now closed quickly. Taylor retyped the accounting drafted by Fiscalini, Ernest signed the accounting for himself and Julio, and Taylor then submitted it to the probate court on June 20. A hearing on the matter was scheduled for Monday, June 30.

Then came a second flurry of activity on June 28, the Saturday preceding the hearing. Robert Fowler, a sixty-eight-year-old Modesto lawyer, prepared a document that he then filed with the court before the hearing Monday morning. Called Joe's "Objections to the First and Final Account," it argued that in addition to "the sum of $14,812.83 owing by E. & J. Gallo Winery" for the loan of his stock proceeds, Joe also was "entitled to the further sum of $25,000.00 as his portion of the profits derived from the operation of said winery through employment of this objector's [Joe's] funds." (What relation this figure had to the designated one-third interest in the E. & J. Gallo Winery or the $16,492.26 figure next to this listing was not explained in this document either.)

On July 2, Judge B. C. Hawkins signed an Order Modifying and Settling Account Directing Payment. He stated first that Ernest and Julio with their attorney, Taylor, and Joe with his lawyer, Fowler, had all appeared in court on Monday, June 30, and having considered the documentary evidence, the judge concluded: "That the account of said guardians of their administration of the estate of said minor as rendered, is in all respects full, true and correct, excepting that said guardians are hereby found to be liable to said minor in the sum of $20,000, in addition to the interest upon said proceeds credited said minor. . . . That said sum of $20,000.00 represents earnings realized by said guardians in the conduct of their business under the name of E. & J. Gallo Winery from and upon the proceeds received by them from the sale of stock of said minor sold by said guardians which proceeds were commingled with the personal capital of said guardians."

Hence, Ernest and Julio were ordered to pay the additional sum of $20,000 to Joe "in full and complete settlement of the liability and obligation of said Ernest Gallo and Julio R. Gallo."

The documents seemed to indicate a dramatic change in Joe. No longer submissive, he had challenged his brothers in court and won. He had questioned Ernest's presentation of the facts and acted in his own best interests, and the court had agreed. The $20,000 was his reward for asserting his independence. He was, one would have thought, out from under Ernest's thumb.

But when these court records were revealed nearly fifty years later, Joe would insist that he had known nothing about them. He said he had never received an accounting of his guardianship estate from Fiscalini; he had never raised objections or hired a lawyer to represent his claim in court; he hadn't attended a hearing, nor was he even aware of a legal procedure closing his guardianship; and finally, he said, he had never received $20,000 as a result of challenging his brothers.

"It would have been unthinkable for me to take my brothers to court," he declared. "That would have embarrassed them and would have shown lack of respect and ingratitude on my part. Nothing was further from my mind. I didn't know about my inheritance, and I didn't know about the sale of any stock. I wasn't aware that they had 'borrowed' my money, and besides, if I had been asked about it, I would gladly have given them the money outright. I would certainly never have hired a lawyer—I didn't know anyone named Fowler who supposedly represented me—and I wasn't at any hearing that discussed my inheritance."

Julio, too, said that he had no recollection of these events. In fact, as he later confirmed, he was still in the hospital at the time of the hearing and couldn't have been present, despite the July 2 court order which indicated both his and Ernest's appearing in person on June 30. Ernest said he couldn't recall attending the hearing, but added that Joe had been complaining for months.

Documents would later reveal that it was also unlikely that Ernest had been present in court that Monday morning. Alcohol Tax Unit records showed that he had an appointment at 10:30 A.M. June 30, with one of its agents who was inspecting the underground tanks at the home ranch and certifying the winery's inventory. Confronted with this report, Ernest suggested that he might have slipped away from the inspection to appear in court. The agent, however, had logged a two-and-a-half-hour visit during which Ernest answered over sixty questions and signed off on the completed inventory at one in the afternoon.

Joe and his attorneys later contended that the closing of the guardianship had been arranged by Taylor and Ernest to preclude any later legal action by Joe. Since Joe denied ever seeing these documents or attending a hearing, they came to believe that the "record" had been choreographed to sanction what seemed an irregular or at least an ambiguous accounting. They pointed to several facts to support their argument: While the court required that Joe be advised of the final accounting and the June 30 hearing in writing, it was later shown that the letters were addressed to him at the winery, not at his Maze Road home, and the certification indicated only that they were delivered to the winery's office, not to him personally.

Although Ernest insisted that Joe had examined the final accounting and was displeased, thus prompting him to hire a lawyer, the document purporting to be Joe's objections in fact showed an inaccurate birthday for Joe—September 9 was listed, not September 11. A point in Joe's favor was that if he had actually read the document, he would probably have noticed and corrected the error.

While Joe claimed that he had never known, much less hired a lawyer named Fowler, Joe's attorneys found evidence that Taylor and Fowler were colleagues on the Modesto Planning Commission and also were on opposing sides of several lawsuits during the summer of 1941. Ernest had also met with Fowler when he had been the city attorney in 1939, and Taylor had corresponded with him in Ernest's name. Joe's attorneys believed that it was possible that on the Saturday preceding the hearing, Taylor had asked Fowler to perform a mere formality of preparing a document and filing it; if he were told that Ernest and Joe had already reached a settlement but Joe needed a lawyer to document his claim, Fowler might have prepared the objection according to Taylor's instructions simply as a favor to his colleague. (The document showed no notice of service to either Taylor or Ernest, leading to the speculation that it had been simply handed to Taylor either in Fowler's office or before the hearing.)

Joe's lawyers' conjectures were further supported when the Gallo Bros. Ranch ledgers showed a payment of $25 to Fowler for his services, leading them to contend that Ernest had paid the lawyer. It was a small fee, even in 1941, and suggested that Fowler had spent little time investigating Joe's supposed objections. (Indeed, if a lawyer had actually computed the profits due Joe from his stocks, he would have needed more information about the winery's finances. But in his one-page objection, Fowler did not explain the basis for the $25,000 claim or the $20,000 settlement figure, nor did he address or define the listing of one-third of the winery as an asset and the accompanying $16,492.26 entry.)

Typing and court filing, not investigating and litigating, would seem to have been the services for which Fowler charged, Joe's attorneys concluded. The winery, however, suggested that Fowler might have been paid more—perhaps out of Joe's award—but apparently Fowler's files had been lost, and neither side could prove their speculations about Fowler's role.

Joe's attorneys argued that only Fowler and Taylor needed to attend the hearing and that they could simply represent to the court that Ernest and Joe had reached a compromise of $20,000 as a settlement of the $25,000 claim. The document was typed on Taylor's stationery, the judge then signed it, and it was filed in the record as the official court order. Joe's attorneys contended that there had been no real dispute or hearing before the judge, since Taylor himself had already designated the payment and prepared the court order for the judge to sign and fill in the appropriate date.

How then did the court order indicate the presence of the three Gallo brothers when in all likelihood none was there? According to Joe's lawyers and their probate expert, probate court procedure at the time allowed for this: Stenographers did not take notes in probate court hearings except at the request of one of the parties. Instead, the judge's clerk copied into his minutes the written order prepared by counsel for the judge's signature. Since Taylor had written the order, asserting the presence of all parties concerned and indicating a payment of $20,000 as settlement, this became the official record of the hearing. On July 2, then, Judge Hawkins signed the order, a documentary record had been created, and the guardianship estate was closed by the court, which gave the transaction the status of res judicata, the matter adjudicated and settled, and no longer vulnerable to further legal action.

Even after the official closing of his guardianship estate, Joe's money and inheritance remained part of the Gallo Bros. Ranches ledger that Ernest had established in 1936. Although Joe later denied that $20,000 had been paid to him, he nevertheless also confirmed that he rarely gave his finances a second thought; he was happy to have Ernest and Fiscalini, the winery accountant, handle all the books. As far as he was concerned, what he had inherited from his parents was part of the family's holdings from which he could draw when needed. All he had to do was ask—that had always been the arrangement and in his mind it was the way it should be. His brothers were generous (after all Ernest had given him a car) and anyway, for the time being, his salary of $300 a month from the winery was more than adequate.

Joe's lawyers would later speculate that Ernest, Taylor, and Fiscalini may have had further doubts about this court transaction, because another guardianship accounting prepared by the accountant would later be produced from the winery's files. This accounting was attached to a covering letter from Fiscalini addressed to Joe at the winery and dated February 24, 1941. This report, however, differed from the accounting filed with the court in June. In it Fiscalini explicitly corrected and explained in attached "exhibits" the discrepancies between valuations and assets listed on Joe, Jr.'s guardianship estate and Susie and Joe, Sr.'s probated estates which appeared in the June 14 accounting submitted to the court.

When this amended accounting came to light many years later, Ernest contended that this was why Joe had been complaining for months. Yet he couldn't explain why Fiscalini, if he had prepared this accounting in February at much greater length and with more accurate figures, hadn't given this report to Taylor to file with the court in June, or why the June accounting that was filed with the court did not reflect the corrections that Fiscalini had made in the supposedly earlier accounting. The questions surrounding these two accountings, Joe's lawyers would later argue, lent more weight to their suspicion that the closing of the guardianship account had been arranged to prove that Joe had been given a full accounting, had stated his objections, had been given his day in court, and thus could no longer raise the issue of his inheritance.

Whether Julio's hospitalization had been related to the closing of the guardianship estate could not be determined. He seemed too upset by memories of this period to answer questions with any clarity, although his attorneys contended that his illness was caused by overwork, not by the guardianship issue. Joe's attorneys, however, had to wonder if Julio had been so troubled by the prospect of closing the guardianship estate that it had revived his anxiety over his parents' deaths and contributed to his collapse that spring.

Indeed, when Julio returned to the winery, he told employees that on his doctor's advice he had to stay away from the business and legal side of the Gallo enterprise. He now began to spend most of his time in the vineyards, although he still supervised the winemaking. From that time forward, he left Ernest to handle business and legal matters, and he concentrated on wine production.

That had always been the informal organization of the winery, but by the fall of 1941, it was clearly defined. Although Ernest would always intrude upon the production department, Julio no longer had to participate in Ernest's sales and marketing and whatever other plans seemed to perturb him. Hence the famous Gallo division of labor originated more out of concern for Julio's well-being than from their fabled exchange of boasts. Julio's vow to "make all the wine you can sell" and Ernest's pledge "to sell all the wine you can make" was a way to preserve Julio's health.

During 1941 Ernest had carried on with his plan to build a wine empire. As if to mark a new era for the winery, he developed another Gallo wine label, substituting a cartoon of "Bacchus," a pudgy, toga-wearing Roman bearing the title "Father of Wine," for the rooster logo. The tag line, "It's thermalized" (as if temperature control were unique to Gallo) replaced Ernest's personal guarantee that he alone approved all wine produced. And at the top of the label ran the new slogan:

BY GOLLY! BUY GALLO!
JOLLY OLD GALLO

In March 1942, Ernest applied for his first trademark in the Gallo name and asserted in his application: "The trade-mark has been used continuously and applied to the goods in the business of the applicant and the predecessor of the applicant, Joseph Gallo, since 1909." Why Ernest chose the year 1909 was puzzling. His father and uncle's wine company had been in existence since at least 1907; in 1909 Joe was running his hotel in Jackson. Perhaps Ernest fixed on the 1909 date because it was the year of his birth. But the implication of Ernest's statement seemed clear: "The goods in the business of the applicant" was wine, and hence the statement suggested that the goods "in the business of . . . the predecessor of the applicant" must have been wine as well. (In the 1988 case, winery attorneys argued that the application should not be interpreted as Ernest's admission of continuing his father's business and trademark, since Ernest prepared the statement himself and was "unaware of the legal subtleties.")

Ernest's assertion would come back to haunt him, but in 1942 he tried to ensure that the Patent Office would see no reason to object to the Gallo name as a trademark on wine. Establishing prior use by his father since 1909 would buttress his and Julio's right to what was a fairly common Italian surname as a trademark.

Ernest had also envisioned an extensive selling campaign to push

Gallo into new national markets. But after the bombing of Pearl Harbor and the country's entry into World War II, he was forced to change his plans. While the marketing campaigns were stalled, the war effort offered the winery other opportunities to develop and expand.

First Ernest bought twelve railroad tank cars and formed the Gallo Tank Lines Company. The minutes for the new company's first meeting in March 1942 reported that Amelia was acting chairman, that Aileen and Julio both attended, and that Ernest was elected president. Neither Amelia nor Aileen recalled any such meeting, and Julio could not have been present, because, as he would later confirm, he was in the hospital again.

Acquiring tank cars was Ernest's next step toward creating a vertical organization of subsidiaries to reduce the total cost of wine production, bottling, shipping, and selling. He also transferred all of the winery's shares, assets, and its recently licensed trademark to the new company, a transaction that both increased the number of shares in the company and effectively put the winery at a further remove from the Gallo Bros. Ranch partnership in which Joe's money was still held.

In the beginning of 1942, winery employees noticed that Julio was again conspicuously absent from the winery. Rudy Wagner, who had left the winery but then returned, heard that Julio had been rehospitalized after a bout of nervous exhaustion and that his son Bob had been enrolled in military school. When Julio returned to work two months later, he told Wagner that he would again have to reduce his hours at the winery and spend much of his time out of doors to try to get his health back.

In the spring of 1942, anticipating Julio's convalescence and reduced hours inside the winery, Ernest hired Charles (Charlie) Crawford, a recent graduate in food science from Cornell University (he would later take courses at UC Davis as well). Assigned Julio's responsibilities, he was named "manager of the winery" and "senior vice-president for production." He became Gallo's first employee to assume managerial duties and an executive title, although Ernest would always insist that such designations meant little to him. There would never be a "chain of command" at the winery, and executives reported directly to Ernest and would continue to do so, even as the company grew. Ernest made a point of knowing every detail of every aspect of the winery's operation, and with Crawford replacing Julio, he gained even more control over what nominally was his brother's territory.

But winemaking then was a lower priority than contributing to the war effort. Ernest decided to produce cream of tartar, which was in demand by explosive manufacturers. When wine is fermented, it leaves a residue of argol, what winery workers call "slop"—a crude form of tartar. The winery needed money to convert wine tanks to the processing of argol and the storage of tartar. Joe was still working in the winery, and Ernest approached him with a business proposition.

"You put in $5,000 and you'll get 2,000 shares of the 5,000 we'll issue," Ernest said. "We'll make you director and president of the company. It will be a real opportunity for you."

Joe became president of Tartar, Incorporated, and Ernest appointed Ed Taylor vice-president and Max Kane secretary. Ernest was treasurer, and he and Charlie Crawford actually ran the operation, Joe's position being more titular than actual—since he was about to enter the army.

At the same time, the winery undertook its primary operation for the government—distilling industrial-strength alcohol from molasses. Although he'd quit the year before, Rudy Wagner had agreed to return and oversee the distillery.

"That's when the winery finally made a lot of money," he recalled. "In years before, especially when they'd just built the new winery on Fairbanks Avenue, they were really hard up. I remember creditors lining up at the winery office and delays in our paychecks. As much as I disliked Ernest, I went back to work for him because he promised me such a good salary. They had a government contract for 10 percent plus costs. The more you said it cost to produce the alcohol— torpedo juice we called it—the more the government paid. You can't imagine the costs we put in for! That's when Ernest really started to rake in the dough."

Because of the war, Joe had decided to enlist before he was drafted so that he would have his choice of service. He selected the Coast Guard, and that summer Ernest drove him to the recruitment office in San Francisco.

Joe was rejected, however, because he was found to be color blind. Ernest drove him to the army recruiting office, and he enlisted there. (Ernest and Julio both had exemptions, and Rudy Wagner and other employees wondered why Joe, too, wasn't exempted. They mistakenly believed him to be a partner in the winery and hence entitled to the same deferment the older brothers received for aiding in the war effort, but Joe himself never had any doubt about wanting to serve his country.)

On August 28, 1942, Joe departed for basic training in Biloxi, Mississippi. He was later sent to Lowry Field in Denver where for nearly three years he served as an instructor in the Twenty-first Technical School Squadron.

Before his departure, Joe had also asked Julio to keep an eye out for land to invest in. He had already bought an undeveloped seventy-acre plot that he planted to alfalfa. But like his brothers, he'd grown up raising grapes, and he hoped one day to cultivate vineyards. Soon Julio wrote to tell him that the Tegner Ranch, 160 acres suitable for vineyards, was for sale. Joe knew the property and asked Julio to make the purchase for him. Julio was happy to do so and volunteered to oversee the vine planting. On Joe's next leave, he and Julio drove out to watch the crew of men Julio had put to work grafting new vines.

Later there would be a dispute about who had financed the purchase and the planting. At the time Joe hadn't given it a second thought—he assumed that the cost was deducted from his monies in the Gallo Bros. Ranches account. As for Julio's supervision, he considered it a brotherly favor. Hence he was flabbergasted nearly fifty years later when Ernest referred to the Tegner proper purchase as evidence of his brothers' generosity and his own ingratitude.

During 1943 Ernest and Julio also acquired a new vineyard, this one located in Livingston, about thirty miles south of Modesto. The American Vineyard was owned by shareholders in the Valley Agricultural Company, and as part of the purchase Ernest converted their shares to winery stock, the first and only time that non-Gallos would own such interest in the family winery. The thousand acres of Thompson seedless grapes composed the largest vineyard of a single varietal in the wine industry. During the war the Thompson seedless were dried into raisins for the government, but Julio envisioned an experimental vineyard where he could continue his testing of planting, grafting, and pruning methods. After the war he would replant the property with a selection of varietals with which to develop different blends.

He wrote to Joe about his plans, and Joe often inquired about Julio's work in the Livingston vineyard in his return letters. This vineyard would become central to Joe's life, but the means by which

Ernest and Julio acquired it contradicted Ernest's contention that even while he was in the army, Joe had been offered the chance to become a partner in the winery.

Ernest recalled visiting Joe once in Denver and over dinner discussing "coming into the winery," only to have Joe once again reject the idea, saying that his brothers worked too hard and he didn't want to live like that. Joe remembered no such proposal nor his alleged repeated refusal, and the purchase of the American Vineyard bore him out. Ernest would have been in no position to offer Joe shares since the winery had transferred all of its preferred stock to the shareholders of Valley Agricultural Company, and sixteen thousand common shares were then issued to convert the shares that Ernest and Julio and their families previously owned. Thus, at the time Ernest claimed to have urged him to "come into the winery," the board would have had to authorize the issuance of additional shares before Ernest could make good on his supposed offer to Joe.

But Ernest alleged that Joe's rejection of his proposal in Denver had hurt him, couched as it was in a criticism of his brothers and their hard-driving ways. Joe insisted that he would never have made such disloyal and ungrateful remarks. He claimed that he still did whatever his brothers asked him to do, and on May 15, 1944, when Ernest sent him a legal document for his signature, he signed it without question.

The document granted his power of attorney to his brothers. Ernest needed it because he was once again reorganizing the winery and family properties. On March 4, 1944, he had restructured the E. & J. Gallo Winery partnership as a corporation into which all shares, subsidiary companies, and assets, including the Gallo trademarks, previously held by the Gallo Tank Lines Company, were transferred. At the same time the winery's capital stock was increased from $25,000 to $500,000.

On May 1, 1944, Ernest had reorganized what had been an oral agreement of partnership and a method of accounting into a written operating partnership called the Gallo Bros. Ranches. As he had during the previous decade, Ernest kept this three-partner account distinct from the two-partner winery. In 1936, he had established the ranch ledger, in which he recorded not only the ranch and vineyard properties inherited by all three brothers but also those they individually acquired. When, on May 1, 1944, he structured the Gallo Bros. Ranches partnership in a written agreement, he signed Joe's name, with the notation, "by Ernest Gallo and Julio Gallo, his Attorneys in Fact," even though it wasn't until May 15 that Joe actually conveyed his power of attorney.

Joe was designated as a limited partner in the Gallo Bros. Ranches. Since the closing of his guardianship estate, Joe had left his inheritance in the brothers' ranch account. Now the arrangement was formalized, and as the general partners, Ernest and Julio's shares of profits and losses were computed at 37.5 percent each, their property (including the home ranch, Hall ranch, and Livingston vineyards but not the winery) valued at $760,000. Joe's share was 25 percent, his property assessed at $189,975.78. Ernest and Julio were to be paid a salary "not to exceed $30,000" out of the partnership account, presumably to manage the home vineyards and Joe's Tegner ranch in his absence.

Unknown to Joe, the power of attorney would remain in effect for nearly fifty years (although no actions seemed to have been taken on the basis of this document after Joe's return from the war).

As far as Joe was concerned, when the war was over he would simply return to his job as a winery warehouseman (as he had listed himself in his army application). But he also had to make plans for his new family. Through Aileen he had met a pretty, vivacious Modesto woman on one of his first leaves. Blond, with large brown eyes and a warm smile, Mary Ann was the daughter of David Arata, one of the county's most successful wine-grape growers, who had first shipped with Joe, Sr., and then sold his grapes to Ernest and Julio at the winery. She and Joe had begun dating each other whenever he was home on leave, and soon she began to visit him in Denver, sometimes accompanied by Aileen and Julio, who were all in favor of the romance. Ernest and Amelia, however, hinted that they had reservations.

Their feelings seemed to stem more from class resentment and envy than from personal dislike. Although Mary Ann's father was Italian, he had crossed into the Modesto mainstream by marrying Mabel Coffee. The Coffees were a prominent founding family, and Mary Ann's grandfather "Bud" had been one of the town's leading businessmen as well as a pioneer test pilot. He had been killed when one of his flights ended in a crash, and Modesto's airport and a thoroughfare were named in his honor. While a grape farmer like the Gallos, David Arata had been welcomed into the civic life of Modesto, and his involvement in real estate, the Chamber of Commerce, and the Rotary Club put him at one remove from his immigrant roots. No gossip about bootlegging, family violence, or difficult temperaments lurked in his past, and his reputation for honesty and fair dealing, along with his congenial personality, had won him a seat on the city council.

Coming from this background, Mary Ann grew up with a secure sense of self and always spoke her own mind. Ernest, according to employees, still suffered from a feeling of inferiority and hadn't achieved the social acceptance for which he had always yearned. Yet because of his success, perhaps because of his defensiveness, he was sometimes abrupt and high-handed.

Mary Ann, however, wasn't about to be overwhelmed or intimidated by Ernest. She could see that he expected Joe's instant obedience and loyalty, and she was sometimes annoyed by Joe's submissiveness. While she might understand his attitude, she wasn't happy that Joe played "little brother" to Ernest's patriarchal control of both the family and the winery. After all, her mother—who never minced words—found Ernest's arrogance and lack of social grace rather comical. As she quipped when she saw Ernest or Amelia putting on airs, "I knew the Gallos when they didn't have a spaghetti pot to piss in."

Amelia also seemed jealous of Aileen's friendship with Mary Ann. The two sisters-in-law were often involved in an unstated competition, whether it was cooking or socializing. Amelia appeared annoyed that Aileen's loyalty seemed to be shifting now that she was becoming close to Mary Ann and spoke enthusiastically about her and her family. Joe was aware of the tension between Mary Ann and the Ernest Gallos, but he was glad that his fiancée and Aileen were becoming best friends, "as close as sisters," as Aileen said.

Joe and Mary Ann were married in Denver on February 4, 1945. They had only a few weeks together until he was ordered to the Philippines with the Sixty-third Infantry Regiment. He saw action in Luzon and was awarded several medals, including the Philippine Liberation Ribbon with one Bronze Star. Promoted to staff sergeant, he then was shipped to Korea with the occupation forces, and finally, on January 18, 1946, he returned to the United States and was sent to the Separation Center at Camp Beale, California. He was still awaiting his discharge when Mary Ann gave birth to their son Peter Joseph on January 29, 1946.

During Joe's absence Julio's health had improved. Overseeing the

Livingston vineyard had been just what the doctor ordered. Yet Julio had also lost some control of the production division inside the winery. Often as not, he wasn't told what Ernest was planning, and soon his conflicts with Ernest worsened into angry quarrels. Sometimes Julio threatened to quit and start his own winery elsewhere; sometimes he threatened to force Ernest out.

Joe himself had assumed that his former winery job was awaiting him. "It's going to seem awfully good to get back to work," he had written Aileen just before his army discharge. In his usual self-deprecating way, he had added, "even though I never cared much for work, ha, ha!"

But when Julio and Aileen accompanied Mary Ann to pick up Joe at Camp Beale in February 1946, it seemed that Julio had a new plan in mind.

Minutes after Joe greeted his family, Joe recalled, Aileen pulled him aside for a hurried, private conversation.

"Julio wants you to manage the Livingston vineyards," she whispered. "Really, he needs your help there, and we'd both like it very much if you would agree to take the job."

The proposal came as a complete surprise to Joe, but nothing more was said until later that evening.

"It's true, I do need your help down there," Julio then explained. "Otherwise, I'm away from the winery too much. I'll pay you $20,000 a year to be the vineyard manager, and you and Mary Ann can live in the ranch house on the property."

Joe could hardly believe the offer. When the winery had first bought the Livingston vineyards and Julio had told him about it, Joe had casually remarked that it would be nice to work there. Little did he imagine that there would actually be a position for him and at a salary that was twice what he had earned as a winery warehouseman.

But according to Joe, when he returned to Modesto and visited Ernest in his office, he learned that this brother had other plans.

"I want you to become manager of the winery operations," he announced to Joe.

"What about Charlie Crawford?" asked Joe. "That's his job, isn't it?"

"Charlie's a lying son-of-a-bitch. I want you to take his place."

Joe was stunned. He knew that Charlie had extensive training in chemistry and oenology, knowledge that was far beyond his own experience. Ernest had always thought highly of the man, and he guessed that Charlie had done something to make Ernest angry.

"Look, Ernest, I don't think I'm qualified—" Joe started to reply.

"If you take the job, you can work into an interest in the winery," Ernest now interrupted.

It was the first time, as far as Joe recalled, that Ernest had ever mentioned this possibility (although Ernest later claimed that when he had visited Joe in Denver, he had made a similar offer and Joe had refused). But Joe remembered only this one discussion when he found himself perplexed by Ernest's proposition: Why were his brothers offering him two different jobs, each equally insistent, as if they hadn't spoken to each other about their separate plans? And why was Ernest offering this added inducement of "working into an interest" in the winery?

"But Ernest, I've already accepted Julio's offer of the Livingston job," Joe said. "He asked me to be the manager down there."

Ernest scowled, and then, according to Joe, he explained that he was worried about Julio's health. "I think it would be better for him to stay in Livingston. If you work at the winery, you'll be relieving his burden."

Joe later recalled feeling confused. Julio and Aileen had made the same argument about the Livingston job. If Joe became the vineyard manager there, Julio wouldn't have to split his time between the winery and Livingston. He would be less overworked and the strain would be less. It was only later that Joe would suspect that there was some sort of behind-the-scenes "power play" involved in the two job offers. If he didn't take the Livingston job, then Julio would still have to spend a great many hours outside the winery. If Joe took Charlie's place, then Ernest would have consolidated his control over the winery and kept Julio at a distance in Livingston.

Although at the time Joe didn't understand Ernest's motives, he was surprised to hear Ernest say that Julio was threatening to take over the winery and force Ernest and his heirs out.

"And you know I built this winery, not Julio," announced Ernest abruptly. "So it's crazy for him to be talking like that."

He paused but then continued in a fatherly tone. "You've developed into a very capable guy in the army. Now it's time to think about your future. You could work into an interest in the winery if you take Charlie's job. That's where your future is, not managing the vineyard for Julio."

"No, Ernest," Joe said emphatically. "I've taken the Livingston job. That's all there is to it."

Joe left the office feeling that Ernest had accepted his choice to go to Livingston. What hadn't occurred to him at the time was to ask whether he could still "work into" an interest in the winery by taking the Livingston job. But since Ernest hadn't suggested it, he didn't ask. As he said later, he felt that Ernest and Julio "could choose what sort of offer they might give me and make whatever arrangements they felt were best."

Years later, Aileen and Julio would both insist that soon after Joe's return, Julio had pressed him to "come into the winery" both over lunch and standing in the driveway. Joe rejected the offer outright, they said, even angrily when Julio repeated the proposal as Joe was about to leave. Ernest also described a discussion he had with Joe, outside in his driveway, in which he also recalled using the phrase "come into the winery" as well as "work into an interest." When asked what he had meant by this phrase, Ernest later said, "I'm sure I didn't think of giving him a one-third interest. . . . Because after all the winery was something that Julio and I built and Joe had no part in it. . . . It's conceivable we would give him extended terms or a good price but not a gift."

Joe and Mary Ann now set about finding a home in Modesto, but when nothing seemed suitable they accepted Julio's offer of the vineyard manager's house on the Livingston properties. Mary Ann had reservations about living in what she considered "the country," far enough away to make casual visits or social evenings with friends and family difficult. But she seemed resigned to it, willing to wait until they could build their own home or find a house back in town. Joe felt that everything had been settled to everyone's satisfaction. (Joe would later confirm that the original salary offer of $20,000 was soon reduced. "I started at $10,000 a year, and that's what I earned until the day I left," he said.)

During his first three years of managing the Livingston vineyards, Joe brought in successful harvests. Julio had also hired a viticultural expert, Paul Osteraas, a graduate from the University of California at Davis, and together he and Joe brought in the largest crops that the vineyards had ever produced. Hearing how pleased his brothers were, Joe approached Ernest and Julio with a proposal: Would they sell the Livingston vineyards to him? They would still own the recently constructed winemaking operation, he explained, but he would own the grape-growing portion of the business. That way he would work into an interest in the winery, as Ernest had suggested three years before. Joe recalled the discussion:

"How are you going to pay for that interest?" Ernest demanded.

"I'll sell you the crop at the going price," Joe explained, having calculated this beforehand. "I would keep the expenses necessary to run the vineyards but give you all the profit."

"And how long would it take to pay us off?"

"That's hard to say. It would depend on the harvest and the profit each year."

"That's a big responsibility," Ernest objected.

"I already have that responsibility," Joe argued. "And I've brought in good crops and a big profit for you."

Ernest thought it over for a few minutes. Then giving Julio a quick glance, he shook his head. "No, I don't think Julio and I want to sell the winery ranches. We want to keep it the way it is."

Why Ernest rejected the proposal, Joe never asked and in his later recollections couldn't explain it either. But at the time, he simply continued to manage the Livingston vineyards. Like Julio, though, he began to feel the effects of the strenuous schedule. He complained of constant headaches, stomach problems, and aching knees, ailments that were related to spraying the vineyards, constant squatting to check grafting and pruning and grape quality. Nevertheless, he refused to slow down, so anxious was he to bring in the biggest and best harvests and receive his brothers' approval. Above all, he wanted to please them. Despite the drawbacks of the job, despite Mary Ann's irritation with her husband's long hours and their isolation in the country, Joe had no intention of leaving the position. The pattern was established; the "unknown" Gallo brother was satisfied both with his work and with his place in the family.

With the end of the war, the Gallo Winery had a sudden infusion of working capital. If anything accounted for its extraordinary growth in size and sales over the next fifteen years, it was the immediate availability of cash in the late 1940s. One source of income had been the government contracts; however, the huge increase came from a plan devised by Ernest, one which he would later regard as a secret triumph that he liked to share with a few select executives. It became a story that made the rounds of the wine industry to suggest just how brilliant and wily Ernest could be in his schemes to make Gallo number one.

During the war, grape growers' sales and profits had been kept at a minimum by price controls and limits on wine production. Anticipating the end of the war and the lifting of regulations, Ernest and Julio traveled throughout the Central Valley and Napa and Sonoma counties where they asked growers to sign with Gallo. They promised higher prices for the next season's harvest than were yet allowed under the wartime restrictions. Growers were easily convinced. So anxious were they about their future sales, so relieved to be guaranteed a better price, they consigned their grapes to the Gallos at the higher rates.

Once price controls were lifted and wineries were allowed to return to full production, Ernest and Julio's competitors discovered a scarcity of grapes—the Gallos had a lock on almost 75 percent of the crop. The larger companies, particularly those owned by distilleries such as Seagram, Schenley, and Hiram Walker, were forced to buy grapes from Ernest. The winery obviously didn't need all the grapes for which it had contracted, and Ernest could call the shots. He sold the surplus for several times the original contracted cost.

For years people would recall how Ernest and Julio had outsmarted their competitors. The plan had also taught the brothers a lasting and valuable lesson: If you control the grapes, you control the wine industry.

But in the late 1940s, Ernest still had a long way to go to fulfill his dream of becoming the nation's number-one winery. Despite his subsequent denial of ever making the comparison, his employees often repeated his statement that his goal was to become "the Campbell Soup Company of the wine industry." His and Julio's strategy was to mass-produce reliable wines that appealed to the majority of the consumers and were reasonably priced.

It was in this decade after the war that the Gallos adopted and developed the winemaking methods that would become the winery's signature. To reduce the tannic flavor in red table wines—what Charlie Barbera had admired as "the old country" taste—they blended Napa and Sonoma grapes with San Joaquin grapes. They no longer pressed grapes for red wine but used paddles to break the skins, releasing "free-run" juice without crushing the seeds. The result was a lighter—some would say blander—red since seeds and skins had introduced the heavier tannic flavor. (Pressed juice was still used in the distillery to produce spirits for fortified sweet wines, however.) But in both white and red table wines, Gallo was after lighter wines, which consumers seemed to favor, although most wine drinkers continued to prefer sweet and dessert wines to table wines anyway.

Considering corks unreliable, Ernest and Julio used aluminum screw-top caps to ensure consistent taste. (This would eventually become a Gallo stigma but in the beginning of this campaign it was felt that the caps would reassure more buyers that the wine would not go bad from cork leakage.) The winery's cooperage was replaced with epoxy-lined steel tanks, since the Gallos had concluded that the woody taste of barrel-aged wines was not popular among consumers. And they increased their tank capacity to such an extent that the winery began to look like an oil refinery. Ernest and Julio always hated the comparison, but by the early 1950s their production and storage facilities rivaled those of their main competitors—Petri's Italian Swiss Colony, Cresta Blanca, and Guild, which now also owned Roma. And since the wine industry had almost completely changed from bulk wine sales to winery-bottled products, a Gallo bottling plant was built in Modesto and was added to the corporation's subsidiary companies.

But most important, Ernest set out to expand his marketing and sales efforts. After the weeks spent in Los Angeles before the war visiting and observing liquor stores, he considered himself an expert —indeed, an innovator—in marketing wine. He would concentrate on "point-of-sale" promotion, and in a 1963 speech to the Stanford Business School, he recited with pride and heavy emphasis how he had "discovered" the keys to his future success. Having noted that retailers were either "too busy or too indifferent to *vocally recommend* a product very long, even for monetary considerations," he devised a way to obtain their "*silent recommendation.*" He would give Gallo "*dominant exposure* by making Gallo *visually very important* in the store." Such tacit retailer recommendation of the brand, he reasoned, "would give the consumer confidence in buying Gallo."

He began to work out his system of pushing Gallo into a dominant position in the stores. In addition to "distinctive manners of packaging denoting quality," he would have his distributors offer "extra incentives to the retailer to encourage him to buy all sizes and types . . . just load him with enough Gallo wines to absorb his purchasing power and exclude competition." If retailers objected that they had no room in their stores for more Gallo wines or for a new brand, Ernest came up with another device—he would provide a metal rack that held ten cases of Gallo wine.

Each month he would send retailers Gallo posters or "broadsides," announcing the promotion of the month. He added "bottle collars," cardboard cutouts hung around bottles' necks, to attract customers, and he developed a system of shelving. Not only should bottles be dusted and rotated regularly, he urged, but Gallo products should all be placed at eye level—the most visible shelf position.

All of these strategies developed by Ernest in his visits to thousands of retail stores, however, remained more theory than practice until he could hire the sales force necessary to carry out a full-scale campaign. But these ideas would eventually become the mainstay of Gallo salesmanship and would change the method of wine marketing throughout the country.

Just after the war, he concentrated on getting Gallo brands into new markets and finding more distributors. He committed some of his new working capital to a full-scale public relations effort to "build the Gallo brand," and in 1945 he hired John Freiburg, who headed his own advertising agency in Los Angeles. For all Ernest's pride in his self-taught marketing skills as well as the advertising program for Gallo White Port he'd launched with Sam Watt before the war, Freiburg considered Ernest's ideas rather unsophisticated. Having surveyed the Los Angeles area, the winery's key market, Freiburg discovered that Gallo wine still had little brand recognition. "A few stores here and there had [Gallo], but the rest of them were oblivious to it, didn't need it, had no call for it, and were not receptive at all."

To make matters worse, Ernest's first slogan, "By Golly, Buy Gallo" had, as Freiburg put it, "muddied the waters." Already Gallo's image was that of a cheap wine that consumers would buy only for its low price. With that first motto, Freiburg recalled, "It was hard to see where there was any class to the wine or any consumer appeal from a quality standpoint."

What had to be done, he advised Ernest, was to "upgrade the image of the wine and to bring it to the public's attention." He banished the Bacchus cartoon; the second rooster logo that Ernest had redesigned to accompany his new motto, "Something to Crow About," was discarded as well. Ernest seemed to love cornball slogans; sometimes they appealed to the general public, but they did not convey the "image of class and high quality" that Freiburg thought necessary. Instead, Freiburg resurrected the theme of personal attention to quality that Ernest had introduced in 1941, but this time Julio's involvement was included: "Every step in the making of Gallo wines is personally supervised by Ernest and Julio Gallo, two brothers raised in the tradition of the vintner's art."

Although Ernest wanted national recognition, he was still a penny-pincher, watching and approving every expense. Freiburg had to search for the most economic forms of advertising. He finally acquired hard-to-come-by billboard space along southern California highways; he mounted full-page ads in the liquor trade journals to give the impression of full saturation of the markets and Gallo's domination of the field; and he was able to convince *Life* magazine to run a story about the "winery's annual wine-crushing party" in its regular "*Life* Goes to a Party" feature.

The winery had never had an annual crushing party, and the event was staged for the story, with pretty models stomping grapes with their feet and "the Queen of the Crushing" taking a bath in wine. The October 8, 1945, *Life* article conveyed the impression of a successful, lavish and nationally dominant winery. With the four-page article as his centerpiece, Freiburg designed a large portfolio of photographs, some purporting to be of the winery offices (but which bore no resemblance to the ramshackle buildings in Modesto, as he would later recall). He included the new advertising promotions for the "Celebrate with Gallo" national campaign that he and Ernest then launched.

Freiburg had nominally kept his own advertising agency—Ernest had learned that an outside agency had more prestige than an inhouse staff. But he and his employees were installed in offices of the Gallo Los Angeles distributing company and were paid by the winery. Ernest soon advised him that he expected more from him than the creation of promotional material. Visiting Modesto, Freiburg realized that aside from Ernest and Julio, the only other winery executive was Charlie Crawford, who was more involved in production than in sales. Assigned a multitude of responsibilities, Freiburg became the winery's first marketing executive, head of advertising, and sales supervisor, all rolled into one. And as part of his job he was expected to go on the road with Ernest, visiting distributors and retailers across the country to convince them to take on Gallo wine.

Armed with the *Life* article and promotional material, the two men traveled from city to city for three to four months at a time, sharing a room in cheap hotels at night, making calls during the day. They found that liquor distributors were reluctant to take on another brand of wine since it was not a high-selling item. "The only wine sales were usually of sweet wines," Freiburg explained, "which went to the more or less ghetto sections where wine was drunk for the alcohol content." Beer distributors were often more cooperative, and in fact Gallo wine was marketed more like beer than like whiskey. By visiting liquor and grocery stores with their promotional material and point-of-sale displays and convincing owners and managers of the winery's extensive advertising programs, Ernest hoped to persuade the retailers to bring pressure on their distributors to carry Gallo wine. And since Ernest and Freiburg realized that their promotions had to appeal to popular taste, they began to advertise the "Gallo Glacier," advising customers to mix soda with Gallo wine ("add sugar if you use a table wine"). It was the first hint of what would eventually become one of Gallo's most successful products—"pop wines," "specialty wines," and then "wine coolers."

Freiburg considered Ernest one of the most ambitious and driven men he'd ever met—indeed, he said, "The man was just a genius"— but also one of the most suspicious. At night in their hotel room, Ernest would sometimes expound on his and Julio's feelings that they "only trusted family members." Freiburg thought that this had something to do with the fact that "they were Italian" or "the way they were brought up." Late into the night he and Ernest had personal conversations, Freiburg recalled, and he once expressed disappointment that "Joseph did not want to be in the business." (Freiburg apparently did not realize that in fact Joe was working for the winery but reporting to Julio.)

Ernest's distrust of others was deep and basic, perhaps the natural reaction of a man whose parents' deaths seemed an inexplicable and tragic turn of fate that had convinced him that he had to dominate others if he were to control destiny. As one former Gallo sales manager whose training was in psychology remarked, "It was clear from Ernest's comments that he hadn't trusted his father. And if you can't trust your father, whom can you trust?"

Yet Ernest's suspiciousness also seemed to originate more in his sense of his own character than in a fear of the randomness of fortune. Given his propensities to maneuver, control, and conceal, he might easily suspect that others were out to do unto him what he was likely to do unto them. As one former employee would later quip, "Ernest is the embodiment of the Hobbesian view of the world: nasty, brutish and short."

Freiburg himself felt the effect of Ernest's suspiciousness. Soon after hiring on with the winery, he was ordered to employ a man named Charles Kellogg in his nominally independent agency. Kellogg had previously worked for Safeway supermarkets and had little experience in advertising, much less marketing wine. But he was, Freiburg learned, Ernest's brother-in-law, married to Amelia's younger sister Ann. Even a shirt-tail relative was more trusted than a non-Gallo in Ernest's lexicon of paranoia. "I knew why he wanted Charlie [in my agency]," said Freiburg. "Ernest wanted to make sure he wasn't being cheated . . . and Charlie was keeping an eye out."

Planting spies throughout the winery would become central to Ernest's organizational strategy. In later years he would rely on moles inside his subsidiary holdings and distributorships, and some alleged that he even had access to information from former employees in competitors' companies. As a result he seemed to become even more suspicious and distrustful. Traitors might be lurking anywhere, and thus it was necessary for him to create a kind of "family" loyalty among employees. But in the late 1940s, when the winery was still struggling to become a nationally known company, he had to rely on his own devices and desires.

Having spent $762,000 in advertising to achieve $6,300,000 in sales in 1946, Ernest was well on his way to gaining nationwide recognition of the Gallo brand. His strategy was to move from state to state, find distributors to take on his brands, and open that territory's market. Since his distribution and sales territories had so expanded, he hired William MacKay, a San Francisco lawyer, to apply for a second Gallo trademark. (This application also claimed that "the trade-mark has been used continuously and applied to the goods in the business of the applicant and the predecessor of the applicant, Joseph Gallo, since 1909.")

But now there was a problem with the winery's application. In Cleveland, Ohio, someone by the name of Charles Gallo was using the Gallo name in his wine-bottling and distributing company. Ernest had in fact met the man two years before, in 1944.

Charles Gallo bought and bottled bulk wine, selling it under various labels, but all were designated "bottled by C. Gallo Wines." He was touring California looking for new sources of bulk wine (since this method of distribution was giving way to winery-bottled products) and stopped by to see Ernest in Modesto. Ernest explained that the winery rarely sold bulk wine anymore. Noting their common family names, Charles then asked him if he would consider him first when he chose his Cleveland distributor. Charles Gallo then left his card reading "Gallo Wine Company" and said he hoped to hear from Ernest soon.

In 1946, Charles Gallo discovered that Ernest had chosen another

Cleveland liquor distributor to carry his wine. He wrote to Ernest to remind them of their conversation, adding that since their shared name would be a promotional gimmick, he hoped that he would be reconsidered as a distributor for the winery.

Ernest saw only difficulties in their shared family name, but he wrote Charles Gallo a pleasant letter telling him that a mutual friend had spoken to him that morning on his behalf. Since he held the mutual friend "in high esteem," he added, he was asking two of his representatives to interview Charles as a potential Gallo distributor. But the letter was a subterfuge, designed to convince the man to speak openly with no suspicion of any possible legal action.

John Freiburg was assigned to this job (although he would later say he did not remember the incident). According to court documents, he and Gallo's Ohio sales representative arrived at the Gallo Wine Company in Cleveland where Charles Gallo and his son Rocco served lunch and wine and answered all the questions Freiburg asked. Prepared by Freiburg at Ernest's request, the queries went beyond those routinely asked of a potential distributor. Freiburg learned that Charles Gallo had started his wine-bottling and -distributing company in 1936 as an outgrowth of his father's grocery store (also named Gallo) but hadn't registered "The Gallo Wine Company" with the state patent office until 1945. He had never sold wine with a Gallo label but all of his wines bore the information "bottled by C. Gallo." Freiburg then acquired a copy of Charles Gallo's full financial records and elicited numerous "anecdotes" of phone calls from customers asking, "Is this the Gallo Wine Company?"

Freiburg reported to Ernest that Charles Gallo "evidenced a great deal of delight in these calls—amused at the idea that they should be taken for the E. & J. Gallo Winery, producers of Gallo Wine." Ernest was not amused. Armed with the information gathered by Freiburg, he was poised to strike. First he advised Charles Gallo that the winery had a policy of not changing distributors without cause. Then, citing his trademark registrations, national advertising, and licensing of the Gallo name to the Los Angeles and New Orleans distributorships, he ordered Charles to stop using the "notation 'Gallo Wines' or 'Gallo Wine Company.' "

Charles Gallo was incensed—not only at Ernest's deception but also at his arrogance. Gallo was as much his family name as Ernest's, and he would fight for his right to use it. Learning that Ernest's 1946 trademark application was pending, he filed an objection with both the Ohio and U. S. patent offices.

After a further round of threatening letters, *l'avvocato* turned to legal methods—he sued. Fearing the loss of his company and his family name for that business, Charles Gallo fell ill, and on September 7, 1946, he died. But his wife Mary and their son Rocco continued the battle, they, too, refusing to capitulate to Ernest's demands. The suit dragged on for two years with discovery, declarations, depositions, briefs, and motions, but finally in 1949 the case was heard.

Taking the witness stand, Ernest recited family history—a history that forty years later he would deny. But in this 1949 court case he had to prove his right to the trademark on the basis of prior and continuous use. Cross-examined by the defense attorney, Ernest announced that "the name of the brand 'Gallo' has been used since 1909 by the rest of my family; that is, my father. We used 'Gallo' in conjunction with grapes during Prohibition. Millions of cases of grapes were shipped with that brand on it. Our company, the E. & J. Gallo Winery, then continued with the brand in 1933 when we started the business. We always sold wine under the brand name 'Gallo.' "

No ifs, ands or buts about it—Ernest considered the Gallo brand an extension of the Gallo name on "millions of cases of grapes" and on pre-Prohibition barrels of wine. He revealed most of the facts (he did not refer to his father's bootlegging) that should have established Joe, Jr.'s right to one-third of both the trademark and the winery as a continuation of their father's business, but which in 1988 he would deny as significant. Nevertheless, in this 1949 lawsuit Ernest provided a narrative "of prior and continuous usage" to win his claim to the Gallo trademark for wine.

While Mary and Rocco Gallo established that Charles Gallo had used the Gallo name in his Cleveland wine business long before Ernest had brought his wines to Ohio, the court found the prior and continuous use argument compelling enough to rule in the winery's favor. Yet the judge ordered the Ohio Gallos to pay only $300 in damages whereas the winery had asked for $75,000, and he issued an injunction that restrained them from using Gallo alone or with a rooster logo as a trademark. Loath to strip anyone of a family name, the judge allowed them to continue using Gallo as their company's trade name in Ohio. Not satisfied with this finding, Ernest had his lawyer write to the court to request that the Ohio Gallos be ordered to add a first name, such as "Charles Gallo & Son Wine Company" or "Mary Gallo Wine Company."

Nearly forty years later Ernest wouldn't even be satisfied with the addition of a first name. By then he was even more obsessed with having exclusive use of the name Gallo. Of course, his testimony in the Charles Gallo case indicated that his younger brother Joe should have had an equal right to the use of the family name. But when he was later reminded of his 1949 declarations as well as his statements in trademark applications, he insisted they were just "a figure of speech" or a "speech problem." Whatever Ernest's speech problems, Joe's lawyers argued that it was highly improbable that Ernest's respected trademark attorney, William MacKay, would make false declarations either to the Patent Office or to the court. More, they contended that in both the trademark applications and the Charles and Mary Gallo case, Ernest was telling the truth about his father's business and the continued use of the name.

At the time, Joe knew nothing about the Ohio litigation. As manager of the Livingston vineyards, he thought of himself as part of their enterprise even if he wasn't a partner.

In 1950, however, Ernest took steps to put Joe at a further remove from a business relationship with him and Julio. He called Joe into his office and announced that he was dissolving the Gallo Bros. Ranches partnership that he had established in 1944.

"What's the purpose of that?" asked Joe.

"My children and Julio's are growing up," he said. "We want to start passing some of our property on to them. Setting up trusts, that sort of thing."

"What does that mean for me?"

Ernest explained that Joe's property would go back to him in his name and that after an accounting, the money in the partnership would be distributed among the partners. But at the same time, Ernest suggested, Joe could continue to have the winery accountants handle his financial matters. Joe would simply be billed for their time, and this would make matters simpler for everyone, since some property that he and Julio had recently purchased was acquired both in Joe's name alone and in joint ownership.

Joe had also recently bought a new property of his own—a 234-acre spread known as the Escola Ranch. In addition to his inheritance that had remained in the Gallo Bros. Ranches partnership, he had also received a note from "the E. & J. Gallo Winery for $50,000 on demand" after the dissolution of the tartar company in 1948. Joe had never demanded payment but left the note in the ranch partnership account. Ernest said that he would have financial advisors draw up a final accounting and valuation of the Gallo Bros. Ranches partnership. He also proposed that in lieu of some of the money owed to Joe from the account, he would assign him and his children shares in the Gallo Glass Company.

In the course of an outside appraisal of the accounts, Ernest again found it necessary to explain the 1941 closing of the guardianship's estate and Joe's inheritance that had been transferred into the partnership. Now Ed Taylor confirmed in a letter to an outside evaluator that Joe, Sr.'s estate had paid Ernest and Julio a salary of $60 each and that the court had approved these payments in several hearings. In any case, Joe never raised the issue of the previous accounting nor did he object to the dissolution of the partnership. Once again he assumed that Ernest knew best. At the time he felt that Ernest's offer to let the winery accountants continue to keep his books was generous. But later his son Mike would come to suspect that this was also a way for Ernest to keep Joe's accounts under his control even after the end of the partnership.

Soon Ernest presented Joe with another plan—dividing the home ranch vineyard on the south side of Maze Road in which Joe still had a one-third interest. Julio wanted to build a new home, Ernest explained. Ernest would buy 6.06 acres to bring his property to the 70 acres surrounding his home; Julio would buy a 6.73 acre parcel to give him a 70-acre home site. Joe would retain an interest only in the vineyards and the family home on the north side of Maze Road.

Joe had some reservations but finally agreed for Julio's sake and for family harmony. Julio and Aileen's new home was a California ranch constructed of redwood and glass, its large windows looking out across the vineyards. The two brothers now had a family compound with enough acreage that someday their children might be able to build homes there as well. Ernest's driveway was marked by two plain white posts on Maze Road, with only the street number, 1712, not his name, appearing on them. Julio's driveway entered the property from the eastern border of the vineyards on Carpenter Road.

Gardens were landscaped; palm trees, which the town of Modesto was removing to widen a street, were transplanted to sides of the driveway and around the houses. Oleanders and cypresses filled in the hedge, creating a screen from the road, as did the vineyards that surrounded the homes. Ernest's and Julio's residences were soon well-hidden in a private enclave from which the public was excluded and which in later years would be protected by security guards, a high-tech guardhouse, surveillance cameras, and Doberman pinschers.

Once the Gallo Bros. Ranches partnership had been dissolved, Joe was effectively distanced from Ernest and Julio's business and properties. He was already outside the winery, living thirty minutes away, and now was excluded from his brothers' financial arrangements. Without realizing it, he had accepted his exile from his brothers' domain.

CHAPTER SIX

In the early 1950s the Gallo Winery was the largest winemaking facility in the country; yet it still lagged behind Guild and Italian Swiss Colony in sales. Ernest now proposed to build an executive structure to push Gallo ahead. Freiburg and his successor, Neil Shaver, had both left the winery, and now Ernest went looking for a sales and marketing expert.

He found his man in Albion "Al" Fenderson, whom he hired first to help direct sales and advertising. Born outside Pittsburgh, Fenderson first attended Carnegie Tech, then went to George Washington University, where he received his degree in economics. He subsequently went to work for the government, becoming one of FDR's whiz kids on the War Production Board, his specialty the regulation of alcohol distilleries under government ownership or contract during the war. After the war, he was national sales director for Publiker, the major producer of alcohol in the United States. Armand Hammer then bought the J. W. Dant whiskey label from Publiker and in 1950 appointed Fenderson vice-president of his newly formed "United Distilleries of America."

Hammer became one of the largest liquor producers and distributors in the country, and Fenderson was both his youngest vice-president and a recognized expert in liquor marketing and distribution. During the early 1950s, however, both J. Edgar Hoover and Joe McCarthy labeled Hammer untrustworthy because of his previous Soviet associations and extensive business deals in Russia. With government and IRS investigations looming, Hammer sold his distillery business to Lewis Rosenstiel of Schenley Industries, and Fenderson left his job, planning to write about his experiences. He completed a pamphlet about American "ism's" as well as an epic poem. But he was without direction until his sister-in-law in California told him about the two Italian-American brothers in Modesto who were trying to build the largest winery in the world.

Fenderson was interviewed by Ernest in the spring of 1952. Impressed by his reputation and the fact that he had been one of Hammer's right-hand men (Hammer was one of Ernest's heroes), Ernest hired him immediately, sweetening the offer by promising him shares in Gallo distributorships. Fenderson handled East Coast sales out of his home until August when he and his family moved to Modesto.

As wily as his employer, Fenderson became another Ernest loyalist. Short and blond with WASP good looks and a tweedy elegance in dress, he fit the image of upper-class respectability that Ernest would always favor in his executives. Fenderson was assigned the all-important task of attracting consumers to Gallo and away from Guild.

At the time Guild, based in Lodi, marketed the Cresta Blanca, Virginia Dare, and Vino di Tavola labels, and with its extensive national advertising and marketing programs as well as its sponsorship of popular radio and television shows, Guild brand slogans and jingles had become household words. The majority of wine drinkers still preferred dessert wines, but Guild's Vino di Tavola, with its checkered tablecloth label, was gaining in popularity. Ernest wanted to make Gallo table wines competitive.

He did so by raiding Guild's executive staff. In 1954 he convinced Howard Williams, president of Guild and the originator of Vino di Tavola, to come to Gallo, where he was to build the marketing division. Williams then brought Ken Bertsch from Guild to work under Fenderson in sales (later Fenderson concentrated more on marketing, while Bertsch became the national sales director). These three executives formed the nucleus of what would become Ernest's inner circle.

Each brought a special talent. A dapper man with an Adolphe Menjou mustache, Williams was a sophisticated marketing expert who was especially attuned to the wine business after his years at Guild. For all Williams's loyalty, he sometimes joked about Ernest's provincialism and rough edges. Like so many self-taught men, Ernest often assumed that he knew best. That wasn't always so, but Williams knew how to make his case without offending him. He had been responsible for Vino di Tavola's advertising as well as its packaging. Ernest gave him his first assignment: Create another Vino di Tavola for Gallo.

Williams asked Julio and the winemakers in his laboratory division to develop a light, "mellow," red blend. But the real innovation was in the packaging and marketing of the new product. Williams designed an attractive rounded jug bottle and called the wine "Vino Paisano di Gallo." Together he and Fenderson planned a sales campaign to compete directly with Guild's Vino di Tavola and Italian Swiss Colony's table wines.

Ken Bertsch was a tall, stoop-shouldered man who had a temperament fashioned by his experience as an officer in the Army Air Corps. Colleagues said that his "Teutonic" personality and his faith in a military-like organizational structure seemed especially appealing to Ernest. He shared Bertsch's conviction that Gallo salesmen had to measure up with unquestioning loyalty, rote learning, and attention to detail as well as cultivate a "no-excuses, take-no-prisoners" ruthlessness. He became the commander-in-chief's right-hand man, the officer who would develop an army of salesmen and impose discipline and obedience. Like Ernest he detested any sign of weakness. If an employee revealed a chink in his armor, Bertsch lit one of the Bering cigars that he chain-smoked, and with obvious pleasure (some employees called it sadistic delight), he moved in for the kill.

But Bertsch also had an "artful dodger side," commented one former Gallo executive, and earned the nickname "Silky" among his regional sales managers: "When sales figures weren't satisfactory and Ernest would exert pressure by asking probing questions, Ken would 'hit the silk,' as in bail out to save himself, leaving the rest of us responsible for problems." He also had the reputation as a "ladies' man" and was sometimes referred to as the "Lothario of Lodi," where he had worked for Guild. "He sometimes insinuated—rather proudly —that a scar on his temple was the result of an irate husband taking a shot at him," added another Gallo colleague. "But we were never sure if this was true or if he just liked that image of himself."

When Ernest raided Guild for his first marketing and sales executives, he did not create a complex organizational hierarchy. Instead, he installed a select group of court faithful. They were the men to whom underlings would answer, but they, like everyone, would report to Ernest, who remained fully aware of even the smallest details in his sales and marketing departments. He didn't so much delegate authority as make men like Bertsch extensions of his power. And Bertsch, who liked a feeling of dominance and control, did Ernest's bidding for almost forty years until his death, never once faltering in his fidelity.

Other employees would wonder at such loyalty, especially when they had been called on the carpet by Ernest and subjected to one of his angry tirades. But Ernest was a brilliant manager—he recognized both the talents and the weaknesses of his executives. He played off both: He gave them a feeling of confidence and assured them of financial security that they would never find elsewhere. Regional sales managers were asked to note any personal quirks, deviation from conservative dress (facial hair was frowned upon), and any difficulties of their men—their drinking habits, their wives' drinking habits, any sexual affairs, any financial difficulties, any skeletons in their closets. Like J. Edgar Hoover, the winery dealt in gossip; it was the currency of control over employees. In a spy versus spy world, secrets were Gallo's aces in the hole.

Ernest and his field marshals had recruited the first battalion of his army of young men (never women) to push Gallo table wines into retail stores, their goal to outsell Italian Swiss Colony and Guild. According to a former Gallo products manager, Ernest's achievement was to bring "professionalism" to a "primitive" industry. Before this time winemakers were more involved in production than in marketing and sales. Ernest found experienced men in these areas and recruited them from other consumer product companies. They then underwent speedy and intensive training (although the Gallo sales and management courses were not yet formalized), and they were taught the three R's of Gallo salesmanship: rigorousness, relentlessness, ruthlessness. The new foot soldiers were schooled in all the techniques that Ernest had "discovered" during his inspections of thousands of retail outlets, and his conclusions became the modus operandi of his expanded sales force.

Recruits were trained—or indoctrinated, as several former employees called it—in "point-of-sale" (or POS) promotional methods. After completing their training, Gallo salesmen were sent to work in Gallo-owned or independent distributorships (even at independents, they were supervised by winery sales managers). They were expected to make regular and frequent visits to retailers, giving them pep talks (stay on friendly terms, they were instructed, but never tell off-color jokes) and checking the Gallo sales. They supervised the displays, advertising, and shelf facings and made sure that Gallo brands dominated the store's refrigerated shelves, or cold box storage, as it was known in the trade—all strategies to bring Gallo products to the consumers' attention and to suggest the retailer's "silent recommendation of the brand."

In effect Gallo salesmen took over the stores. Owners and managers of retail stores might not have time to do all the things that Gallo salesmen did—stocking shelves, dusting bottles, hanging posters and streamers, setting up display cases, stocking the cold box. For the most part, store owners allowed the salesmen to go about their chores, especially since the Gallo method, combined with extensive advertising, obviously worked—with Ernest's troops attending to their duties, the retailers' sales of Gallo wine increased.

Gallo had a strict schematic for stocking stores with its merchandise: Place Gallo in the best and most visually dominant shelf space (seven feet on each of five shelves—determined to be the largest area the eye can scan); position the most popular brands at eye level; put brands that were likely to be bought on impulse just above belt level; where there is a price advantage to the larger size, shelve jug bottles to the right of the smaller bottles; aim for "total merchandising" so that when customers walk into a store, all they see on the right, on the left, and in front is Gallo.

Some Gallo salesmen employed by Gallo distributorships and independent distributorships admitted that to achieve "total merchandising" they moved—even removed—competitors' merchandise. The Bureau of Alcohol prohibited salesmen from touching the stock of their competitors. Some Gallo salesmen said they did it anyway. "Now all wine salesmen move competitive brands," added one former Gallo salesman, "but in the beginning it was a Gallo innovation. We wanted the Gallo brand to dominate the store both visually and spatially."

Salesmen also reportedly tampered with competitive merchandise. They punctured aluminum caps so that competitors' wine would go bad; they would "back-spin" twist-off caps so that customers became enraged with a brand when they couldn't open the bottle; salesmen routinely carried oil, which they wiped or sprayed on competitors' bottles so that dust would accumulate in a minute, giving the impression that the brand had remained unsold for months. And when Gallo salesmen arranged comparative tastings in stores, they sometimes unscrewed bottle caps of competitors' brands and squeezed in heads of dead mice, mice feces, or cigarette butts.

(This was before tamper-proof caps. When cello-seals—plastic tape to bind the cap to the bottleneck—were introduced, salesmen also carried rolls of it so that they could break seals, add the foreign matter, then reseal the bottle with their tape. The tastings were part of a promotion to convince the public that because only Gallo bottled and sealed its wine at the winery, in a clean and regulated environment, it was the only safe wine to drink. Other large wineries still shipped in bulk to local bottlers and distributors, which did not, the winery alleged, have the same high standards of quality control and hygienic bottling. If at these tastings a mouse head or a cigarette turned up in a competitor's bottle, the word quickly spread, confirming the winery's warnings of what could find its way into wine at bottling companies.)

Sales managers' instructions to new Gallo recruits often included a recitation of BATF regulations that prohibited such "sales tactics." But it was with a wink and a nod, said several Gallo trainees. If the salesmen were to accomplish the Gallo goals, they knew rules had to be broken. If an inspector happened to appear in the store when a salesman was moving or tampering with competitors' bottles, he simply paid for the merchandise as if he were just another customer.

"Sometimes the store owner didn't mind, so we just went in and rearranged the shelves and did what we liked," recalled one former salesman. "After all, we were doing his job—stocking shelves, dusting, arranging displays. But if a store owner objected, we could threaten to shut down his Gallo supply or demand payment of his outstanding bill. Or we sweetened the deal with a few extra cases as a bonus, under the table, of course. But usually we just marched in and did what we wanted to do—like filling the best shelves with Gallo or removing all competitors from the cold box and stocking it only with Gallo. If we thought there were too many bottles of competitors' brands, we took those off the shelves."

According to a former sales manager, salesmen usually paid the retailer for the merchandise, then packed it up in cardboard boxes. Sometimes they took the bottles out in the street and smashed them. Other times they brought them back to the distributorship. "From there they were shipped to the winery where the wine was 'recycled' into Gallo wine, and the bottles were 'recycled' into Gallo bottles," he added. "Whatever way they did it, salesmen knew they had to make Gallo number one."

Whether Ernest knew about these practices was unclear, although most salesmen and sales managers were convinced that at least Ken Bertsch was aware of these methods, and the pressure to perform was clearly felt throughout the sales force.

Ernest read sales figures every day, and a salesman could always expect surprise visits at the stores he handled. "Either our district sales manager or Ken Bertsch or Ernest himself would come to check on us," reported a former Gallo salesman. "If we hadn't met their expectations, if the store didn't pass their inspection, we were gone. On the spot. Like the Red Queen in *Alice in Wonderland*—'Off with your head.' "

It was guerrilla warfare brought to wine sales. Yet Gallo had still not overtaken the number-one position in the industry. Part of the problem was the distributorship system, organized in a three-tier structure and regulated by the Bureau of Alcohol. Inserting the wholesale distributorship level between the suppliers and the retailers in the wine and liquor business was meant to eliminate the crime and corruption that had tainted the industry during Prohibition. But it was especially frustrating for Ernest, since it put him at a farther remove from the consumer. (Procter & Gamble and Campbell Soup could distribute their products directly to retail outlets and customers, whereas wineries had to rely on the cooperation of wholesale distributors to push their products into retail stores and attract the buyers.)

However much Ernest and his new executives developed extensive marketing and sales campaigns, they still had to depend on the wholesalers to implement their ideas and push the Gallo brands. But now that Gallo had enlarged and trained its sales force, Ernest saw a way of extending his influence over distributorships. Distributorships were established in the legal name of others. For example, in 1945 Gallo arranged for A. E. "Bud" Anderson to become the Gallo distributor in the San Francisco Bay Area. The son of E. R. Anderson, who ran Gallo's New Orleans distributorship, Bud had been working in the Modesto winery when he convinced Ernest that he could sell the Gallo brands in the Bay Area. With help from the winery, Anderson built a small warehouse and was named president and manager of "Gallo Bay Sales," and his employees were, for the most part, trained and recommended by the winery. Thus, while the distributorship carried some other companies' wines, his Gallo-trained salesmen concentrated their attention on Ernest's products.

With loyal distributors in both northern and southern California, Gallo dominated the state's wine sales. But other markets were more difficult to capture. Ernest developed a new strategy—targeting one territory at a time and sending in his foot soldiers to prove to distributors that Gallo wines could outsell all others. The Gallo soldiers' assignment was to make wholesalers true believers in the Gallo way.

Once a wholesaler agreed to distribute Gallo wine, Ernest had salesmen saturate local liquor, package, and grocery stores, wherever wine was sold; they worked round the clock, visiting each and every retailer of wine, decorating with promotional material and installing display cases, rearranging shelves and placing Gallo products in dominant positions. Soon distributors and retailers were convinced: The Gallo merchandise in the wholesale warehouse moved twice as fast as that of its competitors. In a few short weeks, everyone was turning profits from Gallo sales. The sales figures made them converts.

Then Ernest would suggest to the distributor that with the expanded Gallo market and increasing sales, he needed to hire more salesmen to represent Gallo brands exclusively. These were usually winery-trained employees whose salaries were at first paid by the winery, but once they agreed, the distributors picked up the tab. The salesmen officially worked for the distributor, but they were supervised by Gallo district and regional sales managers. Ernest was their real boss, receiving daily sales reports from his district managers and making surprise visits to inspect the stores, muster his troops to higher sales, and criticize the distributor if he had failed to give Gallo brands enough attention.

If a distributor was unwilling to go along, the winery knew how to twist his arm: It could threaten to withhold Gallo products, it could terminate the wholesaler on thirty days' notice and find a new distributor, it could demand immediate payment of wine sold to the distributor on credit. Ken Bertsch was usually the messenger to achieve what Gallo wanted, although, according to several distributors, they were sometimes summoned to Modesto to meet with Ernest if he were especially displeased.

The employment of Gallo-trained and Gallo-loyal sales staff gave the winery the extra advantage of having spies inside independent distributorships. Gallo knew in detail what went on at the distributorship level, including the sales and advertising programs of competitors. According to several sales managers, when the winery had established its influence with a distributor, Bertsch would sometimes complain to the owner that he had, for example, a weak manager and demand his termination. Not wanting to lose the Gallo line, the distributor fired his employee and hired one that Bertsch recommended. The winery would then have another Gallo mole in place, an employee who usually had no problem phoning Ernest with reports on the distributorship's sales of other wines or meetings with competitors.

Despite the radical changes he was bringing to the structure and organization of the wine industry, Ernest still did not drastically alter consumers' tastes or how they perceived Gallo. For all the national advertising and promotional saturation, he hadn't captured a large segment of those wine buyers who had begun to favor table over dessert wines but remained loyal to Guild or Italian Swiss Colony, which was now gaining in popularity because of its Vin Rosé. If Gallo was going to win them over, the winery needed a new product. For this Ernest again turned to Howard Williams and Julio and his blenders.

Just as Ernest had established his inner circle, Julio now had his own staff of winemakers and a sophisticated chemical laboratory in which to carry out their experiments. (In 1954, the research program was expanded to a full department.) Charlie Crawford still managed this division, and he recruited graduates of UC Davis's oenology program, who put in apprentice years at Gallo, then often moved on to other wineries. In his own fashion, Julio was just as demanding and intolerant of mistakes as Ernest. Nevertheless, the atmosphere in the production division was more relaxed and congenial than that of the sales and marketing divisions. Every afternoon there were wine tastings, and sometimes Julio served up a *bagna cauda* for his employees, the olive oil heated over a bunsen burner in the lab.

When Ernest was present, the mood changed. Once again it was all business. The Gallo production division was always geared to what Ernest and his staff had decided that the market demanded. Whereas Julio rarely strayed into marketing and sales and claimed to have little knowledge of or interest in this side of the business, Ernest often stalked into Julio's domain and tasted the latest experiments. His comments would sometimes irritate Julio and his staff. Abrupt and critical, he issued orders, and sometimes his orders changed from day to day. Ernest considered himself a wine expert, not for his palate, but for his sensitivity to changing consumer tastes. And now he was sure that Gallo needed an equivalent of Italian Swiss Colony's table wines, especially its Vin Rosé: Capitalize on the Italian theme of its advertising, let the public think that Gallo was the true "little old winemaker" who was featured in Swiss Colony's advertising during the mid-1950s.

The "little old winemaker" behind Italian Swiss Colony at this time was Louis Petri. The son of Angelo Petri, who had been an associate of Joe Gallo, Sr., and Dante Forresti in Escalon, Louis had expanded his father's wine empire, buying up several wineries, including Italian Swiss Colony, and forming United Vintners, which was a cooperative but still run by Petri and his family. He and Gallo had long competed in bulk wine sales, and after the war he shipped more wine East than any other California winery. He even transported wine in his own ship, a tanker with a 2-million-gallon capacity that he had bought and salvaged after the war.

Rumor had it that he had purchased Italian Swiss Colony in the early 1950s just to "beat Ernie to the punch" in the expanding table wine market. Others said that in 1951 Ernest had taken a year's option on Italian Swiss Colony, then let it die and announced, "Why buy it when we can do better ourselves?" Still others said that Ernest decided against the purchase because he envisioned hassles with the growers' cooperative on which Italian Swiss Colony depended for its grapes. In any case, in 1953 Petri and United Vintners had bought Italian Swiss Colony and proceeded to built the brand.

Under Petri's direction Italian Swiss Colony had gained a dominant share of the table wine market. Gallo was more popular in the dessert wine category and in what some called the "misery market," "street wines" or "alcoholic maintenance." Avoiding any reference to the ghetto where Gallo white port, sherry, and muscatel were the brands of choice, Ernest used the euphemism "ethnic" to describe the areas where the winery achieved some of its highest sales. (Employees who snickered that "ethnic" could also mean Italian did so at their peril.) But Ernest's major plan of attack was to cut into the sales of Italian Swiss Colony's table wines.

Deciding that the winery's previous Grenache Rosé was too dry, Williams suggested a slightly sweeter product and called it "Gourmet Rosé" (it was later renamed simply Gallo Vin Rosé). But once again his innovation was in the packaging. Italian Swiss Colony's Rosé had become popular in large part because of its attractive bottle. Williams developed the Gallo "grape decanter," the lower half of the glass etched with a design that suggested a cluster of grapes. Once again his instincts were unerring, since the decanter matched the popular conception of what a wine bottle should look like. Soon his marketing and advertising programs had convinced the public that the Gallo decanter was synonymous with "gracious living," and sales of Gallo's Vin Rosé began to creep up on those of Italian Swiss Colony.

The winery's production capacity had increased in the late 1940s when Ernest and Julio acquired Cribari Winery, a former Basciglia family-owned facility in Fresno. In 1954, Gallo also bought and modernized the Las Palmas Winery located in Clovis, outside Fresno, which allowed growers in the southern San Joaquin Valley to deliver their grapes to Gallo more quickly and in better condition. In 1953 Julio had announced a five-year agreement with three grape-growers' wineries, the 110-member Del Rey Cooperative Winery, the 125-member Napa Valley Cooperative, and the 57-member Modesto Cooperative Winery. Bulk wine provided by these wineries from different grape-growing regions assured Julio of a stable supply of the varieties he needed for blending experiments and new table wine products. He also added a staff to supervise vineyards and viticulture techniques, what would later become the basis for a grower relations department created to ensure a consistent quality of grapes bought from growers throughout the state.

By the end of 1954 the Fresno winery was fitted out as Gallo's major crushing and storing facility, and growers delivered most of their grapes to this plant. The original Modesto operation became the site for blending, aging (both in large tanks and small cooperage), bottling, and shipping, as well as serving as executive headquarters. The Modesto aging cellars now exceeded 20 million gallons, and in Julio's production division, a single blending tank holding one million gallons was installed. (Until recently, Julio believed that blending wines of different vintages achieved a consistent taste and quality and argued against vintage bottling. In the 1950s and 1960s, the Gallos insisted that their huge blending vat—the largest in the industry—was one of the keys to their success. Since it maintained a uniform blend for each kind of Gallo wine from year to year, consumers didn't have to worry about vintages.)

But even with Gallo Vin Rosé's sales, the winery still hadn't displaced Italian Swiss Colony. Now Ernest adopted a different approach: If Gallo couldn't entice wine drinkers away from Italian Swiss Colony, then it needed to find a product to induce non–wine-drinking consumers to try wine. Fancy varietals and quality table wines were obviously not the answer. He assigned Albion Fenderson the all-important task of finding the breakthrough product that would attract new wine drinkers to Gallo.

Like Ernest, Fenderson often made regular inspections of retail stores. He and Harry Bleiweiss, a Gallo sales manager who worked for Bud Anderson in San Francisco (his nickname was "White Port Harry"), noticed that liquor stores in predominantly black communities routinely kept bottles of lemon juice or packets of lemon Kool-Aid next to their white port bottles. Customers bought the lemon juice to mix with the wine, they were told. One day during one of their tours of Oakland stores, Bleiweiss remarked, "What we ought to do is mix white port and lemon juice in the bottle and sell the mixture."

According to Fenderson's later written report, Bleiweiss's remark "was the lightning flash" that in 1957 led to the invention of Gallo's number-one-selling product.

In fact, the idea wasn't as original as the winery would later claim. Italian Swiss Colony was producing a citrus-flavored white port called "Silver Satin." Further, in the mid-1950s, New York's Canandaigua Wine Company had developed Wild Irish Rose, a fortified, sweet grape wine that was at the time the only proprietary brand specifically targeting black consumers, and its sales increased every year.

Fenderson and Bleiweiss returned to the winery and asked Julio to taste the mixture that Bleiweiss now concocted from white port and lemon juice. Fenderson fully expected Julio to find the mixture disgusting and spit it out. But he took one sip, then another.

"Those black guys are pretty good winemakers!" he exclaimed. "The problem with white port is that it's too sweet. What they've done is correct the sugar-acid balance by adding more acid."

Ernest was intrigued with the project as well, and he urged Julio and his winemakers to develop a lemon-flavored wine as quickly as possible. Soon they turned out a clear mixture of lemon juice and Gallo white port with an alcohol content of 21 percent to give customers the desired "buzz." Certain that their blend tasted better than the homemade mixture, Al and Ernest then went out into the field to conduct an informal market survey.

They visited bars and liquor stores in black inner-city areas. Whatever the customers' suspicions of the fastidiously dressed blond and the short, growly voiced Italian, they seemed enthusiastic about the new Gallo product. Ernest was satisfied; Fenderson cautioned that they had to be wary of the enthusiasm since consumers were getting it for free. (The winery also solicited African Americans in Modesto to come to the laboratory to sample the product and to receive free cases of it. Finding the concoction too sweet in the beginning, the tasters knew to bring their own lemons. But this form of marketing survey was discontinued after auto accidents and physical violence resulted, the tasters often leaving the winery drunk and rowdy. Once these sessions became common knowledge around town, the winery stopped using locals to test their experiments.)

Ernest wanted to get the product into stores as quickly as possible. Howard Williams and Fenderson were asked to come up with a name. They suggested hundreds, Ernest nixed them all, including Fenderson's choice: "Cockade."

Nearly a year after the invention of the product, Ernest and his marketing staff still couldn't agree on a name for what Fenderson predicted would be a "blockbuster in the enormous black markets." In the meantime they continued to open up new selling territories, and in the spring Ernest and Fenderson were flying back and forth on the company plane to Texas where they were expanding their distribution. (Ernest now had his own plane, not as a symbol of prosperity but as a cost- and time-saving investment.) At night Fenderson put his mind to the still unsolved problem of the flavored wine's name.

On the morning they flew home from Texas, he announced to Ernest that he had solved the problem. In his deliberate way he outlined his reasoning: that the new name was distinctly American, that it would suggest power, which was desirable in the black market, that it conveyed an image of contemporary styling.

So what's the name? Ernest interrupted, impatient with the prologue.

Thunderbird, he intoned.

That's it! Ernest exclaimed.

Later, winery employees heard varying explanations for the name. Perhaps Fenderson had been influenced by his exposure to Southwest Indian lore through his involvement in Q-V Liquors, Gallo's Arizona distributorship (he was already collecting Navaho and Hopi art and rugs). But, as he suggested in his reference to an "image of contemporary styling," he was most of all referring to Ford's Thunderbird, the sports car introduced in 1954, in order to connote power. (According to a former Gallo salesman, the government prohibited references to the power or "kick" of the alcohol content. The Thunderbird association was oblique enough, however, and could also be explained as a reference to the Las Vegas Thunderbird Hotel, not to a "hot rod" car.)

Although there were a few negative reactions to the selection of "Thunderbird" back at the winery, Ernest was convinced and over-rode the opposition. As he often did when he was in a hurry to get a product onto the shelves, he had the winery's in-house printing department design the label for Gallo Thunderbird, and on May 1, 1957, it was test-marketed and distributed in all the key black stores in Los Angeles, Houston, Shreveport, and New York City. According to Fenderson's account, he and his staff "arranged for street-sampling and Thunderbird parties in colored bars wherever we could."

Gallo salesmen recalled that "street-sampling" was perfected for Thunderbird in the ghetto. Bottles of Thunderbird were left on the backseats of salesmen's cars or were handed out in the neighborhood —the idea was to give away free samples and saturate the market. Empty bottles of Thunderbird were thrown in the gutters of skid row streets to increase product awareness.

According to Fenderson, the distributor in Houston who was handing out samples in the black community reported an amazing sight— people running through the streets yelling about Thunderbird and passing bottles back and forth. "It was almost like a Mardi Gras," Fenderson said. A few days later there was a "massive presampling program in one of the big key black bars in a black neighborhood." It had already been announced that there would be free drinks on "Thunderbird Night," and hundreds of people crowded inside. Behind the bar were cold boxes filled with bottles of Thunderbird on ice.

Fenderson recalled opening bottles and pouring drinks while he gauged the crowd's reaction.

Later he reported to Ernest: "One black guy, a little sleepy looking to me, saw one of the Thunderbird labels floating in the ice chest and asked me if I would hand it to him. He took it, dried it a little bit, folded it up and put it in his pocket." Fenderson asked the bar owner what this meant and recorded his answer: *That means you're in. When these people find a product that they like, they want a copy of the label so that they can be sure to get that product in the stores, because, you see, many of them are virtually illiterate and use the label to buy the product.*

The introduction of Thunderbird in New York City had an even bigger promotional draw. There Marty Taub, head of the Brooklyn Gallo distributorship, had a wonderful idea, said Fenderson. He hired "a local black PR guy" and together they selected "a beautiful white model, attired her in a skimpy Indian costume, and presented her to the retailers in the black market as 'Princess Thunderbird.'" Fenderson added, "The retailers loved her, or would have liked to—and bought Thunderbird accordingly."

The initial marketing was so successful that Gallo went national with the wine in only a few short months. They started an extensive advertising campaign as well. For the first time in the winery's history, expensive television commercials were a major part of its promotion. Cesar Romero became one of Thunderbird's promoters, and staring into the camera, he intoned, "This is Cesar Romero, speaking to you from the Thunderbird Hotel in Las Vegas." Once again borrowing from someone else's name, Gallo advertising pushed images of luxury living by high rollers. While the advertising was not directed at blacks, by the summer of 1957, Thunderbird had been introduced in almost every urban black market in the United States.

Ernest and his spokesmen would later deny that they had so specifically targeted blacks, but Fenderson's report suggested otherwise. Even the winery's famous jingle (usually attributed to Howard Williams) was drawn from jazz slang overheard by Gallo salesmen, what was then called "hand jive"—popular on the street—which also emphasized Thunderbird's appeal to blacks:

> "What's the word?"
> "Thunderbird."
> "How's it sold?"
> "Good and cold."
> "What's the jive?"
> "Bird's alive!"
> "What's the price?"
> "Thirty twice."

At sixty cents a quart, Thunderbird caught on in all major cities except Chicago. Ernest took special delight in telling a story to indicate Thunderbird's success. One day he was driving around Atlanta on a routine inspection of local retail stores.

"I was stopped at an intersection, waiting for the light to change," he told his salesmen. "I saw this black guy walking down the street.

So I called out the window to him, 'What's the word?' 'Thunderbird,' he yelled back at me and practically fell down laughing. Then I knew we had made it." Thunderbird had become an automatic response in Gallo's designated urban black markets.

And as the saying goes, Ernest laughed all the way to the bank. Gallo soon dominated all competitors, including Italian Swiss Colony's Silver Satin. Finally Ernest had succeeded in reaching his goal, not because of table wines, but because of a flavored fortified wine. Thunderbird became so popular that it earned the street nicknames "T-Bird," "Pluck," and "Chicken," and in 1957 the winery's production level was increased to 32 million gallons. With the invention of Thunderbird, Gallo sales finally reached those of Italian Swiss Colony and Guild.

Ernest may have stressed the importance of family, but among the Gallos there was unstated tension. During the mid and late 1950s, Ernest and Julio were barely speaking. As Ernest embarked on his master plan to expand and restructure the winery, Julio chose to withdraw, and other than for necessary business discussions, he avoided Ernest as much as possible. Except for traditional family get-togethers, there was a great divide between the two brothers' adjoining properties, and the "J.R.'s," as Ernest and his inner circle referred to Julio Robert and his family and friends, rarely crossed from their side of the home vineyards to Ernest's.

After the success of Thunderbird, with the family's wealth dramatically increasing in the late 1950s, Ernest often entertained his friends, for the most part the executives with whom he had surrounded himself at the winery and whom he treated like surrogate sons. He gave barbecues almost every Sunday for them and their wives and children. These children were Ernest and Amelia's sons' contemporaries, and while they recalled the "Camelot" atmosphere of Ernest's gatherings, they often suspected that the father was disappointed in his real sons, David and Joey, since they both seemed "pretty out of it."

Ernest and Amelia's older son, David, had first attended the local Catholic elementary school (to which the family contributed hefty sums as well as property). He then went to Modesto High School (a Catholic high school had not yet been built) but, according to contemporaries, he made few friends, since he tended to be erratic—his temper unpredictable and his reactions often strange. Having been raised by Amelia almost singlehandedly, he seemed to cling to her. She indulged his whims and his emotional outbursts. Whatever the source, he seemed to have a deep well of anger, and when his will was crossed, he exploded in tantrums. His interests had an obsessive quality, his compulsive behavior and conversation reminding some winery employees of what they would later label as the characteristics of an "idiot savant."

"David seemed weird and childish," recalled one of his teenage acquaintances. "He was gawky and uncoordinated and was desocialized. He couldn't carry on a conversation—it was like his mind was elsewhere on some pet project. He really should have been Julio's son because he was very interested in winemaking, even in high school. But Ernest wouldn't let him get involved, he wanted him to go into marketing and sales eventually."

Joseph Ernest or "Joey" seemed more stable but not remarkably intelligent. He idolized his father, just as David clung to his mother, and yearned for his approval. But he had to work hard in school just to keep up and never excelled academically. Even at a young age he announced that he would follow in his father's footsteps, but he didn't have his father's quickness. Comparing Ernest's two sons, Neil Sweeney, a former Gallo sales trainer, remarked that David seemed to have inherited his father's temper, Joey his mother's brains.

Often away on sales trips or working long hours at the winery, Ernest saw little of his sons when they were growing up. But when he did spend time with them, he was as stern and demanding as his own father had been. Employees noticed that he rarely expressed affection or showed them much gentleness. When he was home, he disciplined them, grilling them about their schoolwork, openly criticizing them for their mistakes. David could be irritating with his edginess and nervous habits, his facial tics and his whining. Joey was aggravating in his slowness and fear of making a mistake. Ernest would find fault with his sons in the presence of others and even when they were adults. But no one else was allowed to criticize: They were, after all, Ernest Gallo's sons.

Julio's elder son, Bob, was more successful than Ernest's boys. Doing well in school, he was tall and attractive and popular enough to be elected to class offices. In 1952, he enrolled at Oregon State University, majoring in business and technology. Although he would eventually return to the winery and work with his father in the production division, Oregon State did not offer courses in oenology and he could learn about winemaking only by studying food technology. After college he served two years in the navy and was promoted to squadron commander before his discharge in 1958.

On July 5, 1958, he married Marie Therese Damrell, the pretty, dark-haired daughter of Frank Damrell, Sr., a Modesto attorney and Democratic party leader who in 1955 was appointed Superior Court judge. The family was well-to-do and active in the community and in the parish, and Marie attended the College of Holy Names, a small Catholic school in Oakland, before she and Bob were married. Modesto's most prominent citizens attended their wedding. The Gallo family on Julio's side was moving up the local social ladder.

Two years younger than Bob, Susann also attended Catholic elementary school and then went to Modesto High School. "She was a cheerleader and had a reputation for wildness," recalled one acquaintance. "She followed her brother to Oregon State, but we all felt she was going to college to find a husband." Susann's future was in marriage and raising a family, not in working for the winery, even though her contemporaries said she was intelligent and competent enough to have become a company executive. But in college she met James Coleman, and although the family expressed some concern that he wasn't Catholic, he converted and became even more devout than his in-laws, attending Mass every day. He and Sue were married September 1, 1957, and since he had majored in business, Julio eventually asked Ernest to hire him in the winery's sales division after graduation. Both couples settled into family life—Bob and Marie back in Modesto, Susann and Jim in Oregon for the next year.

Aileen and Julio's youngest son, Phillip, was a constant worry. Like David, he was sensitive and temperamental, although instead of exploding in temper tantrums, he withdrew into despondent silences. He suffered from painful skin rashes and preferred to stay indoors and out of the sun. Aileen often consulted doctors about his constant colds and allergies, but nothing they prescribed seemed to help. He liked music and books and could barely tolerate the deer and duck hunting trips that his father and brother and Uncle Joe so enjoyed. Yet he was forced to participate, because it was thought that the experience would "toughen" him up.

Julio was impatient with his complaints and what he considered a lack of self-control and weakness of character. Once Phillip burped at the table, and Julio shouted at him. He burped again, and although he excused himself, Julio flew into a towering rage. Phillip began to sob, and his father ordered him to his room.

Within each family and among its friends, there was talk of the other side's "weird son." Ernest seemed to ignore David's problems but told others that Julio's son Phillip was "too spoiled" and "high strung." Julio and his friends remarked on David's eccentricities, his baby-talk and whining, and suggested that his problems stemmed from Amelia's lack of discipline and indulgence of his every whim.

In 1957, Joe and Mary Ann built a new home on the land that Joe had purchased near the winery's Livingston vineyard. It was a California ranch design of wood and glass that overlooked a rolling meadow in front and vineyards to the rear. Inside Joe paneled the walls with redwood he had salvaged from the winery's old cooperage —a tribute, he felt, to the family's wine tradition. But the old barrel staves were so permeated that the house reeked of wine for months. It became a family joke—you could get tipsy just walking into Joe's living room. It took nearly a year of repeated treatments with an antimildew solution to rid the house of its heady aroma.

They were now settled into the home with their three children, their last, a hoped-for daughter named Linda, born on May 5, 1952. Sons Peter and Mike were much younger than their cousins, but even from an early age they were trained in the Gallo family ways. Although Ernest and Julio were still not on especially friendly terms, they held to the tradition of family gatherings on holidays: Thanksgiving at Julio and Aileen's; Christmas Eve and the ritual *bagna cauda* at Joe and Mary Ann's; Christmas Day at Ernest and Amelia's; and Easter again with Joe and Mary Ann. The pattern was the same: The wives prepared elaborate meals—these dinners were showcases for their specialties—and served them at long dining-room tables. Fathers and sons sat at one end, wives, daughters, and younger children at the other.

Joe's son Mike remembered these dinners as interrogations that everyone had to undergo. Ernest ran them like business meetings, asking his sons and nephews questions about politics and current affairs, often instigating arguments as if to test who was the brightest. If a company employee was present, he suffered an inquisition about winery operations; when Julio's son Bob and son-in-law Jim Coleman went to work for the winery, they were expected to give Ernest instant responses to his inquiries. Once Jim was so rattled by Ernest's questions about sales figures that he could only stammer his answers.

Ernest fired him the next week, and Julio hired him in the production division until he was moved to the glass company.

As David and Joey grew older, they adopted Ernest's role with their cousins Peter and Mike. But Peter had his mother's independence and spirit, and instead of answering their questions, he would tease David and Joey or play practical jokes on them. Ernest sometimes tried to discipline or scold him, but Peter refused to be intimidated. Only eight years old at the time, Mike was aware of tension between Ernest's side of the family and his own. "Ernest was always announcing how smart he was, how much he knew," Mike recalled. "The trips he'd taken, the people he'd met. He treated us as if we were the 'country cousins' or unsophisticated bumpkins." When Peter and Mike were alone with their mother, she laughed at Ernest's and his sons' pretensions, especially when David seemed so odd with his facial tics and sloppy shirts that were three sizes too big. And Joey's playing his father's role was another source of merriment since he was so literal-minded and pompous that he never got anyone's jokes.

Sometimes Aunt Celia came to these holiday dinners, and during the summer she and her daughter Gloria often visited Julio and Aileen for a few weeks. She liked to reminisce and would often tell stories about the old days, about the Bianco's winery, about Joe and Susie. Sometimes she mentioned her former husband, but Ernest and Julio exchanged anxious glances when Uncle Mike's name was mentioned. When questioned about him by his sons, Joe told them that their great-uncle was quite a character, but that he was considered the black sheep of the family; it was clear that Uncle Mike was not an acceptable topic of conversation at Ernest and Julio's tables.

Ever since the Bureau of Alcohol and Justice Department investigations and his prison sentence, Uncle Mike had been exiled from the Gallo family. By 1934 he had found financial backing—some said that Ernest had contributed to get him out of the state—to start a restaurant-hotel business in Hawthorne, Nevada, a midsize town on the highway between Reno and Las Vegas. First called Gallo's Inn (later El Capitan) the establishment was popular with travelers, and Mike had a steady stream of customers stopping overnight for his Italian dishes, formal dining room with white tablecloths and candles, and the card games in the back room. (This was long before either Reno or Las Vegas had become gambling meccas, and Mike would later brag that he was one of the first restaurant-casino owners to bus tourists from California.)

Mike was considered a flamboyant character in Hawthorne, and he became famous for his Prohibition "war stories," of how he ran whiskey and wine throughout northern California, knew famous politicians and gangsters, and had all the cops in his pocket. He was proud of his nephews and talked about what a big business they had built out of his and his brother's operation.

Mike was still a ladies' man with a volatile temper. He had girlfriends, often chosen from among his waitresses, and if any customer paid his particular favorite too much attention, he invited the man to step outside or had his son Mario, who worked as his bouncer, "escort" the customer out the door. His philandering ended his second marriage as well, and after his restaurant and hotel burned down, he and his third wife, Vivian, tried to start again. But in 1942, Mike was found guilty and fined for receiving stolen building materials from a military base and violating rationing orders when he attempted to reconstruct his restaurant.

Mike and Vivian then accepted positions as managers of a hotel-restaurant in Duluth, Minnesota. After the hotel-restaurant was sold, they settled in Gillespie, Illinois, where Mike opened another restaurant-tavern called Gallo's. He was jealous of his wife, who was some thirty years younger than he and whom he suspected of carrying on with other men. One day his worst suspicions were confirmed when she ran away with a boyfriend, but a week later she returned to Mike and begged his forgiveness. So enraged was he that he attacked her with a six-inch carving knife, stabbing her repeatedly in the back as she tried to escape.

Mike ran into the street and waved down a taxicab to drive him to the sheriff's office, where he confessed to the crime. He was sentenced to twenty-five years (his wife's infidelity and the heat of the moment were considered mitigating factors). When he was paroled, he moved to Henderson, Nevada, near Las Vegas, where his son Mario was working as a pit boss in a casino. For the next twenty years Mike lived in a rundown house trailer and earned a little money as a short-order cook. A Las Vegas parish priest who befriended him was appalled by his living conditions.

"We became friends because both our families were from Piedmont," recalled Father Benjamin Franzinelli. "But it was several years before I learned that Mike was Ernest and Julio Gallo's uncle.

The Gallo Winery was by then well known and very big, and I couldn't believe that these two wealthy men would let their uncle live the way he did—that trailer was a shambles. They had cases of Gallo wine delivered, but they never visited, as far as I knew. Mike didn't talk all that much about them. I think he felt bitter that they had written him off, that they felt they couldn't forgive him for things he'd done. He liked to reminisce, and hearing his stories, I felt that while he may have been a bootlegger, he may have blown some bucks, and he may have taken up with a few floozies, in his heyday he was a real pioneer, an early entrepreneur. Look what he did up in Hawthorne with his casino—he was one of the first people to come up with the idea of shuttling customers on buses from California."

Neither Ernest nor Julio shared the priest's charitable opinion. What the priest didn't realize was that Mike's past was more than just an embarrassment. His adventures in bootlegging and his knowledge of the activities of his brother (whom he still called Giuseppe when he reminisced to the priest) contradicted the family's official history. Mike's stories would have undermined the legend of the two brothers' creating their winery from nothing. It was now accepted as fact that the winery belonged to Ernest and Julio and had nothing to do with either their father's or their uncle's previous businesses. The regular delivery of cases of Gallo wine to the trailer door kept Mike's existence secret and his remembrance of things past hidden from the public and the family.

But the priest was correct in assuming that Ernest and Julio were wealthy men. After the extraordinary success of Thunderbird, they earned huge profits, much of which they invested in the improvement and expansion of the winery facilities as well as in its subsidiary companies.

The winery already had a bottling plant, which used bottles bought from Glass Containers. But the need for a glass-manufacturing company that could design bottles to the winery's own specifications became obvious when many customers complained that their Thunderbird "had gone off." Quality control experts in the Gallo laboratory discovered that Thunderbird had no stability when bottles were exposed to sunlight over a period of time. For the time being, the winery began bottling the concoction in beer-bottle-brown glass rather than the original clear glass. But meanwhile, construction of the glass plant was begun while Gallo scientists experimented with a new kind of glass that would be light-resistant and would be used for all Gallo brands.

By September 1958 the $6 million glass factory was in full production. Adjoining the winery cellars, the thirteen-acre plant ran twenty-four hours a day, manufacturing the new Gallo bottles—amber-green and featuring a special glass dubbed "Flavor-Guard" that, according to Gallo's promotional announcements, was invented to "shield wines from injury by flavor-stealing light rays." Although canneries like Hunt had built their own glass plants, Gallo was the first winery to manufacture its own glass for the one million bottles made each day.

The Gallo Glass Company became another part in the winery's vertical organization. Ernest asked his brother Joe to serve as its titular president. This was not an invitation back into the family business—like the other family-owned companies, it was designated as separate from the winery. Ninety percent of the new company's stock was issued to Ernest's and Julio's five children. At Ernest's suggestion, Joe bought the remaining 10 percent for $54,000 and placed it in the trusts of his three children, naming Ernest and Julio their trustees. Bob Gallo went to work in the glass plant as an assistant manager and was later promoted to general manager, reporting to Ernest, while at the same time he apprenticed under his father in winemaking. Jim Coleman also moved into a position at the glass plant.

After the invention of Thunderbird, Ernest became obsessed with flavoring experiments to find another perfect mix that would capture the public's taste and lure non–wine drinkers to wine. (Most flavored wines, like Thunderbird, were also cheap to make, since the wine base came from the least expensive grapes and sometimes from other fruit, such as apples, pears, or berries.) The laboratory began to experiment with flavored wines that were marketed as Gypsy Rose (Thunderbird's red equivalent to compete with Canandaigua's Wild Irish Rose). A peppermint-flavored white port called Twister was developed to cash in on the popularity of the dance that originated at the Peppermint Lounge in New York City (it was thought to appeal to the eighteen- to twenty-one-year-old drinkers, much like menthol cigarettes). But nothing would ever match Thunderbird's success. Thunderbird was still "the word" on the street.

The Thunderbird success would eventually undermine Ernest and Julio's desire for respectability. The winery would have to spend millions in advertising to try to dissociate itself from the "street wine" image. Advertising Thunderbird as an "American Aperitif," trying to move it into white markets, and insisting that "older" consumers drank it for its refreshing taste failed to change the public's negative perception. Even after removing the Gallo name from the Thunderbird label, the required designation of origin—Modesto, California— was a giveaway. And for all the extensive advertising programs to upgrade the image, the Gallo name would still be associated with cheap wines, screwtop caps, and dollar-a-pint bottles sold in skid-row stores.

Despite their denial that they had consciously exploited alcoholics and poor blacks, Ernest and his experts continued to experiment with, produce, and market other flavored and fortified wines—what some Gallo salesmen dubbed "ghetto blasters." (A notable later example was Tickled Pink, a variation on Ripple's Pagan Pink flavor; its radio jingles featured a deep voice with a recognizably southern black inflection.) The winery also targeted Native Americans in the Southwest where Gallo salesmen tried to convert residents from their favorite hip flasks of Garden Deluxe—nicknamed "Blue"—by selling Thunderbird from the beds of pickup trucks driven to the reservations. Gallo then invented a flavored, high-proof wine called Cherokee that was test-marketed in the same area, but Navahos and Hopis laughed at the name as well as the label since it featured a picture of a Sioux in full headdress. (This marketing mistake was matched by the later attempt to sell a fortified product as an "oriental wine" called Hai Tori in the midst of the Vietnam War.)

Gallo salesmen's reports still included a separate category of retail stores designated "ethnic." In the lists of Gallo products distributed to retailers, those shipped in three-eights liter and pint bottles were the sweet, fortified dessert wines and the flavored fortified wines, with "T-Bird," as it was recorded in their reports, the leader. And most of these pint bottles were distributed to "ethnic" liquor and grocery stores.

Having made substantial gains on Italian Swiss Colony with sales of Thunderbird, Ernest now made his influence felt in the industry. He had sneered at the winemakers who were appalled by products like Thunderbird. These winery owners, most of them in Napa and Sonoma, argued for quality, for educating American wine drinkers, for promoting California wine for its taste and class. Ernest couldn't give two screw caps for their snobbishness.

When the California Wine Advisory Board had formed the Wine

Institute after Repeal, Ernest had initially refused to join and pay the requisite dues since the Wine Institute's promotions seemed to have little to do with his goals. Finally, however, Gallo became a member, but Ernest's motto seemed to be, if you can't beat 'em, take 'em over. Since Wine Institute dues are assessed on the basis of a winery's sales, by 1957 the Gallo Winery was one of the major financial contributors to the organization, and that same year Ernest was elected president. He now had the respectable and respected representative of California wineries under his control. For years to come, one Gallo or another would serve either on the institute's board or as an officer, or both. *West* magazine would later state that Gallo still ran the organization "through its de facto proxy, the institute director John De-Luca." In 1990 the Wine Institute became a voluntary organization. Smaller wineries continued to complain that the Wine Institute (and the related California Wine Commission) geared their programs and promotions to Gallo's needs and objectives, and some resigned. That same year Sebastiani left, and in June 1992 Robert Mondavi withdrew as well, also because the institute's policies were too closely dictated by Gallo.

With Thunderbird's success, Ernest and Julio could begin to enjoy their wealth. The children had never wanted for anything—though again Ernest would still penny-pinch, refusing, for instance, to give David and Joey the small change to pay their library fines at school. But he now began to play the stock market, considering himself an expert, and began to accumulate a large private portfolio.

He also treated himself and his family to vacations—trips to Europe, especially Italy, and tours of the Orient (all combined with business, as he began to explore worldwide distribution of Gallo wine). He especially enjoyed deep-sea fishing, and sometimes took his brother Joe as well as winery executives and distributors with him to Costa Rica or Venezuela. He liked to present himself as well-traveled and extremely knowledgeable on any subject. He never spent money on new cars, however; his Cadillacs were always a few years old and dented from minor accidents. Not only was he a notoriously bad driver with poor eyesight (he was already wearing thick glasses), but he sometimes careened home after a wine-tasting session.

When he wasn't away on business trips, wine tasting was part of his daily schedule: He arrived at his office in the early hours of the morning to play the stock market, then he attended to business, conducting marketing and sales meetings throughout the day, phoning his distributors throughout the country for sales figures. In the late afternoon he invited executives and any of the sales managers in Modesto that day to sample wines.

"It was always comparative testing," recalled one former sales manager. "He'd send out for the competitive brands, and then we'd go through those bottles, with everyone, of course, agreeing that Gallo was the best. Then if you were favored that week, Ernest might ask you home for dinner. You were expected to ride with him, and you took your life in your hands. He was always knocking into curbs or brushing against trees. We'd finally get to the house; he'd weave up the steps and throw the door open with a bang. Then you'd hear a voice that would break glass. 'Ernest,' Amelia would shout, 'Have you been drinking again?' "

Amelia also enjoyed the privileges of their new wealth. But, like Ernest, she had her quirks. More than ever she cultivated the image of the down-to-earth farm girl who wasn't impressed with money or status and who spoke her mind without inhibition; her uncensored speech brought the description of her as "The Italian Gracie Allen" from winery employees.

One night at dinner she complained to a sales manager about "a fancy watch" she'd given Ernest that had stopped running.

"I took it back to the store," she continued, her voice rising in what employees had come to call the "Gallo whine." "But they wouldn't do anything for me. They said the watch had been abused. Can you imagine? It just wasn't fair—the watch was only six months old. And we've been doing business with them for years."

The sales manager made sympathetic noises, all the while thinking that Amelia was complaining about a small local jewelry shop in Modesto.

"I argued with them but they just kept saying that Ernest had damaged the watch and so they couldn't do anything about it," she went on. Then she turned and gave the sales manager her wide-eyed, innocent look. "And Tiffany's a respectable store, isn't it?"

Amelia and Ernest also played food critics when they went to restaurants. They especially liked going to San Francisco, usually eating in North Beach Italian restaurants. But they made a great production of ordering their food, asking questions about items on the menu, interrogating the waiters about the preparation of dishes, sometimes even ordering "off the menu."

"I hated going out to dinner with them," recalled another former Gallo executive. "First, everyone was afraid to order until they heard what Ernest was going to have. Then because he's a perfectionist, he frequently found fault with the meal. Amelia, too, would always say straight out when something didn't please her. Waiters would come to the table and innocently ask how the dinner was. Amelia would say things like, 'Oh, some people might say it was fine, but I'll never eat here again.' She had a kind of cruel streak in the name of honesty, and I think Ernest enjoyed that in her. And if the meal or the service wasn't perfect, they felt justified in stiffing the waiter for his tip. I think Ernest especially liked this part—he was so tight with money. Neither of them has very many social graces—they just don't think that manners are that important. It's probably one of the reasons why their son David is so asocialized. As he got older, he adopted the image of the great gourmet, too, copying his father and mother's behavior in restaurants. Only he was three times as bad."

Down Yosemite Avenue from the winery was the Italian restaurant Cote D'Oro where Ernest often took his sales and marketing employees for lunch meetings. The waiters suffered Ernest's demands for many years because of the business the winery brought them. They served Gallo wine and eventually set up a "Gallo" room for winery meetings. The food there mattered only to Ernest; everyone else at the table was too busy with Ernest's interrogations to care much about what they were eating. He had an agenda of questions, the answers to which Ernest already knew better than his men.

"When Ernest wasn't hauling us over the coals, he would snap at the waiters or complain to the manager," recalled another sales manager who suffered through these lunches. "I think eventually Ernest and his henchmen like Bertsch and Fenderson wore out their welcome, and they went through several Modesto restaurants as well. But those meals with Ernest were excruciating. If David was present, he also insisted on specially prepared dishes and instant service; then he would spill food and drink down his shirt, and you wanted to sink through the floor. But Ernest had this attitude—'I'm Ernest Gallo. This is my first-born son. And if I say you accept him, you accept him.' It was an intense, defiant familial pride."

Ernest still yearned to be accepted in the Modesto community. With more social skills, Julio and Aileen were invited to the homes of the town's prominent citizens, and after their son's marriage to Marie Damrell, they were considered part of Modesto's upper crust. Relinquishing his solitary habits, Julio even became a member of the Rotary Club. He also enjoyed boating, and like Ernest, he tried to take a few weeks off each year to go deep-sea fishing. But his favorite weekend activity was working in his organic vegetable garden.

The Gallos had also joined the Del Rio Country Club where Modesto's prominent families socialized. When Ken Bertsch came to work for Ernest, he had introduced the idea of playing golf as a social and business asset. Ernest took lessons and while never very athletic, he managed to acquire a passable game. His brother Joe also played and often made up a foursome with Bertsch and other winery executives. Ernest frequently invited visiting distributors, sales managers, grape growers, or union leaders for a round of golf at the country club as well. He expected winery executives to join the club, and in later years when he began to hire more executives, he enticed them with, "I'll get you into the country club."

Ernest wanted to be the best, even at golf. He took a golfing vacation in Palm Springs where he met a golf pro who helped him with his game. Anticipating a golf tournament at the country club and intent on winning that year, Ernest hired him to come to Modesto and coach him. Despite all the extra training, he could do nothing right on the day of the tournament. When he fell many strokes behind, he became irate and stalked over to the pro. Publicly berating him, blaming him for his poor showing, he fired him on the spot.

The country club also became Ernest's chosen place to entertain his executives and their wives at Saturday evening dinners. Employees dreaded these affairs—stiff and formal, none of the husbands able to relax, the wives treated as all but nonexistent. (There were no women in managerial or executive positions at Gallo, although a few women had now been added to the sales force.) Most employees felt that Ernest was simply advertising his membership; they joked that Ernest was trying to transform himself from "WOP" to "WASP" and pointed out that the new Gallo advertising campaigns featured the same images of "country club" leisure and genteel wealth.

When it came to his boys' college educations, Ernest didn't stint either. Ignoring David's eccentricities, he planned for him to enter Notre Dame University in the fall of 1957. "I don't know if David was bright, but his reactions were so strange that he really couldn't concentrate and never did that well academically," recalled one school contemporary. "Still, it was all settled that he was going to Notre Dame. For many years Ernest made large contributions to the library and building fund, and Joey entered a year after David, in 1958. David, we heard, had a sort of bodyguard/tutor, but even with this help, he and Joey ended up graduating the same year."

Julio's son Phillip should have graduated from high school with David in 1957. But because of his health problems he had lost a year of study and was in the same class as Joey for his senior year in 1958. During that year Phillip's appearance and behavior underwent a dramatic and disturbing change, according to classmates. Before he had been considered a "normal guy," tall, thin, with a handsome face, although he had always seemed "sort of nervous." But suddenly he gained over twenty pounds and his face broke out in large cysts. Students also noticed that his gestures had become "effeminate" and soon he was the target of jokes and cruel remarks. When he tried to sit next to classmates in the sweet shop, they jumped up and pointedly moved to another table. As if in self-defense, Phillip began to flaunt his "swishy walk" and "would wiggle his rear end" when classmates laughed at him as he passed their tables or left the classroom. He was taunted with cries of "fairy" and "homo" and "freak." Later, some students heard that Phillip's bloated appearance, cysts, and gestures were a result of hormonal treatments he had undergone. But at the time they had no idea what had caused the overnight change in the Gallo boy.

Phillip had remained interested in music, but he had become even more quiet, frequently lost in thought, daydreaming and self-absorbed. That spring he seemed to have fallen into a deep depression. His nervous habits and detachment annoyed the family, too, and Julio still scolded him in an effort to form him in the Gallo image. Some relatives wondered if he had suffered some sort of mental retardation at birth; others in the family said his problems stemmed not from brain damage but from an inherited nervous disorder. But one family member had a different view of Phillip's anguish.

By the time Phillip was in high school, Stella Bianco, Ernest and Julio's cousin, had married Bill Dorais and was living in San Francisco. Theirs was a different world from that of the Modesto Gallos. Stella worked for a radio station and Bill, who had been head of the Writers' Project in California, now worked for public television. They counted among their friends writers, artists, and entertainers. Phillip always liked to visit Stella in San Francisco, where he seemed to feel accepted and was able to relax. Stella wore her waist-length hair in a chignon, and when he was visiting, Phillip often begged to brush out her hair for her. She had noticed his effeminate gestures as well, and she concluded that her cousin was probably gay, although she wondered if Phillip even knew the source of his emotional and sexual confusion. At the time society in general was hardly tolerant of homosexuality, and in Modesto and especially within the Gallo family, she thought it would have been considered an unmentionable aberration. If Phillip had any understanding of himself, she reasoned, he must have feared even the slightest admission of his feelings.

Nevertheless, Stella used to tell Aileen and Julio, "Just let Phillip be. Stop pushing him into the Gallo mold. Don't scold him for being different." She even considered suggesting that Phillip come live with her and Bill (they had no children of their own), but she didn't want to appear too critical of Julio and Aileen's handling of the situation.

Stella's mild advice went unheeded, since Julio, like Ernest with his sons, believed that hard physical labor would make men of the boys. Like all Gallo sons, as well as executives' sons, Phillip was expected to work for the winery during the summer, either tending the home vineyards, weeding the gardens around the winery's office buildings, or helping in Julio's production department. But Phillip was often taunted by other field hands or other boys working with him.

Phillip's problems became increasingly evident after his graduation from high school in June 1958. Sons of Ernest's executives and distributors had come to know Phillip during the summers when they had worked in the home ranch vineyards or when Phillip had sometimes dropped in at Ernest's barbecues. Most of them liked Phillip, considering him "nicer," "smarter," and "more fun" than Joey and David. They felt sorry that he was teased a lot because he seemed "different," "gained all that weight," and "developed effeminate mannerisms." In retrospect, they would acknowledge that they suspected he was gay, although at the time and at their age, they said, they didn't really know how to talk about it except to make crude jokes. According to the son of a Gallo executive, during the summer of 1958, Phillip suddenly stopped coming to work at the winery and didn't show up at various social events. The official explanation was that "he was away for a while."

A few months later Phillip returned home. His appearance was even more startling—he was bloated, his breasts even more developed. There was talk that he had been hospitalized and had received hormone treatments as part of a "cure for homosexuality" as well as being prescribed lithium. Julio now put him back to work in the winery's laboratory, where one of the research scientists took him under his wing, and everyone said he seemed to be "getting better."

Phillip still lived at home, and after eating dinner with his parents on Wednesday, October 21, he excused himself and said he was going to bed early. It was only eight in the evening, but he allayed his parents' concern by insisting that he was just tired.

The next morning Aileen arose at six to begin her usual routine. She walked to Phillip's bedroom at the other end of the house to wake him for work. As she knocked on his door, she heard a low groan. She flung the door open and rushed inside.

Phillip was sprawled in a pool of blood on the floor of the bedroom. A .410 shotgun lay at his side. He was still alive, moaning weakly, but the blast from the shotgun had torn open his abdomen. Aileen ran from the room and phoned for the doctor. But by the time the ambulance arrived, Phillip was already dead.

Neither Aileen nor Julio had heard a shot fired, they told sheriff investigators. They explained that Phillip "had been under years long treatment for a mental disturbance," but that "he had improved," was "working as a laboratory technician at the winery," and "appeared in good spirits recently."

Coroner Herbert Paul conducted a brief examination and hearing and concluded that Phillip had died from shock and hemorrhage as a result of the "self-inflicted gunshot." Private funeral services were held at the Shannon Chapel, and Phillip was buried near his Gallo grandparents in St. Stanislaus Cemetery.

Accounts of Phillip's death were broadcast on the morning news, and many winery employees heard about the suicide while driving to work. Winery talk tended to blame Ernest and Julio. The rumors focused on the brothers' stern demand that Phillip work for the winery and on his parents' trying to "cure" his homosexuality. Then again Phillip's death revived speculation about Ernest and Julio's parents' deaths—that because the father had killed the mother, then himself, the gossip went, "mental instability" must run in the family.

"Everyone was talking about a screw loose, a bad seed, and while many people felt sorry for Julio and Aileen, there was also a feeling that there was bad blood in the Gallo family," said one former employee who had worked with Phillip. "Besides, it was fairly common knowledge that Julio browbeat his son and forced him to work in the winery, so people tended to blame him, too. Ernest made things worse by insisting that Julio and Aileen had spoiled Phillip, as if his suicide was proof of the kid's moral weakness. No one really knew why it had happened, what had driven Phillip to suicide. But fairly soon after his death, it was made clear that this was something else none of us should talk about. It was all hushed up."

Julio and Aileen planted a tree in their backyard in Phillip's memory. But his suicide became another family secret, and this Gallo tragedy was also shrouded in silence.

CHAPTER SEVEN

In his grief over his son's suicide and because Aileen was so devastated, Julio began to pay more attention to her and their many grandchildren. He also devoted more hours to his vegetable garden, and with his son Bob donated time and money to a local school for retarded children.

Ernest drew his own moral from his nephew's death: Phillip's suicide could have been prevented through hard work and discipline, he told employees. Ernest would expect his own boys to measure up to his standards of performance when they finished college and came to work at the winery.

In the meantime, he intensified his campaign to open new Gallo territories and exert influence in more distributorships. For all his earlier connections in Chicago, Ernest had been unable to crack the Midwest market. Although he had continued to sell bulk wine to Charlie Barbera and Tony Paterno of the Pacific Wine Company for the first decade after Repeal, Ernest met with resistance when he first started to produce Gallo-bottled and -labeled brands. Few distributors were willing to concentrate on the Gallo brands when Italian Swiss Colony, Guild, and Chicago-based Mogen David were outselling them.

In 1946 Paterno had bought out Barbera, and having been a good friend of Cesare Mondavi, he became his representative and later chose to concentrate more on fine table wines and varietals, although he still bottled California bulk wine as well as kosher wine. In the late

1950s Ernest went looking for a new distributor who would push his brands aggressively. Even though his wines still had limited exposure and popularity in the region, he wanted a distributorship where he could install the Gallo method of operation.

One of the distributors that he considered was the Morand Brothers Beverage Company, which was now being run by Michael J. Romano, Sr., who had worked for the Morands before and during Prohibition and then had become a partner in the company after Repeal.

Mike Romano had been watched by the Chicago Crime Commission and the FBI. A confidential memo in the "Hoodlums General File" noted that Romano had "business dealings with Mario Nuzzo concerning liquor purchases" and that Nuzzo was a known Mafioso and a former Capone associate. Romano had also been investigated because of his letter urging early parole for a known Capone associate, Louis Campagna.

Whatever suspicions there were about Mike Romano, he had continued in the business, and with the help of his two sons, Mike, Jr., and Donald J. (Buddy), he had taken over and rebuilt the Morand Brothers Company into a small, moderately successful operation. (Distributors with limited sales and undistinguished brands were usually the type that Ernest looked for, said Gallo sales managers, because they were "hungry" enough to accede to the winery's demands.)

In 1959, Mike Romano, Sr., was visited, as Mike, Jr., recalled, "by a short, dark Italian and a dapper blond man, who looked very young but was older than he appeared." They introduced themselves as Ernest Gallo and Albion Fenderson. Mike, Jr., and Buddy sat in on the conference and watched as Ernest announced what he wanted from Romano if he were to become a Gallo distributor: The company would have to add eighteen salesmen to its twenty-two-man staff, and these new salesmen would handle Gallo brands exclusively.

But Gallo brands were not yet popular in this territory, and Romano was surprised by the Californian's emphatic demands, especially since it was common knowledge that he was making the rounds of Chicago distributors without much luck. Romano was about to say as much when his secretary interrupted to announce that Ernest had an urgent phone call. Mike, Jr., escorted Ernest to his office next door, then returned to hear his father lecturing Fenderson.

What makes you think you can come in and just take over this market? he asked, his voice loud and angry. *The Gallo brands aren't very well known. You aren't a key brand here, so how can you come in and tell me what to do? Look at Italian Swiss Colony, look at Mogen David!*

He was still shouting as Ernest returned from his phone call. Ernest stopped in the doorway. He looked from Romano to Fenderson and back to Romano, perplexed that the discussion had fallen into such disarray. Romano then turned his wrath on him. *Who the hell do you think you are? This is my company, and nobody, I mean* nobody, *gives me orders.*

Ernest and Al hustled out of the office, Romano's voice booming after them. This was obviously not the distributor for them. For the next year no other distributor in Chicago would agree to Ernest's demands, and Gallo still had only about eleven hundred accounts of about five thousand possible retail outlets. Finally, in 1961, a new distributorship was established, organized under a separate corporation, which had originally been formed in Louisiana and called "Edgebrook" for the Modesto street where stockholders Fenderson, Crawford, Bertsch, and Williams all lived. (According to former sales managers, because these corporations were separate entities, Gallo held to the letter of state and federal laws that prohibited wineries from directly owning distributorships. While second-generation family members and Gallo executives were named as shareholders of such corporations, the winery had operational and financial control, with its accountants handling financial transactions and its sales managers running the day-to-day business.)

Fenderson now undertook to open the Chicago market with an aggressive campaign and an army of salesmen to introduce Thunderbird. With a big push of street sampling among black customers, the Edgebrook distributorship sold fifty thousand cases of Thunderbird in its second month of operation. Italian Swiss Colony sold about ninety thousand cases in the black market, according to a former Gallo salesman who was assigned to Chicago, so it looked as if the winery would finally penetrate this territory. Then a photograph ran in the local newspaper—a man lying dead in the gutter, clutching a bottle of Thunderbird. Gallo suspected a setup, but the picture, and the ensuing talk on the street, killed Thunderbird sales.

After another year of disappointing sales and retailers' resistance to Gallo brands, Ernest turned to the one distributor who had real power in the Chicago liquor and wine business—Joseph Fusco.

Fusco was a notorious figure in Chicago. He ran several liquor distributorships and was quite powerful in the trade, much of his clout derived from his having been "superintendent of Capone's beer and wine delivery force" during Prohibition. As the Chicago Crime Commission often noted in its surveillance of him and his activities, he was a major player in Chicago's underworld. He also owned several distributorships in other states, including California, but his Merit Liquor Company was considered the largest and most influential wholesale company in the Midwest. His reputation for mob tactics followed him, and he was often investigated, not only by the Chicago Crime Commission but also by the Kefauver Senate Committee investigating organized crime.

In 1949, Fusco's Gold Seal distributorship was the exclusive representative of Schenley liquors in the area and was granted a $1 million credit line by Schenley. Fusco had thus been able to expand and increase his power. When he agreed to distribute Gallo wine, he was not about to take orders from anyone, much less a winemaker from California. Ernest had very little choice at this point, and Fusco's control of the liquor industry would indeed help sell the winery's brands.

Much of Fusco's success was attributable to his threatening reputation. In California, he was investigated for forcing retailers to buy his Van Merit Beer in order to receive the other brands of liquor that he distributed (though this was not an unusual selling tactic in the liquor distribution business). In Illinois, the Chicago Crime Commission had kept tabs on his activities, including the many times he had been seen in the company of mob associates. Nevertheless, he remained virtually untouchable, especially when one of his former business associates became a member of the Illinois State Liquor Control Commission. And in Chicago itself, it was said that if Fusco wanted a retailer to buy one of his brands, all it took was a phone call and the familiar sound of Fusco's deep, rasping voice.

Fusco achieved higher sales for Gallo, but he was getting on in years and suffered from a heart condition. He had no sons to succeed him in the business, and it was apparent that when Fusco himself wasn't able to exert his influence, sales would decrease. Ernest still yearned for the same kind of control over his Chicago distributorship that he had in other companies, and, according to former Gallo sales managers, he was often stymied by the strong-willed, powerful Fusco. In 1963, however, Fusco suffered a serious heart attack from which it seemed that he would not recover. Ernest had hired Arthur (Art) Palombo away from Schenley, and he now assigned him the task of finding another distributor in Chicago.

"My father was on a trip to Europe," recalled Buddy Romano, "when one morning I received a surprise telephone call from Art Palombo. We'd known him when he was at Schenley, and now he said he worked for Gallo Winery and that Ernest was again interested in having us distribute his wine. At first we couldn't figure out why— Thunderbird was big nationally, so were Paisano and Gallo Rosé— and we knew Fusco had helped increase their sales. What would Gallo want with us? But Ernest, through Art, was offering us an opportunity to build our business if we took on his brands."

Remembering their father's reaction in 1959, Buddy and Mike tentatively broached the subject when he returned from Europe. They explained that while Ernest still required a separate staff of Gallo salesmen, this time he was adding incentives like extended credit and financing the expansion of their offices and warehouse. His enticement was the one he recited so often to potential distributors: "Invest in my brand, and I'll invest in you." His plan was to move Edgebrook's full sales staff into the Romanos' company and give them the entire Gallo line, "lock, stock and barrel."

Ernest had asked his Chicago people to find out who were "the hungriest young distributors in town." He had heard that Mike, Jr., and Buddy were now virtually running their father's company and looking to expand it. Once the Romano brothers had convinced their father to let them consider Ernest's proposal, they flew to San Francisco where they were met by the winery's private plane and taken to Modesto. Now Ernest changed from the imperious approach and wooed them by entertaining them lavishly. Although he still made the same Gallo demands, he treated the brothers "like family" and convinced them that by establishing a Gallo division, their business would become more prosperous than they had ever imagined. The brothers were impressed by the winery's size and its technical advances and efficiency, by Ernest's detailed knowledge of sales and marketing, and by the profits to be made from Gallo sales.

"Ernest sold us on the winery and on himself," Mike, Jr., said, and he and Buddy returned home ready to establish the Gallo division of the Romano Brothers.

"I think Ernest also liked us because we are an Italian family business," added Buddy. "He has the reputation for being ruthless, demanding, and even vicious, which he can be. But he's also generous, and if you're loyal to him, he's loyal to you. He asks a great deal of you, but if you give him what he wants, he gives back triple. I think of him as a second father, and I never make a business decision without consulting him. He helped build our business until we had a 51 percent share of the Chicago market, and our distributorship has become the Midwest Gallo sales training center. There are so many people in the liquor business who have come through here as Gallo salesmen that we're sometimes called Romano University."

Having reached an agreement with the Romanos, Ernest advised the Fusco distributorship of the change and demanded the return of $350,000 worth of Gallo products that the company had on credit in its warehouse. Much to everyone's surprise, Fusco recovered—some said his anger at Ernest had brought him through—and he refused either to return Ernest's wine or to pay the outstanding account. Although Ernest sued him, Fusco had his own methods. Word on the street was that there was a contract out on Ernest Gallo; Gallo employees were aware that Ernest usually sent Al Fenderson to Chicago to take care of business, or if Ernest came to town, they said, he conducted meetings at the airport, not daring to set foot downtown. Furthermore, it was rumored that retailers had been told that if they bought from the Romano brothers, they could never buy from Fusco's company, and they would lose all their Schenley products. Nevertheless, Ernest eventually won the lawsuit, Fusco died, and the Romanos became one of the most successful Gallo distributors in the country.

The Romano brothers joined the Gallo team at a propitious moment—the winery was on the verge of becoming number one in the country. In addition to Paisano and Thunderbird, the winery had developed Ripple, a slightly carbonated, fruit-flavored wine made from inexpensive Thompson seedless. Its alcohol content was only 9 percent to 11 percent, and it was sold in small beer-size bottles. It was gaining popularity among college-age consumers who previously had favored beer over wine. Gallo's television advertising campaign—Don Kent singing "Come along with me to the wine country" on a rearing palomino—was beginning to catch on, too.

The continued success of Gallo Vin Rosé in its decanter bottle then prompted Howard Williams to create what was called in the industry "line extenders," new products that traded on the success of the original product. He adopted two wines to be marketed under the same theme as the Gallo decanter line: Gallo Rhine Garten (a slightly sweet

German white) and Chianti of California. The latter, according to Robert Huntington, who was the group product manager for the decanter line, was another light red, "essentially a recycled Paisano" and not a true chianti wine.

Huntington had been hired by the winery in 1961, and after completing the training program in Los Angeles, he was moved to Modesto to become a brand manager for Gallo vermouth and several of the natural, high-proof aperitif wines, such as Gypsy Rose, Eden Roc (the name would only later be given to a Gallo line of sparkling wines), and Triple Jack (a fortified apple wine). He was then assigned to the decanter line, which became the basis for the renewed campaign to push Gallo table wine sales above those of Italian Swiss Colony.

"It was with the decanters that Gallo television advertising changed as well," Huntington explained. "The Los Angeles agency, Irwin Wacey, developed the theme of 'The Beautiful Wines,' accompanied by impressionistic, poetic images. Ernest always preferred go-for-the-throat advertising; he wanted instant gratification, and if he didn't see immediate results, he would pull ads after a month. Image building and changing perceptions are a slow process so he was skeptical when the agency first presented 'The Beautiful Wines' program. But their account executive and I finally said we'd stake our reputations, even our jobs on its success. George Frank was our East Coast sales manager. [Frank had been building the eastern seaboard market since his employment by Ernest in 1956.] He was very smart and often critical of the usual Gallo hard-sell ads, but after the new ads ran, he called Ernest to say, 'Now you know what good advertising really is.' After that the decanter wines dominated all the other Gallo table wines and began to move us closer to number one in sales."

Just before Huntington had come to the winery, Ernest had hired Richard (Dick) Witter who had recently received his MBA from Stanford Business School. He had the kind of looks, background, and respectability that appealed to Ernest; he was tall and handsome, and he had family wealth behind him. "I like to hire men who have their own money," Ernest remarked to a sales manager. "I can put them in key positions because I know they're not going to steal the first dime that comes their way at the winery." Witter also had what another executive described as "arrogance born of money and privilege which matched Ernest's disdain for others, and a mind for detail that equaled Ernest's compulsion to control."

Witter was first installed in the marketing division, and in the early 1960s, he expanded and built the Mountain Wine label (its most popular, Mountain Red) Ernest had named on the spur of the moment to compete with Franzia's jug wines. Witter's marketing campaign brought higher sales, particularly among younger consumers, and he soon became one of Ernest's fair-haired executives and a member of the inner circle. Some employees said that, like Fenderson and Palombo, Witter was a surrogate son whose brains and aggressiveness were in dramatic contrast to Ernest's own boys. Witter's talents, they explained, were especially important to Ernest during this decade of rapid change and expansion at the winery.

Ernest's sons David and Joey were still being trained for positions in the winery. They completed their courses in business at Notre Dame in 1962, but before they returned to the winery, Ernest decided that they should attend Stanford Business School. Stanford also became the recipient of Gallo endowments, and Joey received his MBA in 1964, specializing in marketing. David, however, never finished his degree, even though in 1963 Ernest made one of his rare public appearances to lecture at the monthly symposium of the Stanford Business School.

Once again presenting the Gallo legend of two penniless brothers founding a winery and through hard work building it into one of the largest wine companies in the world, Ernest stressed the theme, "Young men's capacities are usually underestimated by most companies." Between the lines he sounded as if he were still fighting the old battle with his father: His father had underestimated him, had never listened to him, had refused to make him a partner in his business. Whatever guilt Ernest may have felt about the last years of his father's life and his conflicts with him, he now seemed to justify his actions by his success, as if by developing the Gallo Winery, he had proved how misguided his father had been not to have taken him seriously. He extolled the virtues of employment by the winery because *he* recognized the talents of young men. And he exhorted the students to follow his example of initiative and ambition "to prove again that young men's capacities are usually underestimated."

Ernest, however, seemed to overestimate his own sons' capacities. He continued to push David, even though it seemed to winery employees that the son could neither succeed in getting his MBA nor operate effectively in the real world. "Suddenly the winery hired several Stanford Business School professors as consultants," recalled one Gallo brand manager, "and it seemed to us that this was Ernest's attempt to curry favor and get them to give David a degree. But to no avail, because David left Stanford in 1963 without an MBA."

David also had to fulfill his military obligations. He joined the National Guard, and after finishing his active service, he was assigned to a reserve unit. Fellow guardsmen remembered the nervous habits that would become his most remarked-upon eccentricities. During lectures he not only ate corn nuts compulsively, but he also unbent a paper clip, inserted one end under his eyelid and slid it back and forth, first in one eye, then the other.

Once David and Joey had both finished their active military service (Joey served six months in the Coast Guard, and then was in the reserves), they were assigned winery jobs as part of their training.

Working in the winery's marketing division, David eventually became brand manager of Gallo's new André champagne. (In 1966, the winery had produced and marketed its first champagne, Eden Roc, the name derived from the fashionable beach resort at Cap d'Antibes and then transferred from the Gallo aperitif wine to which it had originally been applied.) Al Fenderson then developed and marketed André as the winery's less expensive champagne (produced in tanks by the "bulk process," not the traditional *champenoise* method of fermenting in individual bottles). Despite his title, David was actually under Fenderson's direction and Charlie Rossi's supervision. Rossi, who was Ernest's shirt-tail relative and acquaintance from grape-shipping days, was employed by the winery to work in marketing and advertising. Trusted as family and called Uncle Charlie by David and Joey, he trained both brothers at various times during their apprenticeships in merchandising. According to winery associates, however, after Rossi was assigned to the André brand, he became David's "watchdog." Nevertheless, David seemed to assume that the product was his own invention and achievement.

"My parents went to the winery party which introduced the new champagne," Mike Gallo recalled. "David came up to my mother and asked her what she thought of *his* champagne. She said, 'It's okay, David, but I like Franzia champagne better.' The Franzia Winery had just put out an inexpensive champagne, and that was a thorn in Ernest's side, so David was incensed. His mouth dropped open, but he forgot he had just taken a gulp of champagne and it splashed down the front of his suit. That was just one of many incidents that showed how out of it he was. Still, no one either in the family or in the winery was supposed to say anything."

By the mid-1960s David's role was well-defined. While he was assigned an office and a secretary, it was unlikely that he could be given autonomous responsibility. But he was so loyal to his father that he was useful in his own fashion. Ernest allowed him to sit in on marketing meetings and sessions with advertising agencies and tolerated his rude and erratic behavior, almost as if he enjoyed it.

Gallo employees and advertising executives making presentations to Ernest and his marketing division found David's behavior at the meetings particularly unnerving. Not only did he continue to run paper clips under his eyelids; he also tipped his chair so far back on two legs that he sometimes fell over. If Ernest didn't like a proposed advertising campaign, he invariably asked David his opinion. That seemed to be David's cue. Invariably, he would respond, as if programmed, "Gee, Dad, I don't think it's very good." When one advertising executive demanded that David explain his reasons, David burst into tears and complained to his father, "Daddy, that man's not being nice to me."

When David returned to the winery, Joey remained on the road, assigned to one sales supervisor and territory for a few months, then moved on to another. For example, in the mid-1960s he was transferred to Miami as "Florida sales manager" when Ali Bianco had been sent there to establish a Gallo distributorship and intensify Gallo's sales efforts in the state.

Ernest had first hired Ali Bianco in southern California. The son of his mother's brother Walter, the younger brother of his childhood playmate Stella Bianco Dorais, he was family and thus trusted to work for Ernest inside distributorships in San Luis Obispo and Riverside. (These and other distributorships later became a part of Midcal Aluminum, the screw-cap production company, of which David, Joey, and Julio's daughter, Susann Coleman, were the principal shareholders. These distributorships did business under the name of Valley Vintners, and were run and supervised by Gallo sales managers.)

When Ali was moved to Florida, Joey was apprenticed to him and lived with him as well. Ali regaled his sister Stella with stories of Joey's affectations, reporting that before meetings with distributors or retailers, Joey stood in front of a mirror and imitated his father's choppy hand gestures and facial expressions, even down to Ernest's squinting eye. *There, do you think I look enough like my father?* he asked Ali.

Distributors and Gallo managers who were asked to supervise Joey during his field training concluded that the real problem was that while Joey could try to imitate his father, he didn't think like him. He repeated empty phrases of businessese, like announcing that he'd gone into the winery sales division because he had met distributors at a very early age and "identified with this type of people." Distributors weren't quite sure how Joey identified with them; what they did feel was the pressure of having the boss's son on their premises while he was trained by the Gallo managers whom Ernest had required them to hire. Joey also spent time in southern California where he was put in charge of the then independent Gallo distributorships in San Diego and Riverside. Later, recalling his position at the two companies, Joey declared that he "was on the winery payroll interfacing with those independent wholesalers."

What "interfacing" actually meant at the time was extending Gallo's influence within the distributorship and reporting to Ken Bertsch about the company's owners, their finances, their commitment to Gallo brands, and if the distributorship carried other wineries' products, information about competitors' programs and sales.

It was natural, too, that Joey should be sent to the Romano brothers in Chicago for more experience. Named Illinois state manager, he again functioned as Ernest's agent within the distributorship. He also went through the training program there, and Gallo managers who lead the seminars assessed Joey as "limited" and "unimaginative." He seemed plodding and indecisive, as if he were afraid he'd make the wrong decision and be taken to task by Ernest. Yet since Mike and Buddy Romano considered Ernest a second father, they lavished attention and praise on Joey, and Joey said they were "like family" to him during his stay in Chicago.

The Romano brothers must have seemed like doting parents to Joey compared to the way Ernest treated him. While he ignored David's weird behavior, he was relentlessly and publicly critical whenever Joey flew home to the winery for sales meetings. Sales managers cringed when Joey was present and Ernest put him through his paces to test his knowledge.

"Ernest is hard on everyone," commented a district sales manager, "but I don't think I've seen anyone emotionally brutalize his kids the way Ernest brutalized Joe. I think he felt that if he were incredibly demanding, his son would develop according to his expectations. Ernest was oblivious to the damage he was doing."

Enough people had witnessed Ernest's repeated humiliations of

Joey that a few of them even gently suggested that the son might perform better if Ernest didn't berate him so frequently.

"You know, Ernest, maybe you could try another approach," commented one of the regional sales managers assigned to train him. "Perhaps Joe would be more willing to learn if you weren't always so hard on him."

Ernest shook his head. "You don't understand. It's the most difficult thing in the world to raise a successful child if you have money."

It was the same moral Ernest had drawn at the time of Phillip's death, and during the 1960s he continued to refer to the tragedy to justify his demands on his son.

But Ernest's treatment of Joey seemed so excessive that there may have been an unconscious motive to undermining his son's confidence. Ernest had felt that his own father had kept him in a subservient position and forbidden any challenge to his authority and dominance. But as a young man Ernest had been convinced that he was more competent, more ambitious, and bound to be more successful than Joe, Sr., and he had set out to prove this with extraordinary drive and single-mindedness. Now that Joey was an adult and expected to play a role in the winery, Ernest seemed to insist that his own son could never surpass him in brilliance or achievement, much less usurp his position or power. Perhaps Ernest's lingering antagonism toward his father compelled him to prove over and over again that no one could measure up to him—especially not his sons.

After Phillip's suicide, Julio had once again found it comforting to confide in his brother Joe when he made his routine inspections of the Livingston vineyards. Whether it was his usual annoyance with Ernest, whether he was upset by Ernest's comments about Phillip, or whether he was reassessing his life after his son's death, Julio often mentioned to Joe that he was thinking of making a change.

"Julio says he wants to split up the winery," Joe told Mary Ann after one of his brother's visits. "But he says Ernest won't discuss it. He just gets angry and says, 'You split it, you decide.' "

"What does Julio want to do instead?" Mary Ann asked.

"He doesn't know," Joe replied, shaking his head. "Sometimes he says he'll buy a winery up north, in Napa or Sonoma. I told him I thought that was a good idea, because then he could make wine the way he wants to do it. Or he could take some of the vineyards here and build a small winery. But he just can't make up his mind. Whenever I suggest something or agree with his idea, he has all sorts of reasons why it wouldn't work. He's just getting more and more unhappy, and I'm beginning to worry about his health."

But if anybody could calm Julio down, Joe could, and he now urged Julio to retreat again, just as he had before. If Julio couldn't make up his mind to leave the winery, then he should stay well away from Ernest and try to ignore the things that bothered him. Within the year Julio seemed to have accepted the situation once again, and his complaints about Ernest tapered off. The rumor among the winery's executives was that they had finally buried the hatchet. Indeed, the two brothers seemed to announce this when Julio made a rare appearance at one of Ernest's inner circle dinners and the two of them together barbecued a tuna for the guests.

Julio had depended on Joe in his times of trouble because of the three brothers Joe seemed the most satisfied with his life. He enjoyed his work managing the winery's Livingston vineyards, and since he reported to Julio, he rarely had to suffer Ernest's tirades or complaints. Nevertheless, he still put in very long hours, eager as ever to please both his brothers.

From the very beginning of his employment by the winery, he had bought cattle and, with his brothers' approval, grazed them on the unplanted areas of the property he managed. Although his brothers had refused to let him purchase the Livingston vineyards, in 1948 they sold him the unplanted half of their vineyards adjacent to the Livingston vineyards where Joe grazed more cattle and planted vineyards of his own. In 1950 he bought the Escola Ranch, which included both pastureland and a hundred-cow dairy. For about a year he ran the dairy as the Joseph Gallo Dairy, but then converted the operation to the Joseph Gallo Feed Lot, which purchased, fattened, and sold cattle.

In 1955, on the advice of Jon Shastid, a lawyer and financial wizard whom Ernest had recently hired at the winery, Joe formed a cattle company. Shastid suggested, in fact, that he call it Gallo Cattle Company. Neither Ernest nor Julio registered any problem with the name at the time, and they most often referred to Joe's separate business interests as Joseph Gallo Vineyards.

By the early 1960s Joe Gallo's name was well known at livestock auctions throughout California, his cattle all identified by his "JG" brand. For the most part he hired his own ranch hands, but sometimes, with Julio's approval, crews from the winery vineyards worked on his ranches. Then the winery accounting office deducted their pay from Joe's sales of grapes to the winery. It was a comfortable, friendly arrangement, and he continued to purchase more land, eventually increasing his holdings to over four thousand acres of vineyards that over the years he replanted to French Colombards and Chenin Blanc, the two wine grapes that Julio most favored for white wine blends and lower-tier brands and that he bought from Joe every harvest. Joe was establishing his own trade name both for cattle and for wine grapes; neither Ernest nor Julio complained about his activities.

Joe seemed to have all that he had ever desired—a satisfying, albeit demanding job for the winery, his own vineyards and livestock ranches, and a beautiful home where he and his wife and children lived comfortably. His wealth couldn't compare with that of his brothers, but he was affluent enough to provide Mary Ann and their children with pleasant luxuries.

But Mary Ann wasn't happy. She felt stifled by living in the country, and especially now that her children were growing up, she wanted more to occupy her time. Joe still put in long hours, his working day often extended by having to attend to his own properties after finishing at the winery's vineyards. The only social life he seemed willing to have was one that revolved around Ernest and Julio and sometimes other winery employees like Charlie Crawford and Ken Bertsch, with whom he played golf. Mary Ann enjoyed seeing Aileen and Julio, but she often resented Ernest's imperious demands on the family's time. Yet Joe seemed content to have their life constricted by his brother, and to her it seemed ironic that he would advise Julio to ignore or withdraw from Ernest when he seemed incapable of resisting himself.

"My mother was never swept off her feet by the idea of being part of the Gallo family," said Mike Gallo. "She was a real scrapper and very independent, and she disliked the idea of everyone around a dinner table kow-towing to Ernest. She was much closer to Julio and Aileen—she and Aileen thought of themselves as sisters, and she was close to Aileen's daughter Susann Coleman, too. They often took trips to San Francisco together to go shopping or see a show. But that didn't solve the problem of feeling isolated in Livingston and not being able to pursue the things she cared about. It was neither Merced nor Modesto, and she and my father had very little social life outside the family and winery associations. He was a workaholic—despite what Ernest and Julio would later say—and part of that was due to his feeling that he had to prove himself to his brothers."

"For many years my mother went along with the expectations of the Gallo brothers," recalled Linda Gallo Jelacich, Joe and Mary Ann's daughter. "She was a very good cook, but when we were giving one of those big holiday family dinners, Dad was always nervous that everything should be just right. That always put her under a lot of pressure. Many guests were invited to our annual Easter barbecue— in addition to family, some members of the winery inner circle always came. Maybe it was twenty, twenty-five guests at the table. My father usually roasted lambs over an open fire, and my mother would make the pasta. Amelia and Aileen always headed straight for the kitchen, looking in pots, tasting sauces, criticizing. Finally my mother began locking the door on them to keep them out.

"My father was always so anxious to please Ernest," Linda continued, "and, of course, Ernest always discovered something to criticize and little to praise. He thinks of himself as an expert—and he is a very good cook, but so were my mom and dad. But that didn't make those family dinners very pleasant. I just remember a feeling of tension. Either it was Ernest finding fault with the food or interrogating people about winery business or getting other guests into arguments over politics. He just liked to start things going, get people arguing. Sometimes my mother would joke about how weird and selfish Ernest was. Like the times we were summoned to his house for dinner and when we arrived, we would have to wait while he had his hair cut in the dining room by his personal barber. But after a while my mother was just exhausted by the family demands and was fed up with living out in the country."

Mary Ann had begun to spend more and more time in Modesto doing volunteer work, going to parties, and finding her own circle of friends. She became increasingly aware of how limited she found the Gallo confines. She withdrew even more from Gallo demands and expectations and openly rebelled by creating her own separate world. In 1962, she decided that she had to act on her feelings and make a new life for herself, and much to Joe's dismay, she left him and moved back to Modesto.

Joe was stricken and at first angry; he sued for divorce, insisting that Peter and Mike remain with him in Livingston, where they would be able to learn farming. Linda, he agreed, should live with her mother in Modesto.

As Linda later recalled, her mother had told her that when Aileen and Julio were told of the impending divorce, they were extremely upset. Aileen especially didn't want to take sides—after all, Mary Ann was her best friend, and she urged her to try to reconcile.

Ernest's response, according to Linda's impression from her mother, was to find Joe the best lawyer available. "My mother thought that Ernest was worried about the financial implications of the divorce," said Linda. According to her and Mike, Ernest wanted a lawyer who could handle any problems because many of Joe's property transactions and holdings were entangled with his brothers, and his accountings were done by the winery's financial offices.

Ernest had previously met C. Ray Robinson, one of the Central Valley's most powerful attorneys and landowners, and he asked Robinson, as a personal favor, to handle Joe's case. Robinson agreed, and John Whiting, then one of Robinson's associates, was assigned to represent Joe in the proceedings.

Whiting and Joe took to each other from the start, and before long they became friends as well as lawyer and client. A balding, burly man then in his late thirties, Whiting had grown up in Pleasanton, where his father had managed the racetrack. He loved raising horses and had even headed Livermore's annual rodeo when he practiced law there. He and his twin brother had both gone to Stanford Law School, and John would be devastated when his brother, whose hobby was flying, died in a plane crash several years later.

"By then Joe and I were already good friends, but when my brother died we became very close. It was as if he took the place of my brother," Whiting explained. "But we had liked each other almost immediately when I started working on his divorce. I could see that he was really upset by the whole thing. I don't know if he and Mary Ann could have gotten back together, although she was seeing another man by then. I think at one point Joe wanted to try but his pride kept getting in the way."

Whether out of his love for litigation or to strengthen Joe's resolve, Ernest attended the 1963 divorce proceedings. His close attention to her parents' divorce aroused Linda's suspicion, so much so that she came to believe that her father and mother might have reconciled if it hadn't been for Ernest.

"My mother told me that there was a time when both of them thought they wanted to give their marriage another try," Linda said. "I don't know if that was ever possible, but I felt Ernest kept saying

The Bianco sisters, Susie (above) and Celia (below), with their mother, Virginia, on their front porch in Hanford, California, where they were courted by two brothers who owned a wine company, Giuseppe (Joe) and Michelo (Mike) Gallo.

(Left) Despite parental disapproval, Susie married Joe in a 1908 civil ceremony, and Celia and Mike were wed a year later.

Born in 1909, Ernest Gallo lived with his grandparents, Virginia and Battista Bianco, after Julio's birth in 1910 and when Susie left Joe and filed for divorce.

26336
Mike Gallo — Age 26
Grand Larceny — 5 yrs.
San Fran. — Nat. Italy
3-25-1913

4

One of Mike's "bunko schemes" landed him in San Quentin, but he went on to become a "kingpin bootlegger" during Prohibition.

5

Gallos and Biancos at one of their frequent family gatherings, about 1920: (rear, l–r) Susie's brother, Walter Bianco; Joe Gallo, Sr.; two unidentified men; Mike Gallo; (middle, l–r) Walter's wife, Lydia; Susie, holding Joe, Jr.; Celia; (front, l–r) Ernest; Walter and Lydia's daughter, Stella; Julio.

(L–r) Julio, Joe, Jr., and Ernest dressed alike for Ernest's 1931 wedding to Amelia Franzia, daughter of the founder of the Franzia winery in Escalon. They pose in front of the original Gallo home, which stills stands on Maze Road in Modesto.

Ernest and Julio stenciled the Gallo name on barrels of bulk wine for sale immediately after Repeal in December 1933. They filed for their first trademark in 1941, citing their father's prior usage of the Gallo name on wine.

In the following decades, Ernest and Julio built the largest winery in the world. Its acres of holding tanks in Modesto resemble an oil refinery.

After the war, Joe, Jr., became the manager of his brothers'
Livingston vineyard and married Mary Ann Arata; in 1954
they took a rare vacation on a cruise to Hawaii.

9

In 1966, Ernest and Julio constructed more regal
headquarters in Modesto. Separated from the rear acres of
holding tanks by parklike surroundings, the building was
known as "Parthenon West" and "Temple on the
Tuolumne" (Modesto is on the Tuolumne River).

10

A display of Gallo wines from 1967 to 1968, representing about
half of the winery's full line of products.

Julio (l)
and Ernest Gallo (r),
1967–68.

13

Divorced from Mary Ann, Joe married Patricia Morgan Gardali (center) in 1966. Julio (l) stands behind his wife, Aileen, whom he married in 1933, with Ernest behind wife, Amelia. Patricia soon learned the depth of Joe's feelings for his older brothers.

Despite his eccentricities, Ernest and Amelia's older son, David Ernest, is the heir apparent in Gallo's marketing division. He met his wife, Mary, through a local priest, and they have two children, Theresa and Christopher, with whom they posed in 1976.

14

15

Ernest's other son, Joseph Ernest (Joe E. or Joey), has been groomed to succeed him in sales, but, like David, he is considered a pale imitation of his father. Only after David found a wife could Joey marry Nicaraguan-born Ofelia; they have three children, Stefanie, Ernest, and Joseph, Jr.

16

Long ago, on doctors' orders, Julio left marketing and sales to Ernest and concentrated on grape growing and winemaking. He calls himself a "simple farmer" and now devotes much of his time to the new Sonoma vineyards.

In 1978, underground cellars the size of two football fields, with storage for 2.6 million gallons of wine, were excavated to the side of the administration building and large casks of imported Yugoslavian oak were installed.

17

Julio expects his son Bob (center) to take over the production division.
He and Bob and grandson Matthew discuss the relandscaping of Gallo's
recently acquired Asti vineyards in Sonoma County.

In addition to their Modesto, Livingston, and Fresno facilities, Ernest
and Julio now own a winery in Sonoma. Like their other plants, it is
closed to the public and bears no "Gallo" sign.

20

Ernest often entertains his inner circle of loyal executives and
their families at barbecues in his backyard. Gathered here are
(l–r) attorney and investment adviser Jon Shastid and wife,
Natalie; first national sales director Ken Bertsch and wife,
Elinor; marketing maven Albion Fenderson and wife, Lynn.

21

22

Richard W. Witter (left), in 1967–68, vice-president of sales for the
western region, who later became director of sales and one of Ernest's
most trusted advisers.

Howard E. Williams (right), the developer of Paisano, Gallo decanters,
and Vin Rosé, and Gallo's vice-president of marketing development, in
1967–68.

One of Ernest's favorite sports is deep-sea fishing. With him (third from left) on a fishing trip in Costa Rica are (l–r): A. E. (Bud) Anderson, Gallo's San Francisco distributor; Joe; and Richard Witter.

A "shirt-tail" Franzia relative and long-time winery employee, Charles "Charlie" Rossi (here with wife, Maria) became "Carlo Rossi" when a Gallo line of jug wines and a vineyard were named for him. He and Ernest like to reminisce about the "good old days" during Prohibition.

25

The Gallo men are avid hunters. When Joe and youngest son,
Mike, then fifteen, shot their limit of deer the first weekend of
the 1965 season, they were featured in the local newspaper,
The Livingston Chronicle.

Joe and Mary Ann's eldest son, Peter,
joined the Army in 1966 and was sent
to Vietnam as a first lieutenant,
where he died in 1968.

26

After Ernest and Julio terminated Joe as their vineyard manager in 1967, Joe developed his own vineyards, cattle ranches, and dairies. In June 1983, he established the Joseph Gallo Cheese Company, and this sign on Route 140 in Atwater is one of several marking his extensive agricultural enterprises.

Joe's cheese plant stands across from one of his several dairies. His twenty thousand head of dairy cattle supply Grade A milk to the cheese-making facility.

Headquarters of Joseph Gallo Cheese in Atwater is a turn-of-the-century farmhouse renovated by Joe and his son Mike. In the background are the cheese plant and dairy.

30

Joe and his cheeses. Joe's use of his own name on his cheese labels provoked Ernest's wrath and his and Julio's complaint of trademark infringement. Joe's lawyer, John Whiting, then discovered documents suggesting that as a boy Joe had been denied his inheritance.

Joe was forced to change his label from "Joseph Gallo Cheese" to "Joseph Farms Cheese," but Ernest still wasn't satisfied.

31

Gallo salame label: the trademark that Ernest and Julio secretly acquired for $2 million and then was at issue in their lawsuit against Joe.

32

After the lawsuits were filed, Ernest and Julio and their
families stopped coming for the traditional Christmas Eve
bagna cauda at Joe's home: (rear) attorney John Whiting,
Patricia and Joe, Kenny and Linda Gallo Jelacich (holding
daughter Ann Marie), Sherrie and Mike Gallo, Kay and Sam
Gardali; (front) Micah, Tiffany, and Peter (Sherrie and Mike's
children), Brett and Gina (Kay and Sam's children).

John Whiting (above) asked attorney
Denis Rice (r), of the San Francisco firm
Howard, Rice, Nemerovski, Canady,
Robertson & Falk, to join Joe's legal
team. Rice and associates presented Joe's
case in the 1988 trial.

Patrick Lynch (r) of the Los Angeles firm
O'Melveny & Myers, and Oliver
Wanger (below) of Fresno's McCormick,
Barstow, Sheppard, Wayte & Carruth,
represented Ernest and Julio in their
lawsuit against Joe. In 1991, Wanger was
appointed to fill Judge Edward Dean
Price's seat on the federal bench.

Now retired, Judge Edward
Dean Price, U.S. Eastern
District Court of California,
was assigned the Gallo case
from 1986 to 1988. A few days
before trial he recused
himself.

38

39

When Price stepped down, he
turned the case over to Judge
Robert Coyle, who had been
a partner in Wanger's Fresno
firm until his appointment to
the federal court in 1982.

things to upset him so that my father wouldn't forget his hurt. Ernest seemed to think that the Coffees and the Aratas had looked down on him, and I suspected that he kept stirring up my father's anger at my mother, even though the Gallos always talked about divorce in general as a real disgrace in the family."

With the divorce made final in 1963, Mike and Peter remained with their father, while Linda stayed with Mary Ann. "My mother then married Dr. Sam Klor, an ob-gyn in Modesto," said Linda. "I liked him as a stepfather, and I got along very well with the three children he had from his previous marriage. I think my mother was happier. I would see my father and brothers almost every weekend and on holidays. The reason that Mike and Peter stayed with my father was so that they could learn about ranching and grape growing. Peter was just finishing high school, Mike was just starting, but the idea was that they would eventually follow in my father's footsteps and become farmers. That was always the Gallo tradition—sons continuing what their fathers did. My brothers were supposed to go to college—Peter went to Cal Poly that year—and learn more about raising grapes and the farming business. Then they would come back and help Dad."

Despite the upheaval following the divorce, Joe and his family adjusted. Joe continued to build his cattle business and extend his vineyard holdings. His success was small compared to that of his brothers, but he was happy that he could share it with his sons.

During the mid 1960s, Ernest's attention was focused on building a new winery headquarters, one that would proclaim Gallo the leader of the wine industry. Before, he'd been content to put most of the profits back into storage facilities, laboratory and equipment, and subsidiary companies. But having won the annual Merit Award from the American Society of Enologists in 1964, a tribute to "an individual judged to have been of exceptional service to the wine industry," he seemed to swing to the opposite extreme.

He envisioned a spectacular structure to announce his company's importance and respectability. Whether Julio felt ignored by the Enologists' award to Ernest alone, he didn't say, although he made it clear that he "sure as hell didn't want a fancy office." But Ernest was not to be dissuaded, and the convincing argument was that along with the $2.5 million headquarters he proposed, he would also build a new laboratory for Julio and his staff.

To be constructed on the Gallo property to the west of the old offices, the thirty-foot-high, two-story structure was designed by San Francisco architect John Bolles. Classically inspired, the plans showed imposing arched columns, an enclosed central courtyard, and an arcade around its perimeter. Three of its four sides would be completely windowed, and the walls and arches would have a hint of greenish cast to be produced by mixing ground glass from Thunderbird bottles with the concrete. Measuring 81,600 square feet, it would be the largest office building serving any winery. "The new building will be an architectural ambassador for California's wine industry," Ernest announced to the press. In his enthusiasm he also quoted the architect's goal to create an "image of cool grace, beauty and refinement which should be the connotation of a leader of the wine industry." And, finally, Ernest added that a visitors' center would be built as well.

Whether Ernest originally meant what he said—that he would encourage visitors after so many years of secrecy—was never clear. The winery also requested the closing of Fairbanks Avenue, which ran through the property, at the same time promising a Gallo Tourist Center and a grape arboretum for the public. While some citizens complained that they needed to use Fairbanks Avenue as a thoroughfare, the town council unanimously approved the plan. When the building was completed in March 1966, there was neither a visitors' center nor a gracious welcome to tourists. Not even a sign announced to the public that this was the Gallo Winery. Fairbanks Avenue was closed, and a few months later the winery constructed a chain-link fence and gate across Oregon Drive, closing off the road without town permission. (The board of supervisors eventually approved this construction after the fact.)

To ensure that no outsiders trespassed on winery property, an elaborate security system with television monitors throughout the buildings and grounds was installed and a guard staff hired. Heading the security force was a former Modesto cop who had made his reputation as an instructor of the police force in Saigon. The winery was effectively sealed from the public, although when the Gallos applied for town approval of the plans for a new research laboratory in December 1967, Bob Gallo again announced that the two one-story precast buildings would also include "the most up-to-date tasting room facilities in the world."

The winery addition was to house a new laboratory, expansion of the bottling operation, and a warehouse, as well as the offices for the grower relations department and quality control division. But once these buildings were completed, the Gallo brothers reverted to secrecy again. No outsider could go further than the front steps of the administration building without being confronted by a security guard, and although later the winery would sometimes allow the inner courtyard of the "temple"—as the headquarters building was now known—to be used for charity benefits such as a concert or an art show, its parklike, landscaped grounds were closed to the public. When reminded of their promises of a "visitor center" or their "wine-tasting room," the brothers' replies were defensive: These were for their designated guests, not for tourists who might drop by to see the winery and taste its wine.

The town accepted the Gallos' donation of a narrow strip of land for a public park on the western border of the winery property next to the creek. The winery then began grading and paving over the creek behind the facility for a parking lot. (A few months later Bob Gallo had to defend the Gallo Glass Company against charges that the company had illegally filled in the creek, insisting to the investigating Wetlands Commission that the creek had been dry and already partially filled when the property had been acquired.) Despite the earlier complaints about the closing of the thoroughfare, the new park site and running creek on the west side seemed satisfactory to the town. This was not surprising—the Gallo Winery was responsible for the largest annual payroll in the area, an estimated $7.1 million, and employed more than two thousand local citizens.

Ernest seemed to adopt a different personality with his new headquarters and rapidly increasing sales. He relinquished his notorious stinginess and hired Andrew Delfino, a well-known interior designer from San Francisco, to decorate his second-story corner office. He created the look of an English gentleman's library—including a crushed green velvet sofa. Ernest filled the bookshelves and tabletops with his collection of roosters—ceramic, glass, and wood figures to honor the Gallo name.

Julio's office was placed on the first floor, directly under Ernest's. (The location might have been symbolic, but it was also convenient, close to the laboratory and grower relations offices.) Julio still insisted that he didn't want a "plush" office but accepted the solid oak desk and wood-worked harvest scenes as suitable for him. He spent most of his time in his new laboratory anyway, which, he said, was "the culmination of a lifetime of work." There his scientists had the most highly sophisticated blending and analysis equipment available as well as a bacteriological laboratory and an interior room 100 percent free of vibrations so that microbe testing and scale balances would be extraordinarily accurate. One winemaker estimated that the Gallo laboratory put the winery technologically ahead of their competitors by fifteen years.

As the new winery facility was being designed and built, Ernest at last seemed to feel he had gained respectability, his success bringing him recognition as a man to be reckoned with.

"I think it was about that time that he began to consider himself and his family as part of the American elite," recalled one former employee. "We began to hear all sorts of references to the Kennedy family, sort of implicit comparisons between the Gallos and them. We all thought that was pretty funny, since it was a well-known fact that Joe Kennedy, Sr., had made a lot of money rum-running during Prohibition. But, of course, Ernest would never openly admit his family's connection to bootlegging."

Unlike Julio and Joe and their families, Ernest did not particularly enjoy roughing it in the wilds. But in the summer of 1966 he surprised everyone by announcing that he was planning a rafting trip down the Colorado River through the Grand Canyon. He invited some of his colleagues in the winery and friends who were distributors to accompany him, along with Amelia and David. He also asked Joe to bring his new bride, Patricia, and her nine-year-old son Sam as well as Joe's children Mike and Linda. (Peter was then in the Army. Julio and Aileen did not join the expedition.)

"I'm sure Ernest came up with that idea because *Life* magazine had just run a cover story about the Kennedy clan taking that same rafting trip," Mike recalled. "By then he had all these delusions of grandeur —not only building the temple in Modesto, but also thinking that the Gallos—or at least the Ernest Gallos—would become a leading American family. He had political connections that he often bragged about, and he sometimes suggested that his son Joey would eventually go into politics."

The trip was elaborately planned with no expense spared. Their guides took them down river, each day arriving at a designated campsite. And every morning the winery's private plane would circle the location to drop provisions.

"But most of all, the plane was there for Ernest," said Mike. "Each day Ernest's pilot radioed down to him to give him the latest stock market quotations. Ernest then called back what stocks should be bought or sold. Then the pilot gave him any winery sales figures that Ernest had requested, and he replied with instructions about them, too. Here we were in this beautiful natural setting, but Ernest was like an addict. He couldn't survive without his daily fix of stock market prices and Gallo sales totals."

Once Ernest returned home, he proclaimed himself an expert on the beauty and ecology of the region. He dictated letters to politicians, then released them to the press, to announce that the rafting trip had convinced him to oppose the proposed construction of two dams on the Colorado River.

"I have traveled widely, and have seen most of what may be considered the well-known natural wonders of the world," he wrote by way of establishing his credentials. "Nothing I have seen is comparable to the canyons through which the Colorado River runs, a part of which is known as the Grand Canyon. Nowhere else does one see the billions of years of our earth's history in majesty, glory and splendor."

Noting the well-publicized letter, employees and neighbors of both the Fresno and the Modesto wineries were amused by Ernest's sudden ecological concern. (In fact, the Gallo Glass plant was asked several times to clean up its "dumping" mistakes when townspeople discovered contaminated bricks from the company's kilns on their properties.) The air around the Fresno winery was usually heavy with odors released by the grape-crushing and winemaking processes, and there were complaints about the standing pools of grape residues on all winery properties. According to former sales managers, Gallo salesmen in various locations throughout the country who were assigned to pick up Gallo bottles that were defective or had gone bad sometimes tossed them into lakes and rivers until citizens complained.

During the rafting expedition Joe's new wife Patricia was more impressed by the family dynamics than by Ernest's attention to nature. She had been working as Charlie Crawford's secretary when in 1965 Joe had come to the winery to see Jon Shastid. Shastid's office was near Patricia's desk, and waiting to see the winery lawyer and financial advisor, Joe had struck up a conversation with her; two days later they had their first date. She was also divorced, having been married to Sam Gardali, an artist who had been employed by the winery in the merchandising and display department, with whom she had her son Sam.

A bright, good-natured woman with red-blond hair and blue eyes, she was taken by Joe's warmth and sense of humor, although he seemed somewhat shy as well. "Joe and I had an instant attraction to each other," Patricia recalled, "and it didn't take us long to realize that we would be happy together. We shared many interests, and I admired his honesty and his wit, even his ability to laugh at himself when the joke was on him. He accepted Sam right away, too, and I saw that he would be a loving father and make no distinction between 'his' children and 'mine.' In short, he was handsome, great company and I was in love with him.

"Of course, I soon realized how much Ernest controlled everybody in that family, but especially Joe," Patricia continued. "I began to understand how much Joe had missed in the way of family love and warmth when he was raised by Ernest. Joe never complained, but it's one of the reasons why he sometimes found it difficult to express his feelings. That just wasn't allowed around Ernest—so many things had been taboo after their parents' deaths. Even when he was an adult, Ernest was still like a stern father, issuing orders and expecting Joe to obey without hesitation. And Joe was absolutely devoted to his older brothers and would do anything to please them."

Ernest's demands on Joe were especially apparent when Joe and Patricia decided to get married in early 1966. They planned to drive to San Francisco on Saturday, February 12, for a small ceremony at John Whiting's apartment. "A few days before the date, Ernest phoned Joe," Patricia explained. "He announced that he needed him to make up a golf foursome with some big grape growers from Visalia. So Joe asked me if I would mind if we put off getting married for a day. I knew that there may have been a legitimate reason for meeting with the growers, but still it seemed abrupt. Of course, I agreed, even though it meant getting married on the thirteenth. It became a joke with us, but it certainly showed me how much Joe was willing to bend to Ernest's needs."

But it was during the raft trip that she saw just how strong Joe's ties to Ernest were and how deep they went. One day the group stopped for lunch. The guides had brought along rubber inner tubes, and everybody was taking them out and riding the rapids for a short stretch down the river. The idea was to start upstream, then end up at the base camp. But when Ernest's turn came, he went shooting past the camp.

"Joe was really upset when he saw that Ernest couldn't get to the side of the river," Patricia recalled. "Everyone was saying, 'Don't worry, he'll be all right. He'll hit the bank at the next turn. He'll come to shore there.' But Joe was yelling at the guides to take the boat and go after him. They kept reassuring him. Finally he shouted, 'But you don't understand, THAT'S MY BROTHER!' And that's the way it was—a very basic, almost primitive emotion."

During their courtship Joe had told Patricia, "You realize, don't you, that I have no part in the winery? I just work for my brothers." She assured him that she was well aware of this, since as a secretary for Crawford she had seen lists of the winery's shareholders. Nevertheless, it did not occur to her to ask him why he was not a partner. He stated it as a given, a fact of life. "Besides," she added, "it wasn't important to me and had no bearing on how I felt about him."

Patricia soon learned that the change of their wedding date wasn't an isolated example of Ernest's demands. In fact, in the course of his Livingston vineyard work, Joe had invented and patented a mechanical grape-picking device. Several years before his marriage to Patricia, Joe was asked by Julio if he would turn the patent over to Ernest's sons. Joe said he would think about it, feeling some reluctance. At a party several days later, Mike recalled, Ernest cornered his father. He pulled up a chair within six inches of Joe, "so close that their knees were almost touching," said Mike, "and then leaned forward to make his point." As his father told Mike later, Ernest then said, *Julio tells me you'd like to give that patent to David and Joey.*

Joe was confused. He'd only told Julio he would consider the idea, but with Ernest's approach he felt almost compelled to accede to the request. Later he would see this as a pattern: Julio's approach as the messenger for something Ernest wanted, then Ernest's subsequent insistence that he had heard from Julio that Joe had made a decision, almost implying that Joe had suggested it in the first place. When Joe hesitated at the party, he recalled that Ernest pushed even harder. Loath to dispute it further, Joe said he had agreed: "Take it, it's yours. Your sons can have it."

Several years after Joe's marriage to Patricia, Ernest announced that David wanted the San Francisco apartment building that Joe, Julio, and Ernest had inherited through their mother from their Bianco grandparents. Although Joe was at first reluctant, he finally gave in to Ernest's argument for David's wishes, since it seemed that Julio had already consented. Once again, Joe felt he couldn't refuse for fear of alienating his brother.

Joe had already seen that resisting Ernest's emphatic demands

could lead to unpleasantness. Ernest was in the process of reorganizing the winery's financial structure. The Gallo Glass Company was to
be merged with the winery and all glass company stock converted to
winery stock, including the 10 percent share that in 1957 Joe had
purchased and placed in his three children's trusts, of which Ernest
and Julio were still the trustees. In the fall of 1965, Julio telephoned
Joe and announced that he and Ernest wanted to buy back the children's glass company stock.

We'll pay $30 to $40 a share, said Julio. *We're going to merge the
glass company with the winery so we want to convert all that stock to
winery stock.*

Sure, that's fine, replied Joe, thinking that the offer meant that the
investment would show a good return.

Julio relayed Ernest's request that Joe come to Modesto the following morning to complete the paperwork.

As Joe later recalled, things seemed turned on their head when Joe
arrived at his office.

I understand you want to sell your glass company stock, Ernest said.

I don't necessarily want to sell it, Joe replied. *Julio told me that's
what you wanted. In fact I'd just as soon keep the stock.*

That's not possible, Ernest interrupted. *We're going to merge, so
you can't keep it.*

*I don't mind if you merge, but why don't we just leave the invest-
ment the way it is?*

No, that won't work. You have to sell it.

According to Joe, Ernest insisted that Joe's children's glass company stock could not be converted into winery stock. He argued that
this would give them only a small percentage of the winery. More, he
didn't want anyone "outside the family" (meaning outside his own
and Julio's families, or "any third party," as he later would put it) to
have winery stock, which might disrupt the "equal ownership of the
two brothers." Joe recalled that he also demanded a guarantee from
Joe that his children would not at a later date sue Ernest and Julio,
the children's trustees, for selling the stock.

*We want you to indemnify us with a letter saying you'll be respon-
sible for any legal costs and any added payment if ordered by the court,*
he said.

But this time Joe challenged Ernest's demand.

*I'll sell the stock, but I want you to pay the income tax on the stock
profits so that we net $40 per share,* said Joe, his voice becoming hard.

And I won't sign that guarantee. With that he stomped out of the office.

The next morning Joe was doing the rounds of the Livingston vineyards when Julio drove up.

Ernest is in a very bad way, he told Joe. *I've never seen him so upset as when you walked out on him. He sent me here to ask if you'll come down to the winery and meet with him again.*

I think maybe it's his turn to come up here, said Joe.

But the next day Joe had a change of heart. He hated to think of Ernest upset. Despite his first angry response, he decided to smooth Ernest's ruffled feathers, and as he recounted later, he arrived at the winery unannounced. Ernest was just leaving to drive to his house to watch the shooting of a Gallo advertisement. This one was to feature models posed next to antique cars in Ernest's driveway. In a great rush, he told Joe he could only talk to him on the ride out to Maze Road.

The first few minutes in the car Ernest stared straight ahead as if he were concentrating on his driving.

You don't have to pay me anything for the stock, Joe said quietly. *Just forget it.*

No, that's not possible, Ernest snapped. Joe obviously didn't understand the legal steps that were required to complete the transaction. But at least he had agreed in principle, and now Ernest repeated that he would pay a fair price; in the meantime, he told Joe, they would also need his former wife Mary Ann's permission to sell the children's stock.

When Joe telephoned Mary Ann to explain what Ernest and Julio wanted, she resisted. The initial offer of $30 or $40 a share seemed low to her, especially when the transaction was meant to keep her children from having an interest in the winery, shares that could presumably be worth much more to them in the long run. She dug in her heels and contacted a lawyer, and in November 1965 she filed suit on "behalf of her minor children" to prevent the sale and demand an outside assessment of the stock's worth.

It was a preemptive strike, and it worked. Ernest had to offer $650,000 for the children's 216 shares—vastly more than the $8,640 he had proposed—since this was the fair market value assigned to them by a San Francisco securities expert. Having forced Ernest's hand, Mary Ann withdrew her suit and notified the court of her permission for the sale. A court hearing was held. According to Joe's recollection, at Ernest's request he testified that he felt the sale was in his children's best interest. The judge approved the transaction, and Ernest and Julio issued promissory notes of $216,666.67 each to Peter, Michael, and Linda, due to be paid in installments between January 1, 1970, and July 1, 1971.

Ernest and Julio got what they wanted—all the shares in the winery were once again held only by them and their families (although there were exceptions—Celia Bianco and Aileen's mother both retained winery stock, for example). But the transaction had proved to be much more costly than they had expected. And whether it was Mary Ann's doing or not, it seemed that Joe was not as malleable as he had been in the past.

If there was lingering resentment after this conflict, Joe couldn't say; he felt that, at least on the surface, the brothers has resumed their usual relationships. But in the spring of 1967 Ernest was away on a trip when Julio drove to Livingston and took Joe aside for a meeting. As Joe recalled, at first he beat around the bush: Didn't Joe have a lot to do now that he had his own cattle ranches and vineyards? Did he have enough time to do all that was needed at the Livingston vineyards? Wasn't he asking Paul Osteraas, the winery's viticultural expert, and Bill Heuer, the assistant vineyard manager, to take on too many extra duties?

According to Joe, he was surprised by Julio's questions. He was sure that he hadn't reduced his hours supervising the winery's vineyards. He took care of his own ranches and vineyards only when his winery duties were completed, and he had hired his own foreman to follow his instructions.

But Julio became insistent. He claimed that he often couldn't find Joe when he had driven down from Modesto to inspect Livingston; he didn't like having to leave instructions for Joe with Osteraas or other vineyard workers. And sometimes he'd criticized Joe's viticultural methods, and Joe had been slow to change his techniques. Joe listened quietly to his brother's complaints, all the while wondering why Julio had never mentioned these problems before. Or how it was possible to have had so many conversations with Julio, so many moments of Julio's confiding his irritation with Ernest, for example, when he had been so conspicuously absent or hard to find. Or if he had so fallen down in his job, why hadn't the winery vineyards' annual yield decreased as well?

Anyway, Joe, we feel that you'd be happier on your own, Julio concluded. *Isn't that what you've always wanted? Now you have the land and the cattle to do it, and, of course, you can continue to sell your grapes to us.*

I'd rather keep working for you, Joe replied quietly. He rarely cried but now found himself weeping. *You know, Julio, I've always wanted to be a part of the winery . . .*

I know, said Julio. His voice trailed off as if he were unable or unwilling to comment further on Joe's remark. After a moment he added, *But this will be the best for all of us. Think of it as a mutual decision.*

When Joe later recalled the event, he said he hadn't tried to argue Julio out of the decision. In some ways he felt he had no rights "beyond those of an ordinary employee" since he had never been led to believe that he had any claim to a share or ownership interest in either the Livingston vineyards or the winery. Nevertheless, he hoped he could change his brothers' minds. He waited until Ernest returned from his trip, and as he remembered, he went to Ernest's office to try to convince him that he wanted to continue working for the winery in Livingston. Although Ernest would later declare that there had been a growing feeling of dissatisfaction with Joe, which he and Julio had discussed, Joe felt that during their discussion, Ernest treated the decision as if it were a *fait accompli* and something Joe himself desired. Ernest then repeated Julio's remark that it would be best for all concerned for Joe to devote himself to his own business. According to Joe, Ernest had then added, *You can always come to Julio and me for advice, and you can still use our accountants for your operations.*

Patricia and the children realized how upset Joe was, but the rest of the family heard only that Joe had decided to devote himself full time to his own ranches, and that all three brothers were happy with the new arrangement. Despite Ernest and Julio's repeated explanation that it was a "mutual" agreement, Joe would always perceive it as a unilateral and painful decision made with no warning. "I felt it just came out of the blue," he said later, remembering how much it had hurt him.

"I knew my father was disturbed when his brothers told him he should quit working for the winery," said Mike. "But he didn't let it show, he just played along with the family script that everyone should act as if nothing was different. I think he was glad when Ernest said the winery accountants would continue to handle his financial affairs because their businesses and properties had been so tied up together.

In fact, it wasn't until 1978 that Ernest told my father that he should hire his own accountants and his financial and legal records were returned to him. Now I wonder if there wasn't a reason for the timing, because it was then that Ernest was getting involved with the lawsuit against Gallo Salame. Perhaps that was why it became important to change the arrangement and separate my father's businesses and accounts from what Ernest was doing in his court case against Gallo Salame."

After his initial confusion and depression, Joe found that devoting his time to his own businesses was a relief. By the end of 1967, he had built an adobe block office on the Escola Ranch near his home on West Vinewood Road in Livingston. In front of the office he placed a large sign, announcing Joseph Gallo Vineyards, and for the next twenty years ran his grape-growing, cattle, and other companies from there. He was still a workaholic, but his hours were now somewhat shorter and his schedule wasn't determined by his brothers. Gradually he was able to forget the pain caused by what he considered his brothers' rejection.

In the next months he expanded into a new business, raising and selling dairy replacement heifers, known as "springers," and soon "Joseph Gallo" heifers, branded with JG, were in demand at livestock sales and auctions. In 1968, he purchased a nineteen-hundred-acre ranch in nearby Merced on which he raised forage crops, and then he was able to acquire five ranches south of Livingston in Atwater. He combined these two thousand acres along Highway 140 into one ranch and posted a large sign at its entrance to designate it Joseph Gallo Blue Heron Ranch. Just down the highway he bought and developed a thirteen-hundred-acre ranch, and another sign went up: Joseph Gallo White Crane Ranch.

During these years of personal turmoil for Joe and his family, the Vietnam War had escalated. When Peter finished college, he had planned to help his father on the ranches and with the new cattle business. But along with many of his contemporaries, he was due to be drafted. Much like his father in World War II, he was convinced that it would be better to enlist than be drafted. Despite the privilege and wealth of the Gallo family, despite influence with local politicians who might have helped a Gallo son avoid military service in Vietnam, Peter agreed with high school and college classmates who thought it was their duty to serve their country. The family could only hope that he would be posted in Germany.

Peter joined the army in February 1966. After basic training he was sent to officers' training school and graduated as first lieutenant. He came home for Christmas in 1967 and almost immediately afterward his unit was assigned to Vietnam, where he was promoted to commander of a personnel carrier tank in the Fifth Cavalry Unit of the Ninth Infantry Division. He was wounded by shrapnel once, receiving his first bronze star, then returned to active duty. At the end of March 1968, during the Tet Offensive, his company was ambushed near Da Nang. Helping his men out of their burning tank, he was killed by a second round of fire but was listed as missing in action until June when army officers arrived in Livingston to announce that he had died on March 30. Posthumously awarded another bronze star and two Purple Hearts, he was buried in Arlington National Cemetery.

Joe nearly collapsed with grief. The previous year he felt he had lost his brothers; now he had lost a son.

"We were all devastated," said John Whiting, "but particularly Joe and Mike. Pete was such a special kid, almost like a son to me, too. Joe had always dreamed of Peter and Mike working with him as a team, and now that dream was shattered. His death was just so tragic for everyone, and I still miss him."

"It was very hard on all of us," said Mike. "For me it was unbelievable that my brother was gone. I had always looked up to him, especially since he was five years older, and I saw the way he was always his own person, always a rebel. I think he got that from my mother. He was very athletic and very strong and had a great sense of humor. From him I learned that you had to stand up for yourself and what you believe in."

With Peter's death Mike made certain decisions about his life. He would do all that he could for his father to relieve his sorrow. Instead of going away to college that year, he stayed at home and attended Merced Junior College. He made promises to himself: He knew how vulnerable his father was; he didn't want his father hurt again; he wouldn't let his father and his dreams collapse. They would build their future together. The bond was strengthened by the loss of Peter, but throughout the next ten years it deepened into an equal partnership and mutual respect that would sustain them in the face of later adversity.

CHAPTER EIGHT

"The winemaker is a warrior," Ernest likes to announce, citing an old Italian proverb. It was during the mid-1960s that he intensified his attack on the competition by opening and dominating new sales territories. His master plan was to build a powerful network of distributorships across the country.

Dick Witter now moved from marketing into sales; this was where the action was, where Ernest was focusing his attention, and where Witter could best make his influence felt. While Bertsch remained the drill instructor of the sales division, the sergeant who implemented Ernest's orders and trained the Gallo army, Witter became the field general who could bring new ideas and battle strategies to his commander-in-chief's campaigns to capture the market. Ernest needed the talents of both executives, and when he promoted Witter from the western sales territory to national sales manager, he gave Bertsch the title director of sales. Titles were never that important to Ernest, and according to employees who reported to both men, over the years Ernest cultivated a power struggle between the two, although eventually Witter emerged the winner.

In the drive to open more sales territories across the country, Ernest encountered the problem of "monopoly states" where liquor and wine were sold only in state-owned package stores. And there were still many "dry" counties where the sale of wine and liquor was prohibited.

In monopoly or control states Ernest had to make sure that his wine received distribution and shelf space in the government-owned stores. In "dry" counties Ernest needed to overturn the Prohibition laws, and each effort required the cooperation of local politicians. The sales battle plan included wooing state and county officials who could smooth the way for Gallo.

"One of the things sales managers were instructed to do," recalled a former employee, "was to contribute heavily to politicians' campaigns. This was true in general—from the federal level to the local Modesto level—but it was especially important in those areas where we were either trying to break into the state-controlled package stores or where we were trying to change the laws and regulations impeding the sale of wine. This took lobbying and maneuvering and, of course, a lot of money. It became part of our sales and executive training— how to enlist politicians to the Gallo cause, how to get legislation passed that benefited us by burying what we wanted in riders to non-controversial bills. Or we learned the tactic of calling for votes just before the end of a session when everyone was in a rush to leave and wasn't paying much attention."

Ernest had wanted to sell wine the way Campbell sold soup, but he was frustrated by the restrictions governing the sale of alcohol. He now put Art Palombo in charge of sales in state-controlled markets. Having worked for Schenley, having dealt with the tough former Capone leader Joe Fusco and his distributorship, and having helped convince the Romano brothers to become the winery's Chicago distributor, Art was thought to have good "lobbying" skills. Ernest assigned him the title vice-president, sales for monopoly states. He was considered the Special Markets Intermediary, who was to develop relationships with politicians in whose districts Gallo wine had to be sold through a state board. He was also asked to turn "dry" locales "wet."

"Ernest really took to Art," commented one of his colleagues at the winery. "Maybe their Italian backgrounds drew them together. He was another surrogate son. With Art doing what had to be done behind the scenes, miracles happened with the Gallo line. Art was another one of Ernest's loyal henchmen, and he devoted himself to getting Gallo wine into counties and states that had been closed before."

In the 1960s and early 1970s Ernest also extended his influence over distributorships by installing more Gallo men as separate sales forces. With so many more recruits needed, he created a formal Gallo training program.

A number of people had led the more informal seminars over the years, including Lloyd Thornton, Legh Knowles, Robert Huntington, and Art Palombo. But in 1968 Neil Sweeney, a Ph.D. specializing in educational psychology and management skills, was asked by an executive head hunter, "Do you think you can work for somebody who has absolutely no appreciation for human values, who is a pure autocrat, who will drain you of everything you've got?"

"It might be interesting," Sweeney replied with a wry smile. "Who is it?"

"Ernest Gallo."

Sweeney was curious enough to agree to an interview, first with Dick Witter, then with Ernest Gallo at the winery headquarters.

"I met Ernest in December 1968," he recalled. "He was dressed very formally in a conservative three-piece pin-striped suit. My impression was of an intense, neurotic man. He exuded a basic dissatisfaction with the status quo; he seemed driven—overdriven—and conveyed a sense that nothing was ever good enough. He phrases questions to get specific answers, and he wants to find out if you will work hard for him and if you will be loyal. Bottom line, he wants to know if he can trust you. I suppose that comes from his background. Can I trust my father when he kills my mother? The answer has to be no, so he really can't trust anybody."

Sweeney accepted the assignment to organize the training programs, first in Los Angeles, then in the Midwest. He was installed in an office at the Romano brothers' newly constructed headquarters, a modern showplace building and expanded warehouse. According to Sweeney, in unguarded moments, Buddy sometimes remarked that a million-dollar, no-interest loan from Gallo had given them all such nice offices. Such loans were one of the methods by which Gallo gained leverage in distributorships (and from which it was later prohibited by the FTC). Sweeney joined Gallo salesman Jack Donahue to organize the new program.

"Jack had immense talent," said Sweeney. "It was a great tragedy when he died in that Chicago American Airlines crash a few years later. We combined his practical experience with my theories of management to create the first Gallo sales manual. At first we developed it without Ernest's knowledge. We put quizzes at the end of every chapter, which later became famous among recruits, who attributed them to Ernest and his desire for militarylike training. Finally, both Witter and Bertsch approved, and then so did Ernest—and this became the famous 'Big Red Book,' the manual that all Gallo trainees have to memorize."

While Sweeney considered Ernest a brilliant executive in many ways, he became increasingly aware of the cutthroat atmosphere and inhuman approach to employees. He recalled that in 1969, three weeks before Christmas, Bertsch ordered him to terminate two long-term Gallo sales directors.

"George Frank, the director of Gallo Sales on the East Coast, had refused to fire them," Sweeney said. "So Ken Bertsch gave me the mission."

When Sweeney returned from the assignment, he was so furious that he marched into Bertsch's office.

"I just want to tell you how I feel about you after what I just did," Sweeney said. "You must be the meanest SOB on the face of the earth."

"You can't talk to me like this," Bertsch shouted. "I run this place."

But Sweeney stood his ground and voiced his complaints, not only about having to fire good employees but about the winery's atmosphere of hostility and in-fighting. What he didn't know until later was that Gallo had been ordered by a federal court to terminate these employees. When an independent Florida distributor had refused to fire his own sales manager and replace him with a Gallo-trained executive, Ernest had abruptly switched to another wholesale house. The distributor sued, and the judge ruled against Gallo, enjoining the winery from such practices and requiring it to terminate the district supervisors.

Despite distributors' complaints about Gallo practices, Ernest continued his march across the country, and by the late 1960s and early 1970s, his power in the wine industry was greater than that of any other wine producer. His expanded markets were one of the major reasons why in 1967 Gallo table wines finally outsold rival Petri and United Vintners' Italian Swiss Colony table wines. Although no other single Gallo wine matched Thunderbird's sales, the decanter line accounted for the highest sales in table wines, especially Gallo Vin Rosé, which in 1967 had become the first table wine in industry history to ship more than one million cases in one year.

"Ernest then came into my office carrying a sheet cake," recalled Robert Huntington, the decanter line product manager. "It was decorated with the message, 'Congratulations, Bob, on your one millionth anniversary!' He was so jubilant."

In addition, Ernest's campaign to lure beer drinkers to wine had succeeded, because of Ripple's continued popularity and the new brands the winery introduced during the 1960s. Gallo had long produced berry wines—sweet, syrupy concoctions that initially were developed to compete with Mogen David and Manischewitz. (The winery had earlier experimented with a sweet wine developed expressly for women, but Gallo-ette had met with little success.) In 1967 Gallo developed the Boone's Farm line of concord grape, loganberry, blackberry, and apple flavored wines, lighter in alcohol and slightly effervescent. (Charlie Crawford had invented the term "mouth feel," having discovered that sweet wines had a less cloying, more appealing taste when carbonation was added.) Boone's Farm was marketed as a "fun," "youthful" wine, and as it became more and more popular among college-age drinkers (reaching its peak about 1970), it added significantly to Gallo's sales. Not only did Ripple and Boone's Farm eventually lead to the Bartles & Jaymes wine coolers, but they also converted a new segment of consumers to table wines (those who would then switch from the "soda pop" wines to the "fighting varietals"—Chardonnays, Cabernet Sauvignons, and white Zinfandels priced in the $3 to $5 range to appeal to younger, "upmarket" wine drinkers in the next decade).

Ernest's success in achieving the number-one position in table wine sales reflected a change in the industry as a whole. In 1967 table wines in general outsold dessert wines. That year the Wine Institute reported that California table wine shipments increased by 14.1 percent over the previous year while dessert wine shipments declined by 4 percent. This was the trend that Ernest had worked for during the past decade. But he was also clever enough to realize that in order to remain number one Gallo had to develop more brands—not only to compete with itself (just as Procter & Gamble manufactures competing products), but also to extend its appeal to the new and more knowledgeable drinkers of table wines. The winery then entered what employees have called Gallo's most creative and exciting period, both in product development and marketing.

Some winery executives were allowed to order cases of wine at no charge for their personal use, and Ernest noticed that those who seemed to have more sophisticated tastes requested Gallo's robust reds like Barberone and Burgundy Pastosos. "That lop-sided popularity among his executives—even those of us who were not Italian—wasn't lost on him," explained Robert Huntington. "He realized that Gallo needed a more full-bodied red than Paisano or the decanter line's Chianti of California. And that's when Julio and his winemakers came up with Hearty Burgundy."

The new blend was produced by adding more wine from Napa and Sonoma varietals to the winery's usual supply made from Central Valley grapes. With its base of Petite Sirah and Zinfandel (Julio's favorite grape), Hearty Burgundy was praised by wine critics for its depth and complexity. Given the winery's emphasis on consistent quality and moderate pricing (even though with this wine it meant a smaller profit), Hearty Burgundy even gained popularity among "wine snobs," who usually scorned the Gallo label. Because of the previous success of the decanter line, Ernest, Fenderson, and Witter then proposed to create "line extenders," premium wines to build on Hearty Burgundy's success. A chablis had been made from French Colombard and Chenin Blanc grapes, and in 1969 it was renamed Gallo Chablis Blanc by John Selecky, one of the winery's younger brand managers.

Ernest and Witter now saw the need for another rosé. The message was sent to Julio's first-floor production division—as was often the case at Gallo, marketing and sales ideas prompted experiments in the laboratory. There the staff, more than a hundred UC Davis and Berkeley Ph.D.'s, produced a mixture of Gallo's original Grenache Rosé and Muscatel. The new wine was rushed into test markets, but it was a resounding flop.

Witter was still convinced that a new pink wine should do well. What was missing? What had been the trends in the last few years? Finally he had his answer—what did champagne and Cold Duck and Lancers, the latest popular wines, all have in common? Bubbles, of course. Witter now had the laboratory add more sugar and pump in carbon dioxide. (As with any of the winery's carbonated products, pressure was kept at about four pounds per square inch—psi—since wines carbonated at six or higher psi were subject to a champagne tax, a much higher rate per case.) Witter then called Ernest and Al Fenderson into his office. He unscrewed the metal cap from the bottle and let them smell the aroma; he poured them each a glass. It was slightly sweet and pink and bubbly—a soda pop of table wine, just what the public wanted.

"We'll call it Pink Chablis," Witter suggested. The name was reminiscent of pink champagne. It would have a youthful appeal, and Chablis would attract the more sophisticated wine drinkers as well, even though the designation wasn't accurate by any purist's standards. With its usual efficiency, the winery produced, bottled, labeled, and distributed the new wine in a month. An intense advertising campaign soon had Gallo Pink Chablis outselling all the competitive rosés, and the following year it was called America's favorite table wine.

By 1971 the winery was marketing the three wines together as Gallo's Gourmet Trio, and this premier line kept Gallo number one in sales at the high end of the spectrum. Witter now concentrated his full attention on sales and the distribution system, and "Skip" McLaughlin was placed in charge of these brands. Gallo still racked up large sales from Thunderbird and its lighter flavored wines, although Ripple, with its "ring-a-ding flavor," would draw negative publicity when Redd Foxx on *Sanford and Son* began to joke, "Let's get ripped on Ripple."

The winery's Mountain Wine label had also won a large following among younger wine drinkers looking for inexpensive jug wines. But Gallo hadn't been happy when a Berkeley commune in the late 1960s dubbed itself "the Mountain Red Tribe," after its favorite jug wine.

In the early 1970s, however, the Mountain Wine brand was extended and became the winery's second-tier, generic table wine. At the same time, Gallo decided to change the name: The new label now read "Made and Bottled by Carlo Rossi Vineyards," after Gallo relative and employee Charlie Rossi. The family connection came in handy. Pietro Carlo Rossi was the original founder of Italian Swiss Colony and his name was well-known in wine circles; Martini and Rossi brands were popular, too. The winery's Charlie Rossi was no relation, but the Carlo Rossi label resonated with the other names to suggest a long Italian tradition of winemaking. Charlie was soon calling himself Carlo in public, and the fiction of him as an independent vintner was sustained by the posting of a Carlo Rossi sign at a local vineyard. While the marketing of Carlo Rossi wine suggested a separate winery, the required label designation of Modesto as its place of origin confirmed that it was a Gallo enterprise, one that became another profitable brand for the brothers' winery.

One last development accounted for the remarkable success of the winery during these years. Gallo's influence over wholesalers and retailers was matched by its domination of California's wine grape growers in a program of contracts that Ernest and Julio devised in 1967.

As the brothers had learned after the war, to control the industry, you had to control the grapes. Stabilizing the winery's supply of grapes, especially varietals, became necessary as Gallo developed and extended its lines of table wines. Dessert wines and Gallo beverage wines were produced, for the most part, from the less expensive, sweeter, and more abundant Central Valley grapes—the common Thompson seedless, Tokay, and muscatel varieties. Thompson seedless grapes were especially popular with grape growers, since surplus harvests rejected by the wineries could either be sold as table grapes or dried and sold as raisins.

Nevertheless, while Thompson seedless grapes were less expensive, they did not make especially good wine. Julio favored French Colombards, Chenin Blanc, and Sauvignon Blanc for whites, and Zinfandel, Cabernet Sauvignon, and Petite Sirah for blending reds. Now that the winery was concentrating on table wines and improved blends, it would require a larger supply of varietals, and it would need to ensure that the grapes were of consistent quality. The answer was to begin at the source; enlist growers in the effort and lock them into a commitment to Gallo.

Experiments in planting, cultivating, and harvesting undertaken at the Livingston vineyards had resulted in methods that Julio predicted would lead to better grapes. In 1964 he had established the grower relations department, and for three years the winery had been advising growers who sold to Gallo on new viticulture techniques. In 1967 Arnold Scheer became the head of the department. He was a graduate of Davis who had taught viticulture at San Luis Obispo State College and had been an instructor of Joe's son Peter. While Joe was still manager of the Livingston vineyards, he had invited Scheer to observe the winery's viticultural experiments. The two men had become friends, and Joe introduced him to Julio, who then convinced Scheer to leave teaching and come to the winery. Scheer and Julio devised a pamphlet that they circulated to their growers, and every day they and their staff visited vineyards, often flying from location to location in the winery's helicopter—their main mission to urge growers to replant their vineyards to the varietals that the winery wanted for its table wines.

They met with resistance. Central Valley soil and climate had never been considered as favorable for the dry varietals as they were for the sweet. But Ernest and Julio devised a plan to overcome the growers' reluctance. In October 1967 Ernest announced a new program to induce replanting and long-range commitments: fifteen-year contracts to growers in San Joaquin, Stanislaus, Merced, and Fresno counties who were willing to replant or regraft their vineyards from common to varietal grapes. In exchange the grower would be guaranteed $75 per ton for varietal grapes or the market price, whichever was higher. Ernest argued that the guaranteed floor price of $75 was much better than the $47.50 per ton that was usually paid for the common varieties and would reduce the risk in replanting a vineyard.

Some growers reacted with skepticism. They pointed out that the varietal grapes had actually brought in $80 per ton that year. And since Gallo was so large and effectively controlled the grape market each year, it would always be able to keep the price at the $75 floor guarantee. Thus the winery would be able to buy varietals at a comparatively low cost for several years.

Growers also worried about replanting entire vineyards. While Julio insisted that the Livingston vineyard experiments proved that table wine varieties could be grafted onto common wine grape rootstock, University of California studies reported only limited success. Growers might have to pull out their old vines and fumigate the soil to eliminate possible disease or nematode problems, then completely replant with resistant rootstock. A total replanting would cost an estimated $700 to $800 an acre and it would be three years before the new vines began producing, four or five before the vineyard reached full yield. And then, growers argued, the cost of harvesting varietals was higher—not only was the tonnage per acre lower than for common varieties, but also the bunches were smaller and took longer to pick, raising labor costs as well. They calculated that it would cost about $75 per ton to grow varietal grapes, and concluded that the proposed Gallo floor price wasn't as generous as Ernest and Julio claimed.

Despite the resistance, many growers finally accepted Gallo contracts. It was an offer they couldn't refuse: The contracts would give the growers security; those who remained with the common varieties would have a difficult time selling their harvests in the future. The winery was shifting its emphasis to the better varietal table wines, and since it bought more grapes than any other winery, the handwriting was on the wall. As Gallo went, so went the rest of the wine industry, although not all wineries preferred the varietals Gallo favored. The arguments were persuasive, and in only two short years California vineyards planted to varietals doubled to nearly 170,000 acres, and Ernest and Julio controlled the majority of them with their contracts and grower relations' supervisory role.

By the late 1960s Ernest and Julio had covered all the bases. They developed new wines that caught the public's attention, they controlled grape production, and they dominated marketing and sales nationally by installing the Gallo method within the distribution system. Having risen to number one, they now had the profits and power to go upscale. Finally, respectability and respect seemed within the Gallo grasp.

Ernest and Julio were crowned the kings of wine by a *Time* magazine cover story in November 1972. But Ernest still fretted about the Gallo image. Despite the article's praise for the brothers' numerous achievements, Ernest was annoyed by the references to "pop wines" and the assertion that Gallo's six brands accounted for 90 percent of the 60 million gallons of pop wine sold in 1971. He commissioned one market survey after another, looking for ways to give Gallo a different image.

Ernest called in marketing consultants and spent thousands of dollars on brand mapping surveys. These showed that Gallo had a more negative image than Almaden, Paul Masson, Inglenook, and Taylor California (AMIT)—hardly boutique wineries but not burdened with a "street wine" reputation or Thunderbird jokes.

"Not an hour went by when someone wasn't discussing this problem, because this was when all the wineries had started to emphasize table wines," a former Gallo sales manager explained. "We were trying to move our bottles into the better table wine shelf positions and a lot of retailers were resisting. Ernest had made his fortune from the high-alcohol, low-grade stuff. Of course, he refused to acknowledge that it was rotgut and would insist with absolute conviction that Gallo made the best wine in the country and all we had to do was change the way it was perceived by the consumer."

Gallo was being challenged by one of its chief competitors in the upscale market, and Ernest was convinced that the public was attracted by the other winery's "classier labels." He asked his marketing men for ideas, but nothing satisfied him.

"Finally, at one of our many meetings Ernest unveiled a storyboard of labels," recalled Paul Merrigan, who was then a Gallo regional sales manager. "We couldn't believe it—they were first-run proofs of the upgraded parchment labels that another winery was about to introduce on its table wines. Ernest didn't hide where they came from, but proudly announced that they had been supplied by a former Gallo employee who had gone to work for the competitor. Ernest proclaimed, 'This is the image we need for our product,' and with the winery's usual efficiency, we had our new lookalike parchment labels on bottles and in retail stores even before the other winery."

Another competitive winery with which Ernest had close ties was Franzia. His in-laws' winery had been bought by Coca-Cola Bottling of New York in the early 1970s, but when Coca-Cola did not fare well in the wine business, Art Ciocca, a former Gallo group product manager and Ernest loyalist, organized investors to buy it. Ciocca became Franzia's CEO, and Ernest and Joey then mounted a matchmaking campaign to bring him and Carlyse Franzia, a granddaughter of the Franzia Winery's founder who worked for Gallo in Los Angeles, together.

"It was a happy arrangement," another former sales manager recalled. "Art was head of the Franzia Winery, had never married, and was much older than Carlyse. But fortunately for everyone, Art and Carlyse fell in love and decided to marry."

Paul Merrigan recalled that several months after the marriage, he was at a dinner in Ernest's home: "Amelia went into her usual complaint that Ernest had driven the Franzias out of the winery business. This time Ernest growled, 'What are you complaining about? Carlyse married Art, so I got the winery back for your family, didn't I?' "

During the 1960s, neither of Ernest's sons, David and Joey, had married. With no grandchildren and employing a staff of servants in addition to a cook, Amelia had very little to occupy her time.

According to winery employees, it was during this period that Amelia took up shopping with a vengeance. Ernest had put a limo and a chauffeur at her disposal, and she made frequent trips to the most expensive shops and department stores in San Francisco. Suddenly Ernest began to receive impatient telephone calls at his office; bills were long overdue. Store managers were polite, but all the same they were anxious about the long-unpaid accounts. Ernest drove home and confronted Amelia: What had she done with all the bills that must have been sent? Why, she'd just thrown them away—she hadn't wanted to upset Ernest. What about all the things she had bought? Well, she'd hidden the boxes in closets.

New rules were imposed—Amelia's bills were to be sent directly to the winery's accounting department. Ernest was so astonished by his wife's behavior that he told winery associates about the incident, shaking his head at his wife's attempt to conceal her purchases and the mounting bills.

In contrast to Amelia, Aileen filled her time with grandchildren. (Bob and Marie had seven children and Susann and Jim had eight children by 1972.) Finally, in 1970, Ernest and Amelia's sons began to think of marriage. Joey, had come back to the winery as vice-president, sales, and he then met Ofelia Carrasquilla, the twenty-year-old younger sister of a woman he had once dated at Stanford, who had come from her native Nicaragua to study in the United States. Ofelia was warm and lively, and Joey began to court her as enthusiastically as he'd once courted her older sister. Soon they became engaged, even though Ernest expressed his lack of enthusiasm for the match.

There seemed to be an unwritten rule that the older son should marry first, and at Amelia's request family, friends, and winery associates started hunting for a wife for David. "I think they had every priest and nun in the area looking," commented one former winery employee. Finally David announced to winery colleagues that he was getting married, too. He explained to them that he had found a wife "the old-fashioned way," through a priest in Escalon whom he knew and whom he had asked to find "a nice Catholic girl who wanted to raise a family." It was at the beginning of the women's movement, and David informed people at the winery that he didn't want a woman with "those crazy ideas," rather one who desired nothing more than to be a good wife and mother. And the priest, he said, had found exactly what he was looking for—Mary Costa, the daughter of a Portuguese farm family in Escalon. Amelia seemed to approve of the choice as well, although she made a point of telling people that Mary had her own money. "She didn't want people to think someone was marrying her son only for his money," a former Gallo employee recalled, "and then she remarked that Mary would look good as soon as she got some I. Magnin clothes."

Once David was taken care of, Joey and Ofelia could proceed with their plans—a family wedding in Managua, Nicaragua. They then returned to live in the "gazebo," the small summer cottage behind Ernest and Amelia's home, while Ofelia was tutored in the English language and in Italian cooking. Winery workers and family members were struck with the irony of Ernest's sons' choices. Both Ernest and Julio openly expressed prejudice against Hispanics, remarking that Mexicans were lazy and dumb, couldn't be trusted, and couldn't be taught anything. Mike Gallo also thought it was ironic that David had married a Portuguese-American woman, since his father had told him that Ernest had forced him to break up with a high school girlfriend because she was of Portuguese descent.

The births of Joey and Ofelia's children during the next several years, however, overcame whatever disappointment Ernest may have felt about the marriage—the first a daughter named Stefanie Amelia, the next a son named for his grandfather (the family called him Ernesto), and finally another son, named Joseph, Jr. In 1972, David and Mary presented Ernest and Amelia with a second granddaughter, Theresa, and another grandson, Christopher, was born two years later.

Following his termination by Ernest and Julio, Joe Gallo still worked long hours. But there was a mellowing to him, as if his son Peter's death had reminded him of the importance of affection and the need to express it, and he took more pleasure in his family. His new wife, Patricia, saw how much Linda, Mike, and stepson Sam helped to console him after Peter's death, and Joe began to allow himself moments of laughter and relaxation. He and Patricia made more trips into San Francisco for dinners and shows; they took up bridge, and Joe even won several tournaments. They planned vacations and took tours of Europe. They visited Fossano and Asti, the villages where his parents had been born, but failed to find any Gallo or Bianco relatives still remaining. (They even had a good laugh when upon their return they were stopped by customs agents who were sure that this Joseph Gallo was the notorious mafioso, "Crazy" Joey Gallo.)

No longer having to take orders from Ernest and Julio, Joe went to his office every day, and along with Mike and Sam made daily inspections of the ranches. (Mike was now studying viticulture and oenology at Fresno State, Sam was enrolled at Stanislaus State, and both lived at home.) Later, when Mike moved to Fresno State, Linda Gallo met and began dating his roommate, Kenny Jelacich, the son of a Croatian immigrant family in Visalia, who was also studying agriculture and viticulture. (They were married in 1977.)

In 1972, Joe bought another two-thousand-acre ranch along Highway 140 and named it the Joseph Gallo Cottonwood Ranch. Joseph Gallo ranch signs now dominated the two-lane road, and with his father's heifer and grape-growing businesses becoming so extensive, Mike left school in 1973 to manage his father's ranches. At twenty-three he was ready to settle into work, and he soon met the woman he would eventually marry.

Sherrie Spendlove, the daughter of a Merced family, was eighteen when she first went out with Mike on a blind date. "I had a rule never to go on blind dates, but my friend kept arguing. Finally I asked who he was. She said, 'Mike Gallo.' I was even more opposed, the Gallos had such a reputation in this area. But she told me, 'He's not one of *those* Gallos, he's a nephew. His father and he are ranchers, separate from the winery.' "

At last agreeing to the date, Sherrie found herself pleasantly surprised, and they continued seeing each other for the next few years, as Sherrie completed her college degree in French literature, and they were married in 1977. Even prior to their marriage, Sherrie was made aware of Gallo rules.

"Sometimes Mike and I would have plans for a Saturday night," she recalled. "At the very last minute I'd hear that we had to change them because either Ernest or Julio wanted us to come to dinner. At first I complained, but then I realized there was no point. That's the way it had always been; it was expected of Joe, and then it was expected of Mike."

After 1972 Ernest planned a new program of personnel recruitment. "We're the biggest, why not recruit the best?" he announced to Paul Merrigan. Instead of hiring recent college graduates and bringing them up through the sales training program, he now wanted to attract M.B.A.'s as well as executives from other large consumer product companies. His goal was to structure a middle management level of executives, something that had been missing in the Gallo organization.

Paul Merrigan had come to Gallo in 1970 from Warner Lambert, and with extensive experience in marketing and sales had been quickly promoted to division manager, even though at five-feet-nine he did not fit the image Ernest usually sought in his managers and executives. "When Dick Witter first interviewed me," recalled Merrigan with a laugh, "he told me that I was too short for the organization. I replied that at least I was taller then Ernest. For whatever reason, they chose to overlook both that remark and my height and hired me anyway."

Merrigan was later promoted to western regional sales manager. "It was an absolutely crazy time of enormous expansion and intense effort at the winery," Merrigan explained. "I had about 350 people working for me. We were growing 40 percent to 50 percent a year in some areas and introducing new products with phenomenal success. In 1970, Boone's Farm apple wine had become the best-selling single wine of any kind in the United States. Then we introduced Boone's Farm Strawberry Hill and later Country Quencher. We were expanding André and launched Gallo Champagne, which replaced Eden Roc. We introduced Madria, Madria Sangria and another fortified wine, Night Train Express, which became another street wine favorite. Meanwhile we were also pushing the new Gallo varietals, trying to move them out of cheap wine into the elite section of stores."

"All the best" didn't always yield the desired results among the new staff of M.B.A.'s. According to Merrigan there was an exceedingly high turnover rate among these employees. M.B.A.'s weren't enamored of the required sixteen-hour days of visiting retail stores. Vicepresidents recruited to middle management from other companies were even more frustrated: They found a glass ceiling between them and the upper echelon, and they complained that information was kept from them, that they were spied on, and that their creative ideas were coopted by Ernest's faithful inner circle, who failed to give the younger men credit.

The atmosphere in Gallo headquarters was one of hostility and suspicion, according to the many employees who were hired, then fired—usually forced to resign rather than formally terminated—during the early and mid-1970s.

Sometimes executives were hired away from another wine company in order to weaken or undermine the competition. For example, the innovator at Mogen David who had developed its most popular product, The Little Brown Jug, was recruited by Gallo. While Ernest and Bertsch publicly extolled the man's marketing genius and assigned him to manage Valley Vintners in San Diego, Bertsch took Merrigan aside to advise him of the private agenda. Merrigan was to withhold all vital information from the new executive; he was to keep Bertsch informed of every mistake made, each loss in sales. In short, Merrigan was told to ensure the new man's failure. Six months later, Merrigan recalled, he received a phone call from Bertsch. "I'm on my way to San Diego," he announced. "Get out of range." The new man was summarily fired, and according to Merrigan, his standing in the wine industry was undermined.

Ernest still analyzed all sales figures, distribution reports, and marketing trends and, with a few pointed questions, could discover which sales managers didn't have the same grasp of the material. He had an established drill to test his employees. When he, along with Witter and Bertsch, didn't like what they saw in a sales report, sales managers were ordered to fly to Modesto immediately. They were to wait at the winery until summoned to a meeting, usually by Ken Bertsch. Bertsch was proud of his technique—"zero preparation"—because all managers were expected to know the answers to any questions that might be asked about the retail stores in their area, distributors, population trends, housing starts, ethnic patterns, anything that affected the market. At some point Ernest joined the meeting—by arriving in the midst of the questioning, he could avoid any pretense of social amenities. (According to employees, he also had a button under the conference table with which he could signal his secretary to summon him if he wished to leave before the session was over.)

After the meeting Bertsch and Witter met with Ernest and dissected the subject. Any sign of weakness—a stammer, a sweaty brow, deviation from Gallo conservative dress—was noted, especially by Bertsch, who was finicky about outward impressions. Ernest and Witter were more pragmatic, analyzing numbers and the employee's presentation.

"The worst sin was to try to bullshit Ernest," said Merrigan. "He disemboweled by the numbers—not in dollars but in warehouse depletion reports, because as he once told me, 'We don't want anyone to know how much money is actually changing hands.' If the message was bad, he wanted to know it. He only killed the messenger when he failed to give an accurate report."

Despite Ernest's desire to raid executives from other companies, Ken Bertsch was eager to find their weaknesses. He seemed to enjoy humiliating the newcomers, and some felt that this was his revenge for having lost to Witter in the power struggle for Ernest's favor. Bertsch wanted people to know he still had authority.

Once he hired the former president of a major consumer products company in New York. The new recruit spent three months in the Los Angeles Gallo distributorship to learn the wine business. He had sold his house in New York and the day after Bertsch came down to observe him on the job, he was scheduled to fly home to move his family West. Merrigan drove them from retail store to retail store while Bertsch grilled the man on competitive products, pricing, methods of marketing, and retail store conditions. It soon became evident that the new executive was still feeling his way and had much to learn. According to Merrigan, they were traveling south on Figueroa Street, near the Los Angeles Memorial Coliseum, when Bertsch lit up one of his Bering cigars and ordered Merrigan to pull over.

When the car was stopped at the curb, Bertsch bounded from the front seat, opened the rear door, and gestured for the new man to get out. The confused executive stood on the curb as Bertsch reached into the backseat and pulled out the man's briefcase and jacket.

"You can get a cab to the airport from here," he barked. "Go home. Don't do anything until you hear from me."

He hopped back into the car, slammed the door, and told Merrigan to get moving. Bertsch ignored the fact that he had marooned someone in a dangerous neighborhood and simply began to discuss another business matter. He never mentioned the recruit again until Merrigan dropped him off at his hotel.

"A lot of them are pretty, but they're dumb," he announced.

One of the assignments that exasperated Gallo managers and executives was "taking care of David." Most often he was sent out on inspections of retail stores with "Uncle Charlie" Rossi, who seemed best able to keep him in line. Paul Merrigan also had to deal with David several times, and he recalled one incident in which David's participation was particularly difficult.

One morning Ernest had called Merrigan into his office.

"Paul, I'd like you to take care of some family matters for me," he said. "I have an old uncle living in Henderson, just outside Las Vegas. Since that's in your territory, I want you to deliver wine to him and check that he's okay."

It wasn't until he actually visited this "old uncle," Mike Gallo, and listened to some of his stories that Merrigan realized that this was the man about whom there had been gossip at the winery.

"After visiting Uncle Mike, I understood the connection," said Merrigan. "He was Ernest and Julio's father's brother and an infamous bootlegger during Prohibition. He was living in a rusted-out house trailer, and Ernest wanted me to make sure he had enough wine. He must have been in his early eighties at least, and pretty battle-scarred by then. I would visit him about once a month, bringing him his supply of his favorite cream sherry and Paisano, and I'd sit with him while he reminisced about the old days and his successful nephews. He often said, 'We never thought when we started'—and I assume he meant he and his brother—'that it would turn into this, because back then it was just a good way of making money, raising grapes and selling wine.' He'd make oblique remarks about some of his problems with the law—like how the San Francisco police gave him a hard time about 'some investment scheme,' or how the Oakland police had given him a lot of shit, or how he had other troubles in Port Richmond, when he was making a delivery and tried to outrun the cops.

"He sometimes mentioned his brother Giuseppe and Susie, Ernest's parents. 'That was just such a terrible thing,' he said, 'the shootings, and it was very hard for Ernest and Julio to accept what had happened. But, of course, I wasn't around a lot'—I guessed that he was in jail—'and then I got my restaurant in Hawthorne.' He gave the impression that he accepted being the black sheep of the family, that he knew he had been exiled because he was an embarrassment. I enjoyed hearing his stories, though he tended to ramble, and he was so pleased that Ernest had asked me to visit him—Ernest's attention to him, even if it came through me, meant a great deal to him."

One Monday when Merrigan had concluded winery business and was about to pack up Mike's supply of wine at the warehouse, the Las Vegas distributor stopped him.

"Haven't you heard?" he asked. "Mike was buried on Saturday. Father Franzinelli told me about it. Didn't the family know?"

Merrigan was sure they didn't. He phoned Father Franzinelli, the parish priest whose church Mike attended regularly and who also had taken an interest in his welfare. The priest confirmed Mike's death and also asked why he had heard nothing from Ernest or Julio.

"Mike had always accepted the 'don't call us, we'll call you,' arrangement," Merrigan said, "so the priest didn't know how to contact the chairman of the Gallo Winery on a weekend. It was left to me to tell Ernest. I phoned his secretary, Ouida McCullough, who said he was 'tied up.' I asked her to give him the message that his uncle had died. She put me on hold, then came back to say, 'Mr. Gallo would like to know when the funeral is scheduled.' 'It was Saturday,' I told her. 'Ask Ernest if there's anything he wants me to do.' "

Ernest had no instructions. Two weeks later, however, Father Franzinelli phoned Merrigan.

"All Mike ever talked about was how proud he was of his nephews. I can't believe they haven't acknowledged his death. Didn't you tell them?"

Merrigan reassured him that he had, and then ordered several cases of Gallo wine delivered to the church for the spring festival. He informed Ernest of the phone call, reporting as well the several that followed when the priest continued to hear nothing from Ernest or Julio.

"The priest took a personal interest in your uncle," Merrigan again advised Ernest, "and he's upset that the family still hasn't been in touch."

Ernest nodded but made no reply, and Merrigan left it at that. A month later, on a Sunday afternoon, he received a phone call at his Los Angeles home.

"Paul, this is Charlie Rossi," the caller announced. "Meet me at San Francisco airport tomorrow morning. You're supposed to fly with us to Las Vegas to introduce us to this priest who was Mike's friend."

" 'Us? Oh God, he must mean David,' " Merrigan recalled thinking. "When Ernest sent David out of the winery, Charlie usually went along to hold his leash. But sending him down to Las Vegas seemed very bizarre. Perhaps it was a message of contempt for Mike and the priest; or maybe David—who tended to get dramatically sentimental about so-called family ties—was insisting on it. But I reassured myself that at least this was a mission that didn't have anything to do with business, so I didn't have to worry about David's screwing up."

Merrigan drove them from the Las Vegas airport to the popular downtown restaurant where he had reserved the best table and where Father Franzinelli and the Las Vegas distributor were to meet them.

The priest was introduced to Charlie and David, and the conversation was friendly. David tried out his Italian phrases, Charlie chimed in, and it was old home week. After the waiter took their orders—with David asking how dishes were prepared, ordering an appetizer, then sending it back—the conversation turned somber.

"Your great-uncle Mike was a prominent member of our parish," Father Franzinelli said to David. "He was very popular, and he always told people how proud he was of his family." He paused. "So we were wondering if you didn't want to do something more for his grave site. He only has one of the small, plain markers, and we thought the family might want to put up a stone, some kind of memorial—"

"What do you mean?" asked David, his face red, his eyes glaring. "You're talking money, aren't you?"

"Well, just $600 for a suitable headstone," the priest began. "That's probably all it would cost."

"It's money, that's what you're after," shrieked David in his falsetto voice. "God damn it, he wasn't a close member of the family! And you get me down here to hold me up for cash! That's all anybody wants from the Gallos—money, money, money. Who the hell do you think you are?"

David continued to shout; neighboring conversations ceased as the diners watched the scene. The mortified priest stood up and politely excused himself. Merrigan and the distributor slipped the manager some money and hustled David into the car and back on the plane. During the entire flight home he was still muttering about all the people who tried to take advantage of the Gallos.

Merrigan was fuming, and failing to reach Ernest directly, he told Bert McGowen, a winery sales executive, to relay a message: "Tell Ernest that I don't care if David is his son. Don't ever send that asshole out my way again."

The next time Merrigan was in Modesto, Ernest asked for a full report. Merrigan described how David had misunderstood the priest's request. Father Franzinelli was simply explaining that if the family wanted to replace the plain marker with a headstone, he thought it would cost about $600. He wasn't asking for money for the church. But even if he had been, there was no reason for David to run amok. He had caused a scene, he had behaved irrationally and had seemed almost on the verge of violence in the middle of a popular restaurant.

Ernest listened but made no comment. As far as Merrigan knew, no headstone was ever placed on Mike's grave, although he was later asked to find a position for Mike's grandson at Gallo's Valley Vintner distributorship in Riverside. There he worked as a mechanic, but next to his Gallo name in personnel records was the indication "no relation."

Apparently Ernest did nothing to try to curtail David's outbursts. At one meeting after another he was disruptive, and Ernest seemed oblivious to the discomfort of others at these sessions. Some might say that this was simply tolerance of a son whose deficiencies were obvious. Others concluded that it was part of Ernest's arrogance: my employees do what I say, even if it means babysitting my son. There was no use complaining about David's late-night phone calls to berate a sales manager or a distributor for not selling enough of his André Champagne. (Ernest, however, would later pay a settlement to a recently terminated employee who claimed David had phoned and yelled at him, informing the man that he had been fired because of his public opposition to a Modesto convention center that the Gallos favored.)

Nor was there any point in telling Ernest that David's presence on a sales trip alienated retail owners. It became common knowledge among the sales managers that when David was foisted on them for a visit in their territory, they could do nothing but try to reduce the havoc he caused. But "David stories" became legion, and, as one former Gallo sales manager added, he became the focus for much of the hostility that was actually directed at Ernest.

But a southern California sales manager, recalling one of many anecdotes, said that David usually deserved the criticism he received. "One time I was told to introduce David to some local Gallo retailers at lunch in Newport Beach," he explained. "Having been at these lunches before, I got to the restaurant ahead of time and slipped the manager $50. 'Someone's joining me,' I said, 'and he's a bit eccentric. He'll come in and want to order immediately; he'll ask how you cook the dishes, and then he'll demand his food in five minutes. Can you handle this?' The guy agreed, and sure enough David pulled his usual stunts about the menu. By the time the waiter had taken the last order from our group, David was already yelling for his food. Because they'd been forewarned, they brought him his appetizer immediately, so that kept him happy. Then he proceeded to guzzle wine and spill it down the front of his shirt and on the table, all the while getting louder and louder. When we left, I was so embarrassed that I gave the manager another $50."

Ernest, however, continued to voice his expectation that Joey and David would be his successors and would someday run the winery. David had a title but little autonomy; Joey had more responsibility and power. But Ernest still criticized him unmercifully, especially in front of other sales executives.

At a meeting called to discuss Ernest's unhappiness with the performance of the winery's Reno and Lake Tahoe distributor, Paul Merrigan presented his analysis of the situation. However, he recommended that despite the drop in sales, Gallo should remain with the present distributor and find ways to motivate him to achieve higher sales and to add more Gallo salesmen to his staff.

Ernest listened to the presentation, then, as was his method, he asked each participant how *he* would solve the problem. "Now, Joe, what do you think?" he asked, turning to his son last.

"I think we should change distributors and go with the Franzias," Joey replied. "They're family and they'll do what we demand. You can always ask more of family than you can in a business relationship."

No one said a word. Like David, Joey often fell back on the cliché of family. Ernest often mouthed the same sentiment, but anyone in the know realized that Ernest never had the same impulses about family when it came to business and the bottom line. It was true that a Franzia family member had a distributorship in Reno, principally to market Franzia brands, but it was considered a small operation. Instead of saying as much, Ernest proceeded to interrogate his son.

"Do they currently have somebody regularly calling on the casinos?"

Joey didn't know.

"Do they carry any other lines besides Franzia?"

Joey had no reply.

"What are their sales figures? What's their trend, up or down?"

Again and again Joey had no response to his father's pointed questions. Tap, tap, tap went Ernest's pencil, as he repeatedly exposed his son's ignorance.

He then called on Merrigan with the same questions, answers to which Merrigan could readily provide. After hearing his replies, which only confirmed that the suggestion of switching to the Franzia distributorship was ridiculous, Ernest turned back to his son.

"God damn it, Joe! When are you going to learn not to speak out on something when you don't know what the hell you're talking about? I expect my sales directors to know these things. What the hell is wrong with you? I sometimes think I've raised an idiot."

On and on Ernest went. Joey's chin sank lower and lower, and his face grew paler and paler. Even the most Ernest-hardened executives were appalled by the father's tirade, his no-holds-barred destruction of his son.

Finally Ernest adjourned for lunch. As was the custom at these meetings, everyone waited to see whom he designated to join him. That day he escorted Ken Bertsch, Paul Merrigan, and Joey out to the company's chauffeur-driven car.

"You ride in front with the driver," Ernest ordered his son, as if he were banishing a two-year-old to his room. Bertsch and Merrigan sat in back with Ernest.

"What do you think of this situation?" Ernest said to Bertsch, who had been noticeably silent during the morning's meeting.

"I think Paul's summary is correct," replied Bertsch, glancing at Joey, who could hear every word of the conversation. "We should stay with our Reno distributor."

Ernest waved his hand impatiently. "Of course, Paul's correct. I mean, what's your excuse for Joe not knowing this? How come he couldn't answer my questions? He should know this stuff as well as if not better than the other sales supervisors. You'll just have to train him harder."

Ernest's solution to the problem was to assign Joe to other sales executives, who were supposed to bring him up to their level of knowledge and experience.

"The problem was that Ernest was always trying to stimulate and inspire his son through harassment and embarrassment," said Merrigan. "Ernest palmed him off to his executives and then compared him to these older men who had three times the experience and four times the brains. But even if Joe had the intelligence to learn from these guys, he was not about to be receptive after his father's treatment. His response, understandably, was to become defensive and at the same time work harder and harder to emulate his father's outward arrogance. David was tiresome, but the way Ernest treated Joe was the real problem in terms of the future of the company."

Ernest's deeply held conviction was that even though the winery had become a large and complicated corporation, it was still a "family business." No matter what, a Gallo would remain at the helm.

Once Ernest said as much to Dick Witter, according to personnel consultant Bernie Weiner and several winery executives, who heard the story. Witter was the man Ernest most trusted, someone he considered closest to himself in terms of brains and competence. Some said that he was another surrogate son who had displaced Fenderson and Bertsch as "most favored." But a surrogate wasn't good enough. At one point Witter had grown disheartened. For several years he had lead the sales and distribution campaigns; he had devoted himself to the winery's crusades, and in a meeting with Ernest, Witter raised the question of his position in the company.

Ernest was confused. Wasn't Witter happy?

Of course, I'm happy, Witter reportedly told Ernest. *But I'd like to know what the future is for me. I mean, when you're not running the winery anymore.*

What are you getting at? Ernest snapped, as if the idea were an impossibility.

Just that I'd like to think that someday I could become chairman.

Ernest stared at him as if he'd lost his mind. *I know you'd make a great president of any company,* he said. *But don't you realize, for this one you have the wrong last name!*

Ernest's insistence on his sons' legacy, his refusal to admit their limitations, began to undermine his organization. According to winery employees and consultants, Ernest's sons had shown that they could not solve the problems created by the winery's growing size and its lack of good middle management. As Bernie Weiner remarked, "David and Joey seemed to want to prove just how far the apple can fall from the tree."

Ernest, however, seemed to feel that he had everything well in hand, including the future of his sons and the winery. But in the next few years he would learn that no matter how much control he thought he exerted over others, fate still held a few surprises. As the winery began to suffer from internal conflict, rapid personnel turn-over, and stalled wine sales, two new opponents appeared on the scene. Despite Ernest's vision of himself as a warrior, neither antago-nist would yield without a fight or without inflicting painful wounds.

CHAPTER NINE

I'*ll lose the ranch before I knuckle under to that SOB,* Ernest shouted, slamming his fist on his desk and staring angrily up into the faces of Al Fenderson and Dick Witter.

They didn't have to ask who had provoked Ernest's wrath. "That SOB" was César Chavez. It was the fall of 1973, and Ernest was already feeling the pinch of Chavez's national boycott against Gallo Wine, organized that June after the winery had signed a four-year contract with the Teamsters to represent its vineyard field hands.

Ernest had in fact liked César Chavez when Chavez had first started rallying farm workers to unionize. In 1967 Chavez's United Farm Workers Organizing Committee (the farm labor subdivision of the AFL-CIO, initially called UFWOC but later known popularly as UFW) had already won the right to represent a majority of grape pickers despite many growers' opposition. In 1966, threatened by a boycott, Schenley Industries had signed a contract with UFWOC, bringing its vineyard workers into the farm union, and in the follow- ing year, more and more grape growers were being pressured to sign similar contracts. While the Gallo Livingston vineyard's grape pickers were actually few (only about one hundred full time, six hundred during harvest), Chavez was eager to bring them into the union.

"In the beginning Ernest admired Chavez," recalled Neil Sweeney, who was then still the Gallo training director. "He thought that a powerful union would help him keep his field workers in line. He had met with Chavez and the UFWOC organizers and had agreed to allow his grape pickers to hold an election. Ernest saw Chavez as much like himself, driven, disciplined, inspiring loyalty and hard work. So in 1967 when he announced that the winery would allow its vineyard workers to vote for unionization, he let other growers know that he was supporting Chavez. That was an important gain for the UFW in the face of so many larger growers' resistance to Chavez."

But that same year the Teamsters also entered the fray. The Teamsters had first supported Chavez, but then Einar Mohn, director of the Western Conference of Teamsters and an adversary of the Teamsters' president, Jimmy Hoffa, tried to increase his power by recruiting California farm workers and bringing them into the union as his supporters. His organizers began to challenge Chavez in the vineyards, Gallo's included. Ernest's problem was compounded by the fact that many employees of the winery and its distributorships were already represented by the Teamsters. Because winery truck drivers would refuse to cross the picket line, the union expected Ernest to sign his vineyards over without holding an election.

Ernest had good relations with the Teamsters, but he now went to court, complaining that the winery was "caught in a jurisdictional dispute" between the Teamsters and the AFL-CIO, and in April 1967 he won a restraining order against further picketing by the Teamsters. In May he presented a petition to both unions in which his farm workers demanded an election and asked the State Department of Labor Relations to appoint a conciliator to solve the dispute. On August 7, sixty-eight of the one hundred year-round Livingston vineyard workers authorized the UFW to represent them, and the winery signed a three-year contract with Chavez. In addition, the Teamsters and the AFL-CIO agreed that the UFW would represent only field workers, while the Teamsters would represent only employees of canneries, creameries, frozen-food-processing plants, warehouses, and markets. Each union pledged not to raid the other's membership.

Thus, while Chavez was fighting many other grape growers—both table and wine—and his union was picketing vineyards throughout California and boycotting nonunion table grapes nationally, the Gallo vineyards were free of conflict. Chavez elicited a great deal of public sympathy for "La Causa," with people from labor, churches, and universities often joining the picket lines and supporting the boycott of nonunion lettuce and table grapes. The grape strike was part of the liberal political agenda in these years, with Chavez's unionization of farm workers gaining strength from the general antiwar, antiestablishment, and anti-Nixon movement and mood. In 1970 Ernest signed another three-year contract with the UFW.

In the spring of 1973, when this contract expired, Ernest did an abrupt about-face and entered into negotiations with the Teamsters. Under the new leadership of Frank Fitzsimmons, the Teamsters began to organize farm labor again, the campaign prompted, it was said, by Fitzsimmons's close ties to Nixon. California agribusiness was a powerful lobby behind Nixon, and it saw Chavez as its enemy, too. Get Chavez, was the cry, and Charles Colson, of later Watergate fame, drafted memos to the Teamsters instructing the union to do everything in its power to undermine Chavez and the UFW. The Teamsters then mounted aggressive attacks on many vineyards where UFW contracts were about to expire, and Ernest and Julio's field hands were a prime target.

The Gallo contract was important to Chavez—not for the number of workers but for its symbolic value. When the contract first expired, Ernest opened negotiations with the UFW by announcing that he was dissatisfied with the way the union was run. His main complaint —one that was common among other growers—was that Chavez's insistence on a union-run hiring hall was impractical and especially unwieldy for the Gallo field hands. Since Livingston employed permanent workers, as well as teams that had returned every harvest to his vineyard, Ernest argued, it was unfair for Gallo to have to go through the hiring-hall assignments. Further, he said that while he admired Chavez, found him "an honorable man," and had always been in favor of unionization, he felt that Chavez's assistants, who actually ran the hiring hall and the day-to-day operation of the union, were disorganized, inefficient, and unreliable. His vineyard managers had complained that they couldn't get quick responses or get through to union leadership for consultation or speedy decisions.

"Ernest's complaints made sense in terms of his own personality, in terms of his own system of management," Neil Sweeney commented. "He could deal with a strong leader, but he wasn't at all interested in Chavez's emphasis on a democratic union, one in which everyone had a voice. He hated the fact that he was treated like just another grape grower, not someone who could have Chavez return his calls in an instant."

When UFW representatives entered into preliminary discussions with the winery about the renewal of the contract, they realized that Gallo spokesmen, and particularly Frank Brennan, the winery's senior counsel (and brother of Supreme Court Justice William Brennan), considered the hiring hall the sticking point. It was a pattern Chavez had often seen in recent months—growers unwilling to compromise on one issue to justify turning to the Teamsters.

"What happened at Gallo was pretty much like the other growers," Chavez explained to the press. "They always found one item where they refused to give during negotiations."

A month later Ernest announced that he had entered negotiations with the Teamsters. The Livingston vineyard workers then went out on strike. Joined by several hundred UFW supporters, they picketed in front of the winery as well as at the Livingston vineyards, and with Chavez himself leading the march, they convened in a Modesto auditorium to rally support.

The winery sent Al Fenderson to the meeting to hear what Chavez was planning. He arrived with his son and daughter-in-law and sat among the crowd of more than three hundred supporters. But when a *Modesto Bee* reporter recognized Al Fenderson as a Gallo executive and pointed him out to UFW leaders, people began to move away, leaving the three Fendersons surrounded by thirty feet of empty seats. Chavez announced that if the winery went ahead with its plans to stage an election from which striking UFW workers would be excluded in order to guarantee a Teamsters victory, Chavez would organize a nationwide boycott of Gallo products.

As a result of this threat, Chavez became the SOB to whom Ernest would never capitulate. With the Teamsters' help, the winery then hired other vineyard hands—strikebreakers or "scabs"—who proceeded to hold an election in which these new Livingston workers voted 158 to 1 to have the Teamsters represent them. The winery signed a four-year contract, claiming that it was only following its employees' preference. While Chavez announced that this was a sweetheart contract that "lowered salaries and benefits and eliminated fair hiring and firing practices," Ernest touted it as "the highest-paying and fairest farm labor contract in America." Almost overnight he and Julio and the Gallo Winery became the national symbols of the oppression of farm workers.

The employees at the Livingston vineyards who had gone on strike were permanent, year-round employees to whom the winery also furnished housing. After bringing in non-UFW crews and allowing Teamsters to patrol the picket lines, the winery then tried to have striking families evicted from their homes. When the sheriff arrived to evict one worker—he was a Gallo employee who had been fired before the strike, according to the winery—the other workers staged a sit-in. Chavez couldn't have paid for better publicity—in UFW press releases published in major California and national newspapers, he announced that the wealthy and powerful Gallo brothers had not only betrayed their own "loyal employees, some of whom had worked in the winery's vineyards for fourteen years, they were also causing whole families, with a total of four hundred children, to become homeless."

A month later when harvest began and more non-UFW grape pickers were brought in, the situation became explosive. Not only were local cops called, but Ernest sent thirty winery security guards to patrol the picket lines. Teamster-hired bullies shouted obscenities and muscled picketers; shoving, fist-fights, and rock-throwing followed, and the cops made a mass arrest of UFW members and sympathizers for trespassing. With priests and nuns on the picket line, with Teamsters given free reign, with sixty UFW arrests, the press jumped on the story. This wasn't the image that Ernest wanted to project, and yet he seemed intent upon confronting Chavez.

If the public didn't like what it saw on the news, it had a way to voice its displeasure. Targeting Gallo as the symbol of oppression, the UFW organized a national campaign: "Boycott Gallo Wine" was a slogan that allowed people across the country to take a simple positive action. Chavez's union then filed a $100 million class action suit against the Teamsters and table grape growers in Coachella. While Gallo itself wasn't even mentioned in this lawsuit, the assumption (repeated in the media) was that Ernest and Julio Gallo were the leaders of the crusade to defeat Chavez. The Gallo boycott gained strength through ignorance. Not many people nationally knew the details of the union struggle in the fields of California, yet Gallo was a name they recognized and an easy target for general support of farm workers.

Joe Gallo was drawn into the battle, too. In this instance, ironically, he was perceived as a partner in the winery. According to John Whiting, when Ernest had decided not to renew the UFW contract, he phoned Joe and Mike and told them that he expected them to sign a union contract with their workers, something they had never done before. "Ernest said, 'Just let the Teamster organizers come in,' " Mike recalled. " 'Those guys will handle everything.' We never signed, but Ernest later sent Teamsters over to our vineyards. John

Whiting was doing our legal work, and we got locked into the dispute when we hadn't wanted any part of it. There was no benefit to us from the winery's sending the Teamsters in, only all the hassles with police and lawyers."

By February 1974 the national boycott of Gallo was in full swing, and in California UFW supporters had mobilized picket lines in front of Gallo distributorships, as well as major retail liquor outlets and grocery stores. Ministers, priests, liberal politicians, celebrities, and college students all voiced their support of Chavez and their opposition to Gallo. While Ernest insisted publicly that the boycott had no real effect on the winery, Gallo's national sales slipped by 7 percent in 1974. Ernest and his executives and legal experts focused on devising strategies to combat the boycott. Meanwhile they devoted less attention to developing new products and marketing strategies. Almaden was gaining a larger share of sales while Gallo crusaded against Chavez both in court and in the press.

Nevertheless, the boycott and demonstrations continued (the arrests only sparked more sympathy) and Gallo sales continued to fall, even by as much as 30 percent in certain areas and among specific consumer groups. College students particularly supported the boycott, and since they had been the major consumers of Gallo's "pop" or beverage wines, the winery saw a dramatic decline in these high-profit sales. "That's when Ernest organized a special group of his salesmen," recalled a former Gallo sales trainer. "These were trainees out of Los Angeles who were closest in age to the students. They were assigned to visit college campuses to explain the Gallo position and urge students not to boycott our wine."

Students were hardly convinced, more because of the "unhip," conservative appearance of Gallo salesmen than because of understanding the dispute. Gallo representatives on campuses were as unwelcome as Marine recruiters. During the 1974 graduation ceremonies, UC Berkeley students held a public "trial" and convicted Frank Fitzsimmons and Ernest and Julio Gallo of "crimes against the people."

In his effort to explain his actions, Ernest also directed his regional and district sales managers to appear at liquor store demonstrations to talk to the media.

"Ernest wanted a daily report on the demonstrations, so every day we went down to those picket lines," recalled Paul Merrigan, whose region included some of the most heavily picketed stores in southern

California. "I thought it might be helpful to try to reason with the reporters who were usually there, and I had written memos to Ernest about this. The amount of rhetoric and hype on both sides was unbelievable. The winery had certainly screwed up, but I also felt that the press was mindlessly sympathetic to Chavez and that some of the winery's complaints about the hiring hall and the ineptitude of local UFW organizers were justified. Still, I don't think anyone realized at that point that there were only about 150 permanent, maybe 500 harvest vineyard workers, involved. People just assumed that Gallo hired more vineyard workers than anyone else. A lot of the bad stuff like the rock throwing and even shootings in places like Coachella were attributed to Gallo. That, of course, spurred the boycott against Ernest and Julio, especially in southern California. Grapes, whether they were wine or table, became synonymous with Gallo, and Ernest became the target for everyone's antagonism. Of course, it didn't help when Ernest went on 60 *Minutes* and looked like the complete villain."

According to Merrigan, when Ernest was interviewed by Mike Wallace, he squinted and resorted to his usual habit of responding to questions with abrupt, rhetorical questions. He refused to explain why workers had been evicted from their homes, insisting that the workers themselves had chosen the Teamsters. Flaring indignantly when reminded that the only workers who voted were strikebreakers, Ernest was perceived as shifty and dishonest. "He came across as the heartless owner of a big, impersonal, uncaring corporation that was eager to enslave the poor Mexican-American migrant workers," added Merrigan. "Gallo became to the farm workers' struggle what Dow Chemical was to the antiwar movement."

The man who had insisted on secrecy now began to grant interviews to print and television reporters in an attempt to win public support for Gallo's position. The winery's advertising budget was doubled, and full-page advertisements stating "the Gallo side of the story" and denying UFW charges appeared in newspapers and magazines across the country.

Gallo distributors were also expected to lend a hand in presenting the winery's side of the dispute. Ernest assigned Angelo (Buff) Bufalino, who had been the head of the Gallo distributorship in Los Angeles since 1959, to lead the national public relations effort. Bufalino had been an Ernest loyalist ever since he joined the company as a salesman in 1952. As Bufalino confirmed, "Ernest has always treated me like family." But when Bufalino became involved in the Gallo publicity campaign during the Chavez dispute, winery colleagues wondered if Ernest was also putting Bufalino's family connections to good use.

Bufalino was the son of Italian immigrants in Pennsylvania and a cousin and good friend of William (Bill) Bufalino, the Teamsters' chief counsel and confidant of Jimmy Hoffa, who had acquired the reputation of "a skillful lawyer who specialized in mob work." (William Bufalino was also a cousin of Russell Bufalino, usually identified as "the northeastern Pennsylvania Mafia boss.") Angelo Bufalino openly acknowledged his relationship to his cousin Bill: "We were very close until his death in 1991, more like brothers than cousins. In fact, he was the godfather of one of my daughters." According to Paul Merrigan and others, winery sales managers speculated that since Gallo needed more forceful efforts and new strategies from the Teamsters to help combat the boycott, Buff might have taken the requests directly to Bill at the top. Bufalino, however, insisted that his trips to Washington, D.C., which several district sales managers noticed during this period, were Gallo publicity junkets to the East Coast and had nothing to do with consulting his cousin on the winery's behalf. "Bill was part of the International Teamsters Union, and had nothing to do with what was a West Coast dispute," he added.

Since he seemed to be making no headway with the media or a national audience, Ernest launched a new, more professional public relations campaign. Walter Bregman, formerly with the Norman B. Craig Agency, had come to the winery to head the in-house advertising program. Now he was reassigned to the anti-Chavez team. Soon, whenever a statement by Chavez was published, Bregman, identified as a winery vice-president, followed with a letter to dispute the UFW position.

Ernest also hired a press spokesman to work under Bregman. A New Yorker like Bregman, Dan Solomon had worked at NBC before becoming a public relations advisor to the California Canners and Growers. When he moved to the winery in 1974, his first assignment was to introduce the new Gallo varietal wines. But then he was asked to join Bregman in issuing press statements and writing open letters to refute UFW allegations and counteract the Gallo boycott.

The public wasn't persuaded, so Ernest turned to legal action and had his lawyers file numerous lawsuits against demonstrations in front of liquor and grocery stores. As he explained in an interview: "We believe we have turned the other cheek too long. . . . This has subjected us to vilification and character assassination." His remarks were perceived as self-serving and insensitive, especially when he went on to claim that the boycott had not affected his latest project, Gallo's premium varietals, sold, he added, at a lower price than varietals of any of his competitors. But his pride in his product backfired. Consumers reasoned that Ernest could afford to keep the prices of his best wines low only because he was profiting from poorly paid vineyard workers.

When these efforts didn't put an end to negative publicity and declining sales, Ernest went back to the Teamsters. The Teamsters then found another way to hamper the Gallo boycott. They could intimidate those stores that had removed Gallo from their shelves for fear of losing UFW-sympathetic customers. The Teamsters had truck drivers, delivery men, warehouse employees, a squad of union members who could impede the delivery of products from other companies. With its power, the union could exert more influence by threatening nondelivery of other consumer goods, thereby forcing retailers to return Gallo to their shelves.

According to Paul Merrigan, the Teamsters went even farther in one instance. A small chain of grocery stores in the Ventura area of southern California had stopped selling Gallo products. Its owner was Hispanic, as were most of his customers, and since they were enthusiastic supporters of Chavez, he pulled Gallo off his shelves and refused to take any deliveries from the Gallo distributor. In this territory and in these stores particularly, Gallo had lost a great deal of business. Ernest was aware of the decline and phoned Paul Merrigan every day to find out where the picketing was concentrated and what the daily sales reports were. Merrigan told him that the successful boycott at this chain of grocery stores was having a noticeable effect.

As Merrigan recalled, one morning Ken Bertsch phoned him. "We can get some help on this from the Teamsters," Bertsch said. "I want to you to go see them."

Merrigan set up a meeting with a Teamsters official. When Merrigan was ushered into the Teamsters' regional office, the heavyset man remained seated, his feet on his desk. He gestured to Merrigan to take the chair in front of him.

"So you guys are having trouble in my district, huh?" he growled out of the side of his mouth. "What's your biggest problem?"

"There's one chain of stores where we usually do about 20 percent of our base volume," Merrigan explained. "The owner has removed all Gallo products from his shelves, and because of the boycott he won't let us back in."

"Oh, yeah, I know him," the official said as he picked up the phone and dialed. When he heard an answer from the other end, he shouted his name and his title into the phone.

"Yeah, that's right, from the Teamsters," he repeated. "Now listen here. You know those nice new trucks you got? How'd ya like a pickaxe through the grill of 'em tonight?" He paused, then: "Okay, so you get that goddamn Gallo back on your shelves, or you're gonna be real sorry."

Merrigan was astonished by the phone call. But the threat worked —within a day Gallo was back in this chain of stores. Merrigan could see how effective the Teamsters could be when called upon for help. Besides, he said, he would never forget leaning back in his chair and looking up at the ceiling as the Teamsters officer made the phone call. Above the desk was a large hole in the ceiling. When the man hung up the phone, he noticed Merrigan staring upward. Without a word, he reached into his desk drawer and pulled out a gun. He aimed it at the ceiling and mock-fired the weapon to show how he had shot out the plaster.

"With some people you just have to make a point," he said with a laugh.

Whenever Gallo won an injunction against demonstrations at distributorships and retail stores, the UFW would appeal. Chavez's lawyers soon began to win when higher judges ruled that the local injunctions violated demonstrators' First Amendment rights. Then not only did UFW lawyers file several class action suits against the Teamsters and Gallo (the major one in January 1975 was a $225 million federal antitrust suit), but they also demanded free television ads under the Federal Communications Commission's fairness doctrine. With Gallo spending millions on commercials, they reasoned they should have equal time.

When that gambit wasn't successful, the UFW filed complaints with the Federal Trade Commission, charging that the Gallo name had been removed from several winery products in order to fool consumers, brands such as André, Boone's Farm, Carlo Rossi, Paisano, Ripple, Thunderbird, Twister, and Tyrolia, which were made by Gallo but did not bear the family name. Indeed, Ernest had long ago chosen not to assign "Gallo" to his lower-tier, proprietary products, not as a result of the boycott but in order to market multiple brands and give the appearance that these were not Gallo products. The FTC agreed that the winery hadn't suddenly adopted this strategy to trick consumers. Still the complaint benefited the UFW; consumers now were alerted that wine labeled as "produced and bottled in Modesto, California" was a Gallo product to be boycotted.

Al Fenderson and Joey, however, devised a new advertising campaign to undermine the boycott. Since Gallo sales among Hispanics had declined dramatically, they created a television commercial to suggest that Gallo's "Spanish wine," called Madria, Madria Sangria, was not a Gallo product. They enlisted Ofelia, Joey's wife, who with her Spanish accent could sound convincing when she spoke about her "family" as winemakers. She was coached to say, "My hosband and my oncle make Madria, Madria Sangria in the Spanish tradition." The television commercials were aired nationally. The UFW immediately filed suit against Gallo, and the FTC initiated an investigation. The winery pulled the commercial, however, and the investigation was apparently discontinued.

During the summer of 1973, the UFW had lost 95 percent of its contracts with grape growers without much attention paid by the public. By the end of 1974, however, the boycott against Gallo had revived enough popular support for Chavez that Fred Ross, who headed the northern California boycott operation, proposed a massive demonstration against the winery in early 1975. The UFW's original march on Sacramento in 1966 had brought out thousands of sympathizers, and media coverage had drawn national attention to Chavez's cause; Ross hoped that a march on the Gallo "temple" in Modesto would do the same.

On February 22, 1975, when the march on Modesto began with a rally in San Francisco's Union Square, a large banner was unfurled across three windows of the St. Francis Hotel: "Gallo's 500 Union Farm Workers Best Paid in U.S. Marching Wrong Way, Cesar?" The winery was responsible, of course, but Chavez pointed out that Ernest Gallo could afford to rent three rooms in an expensive hotel just to unfurl a banner for ten minutes, "while our striking workers have had nowhere to live for the past two years."

Marchers walked to Modesto from San Francisco, Stockton, and Fresno, and on Saturday, March 1, they converged more than ten thousand strong in front of the Gallo Winery entrance on Yosemite Avenue. Ernest and Julio did not make an appearance, although it was rumored that Ernest was in the winery (he later held a press conference in a downtown Modesto restaurant). Another gigantic banner hung down one side of the winery's operations building, the only Gallo structure visible from the street: "Gallo asks UFW to support NLRA-type law in Sacramento to guarantee farm workers rights."

Having heard that Ernest was in the winery, Chavez addressed him directly: "Mr. Gallo, give the workers the right to vote. Let them decide for themselves who should represent them. . . . If you let the workers vote, we pledge ourselves that if we lose, we will call off the boycott and they can live happily ever after." He had the crowd cheering when he announced that Gallo had increased its advertising budget from $6.5 million to $13.5 million annually but that sources inside Gallo estimated that sales had dropped by 30 percent since the beginning of the boycott. (This figure was accurate only in specific areas, not nationally, according to Gallo salesmen.)

Several months later, the California legislature passed a bill that called for supervised elections in the fall of 1975 so that farm workers could fairly choose their union. It also detailed rights of farm workers that met with UFW approval: the right to a primary boycott, the right to secret elections, and the right of striking workers to vote in these elections. It prohibited employers from firing employees who declared for one union or another and, particularly, from telling employees to vote for the Teamsters or any union or risk termination. The state Agricultural Labor Relations Board (ALRB) was established to oversee the elections.

But neither the legislation nor the September 11 vote at Ernest and Julio's Livingston vineyards quelled the battle. The Teamsters nominally won by a margin of 223 to 131, although 198 additional votes for the UFW were challenged by the Teamsters, who claimed that they were not actual employees; the UFW asserted that these were striking Gallo workers whose voting rights were protected under Governor Brown's legislation.

After its investigation, the ALRB issued a complaint alleging unfair labor practices, including "multiple instances of surveillance," not only against the winery but against Joe as well. At both Ernest's and Joe's vineyards, the Teamsters and the UFW had been given access to field hands. But because of the allegations that winery officials were also on hand taking photographs of workers, the board set aside the election results.

The dispute remained in the court for three more years. On March 10, 1977, Fitzsimmons and Chavez announced that they would both drop jurisdictional disputes over any farm where the union elections were certified by the ALRB. Conspicuous among those farms where the dispute was not settled were Ernest and Julio's and Joe's vineyards. But the Teamsters then withdrew from their campaign and agreed not to compete with the UFW in organizing farm workers. Chavez seemed content to allow the courts to decide the outcome of the Livingston election, and gradually the Gallo boycott faded away until on February 1, 1978, Chavez formally declared its termination.

On December 9, 1978, ALRB Judge David Nevins announced the board's finding that Gallo had engaged in unfair labor practices during its union election in 1975. According to his statement, evidence showed that "Gallo had illegally supported the Teamsters Union, had harassed UFW organizers, had used surveillance and security guards to intimidate workers talking with UFW organizers, had broken up a major UFW meeting, and fired two UFW sympathizers." Rather than rule on the challenged workers' votes, he ordered a new election.

Gallo disputed these findings and appealed, and another two and a half years went by before the Agricultural Labor Relations Board reaffirmed the decision and ruled 3–0 that the 1975 election should be set aside because "Gallo's conduct reasonably tended to deprive employees of a free choice and thereby tended to affect the outcome of the election."

But by then nobody seemed to care. Chavez and the UFW had entered a quieter phase, and public attention and media coverage had waned.

At the same time that Ernest was countering the negative publicity with public statements and extensive advertising, he applied even more pressure on his independent distributors to increase their sales. He was convinced that Gallo methods could overcome any boycott if his men just worked harder and the independent distributors gave more attention to Gallo products, even hiring more Gallo salesmen if necessary.

Ernest remained sure that the winery's success depended on its dominance of distributors, "the middle man" between the producer and the retail buyer in the three-tier wine distribution structure. The most obvious solution was to acquire more distributorships. They would be owned by family members or Gallo executives and would have Gallo loyalty. Their financial affairs would be managed by the winery, and they would be staffed by winery-trained personnel, who would implement all of Gallo's merchandising programs.

Another technique was to continue to convince independent distributorships to hire more Gallo salesmen and to demand a greater compliance with the winery's recommended programs, even persuade these distributors that they couldn't adequately represent Gallo brands if they were handling other wineries' products. Thus, during the 1970s, Ernest and Witter flung the winery's net wider, opening up more markets, enlisting additional wholesale houses in the Gallo cause and acquiring more distributorships through separate but winery-related corporations.

The decline in sales prompted by Chavez's boycott came just at the time when the winery was introducing its first varietals, and the program to move these Gallo wines onto fine wine shelves was as intense as any sales and marketing campaign in the winery's history. It required the cooperation of wholesalers, but among the winery's close to five hundred distributors, there were many who retained complete independence.

In the late 1960s, Ernest, Witter, and Bertsch had reorganized the sales system into two separate winery sales teams, Gallo Sales and Vintage Sales. Gallo Sales teams handled only Gallo-labeled merchandise, such as the Gourmet Trio and the varietals, those wines that Ernest and Julio endorsed with the Gallo name. Vintage Sales teams handled everything else—the proprietary brands and second-tier generics. Except for the smallest wholesale houses, distributors were required to have as many winery salesmen as needed to implement this two-pronged approach.

If a distributor's sales were unsatisfactory, if the wholesaler refused either to take on more Gallo salesmen or hire a Gallo-selected manager or engage in designated activities to raise sales, the winery could cancel its contract (which allowed for termination with a thirty-day notice) and move to another distributorship. In the fevered pitch of the mid-1970s campaign, Gallo executives went much farther than they had ever dared to insist on their demands.

"It wasn't subtle at all," recalled one former regional sales manager. "Usually it started with the winery telling the distributor either to add more Gallo salesmen or expand his warehouse space and in return he would be given credit extensions—say sixty days instead of thirty days

—so he could sell his inventory twice before having to pay the winery. Then, if Gallo was unhappy, a letter would go out from the winery, usually coinciding with a crisis in the man's life, like a divorce, or a death, or an automobile accident, or tax problems, and the distributor was informed that his credit had been reduced to fifteen days, so 'as of this date, you owe us x dollars payable immediately.' Some guys went home and shot themselves. One California beer distributor, who had taken on Gallo and then ruined his business by being forced to build a new warehouse and to hire more Gallo salesmen, did just that when Ken Bertsch told him to pay up his bill; others sold their distributorships to Midcal Aluminum's Valley Vintners chain, which was usually what they were after in the first place."

Yet during the mid-1970s, in the face of the increased pressure of the UFW boycott, enough independent distributors complained about Gallo's practices to the Federal Trade Commission that the FTC undertook an official investigation of the winery's alleged intrusion into the distributors' business and alleged illegal practices of its sales force.

With the FTC investigation under way, Ken Bertsch took on a new task. "Oh, God, here comes Ken the Torch," sales managers would shout when Bertsch appeared in their offices.

"The winery couldn't risk telling its employees in writing what records they were supposed to get rid of," said another former sales manager who had several visits from Bertsch in his office at the Los Angeles sales headquarters. "Instead Ken just marched in and rifled our files. Then he burned the papers and reports either in a wastebasket or he took them outside to the parking lot and set bonfires in the dumpster."

Later, according to another manager, Bertsch upgraded his technique—"he carried a portable paper shredder with him."

Whether Ernest knew about Bertsch's actions was unclear, but the destruction of Gallo records and files continued for several months. Nevertheless, the Federal Trade Commission gathered enough evidence to draft a preliminary complaint, a copy of which it sent to the winery. An outside lawyer, Elliot S. Kaplan of the Minneapolis law firm Robins, Davis & Lyons, was hired to aid the winery's legal division in its defense. But eventually Gallo decided to settle the conflict and signed a consent order prepared by the Federal Trade Commission with the added proviso that this did "not constitute an admission by respondent that the law has been violated as alleged in such complaint."

Although the FTC acknowledged that the winery had ceased many of its alleged illegal activities in 1970, it still charged that Gallo "has used its dominant position, size and power to lessen, hinder or restrain competition in the sale and distribution of wines in the United States by engaging in various unfair acts, practices and methods of competition, including, but not limited to, the establishment and maintenance of exclusionary marketing policies and their enforcement through coercion of distributors." Among those practices specifically banned by the consent order were requiring financial statements from wholesalers, the guarantee of all or any part of any loan for a wholesaler, or the assuming of all or any capital expenses of the wholesaler, and the punishing of any wholesaler for dealing in wines of other companies. Finally, it prohibited the winery's "reciprocal" contract condition that allowed Gallo to change prices for merchandise already in distributorship warehouses according to prices that the winery charged in other states. (If prices came down elsewhere, a wholesale house was supposed to have the bill for its Gallo inventory reduced. But according to Paul Merrigan, the winery used this "reciprocal" clause in its contract against uncooperative distributors to raise their outstanding bill by citing the highest prices for Gallo brands, most often those in Alaska.)

The FTC further stipulated that for the next ten years the winery had to allow FTC investigators monthly inspections of its correspondence and transactions with distributors. The word went out to the Gallo sales executives: Put nothing in writing. If that was impossible, keep nothing in the file longer than thirty days. And according to Merrigan and others, just to make sure, Ken Bertsch continued to check everyone's files and either torch or shred anything older than thirty days.

"We couldn't even keep any personal things like mementos from the years we had worked for the winery," said a former sales manager. "Everything had to go, and you were always filling the winery's new burn bags at the end of the day."

"It was just a terrible way to run a business," recalled Paul Merrigan. "At the same time we had this tremendous expansion, this huge sales push for the varietals, and suddenly we were forbidden to keep any records. I'm sure a lot of the winery's history has gone up in flames just because they became so worried about any outsider—and especially someone from the government—seeing documents. And things became even more problematic after the FTC's consent order, because the winery's executive structure then changed."

At the time of the FTC investigation, Dick Witter had become increasingly restless. As Gallo employees recalled, not only was he fed up with having to deal with David and Joey—as Amelia sometimes blurted, "He just can't get along with the boys." But also the changes required by the FTC order made it difficult to run the sales programs with his former effectiveness. Further, there was a limit to how far he could go in the winery, and it seemed time to move on. Ernest was upset by the prospect of losing him, and he took Witter and his wife Bonnie on a round-the-world tour to try to convince him to stay or to transfer into Gallo's international sales division. But to no avail, and Witter made plans for a career change.

"I'm sure Dick got a very nice golden parachute when he left," said Bernie Weiner, who was a personnel consultant to the winery at the time. "He remained loyal to Ernest and never went to work for another winery, even though plenty of competitors wanted him. He remained a consultant to Ernest, and for a while Ernest so hoped that Dick would return that he kept his office vacant and didn't find anyone to take his place in his inner circle."

Witter's departure left more than a vacant office; it threw Gallo's executive structure into disarray. Joey assumed more responsibility and more authority, but according to Gallo sales managers, instead of rising to the occasion, he undermined what had been the unique strength of his father's organization. Compared to other corporations, Gallo's line of command had been extraordinarily simple and efficient —precisely because of Ernest's style of leadership, employees said. Because Ernest kept such close watch on all departments, employees could go directly to the top with problems, questions, or ideas, either to Witter, Bertsch, Fenderson, or Ernest himself. They knew that rather than meander through a maze of middle management bureaucracy, they would receive an immediate direct response, either in person or in overnight memos from "MiCom," the winery's "Modesto Intercom" label indicating its upper echelon origins.

But Joey now expanded his circle of loyalists. What had been a direct route to the top was detoured through Joey and his ally, Peter Conway, a marketing executive imported from Procter & Gamble by his old friend Walter Bregman. Ernest seemed to sanction the change in the organization, even putting Conway in charge of Vintage sales and marketing, and later moving him up to vice-president of marketing.

A number of the winery's older executives felt burdened by having to deal with Joey and his followers to get their messages through to Ernest. Since they had been the ones who had trained Joey and to whom Ernest had compared his son unfavorably, Joey seemed to have lingering resentment. Ernest was ill, then recuperating from an operation during some of these months, according to winery employees. When he was back at work, he often seemed distracted, and perhaps as a result of the FTC decision, perhaps because of Chavez's boycott, he seemed to spend as much time in the legal department as he did in sales and marketing meetings.

Finally, his senior and loyal sales executives, the managers who had been the core of his distributorship system, men like George Frank on the East Coast, Frank Zavell in the Midwest, and Paul Merrigan on the West Coast, found it frustrating to work with Joey and what many described as his "groupthink."

"Joey and his circle perceived us as threats to them," said Merrigan, "and it was becoming more and more difficult to get our jobs done. Finally I decided to resign and I went to see Ernest. He didn't want me to leave, and we talked about the difficulty with Joey and his cohorts. Ernest said that he understood that Joey had to hire his own men and build up his own team. He suggested that I be patient, that there were other things I could do for the company while the dust settled. But at that point I was burnt out with Gallo—Chavez and the FTC and the winery's expansion combined, those years had been just too hectic and chaotic."

When George Frank resigned, he, like Witter, remained a consultant to the winery—he was one of the few salespeople whose understanding of the wine market Ernest trusted as much as his own. Other people who left, however, were "strongly advised" by Ken Bertsch to seek jobs outside the wine industry. Not at all confident that these men would act in the winery's best interests when employed by another winery, Gallo did not want them in any position where their knowledge of its sales and marketing programs would aid a competitor. (Several of them refused to obey the order and then were made aware of the winery's power when they had the impression, sometimes confirmed by prospective employers or distributors, that they were "blacklisted" in the wine industry after Gallo's intervention.)

During the mid-1970s, Gallo sales leveled off and remained at $850 million with no increase. Employees said they felt a lack of creative thinking and progressive ideas in the company—what had before given Gallo its dynamic and forward-looking quality. They had the distinct feeling that the winery was beginning to lose its edge on other wineries. But instead of remedying problems, Ernest seemed preoccupied with a new concern.

Ernest had insisted that Chavez's boycott and demonstrations hadn't bothered either the winery or the family. In June 1975, however, Julio was to receive the American Society of Enologists Merit Award at their annual meeting at the St. Francis Hotel in San Francisco. Finally earning recognition for his contributions to the wine industry eleven years after Ernest had won the same prestigious award, Julio chose not to attend the ceremony. He had been advised that UFW demonstrators would turn out in droves and despite having a bodyguard assigned to escort him inside, he decided to stay home in Modesto while the demonstrators burned him and Ernest in effigy.

Hostility prompted by his brother's actions was extended to Julio even though he insisted that he had always treated his workers well—for example, eliminating "stoop" labor by having his engineers develop a machine that allowed grape pickers to sit in padded seats on a motorized platform that moved slowly through the rows of vines. (He was opposed to mechanical harvesters because he felt that they harmed the grapes; the new machine, he concluded, would save the grapes as well as workers' backs.)

Nevertheless, while he wasn't actively involved in the dispute with Chavez (although his son Bob had earlier claimed to be a friend and supporter of Chavez), Julio became embroiled in conflicts of his own when grape growers complained that he and his staff indiscriminately downgraded their harvests and paid less than agreed-upon prices per ton.

"Julio and his grower relations people really put us through it every year," said one grape grower. "We had a floor price for varietals, but if Julio decided that our grapes didn't look right, he'd assign them to the Carlo Rossi program or to their cheaper wines. This downgrading had very little to do with scientific evaluation—it was usually something arbitrary, like the way the light hit the grapes. But a lot of us suspected that downgrading went on when the winery found it had too large a supply of a certain kind of grape. Then Ernest and Julio didn't want to pay the face value of our contracts, and downgrading was the loophole to let them out of it."

Later a few growers would file formal grievances with the State

Department of Agriculture in which they alleged that "arbitrary downgrading" had continued since 1977. The state ruled for Gallo, since the growers had no written contracts that listed standards to be met, but Julio and his grower relations department were also directed to include such standards in future contracts in order to avoid such complaints. State inspectors, to be paid by Gallo, would also supervise the grading procedure when grapes were delivered to the winery. (Despite these conflicts and continued complaints from growers, most feel they have no choice but to sell to the winery since in 1991 it bought 48 percent of the state's annual wine grape harvest.)

As if to counter the negatives in the 1970s, Ernest and Julio stepped up their charity work. In April 1976 Julio bought the McHenry Mansion in Modesto for $150,000 and gave the Victorian landmark to the city to be restored as a museum. A year later Ernest made his first public announcement of a charity donation, a $400,000 gift to finance the construction of a medical education building at Modesto's Memorial Hospital North. He conceded that this was the first grant that the Ernest Gallo Foundation had ever publicized, but declined to name other recipients of Gallo contributions.

But nonprofit foundations are required to file annual financial statements with the state. Records showed that Ernest and Julio had contributed large sums to Fresno State for its viticulture and oenology programs (as well as for a new football stadium) and to the University of California at Davis to fund viticulture and oenology research and to endow the Maynard A. Amerine Professorship. (Amerine had been a classmate of Julio's at Modesto High School and had been chairman of the department over the years, as well as a winery consultant.) Ernest also gave $210,000 in 1975, and $100,000 in 1976 to Stanford University Medical School and $10,000 to Notre Dame and $7,000 to the Stanford University Business School in 1976.

Around the time of the UFW activity at Gallo, Ernest also took a greater interest in politics. One of the politicians whose career Ernest followed was Alan Cranston, and in 1968 Ernest supported his successful campaign for senator. In ensuing years the Gallos contributed large amounts of money to him by parceling out contributions under individual family members' names. This way the Gallos remained within the limits imposed by new campaign contribution regulations.

In 1978, Senator Cranston lobbied for and guided through Congress a tax bill that later was called the Gallo Wine amendment. The Gallos had become concerned that in the event of Ernest's and Julio's

deaths, current estate tax laws that gave tax relief to family corporations with fewer than fifteen members would not apply to the Gallos
because of their many offspring. A tax amendment was drafted by
winery counsels Frank Brennan and Jon Shastid, working with the
Gallo's Washington, D.C., law firm (in which Robert Strauss, President Carter's trade representative, had been a partner before entering
government). The proposed amendment would extend the provisions
to the Gallo corporation (as of 1973, reorganized as a Delaware corporation called "Dry Creek") and allow Ernest's and Julio's more than
fifteen heirs to spread their payment of estate taxes over ten years.

Alan Cranston enlisted Representative Joe D. Waggoner of Louisiana, head of the House Ways and Means subcommittee that dealt
with estate taxes, to sponsor its passage.

The amendment wasn't designated by the Gallo name when it was
approved by Waggoner's subcommittee on May 19 and came before
the Ways and Means Committee on June 17, 1978—just as the House
was preparing to adjourn for the summer holiday. (Three committee
members were congressmen from California, and as they later confirmed, none of them had been told that this bill had been tailormade
for the Gallos.) The Treasury Department criticized the provision,
not for the Gallo connection but for the potential loss of revenue.
Cranston gave the bill a "timely assist," according to press reports,
when he sent his top legislative aide to appeal to Treasury to withdraw
its opposition. Successful there, he raced back to the Hill and announced the Treasury's change of position. Only twelve members of
the Ways and Means Committee were present, and although nineteen were needed for a quorum, the bill was passed by a voice vote.
"Bells were ringing for a vote on the House floor," said one congressional aide, "and some members were walking toward the door when
the bill was approved."

When winery employees read about the passage of the amendment
in Congress, they recalled how they had been advised to handle legislative matters. "When we were lobbying politicians to help us in a
dry or a monopoly state," said a former Gallo sales manager, "the
plan was to have a politician introduce our bill just before the end of
a legislative session. Everybody would be in a rush to get home and
didn't want to sit around and debate. So we'd get our bill through just
under the wire, and that's exactly how the Gallo tax amendment was
passed."

The following October, Cranston used a similar strategy for passage by the Senate. At six in the evening, at the close of a rare Saturday session called to approve the entire tax legislation to be sent to President Carter for his signature, Cranston won approval of the amendment from only a handful of senators. The California senator did not inform his colleagues that the proposed tax bill rider was designed to provide "substantial benefits" to the Gallo family of California. Senators were then startled to hear Senator Bob Dole state that the provision "has been referred to as the Gallo Wine amendment." Congressional critics contended that the bill had been rushed through without adequate consideration. But Cranston continued to defend the measure, insisting that the amendment would benefit "all large, multi-generational families." He also denied that Ernest and Julio's $3,250 contribution to his reelection campaign had anything to do with his assisting the passage of this amendment with little or no discussion and without identifying the Gallos' interest in it.

The contribution from Ernest and Julio Gallo that had been listed in 1974 public records was small potatoes compared to the financial support that would be reported under individual names of other Gallo family members and executives over the years. For example, a two-year study by Citizen Action, a public interest group based in Washington, D.C., showed that the Gallos contributed more money to federal candidates in 1989–90 than any other American family and more than all but ninety-three of four thousand formal political action committees. Included in the $294,100 given in one year was what the study termed "the single biggest family payday," when on April 13, 1989, Cranston received twenty checks, each for $1,000, from ten Gallo family members ($2,000 being the limit for campaign contributions from individuals). Among the largest contributions from family members were those from Aileen and Amelia, listed as "housewives," who also contributed large sums to the Democratic party and its "get-out-the-vote" campaign in California led by Cranston's son Kim.

(Political analysts considered Kim Cranston's "get-out-the-vote" campaign to be a major factor in the senator's narrow victory in his last reelection. Charles Keating, Jr., had given Kim's group a check for $500,000 in addition to his hefty contributions to the senator's campaign. As the Keating–Lincoln Savings & Loan scandal would later suggest, Cranston did seem willing to exert his influence on behalf of those who contributed heavily to his campaigns, although he continues to deny any wrongdoing in this regard.)

With the passage of the Gallo Wine amendment in 1978, Ernest and Julio not only won financial advantages, but also, when the news of it broke, were perceived as extraordinarily influential. Their intimidation factor trebled. "Don't mess with the Gallos" became the motto in the Central Valley. "They're so powerful they can even get a tax law written for them."

But once again, Ernest and Julio couldn't control fate. In another tragic turn of fortune, their theoretical concern about estate taxes became a practical matter only three weeks later. On November 1, 1978, Mark Gallo, Bob and Marie Gallo's sixteen-year-old son, died. A junior at the Catholic High School, Mark was a popular, athletic boy, when he suddenly fell ill with a high fever and muscle spasms. He was flown to the Stanford University Hospital where he was diagnosed with a rare muscle disease, but specialists there couldn't save him.

Almost immediately Mark's death provoked a conflict with the IRS. Bob had been named executor of his son's estate, but as usual the winery's financial department handled his business affairs. The estate tax returns were filed promptly, and included in the estate were Mark's 1,178 shares of Dry Creek Corporation Class J (for Julio) common shares. The winery accountants assessed their value at $290 per share, $341,620 total, and Bob paid a tax of $77,583 on the holdings. The government responded with a notice of a $347,871 deficiency, having valued the stock at $1,043 per share for a total value of $1,228, 654.

The ensuing tax-court case also confirmed that the Gallo dispute with the UFW and the 1976 FTC Consent Order had hurt the winery during the mid-1970s. Indeed, the winery's experts justified their lower stock valuation by insisting that Gallo "had not kept pace with the industry" and that "for the first time in its history, [it had] confronted effective marketing competition," because "distributors that had previously sold only Gallo wines began to sell wines of competitors as well."

The winery's experts conceded that Gallo's introduction of varietal wines had been hindered by its reputation "as a producer of inexpensive and lower quality wines." Adding that the "image problem impeded attempts by Gallo to compete with the popular price producers in the table wine market," Gallo informed the court that all winery products introduced between 1972 and 1978 were "failures." Although the winery planned to improve and reintroduce its line of varietal table wines, the experts advised the court that Gallo "was pessimistic concerning the success of the line" because of its surveys, which confirmed the winery's continuing image problem among consumers.

Ernest rarely tolerated disparaging remarks about Gallo and its poor image. In the tax case, however, he apparently accepted these negative assessments. The court, too, was convinced, since in 1985 it finally ruled against the IRS and in favor of the lower valuation of the winery's Dry Creek stock.

One day in 1979, Ernest read an article in the business section of the *San Francisco Chronicle* announcing that Consolidated Foods had bought the Gallo Salame Company. Consolidated Foods was a large food conglomerate, better known to the public as Sara Lee. Ernest had in fact met the CEO of the company, one Nathan Cummings, and now he considered it a possibility that Cummings had bought the salami company only to acquire the Gallo name and trademark.

For many years the legal department had been instructed to "challenge any use of the 'Gallo' name that came to their attention." After the Charles and Mary Gallo wine case in Ohio, the winery's lawyers had made official complaints against various companies using the Gallo name on their products—from coffee to beer to lingerie. Usually these were foreign firms, or the companies were so small that they backed down when the legal guns took aim. Ernest, however, had made one exception to his legal instructions.

As he later recalled, in the mid-1960s he had been shopping in Molinari's delicatessen, one of his frequent stops during his visits to San Francisco's North Beach. There he had spotted a package of dry Italian salami with a label featuring a cable car in red and green and in large black print the name GALLO.

What's this? sputtered Ernest, rushing up to the man behind the counter. *Where did you get it?*

It's from a local salami factory, the man told him. *An Italian family makes it.*

Ernest bought a package of Gallo Salame and sampled it. He said he didn't like it as well as Molinari's own salami, but also mentioned to Julio that a company in North Beach was making and selling "Gallo Salame." Neither brother seemed unduly concerned, assuming that it was "a small Italian family's local business." The "small family business" had a large factory with a visible sign across the street from

Ernie's, the well-known restaurant in North Beach where both brothers sometimes dined. Moreover, as Julio later confirmed, Aileen had brought home a package of Gallo Salame from a Modesto supermarket—the company obviously distributed beyond North Beach. Yet neither Ernest nor Julio had raised any objections.

Later Ernest would insist that he hadn't objected to the name at the time because "it was limited to the North Beach, people in that neighborhood [who] know that it is made by this Italian living there. I don't like going after somebody of Italian extraction trying to make a living." (The Gabiatti family had founded and owned the company; the Gallo name had been chosen simply because it was a common Italian name.)

After reading the business article, Ernest was adamant about suing Gallo Salame for trademark infringement. It was not only a question of confusion, he asserted, it was a ploy by Cummings to take over the Gallo name. To underscore his suspicions, Ernest explained that he had met Cummings in Greece when they had both been on cruises and had been introduced by a mutual friend, Gallo's Boston distributor John Pappas. Ernest recalled that he and Cummings had enjoyed each other's company and promised to get together once they returned from their vacations. Cummings invited Ernest to visit him in New York "to see his collection of Asian art."

When Ernest was next in New York, he accepted Cummings's invitation to come to his Waldorf Towers apartment. During the visit, Cummings casually asked if Ernest would ever sell the winery. As Ernest later described his response to the question, he seemed to have reacted like a naive young woman invited by a playboy to "come up and see my etchings." By his own account, he was upset and proclaimed in an angry voice that he would never, never sell. Cummings dropped the subject. But without realizing it, he fueled Ernest's suspicions by later remarking that he would like to see the Modesto winery. Although Cummings merely commented that he was "interested" in the wine business in general and wanted to observe the world's largest winery, Ernest seemed convinced that the man was out to raid his business. During the next year Cummings made several attempts to schedule a California visit, but Ernest repeatedly put him off.

Then, remembering Ernest's interest in his art collection, Cummings inquired if Ernest would be interested in a trip to China that he was arranging. Ernest hedged, and the trip never came about. In retrospect, Ernest insisted that this was further proof of Cummings's ulterior motives. "After all, it was rather strange that a man in his position took such a great interest in me," he said by way of explaining his reasons for filing a trademark infringement suit against Gallo Salame after so many years. He still suspected that Cummings and Consolidated Foods had bought the salami company not only to acquire the Gallo name but to threaten or injure the winery.

But the winery's suit was problematic, since neither Ernest nor Julio had recorded any complaint about the Gallo Salame label for over twenty years. In fact, Gallo Salame had registered its federal trademark in 1968 without any objection from the winery. Nevertheless, Ernest still wanted to pursue the case. First he hired a battery of outside lawyers: Beverly Pattishall of Chicago's Pattishall, McAuliffe & Hofstetter; Elliot S. Kaplan of Robins, Zelle, Larson & Kaplan in Minneapolis (he had negotiated the winery's signing of the FTC Consent Order); Bruce L. Davis and William McKee from San Francisco's Orrick, Herrington & Sutcliffe; and finally James H. Barstow and Oliver Wanger of the Fresno firm McCormick, Barstow, Sheppard, Coyle & Wayte.

Frank Brennan was then kicked upstairs from general counsel to senior counsel, and Ernest hired Jack Owen, a young attorney from the San Francisco firm Owen, Wickersham & Erickson, to replace Brennan as general counsel and head of his legal department. William D. Henderson, another winery in-house counsel, also went to work on the complaint.

Owen's letters to Consolidated Foods went unheeded, and when neither Cummings nor Gabiatti, who remained the president of Gallo Salame, would yield their right to the trademark, the winery filed a lawsuit against them in Federal District Court for the Eastern District of California, located in Fresno. Judge Myron D. Crocker was assigned the case. Gallo Salame responded through their attorneys Stephen Bomse and Marie Fiala, of the San Francisco firm Heller, Ehrman, White & McAuliffe, and Nicholas Dibiaso, from Thomas, Snell, Jamison, Russell, Williamson & Asperger in Fresno.

From the beginning, Julio expressed his opposition to the lawsuit. He had no desire to become involved or to give a deposition, much less testify in court. But Ernest wouldn't drop the suit. Managers at the winery noticed how absorbed he had become with the case, how obsessed he was with proving that the Gallo name was synonymous with wine, and only wine. He began to sound as if he spent his time memorizing trademark law, and even at family dinners he held forth. In public Julio muttered his disapproval of the suit: Joe later recalled that at a family barbecue he had asked Julio why Ernest was so caught up in the case. "It's just bullshit, Joe," he heard Julio exclaim. "The whole thing is bullshit."

Joe supposed it was Ernest playing *l'avvocato* again, and the few times that Ernest mentioned Gallo Salame and spouted his feelings about Cummings, he found him so boring that he stopped listening. Independent and successful in his dairy and cattle business, Joe wasn't really interested in the details of the lawsuit. He did agree to the winery's request to have his deposition taken. Like his brothers, he had seen Gallo Salame in the stores for years, had even bought it and eaten it, but agreed that he had never heard any objections from anyone in the family before. Only later Joe would realize he should have been attentive to the details of the case and Ernest's motives for bringing the suit.

Meanwhile, because of Julio's objection to the suit and his dread of testifying, Oliver Wanger, the winery's Fresno attorney, petitioned the court to exempt him from testifying, citing a weak heart (he had suffered a mild heart attack a few years earlier) as well as other vaguely described "nervous" problems. Although the court received letters from Julio's physician as well as from a geriatric specialist, the other side disputed the severity of Julio's afflictions by describing the active daily schedule he routinely kept. Finally Judge Crocker ruled that Julio would be required to give testimony both in court and in depositions, but under a doctor's supervision and only for two hours a day with numerous breaks.

Each side filed and refiled and argued and counterargued for close to two years. The Gallo Salame lawyers were often frustrated by the winery's response to their discovery motions, by gaps in records and documents, and by what they asserted were "delay tactics." But finally, in June of 1981, Julio and Ernest were deposed.

For all Julio's apprehension, his deposition went easily. (At the last minute his attorneys waived having a doctor present.) Julio claimed to have only vague recollections of events in the winery's business history, having rarely been involved in the registration of trademarks or even the choice of labels for their wines. He could tell his questioners, for example, that Thunderbird was no longer made from white grapes but from apple or pear juice, but he had no idea when or why the Gallo name had been dropped from the Thunderbird label. He had never heard of any of the winery's lawsuits against other companies using the name Gallo, not even the Charles and Mary Gallo case in the 1940s, so he couldn't confirm what Ernest had done to protect the Gallo trademark.

Nevertheless, he did concede that his brother had remarked on Gallo Salame about fifteen, even twenty years before. No, Ernest hadn't been upset when he had seen the product then, Julio said. He had just explained that "some Italian in the North Beach area made it." And there had certainly been no mention of doing something about it, not until Ernest had arrived in Julio's office to announce that Consolidated Foods had bought the company. (Ernest had never before referred to Nathan Cummings or his alleged interest in buying the winery either, Julio added.)

Ernest was questioned at greater length, and once again he recited his version of family history to prove that the Gallo trade name had been in existence long before the salami company had chosen to use it. His father, he said, was in the wine business starting in either late 1906 or 1907 (he seemed to forget that 1909 was the official date listed in his trademark application), and he had remained in it until Prohibition, at which time he bought a vineyard. Then he shipped grapes, also under the Gallo name. When Prohibition was repealed, Ernest continued (once more forgetting his third brother's existence), "We spoke, my father and my brother and I, about going into the wine business." But when his father passed away, he said, "My brother and I inherited all of his property," and then they formed a "partnership" and called it "E. and J. Gallo Winery."

Ernest spent a great deal of time insisting on consumer "confusion" in the marketplace and that this diluted the winery's trademark. Several times he referred to salami as a less than "premium" product, while Gallo wine had spent millions in advertising to promote its "premium" wines. The continued assertions that salami in general was considered low class and Gallo Salame infinitely inferior to Gallo Wine finally provoked overt antagonism. Stephen Bomse, one of Gallo Salame's attorneys, now attacked the winery image.

Was Mr. Gallo aware of a disease known as alcoholism? Ernest at first hedged, then said that he thought it meant, "Some people can't tolerate alcohol." It was not a case of "drinking too much" or being "addicted" to alcohol, as far as he was concerned: It was more a chemical intolerance.

Then Bomse went for the jugular: "Have you ever heard the term 'wino'?"

"Yes, I have," Ernest replied angrily. "And I think that these are people who are uninformed, uneducated, who use that term. . . . I have nothing but contempt for anyone who uses that term."

Bomse ignored the remark. "Didn't the public associate Gallo Wine with winos?" he pressed.

Although Ernest disputed that the term was associated with any one winery, Bomse started to ask if the Gallo Winery had conducted a survey about this issue. Suddenly one of Ernest's attorneys interrupted, announcing that he had to leave to catch a plane. It was at least ten minutes before the scheduled 3:00 P.M. close of the session —agreed upon at noon because of the attorney's anticipated flight— and Bomse registered his strong objections. To him it seemed "absolutely transparent" that Ernest and his lawyers wanted to stop the deposition when he raised questions about the winery's negative image. Because of the attorney's departure and a continued angry exchange among the remaining attorneys, the subject was not pursued.

In fact, though, the court was not very interested in either the winery's previous use of the trade name and consumer confusion or the wine or salami's alleged negative images. As the case progressed, Judge Crocker focused on the problem of *laches*—under the law, failure to take any action for several years might bar the party from bringing a legal proceeding. The winery had expressed no objection to the Gallo Salame name, much less filed any legal action, for twenty years, which certainly raised this issue. Ernest's rationale that it was a small company, that he didn't like to interfere with an Italian family business, was hardly convincing, since the winery's legal staff had several times forced small companies, even Italian companies, to stop using the Gallo name. As Judge Crocker seemed to concentrate on Ernest and Julio's delay, it seemed possible that he might even rule that Gallo was barred from pursuing its complaint.

Ernest's response to the prospect of losing the case was to buy the trademark. As he later explained, "Because we had waited so long to bring this action, [we realized] we had better try and make some kind of arrangement." It was by now the spring of 1983, and his attorneys were ready to "make some kind of arrangement." The winery offered to purchase the trademark, then lease the trademark back to Gallo Salame "royalty free." Thus the Gallo Winery would acquire the trademark as its own without acquiring the business. Ernest had no intention of making salami; all he wanted was the legal basis for claiming that he owned the Gallo name.

Within the next few weeks the winery lawyers held several conference calls—Wanger in Fresno, Owen in Modesto, Kaplan in Minneapolis, Pattishall in Chicago. They needed to work out a settlement that covered all the legal requirements for buying a trademark. Granted Ernest simply wanted the name, but the purchase and the license had to show that the Gallo Winery would become the owner of the trademark and hence exert certain controls over the way the salami company ran its business as well as how it conducted quality control and organized its marketing and distributing.

Despite Ernest's anxiety, Consolidated Foods was more interested in the marketing of the popular salami than owning the name. Ernest's lawyers proposed that the company could run its own business, but with written rules for quality control, and could continue to use the Gallo name with certain restrictions applied to the label and limitations on its geographical distribution and its advertising. In return, Ernest agreed to pay $2 million for the trademark. The winery received no salami recipes, nor did it acquire distribution or sales records. The quality control condition would be taken care of by the winery's hiring a consultant who would make at most three factory inspections a year, scheduled in advance. Gallo Salame agreed to the offer. For $2 million, the lawsuit would disappear, and Ernest Gallo would own the Gallo Salame trademark.

The attorneys for the winery and Consolidated Foods informed Judge Crocker of their settlement, and he closed the case. At the request of the winery, he also sealed the documents and files of the lawsuit. Ernest's purchase of the Gallo Salame trademark was to remain hidden from outside scrutiny. When later asked to confirm that he "kept the whole arrangement secret," he responded, "All of our deals at the winery we try to keep private."

After nearly three years of litigation, in a few short weeks and by June 8, 1983, Ernest had achieved an expensive settlement. Only later would his decision to buy the trademark raise the question of a hidden agenda. Was the Gallo Salame trademark worth $2 million not for its own value but because it gave Ernest the basis for combating what he perceived as another threat? Had remarks at family gatherings as well as an invitation to a party on June 12 prompted him to sign a settlement less than a week before, just so he would have the ammunition with which to attack a new and potentially more powerful adversary?

PART THREE
THE FEUD

· ·

CHAPTER TEN

Joe and Mike Gallo had sent invitations to their open house and barbecue to the entire Gallo family as well as to winery executives, friends, neighbors, and media representatives. On June 12, 1983, nearly a hundred people gathered at Joe's Cottonwood Ranch on Highway 140 in Atwater for the festive occasion. Under a large tent set up in front of Joe's dairy, the guests enjoyed an abundance of food and wine—all the best Gallo varietals—to celebrate the official opening of the Joseph Gallo Cheese Company.

The cheese plant had been a year in the planning and construction. In 1982 Joe and Mike had decided that manufacturing cheese might solve their surplus milk and pricing problems. After touring cheese companies in Wisconsin and California, they felt encouraged to pursue the idea. They hired Gene Goetsch, an expert cheesemaker from Wisconsin, and built a modern plant with the most up-to-date equipment across from the dairy.

During that year Joe had often mentioned the progress of his cheese company at family get-togethers. Julio had been enthusiastic, but Ernest had shown little interest, or so it seemed. Only once had Amelia taken any notice. In the spring of 1983, Joe and Patricia had accompanied Ernest and Amelia to a dinner in San Francisco. They were chauffeured in Ernest's limousine, and on the way Joe was describing the final steps of completing the cheese plant and putting it into operation.

"What are you going to call your cheese?" Amelia asked.

"Joseph Gallo Cheese," replied Joe without hesitation.

"Why are you going to call it that?"

"Because it's my name," said Joe.

Amelia only nodded, as if this seemed as logical to her as it had seemed to Joe and Patricia and Mike when they had chosen the name. Ernest said nothing. In retrospect, Patricia would wonder if Ernest had told Amelia to ask the question. It was a technique that, she had noticed, the two had perfected over the years. Amelia would ask "in all innocence" for information that Ernest had a compelling need to know. But Ernest had made no comment—not then or even later when Joe sent him and Julio cheese from his plant's first production run in gift boxes labeled Joseph Gallo. Julio had not remarked on the name either.

Julio and Aileen were away and unable to come to the cheese plant opening that June, but midafternoon Ernest, Amelia, and David descended on the gathering in the winery's helicopter. Ernest said he could only stay for a few minutes—he was on his way to another appointment—so Joe first showed him around the cheese plant. As Joe recalled, he explained the process as he guided him from the pasteurization area into the cheesemaking room with its gleaming stainless steel equipment and on into the small refrigerated storage room. This storage room was only temporary, until they built a larger warehouse, Joe remarked, as he ushered Ernest through the narrow passageway between the floor-to-ceiling shelves packed with boxes, all labeled Joseph Gallo Cheese. Although Ernest would later have a different version of their conversation, Joe remembered this as a quick tour before they returned to the tent to mingle briefly with the other guests before Ernest's departure.

Joining his father and uncle, Mike thought he'd never seen his father as happy and proud as he was that day. Here was something his father had built himself, and Mike was sure that after all the years of trying to prove himself to his brother, Joe had impressed Ernest with his enterprise and accomplishment. Ernest seemed to suggest as much when he offered his congratulations before he and David boarded the waiting helicopter.

Later that afternoon, John Whiting, Joe's lawyer, was standing outside the tent. He was in an especially cheerful mood, having helped Joe with many of the legal arrangements that had to be made before the cheese plant went into production, from permits and state inspections to choosing the name for the cheese. He was talking to Jon

Shastid and Bill McKee, two of the winery's attorneys with whom Joe had been friends for several years. From above they heard the droning sound of a motor, then saw a small plane begin to circle the gathering, pulling a trail of letters.

A pilot who had cropdusted for Joe for nearly thirty years had decided to celebrate the cheese plant opening by flying over with the banner. He had attached the letters to spell out, "Good Luck, Joseph Gallo Cheese." But on his first takeoff, the "J" had been torn; he had landed to fix the banner, but with no more J's available in his supply of letters, he had resorted to a shorter message.

Whiting stared up at the plane as it continued to circle, the letters fluttering behind. "Good Luck, Gallo Cheese," the banner now read.

Whiting turned back to Shastid and McKee. "Well, there's a lawsuit, boys!" he said with a laugh.

The two other lawyers thought it was a good joke, too.

At the same time that Joe had begun to build his cheese plant and promote his product, Ernest and Julio again turned their attention to upgrading the Gallo image. Intensifying their efforts to move into cork-finished and vintage-dated varietals, they had completed an underground cellar and installed 650 imported oak casks for aging their Chardonnay. Julio and his son Bob had bought the Frei Brothers Ranch and Winery in Sonoma in 1977 and were now developing the two-thousand-acre site with varietal vineyards and planned to build a small winery there.

When "the New Gallo Program" didn't improve sales (now only one in four instead of one in three bottles of wine sold in the United States was a Gallo brand), Ernest blamed his advertising agency. Tired of Ernest's complaints, Young & Rubicam suddenly resigned the account (taking on United Vintners, Gallo's main competitor, as a client instead), and for over nine months Ernest looked for another agency. Noting that the winery had gone through fifteen agencies in the past twenty-five years, *Adweek* called Gallo "the least desirable account in the advertising business" and commented that Ernest was "a one-man show who insisted on supervising every aspect of his company's advertising." But finally, Needham, Harper & Steers, Inc., a Chicago-based agency, took on the Gallo premium lines while Hal Riney, creative director and head of western operations for Ogilvy & Mather, designed a new campaign for Gallo varietals. He won Ernest's approval with his elegant television commercials accompanied by Vangelis's musical score (reminiscent of his *Chariots of Fire* theme) and the new winery slogan: "All the best from Ernest and Julio Gallo." Ernest could brag that this was "classy"—one of his favorite adjectives—and he began to sign his letters, "All the Best."

While table wine sales were stalled, Gallo developed a new product that quickly dominated the market. Aware of the extraordinary success of "California Cooler," created by R. Stuart Bewley and Michael Crete in 1981 (then sold to Brown-Forman in 1985), the winery entered the wine cooler market with a vengeance and a new brand—Bartles & Jaymes. Ripple, Boone's Farm and Gallo's other "pop" beverages had been the precursors of wine coolers; even the folksy promotions for Boone's Farm, designed by Pat McHenry at Gallo, pointed the way for the new label. But it was Hal Riney who devised the characters of Frank and Ed as the pitchmen for Bartles & Jaymes and the "Thank you for your support" campaign. (Contrary to some popular sentiment, Frank and Ed were not supposed to resemble Ernest and Julio; indeed, many consumers didn't realize that Gallo produced Bartles & Jaymes.) But between the strong advertising and marketing campaign and Gallo's typical merchandising push and sales force penetration, Bartles & Jaymes was soon outselling both California Cooler and Seagram's new Golden Wine Cooler (despite its television commercials featuring Bruce Willis).

Riney then established his own advertising agency in San Francisco, taking the Gallo accounts with him. Ernest and Julio added another high-profit product—a white zinfandel—which other wineries had already discovered as a sure-fire success. Basically another "pop" wine, this blush wine cost little to make (aging is not required) but could be sold as an upscale, cork-finished varietal at a higher price; indeed, it quickly became the yuppie wine of choice, and Riney targeted this audience and its yearning for "gracious living" in advertising strategies as well. Nevertheless, other wineries' white zin at first remained more popular than Gallo's among consumers. The winery was playing catch-up in this category, although in the mid-1960s, Dick Witter had developed a white chianti. Gallo could have been ahead of the times, but the product then had no success and had been dropped almost immediately.

In general, sales of premium varietals still weren't taking off as Ernest and Julio had hoped, even after the winery had put great effort into improving these wines and had received approval from wine

critics. Part of the problem remained the Gallo image—the association of the name with cheap wines like Thunderbird and Night Train
Express. But the wine industry as a whole had also begun to suffer in
the early and mid-1980s. With the revived emphasis on fitness, with
increased attention to problems of alcoholism, fetal alcohol syn-
drome, and drunk driving, consumers were buying less wine. The
Gallo brothers had led the way in popularizing wine, but they too
were hit hard. After the previous decade's boom in sales of low-alco-
hol wine (increasing from 294.2 million gallons to 531.1), wine sales
leveled off (except for wine coolers), and in those categories crucial
to Gallo, like generic jug wines, sales began to decline by 2 percent to
3 percent a year.

Whether he was trying to improve his image or was acknowledging
the new attention to health with which the wine industry had to deal,
Ernest gave $3 million to endow the Ernest Gallo Clinic and Research
Center at the University of California Medical School in San Fran-
cisco. It was one of the few major charitable contributions of the
Gallo family that was publicized.

Ernest had also set out to convince the FTC to lift its consent
order, which had restricted Gallo's activities within distributorships.
Insisting to the commission that the order was "outmoded," he argued that Gallo was no longer "the dominant wine firm." In fact, in
1981 the winery was still number one in sales, shipping 131 million
gallons of wine, compared to United Vintners' 50 million. But his was
only a "family winery," Ernest claimed, trying to compete with large
corporations like Heublein, Seagram, and Coca-Cola. By this time
many of Gallo's competitors had adopted some of Gallo's techniques
to control the distribution system, and in May 1983, the FTC agreed
that the market had changed enough to justify lifting the ten-year
restraining order three years before its expiration.

After the winery was released from the FTC order, several independent distributors of Gallo Wine complained about the winery's practices. The Pappas Company in Boston, Premier Wine and Spirits in
Sioux Falls, South Dakota, and Rutman Distributing Company in
Cleveland all sued Gallo, charging the winery with violating federal
antitrust laws. These cases remained in federal court for several years.

Despite the release from the FTC restrictions, in 1984 winery sales
were still stagnant, and neither new advertising programs nor new
Gallo distributorships had changed the way the public thought about
Gallo and its attempt to go upscale. Perhaps that was why Ernest

seemed so defensive and irritable lately, employees speculated; perhaps his obsession with the Gallo name had intensified when, for all his efforts, consumers still considered Gallo and fine wines a contradiction in terms. And as Joe would later wonder, perhaps Ernest was also looking for another reason to explain the public's lack of enthusiasm for Gallo varietals when he seemed to blame Joseph Gallo Cheese as part of the problem.

In late August 1984, Ernest arrived at his office early one morning, even at seventy-five eager to begin a full schedule of meetings and telephone calls. But, as he later recalled, his plans were soon disrupted when one of his salesmen stopped by his office to announce that he had something important to show him.

He placed a package of cheese on Ernest's large mahogany desk, explaining that he had bought it the previous evening in a local grocery store.

Ernest still held the unshakable belief that the name Gallo belonged exclusively to him and that only he and the winery were entitled to use it.

But here was the name Gallo on a piece of cheese sold in a grocery store! Joseph Gallo Cheese, the label read. It was like waving a red flag in Ernest's face. No one was going to trade on his name, no one was going to "ride on his coattails," as he put it, not even his brother. He would put a stop to it immediately.

Although Joe was planning to move his headquarters soon, the office from which he still ran his various businesses was set on a knoll overlooking his Livingston vineyards. Constructed after his brothers had terminated him, it was a one-room, adobe-block building in which were placed two oak desks, one for himself and one for his son Mike, who was now thirty-four and a full partner in Joe's vineyard, cattle, dairy, and cheese operations.

Mike was out doing his rounds of the ranches; Joe sat at his desk studying reports of this year's grape harvest. Just turned sixty-five, he was healthy and robust, his tanned face serene as he looked across his nearby vineyard. Its heavy clusters of French Colombard grapes were almost ready to be picked and hauled to Ernest and Julio's Fresno winery. Joe generally sold about twenty thousand tons of wine grapes to his brothers each year. Now the air was sweet with the aroma of their ripeness, and Joe was sure that this would be a bountiful harvest, coming in with excellent sugar content.

Adding to his satisfaction were the reports from the cheese plant— sales of bulk cheese in forty-pound blocks to supermarkets had been steady for the previous year and a half, and after the spring of 1984, when he had begun to market packaged cheese for consumers under his own label, retail and bulk sales had risen every month and in total were approaching $30 million for the year.

The ringing of the telephone interrupted his paperwork. While he employed a secretary at the cheese plant, he was not a man who stood on ceremony or enjoyed status symbols, and he took the call himself.

"Joe, I'm shocked," came Ernest's gravelly voice over the line. "One of my people just brought in a package of your cheese that he saw in the grocery."

"Yes?" Joe replied, uncertain why his brother was agitated. After all, cheese with the Joseph Gallo label had been sold in grocery stores and supermarkets in Modesto and Turlock since the previous March.

"We have a real problem with your label," Ernest continued. "Because of that agreement we made with Gallo Salame."

"What do you mean?" Joe said, his voice slow and measured as if to counteract Ernest's staccato of righteous indignation. "What does that have to do with me? It's my own name."

"But our agreement with Gallo Salame means we have to protect the trademark."

"I don't know what kind of deals you made with them. We've been making this cheese for a long time, and you must have known about it."

"Well, it's a problem. We need to meet. You and Mike come up here, and we'll discuss it."

As Joe later recalled, he agreed to see Ernest the next day, and they ended the conversation. Because his lawyer John Whiting was out of town, Joe couldn't contact him. But when Mike returned to his desk, Joe related Ernest's message—"something about a problem with Gallo Salame"—and told him about Ernest's demand that they appear at the winery for a meeting.

According to Ernest's recollection, however, the telephone conversation had continued for several minutes. In Ernest's version, he had reminded Joe of statements that Ernest said he had made to Joe at the cheese plant opening in June of 1983.

"Don't you remember when we finished the tour, I asked you then if you were going to sell cheese with your name on it," Ernest recalled asking Joe. "And you promised you were only going to sell in bulk, not to consumers with your label on it. I told you it was all right to use your name as long as you were just selling bulk cheese. But otherwise we would have a problem with Gallo Salame because of the settlement we'd just worked out. I also said that if it was just bulk cheese, all you had to do was write me a letter. But you never did, and now you've broken your word."

Ernest also insisted that he had made a second phone call, in which he repeated his statement of the problem and Joe's supposed promises. When Joe later heard his brother's version of these speeches, he claimed that Ernest had made none of these comments. According to Joe's recollection, during the cheese plant tour Ernest had said nothing about the Gallo Salame settlement's implications for his label, nor had he, Joe, ever agreed not to sell consumer cheese. He suspected that what Ernest called his "promise" was created in retrospect. Joe claimed that if Ernest had asked him, he would have said quite the opposite, that it was natural to go from selling in bulk to consumer packages, just as Ernest and Julio had moved from bulk wine in the 1930s to winery-bottled and -labeled products in the late 1940s.

Mike Gallo, too, later doubted that his uncle had made such statements, since he was sure that his father would have mentioned them to him, both at the time of the cheese plant opening and when telling him about Ernest's phone call and request for a meeting.

Joe and Mike arrived in Ernest's office the next day for their scheduled appointment. Julio was there as well, and after the usual pleasantries, Ernest busied himself carrying chairs to the entrance area of his office. He positioned two chairs side by side next to the door; facing them, and a yard away, he placed two other chairs side by side.

"You and Mike sit there," he said, pointing to the two on the right. "Julio"—he beckoned to his brother, who had been hanging back by the window—"you sit here next to me and opposite Mike. Joe, across from me."

"Here he goes again," Mike recalled thinking to himself as he took his assigned seat. His father had told him that when Ernest had demanded that he sell his Gallo Glass Company stock back to the winery, Ernest had pulled up a chair directly in front of him, placing it so close that Ernest's knee was positioned between Joe's. Joe had remarked to Mike at the time that this seemed to be Ernest's method of intimidation. Today he was doing the same thing with the seating arrangement—it wasn't just a face-to-face meeting, it was an in-your-face meeting.

Julio had moved slowly to his chair, his shoulders slumped, his head down. He gave Joe and Mike a quick tentative smile as he took his seat, but then stared at his lap. Ernest sat down, folded his hands on his knees, and leaned forward.

"You know, Joe, if it were up to me, I wouldn't be worrying about the name," he said. "It's all Gallo Salame—that's the real problem."

"I don't see how that should concern me," Joe repeated once more. "That was your doing—" He glanced at Julio, hoping that his brother would agree. Julio would not meet his eyes, and Ernest interrupted.

"But I explained to you about the license. We have to protect the trademark. If you use the name, you have to ask our permission. If you don't, Gallo Salame might force us to sue."

"Then why wasn't I consulted?" Joe asked. "Why did you agree to that in your settlement with them when you knew I had already started the cheese company?"

Ernest shrugged aside the question, then adopted a conciliatory tone: "Look, the thing for us to do this morning is to try to figure out a way of solving the problem with Gallo Salame."

Mike hadn't said a word as he watched his father and his uncles. He found it hard to believe that the real conflict was with Gallo Salame. After all, during the past year, well after Ernest had acquired the Gallo Salame trademark, he and his father had bought salami wholesale from the company as they experimented with adding bits of salami to one of their cheeses. If Gallo Salame hadn't like the Joseph Gallo name, why hadn't the company complained directly?

As Ernest continued to lecture Joe on the Gallo Salame license, the long and expensive lawsuit they had undertaken to acquire the trademark, Julio became increasingly upset. He must realize that Ernest is trying to pull something here, Mike thought. Mike was already convinced that for all the talk about Gallo Salame, it was Ernest who wanted exclusive control of the name and didn't want Gallo on anything but wine. Ernest wasn't admitting that today, however; instead he was insisting that Joe had to satisfy the terms of the Gallo Salame license.

"I still don't think that's my problem," Joe said flatly. "The license doesn't change the fact that Joseph Gallo is my name, and I can use it on my own products. I'm sorry *you* have a problem," he added, softening his tone.

"I'll have Jack Owen call Whiting," Ernest snapped. "We have to work out a solution."

Julio now began to weep, at first quietly, then openly sobbing.

Ernest glanced at him, pulled back his chair, and abruptly left the room.

Julio now looked up at Joe, his lips trembling. "You know the last thing our mother said to me before she died? She said 'All I want is for you boys to work together . . . to get along . . .' "

He shook his head, weeping again.

"I know, I know," said Joe as he and Mike left the room.

Why this conversation had resurrected Julio's memories of their parents' deaths, including their mother's last words, Joe didn't understand. Nor could he explain Julio's tears when Mike asked about them on the drive home. Julio's reaction to the label dispute seemed excessive to both father and son at the time. But two years later they would speculate that the emotional outburst had been prompted by thoughts of the brothers' inheritance.

On August 15 John Whiting received a phone call from winery attorney Jack Owen.

According to Whiting, after a few words of greeting, Owen got right to the point: "We have a big problem with our respective clients, John."

"What's that?" asked Whiting, perplexed. He had been out of town for several days and had heard nothing about the dispute or about Joe and Mike's meeting with Ernest.

"It's a problem with our Gallo Salame settlement," Owen announced, "and with your client."

"What does Gallo Salame have to do with Joe?" Whiting was still in the dark, since Joe had never mentioned anything about the winery's suit or the settlement with Gallo Salame to his lawyer.

"You see, the winery entered into a license agreement with Gallo Salame, and we have to protect the trademark," Owen explained. "The winery itself doesn't mind that Joe uses his name, but the license makes that a problem. It will cause much publicity and embarrassment if Joe doesn't help us solve this difficulty. So, please, talk to Joe and see if we can work something out."

Whiting still didn't get it, since he was sure that the law permitted Joe to use his own name. He asked Owen to send him a copy of the license and any legal authorities on the subject so that he could see why the winery was insisting that Joe's label was precluded by the Gallo Salame license.

Whiting immediately drove out to Joe's office to find out what this was about. After hearing Joe's account of the phone call and meeting with Ernest and Julio, Whiting still felt that they were on solid legal ground.

"Hell, it's Joe's name!" Whiting exclaimed, recalling the certainty of his position. "It's his right to use it."

Putting Joe's name on the cheese label had been neither a casual nor a rash decision. Whiting said he had researched the question and had concluded that the use of a person's own name was a basic principle of law and was even protected by the First Amendment. According to Whiting, Joe had no desire to "confuse" the consumer—in fact, just the opposite. Whiting believed that his full name along with the Atwater location of the cheese plant and the picture of cows and a dairy on the label would make it clear that this was Joe's own enterprise and his own product. Joe himself didn't want to be associated with the winery—after all, their Thunderbird and Night Train Express street wine reputation wouldn't help his cheese. Whiting had concluded that Joe's full name, which he had been using as a trade name for well over twenty years, and his label were distinctive enough to avoid any confusion with the winery.

Why Ernest was choosing to make an issue of it now, Whiting couldn't determine. He wondered if Ernest's insistence on the Gallo Salame agreement were a smokescreen. A day later, when Whiting received a copy of the license, he felt that his suspicions were confirmed. As far as he was concerned, the license had nothing to do with Joe's use of his own name. And the case law cited by Owen, he felt, had little to do with the issues at hand.

On October 15, Whiting accompanied Mike and Joe to another meeting with Ernest and Julio. No one said a word in the car. "We were all tense, as if we were going to an execution," Whiting recalled.

Suddenly, into the silence, Joe quipped, "Well, boys, I can tell you right now, this isn't going to be fun."

Whiting and Mike burst out laughing at Joe's wry comment. Whiting had met Ernest on social occasions, but as Joe now reminded him, "You haven't faced Ernest in a situation like this."

They were shown into the conference room where Ernest and Julio were waiting. This day attorney Jack Owen attended as well and took a chair across the table from Whiting. Owen was in his mid-thirties, a tall man given to paunch whose collar-length blond hair was swept back from his round face.

While Ernest took a chair directly opposite Joe and Mike, Julio sat to their right and at the end of the table, his chair pulled slightly back, his posture suggesting his reluctance to participate. Nevertheless, when Ernest glanced in his direction, he roused himself and opened the meeting.

"Joe, I want you to know that the winery has no objections to your using your name," Julio began. "As far as we're concerned you can use your name all you want. But the problem is with this Gallo Salame agreement. If you continue to use your name, it could force us to sue you, and that could cause us a lot of embarrassment and adverse publicity."

"How much cheese are you now selling retail, Joe?" Ernest interrupted.

Joe could give him only a general figure—about $4 million to $5 million, he thought.

"Maybe you could phase out your name over several years," Ernest proposed. "You would reduce the prominence of Joseph Gallo on the label and gradually stress the importance of another name. We've done that at the winery very successfully."

"I still don't see why Gallo Salame hasn't complained to me if my label is causing them concern," Joe replied. "I've been buying salami from them for the last year."

Ernest looked surprised. Then: "Well, maybe you could be licensed by us like Gallo Salame."

Whiting ignored the remark. He felt the best strategy was simply to listen.

"Maybe a disclaimer would work," Ernest suggested after a few more minutes of silence.

"What's a disclaimer?" asked Joe.

Owen explained that a notice on the label would indicate that there was no connection between the two companies. "Something like, 'not affiliated with the E. & J. Gallo Winery,' " the attorney added.

"Wait a minute," Whiting objected. "I thought the problem was Gallo Salame, not the winery. Why are you suggesting a disclaimer involving the winery? Besides, has there been any evidence of confusion between the winery and Joe's cheese?"

After a long silence, Ernest asked Owen if he'd had any reports.

"I don't know of any," the counsel replied, "but if there are, they'll be in my file."

"Well, Joe hasn't seen any confusion either," said Whiting.

Repeatedly, though, Ernest returned to the theme: What plan could they and Joe together devise to get Gallo Salame off the winery's back?

Whiting reiterated that legally he felt that the Gallo Salame Company could not come after Joe, because he was using his full name, Joseph Gallo—that and the label were distinctive enough to eliminate confusion.

"Well, we stopped Mary Gallo in Ohio," said Owen, "and we prevented a Sam Gallo from using his name, too. Remember that, Ernest?"

"Right, down in Louisiana, that guy who wanted to sell Gallo coffee," replied Ernest.

Ernest and Owen continued to discuss various trademark infringement suits that the winery had won. Whiting was unfamiliar with them, but the dialogue sounded rehearsed to him, as if Ernest and Owen had planned this exchange to undermine Whiting's assurances to Joe that he was on firm legal ground.

Finally, Ernest said, "Joe, why don't you get the opinion of another lawyer? Let's see what he has to say."

Whiting had some experience in patent law, but he felt it was reasonable to consult another attorney who was a trademark specialist. The meeting closed on friendly terms with Owen's promise to send the license agreement with Gallo Salame, along with supporting documents and the names of lawyers who had worked for the winery in the past.

Joe left the room with Mike, Whiting and Owen following him. But suddenly Ernest rushed out the door and pulled Joe back into the conference room alone.

Much to Joe's surprise, Julio now began to talk.

"Look, Joe, we gotta solve this!" he exclaimed. "Otherwise it could turn into something—something that would hurt the family."

"We have to stick together on this," Ernest echoed his brother. "We must work it out—if there's a lawsuit the publicity could get very embarrassing."

"I'll do anything as long as it doesn't damage my business or my family," replied Joe, but refused to make a further commitment.

On October 16, 1984, Jack Owen sent a more detailed license and the list of lawyers, along with copies of the winery's various trademark registrations and the judgment in the trademark infringement suit that Ernest had brought against Mary and Charles Gallo in Ohio in 1947.

Whiting contacted several lawyers, who, after studying the documents, reported that they believed that Joe's right to use his own name was fundamental and protected by the First Amendment. Whit-

ing then turned to two other lawyers considered leading specialists in
the field of trademark and patent law—Al and Thelma Herzig, husband and wife partners in a Los Angeles firm who together had handled complicated trademark and patent cases across the country,
including extensive litigation for the Mattel Toy Company.

On October 25, 1984, Al Herzig sent Whiting a letter explaining
that he had reviewed the documents provided by the winery (including the license agreement between E. & J. Gallo Winery and Consolidated Foods Corporation concerning Gallo Salame) as well as
various cases relating to the right of a person to use his personal name
as a trademark or trade name.

"Based upon all that we have examined," he concluded, "it is our
opinion that Joseph Gallo has the right to utilize the name 'Joseph
Gallo' on or in connection with packaged cheese products. The cases
strongly state that the right to use one's personal name in connection
with a trademark and trade name is protected by the courts and in the
absence of fraud or intentional deception, the courts will permit the
utilization of a trademark or trade name which is a person's real name
in his trade or business. This is especially true when we consider that
Mr. Gallo has used his personal name for many years to identify
his various farming operations and farms including his dairy which
might be expected to produce and sell among other dairy products,
cheese."

On October 30, Whiting sent Ernest a copy of Herzig's opinion.
Ernest had no reply until November 30 when he wrote Joe to inform
him that Gallo Salame had now demanded that the winery take steps
to stop the use of "Joseph Gallo." Later Whiting learned that, contrary to Ernest's statement in this letter, it wasn't until December 13,
1984, that Gallo Salame company and Consolidated Foods were actually made aware of the Joseph Gallo cheese label conflict. And then
it was only because Jack Owen had written a letter to Consolidated
Foods' general counsel alerting the parent corporation to what Ernest
had been calling Gallo Salame's problem with Joe's label. Indeed,
John Whiting saw Ernest's hand behind a February 14, 1985, letter
from Consolidated Foods to the winery, a copy of which Ernest then
forwarded to Joe on March 5. As Ernest had often predicted, Consolidated Foods was now claiming infringement of the Gallo Salame
trademark by the Joseph Gallo label and asked the winery to take legal
action.

Whiting was now certain that the letter was part of Ernest's strategy
to make Joe think that a court battle was inescapable if he didn't

accept a license agreement. "That was what Ernest seemed to be pushing for," Whiting recalled. "Ernest wanted Joe to assign him his Joseph Gallo trademark. The winery, with Joe's assistance, would no doubt register the mark and then, like the agreement with Gallo Salame, would grant him a royalty-free license for the use of his own name in his trademark."

Indeed, on April 19, 1985, after another month of silence, Ernest sent Joe the draft of a license agreement, which, he said in his cover letter, Gallo Salame had tentatively approved. The draft indicated the restrictions in labeling and advertising that would distinguish Joe's cheese from both Gallo Salame and Gallo Wine. It then stipulated that in addition to conforming to all applicable governmental quality standards, Joe's cheese and cheese plant would be subject to inspections by winery inspectors. The final condition read, "We may terminate this license if you fail to comply with its terms. This license is non-assignable."

Whiting and Herzig both concluded that the quality control and nonassignability conditions were unacceptable. Herzig was particularly adamant, he recalled. "The quality condition and inspections coupled with the threat of termination meant that Ernest could close Joe down," the lawyer said later.

On May 1, 1985, Joe wrote to Ernest to reassure him that he would never sell alcoholic beverages under the Joseph Gallo label and that he would do everything described in the first part of the proposed license so that neither his label nor his advertising would show any similarity or connection to Gallo Salame or the winery. In fact, in early 1985, he had sent letters to his cheese distributors, reminding them that only the full name "Joseph Gallo Cheese" was to be used, never the shorthand "Gallo Cheese," and he had advised them that they were to indicate in the strongest possible terms that the Joseph Gallo Cheese Company and the Gallo Winery were entirely separate entities. But while he was willing to accommodate Ernest and Julio on these matters, he informed them that he did not want to take a license.

Ernest's reaction was to wait a month, then call for another meeting, this one on June 21, when he had returned from a trip to the East Coast. Joe, Mike, and Whiting again drove to the winery and sat down with Ernest, Julio, and Owen in the conference room.

"Why can't you help us out with the Gallo Salame problem so we won't have to sue you?" asked Ernest.

"But the license doesn't actually say you're forced to sue," interrupted Whiting, tired of hearing Ernest's excuse that the problem was all due to Gallo Salame. "I've read this thing now, and it says you only have to defend them and the trademark if Joe is shown to be infringing. Before it ever gets as far as a lawsuit, you can have the issue arbitrated. And I'm convinced that if it were arbitrated, the arbitrator wouldn't find that Joe was either infringing or diluting."

"I don't know, John," Owen interrupted to repeat what had become his refrain: "We stopped Mary Gallo, we stopped Sam Gallo. We've worked long and hard to protect the winery's trademark, and the license agreement requires that we do the same for the Gallo Salame trademark."

"But the license may well be a naked assignment," Whiting objected. "Since no goodwill was transferred, it may be invalid."

"But Joe's use of his—I mean putting *our* name on his label— dilutes our trademark, Whiting," Ernest objected. "Because of this license, we have to protect the Gallo trademark from dilution."

Once again Whiting reminded Ernest that he had previously claimed that the problem was with Gallo Salame, not with the winery.

"That's right," said Ernest. "So the obvious solution is for Joe to take a license from us." He paused, turning to Joe. "Or maybe you could buy Gallo Salame. It's for sale, I hear, and that would solve all the problems."

Joe ignored the suggestion. "I told you, I don't want a license," he repeated firmly. "That's definitely out, because your quality-control conditions give you the power to shut me down."

"But you know we'd never do that!" exclaimed Julio. "We would never shut *you* down."

Mike had noted the emphasis on *"you,"* but it wasn't clear until several months later what Julio's remark might imply. Instead, Mike listened while his father patiently explained to his brothers that the cheese plant underwent regular and rigorously enforced inspections by government agencies.

"Has it occurred to you," Whiting now intervened, "that with a license the winery exposes itself to liability? If you're responsible for the cheese quality and there were ever any problem, you would be vulnerable. Do you really want a license that exposes you unnecessarily?"

As far as Whiting could tell, this question, as well as his other remarks, fell on deaf ears. "I wasn't worried about the quality of Joe's cheese," he recalled. "I just hoped that this would dissuade Ernest and Julio from pursuing the license idea. We hadn't even discussed the nonassignability condition, but giving the winery the power to shut down Joe's company was simply unacceptable."

When the others left, Joe stayed behind with Ernest and Julio. Ernest now offered the plan he had suggested at the first meeting: If Joe gave his cheese trademark to the winery, the winery art department would redesign the label, and the marketing people would help phase the label out over a period of time and push the newly labeled cheese into supermarkets.

Joe thought a few minutes. The use of his name wouldn't be so important as long as he had experts transforming and then building up a new label. Aided by the winery's renowned marketing talents, he would have wide enough distribution to compensate for the change.

"And we can also work something out on your grapes," Julio proposed. "We can set a guaranteed price for your vineyards that aren't under contract."

This suggestion was welcomed by Joe. Aside from his original property in Livingston, he did not have written contracts on his vineyards. He had also accepted Ernest and Julio's encouragement to buy more vineyards and plant or replant them in the varieties of grapes they favored. Coupled with that was his feeling that Julio's grower relations department sometimes arbitrarily "downgraded" his grapes, then cut the previously agreed-upon price per ton. Furthermore, his land was assessed at a lower price without a winery contract.

"Okay, that sounds reasonable," Joe said finally. He shook hands with Julio, then with Ernest, who added that he would have his "legal people work out the fine details." He also asked Joe to send him a financial report "to put them in the picture."

Joe met Whiting and Mike at the car. They were surprised to see him smiling. On the drive home, he explained the oral agreement that he and his brothers had reached. As far as Joe was concerned, everything was resolved; he assumed that his brothers were happy with the arrangement as well, and they had all shaken hands on the deal.

Whiting prepared the financial report and sent it to the winery. In early August, Ernest called another meeting to discuss the details of the settlement.

"We can't go along with this," Ernest said flatly at the beginning of the meeting. As far as Joe was concerned, his brothers had gone back on their word. Angry and disappointed, he stalked out of the conference room.

Over the next several weeks, Joe, Ernest, and Julio talked on the phone but made no headway. Joe sometimes lost his temper, feeling that every time he thought they had reached an understanding, the terms were changed in their next discussion. Ernest continued to pressure him, repeating that he would have to sue. At one point Joe exploded, "Have at it!" and slammed down the phone.

On October 28, 1985, Ernest called Joe to inform him that he was sending him the complaint he was going to file unless Joe accepted a license. His covering letter said that since there was still no agreement on a satisfactory license, he was enclosing the proposed complaint so that Joe would have time to think it over. Ernest would be away in Italy until November 15 and would phone Joe upon his return. He signed the letter, "All the best," and enclosed the draft of the lawsuit.

The proposed complaint was a simple claim of trademark infringement and contained no charge of "dilution" or poor quality. Still, Joe and Mike were surprised that Ernest had gone this far in the midst of their continuing attempts to reach an agreement. Whiting felt it was a lever to get Joe to accept the winery's terms for a license.

Joe was so upset that he phoned Julio. The brothers agreed that they wanted nothing more than to avoid a lawsuit. They now spoke almost every day, trying to reach a settlement in Ernest's absence. Julio repeatedly tried to reassure Joe that the winery would not use the quality-control condition to close him down. He renewed his offer —that if Joe would accept the license, he would give him written grape contracts for all his vineyards. Joe was relieved that by the time Ernest returned from Italy, they seemed to have reached an understanding. Joe wrote Ernest in early November to explain his and Julio's agreement, at the same time reminding him that the license would have to cover the eleven western states.

But again, when Ernest sent Joe the proposed license on December 23, 1985, the conditions had changed. This one listed even more restrictions of labeling and advertising and limited marketing of the cheese to California. The quality-control demands were even more stringent, and a last condition prohibited Joe from transferring the license to his descendants.

Whiting was most perturbed by the new conditions listed under "quality control." Again, if there were any problems, the winery would have the power to withdraw the license immediately. Whiting began to wonder if this was in fact what Ernest had been after all the while? Was this all a ploy to shut down Joe's company? Whiting didn't believe in coincidence, and now he wondered if Ernest had pushed for the June 8, 1983, agreement with Gallo Salame because he knew that four days later Joe was officially opening his cheese plant. Had Ernest paid $2 million to acquire the Gallo Salame trademark in order to use it as legal leverage against Joe?

"It wasn't enough for Ernest to want to take Joe's name away," Whiting later exclaimed. "Then he wanted the power to put him out of business."

Mike's response to the new license was also unequivocal. "We kept struggling to work out a solution," he said. "I felt my father was being led up the garden path. He had agreed to change his label to accommodate his brothers. But then they would withdraw everything they had agreed to. I think with that second license, he and I both began to believe that what they really wanted was to control our business, even shut us down if they could."

Joe was so distraught by this suspicion that he phoned Julio at his vacation home in Pebble Beach on New Year's Eve. Julio tried to calm him down, and in the next several weeks, they again talked frequently, with Julio continuing to reassure Joe, "We'd never shut *you* down, we can work it out, we'll find a solution." He told Joe that he would talk to Ernest about changing the terms in the license, and that in a few days he would let Joe know the price he would set in the fifteen-year grape contracts.

But then Julio called Joe back to say that Owen had informed him that the grape contracts couldn't be part of the license agreement. "The only way you can get the written contracts is to sign the license," Julio explained.

After Julio and Joe failed to come to terms, Ernest called Joe.

"Look, Joe," he said in a placating tone. "We trust *you*, we know you care about quality, so we would never shut *you* down. But after you there's only strangers, and they may not care about quality."

"I was shocked by that remark," recalled Mike, who had been a party to Ernest's phone call. "Ernest knew that my father wanted to make sure that a license could go to me and Linda after his death. And here he was calling me and my sister 'strangers.' We would be the ones inheriting the business, but to him we were strangers. It showed just how much he thought about family, or at least our family."

After Ernest again phoned to demand an agreement, Joe decided he'd had enough. He called Whiting into his office on January 21, 1986. "I'm sick and tired of this whole thing," Joe said, handing his attorney Ernest's first draft of a license. He told his lawyer to accept the quality-control inspections as long as he would be given time to remedy a legitimate problem, but to add that the license would be transferable.

"Just put in what will protect us," he said to Whiting. With these instructions about the two qualifications to be inserted, Joe signed the first license Ernest had proposed, hoping that his compromise on inspections would convince Ernest to change his position on assignability. Give a little, take a little, he thought, and maybe this will finally be settled.

The next afternoon Ernest phoned, having heard that Joe was signing the "earlier" license.

"Where in the hell did you get that damned thing?" Ernest shouted, as if he had forgotten that he had written it. "Gallo Salame won't go for that! It's not acceptable. It says nothing about limiting the states where you can distribute the cheese. You better put that in."

"I won't do that. You're restricting me again."

"How am I restricting you? Gallo Salame used to be national, now they're in eleven states. You'd be in three states."

"Before you said one state," Joe objected. "Everything keeps changing. I don't want any limit in the license agreement."

"Well, you better put that condition in," shouted Ernest. "You just better do it!"

"No, I'm sending it this way."

Ernest received the copy of the first license with the provisions that Whiting had noted in a covering letter.

"This is it!" rumbled Ernest's voice into the telephone when he called Joe on February 3, 1986. "We're further apart than ever before."

"I don't understand," replied Joe, trying to remain calm. "I compromised. I'll allow you to inspect, but you can't close me down without giving me time to fix any problems."

"No! We have to be able to cancel the license if there's any problem. And we can't let you transfer the license. That's the only way we can protect our trademark—"

"It's my name," Joe interrupted, realizing that again the so-called problem with Gallo Salame was really a problem with the winery's trademark.

"We're too far apart. We'll just have to go to court." Ernest slammed down the phone, and on February 16 he wrote Joe a formal letter. The threat was clear—either Joe accepted the terms Ernest wanted in the license or Ernest would bring suit.

Joe felt that a lawsuit would be terrible for the family, just as Julio and Ernest had insisted in their first meetings. On March 12 he wrote Ernest and sent copies of the letter to other family members. He stressed in his letter that a lawsuit would be a "disaster" for the winery and the family because of the ensuing publicity and embarrassment. He said he still wanted to work out a solution to avoid going to court, and he hoped Ernest and Julio would try to reach an agreement with him.

But the letter prompted another angry phone call from Ernest.

"What the hell do you mean by this 'disaster' remark?" Ernest demanded.

"Just what you said in the beginning. A lawsuit will be embarrassing for the family. That's why I want to reach a solution. I told you the few things I needed in the license. Why won't that work?"

"Well, we're too far apart on the conditions," he repeated and hung up.

Julio rang almost immediately. "What did you mean, sending that letter about a 'disaster' and 'embarrassment'?" he also demanded.

Joe explained again. He had only repeated what Julio had said before. He knew how much Julio disliked the idea of publicity.

"Then why won't you sign the license?"

"I did," said Joe. "It's just that Ernest won't accept what I need to protect my business and my family."

"Well, you know, I don't want a lawsuit."

"Then why don't we go back to your first proposal," Joe suggested on impulse. "I would let the winery change my label, then phase it in and help put it into distribution. And you would give me the grape contracts."

"I don't know why that won't work," said Julio with enthusiasm. "I'll call Ernest."

That afternoon, Ernest surprised Joe with a quick phone call to agree to Julio and Joe's proposal. "Come up here tomorrow afternoon, and we'll work out the details," he said.

Joe was tired of snapping to whenever his brothers demanded a meeting, and he said he couldn't come until the following week, March 21. On that day, Joe, Mike, and Whiting drove to the winery and were escorted into the conference room. Ernest, Julio, and Jon Shastid awaited them.

Ernest began this meeting. "What did you *really* mean by that remark in your letter?" he said, staring angrily at Joe. "What do you mean, this will be a disaster for the winery and the family?"

Joe looked perplexed. "Only what you and Julio said in the beginning."

"What did he mean, Mike?"

Mike looked at his father and shrugged. Neither understood what was bothering Ernest. "Just what he said," he replied.

"Come on, Whiting, what did he really mean?" Ernest scowled.

"He was only repeating what you and Julio had said before. A lawsuit would mean publicity. Now," Whiting went on, "can we get down to the proposal?"

But Ernest and Julio proceeded to rescind every proposal they had previously made, from helping Joe to market his cheese to negotiating a new grape contract.

Furious with his brothers, Joe gestured to Whiting and Mike that he was leaving. Whiting, too, felt that they were back to square one, and he followed Joe and Mike to the door.

"Wait a minute, Whiting," Ernest called out. "We need to know what Joe meant by saying this would be a disaster."

"He already told you," replied Whiting. "He was just repeating what you had said about a court case with a lot of publicity."

Ernest still didn't seem satisfied, but Whiting hurried down the stairs after Joe and Mike. In the car, they discussed Ernest and Julio's strange reaction to Joe's March 12 letter. They were all mystified by Ernest and Julio's outrage, but came to no conclusion.

They were silent the rest of the way home, although it was Joe who finally lightened the mood.

"Jesus, I'm never going to write another one of those letters!"

On April 17, 1986, Whiting's phone didn't stop ringing. Reporters were calling to ask for his comment on the complaint just filed by Ernest and Julio against their brother Joe and his son Mike. The famous Gallo brothers had taken a step that placed them squarely in the media's spotlight. The two who had guarded their privacy so vehemently had gone public. Whiting was listed in the complaint as the defendants' attorney, but it was the first he had heard that the winery had actually gone ahead with the threatened lawsuit. And now the journalists wanted to hear the reaction of the "unknown brother": What did Joe have to say about his brothers' allegations that Joseph Gallo Cheese was a health risk? This was the scoop, this was what attracted the media. Not only were the brothers feuding—that was juicy enough, given all the secrecy surrounding the family—but Ernest and Julio were also charging that Joe made rotten cheese.

Since quality control hadn't been part of the original proposed complaint, Whiting concluded that the new accusation to which the press had been alerted was designed to attract this kind of publicity. He was furious. Even though he had not yet seen the filing, he reminded reporters that Joe's cheese had won several statewide awards. But he knew that his comments would be overshadowed by the suit's allegations about Joseph Gallo Cheese and the suggestion of a full-scale family feud.

"I thought at the time and I still think that these allegations were calculated to hurt if not destroy Joe's cheese business financially," Whiting recalled. "I was pretty disturbed, and I knew it would really upset Joe, not only that these claims would be stressed in the news stories, but also that his brothers would say such things. These charges were widely publicized, though I didn't see how they were germane to a complaint of trademark infringement. But I suppose that was the point—Ernest and Julio needed to convince the public that there was a reason for suing their own brother. Otherwise, most people would say, 'It's his name, why can't he use it on his cheese?' But if you claim it's a health hazard, they might be more receptive."

The winery had brought in the heavy artillery. Gallo not only enlisted Oliver Wanger, a partner in the Fresno firm of McCormick, Barstow, Sheppard, Wayte & Curruth, who had been involved in the Gallo Salame case; but it also recruited Patrick Lynch, a litigator from the prominent Los Angeles firm of O'Melveny & Myers.

Lynch had attended Loyola of Los Angeles as both an undergraduate and a law student, and the day after he received his law degree in June 1966, he had joined the O'Melveny firm. He was tall and thin, and his pale, blue eyes and scholarly glasses belied his aggressiveness. He specialized in antitrust litigation and was known as a scrappy courtroom fighter. Outside the courtroom, he was more relaxed, and with twelve children (ten of their own and two adopted), he and his wife were active in community affairs in South Pasadena, where they had lived for many years.

Jack Owen had previously consulted Lynch about pending antitrust matters for the winery, and when the conflict with Joe arose he had asked Lynch to prepare the complaint. Not only did Lynch raise the issue of Joe's refusal of quality control by the winery, he also hypothesized dire consequences on the basis of a recent Jalisco Cheese Company listeria outbreak in which several people died.

"When I first heard about the conflict, I felt that it was a slam dunk trademark infringement suit except for the emotional overlay of the family controversy," Lynch later explained. "The right to use one's own name is an area of some ambiguity in trademark case law. But with a trademark as powerful as Gallo and a product as closely allied with wine as cheese, it seemed clear to me that it was trademark infringement. As far as the allegations about poor quality went, I don't think any person in litigation would knowingly ignore the issue of quality when you're trying to stop somebody from using their name. We had heard that the cheese plant had failed state inspections, and we felt it was important to bring this to the court's attention, even though we were talking about a brother's company."

John Whiting, however, insisted that Joe's cheese had never been cited as a health risk and that the allegations of poor quality were nothing but a legal strategy to make a stronger case for an injunction against Joe's use of his name. He recalled a conversation that seemed to confirm his belief. Whiting, Lynch, and Wanger had met in Wanger's Fresno office to try to arrive at a settlement before going to trial. "At one point I asked Lynch why he had made all these baseless charges against Joe's cheese," Whiting said. "That's when he told me, 'I'm not so naive to think that a jury of twelve people would want to take away a man's name.' He knew that the ordinary person off the street has an instinctive feeling about the right to your own name. So he was confirming that he put in all the references to the Jalisco food poisoning and Joe's cheese as a health risk to convince people that there was a reason for Ernest and Julio to sue their brother to take away his name. But once those allegations were made public, it became even harder to reach a settlement because Joe was so upset."

Even though Joe couldn't understand why Ernest would rather go to court than compromise and settle, Mike Gallo thought he knew what the real issue was. Ernest's remark about Joe's trademark going to "strangers" (meaning him and his sister, Linda) convinced Mike that Ernest wanted the "Joseph Gallo" name for *his* son Joe, and grandson Joe, Jr.

"Maybe Joey wants to put his or his son's name on a bottle of wine someday," Mike recalled thinking at the time, and then felt that his speculation was confirmed by Julio.

After the lawsuit had been filed, Joe had become increasingly worried about the fate of his grape harvest the following autumn. He telephoned Julio and arranged to meet with him and his son Bob at the Foster Farms restaurant in Livingston. Joe brought Mike and Kenny Jelacich, Linda's husband, who now worked as a manager of Joe and Mike's ranches, to the lunch meeting as well.

"What am I supposed to do, bulldoze my grapes?" Joe began. He assumed that because of the conflict, Ernest and Julio would refuse to buy his French Colombards—and only a few other wineries used this variety in their white wines.

"No, no, don't do anything like that," said Julio. "The lawsuit has nothing to do with it—you'll still have a home for your grapes."

Joe was reassured, and now, without Ernest present, Joe hoped that Julio would be more honest about his feelings.

"What would you do if you were in my shoes?" Joe asked. "Wouldn't you want to use your own name?"

"It's funny, Joe, I always thought the name 'Gallo' was hard to sell," Julio mused. "I even thought we should have used a different name in the beginning." He paused, and then, according to Joe and Mike, he added: "But it's really the other side of the family that's causing the problems. Since you're just beginning to market your cheese, there must be plenty of names you could use. Maybe if you found another name—like Mike and Linda Gallo, or M & L Gallo or J & M Gallo— then there wouldn't be a problem."

Mike and Joe exchanged sidelong glances. They were both surprised that Julio would put it so bluntly—the real problem *was* the first name, not the Gallo name alone. No wonder Ernest refused to agree that the license of the Joseph Gallo trademark would be transferable. Although Julio would later have a different recollection of this meeting, Joe and Mike came away convinced that Ernest wanted the Joseph Gallo name (and trademark) to become exclusive to his son and grandson after Joe's death.

Julio later sent a letter confirming his statement that he would continue to buy Joe's grapes. Nevertheless, tension in the family was growing. Outsiders thought the lawsuit was "nothing," a business dispute at most, but one that would be settled before it ever came to trial. Some even thought the conflict was a publicity stunt. But after the winery complaint had been filed, lines of allegiance were drawn, and while remaining formally polite to each other, family members began to keep their distance.

"It was only at my mother's funeral that I realized how serious the fight had become," Linda Gallo Jelacich recalled. Mary Ann had been suffering from cancer for a year. Aileen and her daughter Susann Coleman had continued to visit her during her illness. Despite the growing conflict in the family, the three women had remained close. But by the time of Mary Ann's death and her funeral, on May 19, 1986, the winery's lawsuit had been filed.

"After their initial disputes following the divorce, my father and my mother had been on amicable terms, and the rest of the family knew this, so I was surprised that Ernest didn't come to the funeral," Linda said. "Amelia, Joey, and David came to the church, but they didn't return to my house for the reception afterward. Aileen and Julio and Bob and Marie did come, but they kept to themselves and sat outside in the backyard at a separate table under a tree. The few times I saw my dad with Julio, they seemed very tense and strained."

Whiting also realized how upset Joe was by the turn of events. While he had one meeting with Lynch to discuss a possible out-of-court settlement (according to Whiting, the winery was now offering to buy Joe's trademark for even more than they had paid Gallo Salame, then license it back to him), they still could reach no agreement. Since there seemed to be no resolution in sight, Whiting enlisted the Herzigs to help prepare Joe's defense. He also engaged Richard Fine, a Los Angeles antitrust attorney, to work on a counterclaim based on antitrust issues.

Whiting also acquired copies of the original E. & J. Gallo trademark applications from the United States Patent Office. These all stated that the trademark "has been used continuously and applied to the goods in the business of the applicant and the predecessor of the applicant, Joseph Gallo, since 1909." The goods of the applicant—the E. & J. Gallo Winery—were wine, of course. Whiting was struck by the obvious implication that Joe's father had been in the wine business as well. He immediately telephoned Joe.

"What business was your father in?" he asked.

"He was in the grape-shipping business."

"Did he ever have a winery?"

"No, no. He was a grape grower and shipper."

"When did he die?"

"In the early thirties, I think. I was twelve or thirteen. My mother died at the same time."

"Where?"

"In Fresno. That's where we were living then."

"Was it an automobile accident?" asked Whiting. He was shocked when Joe told him about their deaths. Whiting now pushed to know more: Where were the estates probated?

Joe said he had no idea; he wasn't even aware if they had left a will. "Besides, what's this got to do with anything?" he snapped.

For the moment Whiting left it at that, although he wondered if the father's business and trademark were part of his probated estate. But given Joe's insistence, Whiting decided that the 1909 date in the winery's trademark registration had no substance—that it was simply a way by which Ernest and Julio established an artificial early date of first use and claimed continuous use.

But then Whiting read the Gallo Salame case file as well as documents from the winery's earlier suit against Charles and Mary Gallo. In both, Ernest again asserted the prior and continuous use of the trademark since 1909. Perhaps he was still trying to confirm an "early use" date, Whiting thought. Still, he would like to see the probate of the parents' estates, yet he found no court records in Fresno.

On May 22, 1986, he met with Joe again. Joe was unusually silent, and while trying to boost his morale, Whiting realized how depressed his friend and client had become.

"Joe didn't have to say it," recalled Whiting, "but I realized how sad he was. Driving away from his office, I started to do a mental inventory—had I done everything to investigate my friend's legal position? I reviewed in my mind the trademark registrations, the other lawsuits, my previous conversation with Joe about his parents. But I still couldn't find any records of their estates."

It suddenly occurred to him that the probate records might be in Modesto. On impulse he turned north on Route 99 and drove directly to the Stanislaus County Courthouse. What he found there utterly astonished him.

"It was a spur-of-the-moment decision to go search for the files there," he explained. "All I was thinking was, have I done everything I can for Joe? When I sat down and read through the microfilmed records of the parents' probated estates, I had questions. But when I got to Joe's guardianship estate, which he had never mentioned, I nearly fell off my chair."

. . .

It took several hours to read and reread the parents' estate papers as well as the court records of Ernest and Julio's guardianship of their younger brother Joe. What first struck Whiting was Ernest's petition to continue his father's business and to be allowed to crush the estate grapes and store it as juice, as permitted by Prohibition law. While the court had approved this request, the listing of Joe, Sr.'s assets in the probated estate showed no mention of the father's business, even though it seemed to be the genesis of the winery.

Joe should have inherited the business as well, Whiting concluded, finding that Joe's mother's will made that specific, and that the court-ordered distribution of both estates' assets included the usual omnibus clause providing that unlisted or unknown property also passed to the three sons equally. Whiting was also surprised to find no notices of mailings to Joe, Jr., in the records. Turning back through Joe, Sr.'s file, he discovered that Ernest, as the executor of his father's estate, had obtained an order of the court waiving this legal requirement since Joe was a minor and living with his brothers.

He then read Joe's guardianship file. It was a meager one, he thought. Ernest and Julio had never filed an initial inventory, nor had they submitted annual or biannual accountings, which, from his own legal experience, he knew were required by the court. Again, there were no affidavits of mailings to Joe, and his only participation seemed to have been his consent that his brothers serve as the guardians of his person and estate.

This all seemed highly unusual, but it was the final document—the Petition to Terminate the Guardianship—that took Whiting's breath away. The First and Final Account, filed after Joe turned twenty-one, listed the assets of his guardianship estate. There among his properties was the shocker: "an undivided one-third interest in E. & J. Gallo Winery" with the sum of $16,492.26 to the right of the listing. This, Whiting concluded, indicated that Ernest and Julio had conceded and the court had verified that Joe owned a one-third share of the winery as part of his inheritance after his parents' death. The final document in which Joe, through an attorney named Fowler, had filed objections to the First and Final Account made no sense to Whiting, however, nor did the ordered payment of $20,000 for profits on the "loan of Joe's stocks."

By the second and third rereading, Whiting was convinced of what had first seemed unbelievable. The continuity of evidence seemed overwhelming: Ernest and Julio had continued their father's business with a court order, transforming it into a winery in which Joe should have had a one-third interest. Whiting made copies of the relevant pages then sped to Joe's home in Livingston.

"On the drive down, I went over everything I had just read," recalled Whiting. "What seemed strangest was Joe's hiring an attorney and receiving $20,000. Given the trust and confidence Joe had placed in his brothers—to an extraordinary degree, I'd always thought—I couldn't imagine Joe complaining about Ernest and Julio using his share of stock or hiring a lawyer to sue them. Besides, since the final account indicated that they were going to pay Joe interest for the use of his money, why had Fowler asked for an additional sum of $20,000 as profits? How would they even determine what profits were due without an examination of winery accounts? It just didn't add up, and I wanted to hear what Joe would say."

Joe was returning from the cheese plant when he saw Whiting waving him down from the shoulder of the road in front of his driveway. Sensing his lawyer's urgency, he pulled to a stop and joined Whiting in his car. Whiting explained what he had just found in the courthouse.

"All the while, Joe stared at me as if I were nuts," Whiting recalled. "Maybe he thought I was just trying to make him feel better. But I told him that I'd found the records of his parents' probate and his guardianship. He said he'd never heard of their existence."

Whiting showed Joe the court order that allowed Ernest to continue their father's business, then placed the guardianship account in front of him.

"What about this?" Whiting pointed to the entry indicating a "one-third interest in the E. & J. Gallo Winery."

"That's ridiculous!" Joe exclaimed.

"But you see what this says?" Whiting persisted. "You had a one-third share in the winery."

"But a one-third interest would have been worth a lot more than $16,000."

"How do you know what it was worth in 1941? Do you know how much debt the winery had at the time? Or how much profit it made?"

"Of course, I don't know what it was worth," Joe replied. "But if I had owned an interest, my brothers would have told me."

"I can only go by what it says here," said Whiting, unwilling to voice his own suspicions. "Did you ever hire a lawyer to sue your brothers or complain about the use of your money?"

"Hell, no!" Joe shouted. "What are you talking about? I was living with them, working for them."

Whiting then showed him the objections filed by attorney Fowler. Joe read through them, all the while shaking his head. "What does it mean?" he asked finally.

Whiting explained that according to this document, Joe had in effect sued his brothers and won $20,000 in a court order.

"This is crazy!" Joe exclaimed. "I've never heard of Fowler. The only attorney I knew was Ed Taylor. And I *never* sued my brothers!"

Whiting gave Joe the documents to read more thoroughly. Late that night Joe called him and asked him to explain them again.

"I just don't understand, John," sighed Joe, after listening to the explanations. "I've never seen or heard about any of this. But I'm damned sure I never hired a lawyer and went to court against Ernest and Julio."

Whiting knew that Joe was shaken, and he agreed to meet with him and Mike the following day to discuss the new discoveries. For the next two days, he not only described his interpretation of the documents, he virtually cross-examined Joe about his past, what he remembered about these documents and the guardianship proceedings.

"Joe was very pale and upset, but he was sure of his memory, and I was convinced that he knew nothing about his parents' estates or the court hearing about his guardianship," Whiting later explained. "All of this hit him like a ton of bricks, especially the part about his supposedly suing his brothers. He had never seen his mother's will either. It was in her handwriting, and I know that really affected him."

Whiting began to suspect that, contrary to the often repeated story that Ernest and Julio had started the winery themselves, they had actually taken over their father's business, continued it, and then claimed it as their own. In fact, Ernest had admitted as much, Whiting insisted, citing the petition to the court "to continue his father's business" by crushing the grapes into juice and storing it under governmental authority. He also theorized that since Joe claimed to have been completely unaware of these court filings, Ernest and Julio might never have intended to notify him of his "undivided one-third share of the E. & J. Gallo Winery."

Whiting figured that the reason this asset was included in the guardianship account was to answer any questions that the "continuation" petition might have raised with either a probate court judge or a clerk. "That entry avoided problems with a judge who might look at the file and wonder what had happened to Joe's share of his father's business, which Ernest as executor had continued with the court's petition," said Whiting. It struck Whiting as strange that Fowler had prepared Joe's alleged objections to the guardianship accounting on the Saturday before the Monday hearing. Since Joe denied hiring Fowler or suing his brothers, Whiting speculated that the documents had been prepared to establish that the court had already approved the accounting and a payment to Joe, thereby precluding any possible legal action in the future.

"On paper it looked as if Joe had had his day in court," Whiting later explained. "He appeared to have received the assets in his guardianship estate and a settlement of $20,000 for the loan of his stock to the winery. Thus any future claim by him would have been barred. And in the back of my mind I wondered if this was why Ernest and Julio had become so upset when Joe had written his letter saying that a lawsuit would be a 'disaster.' Did they suspect he'd already discovered these files?"

Joe resisted Whiting's interpretations. His lawyer's speculations might be plausible, but he wanted to hear what Ernest and Julio had to say. He could hardly believe that they had kept all this a secret from him or that they didn't have a reasonable explanation for these documents.

Joe arranged for a private meeting with his brothers. On the morning of May 28, he once again sat at the winery's conference table. Now he was alone, facing Ernest and Julio across the table. Instead of beginning the meeting as he had done in the past, Ernest waited. Joe looked from Ernest to Julio and cleared his throat.

"Shouldn't we get to the matter of my one-third interest in the winery before I get much older?" he said.

"What? You mean you want"—Ernest gestured toward the window that looked out over the winery's grounds "—a piece of this?"

"That's exactly what I mean," Joe said.

"You must be kidding. You know you don't own an interest in the winery. You've had nothing to do with it. Where did you get such a crazy idea?"

"My lawyer has found papers in the Modesto courthouse," Joe replied. "They indicate a one-third interest in the winery."

"What papers?" Ernest demanded.

"Mainly the guardianship papers," Joe said. "I'd like to know what they mean."

"Stop talking in riddles. Where the hell did you get this idea?" Ernest was almost shouting now.

"It's all there in black and white," Joe said. "Right in the courthouse, plain as day. It says I was entitled to a one-third interest. Send somebody down to the courthouse, and they'll find the same thing."

Ernest glanced at Julio. Neither said a word.

After the tense silence, Ernest insisted, "There's got to be a mistake. You know I offered you an interest in the winery and you turned it down."

"You never offered me a third. After I got out of the army, you said that if I took the job with you in the winery instead of in Livingston, I could *work into* an interest. When I took the Livingston job, you never mentioned it again, and you certainly never indicated that I should have inherited a third from our father."

Joe waited for Julio to say something but he simply stared at the table.

"After all, we bought and developed the Tegner Ranch for you," Ernest began to argue, "while you were in the army."

"Yes, you did," Joe agreed, choosing not to debate this for the moment. It wasn't really the point anyway, he thought to himself. Whatever his brothers had done for him—whatever he had done for them over the years—didn't explain the court documents. But Ernest refused to discuss the guardianship records. He simply repeated what he'd done for Joe, as if Joe should consider it an act of charity, perhaps even recompense for not being a partner in the winery. Joe found himself perplexed that Ernest neither explained the documents nor refuted Whiting's interpretation. Rather, he seemed to be calling him an "ingrate" for raising the issue.

Julio still remained silent. Joe had to wonder if his brother's hospitalization in 1941 resulted from his awareness of the guardianship proceedings. Was Julio worried that the conflict over Joe's trademark would bring these documents to light? Was that why he had recalled their mother's last words at their first discussion of the cheese label? Julio again seemed distraught, but he didn't intervene as Ernest continued to lecture Joe about his "ingratitude."

"Send somebody down to the courthouse," Joe interrupted. "Have them look at those files." He rose from his chair. "Then maybe you can tell me what this means."

On June 9, Joe sent Ernest a letter to confirm in writing that his attorney, while researching papers for the trademark case, had discovered a document in his guardianship file that "stated that I was the owner of an interest in the winery."

Alerted that Joe was seriously going to pursue the matter, Ernest sent Jon Shastid from his legal staff to look at these records. On June 19, Shastid met with Whiting to explain Ernest's interpretation of the documents. Shastid insisted that the designation of "one-third interest in the E. & J. Gallo Winery" indicated only the amount of money owed to Joe by the winery.

Producing pages from early winery and Gallo Bros. Ranches accounts, Shastid argued that this was simply an accounting procedure to give Joe his one-third share of what the winery owed the Gallo Bros. partnership. Whiting disagreed, pointing out that the court record didn't designate it that way. Why would there have been the additional assigned sum of $20,000 in the court order if Ernest and Julio were simply paying him a specific debt shown in the brothers' ranch account? Why list a "one-third interest" in the winery as one of Joe's assets and then have a separate court-ordered $20,000 settlement? And on what basis had the sum of $20,000 been computed, since that sum supposedly represented profits earned by Joe's money "loaned" to the winery?

After his discussion with Shastid, Whiting was even more persuaded that Joe's alleged objections and the court order had been orchestrated to bar Joe from any future claims. (In fact, Shastid claimed to have no knowledge of Ernest's petition to continue the family business.) "What really convinced me was a document that Shastid left on my desk," recalled Whiting. "As we discovered later, the winery held Ed Taylor's old files. This document was not the actual court order filed in the case but an earlier one drafted by Taylor, which showed a payment of $15,000, not $20,000. I concluded that Taylor had drawn up the judgment before the hearing, before the judge would presumably hear evidence supporting Joe's alleged suit for $25,000. This draft of the court order that Shastid had in his file suggested that Taylor himself was deciding on the payment, not the judge, and before the supposed hearing."

At Joe's request, Whiting contacted other attorneys, who agreed with his conclusion from the documents that Joe should have inherited one-third of these assets, including a one-third interest in both the winery and the Gallo trade name and trademark.

At seven o'clock one morning a few weeks later, Ernest phoned Joe. "I want to have a meeting," he announced.

"When?" Joe asked.

"I'll be right down."

It was raining, a soft early summer shower, but when Ernest arrived Joe took him through the living room and outside where they stood under the eaves of the overhanging roof. Joe stared across the lawn that sloped down toward the driveway and road. Two colts were frolicking across the grass. He watched them as he waited for Ernest to speak.

Ernest paced back and forth, and soon his words came rapid fire.

"Believe me, Joe, you and your attorney are all wrong. It wasn't a third interest," he repeated. "It was what Shastid told Whiting—just money that was owed to you—er, rather a third interest in the money owed to the estate, you know, what we called the Gallo Brothers Ranches, from the winery."

"I don't see it like that," Joe said. "If it just meant that, why didn't it say so? Why did it say 'one-third interest in the winery'? Why didn't it say anything about Gallo Brothers Ranches? Our father's estate included his business. The business that the court document says you continued, and which I should have inherited one-third of."

Ernest was exasperated; he made choppy gestures as he continued to pace the porch.

"You know that Father was only in the wine business in a limited way before Prohibition," he said. "And that terminated with Prohibition—"

"I remember he told us that he bought wine in barrels and sold them to restaurants," Joe agreed.

"That's right," said Ernest. "Father came to the Bay Area and worked for a restaurant. Then once or twice a week he took a truck to Hanford—down to our mother's family winery—and brought back a load of wine for the restaurant. And that was the extent of Father's wine business, which was really not a wine business at all."

Joe was silent as Ernest went on to add that their father's grape business had been a small one, too, and that the name Gallo hadn't meant anything. Over the years Joe had heard only bits and pieces of the family history. However, given what Ernest had said in his trademark applications and lawsuits, Joe had to wonder if his version of history changed according to his current needs. In the documents Whiting had shown him, Ernest had testified to prior and continuous use of the Gallo name; he hadn't called their father's wine or grape business "small" or "limited," and he'd certainly tried to convince the court that the Gallo name had been significant in both businesses.

Nevertheless, Joe simply let Ernest go on, since he was curious how Ernest would now describe the past, about which he had rarely talked before.

"And then with Prohibition Father went into the grape-shipping business," Ernest said. "He shipped wine grapes back East—you remember—but then with the Depression he began to lose money. When it looked like Repeal was coming, I was all for going into the wine business, and I discussed the idea with him several times—"

"I don't remember that," Joe interrupted.

"You were too young."

"We were down in Fresno, but you and Julio were still up in Modesto. I don't remember you coming down to talk to Father—"

Ernest waved his objection aside. "We talked about the matter several times. Sometimes I thought Father was interested, sometimes he said that he was unable to do it. You remember how sick he was, how upset he was about his financial losses. So he couldn't make a decision. He was moody and uncommunicative; I thought he was irrational."

"I don't think he was that bad," Joe countered, his memories of their father at odds with Ernest's portrait of a morose failure. He certainly remembered conflicts between his older brother and their father, but he didn't recall his father as sick or worried about money before his death.

"If he hadn't died, maybe he would have gone into the wine business," Ernest conceded. "After all, it was a family tradition. But when he died, I was the one who did it. Julio and I, and you know you had nothing to do with the founding of the winery."

Joe was silent again. Hearing Ernest reminisce about their father was strange to him. After their parents' deaths, the brothers had rarely spoken about them. Now Ernest was handing him his history. The irony, of course, was that even in this version, Ernest was giving him reason to suspect that the winery had been a continuation of his father's business, that if he had lived he might have started a winery himself.

While Joe didn't know all the legal ramifications, he guessed that the court had confirmed a "one-third interest" because Ernest and Julio had used their father's estate and property to start the winery. He now said as much to Ernest, who again turned hostile.

"What the hell are you talking about, Joe? Don't you understand? It was our hard work, our effort that built the winery."

"But it should have been listed as our father's business that we *three* brothers inherited and continued," Joe said.

"You're blackmailing me," Ernest shouted. "You're forcing me to pay off your debts. You don't really believe you have an interest in the winery. It's the lawyers who are making you say this."

"Not at all," argued Joe. "I just don't understand why you told the court things you never told me when I was growing up. I always trusted you, I never asked questions, even though I always wondered why I wasn't a partner in the winery—"

"This is outrageous," Ernest shouted again. "It's extortion. But you're bound to lose. With all those attorneys' fees, you're going to be worse off than you are now!"

"I have nothing to lose. My lawyers will take this case on contingency."

Ernest turned on his heels and marched through the house and out to his car.

According to Whiting, after the discovery of the court records and Joe's refusal to accept Shastid's explanation, Ernest aggressively pursued a cash settlement. Joe, however, was unmoved by the offers.

Over the next weeks, Whiting spent long hours with Joe, who now talked much more freely and openly about his parents and his childhood than he ever had before. He was deeply wounded by what he regarded as his brothers' deception and their refusal to answer his questions about the guardianship estate and accounting. But what seemed to upset him most was seeing his mother's will. He now believed that his parents' wishes had not been honored by Ernest and Julio.

"Joe kept a copy of his mother's will on his desk for months," Whiting recalled. "He often picked it up and stared at it, and then he would reminisce about his mother and father and the deep love he had for them. He seemed to feel that he was fighting as much for his parents' right to dispose of their property as they saw fit as he was for his one-third interest in the winery and his right to use his name."

Thus while Ernest was urging a cash settlement, Joe's memories of his parents had strengthened his resolve to pursue the claim of his inheritance.

CHAPTER ELEVEN

Once Joe had decided to sue his brothers for a one-third share of the winery, Whiting felt that he should enlist the assistance of other attorneys, not only because of the complexity of the counterclaims but also because of the time and staff that Pat Lynch and O'Melveny & Myers would undoubtedly assign to the case. Whiting and Joe and Mike met with two San Francisco lawyers, Jess Jackson of Kendall-Jackson and Denis Rice of Howard, Rice, Nemerovski, Canady, Robertson & Falk, a firm with resources comparable to those of O'Melveny. Jackson and Rice agreed to work on the case together; trademark specialists in Rice's firm would focus on Joe's defense in the winery's infringement suit, Jackson on the counterclaim.

On July 31, 1986, Jackson filed Joe's counterclaim against the winery. In his brief, Jackson asserted that Joe was entitled to legal damages amounting to either one-third of the appreciated value of the winery or one-third of the winery's historical and future profits as well as one-third of the royalties lost as a result of Ernest and Julio's misappropriation of the Gallo trademark. Whichever way the damages were calculated, he claimed that Joe was entitled to well over $200 million.

"Usually I love cases that have windows on history," O'Melveny & Myers attorney Pat Lynch said, recalling his reaction to the filing of Joe's counterclaim. "But I thought this was an unfair, ugly charge because it came so late in the lives of the brothers. It had a soap opera quality to it, and it was rough to confront. I don't want to speculate on the motives for it."

Joe insisted that his decision to go ahead with the counterclaim had not been an easy one. From the outset, Whiting had explained what a suit like this would entail. It wasn't just the time and money involved, there was the publicity to consider. Ernest had always kept the winery and the family tightly under wraps. A court battle delving into the past would undoubtedly attract press attention. And there would be the emotional upheaval. The court case was bound to become a real family conflict, and it was quite likely that Joe and his brothers would never be on speaking terms again. But Joe felt compelled to pursue it.

Perhaps more than anyone, Patricia Gallo understood the high emotional cost of Joe's lawsuit against his brothers. She knew how closely he was tied to Ernest and Julio, how much he had looked up to them and admired them throughout his life. Having been secretary to winery vice-president Charles Crawford, she also knew how ruthless the two older brothers could be when they were united against a common enemy.

Patricia realized that discovering these facts about his inheritance and pursuing a lawsuit would mean a dramatic transformation in Joe's life. She sensed that Joe had suffered after the death of his parents more than he had ever let on. For a thirteen-year-old boy to lose his parents must have been tragedy enough. But because their deaths were a forbidden subject in the family, she guessed that he had never been allowed to mourn them and come to terms with their deaths. She wondered if reviving his grief would be too painful. Nevertheless, if he felt he had to do this, she would stand behind his decision.

How deeply this affected Joe was never more apparent than when *The Wine Spectator* ran an article about his lawsuit and printed a photograph of his mother's hand-written will. Although it was a public document, Joe was furious when he learned that Jess Jackson, his own lawyer, had made it available to the magazine, since he considered it an invasion of his mother's privacy.

For this and other reasons, according to Whiting, Joe requested that Whiting dismiss Jackson and ask Rice and his team of lawyers to help with the historical investigation that would be necessary to build the case for the counterclaim.

The investigation of the past wasn't a simple task. Whiting hunted down public documents, tracing the Gallo family's origins in Oakland and Hanford, Jackson and Escalon and Modesto. Howard, Rice associates spent weeks sifting through the winery's records, which, after much wrangling and many delays, were finally provided. As each new fact was unearthed, as record upon record came to light, the Gallo family story began to emerge from the brothers' silence.

Julio soon learned that he would have to break that silence. Once the lawsuit was filed and assigned to Federal Judge Edward Dean Price, the brothers' depositions were scheduled for early February 1987. On February 9, while being prepared for his deposition, Julio showed such symptoms of distress and illness that Pat Lynch, who later confirmed that his client's "health was a concern," called in Dr. Leon Epstein, a specialist in geriatric psychiatry at the University of California Hospital in San Francisco. The doctor examined Julio the next day. Lynch then petitioned the court to excuse Julio from testifying for medical reasons.

In the meantime Bob Gallo had also telephoned Joe to tell him how upset his father had become at the thought of giving a deposition. Could Joe not force Julio to testify? he asked.

Joe said that he sympathized, but would have to talk to his lawyers about it.

When Joe repeated the substance of this phone call to his attorneys, they were unwilling to excuse Julio. They believed that because the counterclaim involved so much of the past and in particular the guardianship estate accounting and hearing, it was crucial to have Julio's recollections. The attorneys were aware that Julio had tried to withdraw from the Gallo Salame case on medical grounds as well, and they wondered if he were now repeating the pattern. It was better, they argued, to have the medical experts examine Julio and file their reports so that the court could make its own decision.

On February 11, the day after Julio had been examined by Dr. Epstein, Bob realized that his father was still upset and tracked Joe down at the Clift Hotel in San Francisco where he was staying while he had conferences with Denis Rice. He asked Joe to meet with him and his father to try to resolve their differences.

Joe agreed, though not without some concern about talking to his brother out of the presence of his lawyers. Still, he thought that without Ernest, Julio might be more willing to compromise.

Bob and Julio arrived at the Clift Hotel at one o'clock and joined Joe at a table in the corner of the crowded dining room, Joe in the middle, Julio and Bob on either side.

"This is too hard on my dad," Bob said immediately. "We have to work this out."

Joe glanced at Julio, who seemed to be mumbling, "We gotta get this thing settled. We gotta get it settled." Joe wondered if Julio was putting on an act. Even when Julio had been upset at other times, he had never rambled like this. Joe couldn't believe that his brother would be this inarticulate when he was also asking to reach a settlement.

Joe found it so difficult to hear Julio that he suggested that they go to his room. Upstairs, Joe positioned a chair across from the sofa where Bob had taken a seat; Julio sat in the armchair at the end of the coffee table and at right angles to both Bob and Joe. Bob took on the role of negotiator, and he now asked Joe to outline the points of contention in the trademark case. Joe explained what he had repeatedly discussed with Ernest and what he had refused to accept in the proposed agreement: the nonassignability of the trademark, distribution limitations, and the winery's power to close him down.

"Well, if that's all you're asking for, I'm sure Ernest would go for that," Julio burst out.

"But those are the things he wouldn't agree to before," Joe said. He ticked them off again, reciting the list of Ernest's objections, but with each item, Julio said, "I'm sure Ernest will accept that if that's what you request now."

"I don't think you understand, Julio. For the last two years every time we nearly got this settled, Ernest brought up one of these objections. I don't think I can trust Ernest, and after all that's happened, I think he'd find a reason to close us down."

"No, no, Joe, you don't have to worry," Julio insisted. "You can trust him, I'm sure of it."

Bob now proposed an agreement very much along the lines that Joe had originally accepted, with the notable exception that Ernest would not be able to close the plant.

Joe said that he could live with this settlement, but that there was the matter of the counterclaim—the trademark and what he should have inherited as well. Once again Bob asked him to explain in more detail what this side of the suit involved. Joe gave a brief summary of the documents that John Whiting had discovered and why he was suing for one-third of the winery.

"But you realize you don't have any interest in the winery!" Julio intervened. "You never had an interest," he added, his voice rising.

"Well, you never told me I did, and you never told me I didn't," said Joe.

"But we built the winery—"

"Let's drop the subject," said Joe. "This isn't the time to prove that you're right or I'm right. We're here to see if we don't have to go to court to decide it."

"That's right," interrupted Bob. "So here's our offer, Joe. Ten million dollars plus a license for your trademark, and in return, you'll drop the counterclaim."

According to Whiting, less than a year before, Ernest had offered Joe ten million dollars to settle the trademark dispute "just so we can all avoid the publicity." Joe had agreed, but two days later Jon Shastid had phoned and rescinded the offer, explaining that Ernest had decided that the settlement figure was out of the question.

"Maybe you don't realize it, Bob," Joe now said, "but I was offered that same amount just so Ernest and Julio could avoid publicity."

"We've already had the publicity," Bob snapped.

"So that's it?" Joe asked, looking at Julio for confirmation.

"That's all there is to it," Julio agreed. "That's all we're interested in doing."

"Okay, that's the end of it," said Joe. "No more talk about it." He moved his chair back to the other side of the room and stalked toward the door.

"No, wait," Julio said, rushing to block Joe's exit. "Come back, sit down."

Joe sat on the edge of the bed and sighed. "What is it now? What else do you want to do?"

Julio paced the room for a few minutes. Then he stopped in front of him.

"Would you take twenty million?"

Joe thought a moment. "That seems reasonable, as long as we can work out the trademark agreement and figure out the tax questions and lawyers' fees."

"I don't think Ernest would go for that," Julio objected.

"Then settle your half of the case yourself."

"That's impossible," said Julio. "But let's just see what Ernest says."

Joe agreed to have Whiting and his San Francisco attorneys calculate the fees involved at that point and also the taxes on the settlement sum. As Bob and Julio departed, Joe promised to call Bob within the week to give him the additional financial information.

But the following week when Joe phoned, Bob cut him short.

"Ernest's side of the family has rejected the whole deal. They don't want to go along with this settlement. But I'll keep working on it and be in touch."

A week later the answer was still the same: "Ernest's side of the family said no."

Bob made one last brief phone call to Joe to say that the settlement had fallen apart and there was no hope of changing Ernest's mind. Once again, Joe felt abused. Irritated that Julio wouldn't break free and settle on his own, he distrusted him as well, especially when the winery's lawyers were petitioning the court to excuse him from testifying.

After Dr. Leon Epstein filed a report of his February 10, 1987, interview with Julio to support the winery's motion, Joe's attorneys filed a brief informing the court that the day after the psychiatrist's examination, Julio had driven to San Francisco with his son Bob and had conducted a "settlement conference" on his own. They reminded the court that Julio had tried to use a medical excuse to exempt himself from a 1981 deposition in the Gallo Salame case, although he had then complained of cardiac problems. They were compelled, they said, to request an examination by their own appointed psychiatrist, Dr. Joe Tupin, a professor of psychiatry at the UC Davis Medical Center in Sacramento.

Judge Price agreed, but it wasn't until November 4, 1987, that Dr. Tupin examined Julio in the presence of Dr. Epstein. Neither doctor, however, questioned Julio about any events before February 10, 1987, the date of Dr. Epstein's first interview with Julio. Although the doctors' observations were in basic agreement, Dr. Tupin disagreed with Dr. Epstein that a deposition would endanger Julio's health and well-being.

The issue of Julio's health had stirred another controversy. The winery lawyers moved to have all such reports sealed and oral arguments closed to the public. They insisted that the public's right to know was balanced with the right of privacy, and in this instance an open record would "needlessly expose litigants or witnesses to loss of their privacy, shame or embarrassment."

Joe's attorneys contended that the question of Julio's testifying should be part of the public record. Not only had the lawsuit been brought against Joe in Julio's name as well as in Ernest's; but also Julio's distress seemed to be exacerbated by those aspects of family history on which Joe's counterclaims were based. If his anxiety was heightened by his fear of giving "the wrong answers," as had been reported to the judge, then Julio's recollections should be heard in open court.

The McClatchy News Service and the New York Times Company

(acting for its newspaper, the *Santa Rosa Press-Democrat*) objected to the proposed closing of these proceedings and the sealing of documents as well. Judge Price ruled against Howard, Rice and the press and closed the November 10 hearing on Julio's medical condition. But he made a point of insisting that the rest of the case would remain open.

After hearing the testimony of the medical experts in camera, Judge Price issued his Memorandum Decision on December 17. He rejected the winery's petition to exempt Julio from having his deposition taken, concluding that it would be unfair to allow "one who starts litigation . . . to withhold his or her knowledge from the adversary or from the trier of fact." He noted as well that a petition for a medical excuse for Julio had been filed in the salami case ("on that occasion, the complaint was with the cardiac system—here, however, the emphasis was on the psychiatric well being of Julio Gallo," he wrote). He added that, in the salami case, Julio seemed to have waived the court-ordered medical supervision and completed his deposition without any problem. He also seemed swayed by the knowledge of Julio's trip to San Francisco to discuss a possible settlement with Joe—without benefit of counsel or "medical personnel"—only the day after he had evidenced stress and anxiety to Dr. Epstein.

At the same time, Judge Price addressed what he noted had been represented to the court as Julio's fear of not performing "well" or giving the "wrong answers": "An honest answer of 'I don't remember' is better than a guess which is designed to conform to a pre-arranged strategy of counsel," he instructed. He ordered that before the deposition Julio would decide whether he would "enter upon a routine of drugs and/or psychotherapy or both as discussed by Doctors Epstein and Tupin." A medical attendant would be present at all times during the deposition, and there would be rest periods after every half-hour of questioning.

Finally, Judge Price expressed his anger at "whoever issued [the] order" instructing the two doctors not to question Julio about events before February 10, 1987. No one was sure where this prohibition originated, and the judge commented that it had been a "great disservice to the patient and to the court."

Finally, a year after they were first scheduled, the three brothers' depositions began in mid-January and continued through the first weeks of March 1988. Each brother's deposition was characteristic of his personality.

Ernest was controlling, answering questions with questions and claiming not to recall certain events, even when shown documents to refresh his memory. In response to some questions, Ernest's answers were inaccurate, which Joe's attorneys did not realize until later. For example, Joe's attorneys wanted as much information as possible about Joe, Sr.'s grape-shipping business and the Gallo label used on his grapes. When asked if any of the grape dealers to whom he and his father sold their product was still living, Ernest said no, although later it was confirmed by Chicago grape dealer Paul Alleruzzo that not only had "Ernie" remembered him and supplied his name to his lawyers, but he had been interviewed by a researcher employed by O'Melveny & Myers, six months earlier. But at the time of Ernest's deposition, the Howard, Rice attorneys had no basis to refute Ernest's statement. Nor did they realize that Alleruzzo was alive and recalled Joe, Sr., and Ernest as "large shippers" and the Gallo label as important to his grape customers.

In the face of questioning about some events, Ernest said he didn't remember them very well. But when asked about certain incidents or conversations, particularly those that involved the guardianship estate, he seemed to recall them in great detail. For example, while he said he did not remember attending Joe's guardianship hearing, he declared that Joe had complained long and loud about the accounting and had hired a lawyer. Here he gave an extended narrative and said that Julio and he had been irritated when they had been forced to pay Joe $20,000. Yet he still could not explain why the court order showed him and Julio present when Julio was in the hospital and he, according to documentary evidence, was meeting with a BATF inspector.

He was most emphatic about two subjects: First, his father had been stern and hard and had made sure that his two older sons put in long hours with little recompense. He was stubborn and set in his ways, Ernest asserted, and in his last years had become so morose and depressed that he had finally refused to make a decision about starting a winery. The theme of this testimony was clear—the father was sick and poor and had made so many bad decisions throughout his life that he could not have provided any basis, background, or business from which his sons could have developed a winery.

Second, Ernest provided detailed narratives of all the conversations in which Joe had supposedly refused to "come into" or "work into" an interest in the winery. He elaborated the alleged discussion after Joe had returned from the army. This seemed to prove to him that Joe not only wasn't a partner but had refused to become a partner.

In contrast to this extended testimony, Ernest had little to say when asked about documents Joe's lawyers showed to him to raise the question of his credibility: for example, his denial to the Bureau of Alcohol that Mike Gallo was a relative; his story to the BATF inspectors that he knew nothing about the brandy incident; his explanation to the BATF that he and Julio, not their father, had built the underground tanks at the Maze Road ranch. And finally he now disavowed his assertions in the winery's trademark applications and earlier court cases that his father was the predecessor user and that the Gallo name had been been in continuous use since 1909. He offered few remarks to explain why his testimony seemed to change with the circumstances.

If Ernest seemed to stonewall, Julio simply faded like the Cheshire Cat. The lawyers seemed to treat him with kid gloves. On several occasions, when they appeared to come close to probing either the parents' deaths or the coincidence of his 1941 hospitalization with the settlement of Joe's guardianship estate, he became incensed and upset. Dr. Epstein asked for a break, and the lawyers retreated. In response to questions about Ernest's statements in the winery trademark applications and previous court cases, Julio insisted that he had no knowledge of many of the business transactions and legal documents that he was shown. While Ernest was asked to explain contradictions between his recollections and the records, Julio said that he had taken no part in preparing official applications or legal statements. For someone who supposedly was an equal partner in the winery, he seemed to have played no role at all in the business and financial affairs of the company and the family. Wine and grapes he could talk about; but, as he reminded his questioners, on doctors' orders he had stayed well away from Ernest's concerns.

Julio claimed that he had one distinct memory: that just after his return from his World War II service, when Joe had lunched with Julio and Aileen, he had refused Julio's offer to "come into" the winery. Yet his language was so similar to Ernest's that Joe's lawyers suspected that the brothers had prepared the story to support their contention that Joe had repeatedly rejected a winery partnership (even though Ernest conceded that the offer did not mean a "gift" or a definite one-third partnership).

In his deposition Joe disputed that he had ever had such discussions with either brother. Instead, he recalled his conversation with Ernest in his office when Joe had refused to replace Crawford and announced his decision to take Julio's job offer at the Livingston vineyards. Confronted with the documents and records that he had never seen before Whiting's discovery of the guardianship estate hearing, Joe insisted that he had no recollection of receiving an accounting, hiring a lawyer, going to court, or even receiving money from a court judgment. But since he claimed "not to remember" these events, his testimony was less forceful than if he had explicitly denied that they had occurred. (Although the implication was often that he would have remembered these crucial incidents if they had happened, he did not state his denials outright, a habit of speech that would later have negative consequences.)

The depositions made evident what Joe's lawyers would encounter when arguing the counterclaims: secrecy, contradictory recollections, failures of memory, lack of knowledge, facts lost to the passage of time. The winery's records were of little help either—in fact, the Howard, Rice attorneys were still wrangling with O'Melveny & Myers over what had been omitted from the files and what had still not been released in discovery.

As their preparations for the trademark infringement part of the case proceeded, John Whiting and Al Herzig maintained that Joe's defense was a simple one—that Joe's use of his own name in his business was a right of commercial free speech protected by the First Amendment and reasserted in recent Supreme Court decisions. They felt that the issue of possible confusion between Joe's cheese and Ernest and Julio's wine could be decided on the precedent of the "*Friend* Decision" in the Ninth Circuit Court of Appeals. The case involved a large, national stationery supplier in Ohio, called the Friend Company after the name of its founder. Breaking with his father, the founder's son had then established his own stationery supplier in California, also calling it Friend and listing a post office box in the same town as his father's original company. The court found that the son was intentionally trying to confuse the consumer; yet, reluctant to take away the son's right to use his own name, it ordered him to use both his first and last names and a different mailing address to avoid confusion with the original company.

Whiting was sure that Joe's defense could be based on these two points of law, and a classic trademark defense, namely, proving no likelihood of confusion and long-time acquiescence by the winery to Joe's use of his name in his businesses. Winery attorneys Pat Lynch and Oliver Wanger were mounting a full attack—a survey to establish the likelihood of confusion between the products and an expert witness to inspect Joe's production records and evaluate his cheese. Howard, Rice responded in kind, hiring its own polling expert to refute the winery's survey as well as a cheese expert to provide his own analysis of Joe's product.

Whiting and Herzig, however, wanted to focus on the First Amendment issue and the *Friend* precedent and were concerned that the case would be swamped by citations, survey results, and scientific analyses. (The Gallo brothers' lawsuit had already accumulated so many documents that they filled two separate storage rooms in the courthouse.)

By then, however, Whiting and Herzig said that they had been squeezed out of the case. According to Whiting, Howard, Rice attorneys had even asked him as well as Joe and Mike to let Herzig go, but Joe had heatedly refused. Whiting felt that the San Francisco attorneys ignored his and Herzig's opinions and failed to keep them informed of all that was happening in the case. No longer running Joe's team, Whiting, however, deferred to the Howard, Rice firm's strategy. These attorneys thought that the trademark case was a cinch—at most the court would order a disclaimer on Joe's label—and that the best defense was to refute the charges of confusion and poor quality with their own surveys and cheese experts.

The disagreements among Joe's attorneys became evident in the pretrial hearings and oral arguments. Judge Price was already impatient with the lack of cooperation from both sides' lawyers, the complaints of withheld documents, and the allegations of bad faith. Now he seemed irritated with the apparent disharmony of Joe's lawyers—they sometimes appeared to be presenting two different cases. During an oral argument for pretrial motions, Herzig tried to reintroduce the free speech issue and *Friend* decision precedent, which he felt had been slighted by Denis Rice. Judge Price denied him the opportunity. Sitting in the rear of the courtroom, Whiting shook his head in exasperation at the ruling. Judge Price ordered him outside.

When *E. & J. Gallo Winery* v. *Gallo Cattle Company* had first been filed in the United States District Court for the Eastern District of

California, Judge Edward Dean Price was assigned the case by the court's ordinary random method of selection. His hearing the case, however, would later become a subject of some dispute. Three judges were available to sit in the Eastern District—Price, Judge Robert Coyle, and Judge Myron D. Crocker, who had presided over the Gallo Salame case. Crocker was by then a "senior judge," semiretired but still presiding in cases when the calendar caseload or the subject matter of the suit made it either necessary or appropriate. As Judge Crocker himself confirmed, he sat "when asked" by either the court clerk or other judges in the district.

In fact, Judge Crocker's assignment to the winery's suit against Joe might well have been appropriate. Under the federal court's Local Rule 123, all attorneys are required to inform the court when they have reason to believe that a new lawsuit is related to a previously filed action. The court may then reassign the case to the judge who heard the prior suit.

Since the winery's trademark infringement suit against Joe involved the same trademarks that had been at issue in the Gallo Salame case, a related case notice should arguably have been filed by Joe's lawyers and the winery's lawyers. Alerted to the related case, Judge Price could then have transferred the case to Judge Crocker.

Neither Whiting nor Rice filed a notice of related case, apparently because they lacked the complete records of the salami case (it was still under seal). According to attorney Al Herzig, he later raised the question with his colleagues, but at the time they seemed not to realize the significance of the cases' related issues.

Wanger's firm had represented the winery as local counsel in the Gallo Salame case. But Wanger and Lynch would contend that the cases were not sufficiently related to require a related case notice (although in a different context Judge Coyle would disagree with their assertion). In a later statement to the court, Herzig would implicitly argue that they had reason to assert the lack of connection and not file a related case notice: In his deposition Ernest had testified that the salami case had been settled, in part, because he and his attorneys were concerned that Judge Crocker might rule against the winery because of its delay in filing the case. They had no reason to believe that he would be more sympathetic to their suit against Joe.

Nonlawyers in the community also had reason to wonder about Judge Price's participation in this particular case. As the *Modesto Bee* chronicled each new motion, charge, and countercharge, one of the persistent questions among Central Valley residents was why Joe's attorneys hadn't asked for a change of venue, or at least another judge.

Judge Price was reputed to be hard on lawyers, especially unprepared federal prosecutors. He scolded attorneys and sometimes threw their cases out of court when irritated. (In one instance, the court of appeals reversed Price's ruling of prosecutorial misconduct, then took the unusual step of remanding the case to a different judge because Judge Price was deemed "disproportionately harsh" in dismissing the case.) Yet according to the *Fresno Bee*, there was one exception to Price's impatience: the winery's counsel, Oliver Wanger, of McCormick, Barstow, the leading Fresno law firm.

Wanger was well known locally. He was handsome, with large blue eyes and graying wavy hair. He was one of two adopted sons of "Ziegfeld girl" Justine Johnson, the first wife of movie producer Walter Wanger. (Although Wanger and Johnson were divorced by the time of the adoption, and Wanger had married Joan Bennett, the two boys took Wanger's name. It was Walter Wanger, who in 1951 scandalized Hollywood by shooting Bennett's agent and lover, Jennings Lang, in the "pelvic region," as headline stories at the time euphemistically put it.)

Oliver Wanger had come to Fresno as a young boy to spend his summer vacations on a ranch, and after law school at University of California's Boalt Hall and a stint as a Fresno County district attorney, he joined the McCormick, Barstow firm. Having often appeared before Judge Price, Wanger was called his "favorite attorney." But Wanger disagreed. "I've been dinged in his court too," he insisted in a *Fresno Bee* interview, adding that the judge "has a better grasp of cases than most attorneys, although sometimes he can be indiscreet."

Judge Price had extensive personal and professional connections in Modesto. He was born in 1919 in Sanger, another Central Valley agricultural town where grapes were a major crop. He attended law school at the University of California before interrupting his studies to serve in the army during World War II. After completing law school, he returned to the Central Valley and went to work for the Modesto law firm of Cleary and Zeff. Five years later, he founded his own practice, Price, Martin and Crabtree, which specialized in civil law. Along the way he became what he described as a "close personal friend" of Frank Damrell, Jr., a partner in his father's Modesto law firm, Damrell, Damrell & Nelson.

Frank Damrell, Jr., was the brother of Marie Damrell, the wife of Bob Gallo, and through him Price also knew the Gallo family. Furthermore, having had professional and social dealings with the Damrell law firm, Price was also an acquaintance of Davis Grant Vander Wall, a Damrell associate who went on to become a municipal judge and married Julie Gallo, Bob and Marie's daughter (Price attended the 1983 wedding).

After Edward Taylor, Sr.'s death, Damrell had replaced him as the Gallo Winery and Glass Company's Modesto counsel. He also seemed to have been helpful in gaining Price's appointment to the federal bench. Damrell had been a college roommate of former California Governor Jerry Brown, and, according to the *Modesto Bee*, was described "as a close personal friend and supporter of Alan Cranston" by one of Cranston's aides, Roy Greenaway, who added that, given their relationship, it would have been "surprising" if Cranston hadn't consulted Damrell about the judicial appointment. In November 1979, Cranston recommended Price to fill a judgeship in California's Eastern District federal court. Shortly thereafter Damrell gave a fund-raiser for Cranston, and the following morning Price had a meeting with Cranston at Damrell's home.

The ties among Price, Damrell, Cranston, and the Gallos were strong enough to feed the local rumor mills. People remembered seeing Judge Price at social affairs with Julio and Ernest; all three belonged to the Sportsmen of Stanislaus and the Del Rio Golf and Country Club and Julio and Price were Rotary Club members. Stories circulated that in the past the two Gallo brothers and the judge had dined together at the Cote D'Oro, the winery's once-favorite restaurant.

As a result of local gossip, Linda Gallo Jelacich, who lived in Modesto, received several unsolicited telephone calls reminding her that Judge Price was "an old personal friend of Frank Damrell, Jr.," and "had lots of connections to Ernest and Julio." How could Judge Price sit on the case? they asked Joe's daughter. Weren't the attorneys going to object?

Beyond the personal and political connections, Price had also presided over several cases involving the winery before his assignment to the Joe Gallo lawsuit. In November 1982, the C. Pappas Company, Gallo's Boston distributor, had sued the winery in Massachusetts, alleging violations of federal antitrust laws and breach of contract, breach of fiduciary duties, tortious interference with prospective business relations, and violation of the Massachusetts Consumer Protection Act. But Gallo's contract with distributors required that any cause of action be brought "only in a court having jurisdiction at the home office of the winery." Gallo successfully petitioned to have the case transferred from Massachusetts to the Eastern District of California, where it was first assigned to Judge Robert Coyle. On August 10, 1983, however, Judge Coyle stepped down, and he and Judge Price signed the order that transferred the case to Judge Price.

Although no reason for the transfer was stated in the court record, three attorneys for the Pappas Company recalled that it was their impression that the case had been transferred to Judge Price because Oliver Wanger of McCormick, Barstow, the law firm in which Coyle had been a partner, was co-counsel for the winery. Entered into the civil minutes and on the docket in large print was the additional order, "All motions will be heard by E.D.P." This ensured that any motions would be heard and ruled on by Price alone, and if he were taken ill or an emergency arose, the hearing would be rescheduled and not turned over to a magistrate (which would have been standard procedure, especially since Pappas's lead attorneys had to travel from Boston for scheduled court appearances).

In 1985 Judge Price granted the winery's motion for summary judgment, concluding that Pappas had provided no evidence for its claims that it had been terminated for resisting the winery's demands. He ruled that the Gallo distributorship agreement was neither exclusive nor assignable and concluded, "The adoption and compliance with Gallo's merchandising philosophy by the distributor was a condition precedent to being appointed a Gallo distributorship . . . and to the retention of such distributorship."

In 1986 Judge Price heard another case against the winery, this one brought by Premier Wine and Spirits, Gallo's distributor in South Dakota. Premier claimed that Gallo had wrongfully terminated the contract, because Premier's managers refused to perform alleged illegal acts—specifically, "resetting dealers' shelves." It also argued that the winery's requirement of hiring and paying a separate Gallo sales force constituted a franchise fee, and that the thirty-day termination clause was "unconscionable." Again, because of the Gallo contract's "forum selection clause," the case was remanded to California where it was assigned to Judge Price. In this case as well Judge Price issued a summary judgment in favor of the winery.

Judge Price then presided in a 1987 suit that the Winery, Distillery

& Allied Workers Union filed to compel arbitration in the dismissal of striking employees by Gallo, Franzia, and Bronco wineries. (Art Ciocca at Franzia and Fred Franzia at Bronco, like Ernest, had fired workers who had gone on strike.) Price ruled against the union and for Ernest and his in-laws. Two months later the National Labor Relations Board found sufficient evidence to call for a hearing on the alleged "unfair labor practices" of the wineries. The proceeding eventually resulted in the employees' rehiring.

On August 29, 1988, Judge Price issued two decisions in the Joe Gallo case. First, he ruled against Joe's motion for a summary judgment on the winery's trademark infringement suit and ordered the case to go to trial on November 10. At the same time, he granted the winery's motion for summary judgment on Joe's counterclaims. He decreed that there was no basis for Joe's claim that he had been denied his inheritance of one-third of the winery.

The crux of his decision was that the guardianship hearing and the court order instructing Ernest and Julio to pay Joe an additional $20,000 was res judicata, that is, already settled by a judge. In order to set aside these court decrees, Joe and his attorneys had to prove that "the Executors of the respective estates, and particularly Ernest Gallo, the Executor of the estate of Joseph Gallo, Sr., practiced a fraud upon the probate court." Judge Price concluded that Joe had failed "to establish facts that would support that assertion."

Short of conclusive evidence of fraud, it was unclear what would have convinced Judge Price that there was at least a triable issue of extrinsic fraud in the probated estates and the guardianship hearing. Pointing to the court minutes that reported that Ernest and Joe were examined as witnesses at the guardianship hearing, he found that there was "no evidence which would overcome the presumption that the court's records accurately reflect what transpired." He found Joe's documentary evidence showing that Ernest was at that time meeting with a BATF inspector unpersuasive, stating that "It is not at all outside the realm of possibility that Ernest Gallo attended the court proceeding and later met with the official in question. To find otherwise would result in the wildest kind of speculation."

Noting that Joe "does not directly deny that this event occurred," he remarked, "Instead, he claims he has no memory of being in court on that day. Who among us can recall what he was doing on June 30, 1941?"

Price did not address Joe's other statements in his declaration in which he expressly denied hiring a lawyer, receiving a final accounting, or complaining to his brothers, much less suing them ("that would have been unthinkable"). It was equally likely, and more than likely, given Joe's relationship with Ernest and Julio, that he would have remembered if not the date, then the act of suing his brothers and winning $20,000, especially if, as Ernest alleged, it had provoked some dissension and bitterness in the family. Nor did Price comment on Julio's assertions that he knew nothing about these proceedings or a payment of $20,000. Furthermore, the judge made no reference to the counterclaims' arguments that Ernest, not Joe, had paid for a lawyer, that Joe's signature on the document was questionable, that his birthdate was inaccurate, and that Taylor seemed to have prepared the court-ordered settlement before the supposed hearing.

Judge Price then addressed the more general argument mounted by Joe's attorneys: that Ernest and Julio had continued their father's wine and grape business and therefore Joe should have inherited one-third of the "predecessor's business and trademark." His ruling dismissed the existence of Joe Gallo, Sr.'s wine business as "mostly the stuff that family antidotes [sic] are made of." He declared that although the term "wine business" was ambiguous, the winery was not a continuation of the father's business. Despite the fact that Ernest's petition to continue the father's business proposed crushing grapes into juice, he concluded that the winery was a separate enterprise. However, he seemed unaware of changes in Prohibition law in anticipation of Repeal when he explained that a winery could not have been established in the estate's name, because "a petition to start a winery would not receive favor with a probate court in Stanislaus County in 1933."

Having noted that the parents' estates "did not list any wine licenses, or any other indicia of being in the wine business," Price did not comment on the omission of the underground wine tanks from the property inventoried; he simply noted that "Ernest's administration was appropriate and . . . all of the assets of the estate were reported and administered." Further on, however, he concluded that, while Joe and his attorneys "make much of . . . the construction of cement tanks," the purpose of the tanks was in dispute and the two sides simply canceled each other out.

Ernest's testimony in other circumstances seemed to support Joe's contention that the winery was a continuation of his father's business —most notably in the winery's trademark applications and his depositions in both the Charles and Mary Gallo and Gallo Salame cases. Price, however, diminished the importance of these statements by calling them "Ernest Gallo's *post facto* 'puffing' of his ancestors' involvement in the wine business." Thus, while at certain times he chose to base his conclusions on evidence "relying principally on the memory of the oldest son Ernest," here he chose to give little weight to Ernest's statements, even though they were made under oath.

The summary judgment now meant that the trademark part of the case would not be heard by a jury. Because Ernest and Julio were asking for an injunction against Joe but no monetary damages, the winery's trademark suit, under federal court procedure, would be decided by Judge Price alone. And Joe's attorneys were now alarmed that the judge's rulings on the summary judgment motions at least indicated a tendency to give Ernest and Julio's position more credence than Joe's. Indeed, they wondered if this had been the reason why Ernest and Julio had initially decided not to sue Joe for monetary damages.

"It makes sense to try to avoid a jury trial in a case where there is so much emotional intensity," Pat Lynch later commented. "There's an obvious jury appeal to the notion that an individual has a God-given right to use his name as a trademark. Still, I doubt that Ernest and Julio didn't sue for money because they didn't want a jury trial. Although not many trademark owners forgo damages, in this case they did so because it was not their purpose to damage or hurt Joe. Ernest and Julio just wanted to establish that the winery trademark was not there for the taking, by their brother or by anyone else with the name Gallo."

Ernest himself regarded the summary judgment against Joe as a great victory, and David reportedly danced through the winery hallways, popping bottles of André Champagne. Dan Solomon, the Gallo press spokesman, broke his usual silence and confirmed the family's exuberance. Later, however, Ernest curtailed the champagne celebrations, or at least the triumphant exclamations to the press.

In response to Judge Price's decision, Denis Rice filed two motions. First, he moved to stay the winery's trademark case until his appeal of the summary judgment. Second, Rice petitioned the court to have the trademark infringement suit heard by a jury. Judge Price denied both motions and scheduled trial to begin November 15.

A week before trial, Judge Price consented to an interview with a reporter from the *Modesto Bee*. Linda Di Pietro was a staff writer assigned to business stories who had been reporting the brothers' lawsuit for the previous two years. Several times she had requested an interview with Price, but why Judge Price agreed to an interview just before the case was to begin, she wasn't sure. She conducted the interview on Wednesday, November 9, and questioned him about his possible Gallo connections. Price admitted that he had associated socially with Ernest and Julio (but also hastened to add that he had even more frequently attended civic luncheon meetings where Joe had been present).

He confirmed that he had attended Julie Gallo's wedding, and although he didn't expand on his friendship with Frank Damrell, he acknowledged that Cranston had recommended him and that he had had a meeting with the senator arranged by Damrell at the latter's home. According to Di Pietro, she then had the impression that Judge Price suspected that she had further information about possible Gallo associations, because he interrupted the interview to make a surprising announcement: "If any party to this action had any questions, I would have disqualified myself. . . . Both sides seem to be happy with the way I've handled this case, but if any counsel . . . believes they can't get a fair trial in my court, I'll gladly step aside."

The statement would not appear in print until Di Pietro's *Modesto Bee* article was published on Sunday, November 13. However, on the day following the interview, Mike and Joe were meeting with Denis Rice and his associates when they received word that Judge Price was requesting an urgent telephone conference with counsel for both sides. During the subsequent call, Price repeated to the attorneys what he had told the *Modesto Bee* reporter: "If any counsel in this case believes they can't get a fair trial in my court, I'll gladly step aside." He reiterated that if any of them questioned his impartiality, then they should put that in writing and have it on his desk in the morning "so that appropriate arrangements for reassignment of the case could be made."

Mike and Joe did not participate in the call, but the judge's announcement prompted a flurry of activity in the Howard, Rice office. "Rice and his associate Alan Sparer started rushing around," recalled Mike. "We all wanted to disqualify Price, and the lawyers said that the judge had already told them he would step down if they filed a motion to disqualify by the next morning. My impression was that it was going to be a simple motion—that all we had to say was that we were concerned about getting a fair trial. And by that point we were very concerned. But we weren't told that Judge Price would immediately transfer the case to Judge Coyle." Mike and Joe left the lawyers to prepare the necessary paperwork, including an affidavit from Mike confirming his knowledge of the phone calls his sister Linda had received about the Price-Gallo associations.

Sparer drafted the motion to disqualify, in which he cited the connections between the judge and the winery that had led Mike to "have a reasonable belief that [Price] cannot be impartial." Sparer signed it and faxed copies to Judge Price, Lynch, and Wanger on Friday, November 11. Outraged at the last-minute motion, the winery attorneys drafted their response over the weekend and filed their brief at 11:28 Monday morning, November 14. Within a few hours, Judge Price recused himself and ordered the attorneys to appear the following morning before Judge Robert E. Coyle.

The process happened so quickly that only in retrospect was there time to question the circumstances. It was strange that questions from a newspaper reporter had prompted the judge's offer to step down. In his written recusal order, Judge Price seemed to be having it both ways. While insisting that "the Court is not convinced that the defendants' motion states sufficient grounds for disqualification," he nevertheless withdrew from the case. This seemed a judicial equivalent to being a little bit pregnant—either there were grounds for recusal or there were not.

Judge Price's recusal appeared to be a favorable development for Joe. But embedded in a footnote in the recusal motion filed by Howard, Rice, Sparer had declared: "Defendants do not claim that the decisions made prior to this motion show bias or prejudice, and Defendants do not and will not seek to have any such prior decision set aside on that ground."

John Whiting later insisted that he had never seen the motion or this concession until many months after trial. If he had seen it at the time, he said, he would have refused to include it. What was the point of arguing recusal for cause if not to establish grounds for appealing Price's summary judgment? Sparer insisted that the footnote was "necessary," but Whiting said that Sparer never explained why. Perhaps Sparer believed or had been informed that Judge Price would have denied the recusal motion if he had not added the footnote. Whiting, however, disagreed with this strategy, saying, "If you have grounds for recusal, you argue them. If a judge refuses your motion, you ask for a hearing."

The Howard, Rice motion also seemed to imply that Joe's attorneys had already agreed to the transfer of the case to Judge Robert E. Coyle. Describing the conference call in the motion, Sparer wrote that Judge Price had said that they should seek disqualification "without delay in order that the matter could be turned over to Judge Coyle with a minimum of delay and disruption of the calendar of the judges involved."

It seemed a somewhat irregular maneuver. Under usual disqualification procedure, Judge Price would have vacated his summary judgment and returned the case to the clerk to be reassigned. Although Coyle was the only full time judge available, Judge Crocker was a possible alternative, especially since under Local Rule 123 it would have been appropriate to assign him the case in the first place. Instead, Judge Crocker was again overlooked, and the case was rushed into Coyle's courtroom. With no objection from the attorneys, Judge Coyle announced on November 15 that he had already cleared his calendar so that trial could begin on Tuesday, November 22.

In the normal course of case assignments, attorneys usually research a judge's background and previous rulings. Whether the Howard, Rice firm had done so was unclear. In early 1988, however, Judge Price had proposed Judge Coyle to preside over required pretrial settlement conferences. Denis Rice had then rejected the proposal. Judge Price offered only one alternative—a judge in Sacramento. (Once more Judge Crocker had been overlooked when he was not only eligible, but more than suitable under Local Rule 123.)

Whatever his previous reservations about Coyle as a settlement judge, Denis Rice did not voice objections to the transfer or raise any questions about Judge Coyle's former partnership in McCormick, Barstow and its representation of the winery in the Gallo Salame case. It seems, instead, that Joe's attorneys were so intent on disqualifying Price that they were willing to accept Coyle without question.

Robert Coyle was another local boy, born and raised in Fresno. Admitted to the bar in 1956, he, like Oliver Wanger, first served as a deputy district attorney for Fresno County and then joined McCormick, Barstow and was made a partner. Coyle became and remained friends with several members of the firm, including the younger Oliver Wanger. (In some legal circles Coyle was referred to as "Ollie's mentor.")

The McCormick, Barstow firm had handled several cases for the winery, and from 1980 to 1983, one of McCormick, Barstow's cases had been the Gallo Winery's trademark infringement suit against Gallo Salame and Consolidated Foods. Wanger would later say that he was simply acting as a local counsel to file motions and briefs in the Fresno federal courthouse for the Minneapolis and Chicago law firms that were principally involved. But the case files indicated that Wanger was party to almost all conference calls, deposition summons, discovery motions, and briefs, as well as status and settlement conferences, and he had prepared and signed the motion to exempt Julio from testifying. Some of his involvement was standard for all "local" counsel, but Judge Crocker also recalled that Wanger had been an active participant in the case. Furthermore, it seems likely that he had done well enough in the Gallo Salame case for Ernest to take notice so that in 1983, he was asked to act as the winery's co-counsel in the Pappas case. (When Ernest was impressed with an attorney's performance, he made him an active member of the Gallo legal team. Indeed, when the Salame case was settled, the Mc-Cormick, Barstow firm received a bonus for its work on the case.)

Robert Coyle first sat on the federal bench in May 1982. In order to dissolve his financial interest in the McCormick, Barstow firm, he was to be paid an annual sum for his share of the partnership over the ensuing three years. It was only a year later, in June 1983, that his former firm helped negotiate the winery's acquisition of the Gallo Salame trademark.

When in 1983, Judge Coyle stepped down and the Pappas case was reassigned to Judge Price, Coyle at least seemed to have had reservations about presiding in a lawsuit in which his former firm and his former colleague Wanger were involved. Local attorneys report that under ordinary circumstances, judges usually wait two or three years before hearing cases in which their former firms are counsel. After the three-year period, Coyle did preside in some cases involving former McCormick, Barstow clients or his former partners. But not those involving Gallo—subsequent winery cases were assigned to Judge Price. Whether that was the "luck of the draw," or whether Coyle had reasons not to hear winery cases, couldn't be determined.

But Coyle's continued social and business connections to his former partners would raise questions about his acceptance of the transfer of the Joe Gallo case. Very soon after the case had been filed, Coyle had hosted a dinner party that Oliver Wanger attended. According to another guest, Wanger referred to his new Gallo assignment. "It's so great to be working for Ernest again," Wanger was heard to say. "He always treats his lawyers so well." He went on to describe a visit to the winery, a delicious meal, and an extensive wine-tasting session with the Gallos (Wanger fancied himself a wine aficionado).

During the time that McCormick, Barstow was preparing the winery's case against Joe, Coyle continued to have financial ties to members of his old firm. He and one former partner co-owned a vacation condominium; he and another former partner were coinvestors in a number of agricultural properties in Fresno County and the neighboring Madera County, including at least two vineyards. When he came to the bench, Coyle's required annual financial disclosures revealed that his investments and holdings were valued at close to $1.6 million. Many of his investments were made through Pacific Agriculture, a land and agricultural management company that had extensive vineyard holdings and was founded by Donald Howard and Roland D. Ewell, the latter the brother of Ben Ewell, another former partner in McCormick, Barstow.

By accepting the assignment of the Joe Gallo case, Coyle would be asked to rule on the validity of the Gallo Salame trademark sale to the winery, the agreement that his former firm and his good friend Ollie Wanger had helped negotiate. (Joe's attorneys were claiming that this was an invalid transaction, and thus Joe could not be infringing on this trademark.) Nevertheless, at the time of Price's transfer of the case to Coyle, none of the attorneys for either side remarked upon the connection between Coyle's former firm and the Gallo Salame settlement. Whether this would have constituted grounds for disqualification wasn't clear. But in retrospect it seemed strange that at the time of Price's reassignment, neither Judge Coyle nor the attorneys addressed this possible conflict directly and the case went to trial a week later.

When Judge Coyle called the proceedings to order at 9:05, Tuesday morning, November 22, he already seemed irritated with Joe's lawyers. Al Herzig and John Whiting still felt that Denis Rice was ignoring the central argument to be made in Joe's defense—that using his own name was a right of free speech protected by the First and Fourteenth amendments. Herzig had flown up from Los Angeles and tried to file a brief arguing the issue before the trial started that morning. Coyle announced he felt "imposed upon" by the last-minute presentation. Sensing the judge's annoyance, Rice agreed not to include Herzig's brief in the record until "after the evidence has been submitted."

Whiting sat glumly in the back of the courtroom. He felt that Rice's open disassociation from Herzig's motion only sanctioned Judge Coyle's impatience and worsened the antagonism in Joe's camp. Joe had wanted Whiting to lead the team, but Rice had insisted that Whiting was needed as a crucial witness for Joe and hence could not act as principal litigator. As a result, Whiting felt his hands were tied.

Since the Gallo brothers' court conflict had been reduced to the trademark issue, opening arguments centered on the same charges and defenses that had already been presented in the pretrial motions. Wanger did try to enliven his presentation with two new claims. First, he explained that Ernest and Julio's $70 million campaign to promote their varietals (as opposed to their "generic" wines) and upscale their image hadn't met with great success. Now, he seemed to suggest, the winery had a new reason—some might say a scapegoat—for the promotion's failure: Joe Gallo's "commodity cheese" had undermined Ernest's effort to change the way consumers thought about Gallo.

Second, Wanger claimed to have a "smoking gun" that proved Joe's "bad faith usurpation" of the Gallo name in labeling his cheese. He announced that he had documents, which he called "the cheese notes," made by a copywriter in a Fresno advertising agency that Joe had once considered hiring. Wanger asserted that the notes, which referred to the "known-ness" of the Gallo name, proved that Joe intended a "free ride" on the reputation of his brothers' wine. He added that bad faith was evident in that the "cheese notes," provided by the agency, had been "buried" in Joe's old tax files. (Wanger alleged that Joe's lawyers had received the "cheese notes" from the advertising agency and then concealed them among other unrelated records produced by Joe's attorneys during discovery, an allegation that they would later strongly deny.)

In his opening argument, Denis Rice quickly listed the main points of his defense for Joe: Like Wanger, he would call a cheese expert and a survey expert, who would refute the winery's arguments of poor quality and trade name confusion. He would also question the winery's acquisition of the Gallo Salame trademark.

Perhaps still angry at Wanger's suggestion that his team had concealed evidence, Rice then went after Ernest. He quoted from Ernest's deposition in the Gallo Salame case. Justifying his long delay, until 1980, in bringing suit against the North Beach company, Ernest had declared that he hadn't wanted to sue "someone of Italian extraction who had a family-owned business and was trying to make a living."

"But Ernest," Rice countered, "has no qualms about suing Joe, who is also Italian, runs a family-owned business to make a living, and is even his own brother."

Correspondence between the winery and Gallo Salame, Rice continued, indicated that both agreed to "allow" Joe to use his name on his cheese as long as he would accept a license from the winery. In other words, Rice said, Ernest's goal was to acquire both the Joseph Gallo name and control of his cheese company.

Rice then attacked what he must have known was Ernest's sore spot. He pointed out that some wines produced by the winery were acknowledged with the Ernest and Julio Gallo labels, while others were dissociated by omitting the Gallo name altogether. "Just as," he added, "the winery is carefully distancing itself in this litigation from Thunderbird, Bartles & Jaymes, pop wines, and Gallo street wines." (None of the trademarks which the winery was seeking to protect in this case was for the lower-tier Gallo brands.)

As for the cheese's alleged negative effect on the image of Gallo wine, Rice reminded the court that since Gallo wine was synonymous with "jug or cheap wine," Joe had an even stronger reason to distinguish his award-winning cheese from the winery's products.

Finally, Rice became his most aggressive when he assaulted Ernest's credibility. "We will be reviewing with the court the tendency of Mr. Ernest Gallo to state whatever set of facts will achieve a given result at a given moment in time," he said. He went on to list the number of times Ernest had disavowed previous statements or testimony, particularly those instances that Judge Price had excused as "puffing up" the family history. Some would call it lying, Rice said; at the very least the record showed that Ernest had a long history of changing his version of events "to suit his particular needs."

The opening statements of Wanger and Rice set the hostile tone that would pervade the proceedings as they dragged on for the next month, with tedious examinations and cross-examinations of the "experts" about survey methods and cheese testing, about quality control at Gallo Salame and consumer complaints about Gallo Wine.

Hours of court time were devoted to angry arguments between the attorneys over evidence or exhibits. The winery's attorneys often presented new binders of records to the Rice team the night before they were to be introduced as evidence. What certain pretrial stipulations actually meant became a continual source of controversy, until even Judge Coyle noted that he'd never seen a case in which opposing sides could not even agree upon their previous agreements.

The only person who seemed to enjoy these proceedings was Ernest Gallo. When he took the stand, he tended to make speeches in response to Wanger's questions. The direct examination seemed designed to give Ernest ample opportunity to narrate the development of the Gallo Winery, its brands and labels, and its distribution system. His obsession with the Gallo name became clear when he proclaimed that if he didn't stop Joe, he would be unable to stop "other potential infringers, and particularly those whose name happened to be Gallo." He was also adamant that because Joe made "generic cheese," he had undermined the effort to "improve our image to the upscale varietal segment." And because the winery was unable to inspect and control the quality of Joe's cheese, Ernest alleged that there were real health risks to be considered. The "poor quality" of Joe's cheese had him "very much concerned that there could be a risk of a bad batch of cheese going out there and being very injurious to the winery."

When, during cross-examination, Rice touched on sensitive areas, such as Ernest's testimony in the Mary Gallo case, Wanger successfully objected that any references to the use of the Gallo trade name or trademark before 1940 were excluded because of Judge Price's summary judgment. But Ernest flared and almost lost his temper as Rice questioned the quality of Gallo wines. He had seemed comfortable enough when he impugned the quality of Joe's cheese; let anyone denigrate his wines, though, and he became indignant.

First he hedged when Rice asked: "Thunderbird,is a mix of citrus juice and what?"

"Fine white wine," he replied, ignoring the fact that Thunderbird's original base had been Gallo's generic white port; nor did he acknowledge that, according to Julio's deposition, Thunderbird was also produced from pear or apple juice.

Then Rice asked him about various newspaper articles that showed Gallo's vast production and sales of "street wines."

"What do you mean by street wine?" snapped Ernest.

"Cheaper wines used by winos," said Rice.

"And what do you mean by wino?"

"People who drink excessive amounts of wine."

"So what's the question?"

When Rice showed him a *San Francisco Chronicle* article indicating that Gallo led the sales of street wines, Ernest still resisted. Admitting that the report did not help the Gallo Winery image, he added that the story "was unfair." He also said that he did not recall why the Gallo name no longer appeared on the labels of such street wines as Thunderbird and Night Train Express.

Rice further infuriated Ernest by questioning him about a compilation of consumer complaints that included reports of tartrate crystals, possible rat feces, shredded cardboard, broken glass, cockroaches, and worms, all alleged to have been found in bottles of Gallo wine. Ernest was pale with anger and asserted that upon investigation, these complaints had proved to be baseless.

By the end of his second day on the stand, Ernest was so annoyed that in response to one of Rice's last questions, he snapped, "I think you are confused." Judge Coyle reminded him that a "yes" or "no" or "I don't understand the question" would suffice.

Pat Lynch next called Joe Gallo as a hostile witness. The contrast between the two brothers couldn't have been more striking. On direct examination Ernest seemed to have enjoyed elaborating on his answers; on cross, he had been ready for a confrontation and seemed to pride himself on parrying with Rice. Lynch's style was to shoot rapid-fire questions, and Joe had trouble hearing. (Despite Mike's urging, Joe still refused to wear a hearing aid.) There were long pauses as Joe tried to deduce what Lynch had said by lip-reading and logic. Thus, he came across as slow and tense, whereas Ernest had seemed quick and energetic. Too, the emotional toll on Joe seemed greater. He was depressed by the lawsuit, while Ernest seemed to relish the conflict.

Lynch put Joe on the defensive, questioning his supervision of the cheese plant, his quality controls, his knowledge of cheesemaking and marketing. As a result Joe tended to respond with an "I don't recall," rather than leave himself vulnerable to further criticism.

Finally, Lynch raised the issue of "the smoking gun"—the "cheese notes" allegedly hidden in a file of Joe's old tax returns. Patty Johnston Thayer, one of the Howard, Rice lawyers who had also worked on assembling documents, rose to explain to the count that this was a misfiling by the attorneys, not an intentional act by Mr. Gallo. Lynch, however, maintained that the attorneys had purposefully tried to bury the "cheese notes" among the tax papers. Judge Coyle made no comment and simply asked Lynch to resume his examination.

Joe testified that he had never seen the "cheese notes," and that at his one meeting with the advertising executive who had prepared them, nothing had been said about the Gallo name giving his cheese "instant known-ness."

During a recess, Joe became more pointed in his statements: "I never saw those notes, and I would have rejected the idea of playing off Ernest and Julio's label. Why would I want my cheese associated with their wine, when they have such a poor reputation?"

Later, under Rice's direct examination, Joe became more responsive, especially as he described his own career, managing his brothers' Livingston vineyards, then building up his own grape-growing and cattle and dairy businesses and finally starting the cheese company. He had certainly never told his brothers, as they now were claiming, that he didn't want "to come into the winery" because they worked too hard, he asserted. After all, he had also worked hard all his life.

In his re-cross, Lynch tried to impeach Joe's statement by quoting from the letter that Joe had written to Aileen just before his discharge from the army: " 'It's going to seem awfully good to get back to work, even though I never cared much for work.' "

"But at the end of that I said, 'Ha!' " Joe objected, smiling slightly at his remembered joke.

Lynch chose not to get it.

Rice questioned Joe again, then finished his examination by playing a video of the coverage by a local television station of Joe's cheese plant opening. Previously, Wanger had played an excerpt from the same tape to support his contention that people naturally associated wine with cheese. In the introductory segment, the reporter had remarked that it seemed only fitting for the brother of the Gallo wine moguls to make cheese. Now Rice played the entire news segment, during which the reporter had also stressed that the "Joseph Gallo Cheese Company" was entirely separate from the Gallo Winery.

Then, without a pause and with no introduction, Rice added an excerpt from a *Tonight* show monologue.

"Have you heard about the Gallo brothers' family feud?" Johnny Carson asked. "Ernest and Julio are suing their brother for using the name Gallo on his cheese. What do they expect him to call it? Kraft?"

Ernest was not amused.

.   .   .

Ernest conducted another lobbying campaign in the corridor after his brother's testimony, this time remarking on Joe's frequent response of "I don't know" to Lynch's technical questions about cheese. Joe's reliance on his cheesemaker did not square with Ernest's method of running the winery.

"Now do you see what a management problem there is at the cheese plant?" he announced in the hallway to several reporters. "Joe doesn't even know what's going on in his own company. So how can he make good cheese?"

The reporters made no comment.

"How can someone run a company that way?" Ernest rushed on. "It's just a mess. Have you ever seen his cheese plant?"

The reporters conceded that they hadn't.

"Cow manure just a few feet away from the front door," he exclaimed. "And flies and a muddy road. Disgusting!" He marched away to join his lawyers.

Having heard about Ernest's repeated comments, Joe asked Whiting and Rice to prepare a press release, which was distributed to reporters the following morning. If Ernest didn't stop making these scurrilous comments, Joe announced, he would sue for slander. "This kind of attack is driven by the same type of negative strategy that led to the FTC consent order against the winery in 1976," the statement continued. "Only this time, Ernest's malice is being directed against me and my family. . . . I will pursue every step available to protect my family, as well as the reputation of our gold-medal cheese."

Ernest curtailed his hallway comments, but he still attended court every day and frequently wrote notes to winery counsel Jack Owen, who sat beside him. "Court costs, court costs!" he scribbled a few times. The story circulated that Ernest and his legal team intended to prolong the trial. If Joe lost, he might be required to pay the winery's court costs and legal fees. With more than fifteen associate lawyers and paralegals from the O'Melveny & Myers and McCormick, Barstow firms working on the case, both behind the scenes and in the courtroom every day, it was rumored that Ernest was trying to drive Joe into bankruptcy. The winery attorneys denied the speculation, but one day, when Lynch continued to ask a relatively unimportant witness tedious and repetitive questions, Judge Coyle finally interrupted. It had been brought to his attention, he said, that "efforts are being made to delay these proceedings, and I will not tolerate it from either side." With that he ordered Lynch "to get on with it."

When the defense finally presented its case, Rice first called Joe back to the stand. Again, Joe insisted that he labeled his cheese Joseph Gallo because it was his own name, not because he wanted people to think that it was made by the winery. Mike then took the stand to support his father's testimony. He testified that his father had decided on the Joseph Gallo name from the very beginning of his cheese plant operation, and not after an advertising writer had supposedly said that he should trade on the Gallo association by putting his name on the label.

Rice also questioned Mike about the meeting that he, his father, and Linda's husband, Kenny Jelacich, had with Julio and Bob at the Foster Farms restaurant. Mike repeated what he recalled as Julio's remarks: that the conflict was with Ernest's side of the family and that naming the cheese something other than Joseph, such as M & L Gallo, would solve the problem. As a result of Julio's comments, Mike explained, he had concluded that Ernest wanted the trademark "Joseph Gallo" for future use by his son Joe E., even by his grandson Joseph, Jr.

On cross-examination, Lynch again attacked the quality of Joe's cheese by trying to portray Mike as ignorant and inexperienced in cheesemaking, but Mike held his own, and finally Lynch backed off.

Rice's main defense strategy, though, was to undermine the winery's attack on the quality of Joe's cheese. His associate Alan Sparer had already pointed out errors in testing and computation during his cross-examination of the winery's expert. Now Rice called a former Kraft quality control specialist who testified that having conducted his own analysis, he found Joe's cheese "as safe as any comparable cheese . . . and in compliance with applicable standards and regulations."

During cross-examination of the defense's cheese expert, Lynch reintroduced some of the findings of the winery's cheese expert. The following morning newspaper articles repeated the winery's allegations of poor quality, even as Joe's expert refuted them. Joe was distraught over the bad publicity—especially since he was now certain that it was Ernest's intention to put him out of business. He thought his attorneys were playing into the winery's hands. "Stop bringing up quality; don't give Lynch or Wanger a chance to repeat their cheese expert's findings," he told them. Whiting had not liked this approach anyway, and he and Joe now told the Howard, Rice lawyers to remove from the witness list his cheesemaker, quality control manager, and product distributors. They did not want Lynch's hard-hitting cross-examinations to become the occasion for yet another article detailing the winery's allegations.

His hands tied, Rice was left with only three more witnesses. He called his own survey expert Robert C. Sorensen (brother of Kennedy speechwriter Ted Sorensen) to dispute the winery's $75,000 Mervin Field poll that claimed to prove brand confusion among 43 percent of those surveyed. Sorensen's calculations showed a likelihood of confusion at 13 percent, even less if surveys were conducted in areas where Joseph Gallo Cheese was actually marketed, not at random sites throughout the country.

On Thursday, December 15, Rice called his last two witnesses to attack the quality of Gallo Wine. It seemed to be revenge—an effort to give Ernest a taste of his own medicine.

The first, a marketing specialist who had once been employed by the winery to conduct "brand-mapping" surveys, confirmed that Gallo Wines suffered from a poor image compared to competitors and that the winery's attempt to go upscale with varietals was undermined by the public's association of Gallo with cheap street wines.

Then Dan Solomon, the winery's "Communications Director," took the stand. Since he had handled complaints in 1983 and 1984, he was asked to explain the unsavory reports in letters received from customers that had been introduced as exhibits. These files confirmed that the winery often disposed of such complaints either with free cases of wine or in the more extreme instances with settlements (one as high as $10,000). Solomon conceded that these records didn't indicate which complaints had proven to be valid. He himself couldn't remember which complaints were legitimate, although he insisted that the winery's investigations had concluded that most were unfounded. Still, the lack of recorded findings was to Rice's benefit. By the time he was finished with Solomon, Rice had court observers laughing and Ernest livid with anger.

The following morning newspaper articles and a national radio news broadcaster repeated the alleged complaints. For the first and only time during the trial, Ernest failed to attend court that day. Reportedly, he was back in his hotel room, supervising "damage control."

Having forced Ernest to experience what he had inflicted on Joe,

Denis Rice rested for the defense on December 21. It looked as if the trial would be completed before Christmas, just as Judge Coyle had predicted.

But Ernest and his lawyers had only been lying in wait. They had a few more surprises for Joe and his attorneys.

CHAPTER TWELVE

On Wednesday morning, December 22, Joe sat at his counsel table reading the newspaper. The attorneys were in chambers with Judge Coyle to discuss the schedule for closing arguments. Joe was relieved that this ordeal would soon be over. Then he heard excited whispers in the back of the courtroom. He turned to see Julio walking down the center aisle, escorted by three O'Melveny & Myers partners. Joe stiffened; Julio hadn't appeared in court since the opening session, and Joe was certain that he was here today to testify.

After a quick, nervous glance at Joe, Julio bowed his head, as if in church, then slid into the second row of the spectators' section where Ernest had already taken his seat. The three lawyers lined up next to Julio, but he said not a word to them or his brother.

Joe looked back at Mike, who nodded his same suspicion. They had been outmaneuvered. After all the controversy and court hearings about Julio's testifying, Denis Rice had decided not to call him as a witness. The winery lawyers had indicated that they would not put him on the stand either. Joe had still harbored the hope that Julio was an unwilling participant in the lawsuit. Even if the Clift Hotel meeting hadn't worked out, he had felt that Julio's continued absence after the first day of trial conveyed his disapproval of what Ernest was doing.

Now Julio sat staring straight head, sighing, a look of anxiety on his face. Fifteen minutes later Wanger and Lynch exited chambers and with a smile and a nod to their clients, they headed for the corridor.

Ernest and Jack Owen hurried after them for a conference, but Julio did not move.

Ten minutes later, Judge Coyle opened the proceedings, and Lynch called Julio to the stand. He sat hunched in the witness chair, his hands trembling as he identified himself as "self-employed" and the president of the Gallo Winery.

Lynch had Julio confirm that he had been present at the lunch with Joe and Mike at the Foster Farms restaurant in Livingston. Julio explained that he and Bob had gone at Joe's request for a meeting.

Lynch then asked him to describe the conversation he had with his brother. According to Julio, Joe immediately brought up the trademark suit by asking, "What would you do if you were in my shoes? Wouldn't you want to use your own name?"

"I said that I would use another name just starting out with a new product," Julio now explained. "I said, 'There are plenty of other names' "—he paused, but then gained speed as he rushed on—" 'unless you intend to capitalize on all the effort and amount of money we've spent building up our trademark.' "

It sounded like the definition of trademark infringement that Ernest often repeated. (The same language had also been used by Bob Gallo in his deposition when he was asked to describe the conversation at this meeting.)

Julio added that he had then suggested alternatives, such as naming the cheese Bear Creek, after one of Joe's ranches.

"Joe didn't agree, of course, so we went back and forth."

"Did any other subjects come up?" asked Lynch.

"At the end Joe said, 'I might as well dig up the vineyards.' I told him I didn't see what his grapes had to do with the trademark issue. We've always made a home for his grapes, although he didn't have any price minimum on a long-term contract."

Lynch left the last remark hanging, and asked if Julio had told Mike and Joe that Gallo was a bad name, that it was hard to sell, and that he had been opposed to using it from the very beginning?

"No," was his single reply.

Had he suggested using Mike and Linda's names or initials with the Gallo name rather than Joseph?

"No."

Had he said it was Ernest's side of the family that was pushing for the lawsuit?

"No."

And finally, had Julio said that the use of the Gallo name was objectionable?

"Yes, I told him that."

Rice cross-examined briefly and in a gentle fashion. Had Julio told the court everything that was said at this meeting?

"Yes," replied Julio.

After a few more questions and Julio's equally terse responses, Rice asked: "Over the years, have you found that your brother Joe is an honest person—that he tells the truth?"

"Yes," said Julio, his eyes beginning to tear.

He left the stand, and flanked by O'Melveny & Myers lawyers, he departed from the courtroom.

During the following recess, Mike stood in the corridor, his wife, Sherrie, at his side.

"What do you expect him to say?" he asked. "That sounded like Ernest, all that trademark stuff. Julio doesn't talk like that, and he certainly didn't say that during our meeting. I think Ernest is just afraid that people will figure out that he wants my father's name and trademark so that his son can use it. That's what Julio was saying that day, and we were all so shocked by his admitting it that there's no way we wouldn't remember it."

"I just couldn't believe Julio would . . . well . . . lie like that," Joe said later. "And Bob too in his deposition, repeating all that legal talk. Bob is very religious, and I just don't know how he could do this. He and Julio did everything they could to settle the lawsuit so that Julio wouldn't have to testify." His voice trailed off. He seemed as shaken by Julio's action as he had been by Ernest's negative remarks about him and his cheese.

Mike was bitter that his father had been so selflessly concerned about Julio's health. "He didn't want to upset Julio," he explained, "and he didn't want the lawyers to call David and Joey either, which might have embarrassed Ernest. But we thought Julio would do anything not to testify, so we didn't expect them to put him on the stand at all. I think they brought him in at the last minute just to make it hard for us to really question him."

"We *were* worried about Julio's health—that's why his appearance was so abbreviated," Lynch later commented. "But because of Mike's testimony, there were things attributed to him that we didn't want to let stand. The thing that upset JR—Julio—was the impression that he had told Joe that the lawsuit was just Ernest's doing. So he wanted to make it clear that it was as much his lawsuit as Ernest's. There was the general impression that since Ernest has always run the legal part of the winery, he seemed much more at the helm. But JR regarded it as a personal charge that he had nothing to do with the lawsuit, and he felt he had to testify about that meeting at the Foster Farms restaurant."

After the recess, Lynch called his last witness. The week before, Lynch had announced to the court that Larry Holmboe, a man whom Joe had interviewed and almost hired as a sales manager in the fall of 1983, had come forward to testify. Alan Sparer had deposed him and concluded that Holmboe seemed to have said nothing damaging to Joe's case. The defense then was taken by surprise when Lynch asserted that the man's testimony was significant enough to make him the winery's final rebuttal witness.

Holmboe was of medium height and stocky build; he wore heavily tinted glasses and spoke quickly, in a high, thin voice. Wanger questioned him, and as Holmboe narrated his brief association with Joe Gallo, it became apparent that he considered himself responsible for Joe's decision to use his own name on his label. Through his former wife, Holmboe explained, he had learned that Joe was looking for a sales manager. While he was employed as a food broker, he was interviewed by Joe, and during the meeting, Holmboe said that he had suggested to Joe ideas for marketing consumer-size packages to retailers.

"I told him he should call his cheese Gallo," Holmboe asserted. "He said he couldn't because his brothers wouldn't like it. I asked him why not? He said they weren't in the business together. 'My brothers are at the winery, I'm the farmer,' he told me. That's when Joe went on a little bit about the fact that he and his brothers weren't the best of friends. And he felt that they wouldn't let him use the name Gallo."

Seemingly unaware that Joe had been calling his product Joseph Gallo Cheese since he'd opened his plant in 1983, Holmboe claimed that in a second meeting he had advised Joe to use his first and last names. "I told him that with the name Gallo on the cheese, we would have a better chance of selling it retail because it's a well-known name, a quality name. I said, 'Why can't you use your first name, since your brothers use their first names on a totally different product?' "

"What was his response?" asked Wanger.

"He never really said anything. He just kind of agreed with it," said Holmboe.

Rice objected, but Coyle overruled: "That is the most important question of the entire case."

It was an important question, but Holmboe's answer that Joe just "sort of smiled" was hardly confirming. If Joe had "never really said anything," how could Holmboe know that he had agreed? Holmboe went on to describe another meeting at lunch in Joe's home, where he said they sat in the sort of "kitchen-dining-room area."

At this Joe shook his head vehemently.

A clue to Holmboe's possible motive for offering to testify for the winery began to emerge when he added that the job hadn't come through. He explained that Joe had offered him the $40,000-a-year job with the cheese company. But when he'd asked for a two- or three-year contract, he continued, Joe had sent a telegram refusing the demand. As a result, Holmboe said, he had declined the job. His resentment was more evident as he remarked that he felt Joe had "used him" to get information about cheese pricing and distribution and then had treated him unfairly by rejecting the contract request. "And after all," Holmboe repeated, "I was the one who had given him the idea of using the name Gallo on his label."

Alan Sparer cross-examined the witness, highlighting the crucial matter of Joe's reaction to Holmboe's alleged suggestion of using his own name. Now Holmboe agreed that Joe had just nodded and smiled and said he would look into it. (Sparer was trying to convey Joe's sarcasm—that here was a man telling him to put his own name on a label when in fact he had used it as a trade name for over forty years and was already using it on his cheese. But without underscoring Joe's inflection, the point seemed lost.) Sparer then confirmed that Holmboe had done most of the talking during his meeting with Joe. This obliquely referred to the witness's speech patterns: If Holmboe had spoken as he now did in court, the words tumbling forth at breakneck speed in a high, reedy voice, Joe, with his hearing problem, wouldn't have been able to understand him. A nod or a smile might have been Joe's polite response to the man's barely heard monologues.

Sparer then explored the man's motivation for phoning the winery and offering to testify for Ernest and Julio. Did he feel that Joe had taken his idea, that he'd been picking his brain? Yes, Holmboe agreed, when he had first seen Joe's cheese in the grocery store, he had thought, "By golly, he took my idea." Sparer confirmed that Holmboe could produce no documentation of his story, since, as he explained, he had thrown away his written demand for a contract as well as Joe's alleged telegram. Holmboe went on to concede that he had been reading about the court case in the newspapers, but at first he hadn't wanted to "get involved." Then he had decided that his information "might be helpful," so he called the winery, he said. He couldn't or wouldn't explain why he hadn't phoned Joe, whom he presumably had met, but instead contacted the winery, although he knew neither Ernest nor Julio.

Holmboe finished his testimony and left the stand. During the recess he hovered in the hallway near Ernest and his attorneys—waiting, it seemed, for their recognition and thanks. Joe stared at him from the other end of the corridor.

"I still don't remember him," he said, shaking his head. "I know I talked to some fellow, but I thought he was taller and thinner. And I could barely hear what he was saying today—he talks so fast. It just doesn't make any sense. I would never have said that I didn't get along with my brothers, not to anyone, because we did get along then. And why would I ask a stranger what I should call my cheese when I'd already named it Joseph Gallo?"

Mike didn't recall Holmboe either, although Holmboe had testified that he had been present during two of the meetings. "I always remember faces," Mike said, "and this guy couldn't have spent all that time with my dad. We were still in our old office then, where my desk was right across from my father's. As for eating lunch with my father, that's ridiculous. I eat with him almost every work day, so I would have been with him. Anyway, my father doesn't have a kitchen–dining room. The dining room is separate so I can't believe they ever had that lunch meeting."

With the court back in session, Denis Rice attempted to call Kenny Jelacich to refute Julio's version of the Foster Farms lunch meeting. Judge Coyle sustained Pat Lynch's objection, agreeing that to allow everyone who had been present to testify would mean "we could go on forever and even call the waitress."

Rice was left with no alternative but to bring Joe back to the stand to counter Holmboe's testimony. Joe answered in his usual terse manner: No, he'd never sent anyone a telegram about employment; the closest telegraph office was in Modesto. (The implication was that it was ludicrous to think he'd drive all the way to Modesto, where Holmboe in fact lived, to send him a wire.)

Perhaps because he was uncertain of Joe's answer, Rice did not ask him the crucial question: Had he ever met with Holmboe and discussed ideas for labeling and marketing his cheese? This was left to Wanger.

Had there been any written communication between Joe and Holmboe? the winery attorney asked.

"No," said Joe.

"Have you ever seen him before?"

"No. I've never seen that man before."

And that was the end of the matter as far as Joe was concerned. Yet his emphatic denials were a mistake. If Joe had ever met Holmboe (which he apparently had), he needed to describe the meetings in detail, however brief and insignificant they seemed to him. Instead, with his abbreviated responses, Joe gave the appearance of having something to hide. And this was the worst impression to leave with a judge who had already exclaimed that Joe's reaction to Holmboe's alleged suggestion to use his first name as well as his last was "the most important question of the case."

Rice did not call John Whiting, even at this point. After refusing Joe's demand that Whiting try the case on the grounds that he was going to be a principal witness, Rice never put him on the stand. According to Whiting, he could have chronicled Joe's use of his trade name and how the selection and design of his label had been made with great care to designate Joseph Gallo Cheese as separate from the Gallo Winery. He also felt that he could have shown that these decisions had been made long before Holmboe claimed to have suggested using the Gallo name as a good marketing strategy. Rice apparently disagreed.

"He didn't ask me to testify about any of this," Whiting later remarked. "When I asked why, I was told that it wasn't necessary since my deposition had been offered into evidence. It was only later that I learned that it hadn't been. So my testimony, either in my deposition or what I could have said on the stand, was never used on Joe's behalf."

By noon on December 22, the trial was over except for closing arguments. Even on this issue, the attorneys couldn't agree. Lynch wished to proceed the following morning. Rice objected, preferring to wait until after Christmas. The two firms' legal teams were also fighting about the various exhibits and excerpts from depositions that would be entered into the record. Agreements that had been made before trial were now reargued, and it seemed unlikely that the lawyers could reach a consensus before the long holiday weekend.

"I don't mind telling you, this is the craziest trial I ever saw," Judge Coyle said. "You people shift gears every five minutes. You have stipulations and you can't even agree among yourselves what they mean."

But he did put closing arguments off until after Christmas.

On the following Wednesday, December 28, Ernest was in his usual seat, Jack Owen again at his side. Julio was not present; nor were Amelia, Aileen and Bob, Joey, or David.

By contrast, Joe's family again accompanied him. Now that Patricia would not be called as a witness, she came to court, and this morning Mike and Sherrie also brought their nine-year-old son, Micah.

"You know what I'd like to tell the judge?" he whispered to his parents as they waited for the session to begin. "I'd tell him that they were born with the name, and that we were born with the name, so why can't we all share it?"

Patricia had heard about the derogatory comments that Ernest had made about Joe's cheese in the corridor. If she had thought that Ernest was vindictive during the proceedings, she was now amazed by Pat Lynch's remarks in his closing argument.

Lynch wanted to prove Joe's "bad faith" and his intent to confuse by choosing the "Joseph Gallo label." As his main evidence, he cited Holmboe's description of Joe as "embarrassed" or "shy" at the suggestion of using his own name on his cheese. Then he scoffed at the idea, implying that it was secretiveness on Joe's part, not reticence. "It's hard to imagine Joe Gallo as shy," he said sarcastically.

Patricia groaned; she knew her husband actually was shy, not secretive as Lynch was insinuating.

Lynch continued to stress the alleged potential health problems with Joseph Gallo Cheese. He even resurrected a news story about a case of food poisoning from enchiladas served at a wedding party in southern California. Lynch had never introduced this incident into evidence, but he had made the article available to the press. The article reported that the market where ingredients for the enchiladas had been bought had removed Joseph Gallo Cheese from its shelves (thus implying that Joseph Gallo Cheese had been the cause). The supermarket assistant manager, however, had insisted that he had removed Joseph Gallo Cheese because it was the only cheese left on the shelf. Nevertheless, he said he was sure that it hadn't been used in making the enchiladas. By the time of closing arguments, health department investigators had, in fact, determined that neither cheese in general nor Joe's cheese in particular was the culprit (the food had been left unrefrigerated for twenty-four hours). Lynch, however, was still using the incident rhetorically.

(Later, when told of the market manager's explanation and the health department's findings, Lynch defended his reference to the story by explaining that while he knew the evidence wasn't conclusive, he had also been contacted by lawyers for the party guests about a possible lawsuit against Joe. "They told me it was tainted cheese," he added, "but I didn't know the merits. I don't remember their names, because I told them we didn't want to get involved with anything that disparaged the Gallo name.")

Continuing his closing argument, Lynch went on to make a passing reference to five days of tedious testimony about the testing of Joe's cheese. "But the court doesn't want to hear more of it anyway," he added quickly.

"You got that right," interrupted Judge Coyle.

While little in his closing remarks was surprising, Lynch had a new gambit: He repeatedly called Joseph Gallo Cheese simply Gallo Cheese, as if to engrave the idea of confusion on the judge's mind.

He concluded by arguing that the winery's only relief was a court-ordered injunction. Aware of judicial reluctance to deprive someone of the use of his name, Lynch cited cases in which defendants were allowed to use their names on a product but not as a trademark. For example, he offered, the Joseph Gallo name could appear in small print on the label, but the cheese would be called Cottonwood Ranch Cheese.

"Or O'Melveny & Myers Cheese," joked Judge Coyle.

"Maybe even Denis Rice Cheese," countered Lynch with a laugh as he sat down.

Rice began his summation by noting that the winery had switched its emphasis in the case: It had spent more court time trying to show the alleged "poor quality" of Joe Gallo's cheese than it had proving confusion. He then argued that if the court granted the winery's requested injunction, it would become a landmark case in which a defendant would be precluded from using his name on a noncompeting product.

Reviewing the testimony of Sorensen, the defense's survey expert who had criticized the Mervin Field survey methods, Rice argued that Field's interpretation and tabulations were inaccurate. He pointed out that even when people said that Joe's cheese was *not* made by the Gallo Winery, Field had counted it as confusion since they had thought of the connection spontaneously; or even if they simply mentioned the word "wine" in their response, they were categorized as "confused." He went on to insist that simple word association was not the same as evidence of confusion, but was interrupted by Judge Coyle.

"If I go into a store and see Joseph Gallo Cheese," the judge asked, "and I guess it's made by the winery, is that confusion?" Hardly pausing, he added, "It has to be a guess because I don't have anything else to go on. . . . I just don't understand your expert's theory."

When Rice again tried to explain Sorensen's assessment of word association in the winery survey (wine with cheese, and what he alleged was the leading question, "What other products does Gallo make?"), Judge Coyle again stopped him: "I'm no Ph.D., but I don't see how anyone can't say they are confused."

Rice went on to reassert that the winery's acquisition of the Gallo Salame trademark was invalid, a "naked assignment" and not acceptable under the law. Covering all bases, he argued that the Gallo Winery could hardly accuse Joe's cheese of "tarnishing its image"—it had already been tarnished, he claimed, by the public's association of Gallo with "cheap wine and winos."

When Rice concluded by returning to the central issue of Joe Gallo's right to use his own name, Judge Coyle immediately stepped in. Was it an absolute right? he asked. Would it matter if Joseph Gallo were not his own name?

Rice replied that then the court would be faced with a different question. In this case, the same name was given at birth. Previous Ninth Circuit Court of Appeals decisions, especially that of the Friend case, confirmed that even if confusion or bad faith were proven, a person could use his first and last names.

Coyle interrupted again. "Suppose he sold his name to Jalisco Cheese Company?"

Rice seemed stunned. "I haven't addressed that possibility," he said. Indeed, it was a bad sign that the judge had chosen a hypothetical that seemed to associate Joe Gallo with a major food poisoning case.

"What if he assigned you the use of the name Joseph Gallo?" he asked.

"I don't know," said Rice. "I didn't go into those cases."

Rice had not expected the question. The issue of assignability or sale of the trademark had never been raised during the proceedings, and it wasn't part of the winery's original complaint or request for injunctive relief. Why Judge Coyle had fastened on it now, no one could say. If Joe's lawyers needed a signal that the judge was sympathetic to Ernest's position, his unexpected concern about the future assignability of the Joseph Gallo trademark was it. Ernest had often insisted to Joe and Mike that this condition of the proposed license was necessary because he couldn't let the name go to "outsiders." And even though the issue hadn't been part of the winery's complaint, now Judge Coyle seemed to echo Ernest's position.

Rice still had no response, and the judge looked at him in amazement.

"That's the problem, isn't it?" he said sternly.

Pat Lynch drove the point home in his rebuttal, arguing that the winery had never asked the court to force Joe to take a license but wanted the court to enjoin Joe from using his name as a trademark and having the power to assign or sell it. Lynch then addressed the defense's remarks that stressed the public's association of Gallo with cheap or street wine: If the winery's image were as fragile as Rice had suggested, there was all the more reason to be concerned about the effect of Joe's cheese on consumers' perception of Gallo Wine.

He closed by adding what may have been the saddest comment of the entire court battle and the most revealing of the emotions that had resulted in this family feud. It seemed to suggest Ernest and Julio's lifelong sense of superiority and power over their younger brother: "Joseph Gallo just happened to have the good luck to be born with the same last name that his brothers made famous."

The trial left Joe and John Whiting exhausted and depressed. Meanwhile, the Howard, Rice attorneys prepared the posttrial brief, the recitation of facts and laws, as well as deposition excerpts, which they then submitted as a summary of Joe's defense to the judge. But once again they chose not to argue Whiting and Herzig's contention that Joe's use of his name was commercial free speech and protected by the First Amendment.

According to Whiting, Rice had reassured him that the judge had said that unless the free speech issue was specifically waived, it remained before the court. Amending the pretrial order, as Herzig had attempted to do the first day of trial, wasn't necessary. Herzig remained skeptical, however. He first attempted to file a supplemental brief to add the First Amendment issue to the Howard, Rice findings of fact and conclusions of law. When the winery objected, arguing that Joe's lawyers had "failed to reserve any First Amendment issue in their pretrial statement," Herzig felt that his skepticism was justified. On March 3, 1989, he filed a motion to amend the pretrial statement to conform to evidence to make explicit his First Amendment argument: "To preclude an individual from using a given surname," Herzig wrote, "would be, as a 1942 Second Circuit Court decision put it, 'to take away his identity: without it he cannot make known who he is to those who may wish to deal with him; and that is so grievous an injury that courts will avoid imposing it, if they possibly can.' "

Hearing of this new motion, Rice threatened to quit. He argued with Whiting, he argued with Herzig: The motion would open up a can of worms, he said, leading to a flurry of opposing motions and a long delay before the judge could even begin to consider his decision. Finally, Herzig threw up his hands: Rice could decide. On March 14, Alan Sparer wrote to Judge Coyle withdrawing Herzig's motion, since "we have concluded that the First Amendment issue is already properly before the Court." On March 29, 1989, Coyle ordered "that the case is submitted for decision based upon the pretrial order on file." He added the preliminary ruling that "because the pretrial order does not assert any legal issue involving the First Amendment, the court holds that the issue is not before it in resolving this action."

It was exactly what Herzig had feared. Whether this would have affected the outcome of the case was unclear at this point. But Whiting and Herzig had both felt that Joe had a strong defense going into the trial. "As far as the evidence and the law were concerned," Whiting later commented, "I thought we'd entered the fray with howitzers. During the trial we looked as if we were firing water pistols. I didn't know why and I was frustrated. Still, I hoped that Judge Coyle would follow the lead of so many other judges and at least protect Joe's right to use his own name."

After nearly six months of waiting, his hopes were dashed. On June 19, 1989, Judge Coyle issued his decision enjoining Joe from using his name as a trademark.

"They might as well have shipped Coyle their floppy disk," Whiting complained. Indeed, changing "the Winery" to "the Plaintiff" in the text, Coyle adopted almost all of the winery's contentions as fact. Coyle also ruled that the Gallo Salame trademark settlement was valid and affirmed the winery's argument that the purchase had transferred "information to the Plaintiff sufficient to enable the Plaintiff to continue the business" and that "although Gallo Salame did not provide its recipes, the Plaintiff could have reverse-engineered equivalent recipes. . . ."

What was most upsetting to the defense was the judge's finding of "bad faith" on Joe's part. Coyle accepted Holmboe's testimony and also repeated the winery's allegation that the "cheese notes" had been purposefully hidden. The judge then drew the conclusion that Joe had all along intentionally concealed from his brothers that he planned to market consumer cheese under his name in a "willful exploitation of the fame and advertising of the Gallo brand."

Despite the consumer surveys that confirmed a negative image long before Joe's cheese had even existed, Coyle accepted the winery's claim that the "low-priced, generic image" of Joseph Gallo Cheese "reinforces" the very image that Gallo was seeking to overcome because it "threatens to damage" the winery's attempts to improve the image of Gallo Wine among "traditionalists, who tend to shop for wines in smaller containers, with traditional cork closures and vintage dating." He seemed to give less weight to state and federal inspections and approvals of Joe's cheese as well as his gold medal awards; instead he confirmed the winery's insistence that the cheese posed the risk of "a serious health problem . . . that may injure the Gallo brand."

And last, Judge Coyle renarrated the winery's version of Joe's failure to make an effort to establish his own trademark. He included what had been Ernest's assertion that Joe had been "offered the opportunity to join his brothers as a partner" but "For his own reasons . . . declined to do so." (This allegation was more properly an issue in the counterclaims, in which Joe had disputed Ernest's recollection; it had not actually been argued in the infringement proceedings, and what significance it had in the trademark dispute was unclear. But Coyle adopted Ernest's statement as fact and did not remark upon Joe's denials.)

Coyle did not discuss the argument that a trade name on agricultural products and wholesale products in some cases constitutes use as a trademark (the legal basis for Ernest's claim that "Gallo" had been continuously used as a trademark since 1909). Instead, he concluded that Joe's forty-year-long use of his trade name did not establish a trademark by reasoning that although Joe used his name in various business activities, he had never used his name on any consumer products.

Finally, having already ruled that the First and Fourteenth amendment issues were "not before the court," he did not address what Whiting and Herzig had felt was central to Joe's defense.

On the basis of these findings, Judge Coyle issued a permanent injunction. Not only was the name Joseph Gallo not to appear as a trademark on any label or in any advertisement or published material, but the name itself was not to be spoken or "audibly communicated" in any television or radio broadcast. Joe was allowed to retain his name on his bulk cheese packages, and either Gallo Cattle Company or Joseph Gallo Farms could appear as a trade name on his retail cheese, as long as it was designated in print no larger than twelve-point type and below both the trademark and the cheese variety. And finally, these terms allowing the use of Gallo as a trade name were to "remain in effect only so long as a person whose surname at birth is Gallo is an owner, principal or active participant in the business of defendant Gallo Cattle Co. or any successor or assignee of Gallo Cattle Co."

Whiting was furious as he read and interpreted the conditions. "Do you realize what he's saying?" he stormed. "Joe can't even mention his own name on television or radio? Whether it's a commercial or even just an interview, he can't stand up and say, 'My name is Joe Gallo and I make cheese.' He can't even say he makes something else either. If that isn't a violation of Joe's right to free speech, I don't know what is. Then this thing about having to be born with the name Gallo to be able to use the company's trade name. That means Joe's wife or Mike's wife or even Linda's daughter are denied their rights under this injunction! I can't believe it—he gave Ernest all he wanted and then some."

Joe shook his head in disbelief when he realized the full implications of the injunction. "I guess it's true—Ernest always gets what he goes after. It's always been like that, and it will never change."

Joe was saddened, not simply by the loss of his own name but by the sense that his brothers had so much power and influence that they could deny him his identity—not only his name but also the chance to recover his past from the secrecy that his brothers had imposed. In both Judge Price's and Judge Coyle's courtrooms, his recollections, his assertions, his word seemed to count for little compared to his brothers' statements. And now, on top of that, Judge Coyle had concluded that he had lied and concealed his business from his brothers and shown bad faith by keeping secrets. This, when throughout his life, he had been proud of his brothers, loyal to them, and had never made important decisions without consulting them. Why had he invited them to the opening of the cheese plant? Why had he sent the family boxes of his cheese? It was bad enough to lose the case, but for the judge to call him dishonorable and secretive and even untruthful was an especially bitter pill to swallow.

After the decision, Joe and Mike fired the Howard, Rice firm, and Whiting, assisted by Al and Thelma Herzig and their Los Angeles firm, undertook to handle Joe's appeal of both the trademark decision and the summary judgment in Joe's counterclaims. On July 24, 1989, they filed a motion for a new trial as well as secondary motions to vacate judgment pending appeal, to amend the pretrial statement, and to disqualify Judge Coyle.

But the dissension among the attorneys turned the July 31 hearing of the arguments into a fiasco. The motion for a new trial was fairly pro forma, although Whiting now focused on the issue of Joe's First Amendment rights. Judge Coyle immediately interrupted. Didn't Mr. Whiting remember the first day of the trial when Mr. Herzig had tried to amend the pretrial order, and then the winery lawyers "screamed bloody murder that this was not an issue in this case?" But when asked if they wanted to proceed with the Herzig motion, "Mr. Gallo's attorneys decided it was no, that they did not want . . . to set up a First Amendment issue . . . in this case."

Whiting tried to explain: Yes, he remembered, but "frankly, Your Honor, I don't know why Mr. Rice said no." And then, he agreed, Rice had withdrawn Herzig's posttrial motion because "he felt that the issue was already before the court. . . . There clearly was no intention to waive Mr. Gallo's First Amendment rights or any other constitutional rights."

Whiting continued, arguing that whether or not the question of Joe's First Amendment rights was spelled out, the court was "duty bound to protect those rights."

"Wait, Mr. Whiting," Judge Coyle replied, a sarcastic edge to his voice. "I'm duty bound to say, 'All right, Mr. Gallo, you have two sets of highly competent, highly paid attorneys. They can't agree what the issues are in this case; therefore, it's my duty to do something?' "

Whiting then argued the ways in which he felt the injunction abridged Joe's rights, from restricting the use of his trade name on any product to denying him the trademark on cheese and forbidding him to use his name in radio and television advertising. He also refuted Coyle's finding of confusion, insisting again that since the record is "absolutely devoid of any actual confusion," the court should not "categorize the [Field] survey as the strongest evidence of actual confusion."

Lynch was brief in his response. He claimed that the injunction did not prohibit the use of Joseph Gallo or Gallo as a trade name but only the use of the trademark on cheese. He also pointed out that Whiting was trying to reargue the evidence on confusion, but most adamantly, he insisted that up until the first day of the trial there had been "no contention made . . . that the First Amendment was somehow involved."

When Joe Yanny, a Herzig associate, stepped forward to respond to Lynch and also to raise the recusal issues, Judge Coyle again interrupted. He narrated for the record what he perceived as the confusion and contradictions of the defense lawyers. He read from the first day of trial transcript; he noted Herzig's posttrial amendment, then Sparer's letter to withdraw the motion. He reminded Joe's attorneys of the calls his clerk had made when the filings for these motions were incomplete. He was especially angry that Yanny had apparently submitted an unsigned declaration from Denis Rice, which stated that while he had known that Coyle was a partner of McCormick, Barstow, he hadn't realized that it was during this time that the Gallo Salame suit had been litigated and the trademark sale and license arrangement negotiated. The Howard, Rice firm, however, had then notified the court that the declaration was to be withdrawn, as Denis Rice would not be signing it.

Coyle also noted that while Whiting's motion included recusal issues, the defense had filed no separate motion for disqualification (even though Yanny had indicated that one was forthcoming). Yanny now undertook to address the question in this proceeding. Judge Coyle took the opportunity to say, "I do not appreciate the tenor [of the documents suggesting] that I somehow got this case into this courtroom so I could try it. It was brought to me the day before trial as a result of the defendants' filing a motion to recuse Judge Price, a motion which, I might say, had no merit." He added that he had been unaware that the Gallo Salame case had been handled by his former law firm, but "if I had any knowledge of it, I had long forgotten about [it]."

Yanny, however, argued that a lack of recollection was beside the point. He focused on McCormick, Barstow's involvement in the Gallo Salame case and insisted that Judge Coyle was duty bound to conduct "a searching and fearless moral inventory to see if you had a potential conflict." And if it had "slipped his mind," then Oliver Wanger, Coyle's former partner, who was involved in the Gallo Salame lawsuit and settlement, should have brought it to the court's attention. (He did not add what was also the case—that Joe's lawyers might also have filed a notice of related case, or at least called attention to it when the case had been transferred to Coyle.) Yanny then struck out at the judge's suspected property investments with former partners and his vineyard holdings, asserting that he should make his vineyard involvement public as well as whether he or his partners or both sold grapes to the winery. Judge Coyle looked surprised, but he made no immediate response.

Pat Lynch, however, defended the judge, calling Yanny's statements "pious, arrogant, and utterly outrageous." He argued that Joe's attorneys had all known that Coyle's former firm had handled only "housekeeping" matters in the Gallo Salame case, like filings in the Fresno courthouse. Rice and Whiting had both seen the McCormick, Barstow name on the case documents, he said, and neither had objected to the case's transfer. The matter had been settled three years before the instigation of Joe's lawsuit, he asserted, and hence did not fall under the recusal rules. And last, he pointed out that if Howard, Rice had found reasonable grounds to question the judge's impartiality, "they had ample opportunity to do so." They were compelled to make a "timely complaint," and since they had failed to do so, Joe was now barred from raising the recusal issue. (Later, outside the courtroom, Lynch's language became even stronger when he called Yanny's argument "smear tactics" and "character assassination" and denounced Joe and his attorneys for "judge-shopping.")

On August 3, Judge Coyle denied all motions, although he did extend the deadline for changing Joe's labels. He ruled that his prior partnership during the Gallo Salame case did not require his recusal under federal rules, and he again chronicled the disorganization and problems of Joe's attorneys. He maintained that his decision showed no "inordinate bias and prejudice" and defended using the winery's proposed findings with slight modifications for his own findings of fact as his standard practice.

He made no mention of his property holdings, however. Without referring to the questions explicitly, he noted only that Yanny had failed to file a separate recusal motion. "Hence the time for making such motions is now past," Coyle concluded in a footnote in which he derided the failure to make the motion as "deliberate and yet another example of Defendants' penchant for treating recusal motions as a game of hide the ball."

If Joe hoped to get any relief, he would have to take both his counterclaims and the trademark decision to a higher federal court—the United States Court of Appeals for the Ninth Circuit. But given the ground he had lost with the conflicts among his lawyers, the appeal would have to be doubly persuasive.

John Whiting undertook the task of preparing the appeals brief. When the Howard, Rice firm shipped the files to Merced, he faced a warehouse full of papers with only his wife Carol and a young lawyer from the Herzig firm to help sort them out.

The Herzigs also assisted, and they enlisted Stanley Fleishman, a Los Angeles attorney specializing in civil rights work, to prepare an amicus curiae brief on behalf of Linda Gallo Jelacich and her minor daughter, Ann Marie, to object to what they considered the discriminatory conditions of the injunction. Besides denying equal rights to Linda's heirs (since they would not be born with the name Gallo), Fleishman argued, the injunction ignored the rights of adopted heirs. (Since Kenny and Linda's three-year-old daughter, Ann Marie, had been adopted, she, like any adopted child, would not have been "born with the name Gallo," whatever her adoptive parents' names.) The winery objected strenuously to the amicus brief, and the Ninth Circuit Court of Appeals agreed, advising Whiting to incorporate the "equal protection" objections in his full appeal.

With only a few months to prepare, Whiting begun to work a back-breaking schedule, to the point that his wife and Mike became concerned about his health. Mike, meanwhile, was also worried about his father, who seemed physically and emotionally drained. Nevertheless, he and Joe turned their attention to redesigning their labels according to Judge Coyle's injunction. Their cheese would now be marketed as Joseph Farms, with Joseph Gallo in small script appearing as a trade name.

After the cheese with this new label was distributed to supermarkets, Pat Lynch wrote Whiting to complain that the print size of "Joseph Gallo" did not conform to the injunction and threatened legal action. Whiting responded that the lettering was exactly what the injunction ordered and presumably what Lynch objected to was the fact that "Joseph Gallo" appeared at all on the label, even as a trade name.

"There's going to be no satisfying Ernest now," Whiting exclaimed. He also included Lynch's letter as another basis for appealing the injunction—that the winery interpreted the judge's order as a prohibition against using "Joseph Gallo" in any way.

On January 18, 1990, Whiting filed Joe's appeal with the Ninth Circuit Court of Appeals in San Francisco. It was long and complicated, covering as it did Price's summary judgment and Coyle's trademark decision and injunction as well as the recusal, free speech, and equal protection issues. The winery followed with its response six weeks later. Working with Al and Thelma Herzig, Whiting prepared and submitted the reply brief for Joe and Mike on April 24, 1990. All they could do now was wait until oral arguments were scheduled.

During the months that followed, Joe's mood seemed to improve. Mike, Sherrie, Linda, Ken, and Patricia's son, Sam, and his wife, Kay, had all been attentive, and with the help of Patricia's cheerful optimism, he had emerged from his depression. The label change to Joseph Farms hadn't reduced distribution, and his cheese sales reached $35 million. (This seemed to confirm what Joe and Mike had always stated—that customers bought the cheese not for the Gallo association but for its quality.) He continued to sell his grapes to the winery, and Phil Bava, who headed Julio's grower relations department, congratulated Joe and Mike on their fine harvest in the autumn of 1990. But Joe and his family had no direct contact with either Julio or Ernest or their families. That would have been too painful.

The three brothers now celebrated the holidays separately. No traditional *bagna cauda* on Christmas Eve or Easter barbecue at Joe's, no Thanksgiving at Julio's or Christmas Day or New Year's party at Ernest's for the entire Gallo clan. And while this saddened Joe, there was also a feeling of relief. He and his family no longer felt constrained by the expectations and controls that Ernest had so often imposed in the past.

Joe and Mike had been upset that Julio had testified the last day of the trial, and any hope of reconciliation with his side of the family had been destroyed. Nevertheless, when a serious auto accident involving Julio and Aileen made headline news, Joe and his family at first felt sympathy for everyone involved.

On January 2, 1990, Aileen and Julio had been returning to Modesto from their vacation home in Pebble Beach. Aileen was behind the wheel of their Lincoln Town Car, driving the narrow, winding Pacheco Pass route through the Central range, a highway known for treacherous curves and major accidents. (Several years before, his granddaughter had been driving Julio when the car rolled into a ditch on the same road. She was unhurt, but Julio's neck had been injured). In this accident, Aileen had veered into the opposite lane and struck a Honda Civic. Aileen and Julio suffered bruises and broken ribs. But the head-on collision killed the driver of the Civic, twenty-seven-year-old Sharon Kauk. Her husband, Tim, had a concussion and their three-month-old son sustained head injuries.

"I'm sure Aileen must have been devastated," said Sherrie. "Of any of them, she would feel the most guilty and the most upset at the young woman's death." Worse still, the California Highway Patrol said that since witnesses had observed Aileen swerve into the westbound lane, she could be charged with vehicular manslaughter.

Several days later, Frank Damrell, Jr.—the brother-in-law of Bob Gallo, and the sometime Gallo Winery attorney who had figured prominently in Judge Price's recusal—reported to the CHP that two new witnesses had come forward to say that Kauk's car, not Aileen's, had crossed the yellow line. The Joe Gallo family's sympathy began to wane. "Funny thing how Ernest lucks into these last-minute witnesses," commented Mike. He couldn't help but be skeptical when he learned that one of the two new witnesses lived in Modesto. The witnesses said that they had been several cars behind the Gallos, had left a card in Aileen's purse, but, because they were "in a hurry," hadn't stayed at the scene to talk to investigating officers. Two days later, the Modesto witness contacted the winery, according to spokesman Dan Solomon.

The CHP, however, was not convinced by the new witnesses' version of the accident. Given the comparative weights of the cars and their final resting position in the westbound lane, given the testimony of the drivers directly behind and in front of the Kauk car, investigating officers concluded that Aileen was responsible for the collision.

In February, Sharon Kauk's family filed a personal injury and wrongful death suit against Aileen. Aileen then pleaded no contest to one count of vehicular misdemeanor manslaughter and was sentenced to probation, 350 hours of community service, and a $2,000 fine. (Tests had shown that she wasn't intoxicated, but there was still no explanation for her erratic driving, even from her.)

According to Vincent Ruocco, the Kauk family attorney, a settlement with Aileen and Julio was "expeditiously" reached in November 1990, and the two new witnesses "never became an issue." While the financial terms of the settlement were confidential, Ruocco said that Julio and Aileen, whose depositions he took, were quite upset about the tragedy, and between both insurers' and "their own money," they reached an agreement that also reflected "their concern about unforeseen lasting effects of head injuries to the Kauks' child." As a result of the settlement, on December 7, 1990, Ruocco asked for a dismissal of the claim against the Gallos.

During the months after his and Ernest's suit against Joe, Julio, along with his son Bob, and grandson Matt, had concentrated on the development of the Gallo Sonoma vineyards. In 1989, the winery bought the 600-acre Asti vineyard, once owned by Italian Swiss Colony, for a reported $11 million. (With the Gallo-owned Frei Ranch 625-acre vineyard, the Canyon Creek Ranch 200-acre vineyard, the 360-acre Laguna vineyard and the 100-acre Chiotti vineyard, Ernest and Julio's properties in Sonoma County totaled almost 2,400 acres, about 5 percent of the county's vineyards and more than any other winery in the area.) Julio had always favored "Sonoma reds," and with over 1,200 acres of vineyards already planted, he began to "move mountains" at the Asti vineyard, literally redesigning its topography: scraping topsoil, grading and leveling hillsides to a 10 percent to 12 percent slope to control erosion, replacing the topsoil, conditioning it with lime waste trucked from the Gallo Glass plant—all to prepare for the eventual new planting of Cabernet Sauvignon, Merlot, Cabernet Franc, and Sauvignon Blanc grapes.

Although no Gallo signs marked any of these vineyards, Sonoma neighbors began to hear that Julio and Bob were planning to open a visitors' center at Asti. Whether or not these Gallos were actually going to relinquish the winery's traditional secrecy, their attention to the northern vineyards was part of the winery's even more rigorous campaign to dominate the $5 to $7 range of the varietal market. With the new vines, the Gallos also hoped to enter the $8 to $10 varietal shelves.

Although Julio had complained to a grape grower in Lodi, "I never know what's going on in the winery anymore—they never tell me anything," he seemed happy to devote himself to the perfection of the Sonoma vineyards and the new Gallo vintage varietals. And perhaps, like the Livingston vineyards in the 1940s, his Sonoma project kept him at a welcome distance from the continuing legal conflict. Indeed, he did not appear in court for the oral arguments in Joe's appeal.

Because the earthquake in the Bay Area on October 17, 1989, had so damaged the San Francisco Federal Courthouse, cases had been postponed (files and documents had scattered and had to be resorted) and hearings had been rescheduled at other federal courthouses. Joe's appeal was relocated to Pasadena and was finally heard by Appellate Court Judges Betty Fletcher, Thomas Tang, and Stephen Reinhardt on Friday, December 14, 1990.

Al and Thelma Herzig had by then become members of the Santa Monica law firm of Haight, Brown & Bonesteel and had enlisted the chief of the firm's appellate division, Roy Weatherup, to present the oral arguments in Joe's case. Joe attended the hearing accompanied not only by John Whiting and Al Herzig, but also by Mike, Sherrie, Linda, and Whiting's wife and stepdaughter. As usual, Ernest entered the courtroom with his "family" of lawyers—winery in-house attorneys, Pat Lynch and several other O'Melveny & Myers partners and associates.

While Lynch went through his papers and set up an easel for exhibits, Ernest engaged a new member of the O'Melveny team in conversation. (The young attorney hadn't been present during the Fresno court proceedings, and Ernest seemed to be welcoming him aboard.)

Ernest asked him where he was from. When the young man replied Chicago, Ernest began to reminisce about the weeks he had spent in Chicago in the 1920s selling wine grapes.

The lawyer replied enthusiastically that he had heard of the grape yards from his Polish grandfather. "He used to tell great stories," the attorney added, "all about Prohibition and bootlegging and how everyone was making wine back in those days."

Ernest frowned, then abruptly turned away and took a seat in the

front row of the spectators' section. The young man looked perplexed, apparently unaware of what he had said to irritate the client.

For the next hour, Lynch and Weatherup presented their arguments. Judge Betty Fletcher led the questioning for her judicial colleagues and several times interrupted Lynch during his presentation.
Lynch was defending the injunction, arguing that the prohibition
against Joe's announcing his name in radio and television advertisements was valid. Judge Fletcher seemed surprised: Did the injunction
mean that Joe Gallo could not go on television and tell people who
he was and what he was selling, like the commercials for cars late at
night?

"Are you saying that if Joe Gallo decided to sell Cadillacs, he
couldn't use his name?" she asked.

Lynch seemed startled by the down-home analogy, but took the
question as rhetorical. He insisted that the judge's example was different—the injunction banned any designation of Joe's name as a trademark. Such verbal communication by Joe would suggest that Joseph
Gallo was a trademark.

Then, arguing against Joe's appeal to reinstate his counterclaims,
Lynch insisted that since the guardianship estate had been closed and
settled by a court hearing in 1941, res judicata precluded any further
legal action and thus the summary judgment should not be overturned. He displayed an enlargement of the first and last account of
Joe's guardianship estate. Pointing to the item designating a one-third
interest "in the E. & J. Winery," he reiterated that it indicated only
Joe's one-third share of what the winery owed the father's estate.

Judge Fletcher leaned forward and peered at the line in the accounting, then read the item aloud.

"Well, that's certainly ambiguous, isn't it?" she commented.

For the first time in many months, Joe and his attorneys felt that a
judge had shown some understanding of the counterclaims case.
Judge Fletcher's remarks had given them a glimmer of hope. But
whatever the impression left by the oral arguments, it would be over
a year before the court reached a decision.

With hardly a word to anyone, Ernest left the courthouse quickly, his
chauffeured limousine waiting to take him to the airport. For the next
months he returned to running his wine empire and leading the Gallo
attack on the premium and varietal wine market. As part of his cam-

paign, he gave an interview to Marvin Shanken, editor and publisher of *The Wine Spectator*. Touted as Ernest's first interview in fifty-eight years, the article, which appeared on September 15, 1991, was a repetition of the Gallo official story and of Ernest's usual remarks about the secrets of his success, along with his thoughts about his aims, the future of the company, and the future of the wine business.

He seemed to have an agenda for this rare interview, and Julio, too, had suddenly become accessible to the press, or at least to favored wine writers: The two brothers proudly announced that in the next year or two, they would market an estate-bottled $60 Cabernet Sauvignon and a $30 Chardonnay.

The wine, to be made at their new Sonoma winery, was presented as the pinnacle of their "high-image" campaign for Gallo vintage-dated varietals. Industry insiders questioned the marketing decision when both the national economy and the wine business were in serious slumps. And no matter how Ernest pushed his upscale campaign, he still had to contend with the public's association of Gallo with generic, jug, and street wines. (While the winery had increased its share of the premium market and in 1991, with an estimated 4.3 million cases sold, was listed as number one in varietal wine sales, its largest market share was still in the generic and jug categories, its Carlo Rossi Chablis, Gallo Chablis Blanc, and Carlo Rossi Rhine the top three national sellers.)

Ernest was still trying to change the Gallo reputation (in 1989 he had even begun marketing a Hearty Burgundy Limited Release in smaller bottles to take it out of the jug category). "It's time for a change to Gallo" now accompanied the winery's most recent print and television advertising. (In its Thanksgiving, 1991, "Golden Turkey Awards," the *San Francisco Examiner* again awarded one to E. & J. Gallo's commercials: "Perpetually annoying, this time a setting of sculpted potato curls and steamed fish and yuppie restaurant—whites only, of course—all supposed to 'change the way you feel about Gallo.' In the immortal words of Macaulay Culkin: 'I don't think so.' ")

At the same time that Ernest was heralding his $60 and $30 bottles of wine, Gallo's image took another beating. Two years earlier, after growing complaints about Gallo's Thunderbird and Night Train Express, the winery had proclaimed an experiment to "help reduce alcohol-related social problems" by withholding its wines from retail stores in skid row and ghetto districts for six months. (Retailers, however, reported that they had been forewarned of the planned withdrawal and that they stocked up on their Gallo inventory.) The winery then announced that during Gallo's seven-month absence from stores, drinking habits hadn't changed and thus it returned its wines to shelves.

On September 16, 1991, the day after Ernest's interview in *The Wine Spectator* had appeared, the public was again reminded of Gallo's street wine reputation when *People*, as well as several tabloid newspapers, ran a photograph of Milwaukee "cannibal killer" Jeffrey Dahmer comatose on his bed clutching a bottle of Thunderbird.

The winery was fighting battles on other fronts as well. In November 1990, Proposition 134, an alcohol tax initiative, was on the ballot in California, and Angelo (Buff) Bufalino led the winery's opposition to the measure. Although this campaign was successful, Ernest now pointed out that it might be time for Buff to retire. "There were no hard feelings, and he gave me a wonderful retirement party," Bufalino said, denying a rumor that he was unhappy with the suggestion. (Bufalino remained a part-time personnel advisor to the winery as well as heading his own career consultant business.)

As part of its effort to upscale its image, the winery was also lobbying the Bureau of Alcohol, Tobacco, and Firearms for a change in champagne label regulations. Unless champagne is made by the traditional "champenoise method" (fermenting in individual bottles rather than in steel tanks), it must be designated by the phrase "bulk process." Arguing that the term is "demeaning and degrading," Gallo was seeking to change the label to read "Charmat method." Named after its French inventor, Eugene Charmat, the method is also a bulk process but sounds classier; indeed, champenoise makers and champagne importers charged that Gallo's proposed change was designed to deceive consumers.

According to the *Modesto Bee*, two senators lobbied for the Gallo proposal: Bob Dole, Republican from Kansas, and John Seymour, Republican from California. The senators argued the winery's case in a letter to Deputy Treasury Secretary John Robson only a few days before he met with winery representatives. Federal Election Commission records show that during the previous three years the two senators received a total of $112,000 from the Gallo family. Both senators denied that there was any connection between the Gallo contributions and their efforts on behalf of the winery.

John Seymour had been chosen to fill the U.S. Senate seat vacated by Pete Wilson when he was elected governor of California in 1990. According to Mike Gallo, Wilson had been another recipient of Gallo contributions.

Before leaving the U.S. Senate in 1990 to become governor of California, Pete Wilson had sponsored the nomination of Oliver Wanger to the federal bench in the Eastern District of the United States District Court in California. In February 1991, after his confirmation hearings, Wanger replaced Judge Edward Dean Price, who, like Judge Crocker, now had "senior" status and was semiretired. While Wanger was undoubtedly a high-profile attorney in the area, neither he, Coyle, nor Price had served as judges at other levels. Unlike Crocker, they had all come directly from private practice. With the appointment of Wanger, the two sitting judges in the Eastern District are men who were formerly partners in the same law firm that continues to represent the winery; it is to this venue that Gallo distributors' contracts still require transfer if a legal dispute arises.

After Democratic Congresswoman Barbara Boxer became a candidate for senator, attorney Denis Rice announced that he would run for her seat to represent the Sixth District (predominantly Marin County, where he lives) in the House of Representatives. In mid-November 1991, he launched his campaign by trying to swim the San Francisco Bay from the Marin side to the city, but had to be pulled from the water when high tides kept him from reaching shore. He had consulted a tide book but had forgotten to correct for the change from daylight savings to standard time. In the June 1992 primary, he placed third.

While both sides awaited the appeals court decision, Ernest and Julio made another move against Joe and Mike. In August 1991, Phil Bava, head of the grower relations department, officially informed them that after the 1991 harvest, the winery would no longer buy grapes from Joseph Gallo. Joe had a contract with the winery only for grapes from his original vineyard surrounding his Livingston home. Termination of this contract required a five-year notice, which Bava now also put into effect. Since Joe had no formal contracts for the majority of his vineyards, the winery announced that they would purchase none of these grapes in 1992.

Joe and Mike were astonished; several times during their settlement negotiations in the case, the question of vineyard contracts had been raised. At the very beginning of the conflict, Ernest had threatened to stop buying Joe's grapes if Joe did not accept the proposed license agreement. He had backed off, however, when Joe's lawyers suggested that they would pursue legal action if Ernest implemented this threat. During the Foster Farms restaurant meeting with Julio, Joe had raised the issue. At that time, according to Mike, Julio had reassured him that he would "always have a home for his grapes at the winery" and had later confirmed the statement in several letters.

The winery's decision not to purchase his grapes would have financial consequences for Joe. Most of his vineyards were planted to French Colombards and Chenin Blanc because the winery needed vast supplies of these two grapes for its generic wines. Other than Gallo, few wineries used these two varieties extensively. And few other wineries were large enough to handle the volume of grapes that Joe's many vineyards produced. Because these grapes were more expensive to raise and pick than other varieties, Joe depended on crop loans for expenses, loans that were approved by banks because he had a guaranteed buyer for the grapes.

Mike immediately phoned Phil Bava. Bava seemed reluctant to take his phone call, Mike recalled, and nervous when he gave what sounded to him like a rehearsed explanation. He told Mike that Gallo was no longer interested in buying huge supplies of French Colombards or Chenin Blanc "because generic wines aren't selling anymore. Besides," he went on, "we're not in the welding business. We're not going to keep building tanks just to store all you growers' grapes." (The upscale Gallo approach had apparently affected the grower relations department; Bava's remark seemed to imply that Gallo no longer had much interest in their jug wines and would not be constructing more of their stainless-steel tanks to hold this supply. But the winery's continued domination of generic wine sales suggested that this was hardly the case. Besides, one of Gallo's best-selling wines is French Colombard, which it now bottles and markets as a varietal.)

Although Joe was prepared to fight this latest attack, he was convinced that his brothers were now trying to undermine his business and ruin his financial standing. They seemed intent on obliterating his very existence and severing him completely from both the winery and the family.

Joe's impression was reinforced when he read Ernest's comments in *The Wine Spectator* interview. In the course of his conversation with Shanken, Ernest had explained, "It's traditional between Julio and me, every Christmas Eve, that I go over to his place and we make *bagna cauda*."

Up until the lawsuit, it had been traditional for Ernest and Julio to go to Joe's home for *bagna cauda*. Ernest's statement once again seemed to confirm his willingness to rewrite history—he chose not to mention Joe's name and simply changed the facts.

It was a small detail, but it suggested to Joe and Patricia that Ernest was ready to deny the past and prune him from the family tree. Everyone who didn't fit in with the official story had been excised— including their father and mother, their uncle Mike, and now their brother. The mysteries and ambiguities of the early years had been locked away, so now Joe and his family would be erased from the record.

What Ernest felt about the tragedy of the brothers' feud he didn't say, either in the interview or during his and Amelia's sixtieth wedding anniversary party in 1991. San Francisco advertising executive Hal Riney served as the master of ceremonies for the gala celebration. Three years earlier, after a dispute with Ernest, he had resigned from the Gallo accounts, but he seemed back on friendly terms as he narrated Ernest and Julio's rags-to-riches odyssey. Guests added their own tributes to the brothers' accomplishments. No one doubted the extraordinary achievements of Gallo—what they had done for the wine industry was incontrovertible. Whatever the conflicts, problems, and resentments among employees, distributors, competitors, and family over the years, they were put aside or forgotten in the glow of the evening's festive mood. Once more the Gallo self-creation myth was sanctioned as the true American success story. The rest was silence.

One evening in 1991, Ernest gave a dinner and wine tasting for a group of California winemakers, distributors, and successful businessmen. (Julio was not present—he usually avoided these public relations gatherings.)

During dinner, one of the guests was describing his business partnership with his brother. They had done very well, he explained, and he was sure that the reason for their success was their mutual affection and respect.

Ernest sat at the head of the table, talking to guests on his immediate left and right. But when he overheard the remarks extolling the family business, he suddenly stopped his own conversation.

"Listen, I have a word of advice for you," he interrupted. Startled, the others fell silent. Ernest now shook his finger in warning and called down the table:

"Never trust your brother!"

EPILOGUE

On February 7, 1992, the United States Court of Appeals for the Ninth Circuit issued its opinion in the Gallo case. Written by Judge Betty Fletcher, it affirmed the summary judgment granted to the winery, and finding that "the use of the GALLO name as a trademark on retail packages of cheese was trademark infringement by one of the Gallo brothers," it upheld the district court's permanent injunction against Joe, but limited its scope.

In the matter of the summary judgment, Judge Fletcher supported Judge Price's reasoning that in order to overturn the previous probate decrees involving the distribution of Joe, Sr.'s property and the guardianship estate, Joe had to show that Ernest and Julio engaged in extrinsic fraud. Agreeing with Judge Price that Joe's evidence had failed to do so, she ruled that Joe's counterclaims "were barred by *res judicata.*"

Considering the issues raised in the appeal of the trademark infringement case, Judge Fletcher concluded that Judge Coyle's decision was fully consistent with the Ninth Circuit's *Friend* decision: "The district court properly found that Joseph knew that the winery would object to his use of the GALLO name and that he intended to capitalize on its reputation and selling power." By "limiting the use of Joseph's name only to the extent necessary to avoid public confusion, the district court demonstrated the appropriate reluctance to enjoin all use of a person's name." The earlier disagreement among Joe's lawyers regarding the inclusion of a *Friend* defense thus ultimately proved irrelevant.

As for Joe's appeal on other matters, Judge Fletcher upheld Judge Coyle's rulings that the Gallo Salame trademark agreement with the winery was a valid assignment of the mark, that the winery had proved the likelihood of confusion, and that Joe could not cite his brothers' delay in complaining as a defense, since he had not been "prejudiced by the winery's failure to object to his use of his name in relation to other products and his other business properties."

Joe's attorneys had included a recusal motion in their appeal, arguing that Judge Coyle should have disqualified himself because of his former firm's involvement in the Gallo Salame litigation and because of his joint real estate investments with some of his former law partners, "creating a reasonable question as to his impartiality." Judge Fletcher noted that Judge Coyle's statement that "he was not aware of his former firm's involvement" until it was brought to his attention in Joe's motion for a new trial was "irrelevant if the firm's involvement was such that a person knowing all the facts could reasonably question his impartiality." However, she wrote, "The threshold issue is the timeliness of Joseph's argument." She pointed out that while Joe's attorney Joseph Yanny had raised the issue in his oral presentation of posttrial motions, he had never filed the promised separate recusal motion. She stated that although Joe's attorneys "knew at the time of the transfer to Judge Coyle" that McCormick, Barstow had represented the winery in the Gallo Salame case, they "did not act on that information but waited until they lost on the merits." Hence she upheld Judge Coyle's denial of Joe's posttrial motion for disqualification, concluding that "the unexplained delay for the recusal motion suggested that the recusal statute was being misused for strategic purposes."

It was a sweeping decision against Joe and his attorneys, although they had one small victory. While Judge Fletcher ruled that the district court's injunction was proper and was not an impermissible restriction of free speech, she added that it was "overbroad" in that "the prohibition against audible broadcast advertisements extended to 'other products'" and that "its reach to Joseph's descendants might reach others in unforeseen ways." With these modifications, she affirmed Judge Coyle's permanent injunction.

Joe's attorneys filed a "Petition for Rehearing and Suggestion for a Rehearing En Banc" on February 21. They asked that the full appeals court rehear their appeal of the summary judgment and cited other case law to support their appeal of the summary judgment and the res judicata ruling: "Ernest and Julio are not in a position to hide behind the probate decrees. If appellants are able to prove that the winery was a continuation of a business owned by the parents of the three Gallo brothers at the time of their deaths, then ownership of a third of the winery passed to Joseph Gallo, even if Ernest and Julio converted the assets constituting the business to their own use. These assets, in which Joseph had an interest, gave birth to the winery."

Al Herzig agreed with this argument, but he was disturbed by another aspect of the court's decision. From the beginning, Herzig said, he had called attention to Local Rule 123 and wondered why a notice of related case had not initially been filed and why at several crucial points in the case, including the transfer to Judge Coyle, Judge Crocker had been passed over. In her opinion, Judge Fletcher addressed this issue obliquely when she wrote in her summary of the case, "On November 14 . . . Judge Price transferred the case to Judge Coyle, the only other district court judge in Fresno."

Judge Crocker said that he himself had received several phone calls joking about this statement in the opinion. Indeed, he remarked with a laugh, "I'm going to have to remind Judge Fletcher of my existence the next time I see her." But Herzig took the error more seriously. He felt that the inaccurate statement again raised the question of "the appearance of impropriety" in the judicial assignments in Joe's case. On April 28, he filed a separate declaration as a Request for Judicial Notice of and Correction of Error. He reminded the court not only that Judge Crocker still sat in the Eastern District, but that he had presided in the related Gallo Salame case. He noted that Judge Coyle had conceded that the cases were related (because of the Gallo Salame trademark at issue in Joe's case), and that the judge had said that he could not agree with the winery attorneys' assertion that the two cases "were wholly unrelated." As a result, Herzig proposed that under Local Rule 123, it would have been appropriate to assign Judge Crocker to the Joe Gallo case in the beginning, then later as a settlement judge and, most significantly, when Judge Price had disqualified himself. (He added that with the transfer to Judge Coyle rather than to Judge Crocker, "The appearance of impropriety was even greater," because Wanger had been both counsel for the winery in the salami case and Coyle's "former litigation partner.") He stated that Judge Price recused himself and assigned the case to Judge Coyle, "instead of vacating his [summary judgment] . . . and returning the case to the clerk to be re-assigned to Judge Crocker for trial."

And finally, he suggested, albeit subtly, that the winery might have wanted to avoid Judge Crocker since the settlement of the related Gallo Salame case "could nourish an inference that the winery feared it had not convinced Judge Crocker that [it] had a *bona fide* trademark infringement case against Gallo Salame, Inc." He also cited Ernest's deposition, in which he explained that the winery had decided to negotiate a settlement because "we realiz[ed] we had waited so long to bring this action." And finally, he noted that Judge Coyle had disqualified himself in the Pappas case (presumably because Wanger and his former firm were representing the winery).

On June 22, 1992, Judge Fletcher issued the Ninth Circuit's denial of Joe's petition for rehearing and rehearing en banc. However, she also ordered that her February 7 opinion was to be amended: "the phrase 'the only other district court judge in Fresno' is deleted."

That left Joe's attorneys only with the option of appealing to the U.S. Supreme Court.

Joe, however, had his own feelings about the prospect of another appeal. After Judge Fletcher had ruled against him, he and Patricia decided "to put this case behind us." Joe and Mike believed that they could live with the injunction after the appeals court had narrowed its scope. Besides, Joe had been exhausted by the continuing court battle, especially when it seemed that what he had been assured was a strong case was beset by untimely delays, crucial omissions, and mistakes that cast him in a bad light. The waters had been so muddied by legal squabbling and confusion that it was no wonder he was reluctant to return to litigation.

He and Patricia felt that it was, as she put it, "time to get on with our lives." Similarly, Joe and Mike also decided not to fight Ernest and Julio's decision to stop buying their grapes. "We just realized how much better it is for us to be totally free of Ernest and Julio," Mike explained. "It feels good not to have to think about them or have to be hassled by them. We won't have to do everything their way and then risk having our grapes downgraded and being paid a lower price." Joe and Mike have now contracted to sell their grapes to Vintners International (owners of the Paul Masson and Taylor California brands).

Joe seems emotionally free of his brothers as well. And although Joe and Patricia sometimes wonder if they expended too much time and energy in the conflict, they also say that they don't regret having pursued the case. They are also heartened by the many letters of support they received, not only from people in the Central Valley but from cheese customers throughout the western states. Most people, Patricia reports, have expressed their astonishment that the court has told someone that he can't use his own name on his product. Others have praised Joe for taking on his brothers and refusing to knuckle under to their power and wealth.

"I felt I had to fight for what was right," Joe explains. "Not just for what was mine, but to honor my parents as well."

Indeed, despite the court's ruling against his counterclaims, despite its affirmation of Ernest's and Julio's recollections, Joe himself still believes that the Gallo family history is more complicated than his brothers will ever concede. No matter what the court decided, Joe had retrieved his memories of his parents and made them his own. He could now honor his sense of the family and its past.

In recovering his past, Joe also reaffirmed his sense of identity. No longer defined by his brothers, no longer acceding to their views and their demands, he had been released from the Gallo constraints and was now free to be himself.

Perhaps his grandson, Mike and Sherrie's son Micah, had said it best. After the court's decision, he had at first been upset. Then he announced with confidence: "They took away our name, but we still know who we are."

ACKNOWLEDGMENTS

I am especially grateful to the numerous people who were interviewed, often several times, and who also provided research and documentation for this book. Many of them are cited in the following notes, but there are others who, for various reasons (not the least of which was fear of Gallo retribution), prefer that their names not appear in print. Nevertheless, to all my sources, to all those who assisted me either by name or "on background," I wish to express my deepest thanks and my hope that the book itself makes their participation worthwhile.

This project could not have been completed without the cooperation of county and state libraries, local historical societies, and chambers of commerce throughout California. The information and documents supplied by various research librarians were invaluable, as the following notes indicate. But I'd like to add my special thanks to Ray Silva of the Hanford branch of the Kings County library. Because research for this book involved many legal filings, I also depended on the cooperation of the staffs of the federal courthouse in Fresno and the federal court archives in San Bruno. Thanks as well to the clerks of the courts and staffs of recorder's offices in Alameda, Amador, Fresno, Kings, Los Angeles, Madera, Merced, San Francisco, San Joaquin, and Stanislaus counties. To the Chicago Crime Commission and the Chicago Historical Society library, my appreciation for providing research assistance and facilities.

I benefited from generous help given by colleagues at several newspapers, including Linda Di Pietro and Becky McClure, formerly of the *Modesto Bee*; Patt Morrison and Peter King of the *Los Angeles Times*; Paul Galloway, Bob Greene, Augie Jewel and John Murphy of the *Chicago Tribune*, and Vern Whaley, now-retired *Tribune* photographer.

For assistance in photography research, my thanks to: Edward Guthmann and Sally Kibee of the *San Francisco Chronicle*; Wendy Roberts of the *San Jose Mercury News*; Susan Windemuth of the *Modesto Bee*; Thom Halls and the community relations staff of the *Fresno Bee*; Steve Trousdale of the *Los Angeles Daily Journal*; the staffs of *The Wine Spectator*, the Sonoma County Wine Library, and the California Historical Society.

To editors Bonnie St. Clair and David Currier of *Parade*, Peter Bloch of *Penthouse*, and Linda Mathews, formerly of the *Los Angeles Times Magazine*, my appreciation for their continued interest and encouragement during the writing of this book.

My agents Lois Wallace and Marion Rosenberg were stalwart in their support as well. My thanks to them and to Bob Bender of Simon & Schuster and to Leonard Mayhew for their editorial supervision and assistance.

Other friends and colleagues were helpful in many ways, but most of all I value the sustenance of the friendship and understanding of: Steven Simmons, Ralph Singer, Jack Martin, Jerry Neu, David Fechheimer, Edie and Conrad Reiman, Barbara Grizzuti Harrison, Nick von Hoffman, Sharon Churcher, Tom Goldstein, David Looman, and my brother Dan Hawkes. To others my thanks for what, in various ways, was essential to my well-being while working on the book: Chuck Emerson, for the house on Mirabel in San Francisco (and its resilience during the 1989 earthquake); Dr. Lynn Shannon of Hemingway Cat Hospital in Saratoga for her care of my cat Kate; Dr. William Mills for his medical care after a car accident; the staffs of the Holiday Inn in Modesto, the Hilton Hotel in Fresno, and the Sunset Marquis in Los Angeles for their attentive service during my many and sometimes extended stays; Karen Nobile of Saab and Dick Fehr of Nissan, for transportation during my research trips; the Coulters of Mail Boxes, Etc., of Saratoga, for faxing and copying efficiency; Saratoga Wine and Spirits and Vic's Liquors in Stamford, Connecticut, for keeping me up-to-date on wine news; George and Jim Cooper and Jan Garrod for their tips about winemaking and viticulture; Eleanor Ray for her reminiscences of her late husband

Martin Ray and her unpublished manuscript about his winery and adventures with pioneer vintner Paul Masson.

And, finally, the dedication of *Blood and Wine* to Anita Hawkes and Peter Manso is but a small token of my love and gratitude, of how much they mean to me, and without whom I could not have completed this book.

NOTES

For frequently cited court documents filed in the Gallo brothers' lawsuits, the following abbreviations are used in these notes:

Ernest Gallo's deposition (EDepo)
Amelia Gallo's deposition (AMDepo)
Julio Gallo's deposition (JULDepo)
Aileen Gallo's deposition (AIDepo)
Joseph Gallo, Jr.'s deposition (JODepo)
Gallo Winery's Motion for Summary Judgment (GWSJ)
Joseph Gallo's Opposition to Gallo Winery's Motion for Summary Judgment (JOSJ)
Joseph Gallo's Opposition to Gallo Winery's Motion for Judicial Notice (JOJN)
Joseph Gallo's Motion for Summary Judgment (JGSJ)
Gallo Winery's Opposition to Joseph Gallo's Motion for Summary Judgment (GWOSJ)
Judge Price's Pretrial Order, Sept. 2, 1988 (PTO)
Trial transcript of Nov.–Dec. 1988 proceedings (TT)

PROLOGUE

PAGE
14 *his father had nicknamed him* l'avvocato: According to Joe Gallo interview and JODepo; in EDepo, Ernest said he didn't recall this nickname, but Joe said their father used the term behind Ernest's back.
16 *"Ernest always told us"*: According to Mike Gallo interview.
17 *It is estimated:* Gallo Winery holdings and sales according to *Fortune* (for

example, Jaclyn Fierman's "How Gallo Crushes the Competition" (September 1, 1986), *Forbes* annual listing of "The 400 Largest Private Companies," and the *New York Times*, November 22, 1992.

18 *he accumulated over three thousand acres:* Joe Gallo's properties and sales of Joseph Gallo Cheese, according to Mike Gallo and John Whiting.

20 *"History doesn't do a thing for me":* Ernest's remark to Robert Mondavi, cited in James Conaway, *Napa, the Story of an American Eden* (Boston: Houghton Mifflin, 1990).

O N E

PAGE

23 *Giuseppe, born July 15, 1882:* The story of Giuseppe and Michelo Gallo's emigration to America from Fossano, Italy, is based on their own stories as passed down to succeeding generations and reported in interviews with Joe, Patricia, and Mike Gallo; Stella Dorais; Rudy Wagner; Father Benjamin Franzinelli; GWSJ also summarizes their early years, citing depositions of Ernest, Julio, and Joe Gallo, Jr.

24 *together they ran a badger game:* Described in a later trial as reported in the *San Francisco Call-Bulletin*, June 3, 1913.

25 *they stenciled "GALLO" in red:* According to GWSJ and EDepo, as well as EDepo in Gallo Salame case. "The Gallo Wine Company," confirmed in Oakland telephone directories, Alameda County Library in Oakland.

25 *Battista Bianco was a third-generation:* Bianco family history and Hanford background drawn from interviews with Joe, Patricia, and Mike Gallo; Stella Dorais; Fred Giacomazzi; Jack Lowe. The Kings County Records Office, the County Courthouse, Kings County Historical Society and Ray Silva, research librarian of Kings County Library in Hanford, provided historical information and documentation, including Hanford City directories and maps. GWSJ also includes references to the Bianco family's arrival in Hanford and their establishment of a winery.

26 *"We must work, work, work":* According to Stella Dorais, Battista Bianco's granddaughter.

28 *"I need a button right here":* Recalled by Stella Dorais.

28 *the brothers bought the Central Hotel:* Amador County Recorder's Office confirmed the Gallo purchase of the Central Hotel.

28 *Instead he and Tillie together loaned:* According to Kings County court records in Hanford.

28 *their marriage license read "Galli":* Registered March 18, 1908, in Kings County Courthouse, Hanford, and reported in the *Hanford Weekly Sentinel*, March 19, 1908.

29 You God damned bitch: According to Susie Gallo's petition for divorce, Kings County Superior Court, January 27, 1910.

29 *Celia came to Jackson several times:* Reported in the *Amador Dispatch*, September 4, September 18, and November 20, 1908.

29 *on March 18, 1909, a year from the day:* Registered in Amador County Recorder's Office in Jackson, although the listing shows that his first name, with no middle name, wasn't officially recorded until April 28, 1942, when presumably Ernest requested a copy of his birth certificate for the draft board. His birth (without name) noted in the *Amador Dispatch*, March 19, 1909.

29 *because on August 17, Celia had married Mike:* Registered in Kings County Courthouse and reported in the *Hanford Daily Journal*, August 17, 1909.

30 *ran an advertisement in the* Amador Dispatch: Joe Gallo's Central Hotel

advertised for sale in *Amador Dispatch*, August 27, September 3 and September 10, 1909.

30 *Finally he agreed, paying $2,000:* Sale to Genolio and deed filed August 31, 1909, in Amador County Recorder's Office.

30 *A front-page headline and story:* Genolio's suicide attempt reported in the *Dispatch*, September 10, 1909.

31 *He also purchased land outside town:* Joseph Gallo's purchase of one acre of land registered in Kings County Recorder's Office, January 4, 1910. (Susie Gallo was listed as a co-owner, along with Michele Aragno; on October 26, 1910, Celia Gallo paid 1909 delinquent taxes on the property.)

31 *Battista lost patience and sued him:* Battista Bianco v. Giuseppe and Assunta Bianco Gallo, filed October 22, 1909, in Kings County Superior Court.

31 *Joe began to beat Susie again:* These details are from Susie Gallo's petition for divorce filed in Kings County Superior Court, January 27, 1910.

32 *Julio Robert was born on March 21, 1910:* Registered in Alameda County Recorder's Office, and a duplicate supplied by the California State Board of Health's Bureau of Vital Statistics. (According to the document, his first and middle names were added June 16, 1942.)

32 *to buy the hotel next door:* According to Alameda County deeds.

32 *to dismiss her divorce action:* Filed in Superior Court of Kings County on October 15, 1912.

32 *and filed a second divorce petition:* Filed in Superior Court of Kings County, then transferred to Alameda and dismissed January 12, 1915.

32 *When asked to explain why they were there:* Ernest and Julio's residence in Hanford and their explanations that it was because of Joe, Sr.'s business, according to their depositions; recollections of their Hanford stay from interviews with Stella Bianco Dorais, Fred Giacomazzi; according to GWSJ, Ernest "lived with the Biancos about five years."

32 *Julio's resentment, for example, was expressed:* Recalled by several winery employees who have heard him reminisce about the family. It is also evident in JULDepo: for example, "the father bought wine from my grandfather."

33 *"He's mad at me":* From Celia's testimony during Mike Gallo's trial for running a "bunko ring," reported in the *San Francisco Chronicle*, February 15, 1913.

34 *Mike became the prosecution's star witness:* His and wife Celia's appearance and testimony at Esola's trial reported in the *San Francisco Call-Bulletin*, June 3, 1913, and in case records filed in Superior Court of San Francisco County.

36 *they would brag about their grandfather Bianco and his winery:* In "The Story of Gallo," an official history of the winery: "Ernest and Julio, sons and grandsons of these pioneer California wine growers, learned vine culture and winemaking from childhood." In his deposition, Julio confirmed that this statement referred to their maternal grandfather.

36 *When Ernest came to live with them:* Ernest and Julio's stay in Hanford, including Battista Bianco's penny-candy trick and Ernest's outsmarting him, recalled by Stella Bianco Dorais.

37 *Ernest and Julio resisted the suggestion:* According to EDepo and JULDepo. They also claimed that Battista Bianco's winery was small and insignificant, like "home winemaking," and that they and their father learned nothing from it, according to EDepo and JULDepo, and cited by GWSJ.

37 *In 1912, Hanford declared itself dry:* Background of Hanford's prohibition movement supplied by Eugene L. Menefee and Fred A. Dodge, "Vanishing of the Saloons," *History of Tulare and Kings Counties, California* (Los Angeles, Calif.: Historic Record Company, 1913).

37 *Walter fought the arrest in court:* Record of trial of Walter Bianco, charged with illegally selling wine from the Bianco winery, filed April 17, 1913, in the Justice Court of Lucerne Township of Kings County.

37 *"Probably the quantities run up in the thousands":* According to the trial transcript in which Sheriff Jacobs testified that he saw at least "eight large vats of wine" in the Bianco cellar. (While the sheriff conceded that he did not know how many hundreds of gallons of wine each vat held, it is likely that these were at least several-hundred-gallon vats, if not larger.) Fred Giacomazzi and Stella Dorais both confirm that the Bianco winery made enough gallons of wine to sell barrels to local customers, to distributors such as Joe Gallo, and to San Francisco boardinghouses and saloons, as well as to ship in bulk to the East Coast.

38 *and had added a retail liquor business to:* Joe Gallo's property transactions recorded in the grantor-grantee index in Alameda County Courthouse. Joe's hotel and saloon as well as his liquor-retailing and wine-distributing business listed in Oakland directories, 1912–18.

38 *When Battista died on January 17, 1916:* According to the probate of his estate filed in Kings County Superior Court, January 28, 1916.

38 *the nation's growing Prohibition campaign:* Prohibition background drawn from John Kobler, *Ardent Spirits, The Rise and Fall of Prohibition* (New York: G. P. Putnam's Sons, 1973).

39 *by buying a vineyard in Antioch:* Contra Costa County grantor-grantee index confirms the Gallo property in Antioch.

39 *If anything seemed to harden Ernest and Julio's hearts:* The hardships of the Gallo family's years on the farm in Antioch recalled in interview with Stella Bianco Dorais and in family anecdotes, especially those told by Celia Gallo. Julio and Ernest described these years to winery employees, remarking that they had driven mules and plowed vineyards before they were ten years old. Their recollections are also confirmed in GWSJ, citing EDepo, JULDepo, and AIDepo.

41 *a brother was born on September 11, 1919:* Registered in Contra Costa County Office of Records, September 11, 1919.

41 *San Pablo Bottling Shop:* Mike and Celia Gallo's residence and Mike's San Pablo Bottling Shop confirmed in Oakland directory and Alameda County Records Office. The Gallo family's move from Antioch to Livermore confirmed in interviews with Joe Gallo and Stella Dorais, and in GWSJ, citing EDepo and JULDepo.

42 *that their work days in Livermore would be just:* Livermore documents from Alameda County Hall of Records and County Courthouse as well as the Livermore Public Library, Livermore Historical Society, the Livermore Town Records Office (with assistance from Marjorie Zekerski), the Municipal Courthouse, and the Town Council archives. Historical background and recollections of Joe and Mike Gallo provided in interviews with Judge Joseph Schenoni, Rudy Wagner, and others who recalled the Gallo brothers in Livermore during the early years of Prohibition. Joe Gallo supervised Mike's still in Livermore, according to GWSJ.

43 *One evening his father dropped Julio off:* Described by Bob Gallo in his deposition and to Mike Gallo, Joe Jr.'s son.

43 *Mike's operation distributed brandy and wine:* According to Livermore sources (and confirmed in Mike's later court records). Mike's "clout among cops" recalled by Livermore sources, and Joe, Jr., also remembered that his uncle Mike bragged about the politicians he knew and the influence he had.

43 *By 1921, California was already called:* Historical background from Schaeffer, Paul, D. M. Brown, and J. D. Hicks, eds., "The Prohibition Movement in California, 1848–1933," *The Eighteenth Amendment, 1917–1919* (University of California Publications in History, Vol. LVII, University of California Press, 1976). Stories of Livermore bootlegging compiled from issues of the *Livermore Herald*, 1920–25.

44 *he also became acquainted with Albert Wagner:* Recollections of Albert Wagner, his bootlegging, and his association with Joe Gallo, Sr., provided in interviews with his son Rudy Wagner.

45 *the appraised $18,000 inventory from a 1922 hotel raid:* From the *Livermore Herald*, January 21, 1922.

45 *Mike did, however, have a brush with the law:* Mike Gallo's San Francisco arrest reported in the *San Francisco Bulletin*, November 27, 1922, and the *Livermore Herald*, November 28, 1922.

46 *usually boxing their ears:* According to his own reminiscences as repeated to Joe, Jr., and his son Mike, and confirmed by former classmates.

48 *The next morning, July 6:* Joe's arrest on July 6, 1922, and dismissal of bootlegging charge, December 29, cited by GWSJ. Joe, Jr., also heard the story of the Livermore raid and Mike's "taking care of the problem" from Ernest and Julio, Aunt Celia, and other family members.

T W O

PAGE
50 *70 percent of the state's annual wine production:* According to William Ellis, "Harvest of Change," *National Geographic*, February 1991.

50 *Joe Gallo's newly acquired twenty-acre:* Purchase of the twenty-acre Escalon vineyard as well as a twenty-acre vineyard in Keyes, registered with San Joaquin County Recorder's Office. The family's move to Escalon, the Keyes vineyard purchase, and the vineyards' varieties and yields of grapes confirmed in GWSJ, citing JODepo, EDepo, and JULDepo.

50 *the number of vineyards had increased:* Escalon's total vineyard acreage and railroad cars of wine grapes shipped to eastern markets, according to the *Escalon Tribune*, December 26, 1924. Escalon background provided by local histories collected by the Escalon branch of the Stockton–San Joaquin Public Library.

51 *Alicante Bouschet, the grape variety favored:* According to Ruth Teiser and Catherine Harroun, "The Volstead Act, Rebirth, and Boom," *Winemaking in California* (New York: McGraw Hill, 1983). Before Prohibition wineries used few Alicante grapes, and rarely were California vineyards planted to this variety. In the 1920s, when grape sales shifted from in-state wineries to the Chicago and eastern grape markets, many new vineyards were planted in Alicante Bouschet. By 1924 (when Joe Gallo bought his vineyard in Escalon), Teiser and Harroun note, Alicante was "the 'big name' grape because of its unique characteristics, and prices for it rose faster than for any other variety."

51 *was planted to Carignane:* Characteristics of Carignane and Petite Bouschet, as well as other information about varietals included in this chapter,

were described by Bern Ramey in interviews and in his book, *The Great Wine Grapes, and the Wines They Make* (A Limited First Edition, with color plates, Burlingame, Calif.: 1977). Joe Gallo's second prize for his Petite Bouschet grape at county fair, according to the *Escalon Tribune*, August 29, 1924.

51 *Angelo Petri, for example:* Background of the Petri family drawn from James Conaway, *Napa* (cited above). The Petris and the Cella Brothers, according to Conaway, "fueled many a clandestine winery in the basements of big-city tenements, and made contacts through bootlegging that would continue to pay off."

52 *Joe Gallo knew him from Escalon:* Joe's acquaintance with Petri and Forresti confirmed in interviews with Anthony Ciccarelli and Ted and Ray Cadlolo, sons of Charles Cadlolo, founder of the Cadlolo Winery in Escalon and one-time neighbors of the Gallos. Escalon history, remarks about growers and wineries, and Forresti's background and his friendship with Rafaele Petri, provided by Frank Thornton, *History of the Escalon Community in California* (Escalon Chamber of Commerce, private printing, 1964). The story about Ernest and Petri's refusal repeated by former Gallo employees but unconfirmed.

52 *where he hired Louis Sciaroni:* Founding of Louis Sciaroni's Escalon winery, the Cadlolo Winery, and Charles Cadlolo's purchase of The Valley Inn during Prohibition according to Ted and Ray Cadlolo.

53 *Joe soon had a reputation for producing good reliable wine:* From interviews with Sal Curzi, who recalled his father regularly buying wine from Joe Gallo.

53 *"Hell, no, he was a bootlegger":* According to one of Julio's classmates.

53 *Joe, Jr., remembered one trip in particular:* From interview.

53 *for the San Joaquin County district attorney to file:* Criminal case filed in the Superior Court of San Joaquin County, December 17, 1923. This and other documentation located with the research aid of Sandy Lincoln, records clerk in the courthouse.

54 *he couldn't resist taking his family:* Mike and Celia's trip to Italy described in "Aunt Celia's" reminiscences to the family, and recalled by Joe and Patricia Gallo, Stella Dorais, and Aileen Gallo. The Italian lace tablecloth, given to Susie by Celia, then promised to Joe but retained by Ernest, mentioned by Aileen, first to Mary Ann Gallo, then to Patricia Gallo.

54 *Instead he invested his money:* Joe Gallo's purchase of the Waukeen Hotel in Manteca, as well as his subsequent leases to tenants to manage it, registered in San Joaquin County Recorder's Office, Stockton.

54 *"he had to work harder for his father":* From interview with Mr. and Mrs. Joe Sciaroni. According to Escalon sources, Joe Sciaroni's father, a butcher in town, was also a winemaker selling wine illegally. Sciaroni confirmed that he had learned his own wine- and sherry-making skills during Prohibition from his father and from other bootleggers for whom he also worked (it was practically the only job a young boy could get that paid anything at the time, he said). Sal Curzi confirmed that Sciaroni's father was reputed to be a bootlegger, and the Cadlolo brothers recalled that their uncle Louis Sciaroni, founder of the Escalon Winery, denied that he was related to Joe Sciaroni because of his rumored bootlegging.

55 *He hit two home runs:* Reported in the *Escalon Tribune*, October 3, 1924.

55 *Joe seemed to be a different man toward his youngest son:* Also suggested by recollections of Joe, Jr. The disparity between his and Ernest and Julio's

memories of their father is striking, but in interviews, Joe insisted that he was never struck or disciplined by his father, that he never saw him either violent or out of control, in contrast to Ernest and Julio's repeated descriptions of a stern, temperamental man.

55 *An emigrant from Genoa, Franzia:* History of Franzia Winery and family drawn from Bob Thompson, *Guide to California's Wine Country* (Menlo Park, Calif.: Sunset Books, 1982); John Melville, *Guide to California Wines,* revised by Jefferson Morgan (San Carlos, Calif.: Nourse Publishing Company, 1968); according to AMDepo and repeated family recollections, Giuseppe (or Joe) Franzia met Joe Gallo, Sr., when they traveled together with their grape shipments to Chicago.

56 *The property, purchased from Claude Maze:* Modesto documentation and background provided by the Stanislaus County Hall of Records and Courthouse in Modesto, the Modesto Public Library, Modesto Historical Society, and the McHenry Museum. Joe Gallo's purchase of Modesto rental properties and the Maze Road seventy-acre vineyard in Modesto registered in Stanislaus County Recorder's Office, Modesto. Joe, Jr., confirmed that the family lived in one of their Modesto rental properties while their Maze Road home was being built. He and his brothers recalled the construction cost as about $8,000, and Stella Dorais remembered Susie's asking her sister Tillie to help her with the decorating.

57 *made a point of knowing:* According to Anthony Ciccarelli and Sal Curzi. Joe, Jr., confirmed that the sheriff was a friend of his father.

57 *Founded as a railroad town:* Modesto and Central Valley history drawn from Jeannette Gould Maino, *One Hundred Years, Modesto, California, 1870–1970* (Modesto: Bell Printing & Lithograph Co., 1970); Stephen Birmingham, *California Rich* (New York: Simon & Schuster, 1980), especially the chapter "Valley People," including a brief commentary on Ernest and Julio Gallo; and Kevin Starr, *Americans and the California Dream, 1850–1915* (New York: Oxford University Press, 1973).

58 *he joined the Agricultural Club:* High school yearbooks available in Modesto Public Library and at Modesto High School. (Ernest's senior yearbook was missing from both the library and the high school, but eventually it was made available by a high school classmate.)

58 *Ernest became argumentative:* Descriptions of tension between Ernest and his father drawn from Ernest's later remarks to winery employees as well as EDepo, JULDepo, JODepo.

59 *In fact, the California State Department of Agriculture:* According to the *Lodi Sentinel,* September 25, 1928.

59 *Joe had a local woodworker:* Ernest and Julio hammered together lugs for field-packing grapes and stenciled "Gallo," according to GWSJ. The "Joe Gallo" label with a rooster was confirmed by Chicago grape dealer Paul Alleruzzo.

60 *close to two hundred cars altogether:* According to EDepo and JULDepo, the two-hundred car total was by their reckoning, but they seemed to be underplaying the size of their father's business. Alleruzzo and others recalled Joe, Sr., as a "big shipper," and estimated Gallo shipments as closer to one thousand carloads per season.

60 *Upon arrival in Chicago:* Information about the Chicago grape market and Joe Gallo's shipping provided in interviews with Paul Alleruzzo, son of the founder of Santa Fe Grape Distributors, who had met Joe, Sr., when he was about thirteen.

60 *"Excuse me, mister"*: Alleruzzo's first conversation with Joe, Sr., recalled in interview. In his deposition, Ernest declared that no grape dealer who had known his father and himself in the 1920s survived, according to GWSJ; in his interview with me, Alleruzzo confirmed that he had previously been questioned by a researcher sent by the winery's law firm, O'Melveny & Myers.

62 *The Mondavi and Gallo family histories*: The Mondavi family story described in interview with Robert Mondavi and in Cyril Ray, *Robert Mondavi of the Napa Valley* (New York: Warner Books, 1984). Historical background of the Mondavis, other Italian families, winemaking, and wine grape shipping in Minnesota's Iron Mountain range provided by Lawrence Belluzzo, author of *Dago Red*; Mr. and Mrs. Gene Scaia; Bill Allegrazzo (son of Dominic Allegrazzo, who worked for his uncle, the owner of the Old Wine House where wine grapes were sold to local home winemakers); Bob Tiburzi and Jack Fena, both of Sunnyside Wine, bottlers and distributors of wine in Minnesota; Henry Pappone; James Rodorigo, son of John Rodorigo, who bought grapes from Mondavi and Gallo for the Italian Work People's Cooperative; Quinto Aluni, former police chief of Virginia, Minnesota, whose brother Sam also ran the Italian Work People's Cooperative; Joe Maganini, who later moved to California to work for Cesare Mondavi; Elizabeth Bright, Iron Range Research Center; Dallas Lindgren, Minnesota Historical Society.

63 *"My father told my brother and me over and over"*: From interview with Robert Mondavi.

63 *Joe met Charlie Barbera*: Barbera and Paterno backgrounds provided in interviews with Alleruzzo as well as with Anthony "Tony" Terlato, Anthony Paterno's son-in-law and now president of the Pacific Wine Company in Chicago. Further information and assistance given by Patty Crutchfield, public relations director of Pacific Wine Company.

63 *Another respected grape dealer who became*: Story of the Matkovich family provided in interview with Alleruzzo. Although Ernest did not include Guy Matkovich's name when asked if any Chicago grape dealers could still be contacted, Guy Matkovich was still living. He had gone on to become a judge in Chicago, and the Matkovich and Gallo families continued their friendship for many years. By the time this book was being researched, Judge Matkovich was too ill to be interviewed.

64 *The grape market had a number of "toughs"*: Chicago background and activities of Al Capone and his gang and Genna gang involving wine and the grape market provided by interviews with George Murray, author of *The Legacy of Al Capone* (New York: G. P. Putnam's Sons, 1975); Ed Baumann, former reporter for the *Chicago Tribune*; Al Wolff, "the last of The Untouchables"; Judge Abraham Lincoln Marovitz; historian Herman Kogan; former Chicago wine distributor Roland Wrecher; Edward Bragno of the Bragno Brothers' wine distributorship. Chief Investigator Jerry Gladden provided assistance in researching files of the Chicago Crime Commission. Paul Galloway, Augie Jewel, and John Murphy of the *Chicago Tribune* assisted in background research as well.

65 *"Capone's dago red"*: Vern Whaley, a now retired *Chicago Tribune* photographer, recalled "sports promotion" dinners hosted by Al Capone at which he served his homemade wine and bragged that it tasted "just like the old country."

65 *Joe did not particularly enjoy his six-week sojourn in Chicago*: Confirmed

by GWSJ. According to deposition of Ernest's son, Joseph E. "Joey", Ernest said that Joe, Sr., would lose his temper and walk away and refuse to do business with him any longer. "So pretty soon he couldn't do business with anyone back there, so he stopped going. . . . He didn't like to deal with that group of people."

66   *"They were all big shippers of wine grapes"*: According to interview with Alleruzzo.

66   *"I remember that first year I met Ernie"*: From interview with Alleruzzo, who also provided descriptions of the incident with Capone's henchmen and Jake Matkovich's instructions to avoid them.

67   *One of his favorite stories in later years*: According to a former Gallo sales manager and others.

68   *He was elected to the HiY Club*: Modesto High School Yearbook, 1927, records Ernest's club activities and his honor-roll grades.

68   *When Ernest reminisced as an adult*: According to interviews with several former Gallo sales managers and winery personnel consultant Bernie Weiner.

68   *Even that first season in Chicago*: Ernest's sales pitch to win a grape sale from another shipper recalled by Alleruzzo.

69   *"You always have a sales pitch"*: Alleruzzo recalled this conversation with Ernest.

69   *was of how he handled a customer who complained*: Recalled by son Joe E. in his deposition, as well as by several winery employees.

69   *Joe sent Julio to New Jersey*: Confirmed by GWSJ, citing JULDepo.

70   *Jack Riorda was a fellow Californian*: In a July 1975 article in *Wines and Vines*, Julio recalled accompanying Jack Riorda on visits to Hoboken customers and learning about winemaking from him and the home winemakers. "In the evenings, I [Julio] would visit with our customers and learned their ways of making wine. I knew about metabisulfite and saw to it that these people had a supply for use during fermentation so their wines wouldn't go bad." Riorda also routinely handed out printed instructions on making wine, although he was careful to call the liquid in the kegs "the Juice of the Grape." According to Robert Mondavi, Riorda was an experienced winemaker, who, forecasting the end of Prohibition, amassed a supply of wine to sell when wine distribution became legal. (It was Riorda who eventually asked Cesare Mondavi to become his partner in the wine business.)

71   *"Just think what I could have done"*: Recalled by Patricia Gallo and others.

71   *Joe, Jr., was now old enough*: Joe described his chores, his driving the car, his father's present of a pony, what he referred to as almost "hero worship" of his older brothers, his sense of Ernest and his father's arguments, but puzzlement over Ernest's later descriptions of their father as abusive.

72   *especially now that Prohibition laws applied to wine*: From interviews with winemakers and grape growers, including Robert Mondavi, Anthony Ciccarelli, and Dan Scabica, a Modesto grape grower and founder of the Scabica Olive Oil Company. Background of winery development and winery owners' recollections of late 1920s, early 1930s campaign and plans for Repeal drawn from the Wine Advisory Board–sponsored oral history project for the Regional Oral History Office of the University of California (many of the interviews conducted by Ruth Teiser). (Ernest Gallo's interview is under seal until after his death.)

72   *The Woodbridge Winery had been founded*: History of the Woodbridge Vineyard Association and the Woodbridge Winery, according to Jack Shinn and

Fred Snyde, and also drawn from written recollections of John M. Posey, one of the founders, and the *Lodi News-Sentinel*, May 2, 1958. Shinn and Snyde were among the shareholders who sold the winery to Mike Gallo and Samuele Sebastiani. In 1933, after Repeal, they and others reorganized the Woodbridge Vineyard Association and founded a new Woodbridge Winery. This winery was different from the winery in which Mike Gallo became a partner in 1928 and that Sebastiani acquired solely in his own name in 1930. Supporting documents from the San Joaquin County Recorder's Office and Courthouse, and the files of Bureau of Alcohol, Treasury Department and Department of Special Collections, Shields Library, University of California at Davis.

73 *Virginia Bianco had bought and moved to:* Probate of Virginia Bianco's estate filed in Alameda County Courthouse. Celia's transfer of her stock to Mike and expected shares in the Woodbridge Winery documented in her divorce filing, April 6, 1929.

73 *police records indicated:* John Cherino, aka Severino, was arrested for running a still in the Scott Street house owned by Mike Gallo on June 21, 1928; Severino's involvement in bootlegging cited in two criminal indictments, both of which were included in charges brought in U.S. v. Mike Gallo et al., Case No. 20126-L, filed by the Department of Justice, October 28, 1929.

74 *Born in 1874 in Farneta, Tuscany:* Sebastiani family background drawn from interviews with Sylvia Sebastiani, the widow of Samuele's son August, her son Donald, and Doug Davis, winemaker and manager of the Sebastiani Winery, who also provided a copy of his history of the Sebastianis.

75 *Sebastiani would explain:* According to interview with Sylvia Sebastiani, confirmed by Don Sebastiani, and Doug Davis. All three expressed surprise at the documents recording the Sebastiani-Gallo partnership. They insisted that the Woodbridge Winery was solely Samuele's and that he hadn't bought it until 1930. Indeed, Davis's history of the Sebastiani Winery notes that in 1930, Samuele purchased the Woodbridge Winery, his son Lorenzo managed its production of sacramental wines, and the winery's "stores of brandy," already on the premises, brought a large profit when sold after Repeal.

75 *Mike was known to extol:* According to Paul Merrigan, to whom Mike Gallo later reminisced about his and his brother's "wine business," in which they had a ready supply of grapes for their wine. Joe, Jr., recalled the special 1928 Easter dinner (and still had the menu in his possession), but he could not remember why Mike had given the dinner specifically to honor his parents.

76 *Joe's name began to appear:* Joe, Sr.'s name appeared in lists of growers and shippers who were members and were attending meetings of the California Vineyardists Association and the Grape Growers League (later the Wine Producers Association), both of which were lobbying for repeal of Prohibition laws against wine.

76 *Ernest recalled such meetings:* Ernest's anecdote of grape growers' and winemakers' dinners that he attended with his father later repeated to winery employees, according to Paul Merrigan.

76 *according to Joe, Jr.'s recollections:* Joe, Jr., recalled his uncle Mike's frequent visits to Modesto that spring and his impression that his father and uncle were discussing business more than usual. He also remembered Julio's story about Mike's convincing his father to let him run in the track meet and the ribbons that Julio kept for many years.

77 *"I was only a kid":* From interview with Joe, Jr.

THREE

78 *Samuele and Mike had already received permission:* Filed in Department of Special Collections, Shields Library, UC Davis.

78 *With so much traffic and lights:* Activities at the Woodbridge Winery and remarks by Lorenzo Sebastiani recalled by Rudy Wagner, then working at a nearby winery, as well as by neighbors of the winery.

79 *Two hours later he felt sure:* Mike Gallo's recollections of outrunning federal agents retold to family members, as well as to Paul Merrigan.

79 *John Severino, along with:* The arrest, May 22, 1928, near Martinez, California, of Joe Silva, Pete DeRosi (alias Pete Ozella) and John "Cheavrino" (John Cherino, alias John Severino) recorded in U.S. v. Mike Gallo et al., Case No. 20126-L, Department of Justice. Mike's comments to the officer related in the arrest and investigation report. The files also confirm the continuing investigation of Mike Gallo after the arrest of his three employees, including the June 21, 1928, raid of his Scott Street property and Enrico Castagnasso's testimony that Mike both in person and in writing had several times instructed him to load barrels of wine from the Woodbridge Winery onto trucks for delivery elsewhere. As a result, the investigating officer designated Mike Gallo (alias Tony Bima) as the "major conspirator in this case."

80 *ILLEGAL WINE GANG HUNTED: San Francisco Chronicle,* September 21, 1928. The grand jury indictment on October 9, 1928, the ensuing year's briefs, and evidence reports, filed in the United States District Court, but now held in U.S. Court Archives in San Bruno, California.

81 *On October 20, 1928, Samuele:* Sebastiani's petition to separate his case from those of the others, and his nolo plea, filed in U.S. District Court, October 20, 1928. In interviews with Sylvia Sebastiani, Don Sebastiani, and Doug Davis, they all said they had never heard anything about a 1928 arrest of Samuele and said that they were as surprised by these court documents as they were by his Woodbridge partnership with Mike Gallo.

81 *Nevertheless, in 1928 Joe could afford:* Joe Gallo's purchase of 160 acres registered in Stanislaus County Recorder's Office, Modesto. Purchase of Transamerica Corporation stock confirmed by his and Susie's later estate records in Stanislaus County Probate Court, Modesto.

81 *First Mike announced:* Mike's sale of his share of the Woodbridge Winery to Sebastiani for $40,000 reported in the Justice Department Mike Gallo case file 2026-L and also registered in San Joaquin County Recorder's Office and in Prohibition Office winery records, Department of Special Collections, Shields Library, UC Davis.

82 *To make matters worse:* After the stock market crash, grape prices fell, according to GWSJ, citing EDepo and JULDepo, in which they recalled telling their father, "Don't ship any more grapes" and "There isn't a hope in hell . . ."

82 *Early one morning in late October:* Description of father digging underground tanks and mother telling him it was for Mike and Joe's business, according to Joe, Jr.

83 *"Underground tanks became essential during Prohibition":* According to interview with Robert Mondavi.

83 *Ernest and Julio would later give their recollections:* According to GWSJ, citing EDepo and JULDepo.

84 *The Prohibition Administration had just exempted:* According to August 6, 1929, Commissioner of Prohibition's Circular Letter No. 488, reported in Ruth Teiser and Catherine Harroun, "The Volstead Act, Rebirth, and Boom," cited above.

85 *If Susie had been upset:* According to EDepo, in which Ernest claimed that their mother was disturbed by the building of the tanks. Joe, Jr., however, recalled no such anxiety by his mother or anyone else in the family.

85 *and on April 6, 1929, Celia filed:* Celia Gallo's first divorce petition filed April 6, 1929, and dismissed on April 10, 1929, in the Superior Court of Alameda County.

86 *on January 8, 1930, she refiled:* Celia's second petition was filed January 8, 1930, and the divorce was granted on January 22, 1930. (Descriptions of Mike's behavior and statements to Celia quoted from record of divorce proceeding.)

87 *This marriage lasted until:* Adelaide Gallo's petition for divorce and allegations of Mario's physical abuse filed in Superior Court of Alameda County, October 12, 1933.

87 *a pistol would be confiscated:* In Mike's arrest in 1931, his .45-caliber Colt revolver was found in his car, according to Case No. 1598-M, Department of Justice files.

88 *Celia moved to an expensive apartment:* According to impressions of Stella Dorais, who visited her aunt at her new residence.

88 *In the winter of 1929 Joe ordered:* According to GWSJ, citing EDepo and JULDepo, and from interview with Joe, Jr. According to several Gallo Winery employees, this was one of Ernest's favorite anecdotes that he told in later years to describe how hard he had worked as a young man and how stubborn his father had been.

89 *"That vineyard was always poor":* According to JULDepo.

89 *Sometimes Joe said he would:* Joe, Sr.'s reluctance to make a decision about Ernest's future described in EDepo.

89 *nineteen-year-old Amelia:* Ernest's courtship of Amelia Franzia described in family reminiscences as well as AMDepo. The Franzia family's wariness of Ernest described by a former winery employee who heard the story from Charlie Rossi and others. According to winery employees, Amelia would make sarcastic comments in later years about Ernest's marrying her for her family's winery.

90 *as he later recalled to Rudy:* Pete Cisi's recollection of Joe, Sr.'s chasing Susie and Ernest and Julio through the vineyards, told to Rudy Wagner, who related Cisi's description of the event in interview; scene recreated from this recollection as well as from statements by several winery employees who had heard the story. But like other accounts that describe Joe, Sr., chasing his sons with a shotgun, including the September 1, 1986, *Fortune* article and Stephen Birmingham's narrative in *California Rich*, they seemed to conflate this earlier incident in Modesto with the 1933 events in Fresno. Based on Ernest and Julio's later comments to winery employees about "the troubles," it seems likely that this event precipitated their flight to El Centro in 1930.

91 *At the desk they asked:* Ernest recalled exchange with hotel owner in EDepo and in later remarks to winery employees about El Centro.

91 *He asked one of his distributors:* According to a Gallo sales manager present at the lunch meeting with distributor when Ernest described their flight to El Centro.

92 *Celia relayed their messages:* Stella Dorais and Joe, Jr., confirmed Ernest and Julio's absence for several months, and Susie and Celia's attempt to bring the boys home.

92 *Before they went near the ranch:* Ernest and Julio's visit to Joe, Jr., at school and their questioning of him described by Joe, Jr., in interview and JODepo and confirmed by JULDepo; Ernest did not remember stopping by school to see Joe, but did recall the telephone conversations with Aunt Celia.

93 *including two new ones that:* Property deeds, crop mortgage agreements, and civil court cases filed against Joe Gallo, recorded in San Joaquin County Courthouse, Stockton. (For example, "Minnie Medinger, a widow and incompetent by Helen Kaufman, her guardian, v. Joe Gallo et al.")

93 *After the disastrous 1929:* History of Donald Conn and the California Vineyardists Association drawn from Donald D. Conn, *The California Vineyard Industry Five Year Report* (San Francisco: California Vineyardists Association, 1932), and Ruth Teiser and Catherine Harroun, "The Volstead Act, Rebirth, and Boom," cited above.

93 *A lawsuit filed by the CVA:* "California Vineyardists Association v. Joe Gallo, First Doe, Second Doe, Third Doe and Doe Company, a Corporation; Complaint for an Accounting," filed August 25, 1931, in Superior Court of Stanislaus County.

93 *But was it possible that the grapes:* Speculation that Joe's grapes had been turned into "juice" suggested by grape growers and grape dealers, remarking that in the 1930 grape season, this was an acceptable practice and a more profitable method of shipping and selling grapes (it eliminated the problem of perishability). In his 1987 deposition, Ernest could not recall the lawsuit, and court records did not refresh his memory, although he assumed from reading the documents that it had been an accounting mistake settled by Joe, Sr.'s payment of the balance due to CVA. He was not specifically asked about the account's notation of a "red ink" shipment or the possibility that the grapes had been shipped and sold as juice.

94 *Capone reportedly threatened to kill:* Teiser and Harroun, cited above, report Al Capone's attempts to control the sale of wine grape juice and concentrate, Fruit Industries' distribution of Vine Glo and death threats made in anonymous letters to Donald Conn in November 1930. Capone threats against Conn also reported by the *Chicago Tribune*, November 14, 1930.

94 *the next month Hoover assigned:* A report of the FBI investigation of syndicate attempts to take over the Chicago grape markets is contained in the massive Capone files in FBI archives in Washington, D.C. This aspect of the Capone files was called to my attention by Perry Duis, professor of American History at the University of Illinois, Chicago Circle. His graduate student Doug Bukowski researched these files in the course of completing his Ph.D. dissertation about Chicago's mayor "Big Bill" Thompson and kindly provided copies of the FBI's investigation of Capone and grape shippers and dealers.

94 *Capone's henchmen, Tony Romano:* FBI investigation reports confirm Tony Romano and Manny Schraiberg as Capone henchmen trying to muscle in on grape shippers and dealers. Alleruzzo recalled these two as "Capone's boys," who were giving shippers and dealers trouble in the late 1920s and early 1930s. Chicago Crime Commission records, as well as George Murray in *The Legacy of Al Capone* (cited above), refer to Joe Fusco as supervisor of Capone's beer and wine operations.

95 *he bought a gun—a .32-caliber Smith & Wesson revolver:* Described in EDepo and by Alleruzzo.

95 *"Label it juice or jelly":* According to former Gallo sales managers.

95 *he liked to tell winery associates:* Charlie Rossi's story about meeting Ernest in Virginia, Minnesota, repeated to Paul Merrigan; competition between Gallo and Mondavi grapes confirmed in interviews with Bill Allegrazzo and other Iron Range residents cited above.

95 *telling two of his executives:* According to several winery employees, Albion Fenderson, longtime Gallo executive, has often repeated Ernest's claim that his father had a license to make sacramental and medicinal wine during Prohibition. Charles Crawford also mentioned the license as part of the family and winery history he presented at a Gallo in-house seminar. No such license was recorded, according to Prohibition Office and Bureau of Alcohol files collected in Department of Special Collections, Shields Library, UC Davis.

96 *he liked to brag about:* Mike Gallo's reminiscences about his and his brother's wine business told to Paul Merrigan.

96 *Julio was not sent to New Jersey:* According to GWSJ citing JULDepo.

96 *In 1930 Ernest also:* Ernest told colleagues in the Chicago grape market that he planned to marry Amelia Franzia and go into the wine business, according to Alleruzzo, who repeated his conversation with Ernest.

96 *but was upset that his outfit had come:* According to Joe, Jr., and Patricia Gallo.

97 *they would combine their honeymoon with:* According to AMDepo, family reminiscences, and Alleruzzo.

97 *That October a Kansas City federal judge:* Reported in Teiser and Harroun, cited above.

97 *On August 14, 1931, Mike was:* Case No. 1598-M, Department of Justice files, includes the following records: Lister Ranch arrests of Mike Gallo et al. on April 2, 1930; arrest of Mike Gallo (alias George Bruno, alias Joe Marro) on August 14, 1931, in Albany for driving a truck loaded with six hundred gallons of port and wine; on November 13, 1931, the same truck stopped in El Cerrito carrying nine hundred gallons of wine and two drivers arrested; Mike's December 18, 1931, arrest at home; his Los Angeles indictment, December 28, 1931. The investigation reports describe Mike Gallo's wealth and assets; his prior criminal record, including his prison term in San Quentin for his bunko scheme, a 1912 vagrancy charge, a 1928 arrest for vulgar language, and several other bootlegging indictments (with fines paid or charges dropped).

98 *On January 29, 1932, another:* According to the *Oakland Tribune*, January 29, 1932.

98 *According to Ernest's recollections:* Joe, Sr.'s increased anxiety and inability to make decisions described by GWSJ, citing EDepo, JULDepo, AIDepo, and AMDepo; however, Joe, Jr., did not have the same impression, according to his deposition and interviews.

99 *Then one day he returned:* Joe, Sr., and Susie's sudden and inexplicable departure, their return and move to Fresno described by Joe, Jr. (He was later told that they had been looking for new property "up near Chico" but then had found the ranch in Fresno.)

99 *he had bought vineyards in Fresno:* Registered in Fresno County Recorder's Office, Fresno.

99 *"Maybe Father made an agreement with Ernest":* According to interview with Joe, Jr.

100 *It was old and dilapidated:* From GWSJ and AIDepo and confirmed by Joe, Jr., who also recalled that there was no electricity and no telephone.

100 *they often took him to the movies:* Joe, Jr.'s recollections of Fresno home, going to the movies, and his father from interviews. His memories contradict Ernest and Julio's depictions of Joe, Sr., as morose and depressed. "But Julio only came down twice, and Ernest not at all," Joe, Jr., said in his deposition. In EDepo, Ernest claimed to have visited several times to discuss plans with his father.

101 *he introduced himself and asked:* Julio's meeting and courtship of Aileen Lowe described in family reminiscences and in AIDepo.

102 *Ernest later claimed that he had gone:* According to EDepo. (In his earlier deposition in the Gallo Salame suit, Ernest said that during this year, he and his father had talked about going into the winery business together, implying that there would have been a family partnership had his father not died; in his 1988 deposition Ernest said that his father wouldn't agree to his proposal, and, therefore, he had planned to start a winery himself.)

102 *Ernest also said that when:* Joe, Sr., refused to give grapes to Ernest on a "share basis," and Ernest then refused to go to Chicago that fall, according to EDepo.

103 *In the spring of 1933, Joe:* Recollection of Joe Gallo, Sr.'s, discussion of his problems with neighbor and friend Peter Brengetto provided by the latter's son, Gino Brengetto, who specifically recalled the reference to "his winery."

103 *One day in mid-May, Julio:* Recalled from family reminiscences by Joe, Jr., and Patricia Gallo; GWSJ and AIDepo confirm and describe the visit and car discussion about Julio's parents.

104 *An Austrian immigrant who had shortened:* Max Kane's background from 1938 Bureau of Alcohol investigation. His recollections and the incident of the car in the canal told to and repeated by Joe, Jr., and Rudy Wagner.

105 *had been sentenced to three months:* According to Case No. 23839-S in the U.S. District Court Archives, San Bruno, California, which also records the reduction of his sentence because "wife Irene had suffered a nervous breakdown."

105 *she loaned him only $4,000:* Recorded in probate of Joe, Sr.'s estate, Stanislaus County Courthouse, Modesto.

105 *On June 14, 1933, he filed:* Ernest's letter of application and the June 20, 1933, letter of rejection for his proposed bonded wine warehouse in San Francisco included in Prohibition Office records, Department of Special Collections, Shields Library, UC Davis.

105 *On the same day that Ernest's:* Described in JULDepo and AIDepo. In interview with Joe, Jr., he described in detail his recollection of the visit, which was different from theirs.

107 *"All I want is for you boys":* His mother's last words recalled by Joe, Jr., and Julio many times in family discussions and in their depositions. (Julio, however, sometimes said that his mother's last words were, "All I want is for you boys to get along," but not "work together.")

107 *"Be good, and mind your brothers":* Recalled by Joe, Jr., in interview.

107 *According to Max Kane:* Description of events of June 21, 1933, reconstructed from deputy sheriffs' report and transcript of coroner's inquest made available by the Fresno County Courthouse and the Fresno County Sheriff's Office, with research assistance provided by Don Justice, senior criminologist.

FOUR

111 *He claimed, however, that a* Modesto Bee *reporter:* According to EDepo. (At the time the local newspaper was called the *Modesto News Herald*, not the *Bee.*)

111 *"Don't worry":* According to JOSJ, and interview with Joe, Jr.

111 *In Fresno, Ernest identified:* Joe and Susie's death certificates on file in Fresno County Recorder's Office, Fresno. Coroner's certificates, medical examination records, and coroner's verdict from the Office of County Coroner, Fresno.

111 *"Do you know of any motive for it":* Transcript of coroner's inquest, June 21, 1933.

112 *The* Fresno Bee *ran:* Report of deaths in the *Fresno Bee*, June 21, 1933, and the *San Francisco Chronicle*, June 23, 1933. No story ran in the *Modesto News Herald*, although the two deaths were briefly announced in the Vital Statistics column, June 23, 1933.

113 *The medical examiner, for example:* His report indicated that he had performed examinations, not autopsies, and listed the causes of death as gunshot wounds. Based on the report, it appears that no further detailed examination of the bodies was made and the reason for Joe, Sr.'s alleged poor health was not diagnosed or confirmed.

113 *Wallace Moore, continued to wonder:* According to former colleagues, Moore was especially interested in fingerprints and ballistic analyses and was the sheriff's department expert, having taken special training courses in these investigating techniques.

114 *he thought his own standard Smith & Wesson:* According to EDepo.

114 *If, as Joe, Jr., and Julio recalled:* Despite Julio and Joe's statements to the contrary (JULDepo, JODepo and interview), Ernest insisted that he had visited his parents in Fresno at least twice (EDepo).

114 *Joe, Jr., would also come to realize:* According to interview in which he described contradictions between his own memories and official reports; discrepancies confirmed by John Whiting and Mike Gallo, to whom Joe repeated why his memories of the morning's events were at odds with sheriff's report and Ernest's description in EDepo.

115 *Ernest had then given Max:* Max Kane confirmed that he had been given the family car because "it wasn't worth much anyway." According to John Whiting, Kane later spoke to him and Joe before the 1988 case came to trial, but he was unable or unwilling to recall what had happened on June 21, 1933; he did tell Joe about the prior incident of Joe, Sr.'s car driven into the irrigation ditch, which he thought might have been an earlier suicide attempt.

115 *the account of Peter Brengetto:* Recalled by his son Gino in interview.

116 *because of threats by the "big-city mob":* Sal Curzi recalled the rumors about a syndicate assassination of the Gallos. He was particularly interested, he said, because his older brother, who had been a driver for a "mob bootlegger in San Francisco," had been killed in an unexplained accident outside Fresno. "The sheriff never really investigated that either, I think he was afraid to," Curzi recalled. "But I was sure that the mob staged it—killed my brother, then turned the truck over on him to make it look like an accident—because he was withholding money he was collecting from his deliveries. He had always told me that these were dangerous guys he worked

for and that they had taken over a lot of the bootlegging in the Central Valley."

116 *In fact, Joe's two loans:* Confirmed in Bank of America and Federal Land Bank records, according to JOSJ, which also stated that "the disposition of the $31,000 remains a mystery," citing EDepo and JULDepo.

116 *Susie's brother Walter:* According to interview with Stella Dorais.

117 *mourners spoke of "warding off the evil eye":* Recalled by a daughter of a grape grower who was at Joe and Susie's funeral.

117 *"It was made clear that this subject":* According to Joe interview.

117 *"It was a big, big secret":* According to Joe's son Mike.

118 *The Bureau of Alcohol had:* Bureau of Alcohol's rejection letter as well as John Walsh's letter on behalf of Ernest from winery bonding records, Department of Special Collections, Shields Library, UC Davis. Ernest contacted Forresti, who put him in touch with Washington, D.C., attorney Walsh, who wrote letter quoted in GWSJ and citing EDepo.

119 *he petitioned the probate court:* Ernest's petition, August 17, 1933, and the superior court's authorization, August 28, 1933, to continue his father's business in probate record of Joe, Sr.'s estate filed in Superior Court, Stanislaus County, Modesto.

120 *Julio had previously planned:* According to GWSJ. Julio then decided that with Repeal, "there might be opportunities in the wine business." Neither asked Joe to become a partner or if his share of the estate could be contributed to the founding of the winery, according to GWSJ, citing JULDepo: "Nobody else had an interest [in the winery]. Just Ernest and I were partners."

120 *they had stationery printed:* E. & J. Gallo's new stationery evident in September 27, 1933, letter to supervisor of permits, Bureau of Alcohol, filed in Department of Special Collections, Shields Library, UC Davis.

120 *Ernest and Julio first considered:* According to Ernest's August 14, 1933, letter to supervisor of permits, Bureau of Alcohol, and confirmed by GWSJ.

120 *"grape growers with over 400 acres of grapes":* To supervisor of permits, August 14, 1933, as cited above, and in GWSJ.

120 *But in fact Joe, Sr., had already taken:* In 1932, the winery in an early form may have already existed, as indicated in JOSJ, which claims, "Ernest and Julio filed tax returns for calendar year 1932 showing $2,209.90 net partnership income from 'E. & J. Gallo Winery.' . . . Julio conceded that something may have been going on with respect to the Winery in 1932 (when Joe Gallo, Sr., was alive) . . . [a]lthough the Winery argues that these were in reality 1933 returns." (If Ernest and Julio had tried to start a winery in 1932 or make the existing facilities their own when their father was in Fresno, perhaps this was the cause of Joe, Sr.'s anger at Ernest, his argument with Julio on June 20, 1933, as recalled by Joe, Jr., and his anxieties about his "business" and "winery" in Modesto, as expressed to Peter Brengetto. It may also be why Joe, Jr., recalled that wine was already stored in the Maze Road underground tanks when he returned from Fresno in June 1933.)

120 *Ernest did not list:* Confirmed in "First Account and Report of Administrator," August 24, 1934, and in "Petition for Decree of Final Distribution and Settlement of Final Account," April 19, 1935; both accountings filed by Attorney Edward Taylor in Superior Court, Stanislaus County. It is unclear whether Ernest was required by then-applicable law to list these assets. JOSJ argued that because they were not included in the estate accounting, neither the court nor Joe was put on notice that they existed.

121 *Years later Julio confirmed:* According to JOSJ, while Joe, Sr., had been living in Fresno, he had written to his attorney, Ed Taylor, informing him that Julio had access to the safe-deposit box.

121 *"Going into the winery business was":* From interview with Robert Mondavi, in which he also recalled Jack Riorda's proposal to his father to start a wine business together because Mondavi's many contacts and reputation as a grape shipper would help market the wine that Riorda had already acquired.

121 *At thirteen, he was simply glad:* According to Joe, Jr., interview and JOSJ.

121 *On August 21, 1933, Leonard:* Ernest's denial of knowing or being related to Mike Gallo, the bank manager's and sheriff's comments, meeting in Ed Taylor's office reconstructed from report by Inspector Leonard Rhodes, August 30, 1933. This inspection was required before winery approval could be granted and included a "personnel" and financial investigation conducted on August 28, 1933, and detailed in the report (held in Department of Special Collections, Shields Library, UC Davis). In EDepo, Ernest confirmed that he had told Rhodes that Mike Gallo was "unknown to him," but he could not recall what he had stated in his affidavit. He asserted that Rhodes had asked him if Mike Gallo was involved in the winery, and he had assured him that he was not. He also said that he had never seen his father's unsigned will until Taylor showed it to the inspector, nor did he know why Joe, Sr., had never signed it or what had become of it subsequently. (The unsigned will apparently was not among Ed Taylor's records that were in the winery's possession and were produced during discovery in the 1988 trial.)

123 *Mike had stayed at the Fresno:* According to Mike's later reminiscences to former Gallo employees.

123 *their uncle still came to see:* According to AIDepo.

124 *The parents' estate had played:* According to the financial investigation by Rhodes reported in the same document. Rhodes's report also indicated Ernest's explanation that his father's estate, to which he, Julio, and a third brother were sole heirs, owned more than "400 acres of which in excess of 240 acres of wine grapes make up the home ranch" and "in excess of 200 acres of grapes (wine and table) near Fresno." In EDepo for 1988 case, however, he insisted that the estate had only about seventy-three acres of vineyards producing wine grapes at the time he applied for the winery permit—thirty-three acres on Maze Road, twenty at Keyes, and twenty at Ripon. Ernest would later attribute these differences in his statements to a "speech problem," which led him "to say one thing and mean another."

124 *forced to ask for loans from relatives:* Julio's savings of $900.23, construction of tanks and purchase of equipment on credit, according to GWSJ, citing EDepo and JULDepo.

125 *Their father's estate included:* Ripon vineyard note, foreclosure, and gross receipt from sale for $4,195, listed in Ernest's "First Account and Report of Administrator" of father's estate, filed August 24, 1934, in Superior Court, Stanislaus County; postponement of auction and eventual sale to Julio registered in Records Office, San Joaquin County. According to EDepo, Ernest could not recall that the property was sold to Julio and whether he had paid the money to the estate. According to JULDepo, Julio said that he could *not* have paid that sum of money because he didn't have it at the time. The 1941 Fiscalini accounting in Joe, Jr.'s Guardianship Estate, Exhibits 3 and 8, cited by JOSJ, confirms that the Ripon property "did not go

through [the father's] estate" but credited Joe, Jr., with a one-third interest in its $4,039.13 valuation.

125 *Max Kane became:* According to Rudy Wagner, who also confirmed that his father, Albert Wagner, was "a bootlegging colleague of Joe, Sr.," in Livermore and "that was why Ernest remembered him and offered him a job." Joe Sciaroni confirmed his brief employment in interview.

125 *Yet all these salaries:* That these were debited to Joe, Sr.'s estate evident in Ernest's "First Account" in the father's probate file, as cited above.

126 *a ton of grapes produced:* According to Ernest's own calculations; the $3,525 credit for "sales of grapes" in the estate account would suggest that the estate's vineyards had produced only about 118 tons of grapes. A good vineyard should yield about 3 tons per acre; a poor yield would be 2. According to Ernest's statements at the time, the estate had at least 240 acres of vineyards, and even using the more conservative figure of 2 tons per acre, they should have yielded at least 500 tons of grapes and the estate should have been paid at least $15,000. (In his 1988 deposition, Ernest reduced the number of estate acres producing wine grapes to seventy-three, as noted above.)

126 *but in this instance, too:* Difference between amount owed to estate for grapes indicated by comparing the "First Account" and amount listed in winery's books, according to GWSJ; according to deposition of winery's accounting expert Gene Deetz, he could not explain the disparity, although he conceded that whatever the estate's grape sales to the winery, they were probably listed in the books without actually being paid. If that was the case, Ernest and Julio retained the use of those funds in the winery, which under ordinary circumstances would have been paid out to a grape grower. As JOSJ contends, the estate was operated as a bank, with proceeds from its grape sales thus available to Ernest and Julio and the winery. This question was debated by accounting experts for both the winery and Joe, Jr.; the winery lawyers argued that even if it couldn't be proven that the estate was actually *paid* for its grapes, Joe's attorneys could not "adduce clear and convincing proof that the Winery did not make payment for the grapes" (GWSJ, Reply Brief). At the very least, though, the records for payments to the estate for grapes were unspecific, with the winery accounts at odds with the estate's accounts and with no details of total tonnage or gallons of wine sold.

126 *Ed Taylor wrote:* According to June 12, 1934, letter to the Alcohol Tax Unit of the Bureau of Alcohol, Tobacco and Firearms (by 1934, the Treasury Department agency supervising wineries and hereafter called BATF); BATF reply June 14 informed him of the regulations that would allow the sale of a deceased grower's wine, according to JOSJ.

127 *When he finally made:* According to BATF records, Department of Special Collections, Shields Library, UC Davis, and cited by JOSJ. In his 1934 BATF application, Ernest claimed that he and Julio had constructed the tanks the year before in anticipation of building a winery on the home ranch premises and had modeled them after Italian Swiss Colony's tanks. In his 1988 deposition, cited by JOSJ, Ernest changed his testimony, admitting that he hadn't wanted to reveal "why my father built the tanks" to BATF authorities; he also denied his previous statement that the tanks were like Italian Swiss Colony's concrete tanks (they "weren't as well suited for storing wine," he said), as if he wanted to negate the implication that Joe, Sr., had originally built them to hold wine.

127 *Joe, Jr., recalled:* According to Joe interview and JODepo.
128 *Here, too, Ernest benefited:* According to Robert Mondavi and others, many grape dealers became wine distributors after Repeal. It seems likely that Joe, Sr.'s shipping business established useful contacts and "goodwill" for the sale of Ernest and Julio's wine just as Cesare Mondavi's established reputation as a grape grower and shipper was the basis for first-year sales. As Robert Mondavi explained, wine dealers who became distributors "had always trusted my father and bought his grapes, and they then were eager to buy his wine."
128 *Charlie Barbera and Tony:* History of the Pacific Wine Company provided by Anthony Terlato and Paul Alleruzzo. Ernest's account of selling first Gallo bulk wine to Barbera according to family reminiscences, official stories (e.g., Ernest's 1963 speech at the Stanford University Business School), and GWSJ, citing EDepo, JULDepo, and AIDepo. Inventory of shipments of Gallo Wine to the Pacific Wine Company for several years confirmed in winery letters to the Alcohol Tax Unit, Department of Special Collections, Shields Library, UC Davis.
128 *Ernest headed to the East Coast:* According to GWSJ.
129 *They later explained that:* According to Ernest's testimony in the Gallo Salame case: "We have been using [the name Gallo] from the time my father went into the wine business. . . . [H]e had started the wine business and I wanted to perpetuate the same thing." In the earlier Mary Gallo trademark case, Ernest testified, "We used 'Gallo' in conjunction with grapes during Prohibition. Millions of cases of grapes were shipped with that brand name on it . . . [i]t was a logical and normal thing for us to do to use it on our wine labels" (both testimonies cited in JOSJ). In his 1988 deposition, Ernest not only diminished the number of cases of Gallo grapes shipped, but when asked if using the Gallo name and the rooster on his wine was the "logical thing to do," he replied, "No. I don't think so. Gallo is, as you know, an Italian name" (JOSJ, citing EDepo).
129 *they earned a profit of $34,000:* Cited in Ernest's speech to Stanford Business School. The specific amount did not appear in any of the available early accountings of the winery, according to JOSJ.
129 *the combined estates were valued at:* According to the declaration of Charles B. Stark, Jr., a financial analyst consulted by Joe's attorneys in the 1988 case, who also contended that the estate had more "liquid capital" than Ernest and Julio.
129 *he sold the Fresno ranch:* Documented in probate record, Superior Court, Stanislaus County, and according to JOSJ. Petition to court and permission received to sell some of the estate's Transamerica stock, November 28, 1933, in probate record, Superior Court, Stanislaus County; Ernest's 1935 final estate account notes that it had been unnecessary to sell the stock after all.
130 *"No, I did not":* According to JOSJ, citing EDepo.
131 *"My brother and I inherited":* Ernest's testimony in the Gallo Salame case, cited in JOSJ.
131 *it wasn't until February 1934:* Joe, Jr.'s "Nomination of Guardians," February 2, 1934, Ernest and Julio's Petition for Letters of Guardianship, February 13, 1934, and Anna Lowe's and Teresa Franzia's posting of bond, April 12, 1935. Filed in Superior Court, Stanislaus County, Modesto. (Waiver of Notice Requirements filed in Joe, Sr.'s probate record.)
131 *"But Ernest would often just":* Interview with Joe, Jr.

133 *"From what Joe told me"*: According to interview with Patricia Gallo, to whom Joe, Jr., described the abrupt changes and difficulties in his life after his parents' deaths and because of Ernest's expectations.

133 *"These grades aren't acceptable"*: Ernest's lecture recalled by Joe, Jr. According to JOSJ, "Although Joe's coach told him that . . . his brother's rule against practices was [un]just, Joe said that he never felt there was any possibility of doing anything other than what his brother had directed."

134 *They worked over sixteen hours*: According to AIDepo, JULDepo, EDepo cited in GWSJ. Repeated disclaimers of knowing anything about their husbands' business activities or the meaning of documents they had signed in AIDepo and AMDepo.

134 *Joe found some emotional respite*: According to interviews with Joe, Jr., and his son Mike, and AIDepo.

134 *Later Ernest cited these vacations*: According to EDepo.

134 *Ernest disapproved of one*: According to Mike Gallo, who had been told this story by his father.

134 *son, Robert Julio, born*: Confirmed in Recorder's Office, Stanislaus County, Modesto.

134 *Ernest still set the tone*: According to JOSJ.

135 *As Ernest liked to quip*: According to former Gallo sales manager Paul Merrigan, Ernest's remark usually justified his immediate firing of employees, since he did not believe that they could change or remedy their mistakes.

135 *By 1935 the E. & J. Gallo Winery*: According to the *Modesto Bee*, October 28, 1938.

135 *berating Julio and employees*: According to interview with Rudy Wagner.

135 *"We don't need all his junk"*: According to EDepo.

135 *"Ernest married me for my family's winery"*: Remark made to former Gallo employees.

135 *Completed in 1936, the new winery*: According to the *Modesto Bee*, October 28, 1938.

136 *Ernest continued an "open book" system*: Described in EDepo and JOSJ. Petition to sell the stock filed April 20, 1936, in Superior Court, Stanislaus County. Winery accounts showed credit of monies from stock and land sales, as confirmed by First and Last Account of Guardianship estate, filed June 20, 1941, which noted the "loan" of Joe's shares to the winery.

136 *Make your own goddamned wine*: Julio's repeated remark according to interview with Rudy Wagner, who also recalled Ernest's departure because of illness and the "hush-hush atmosphere" about his absence from the winery. GWSJ and Winery Replies confirm Ernest's illness during these months.

137 *He later regretted how little time*: According to JULDepo and AIDepo. Birth of Susann, May 28, 1936, registered in Recorder's Office, Stanislaus County.

137 *According to the inspector's report*: Inspector's exchange with Julio about Ernest's dye orders reconstructed from report, filed April 25, 1936, in BATF records, Department of Special Collections, Shields Library, UC Davis.

138 *increase the storage tank capacity*: According to the *Modesto Bee*, October 28, 1938.

138 *as Joe recalled, he finally*: In interview and JODepo, Joe claimed that Ernest had told him to give up junior college; in EDepo, Ernest insisted that Joe had dropped out on his own.

139 *"He'd just hang his head"*: According to Rudy Wagner, who also recalled Max Kane's explanation to him that "Joe was a silent partner" and Joe's response to his question of why he put up with Ernest's scolding.

139 *Just before noon on May 15*: Brandy tampering incident reconstructed from interviews with Joe, Rudy Wagner, EDepo, and BATF investigator's report completed July 10, 1939. The case was filed with the Justice Department (Case No. 6217-M), and a copy was sent to the U.S. attorney in San Francisco. Nolo plea entered, fine imposed, and case closed July 20, 1939, according to Justice Department records. According to EDepo, Ernest recalled that "something happened about coloring the brandy . . . something to the effect that they hadn't put enough caramel in it and they added it later. It was no big deal." He asserted that this was not illegal but was "a matter of format of applying for permission." He agreed that Max and Joe had been involved but did not recall that they had been instructed to add caramel, that they had offered to take the blame or that charges had been filed.

143 *he had also honked*: According to Rudy Wagner. During his deposition, Ernest was not asked if he had honked his horn. Wagner had a clear memory of this, since he had found it humorous: "How could Ernest try to deny he knew what was going on when he followed Herd, all the time blowing his horn to warn Max and Joe?"

143 *"Ernest just told him to disappear"*: According to Rudy Wagner; confirmed by Joe's recollection of Kane's later remarks in JODepo and interview.

144 *The story was resurrected*: Reporters asked Joe, Jr., and his lawyers if this was, as rumored, the real reason why he had never been made a partner in the winery. Joe and his attorneys denied the story, and Joe later remarked on the irony of the rumor in interview. The BATF and Justice Department records of the case confirmed Joe's version of the event and showed that there had been no court-ordered ban on his participation in the winery's ownership.

FIVE

PAGE

145 *the Gallo Winery was producing a full array*: According to the *Modesto Bee*, October 28, 1938.

145 *He first considered calling*: According to Ernest's testimony, TT.

146 *The New Orleans company was established*: Confirmed in EDepo and BATF records.

146 *Distillers Outlet, his Los Angeles*: According to EDepo and his testimony in TT.

146 *Ernest set out to learn*: Described in EDepo and his testimony in TT.

147 *Phillip, had been born*: Registered in Recorder's Office, Stanislaus County, Modesto.

147 *"I sometimes go away"*: Recalled by Rudy Wagner.

148 *their first son, David*: Births of Ernest's sons, David Ernest and Joseph Ernest ("Joey"), registered in Recorder's Office, Stanislaus County, Modesto. Construction of Ernest and Amelia's home in 1939 confirmed in EDepo, although Ernest recalled the year as 1941, "the year of my first son's birth" (which was, in fact, 1939).

148 *In the minutes for both*: Minutes of Los Angeles Gallo Wine Company board of directors' meetings, April 16 and May 16, 1941. Cited by JOJN.

149 *But on June 14, 1941*: "First and Final Account," Attorney Fowler's June 28

objection, the transcript of the June 30 probate court hearing, and the judge's July 2 order: Filed in Superior Court, Stanislaus County, Modesto, and cited by JOSJ.

151   *Joe would insist that:* According to JODepo, his Declaration to the court, and interview.

151   *"It would have been unthinkable":* Interview with Joe, JODepo, and JOJN.

151   *Julio, too, said that:* According to JOSJ and JOJN. Julio, Ernest, and Joe were noted as "appearing in person" in the July 2 "Order Modifying and Settling Account Directing Payment," in Superior Court, Stanislaus County. The minutes of the June 30, 10:30 A.M., hearing indicate the attendance of Ernest and Joe (and not Julio), but also make it evident that no clerk was present that day.

151   *Ernest said he couldn't recall:* According to GWSJ, citing EDepo, in which he also stated that he and Julio had been annoyed at having to pay $20,000 because of "some technicality." (If Joe had received an accounting from Fiscalini as early as February and had been "complaining for months," as Ernest claimed, then Julio, who was not yet hospitalized, presumably would have heard Joe's alleged complaints, especially since Joe was living with him at the time. Julio did not recall such complaints.)

151   *Alcohol Tax Unit records showed:* According to "Report of Inspection—Bonded Wineries and Bonded Storerooms," June 30, 1941, filed with the Office of District Supervisor, San Francisco, of the Alcohol Tax Unit; now in Department of Special Collections, Shields Library, UC Davis.

152   *certification indicated only that they were delivered:* According to JOSJ (these records were produced from winery files, not Joe's, during discovery in 1988 case).

152   *While Joe claimed that he had never:* According to JODepo and JOSJ. Who asked Fowler to prepare Joe's objection is in dispute; Fowler and Taylor were colleagues on the Modesto Planning Commission and were on opposing sides in lawsuits, according to the *Modesto Bee* files. Ernest confirmed knowing Fowler (EDepo); Fowler's correspondence with Taylor as Ernest's representative, introduced in JOJN, which also states, "The Gallo Bros. Ranches journal shows payment to Fowler of $25 for the services he rendered," citing the ranch ledger, and concludes, "Therefore, it seems quite likely that Fowler was retained to handle the Transamerica stock issue by Edward Taylor and/or Ernest Gallo."

153   *only Fowler and Taylor needed:* According to Declaration of Joe's probate expert Robert Mills, president of the International Academy of Estate and Trust Law: "It is quite possible that counsel submitted an agreed order to the court," and the clerk's minutes "may in fact have been created by copying a written order . . . prepared by counsel for the judge's signature" (from JOSJ, citing Mills's Declaration).

154   *Fiscalini explicitly corrected and explained:* According to JOJN, citing as well EDepo in which "Ernest couldn't explain."

155   *another Gallo wine label:* The 1941 label with cartoon of "Bacchus" and slogan "By Golly! Buy Gallo!" described by Ernest in TT and depicted in Joint Exhibit 1.

155   *In March 1942, Ernest applied:* Ernest's 1942 trademark application for the Gallo name as trademark on wine (but without the accompanying cartoon or slogan or previous rooster logo) filed March 17, 1942, with the United States Patent Office and granted Registration No. 394,057. According to EDepo and his testimony in TT, Ernest prepared these first trademark

applications himself, citing the continuous use of the trademark by the winery and in the business of Joe, Sr., "the predecessor of the applicant, Joseph Gallo, since 1909."

155 *was "unaware of the legal subtleties"*: According to GWOSJ.

156 *the Gallo Tank Lines*: According to JOSJ, citing EDepo. Neither Aileen nor Amelia recalled the meeting, and Julio could not have been present, as confirmed by JOJN.

156 *Ernest hired Charles (Charlie) Crawford*: Recalled by Patricia Gallo from conversations with him when she was his executive secretary until her marriage to Joe in 1966.

157 *"You put in $5,000"*: According to JODepo and interview and EDepo; minutes of meeting July 15, 1942, and January 15, 1946, cited in JOSJ.

157 *Joe's position being more titular*: According to Joe, Jr., interview and JODepo. (A month after first meeting, Joe departed for basic training. Nevertheless, minutes still recorded his presence, even at a meeting on January 15, 1946, when he was in the Philippines.)

157 *Ernest drove him to the recruitment office*: The drive, the eye test for the Coast Guard, and his enlistment in the army described by Joe, Jr., in interview and in his Declaration for JOSJ.

157 *Rudy Wagner and other employees wondered*: According to Wagner.

157 *Joe himself never had any doubt*: According to Joe and John Whiting. Date of entering and four years in service (three years of which in the Army Air Corps) confirmed in Honorable Discharge papers, February 16, 1946, filed in Official Records, Stanislaus County.

158 *Joe knew the property*: Purchase of Tegner Ranch and later dispute about financing it, according to JODepo, EDepo, and JULDepo, confirmed in interview with Joe and his Declaration for JOSJ as well as interview with Mike Gallo.

158 *The American Vineyard was*: E. & J. Gallo Winery's merger with Valley Agricultural Company (through which Ernest and Julio acquired Valley's American Vineyard and renamed it Livingston Vineyard) recorded October 15, 1943, and cited in JOSJ.

159 *Ernest recalled visiting Joe once*: Confirmed by EDepo and JODepo, although they dispute the substance of their conversation over dinner.

159 *the board would have had to authorize*: According to Denis Rice, Joe's attorney, Valley Agricultural's stock had been converted to E. & J. Winery stock, and "all available stock was issued to accomplish the merger" in 1943.

159 *The document granted his power*: Joe signed the power of attorney without question, May 15, 1944, according to his Declaration and JOSJ. Neither Joe nor his legal representatives has argued that the written reorganization of what had previously been an "oral, unwritten" partnership was unfair to Joe, despite his being unaware of the arrangement. What his lawyers note is that this was another instance in which "This authority from Joe [his power of attorney] was sought in the wake of an event which had already occurred."

160 *Although Mary Ann's father*: Background of the Arata and Coffee families drawn from interviews with children of Joe and Mary Ann: Linda Gallo Jelacich and Mike Gallo, and from Jeannette Gould Maino, *One Hundred Years*, Modesto (cited above).

161 *"I knew the Gallos"*: Comment by Mabel Coffee Arata, recalled by Sherrie Spendlove Gallo, Mike Gallo's wife.

161 *Joe and Mary Ann were married*: Marriage date of Joe and Mary Ann, Joe's

assignment to the Philippine's, and birthday of Peter Joseph confirmed by Patricia and Joe Gallo. Army honorable discharge (as cited above) confirmed by Joe's service record.

162 *Julio had also lost some control:* According to Joe's speculation, JODepo, and his Declaration in support of JOSJ.

162 *"I'll pay you $20,000":* According to JOSJ. AIDepo and JULDepo both confirm that Joe was offered the Livingston job at Beale.

162 *"What about Charlie Crawford?":* From JODepo and Joe's Declaration for JOSJ. (According to EDepo, Ernest did not recall either dissatisfaction with Crawford or making this remark ("Charlie's a lying son-of-a-bitch") to Joe; he did say that he had asked Joe to work at the winery, but placed this conversation not in his office but outside his home, after lunch, in the driveway.)

163 *he was worried about Julio's health:* Ernest's concern about Julio related to Joe, according to Joe's Declaration. According to Mike Gallo, only when Joe recalled this discussion in light of Ernest and Julio's allegations in the 1988 lawsuit did he begin to wonder if this might have been some sort of "behind-the-scenes power play."

164 *whether he could still "work into":* Ernest and Joe agreed that the question of working into an interest by becoming the Livingston manager was never raised.

164 *Ernest and Julio "could choose":* From Joe's Declaration for JOSJ.

164 *Years later, Aileen and Julio:* According to JULDepo, AIDepo, and GWSJ, both Julio and Ernest had offered Joe the chance of a partnership if he were to "come into the winery," which they said Joe refused. Joe disputed their recollections (in JODepo, JOSJ, and his Declaration) and said this didn't make sense since Aileen and Julio also confirmed that the Livingston job had already been offered to him at Camp Beale. Joe's lawyers also questioned why Ernest, Julio, and Aileen recalled supposedly separate conversations with Joe, both "after lunch, outside, in the driveway" and in such similar language. When questioned, neither Aileen nor Julio was sure what "come into the winery" (the phrase used by Ernest) actually meant in terms of a partnership.

164 *"I'm sure I didn't think of giving":* According to EDepo.

164 *"I started at $10,000 a year":* From interview with Joe, Jr., and confirmed by John Whiting. While Ernest later claimed that, as far as he was concerned, Joe had taken the Livingston position as "temporary" until he went out on his own (GWSJ, citing EDepo), Joe recalled, "I certainly had no plans to be 'on my own' . . . and did not regard my job at the winery as an interim job."

164 *Paul Osteraas, a graduate:* According to JODepo and JULDepo, and confirmed by Mrs. Paul Osteraas.

164 *largest crops that the vineyards:* According to Joe's Declaration for JOSJ, in which he recalled Ernest's remark, "[I]f it wasn't for the money made on the ranch, the winery would have lost money that year."

164 *Joe approached Ernest and Julio:* Joe's proposal and brothers' response to "work into an interest in the winery" by purchasing the Livingston vineyard, recounted in Joe's Declaration for JOSJ.

165 *he began to feel the effects:* From interview with Joe and in his Declaration for JOSJ. While Ernest and Julio's depositions in the 1988 lawsuit stress how hard they worked and—by comparison—how little Joe worked, others remember that Joe put in long hours at the winery before the war and man-

aging the Livingston vineyards after the war. Mike Gallo recalled that one of his mother's worries (and sometimes her complaint) was her husband's extended working day, from early morning until late into the evening, which kept them at home in Livingston much more than she would have liked.

165 *With the end of the war:* According to interview with Robert Huntington, confirmed by several "oldtimers" in Napa and Sonoma. While former Gallo executive Dick Witter eventually refused to be interviewed for this book, he did confirm that Ernest had told him that just after the war the winery amassed a huge fund of working capital.

166 *developed the winemaking methods:* Described by Leon Adams in *Wines of America* (New York: McGraw-Hill, 1973, rev. 1985); also "The Story of Gallo," the winery's official history. Mario Ricci, employee of the Gallo distributorship in San Francisco, confirmed the huge expansion of storage facilities after World War II, when, as a recent emigrant from Italy, he, along with many others, was hired by the winery to build storage tanks.

167 *He would concentrate on "point-of-sale":* Innovations described by Ernest as his discovery of "retailers' recommendations" and "point-of-sale" advertising, from his speech to the Stanford University Business School, February 28, 1963. Remarks and examples of early advertising programs drawn from "The Story of Gallo," cited above, and confirmed in interview with Angelo Bufalino, who began in Gallo sales in the early 1950s and was an executive of the Los Angeles Gallo Wine Company until his retirement in 1991. Ernest's description of his first marketing efforts and surveys of retail stores from TT.

168 *John Freiburg, who headed:* Freiburg's recollections of his duties, advertising programs, promotional strategies (including billboards, radio spots, trade publication saturation, wine racks, grape arbor streamers), and his and Ernest's city-by-city visits to distributors for Gallo Wine, according to Freiburg deposition, September 25, 1987. Promotional themes and advertising portfolio described by Angelo Bufalino.

169 *The October 8, 1945, Life:* "*Life* Goes to a Grape Crush," *Life* magazine article, October 8, 1945. In his deposition Freiburg explained that the party had been arranged by him: "I wrote the scenario [for] it." He also conceded that the photographs in the new promotional portfolio of an imposing corporate building bore little resemblance to the actual "little ramshackle office" at the Gallo Winery: "We tried to aggrandize the picture. . . . I take it this photo was furnished to me and I accepted it and put it in the brochure." He was asked if, for all he knew, it could be a photograph of General Motors, and he agreed, "It could be."

169 *"The only wine sales were":* According to Freiburg deposition, cited above.

170 *"The man was just a genius":* Freiburg deposition.

170 *"only trusted family members":* Freiburg deposition.

170 *expressed disappointment that:* Freiburg deposition.

170 *"It was clear from Ernest's comments":* According to Neil Sweeney, who headed Gallo sales training seminars in the 1960s.

171 *"I knew why he wanted Charlie":* According to Freiburg deposition, cited above.

171 *Having spent $762,000 in advertising:* According to Gallo Winery's "Replies to Interrogatories" in 1988 lawsuit. According to winery representatives, "These are conservative estimates" for brands advertised and sold under Gallo label. During Charles and Mary Gallo lawsuit, cited below, Ernest

was shown and confirmed Exhibit 13-A, which also indicated $762,000 advertising expenditure in 1946, and 3 million gallons sold. Wine industry estimates at the time placed the winery's sales at close to $6.3 million.

171 *he hired William MacKay:* San Francisco attorney William MacKay represented Ernest Gallo in the Gallo Winery's 1946 trademark application for "Gallo" (alone), according to February 11, 1946, application Serial No. 496,376 in the United States Patent Office.

171 *Charles Gallo bought and bottled:* Narrative of the Charles and Mary Gallo trademark conflict reconstructed from E. & J. Gallo Winery v. Mary Gallo, doing business as Gallo Wine Company, Civil Action No. 25172, in U.S. District Court, North District of Ohio, Eastern Division, and transcript of court testimony, commencing March 8, 1949.

172 *John Freiburg was assigned to this job:* According to documents and testimony in the above case. Freiburg could not recall his interview with Charles Gallo or his report to Ernest in his 1987 deposition.

174 *Joe knew nothing about:* According to interview and JOSJ.

174 *he was dissolving the Gallo Bros.:* Dissolution of Gallo Bros. Ranches partnership and "$50,000 on demand" note (after closing of tartar company) confirmed in JODepo and interview, EDepo, and by Mike Gallo's recollection of his father's narrative of events to him. Taylor's confirmation of Ernest and Julio's salaries sanctioned by closing of guardianship estate introduced in GWSJ.

175 *But later his son Mike:* From interview with Mike Gallo.

SIX

177 *He found his man in:* Background of Albion "Al" Fenderson from several former Gallo colleagues and employees.

177 *labeled Hammer untrustworthy:* According to Steve Weinberg, *Armand Hammer, The Untold Story* (New York: Little Brown, 1989).

178 *Ernest's provincialism and rough edges:* From a source who knew Williams and commented that, compared to Ernest, Williams was sophisticated: "After all, Howard had been the West Coast manager of Young & Rubicam in the thirties and forties, before he went to Guild; he was brilliant and creative and responsible for developing many of Gallo's most successful products and presentations."

179 *develop a light, "mellow":* Williams's development of "Vino Paisano di Gallo," according to former Gallo employee Robert Huntington and his recollections of Williams, who is now deceased. (Huntington left Gallo in 1970, after ten years as a brand and senior group product manager, and became vice-president of Canandaigua Wine Company in New York.) Vino Paisano di Gallo went into distribution in May 1953, and its trademark (number 599,169) was approved and registered by the United States Patent Office on December 7, 1954. Paisano was developed as a light red or *vino rosso*, because Ernest believed that the general public did not favor heavier table wines. In fact, though, the winery did make two "robust" table reds, Barberone and Pastoso e Scelto Burgundy, which were blended to taste more like Old World wines and to appeal to Italian wine drinkers. These two brands were marketed in half-gallon and gallon jugs, with sales almost exclusively in Italian communities.

179 *Ken Bertsch was:* Story of Bertsch's move to Gallo and descriptions of him and his methods drawn from interviews with several former employees. (Joe

and Patricia Gallo later became close friends with Ken and Elinor Bertsch, and according to them and others, while Bertsch could be intimidating and harsh with his sales teams, in social situations he loosened up and could be "charming" and "affable.")

179 *earned the nickname "Silky"*: According to a former Gallo brand manager. Bertsch's reputation as a "ladies' man" and the story of his scar, according to former Gallo executives.

180 *In a spy versus spy world*: According to regional and district sales managers, who were expected to file reports about their employees; while rating employees' performances, they were asked to indicate personal difficulties, derelictions in speech and dress, extramarital affairs, divorces, and hints of disloyalty or cynicism.

180 *Ernest's achievement was to bring*: According to Huntington.

180 *sales and management courses were not yet formalized*: According to Angelo Bufalino.

180 *indoctrinated*: According to former Gallo salesmen who went through Gallo training seminars. Even though the training programs evolved into more formal and complex seminars, their impression was that Bertsch had originated the "military-like" program and the "indoctrination" methods. The techniques and tactics described for pushing Gallo brands into markets and retail stores are a compilation from interviews with former sales managers who started in the training programs and were promoted through the Gallo ranks.

181 *they moved—even removed*: Tactics such as moving competitors' merchandise, back-spinning caps, spraying with oil, comparative tastings, according to former employees who described both engaging in and witnessing these practices. Nevertheless, they indicated that these were not explicit orders, but that the command, "Do anything it takes to accomplish the Gallo goal," implicitly prompted such tactics.

183 *concentrated their attention on Ernest's products*: According to former Gallo sales manager Paul Merrigan and others.

184 *If a distributor was unwilling to go along*: According to Gallo sales managers and distributors.

185 *to carry out their experiments*: Experiments with new products as well as upgraded and expanded research program described in interviews with winemakers who had trained at Gallo and confirmed by the winery's official commentary, "The Story of Gallo," cited above.

186 *The "little old wine maker" behind*: The story of the Petri family from interview with Anthony Ciccarelli and from account in James Conaway, *Napa* (cited above).

186 *taken a year's option on Italian Swiss Colony*: According to Merrigan, Huntington, and others. They recalled Ernest's almost personal animosity toward Petri, more vehement than his feelings toward any other competitor (although they added that any winery with substantial sales was a thorn in Ernest's side). Some sources attributed the antagonism toward Petri to the unconfirmed story that in the first years of the winery, Petri had refused to help Ernest get a loan from the Bank of America (Petri was a friend of its founder, A. P. Giannini).

186 *Ernest used the euphemism "ethnic"*: According to several sources and confirmed by Gallo distributors' Market Audits, which show the category "ethnic" to designate retail outlets in predominantly black communities.

186 *Williams suggested a slightly sweeter*: Story of Williams's designing and

marketing the "grape decanter," which turned Gallo Grenache Rosé (later Gallo Vin Rosé) into the winery's best-selling table wine, according to Huntington, Merrigan, and others.

188 *Canandaigua Wine Company had developed Wild Irish Rose:* According to Robert Huntington, who in a *San Francisco Chronicle* article, February 27, 1988, also confirmed that 60 percent to 75 percent of the sales of Wild Irish Rose (known as "Red Lady" on the street) were in "primarily black, inner-city markets."

188 *Fenderson and Bleiweiss returned:* Story of inventing and naming Thunderbird, according to report written by Fenderson, copies of which several former Gallo employees retained; they also confirmed Bleiweiss's nickname. Despite awareness of Fenderson's report among employees, the winery has disputed this history of Thunderbird: According to the *Chronicle* article cited above, a Gallo spokesman said that the Kool-Aid story "is a nice myth," but that Thunderbird was "developed by our wine makers in our laboratories." Winery spokesman Dan Solomon added that Thunderbird "has lost its former popularity in the black and skid-row areas" and is now drunk by "retired and older folks who don't like the taste of hard products."

189 *since consumers were getting it for free:* According to several former Gallo employees as well, distributing free samples was a way to introduce Thunderbird and later other "street wines." According to the *San Francisco Chronicle*, February 27, 1988, other wineries also hand out free samples to "skid row's opinion leaders," called "bell cows," to convince them to change brands. As former Gallo marketing executive Arthur Palombo confirmed in the same article, "these were clandestine promotions" (although he did not say which wineries used this method).

189 *The winery also solicited African Americans in Modesto:* Described by a local resident and former Gallo employee in the Thunderbird bottling room.

190 *he had the winery's in-house:* "Gallo Thunderbird label" in use on April 22, 1957, and trademark (number 668,475) registered October 14, 1958, by the United States Patent Office. (The file includes the amendment, January 27, 1964, to remove "Gallo" from the label.)

190 *Gallo salesmen recalled that "street-sampling":* Described by Paul Merrigan, Neil Sweeney, and former Gallo sales managers and trainers. They confirmed James Conaway's repetition in *Napa* (cited above) of the often-told story "of uninhibited sales techniques: strewing selected skid rows with empty Thunderbird bottles as a unique route to product awareness, and the destruction of the competition's aluminum screw-caps by bands of men roving the liquor stores."

191 *"presented her to the retailers":* According to the *San Francisco Chronicle* article cited above, a Princess Thunderbird was chosen as recently as 1988 as part of a promotional campaign in New Jersey, even though Gallo no longer advertises its association with Thunderbird.

191 *usually attributed to Howard Williams:* According to several sources, although some thought that Fenderson may have created the jingle, inspired by jazz slang that he heard during his field surveys in black communities.

192 *Ernest and Julio were barely speaking* (and description of the Camelot atmosphere of Ernest's Sunday gatherings): According to friends of family and former employees.

193 *characteristics of an "idiot savant":* According to Neil Sweeney and others.

193 *But no one else was allowed to criticize:* According to Mike Gallo and others.

193　*Julio's elder son, Bob:* Background drawn from his deposition, Modesto High School yearbook, and interview with Mike Gallo. His marriage confirmed in Recorder's Office, Stanislaus County. Background of Frank Damrell, Sr., and family, provided by *Modesto Bee* clips and family friends.

194　*"She was a cheerleader":* From interview with acquaintance whose father worked for the winery and who met her at winery gatherings.

194　*even though her contemporaries said:* According to family friends and Linda Gallo Jelacich, who recalled remarks made by her mother. (Mary Ann was close to Susann as well as to Aileen.)

194　*Phillip, was a constant worry:* According to interview with acquaintance who worked in the home vineyards with him and heard discussions of the problem.

194　*could barely tolerate:* From interview with Mike Gallo.

194　*the experience would "toughen":* According to Stella Dorais.

194　*Once Phillip burped:* Incident described by Mike Gallo.

195　*told others that Julio's son:* Recalled by Paul Merrigan and others.

195　*built a new home on the land:* According to Patricia Gallo, Joe bought the Frazier ranch where he eventually built his new home. Anecdote of wine-soaked cooperage used as paneling in his new home, from interview with Joe Gallo; the story is also included in Leon Adams, *Wines of America* (cited above).

195　*born on May 5, 1952:* Confirmed by Linda Gallo Jelacich.

195　*Once Jim was so rattled* and *would tease David and Joey:* According to Mike Gallo.

196　*She liked to reminisce:* Drawn from AIDepo and Joe, Patricia, and Mike Gallo.

196　*Ernest and Julio exchanged anxious glances:* Impression of Joe's son Mike Gallo.

196　*some said that Ernest:* From remarks made by "Uncle Mike" Gallo to former Gallo sales manager Paul Merrigan and to people who knew him in Hawthorne: Nevada assemblyman Robert Revert, Holman Barlow, and his parish priest, Father Benjamin Franzinelli, in Henderson, Nevada. Descriptions of Gallo's Inn and El Capitan from Holman Barlow, who also recalled some of Mike's reminiscences about Prohibition adventures.

197　*He was proud of his nephews:* According to Barlow, Merrigan, and Franzinelli.

197　*Mike was found guilty and fined:* According to Justice Department National Archives, Case No. 146-27-12-5.

197　*he attacked her with:* Report of stabbing, confession, and sentencing, according to the *Chicago Tribune*, May 5, 1948.

197　*For the next twenty years Mike lived:* According to Jim Costello (Gallo's Las Vegas distributor), Father Franzinelli, and Paul Merrigan.

197　*"We became friends":* From interview with Father Franzinelli.

198　*The regular delivery of cases:* Confirmed by Merrigan and Costello.

198　*Thunderbird "had gone off":* According to Fenderson's written recollection as well as former employees.

199　*By September 1958 the $6 million:* According to the *Modesto Bee*, October 16, 1958.

199　*Ernest asked his brother Joe to serve* and *Joe bought the remaining 10 percent:* Confirmed by JODepo and interview with Joe.

200　*experiment with, produce, and market:* Description of development of flavored and fortified wines and selling tactics to, for example, American

Indians provided by former Gallo salesmen who participated in promotions. Tape of Tickled Pink commercial provided by Paul Merrigan. Several Gallo sales trainees report accompanying boxing champion Ezzard Charles to publicize Thunderbird in urban black bars.

200 *still included a separate category:* From Market Audits; these records also show that the pint flasks and small bottles of flavored, fortified wines were most often distributed to "ethnic" stores.

201 *Ernest had initially refused:* According to James Conaway, *Napa* (cited above), and others. In 1934 the Wine Institute was formed as the trade association for the California Wine Advisory Board and required state wineries to contribute a percentage of their sales, according to a California State Chamber of Commerce report on the state wine industry. (Since 1990 the Wine Institute is a voluntary organization, but Gallo remains a member and its largest contributor.)

201 *Gallo still ran the organization:* From Glen Martin, "The Biggest, Little Old Winemakers in the World," *West* magazine, *San Jose Mercury-News*, August 19, 1990; small wineries' complaints and resignations of Sebastiani and Mondavi from the institute, according to *The New York Times*, June 27, 1992.

202 *"I took it back":* Tiffany watch story related by Paul Merrigan.

204 *"I'll get you into the country club":* Reported by former Gallo executives and confirmed by Legh Knowles in James Conaway, *Napa* (cited above).

204 *Ernest hired him to come:* According to Mike Gallo.

206 *"Just let Phillip be":* According to interview with Stella Dorais.

206 *since Julio, like Ernest:* Confirmed by Mike Gallo.

206 *There was talk that he:* Phillip's hospitalization recalled by several former employees, who heard gossip at the time, and confirmed by Stella Dorais.

207 *Phillip was sprawled:* Narrative of suicide reconstructed from autopsy report, Stanislaus County Coroner's report, and the *Modesto Bee* article, October 22, 1958.

207 *The rumors focused on:* Recalled by Paul Merrigan and other employees.

207 *revived speculation about Ernest and Julio's parents':* According to Neil Sweeney.

SEVEN

PAGE

209 *and with his son Bob donated:* According to the *Modesto Bee*, February 24, 1967.

209 *Ernest drew his own moral:* According to his comments made later to Paul Merrigan, Neil Sweeney, and others.

209 *In 1946 Paterno had bought:* Narration of Paterno background provided by Anthony Terlato, Paterno's son-in-law and today president of the Pacific Wine Company.

210 *Mike Romano had been watched:* According to Chicago Crime Commission file, which recorded September 1947 "Congressional Inquiry into Methods by which Subjects Obtained Federal Parole." (The investigation was prompted by the release, on August 13, 1947, of four "Capone mobsters," including Romano's friend Campagna, after "serving minimum time on a ten-year sentence.")

210 *In 1959, Mike Romano:* Ernest and Albion Fenderson's first meeting with Mike Romano, Sr., in 1959 recreated from descriptions by Mike, Jr., and D. J. (Buddy) Romano.

211 *Finally, in 1961:* According to Romano brothers and Gallo employees who worked out of this distributorship. Fenderson, Bertsch, and Williams were among the Gallo executives who owned shares in the Edgebrook corporation and its distributorship.

211 *According to former sales managers:* Several confirmed that this corporate structure was established because in most states, wineries were not allowed to own distributorships.

211 *Fusco was a notorious figure:* According to Kobler and Murray, both cited above, and Chicago Crime Commission files, dating from Fusco's first indictment, January 6, 1921, and continuing to his nineteenth, on June 29, 1933, in which Fusco is described as "superintendent of Capone's beer and wine delivery force" as well as "Capone's trusted gunman." With Repeal, Fusco announced that he had "left the racket and got a legitimate job when legal beer came in," but the U.S. Senate–Kefauver 1950 Illinois hearings investigated the Crime Commission's observations of Fusco's continued connections with mob figures and organized crime. According to the Chicago Crime Commission reports, in 1948 Fusco was investigated by the Alcohol Tax Unit and warned for "using syndicate muscle in peddling liquor"; in 1952, Fusco established the Pacific Brewing Company in southern California; he was then investigated for refusing to sell brand whiskeys to retailers unless they bought his Van Merit beer.

212 *In 1949, Fusco's Gold Seal:* According to the Chicago Crime Commission Fusco files and the *Chicago Tribune*, January 7, 1949, and February 19, 1956.

212 *especially when one of his former:* According to the Chicago Crime Commission report on a former partner in Fusco's Cornell Distributing, and the *Chicago American*, October 24, 1961.

212 *all it took was a phone call:* Carmen Bragno, whose family has owned a bottling company and distributorship in Chicago since Repeal (now called Bragno World Wines, Ltd.) and later a winery near Modesto, confirmed Fusco's muscle power and extensive control of distribution in the Chicago area, as did interviews with Ed Baumann, Vern Whaley, Paul Alleruzzo, and Mike and Buddy Romano.

212 *Ernest had hired Arthur (Art) Palombo:* According to Mike and Buddy Romano, who also described Palombo's phone call, Ernest's enticement of "the hungriest young distributors in town," and the subsequent "sense of family" and success of the distributorship.

214 *demanded the return of $350,000:* According to former Gallo sales managers who described the winery's Chicago history, including the rumor of a contract out on Ernest as well as Fusco's threats to retailers not to buy Gallo brands.

214 *prompted Howard Williams to create:* According to Robert Huntington, who also described his tenure at Gallo and the change in the winery's television advertising.

215 *Ernest had hired Richard (Dick) Witter:* Witter's background and contributions to the winery related by former Gallo employees and confirmed by Patricia and Joe Gallo, who have been friends with him and his wife, Bonnie, for many years. Witter himself declined comment. Although he no longer works for the winery, he remains close to Ernest, but he is also a consultant to Joseph Gallo Cheese Company.

216 *he expanded and built the Mountain Wine label:* According to Huntington, Neil Sweeney, Patricia Gallo, and others.

215 *had named on the spur of the moment*: According to Huntington and James Conaway, *Napa* (cited above).

216 *Ernest stressed the theme*: Quoted from his February 28, 1963, address to the Stanford Business School's symposium, "Building a Sales Organization for Gallo."

217 *"and it seemed to us that this"*: According to a former Gallo employee. Neil Sweeney confirmed the general opinion among winery employees that Stanford consultants had been hired to try to help David get his degree.

217 *"My parents went to the winery party"*: From interview with Mike Gallo.

219 *it was unlikely that he could be given*: According to several former marketing and sales managers, as well as Stella Dorais and Bernie Weiner, a personnel consultant to the winery.

218 *David's behavior at the meetings*: Confirmed in interviews with Neil Sweeney, Gary Glasgow, Paul Merrigan, Stella Dorais, Bernie Weiner, and advertising account executives.

218 *later became a part of Midcal Aluminum*: Gallo distributorship records confirm ownership as Midcal Aluminum, d/b/a Valley Vintners.

218 *Joey stood in front of a mirror*: Recounted by Ali Bianco to his sister, Stella Dorais; Joey's habit confirmed by Paul Merrigan: "The joke was that if Ernest developed a facial tic one morning, Joey would have the same tic the following day."

218 *he didn't think like him*: According to Neil Sweeney. A trained psychologist, Sweeney reported that Ernest once asked him to give David and Joey IQ tests. He tested them as part of the training program, which Sweeney was then supervising.

219 *"identified with this type of people"*: According to Joey's deposition in the 1988 lawsuit.

219 *what they did feel was the pressure*: Recalled by Neil Sweeney.

219 *Joey also spent time* and *"was on the winery payroll"*: According to his 1988 deposition (cited above).

219 *What "interfacing" actually meant*: According to Neil Sweeney, Paul Merrigan, and others.

219 *Named Illinois state manager*: Confirmed by Joey's 1988 deposition, as well as by the Romano brothers.

219 *assessed Joey as "limited"*: According to Neil Sweeney and others.

219 *they were "like family"*: According to Joey's 1988 deposition and interview with Mike and Buddy Romano.

220 *"Julio says he wants to split"*: According to Mike Gallo and JODepo.

221 *the rumor among the winery's executives*: According to a former Gallo sales manager, who recalled Ernest's barbecue at which Julio made a rare appearance and grilled a whole tuna, prompting guests to remark that the brothers "had finally buried the hatchet."

221 *In 1950 he bought the Escola*: According to Joe's Declaration for JOSJ, JGSJ, and JODepo, and confirmed by Mike Gallo.

221 *Shastid suggested, in fact, that*: According to John Whiting.

221 *Joe Gallo's name was well known*: Confirmed by Central Valley cattle ranchers, John Whiting, and Mike Gallo.

222 *But Mary Ann wasn't happy*: Narration of Mary Ann's unhappiness from interviews with Linda Gallo Jelacich and Mike Gallo.

223 *he sued for divorce*: According to John Whiting.

224 *Robinson agreed*, and *John Whiting*: According to Whiting, who also described his own background and the development of friendship with Joe during the divorce proceedings.

224 *"My mother told me"*: According to Linda Gallo Jelacich. While Linda suspected that her uncle Ernest was in favor of the divorce, Joe asserted that Ernest played no role in convincing him to get divorced (JODepo). Nevertheless, Joe later confirmed to Mike that in the beginning, perhaps Ernest had stirred his anger enough to prevent getting back together. By the time the divorce proceedings were actually under way, however, reconciliation was impossible. Joe's brothers and their wives publicly expressed disapproval of the divorce, considering it a blot on the family's proper Catholic reputation, according to Linda Gallo Jelacich. (This was the same sentiment later expressed when Celia and Mike Gallo's daughter, Gloria, divorced her first husband, Bill MacKay, and then married Dr. Frank Stangl, and one of Susann Coleman's daughters divorced her husband and took up with one of the family's security guards.) Despite its frequent disapproval of divorce (and according to former employees, it was frowned upon at the winery as well), there were already several divorces in the Gallo family—Celia and Mike, Mike's second divorce, and his son Mario's divorce, and Susie had twice filed for divorce from Joe, Sr.

225 *Ernest's attention was focused*: According to *Modesto Bee* articles, October 6, 1965, April 15, 1966, and "Personal Spotlight" feature, April 24, 1966.

225 *But having won the annual Merit Award*: Reported by the *San Francisco Chronicle*, June 5, 1964.

225 *"sure as hell didn't want"*: Julio's comment quoted in JULDepo and confirmed by Leon Adams for his revised edition of *Wines of America* (cited above).

225 *the plans showed*: Plans for the winery's new headquarters described in *Modesto Bee* articles cited above as well as in Stanislaus County records and Modesto zoning board and board of supervisors meetings.

226 *hint of greenish cast*: Described in the *Modesto Bee*, April 15, 1966, and confirmed by Gallo employees.

226 *"The new building will"*: Quoted by the *Modesto Bee*, October 6, 1965. (The article also confirmed that the Gallo Glass plant had originally cost $6 million to build in 1958, that its capacity had been doubled in 1960, and that Midcal Aluminum and Fairbanks Trucking Company were also located on the winery's Fairbanks and Yosemite Avenue site.)

226 *Whether Ernest originally meant*: The initial stories, as well as proposals before the board of supervisors, all mentioned a future Visitors' Center.

226 *The winery also requested*: According to the *Modesto Bee*, March 15, 1966.

226 *eventually approved this construction*: First proposal considered, then tabled, December 20, 1965. Later approval reported in the *Modesto Bee*, December 21, 1966, which noted that the winery had also closed off Oregon Avenue as well as Fairbanks in order to prevent through traffic: "The E. & J. Gallo Winery yesterday was granted permission to erect a gate across Oregon Drive—after the installation had taken place." (Fairbanks Avenue curved into Oregon on the south side of the winery. The chain-link fence and gate made it impossible for public traffic to continue from Fairbanks to Oregon as a thoroughfare.)

226 *Heading the security force*: According to Mike Gallo as well as Modesto residents and former Gallo employees.

226 *plans for a new research laboratory*: Described by Bob Gallo in the *Modesto Bee*, December 29, 1967.

227 *accepted the Gallos' donation*: Reported in the *Modesto Bee*, December 16, 1965.

227 *Bob Gallo had to defend:* His letter to the State Reclamation Board quoted in the *Modesto Bee*, March 29, 1967.

227 *"the culmination of a lifetime":* Julio quoted in the *Modesto Bee*, December 29, 1967.

228 *put the winery technologically ahead:* According to interview with Bern Ramey, who had worked for several other wineries, started his own winery in Michigan, and turned down Ernest's insistent employment offers. (Now retired, he is the author of books about wine, wineries, and wine grape varietals—see citation above.)

228 *"I think it was about that time":* According to Neil Sweeney.

228 *But in the summer of 1966:* Ernest's raft trip described by Mike and Patricia Gallo.

229 *"I have traveled widely":* Ernest's letter published in the *Modesto Bee*, July 25, 1966.

229 *the Gallo Glass plant was asked:* According to several *Modesto Bee* articles, including summaries of problems, May 23, 1986, and February 24, 1987. The winery had to dig up thousands of bricks (used as heat absorbers in kilns and shown to be contaminated with chromium 6, considered carcinogenic by state health officials), which had been buried on various properties in Modesto.

229 *Joe had struck up a conversation:* Described by Patricia Gallo; she also provided the anecdote about the change of their wedding date, Joe's reaction during rafting-trip incident, and his comment that he worked for his brothers and was not a partner in the winery.

231 *Joe was asked by Julio:* According to Mike Gallo, who described Ernest's moving chair in front of Joe, Ernest's request, and his father's seeing "this as a pattern."

231 *Once again, Joe felt he couldn't refuse:* Confirmed by Patricia Gallo.

232 *that he and Ernest wanted to buy:* Story of Gallo Glass stock dispute according to Mike Gallo, JODepo, EDepo, and the hearing on the Petition to Sell Assets of Gallo Minors Trust in Stanislaus County Superior Court, November 19, 1965; ensuing court order based on November 8, 1965, agreement between Ernest and Julio Gallo (trustees of Joe's children's trusts) and Gallo Glass Company, a Nevada Corporation, as well as the Consent of Guardian . . . permitting sale of Trust Assets, signed by Joe Gallo and Mary Ann Klor, November 19, 1965.

232 *didn't want anyone "outside the family":* According to EDepo, JODepo. Conversation of Joe, Ernest, and Julio about this transaction reconstructed from their depositions.

234 *although there were exceptions:* According to Patricia Gallo, this dispute occurred before she married Joe and when she was still working at the winery. In 1966, a year after the sale of the stock, she saw lists of shareholders that were filed with the BATF tax division. Hence, she was surprised when Joe later told her Ernest's rationale—that only his and Julio's children would hold winery stock; she was aware that after Joe's sale, "outsiders" still owned stock, including Julio's mother-in-law, Anna Lowe, and Celia Bianco. "I realized that Ernest had not been entirely truthful in telling Joe that all [outside] shares had been called in," added Patricia.

234 Anyway, Joe, we feel that you'd: Julio's termination of Joe described in JODepo, EDepo, and JULDepo, from which their conversation is reconstructed. According to Ernest and Julio, they had expressed their dissatisfaction for many months.

234 *now found himself weeping:* According to Joe's Declaration for JOSJ, "I cried on this occasion and was very hurt."

235 I've always wanted to be a part of the winery: According to Mike's recollection of his father's description of the conversation following the termination.

235 *"came out of the blue":* According to interview with Joe and his Declaration for JOSJ.

235 *"I knew my father was disturbed":* Interview with Mike Gallo. His speculation about coincidence of separation of Joe's accounting and books and winery's suit against Gallo Salame seconded by John Whiting in interview.

236 *By the end of 1967, he had built:* According to Joe's Declaration for JOSJ, JGSJ, JODepo, and confirmed in interviews with him, Mike, and Whiting.

237 *Peter joined the army:* According to Patricia and Mike Gallo, as well as Linda Gallo Jelacich.

EIGHT

PAGE

239 *assigned him the title vice-president:* Confirmed by Robert Huntington, although others heard Palombo referred to as "Special Markets Intermediary."

239 *"Ernest really took to Art":* Interview with Paul Merrigan and confirmed by other former Gallo employees.

240 *"I met Ernest in December 1968":* Interview with Neil Sweeney, who narrated his development of the formal training program.

240 *"the famous 'Big Red Book' ":* Interview with Neil Sweeney.

241 *Bertsch ordered him to terminate:* According to Sweeney.

241 *"Ernest then came into my office":* According to Robert Huntington.

242 *when Julio and his winemakers came up:* Development of Hearty Burgundy, Chablis Blanc, and Pink Chablis described by Huntington, Merrigan, and others. Witter would not confirm that Pink Chablis was his creation, but among several former winery sources, it was generally believed that it was his marketing innovation (although winery consumer surveys had perhaps suggested the name, since it was concluded that the name Chablis carried more positive associations than, for example, Sauterne).

244 *the fiction of him as an independent:* See photograph of Rossi next to sign posted at vineyard. Nevertheless, when Charlie Rossi began to inflate his role from brand manager to independent winemaker, Ernest sent him to London to supervise Gallo distribution in England. Mike Gallo recalled that Joey and David laughingly told him, "Charlie doesn't realize it, but he got too big for his britches, and Dad has shipped him to Siberia."

245 *In 1967 Arnold Scheer became:* Background of Arnold Scheer, his employment by the winery, and Gallo's emphasis on certain growing, irrigation, and pruning techniques provided by Mike Gallo.

245 *In October 1967 Ernest announced a new program:* According to the *Modesto Bee,* October 19, 1967, which also described "skepticism of growers." Necessity of growers' agreement to the Gallo plan reported in the *San Francisco Chronicle,* December 8, 1967.

247 *Ernest and Julio were crowned: Time* magazine, November 27, 1972; sales figures quoted from the article.

247 *brand mapping surveys:* Submitted as evidence for JOSJ and confirmed by Richard Boone, Gallo's director of Consumer Research, who testified to "Gallo's negative image" compared to "AMIT" in TT.

247 *"Finally, at one of our many meetings"*: Interview with Paul Merrigan. According to former Gallo executives, Ernest also acquired advance notice of labels through contacts at printing houses that served Gallo as well as other wineries. Because the winery was their largest client, printing house employees were sometimes willing to pass on competitors' labels or promotional material.

248 *Art Ciocca, a former Gallo group product manager*: According to Neil Sweeney, Bernie Wiener, and Paul Merrigan.

248 *had very little to occupy her time*: Amelia's shopping adventures and Ernest's reaction related by winery employees.

249 *he then met Ofelia*: Background of Ofelia Carrasquilla related by Neil Sweeney, who among others recalled Ernest's lack of enthusiasm; Sweeney, however, liked her and became friendly with her after her marriage to Joey. He noted that while Ofelia pronounced her name O-fay-lia, the Spanish pronunciation, Amelia insisted on calling her O-fee-lia.

249 *There seemed to be an unwritten rule*: Confirmed by winery employees who recalled the search to find David a wife and David's remarks.

249 *returned to live in the "gazebo"*: According to Neil Sweeney.

249 *Both Ernest and Julio openly expressed*: According to Merrigan and others who recalled several comments made directly to them in which Hispanics were disparaged.

250 *left school in 1973*: According to Mike Gallo, who also recalled that it was about this time that Albion Fenderson approached him at a family/winery party and asked him what he was planning to do after graduation. "Work with my father," was Mike's immediate response. Fenderson then tried to convince him that he could have a "real future" at the winery, "almost as if he didn't understand or couldn't believe my wanting to be my father's partner," Mike added.

251 *"I had a rule"*: Interview with Sherrie Spendlove Gallo.

252 *information was kept from them*: According to former Gallo employees, marketing and sales executives needed facts and figures, which Ernest regarded as classified information. The complaint was also noted by Anitra S. Brown, "The Genius of Gallo," *Market Watch*, May 1988. Gallo's insistence on secrecy within the company is also confirmed in U.S. International Trade Commission v. E. & J. Gallo Winery, 637 F.Supp. 1262 (D.D.C. 1985): When the winery had refused to answer an ITC questionnaire, the ITC asked the federal court to compel a response. According to the case report, Gallo's counsel told the court that the information sought by the ITC subpoena "is data that Gallo's owners allocate among six independent accountants; and that these bookkeepers, for the express purpose of maintaining intracompany secrecy (let alone extracompany confidentiality), issue their respective quarterly reports directly and solely to the Gallo brothers." The winery's counsel had added during oral argument that not even Gallo's general counsel had a "complete picture of Gallo's operations and business projections." (Gallo eventually disclosed the information requested by the ITC after a confidentiality agreement was reached.)

252 *usually forced to resign*: Personnel records indicated the rapid turnover during these years, and resignation was the euphemism for "termination," according to former managers who said that employees were threatened with being blackballed from the wine industry if they didn't agree to resign.

252 *the innovator at Mogen David*: According to Paul Merrigan, Neil Sweeney, and others.

253 *Bertsch was proud of his technique:* According to interviews with former Gallo managers.

253 *After the meeting Bertsch and Witter:* According to Merrigan, who attended many of these sessions.

254 *he recalled one incident in which David's:* Paul Merrigan provided recollections of "Uncle Mike" in Henderson as well as the story of his death and later funeral arrangements. Father Benjamin Franzinelli and Las Vegas Gallo distributor Jim Costello also recalled the lunch meeting with David Gallo and Charlie Rossi in the Las Vegas restaurant.

257 *Ernest, however, would later pay:* According to the *Modesto Bee*, September 27, 1986.

258 *At a meeting called to discuss:* Related by Paul Merrigan.

260 *in a meeting with Ernest:* Recreated from reports by Neil Sweeney, Bernie Weiner, and others who heard the story.

261 *"David and Joey seemed to want to prove":* Interview with Bernie Weiner.

NINE

PAGE

262 I'll lose the ranch: According to story told by Al Fenderson to Gallo employees.

262 *In 1967 Chavez's United Farm Workers:* Background of UFW dispute with Gallo from Ronald B. Taylor, *Chavez and the Farm Workers* (Boston: Beacon Press, 1975); Jacques Levy, *Cesar Chavez, Autobiography of La Causa* (New York: W. W. Norton & Company, 1975); John Gregory Dunne, *Delano*, revised and updated (New York: Farrar, Straus & Giroux, 1971).

262 *"In the beginning Ernest admired":* Interview with Neil Sweeney. He also speculated that because of Catholic clergy's early support for farm workers, Julio's son Bob Gallo had liked Chavez and his efforts (Bob Gallo had served on several civil rights committees in Stanislaus County as well). Mike Gallo agreed, recalling that in 1967 Bob had said to his father, "I'm good friends with Chavez. Let him come in, sign with him for your vineyards." According to John Whiting and Mike, Joe did not sign with either union.

263 *The Teamsters had first supported:* Teamsters background from Ronald B. Taylor, cited above, and Steven Brill, *The Teamsters* (New York: Simon & Schuster, 1978).

263 *he now went to court:* According to the *San Francisco Chronicle*, April 29, 1967; Stanislaus County Superior Court issued temporary restraining order on same day, confirmed in court records.

263 *On August 7, sixty-eight of:* According to the *San Francisco Chronicle*, August 8, 1967.

264 *Under the new leadership of Frank Fitzsimmons:* Background of Teamsters politics leading to new campaign against Chavez provided by Taylor and Brill, both cited above.

265 *"What happened at Gallo was":* According to Chavez, quoted in Levy (cited above), and confirmed by UFW.

265 *The winery sent Al Fenderson:* According to a former Gallo employee. Chavez's remarks confirmed by the *San Francisco Chronicle*, August 9, 1973.

265 *When the sheriff arrived:* According to the *San Francisco Chronicle*, August 9, 1973, which reported Chavez's remark.

266 *the situation became explosive:* According to Taylor (cited above) and the

San Francisco Chronicle, August 28, and August 30, 1973, which reported arrests of sixty picketers.

266 *a $100 million class action lawsuit:* Reported by the *San Francisco Examiner*, December 9, 1973.

266 *Joe Gallo was drawn into:* Interviews with Whiting and Mike Gallo, who both confirmed that Joe Gallo did not sign with the UFW either in 1967, even though he had been urged to do so by Ernest and Julio, or in 1973. Yet because his vineyards were identified with the sign Joseph Gallo Vineyards, he was picketed because of his name.

267 *Gallo's national sales slipped:* According to state tax records, cited by George Baker in *The New York Times*, July 16, 1974.

267 *even by as much as 30 percent:* According to former Gallo sales managers. While denying any effect from the boycott, the winery still refused to divulge any sales figures and the boycott's effect could only be estimated. (See, for example, the *San Francisco Examiner*, March 12, 1975.)

267 *During the 1974 graduation ceremonies:* According to the *San Francisco Chronicle*, June 7, 1974.

267 *"Ernest wanted a daily report":* Interview with Paul Merrigan, who also described Ernest's appearance on *60 Minutes*.

268 *now began to grant interviews:* For example, to *The New York Times* (cited above) and the *San Francisco Chronicle*, April 30, 1974.

268 *Gallo distributors were also expected to lend a hand:* According to Herb Caen, the *San Francisco Chronicle*, April 23, 1975, Arvin E. Anderson, better known in the winery as Bud Anderson, head of Gallo Bay Sales in South San Francisco, offered payment to employees to send letters supporting the winery to Governor Jerry Brown. Caen reported that fourteen hundred letters were sent to the governor, but Anderson explained, "Not one person would accept payment. They felt it was their duty as loyal Gallo employees to contribute their letters."

269 *"Ernest has always treated me":* According to Angelo Bufalino, who also recounted his background and confirmed his relationship to William (Bill) Bufalino.

269 *William (Bill) Bufalino, the Teamsters':* Backgrounds and relationship of William and Russell Bufalino, as well as their ties to the Teamsters and the Mafia, according to Jonathan Kwitny, *Vicious Circles, The Mafia in the Marketplace* (New York: W. W. Norton, 1979); Ovid Demaris, *The Last Mafioso* (New York: Times Books, 1981); David E. Scheim, *Contract on America, the Mafia Murder of President John F. Kennedy* (New York: Zebra Books, 1988); Michael Dorman, *Payoff* (New York: Berkeley Books, 1972).

269 *"Bill was part of the International":* Interview with Angelo Bufalino. According to Neil Sweeney and others, at the time of Bufalino's remarked-upon trips to Washington, D.C., Gallo colleagues asked him if he were acting as an intermediary between the winery and the Teamsters. Despite Bufalino's repeated denials, the colleagues were not convinced that he played no role, since they had also noticed that Gallo executives seemed to take pride in having direct and immediate access to the Teamsters' highest offices.

269 *Dan Solomon had worked:* According to Becky McClure in the *Modesto Bee*, March 17, 1986. (Until she left the newspaper in 1987, McClure wrote most of the feature articles about the Gallo Winery.) Solomon's main responsibility now seems to be explaining that he as well as Ernest and Julio have no comment. As he quips in the McClure article, "I'm Dan Solomon, the Gallo spokesman, who is unavailable for comment."

269 "We believe we have turned the other cheek": Ernest quoted by George Baker in The New York Times, July 16, 1974.

270 could exert more influence by: Confirmed by Neil Sweeney. The UFW then filed a complaint of an illegal secondary boycott with the National Labor Relations Board, according to the San Francisco Chronicle, April 6, 1974. (The complaint was dismissed on April 19, 1974, the NLRB having found that the Teamsters' action did not constitute a secondary boycott.)

270 one morning Ken Bertsch phoned: According to Paul Merrigan, who recreated his meeting with the Teamsters official and the phone call made in his presence.

271 ruled that the local injunctions: San Francisco Chronicle, July 3, 1974.

271 $225 million federal antitrust: San Francisco Chronicle, January 3, 1975.

271 demanded free television ads: San Francisco Chronicle, August 28, 1974.

271 charging that the Gallo name: This, and the complaint about Madria, Madria Sangria, according to the Modesto Bee, December 17, 1974, and the San Francisco Chronicle, March 3, 1975 (the latter erroneously calling Ofelia "Argentinean").

272 Al Fenderson and Joey, however: Description of Joey and Fenderson's new advertising campaign and coaching of Ofelia provided by Neil Sweeney. After the UFW's complaint was filed, the winery charged that Chavez's organization had gone "too far by attacking members of the Gallo family," according to the Modesto Bee, May 4, 1975.

272 Fred Ross, who headed: According to Taylor, Chavez and the Farm Workers (cited above).

272 "while our striking workers have had": San Francisco Chronicle, February 23, 1975.

272 more than ten thousand strong: Published police estimates, although UFW spokespersons estimated fifteen thousand in attendance, according to Levy, Cesar Chavez, Autobiography of La Causa (cited above). Gallo banner described and Chavez speech quoted in San Francisco Examiner, March 2, 1975. In the Modesto Bee, May 4, 1975, Walter Bregman refuted "UFW's irresponsible accusations." The winery also circulated a pamphlet at shopping centers listing UFW charges and countering with "Facts."

273 the California legislature passed: According to Levy (cited above) and reported in the San Francisco Examiner, June 22, 1975.

273 The Teamsters nominally won: According to the San Francisco Chronicle, September 11, 1975.

273 the ALRB issued a complaint: According to the San Francisco Chronicle, November 13, 1975.

273 On March 10, 1977, Fitzsimmons: Reported in the San Francisco Chronicle.

274 But the Teamsters then withdrew: According to the San Francisco Chronicle, January 3, 1981, when the Gallo Livingston vineyard 1975 votes were retabulated in line with ALRB's designation of eligible voters, the Teamsters still won, but only by a margin of five votes (237–232).

274 Chavez formally declared its termination: San Francisco Chronicle, February 1, 1978.

274 ALRB Judge David Nevins announced: San Francisco Chronicle, December 9, 1978.

274 the 1975 election should be set aside: San Francisco Chronicle, April 21, 1981; the ALRB also ordered the winery to rehire the two workers who had been fired for union activity.

275 couldn't adequately represent Gallo brands: According to Jacklyn Fierman, "How Gallo Crushes the Competition," Fortune, September 1, 1986, when

George Frank was asked about Ernest's attempts to persuade distributors to sell his wines exclusively, he explained, "We never told distributors to throw out Gallo competitors. But we might have asked them how they planned to do justice if they carried two competing brands."

275   *flung the winery's net wider:* According to Robert Huntington and former sales managers and distributors.

275   *two separate winery sales teams:* According to *Market Watch*, May 1988, and interviews with Angelo Bufalino, Paul Merrigan, and others.

276   *the FTC undertook an official:* Confirmed in FTC Case No. 2836 and published Consent Order.

276   *"Instead Ken just marched in":* According to Gary Glasgow, confirmed by other former sales managers.

277   *Gallo "has used its dominant position":* According to the FTC Consent Order, which also presented sales figures that Ernest was loath to make public. Sales had declined in 1972–73, but the winery's share of the market was still 28.8 percent of all wine sold in the United States, and Gallo's 1973 sales of approximately 100 million gallons were twice those of its nearest competitor. Its shares of table wine, sparkling wine, and dessert wine sales were 31 percent, 34.8 percent, and 24.8 percent respectively. Consent Order published August 26, 1976, in "Federal Trade Commission Decisions" (pp. 256–62). Signing of order reported in the *San Francisco Chronicle*, May 20, 1976, which quoted a winery spokesman's denial of the FTC's allegations: "[The] consent order was proposed for settlement purposes only, which did not involve any admission that we violated any law. We're confident we would be able to prove that the FTC charges are without merit." The spokesman added that winery lawyers had warned that defending against the charges would "require substantial attention by our executive staff for an extended period of time," and hence the consent order was signed to "terminate the disruption."

277   *to raise their outstanding bill:* According to Paul Merrigan, who provided an example of the winery's attempt to drive one of the distributors in his region out of business by raising the price of warehoused wine, then demanding immediate payment. In this instance, the distributor came up with the additional money to pay the higher billing and forestalled the winery's attempt to take over the distributorship.

277   *Witter had become increasingly restless:* According to former employees of the winery, confirmed by friends of Witter.

278   *What had been a direct route:* According to a former marketing executive, confirmed by sales directors.

279   *were "strongly advised" by Ken Bertsch:* Confirmed by Paul Merrigan and others.

279   *had the impression, sometimes confirmed:* Robert Huntington, for example, recalled the effect of "blacklisting" when he left Gallo and no other winery would hire him, despite his years of experience. When he and another former winery employee established a wine-marketing consulting company, he was told by distributors that they had been advised not to carry wines represented by his company or they would lose their Gallo contracts. Other former executives reported either not being hired by other wineries or being fired from positions at other wineries because, as they were told by inside sources, Ernest or his representatives, like Bertsch, had intervened.

279   *sales leveled off:* According to winery employees and wine industry estimates.

280 *Julio was to receive:* According to the *San Francisco Chronicle*, June 29, 1975.

280 *by having his engineers develop a machine:* According to the *Modesto Bee*, September 5, 1975, which included remarks by Gallo's engineers, James Fox, who designed the picking aid, and Hayward Hawke, who explained the winery's opposition to mechanical harvesting: "Particles of leaves were torn from vines," and were too small to be removed by the "stemming machine," and as a result flavored the fermenting wine. Mike Gallo confirmed that the winery dislikes mechanically harvested grapes, adding that the Joseph Gallo vineyards were always picked by hand.

280 *a few growers would file formal grievances:* According to the *Modesto Bee*, March 14, 1984, and August 27, 1987, a lawsuit filed by a Lodi grower and a class action lawsuit brought on behalf of members of the Napa Valley Cooperative alleged that the winery's practice of downgrading and underpaying contracts had been going on since "at least 1977." In 1984, a Sonoma grower also filed a grievance with the California Department of Agriculture. According to Jacklyn Fierman, "How Gallo Crushes the Competition," *Fortune*, September 1, 1986, the state ruled in Gallo's favor, but the winery now gives "one-year contracts in Sonoma County that spell out its standards." The Lodi grower's 1987 suit was eventually settled out of court. Other growers expressed general satisfaction with the winery's grower relations department, although they conceded that "downgrading and postharvest price negotiation for growers' cooperatives bulk wine have been a problem." Winery spokesmen have repeatedly denied charges of downgrading, calling such complaints "frivolous and completely unfounded."

281 *continued complaints from growers:* Such complaints, usually off the record, are also described by Glen Martin, "The Biggest, Little Old Winemakers in the World," *West* magazine, *San Jose Mercury-News*, August 19, 1990. According to Mike Gallo, he has heard similar complaints from fellow growers, and contrary to their belief that he and his father have received preferential treatment from the winery, they, too, "have had our grapes downgraded many times over the years, even before our lawsuit with Ernest and Julio."

281 *bought the McHenry Mansion:* According to the *Modesto Bee*, April 17, 1976. Ernest's donation to Memorial Hospital announced in the *Modesto Bee*, December 4, 1977. Listings of Ernest and Julio's charitable contributions from the Gallo Foundations tax records and annual reports, Form 990-AR IRS, and published by Becky McClure in the *Modesto Bee*, December 13, 1981.

281 *parceling out contributions under:* According to the 1991 Citizen Action's study of political campaign funding, which listed the Gallo family's contributions by individual family members.

281 *In 1978, Senator Cranston:* Description of Cranston's presentation, support, "timely assist," and the passage of the Gallo Wine amendment in House and Senate according to the *Los Angeles Times*, June 17, 1978, and the *San Francisco Chronicle*, June 17, 1978, and October 12, 1978. Political columnist Nicholas von Hoffman announced, "Congress passes a bill for the rich" in the *Chicago Tribune*, October 28, 1978, and noted that the Gallo tax break had been buried in a quickly passed (and probably unread) complicated piece of legislation.

283 *But Cranston continued to defend:* Cranston's remarks reported by the *San Francisco Chronicle*, October 12, 1978.

283 *Cranston received twenty checks:* As the Citizen Action report put it, on one day alone (April 13, 1989), "Cranston raked in 20 $1,000 checks from individual [Gallo] family members" (also reported in the *Modesto Bee*, May 22, 1991).

283 *Political analysts considered Kim Cranston's* and *As the Keating–Lincoln Savings:* According to Stephen Pizzo, Mary Fricker, and Paul Muolo, *Inside Job, The Looting of America's Savings & Loans* (New York: Harper-Collins, 1991).

284 *The ensuing tax-court case:* Mark Gallo Estate Tax Court Case decision in *Tax Court Memorandum Decisions,* Docket No. 24465-82, p. 470 (decision issued on July 22, 1985).

285 *One day in 1979:* Reconstruction of Ernest's reading *Chronicle* article, his "discovery" of Gallo Salame, and his earlier reaction to the brand name from EDepo, JOSJ, and TT, in which Ernest's deposition in the Gallo Salame case was cited. E. & J. Gallo Winery v. Consolidated Foods (Gallo Salame), Case No. 80232, filed in U.S. Court, Eastern District, Fresno (original complaint filed October 14, 1980); following 1983 settlement, the case, accession number 21-87-0041, was held under seal at the Federal Records Center in San Bruno, California, until it was introduced as exhibits in the 1988 winery suit against Joe.

286 *Later Ernest would insist:* According to Ernest's deposition in the 1980 suit against Gallo Salame, cited in 1988 GWSJ Exhibits, which also provided Ernest's recollection of meeting Cummings in Greece, visiting him in New York, and his suspicions of Cummings's motives.

288 *"It's just bullshit":* Julio's remark recalled by Joe in interview; in his testimony in 1988 TT, he said that Julio had called it a name he did not want to repeat in court.

288 *Joe supposed it:* According to interview and confirmed by Whiting.

288 *Oliver Wanger, the winery's Fresno:* According to Gallo Salame case file and confirmed by Judge Price's later order compelling Julio to testify in the 1988 case.

288 *Julio claimed to have:* Remarks from Ernest's and Julio's depositions in Gallo Salame case cited in 1988 GWSJ Exhibits, JOSJ, and TT.

289 *Was Mr. Gallo aware of a disease:* From Ernest's deposition in Gallo Salame case, included in 1988 GWSJ Exhibits.

290 *Judge Crocker focused on the problem of* laches: He later confirmed by telephone that he had been surprised that the winery was bringing the lawsuit after doing nothing about the Gallo Salame trademark for fifteen or twenty years.

290 *As he later explained:* According to Ernest's testimony in 1988 TT.

291 *Within the next few weeks:* Settlement conferences, participants, and June 8, 1983, agreement and license recorded in documents of the Gallo Salame case and included in GWSJ Exhibits and JOSJ.

291 *In return, Ernest agreed to pay $2 million:* Confirmed by EDepo, JOSJ, and Ernest's testimony in 1988 TT.

291 *"All of our deals at the winery":* According to Ernest's testimony in 1988 TT.

TEN

295 *"What are you going to call"*: Story told by Joe and Patricia Gallo.

296 *so Joe first showed him around:* Joe's version from JODepo and Joe's testimony in TT, as well as interviews with Joe, Patricia, and Mike Gallo. The substance of the exchange would become a matter of dispute.

296 *Although Ernest would later have a different version:* According to EDepo and Ernest's testimony in TT.

296 *Mike thought he'd never seen:* Interview with Mike Gallo.

297 *"Well, there's a lawsuit, boys!":* According to John Whiting.

297 *Intensifying their efforts:* Reported by the *San Francisco Examiner,* September 1, 1985. According to winery announcements to the press, Gallo had released its first vintage-dated varietals in October 1983 (the *San Francisco Chronicle,* October 13, 1983). Description of the construction of new winery cellar, "as long as two football fields" with storage facilities for more than 2.6 million gallons of wine and installation of large oak casks (made from Yugoslavian oak by Italian coopers), reported in the *Modesto Bee,* January 27, 1987. The area above the underground facilities became the landing pad for the winery's helicopter. Julio and Bob Gallo's 1977 purchase and excavation of old Frei Winery vineyards (Laguna and Dry Creek ranches) in Sonoma County according to the *San Francisco Chronicle,* January 21, 1982, and the *Modesto Bee,* September 7, 1986.

297 *Young & Rubicam suddenly resigned:* The *San Francisco Chronicle,* August 5, 1981. An *Adweek* survey of agencies termed Gallo "the least desirable" and quoted the most common complaint that Ernest was "a one-man show," according to the *San Francisco Chronicle,* April 10, 1982. On May 2, 1988, *The New York Times* featured a piece quoting several advertising executives' complaints about Ernest Gallo, and headlined the article, "The Client Whom Ad Agencies Hate to Love." One executive commented that if he were to write his memoirs, at least one chapter would be devoted to "the trauma and torment" of working for the winery and would be titled, "Sentenced to the Gallos."

298 *Aware of the extraordinary success:* According to former Gallo marketing and sales directors and confirmed in Conaway, *Napa* (cited above) and in Jay Stuller and Glen Martin, *Through the Grapevine* (New York: Wynwood Press, 1989).

298 *even the folksy promotions for Boone's Farm:* According to Paul Merrigan and others.

299 *to endow the Ernest Gallo Clinic:* According to the *Modesto Bee,* April 1, 1983. The headline, however, read "Gallow endows . . . ," prompting the editor of the paper to write an apology, which included a long explanation of how the "typo" had crept in. Others suspected that the "Gallow" reference was no accident and that someone at the newspaper was indulging in "gallows humor."

299 *Ernest had also set out:* According to the *San Francisco Chronicle,* October 7, 1982, which quotes Ernest's argument (filed with the FTC) while noting that *Impact* (a wine-marketing magazine) estimated that Gallo had shipped over 131 million gallons of wine during the previous year. The *Chronicle* confirmed the FTC's three-to-one ruling to release the winery from the 1976 ten-year restrictive order on May 21, 1983.

299 *several independent distributors:* According to cases originally filed in fed-

eral court in Boston, Sioux Falls, and Cleveland (Pappas and Premier lawsuits discussed in following chapter and cited below). According to the *San Francisco Chronicle*, July 7, 1984, when Rutman refused to comply with the winery's demands, Ernest dropped him and took on Wine Distributors, Inc., as his representative. Rutman also charged that Ernest had convinced Art Ciocca to transfer Franzia's Wines to Wine Distributors, Inc. Rutman asked for a permanent injunction preventing Gallo from dropping it as a distributor as well as for $800,000 in damages. (The court ruled in Gallo's favor, but Rutman has appealed.)

300   *In late August 1984, Ernest arrived:* According to EDepo and 1988 TT. Ernest's "discovery" of the label and his ensuing telephone conversation(s) and meetings with Joe and Mike from EDepo, JODepo, TT, and interviews with Joe and Mike Gallo and John Whiting. (Again, Ernest's and Joe's recollections about these incidents differed, and the narrative is reconstructed from both versions as well as from Mike Gallo's recollections.) Ernest's and Julio's recollections of ensuing meetings are not available, since, in the 1988 court proceedings, Joe's attorney Denis Rice moved that these be excluded from deposition and court testimony. The judge agreed, ruling that they were settlement conferences. Mike Gallo later claimed that this added to their problems: "It was at these preliminary meetings that Ernest, Julio, and Owen admitted that there was really no problem with confusion between Joe's cheese and the winery's wine, that it was simply because of the winery's agreement with Gallo Salame. It was only later in the case that the winery began to insist that the problem was 'confusion and dilution.' "

302   *Joe and Mike arrived in Ernest's office:* First meeting with Ernest and Julio and Julio's tears recalled by Mike Gallo. He also confirmed that his father and he could not understand Julio's tearful outburst but that later they thought it might have been because of the disputed inheritance.

304   *"to work together":* Julio would later dispute that his mother had added this phrase, recalling instead that her final words were "All I want is for you boys to get along."

305   *On October 15, Whiting:* October 15 meeting of Joe, Mike, and John Whiting with Ernest, Julio, and Owen according to Whiting and Mike Gallo, and JODepo.

305   *"this isn't going to be fun":* Joe's remark recalled by Whiting and Mike Gallo.

307   *Ernest rushed out the door:* According to Whiting. The separate conversation with his two brothers recalled by Joe, confirmed by Mike and Whiting's recollection of Joe's description of the brief conversation immediately thereafter.

308   *On October 25, 1984, Al Herzig:* Herzig's letter introduced into 1988 court record; his opinion later confirmed by him.

308   *it wasn't until December 13, 1984:* According to 1988 court records and confirmed by Whiting.

309   *Indeed, on April 19, 1985:* Letter enclosing draft of license agreement confirmed by Whiting and testified to by Ernest in 1988 TT.

309   *Herzig was particularly adamant:* According to Herzig.

309   *On May 1, 1985, Joe wrote:* According to Whiting.

309   *on June 21, when he had returned:* Recalled by Whiting and Mike Gallo.

311   *When the others left, Joe stayed:* Described by Joe to Mike, who recalled that "they were surprised to see [Joe] smiling."

311 *"We can't go along with this"*: Ernest's remark and August meeting recalled by Whiting.

312 *On October 28, 1985, Ernest called:* Letter and proposed complaint drafted by Elliot S. Kaplan confirmed by Whiting.

312 *Joe was so upset that he phoned Julio:* Recalled by Whiting and Mike Gallo.

312 *listed even more restrictions:* According to Whiting, who described his speculation about Ernest's motives.

313 *"Look, Joe":* According to Mike Gallo, who described his shock at Ernest's remark.

314 *"I'm sick and tired of this whole thing"* and *"Just put in what will protect us":* According to Whiting.

314 *he called Joe on February 3:* Ernest's phone conversation, February 3, 1986, and his February 16, 1986, letter confirmed by Whiting.

315 *On March 12 he wrote Ernest:* Recalled by Whiting. March 21 meeting at winery described by Whiting and Mike Gallo.

316 *"Jesus, I'm never going to":* Joe's remark in the car recalled by Whiting and Mike Gallo.

316 *the complaint just filed by Ernest:* E. & J. Gallo Winery v. Gallo Cattle Company, Joseph E. Gallo, Michael D. Gallo, Case No. CV-F-86-183-EDP, filed April 17, 1986, in Federal District Court, Eastern District of California, Fresno.

317 *was known as a scrappy courtroom fighter:* According to the *Los Angeles Times*, September 29, 1987. Lynch's background, his hiring by the winery, and his feeling that this was "a slam dunk trademark infringement" from interview.

319 *Joe brought Mike and Kenny:* Described by Mike Gallo and Kenny Jelacich; also recounted in Mike and Bob's depositions, JODepo, JULDepo, and 1988 TT. Julio's subsequent written assurance of grape purchases by winery confirmed by Mike and John Whiting.

320 *"What business was your father in?":* Whiting's conversation with Joe, according to interview with Whiting and his deposition.

321 *On May 22, 1986, he met with Joe again* and *drove directly to the Stanislaus County Courthouse:* According to Whiting's deposition and recollection.

324 *and he agreed to meet with:* Joe's gradual understanding of what the documents meant recounted by Joe and Mike Gallo in interviews, as well as in JODepo and Whiting's deposition.

325 *"Shouldn't we get to the matter":* According to Joe Gallo interview, JODepo, EDepo, and JULDepo. Mike Gallo and Whiting recalled how Joe described the meeting immediately afterward as well.

327 *On June 9, Joe sent Ernest a letter:* According to Whiting.

327 *On June 19, Shastid met:* Recalled by Whiting in deposition and in interview.

328 *At seven o'clock one morning:* Ernest and Joe's conversation at Joe's home reconstructed from interview with Joe, JODepo, and EDepo.

330 *"Joe kept a copy of his mother's will":* According to John Whiting. Mike Gallo confirmed that Ernest had urged a cash settlement, but that his father's belief that his parents' wishes had been betrayed strengthened his resolve to pursue the counterclaims.

ELEVEN

332 *On July 31, 1986, Jackson filed:* In Federal District Court, Eastern District of California, Fresno, Case No. CV-F-86-183-EDP.
332 *"Usually I love cases that have":* Interview with Pat Lynch.
333 *his mother's handwritten will:* Photograph in *The Wine Spectator*, October 31, 1986, accompanying James Laube's article, "Gallo vs. Gallo."
334 *On February 9, while being prepared:* As described in Judge Price's Memorandum Decision, December 17, 1987.
334 *Pat Lynch, who later confirmed:* According to Memorandum Decision; Lynch confirmed that his client's "health was a concern" in interview.
334 *On February 11, the day after:* Description of this meeting reconstructed by Joe Gallo and confirmed by Mike Gallo, who recalled his father's account and the proposed settlement.
336 *But the following week:* According to Whiting.
337 *Dr. Joe Tupin, a professor:* Tupin's academic position and specialty, date of examination by Drs. Epstein and Tupin, and their conclusions according to Judge Price's Memorandum Decision, December 17, 1987.
337 *The winery lawyers moved:* Winery's motion to close hearing, and Howard, Rice and newspapers' objections argued July 13, 1987; transcript of proceedings filed August 6, 1987.
338 *concluding that it would be unfair to:* According to Judge Price's Memorandum Decision, December 17, 1987.
338 *the three brothers' depositions began:* Ernest's deposition taken January 25–29, February 1–4, 8–12, 16–17, 1988; Julio's deposition, February 16–19, 22–26, 29, March 1, 3–4, 1988; Joseph Edward's deposition, January 27–29, February 1–4, 8–10, 1988.
341 *were still wrangling:* Confirmed in the many exchanges of memos filed in the court record.
341 *John Whiting and Al Herzig maintained:* According to interviews in which they also described being "squeezed out of the case."
343 *Under the federal court's Local Rule 123:* "Counsel who has reason to believe that an action on file or about to be filed is related to another action on file (whether or not dismissed or otherwise terminated) shall promptly file . . . a Notice of Related Cases."
344 *Judge Price was reputed to be:* According to the *Fresno Bee*, April 17, 1988.
344 *In one instance, the court:* The *Fresno Bee*, September 14, 1988.
344 *He was one of two adopted sons:* Background of Wanger provided by the Wanger family, professional listings of McCormick, Barstow partners, as well as his remarks to me during 1988 court proceeding.
344 *who in 1951 scandalized:* Story of movie producer Walter Wanger's shooting of Bennett's agent from many news articles at the time, including the *Los Angeles Examiner*, December 14 and December 21, 1951.
344 *"I've been dinged":* Wanger quoted in the *Fresno Bee* article, April 17, 1988, which also refers to his reputation as Judge Price's "favorite attorney."
344 *Judge Price had extensive:* Price's background described in the *Fresno Bee* article, April 17, 1988, and by Linda Di Pietro in the *Modesto Bee*, November 13, 1988.
344 *Frank Damrell, Jr., a partner:* Frank Damrell, Jr. and Sr.'s backgrounds from professional listing as well as the *Modesto Bee*, June 22, 1955, and December 12, 1968.

345 *Linda Gallo Jelacich, who lived:* Confirmed in interview, as well as by "Defendants Motion to Disqualify," filed November 14, 1988.

345 *In November 1982, the C. Pappas:* C. Pappas Company v. E. & J. Gallo Winery, Case No. CV-F-83-296-EDP. (The initials EDP indicated that Judge Edward Dean Price was assigned the case. The original filing, however, showed the initials REC, indicating that Judge Robert Coyle had first been assigned.) The Civil Minute Order transferred the case from Coyle to Price and was signed by the two judges, August 10, 1983.

346 *three attorneys for the Pappas:* D. Peter Harvey, Richard Oetheimer, and Robert Paul confirmed that it was their impression that Coyle had stepped down because of his previous partnership with Oliver Wanger at Mc-Cormick, Barstow.

346 *"All motions will be heard by E.D.P.":* The order appears in large print on the covering sheet of the docket, as well as on page 2, in larger typeface than other docket entries.

346 *granted the winery's motion for summary judgment:* Granted May 23, 1985 (Judge Price's decision, 610 F.Supp. 662). Decision upheld by Ninth Circuit Court of Appeals.

346 *In 1986 Judge Price heard another case:* Premier Wine and Spirits of South Dakota, Inc. v. E. & J. Gallo Winery, a foreign corporation, Case No. CV-F-84-657 (EDP). Winery's Motion for Summary Judgment granted by Judge Price, September 23, 1986 (644 F.Supp. 1431).

346 *Judge Price then presided:* According to the *Modesto Bee*, March 3, 1987, and June 4, 1987.

347 *Judge Price issued two decisions:* Memorandum Decisions in CV-F-86-183-EDP, filed in U.S. District Court, Eastern District of California, August 29, 1988. Findings of Fact and Conclusions of Law, filed October 3, 1988.

349 *"It makes sense to try to avoid":* According to interview with Pat Lynch.

349 *Denis Rice filed two motions:* Motion for Stay Pending Appeal and Bifurcation of Trial Issues, October 12, 1988; oral arguments heard October 31, and Judge Price's denial of motions, issued November 1, 1988.

349 *Judge Price consented to:* Account of attempts to interview, agreement to appointment, and her impression recalled by Linda Di Pietro. The *Modesto Bee* article, November 13, 1988, quotes Price's remark, "If any party to this action . . ." Judge Price's conference call to attorneys according to "Memorandum in Support of Defendants' Motion to Disqualify" and Mike Gallo.

351 *"But we weren't told":* According to interview with Mike Gallo. (The Howard, Rice Motion to Disqualify confirms that Joe's attorneys had, at least tacitly, agreed to the transfer to Coyle during their conference call with Judge Price.)

351 *Mike and Joe left the lawyers:* According to Mike Gallo, neither he nor his father saw Sparer's motion before it was filed, but they had given their verbal approval, presuming they knew the basis for the motion. According to Howard, Rice attorneys, Mike and Joe were fully aware of the terms of the recusal motion and the agreed-upon transfer of the case to Judge Coyle.

351 *the winery attorneys drafted their response:* According to E. & J. Gallo Winery's Opposition to Defendants' Motion to Disqualify, Lynch and Wanger were notified of Rice's intention to ask Price to recuse himself at 5:00 P.M., November 10, only "two business days before the trial . . . was scheduled to begin."

351 *"the Court is not convinced":* According to Judge Price's "Order Transferring Case," filed November 14, 1988.

351 *"Defendants do not claim"*: According to a footnote in Defendants' Motion to Disqualify, cited above.

352 *The Howard, Rice motion also seemed to imply*: Judge Price, too, seemed to imply as much in his order transferring the case. He wrote, "In keeping with the Court's private and public representations, this case is transferred to Judge Robert Coyle."

352 *Denis Rice had then rejected*: According to Mike Gallo and confirmed by Sparer letter to Wanger in court record. (The April 29, 1988, Settlement Conference was eventually heard by Judge Edward J. Garcia in Sacramento, not by Coyle.)

352 *Robert Coyle was another local*: Background of Robert E. Coyle from professional listings, as well as from U.S. Senate Judiciary Committee hearing, March 4, 1982.

353 *When Ernest was impressed*: As Robert Paul, one of Pappas's attorneys, pointed out, when Ernest was impressed with an attorney's work, he tried to hire him. According to Paul, he and Richard Oetheimer were taking Ernest's deposition in the Pappas case, and during a break the winery chairman complimented Oetheimer on the job he was doing. Oetheimer reported the conversation to Paul: Ernest was standing next to him at the men's room urinal and after praising him, added that he would double his salary if he came to work for the winery.

353 *received a bonus*: According to source who confirmed the information with documentary evidence.

353 *he was to be paid an annual*: According to Coyle's 1982 confirmation hearings, in which he explained the terms for withdrawal from his firm. His yearly financial disclosure reports to the Judicial Ethics Committee showed payments from 1983 to 1985 of $21,000, $36,000, and $36,000.

354 *Coyle continued to have financial ties*: Coyle's property holdings listed in his yearly financial disclosures to Judicial Ethics Committee; property investments confirmed in Office of Records in both Fresno and Madera counties. (His investments with former partners continued through 1988.)

354 *valued at close to $1.6 million*: According to the *Fresno Bee*, July 3, 1989.

354 *through Pacific Agriculture*: Background of Pacific Agriculture according to deed and tax records of Fresno and Madera counties.

354 *the proceedings to order at 9:05*: Testimony and descriptions of proceedings in trademark infringement case from Trial Transcript (TT), and from my personal observation, notes, interviews, interpretations.

355 *but Rice had insisted*: According to Whiting.

358 *he added that the story "was unfair"*: That seemed to be Ernest's usual reaction to negative remarks. After the cover story on Ernest and Julio appeared in *Fortune*, September 1, 1986, Ernest was so outraged that he pulled all Gallo advertising (an estimated $650,000 worth) from Time, Inc., publications. According to the *Modesto Bee*, September 11, 1986, Gallo denounced the magazine for its "many vicious and damaging inaccuracies in its treatment of the Gallo Winery and the family." Winery spokesman Dan Solomon cited as inaccurate the story about Ernest and Julio's father chasing them across the field in 1933 and descriptions of David as "occasionally bizarre" and Joey as "uneven."

358 *this was a misfiling by the attorneys*: According to John Whiting, the misfiling may have occurred when the advertising agency delivered its files to his office. At the same time he was compiling Joe's financial records, and his desk was piled with documents when the agency's papers had been placed among them.

359　*During a recess, Joe became more pointed:* Interview with Joe Gallo in court-house hallway.

359　*playing a video of the coverage:* News segment about Joseph Gallo Cheese plant opening, Channel 13, Modesto, June 12, 1983; videocassette and audio portion transcription, submitted to record as Exhibit 10343A.

360　*"Now do you see what a management problem there is at":* Ernest's corridor comments made to me and several other reporters. His comment that there was "cow manure just a few feet away from the front door" was not true; the cheese plant stands across the road from the dairy, and the cow pens are over one hundred yards away.

360　*to prepare a press release:* Press release, "Joseph Gallo Threatens E. & J. with Counter Lawsuit," prepared and distributed to media, December 12, 1988, by Denis Rice.

361　*The following morning newspaper articles:* For example, the *Fresno Bee* and the *Modesto Bee*, December 15, 1988.

362　*The first, a marketing specialist:* Richard Boone, Director of Consumer Research, who, along with Mike Boyd, had prepared brand-mapping reports and image surveys for the winery (including those reports cited above, and entered as Defense Exhibits numbers 5277, 5322, 5308).

362　*Then Dan Solomon, the winery's:* According to TT and Defense Exhibits numbers 5572, 5159, "Consumer Complaints to Winery." On December 16, 1988, the *Fresno Bee* and *Modesto Bee* headlines read, "Gallo Winery Quality Troubles Described," and the article cited the allegations of worms, cockroaches, and "unidentifiable objects" found in Gallo wine.

362　*a national radio news broadcaster:* According to Linda Di Pietro, Wally George had dropped "alleged," which was in her story about the complaints.

362　*Reportedly, he was back:* According to Di Pietro, who was sought out by Jack Owen and asked to contact Ernest by telephone. Apparently Ernest had already complained to her *Modesto Bee* employer, and he now wanted to speak directly to her. Since her story had used the word "alleged," she felt she was on firm ground and refused Ernest's request to print a retraction. The following day, George explained that these were only "alleged" complaints.

TWELVE

PAGE

364　*After all the controversy:* The Gallo Winery had also filed a motion for a court order regarding "Procedures for the Examination of Julio Gallo as a Witness at Trial." (This, again, was sealed.) On November 7, 1988, Judge Price granted the motion, but whatever the procedures the winery's lawyers felt were required, until that morning neither they nor Joe's attorneys had indicated that Julio would be called to testify.

365　*The same language had also been used:* From Bob Gallo's deposition, excerpts of which were included in the court record.

370　*He also felt that he could have shown* and *"He didn't ask me to testify":* According to John Whiting.

371　*"You know what I'd like to tell":* Micah Gallo's comment heard in court-room, and later confirmed by Sherrie Gallo.

371　*she knew her husband actually was shy:* According to interview with Patricia Gallo.

371　*He even resurrected a news story:* Article appeared in the *Los Angeles Daily News*, October 10, 1988. According to Jim Elizarraz, the assistant manager of the supermarket, he said he'd been "pushed like I've never been pushed" by the *Daily News* reporter to say that he had taken Joseph Gallo Cheese off the shelf when the health department first told him to remove all brands of cheese "as a precautionary measure." "Joseph Gallo was the only cheese left to remove because it isn't that popular here," he explained. "It's an Hispanic neighborhood, and people prefer soft cheese for things like enchildas. The reporter threatened to 'give the store a bad write-up' if I didn't say which cheese I'd removed, so I finally told her Joseph Gallo even though I was sure it wasn't the cause. But that's why Joseph Gallo Cheese got slammed in the [first] newspaper [article]." A follow-up story indicated the health department's conclusion that Joseph Gallo Cheese was not the source of the problem.

375 *"To preclude an individual from using"*: Supplemental Posttrial Brief, filed separately by Herzig, January 30, 1989.

375 *Whether this would have affected*: On appeal, the Ninth Circuit later considered and rejected Joe's defense based on the *Friend* decision and the First Amendment.

375 *Judge Coyle issued his decision*: Judge Coyle's Permanent Injunction, filed June 19, 1989, and accompanied by his "Findings of Fact and Conclusions of Law."

376 *"They might as well have shipped"*: From interview with Whiting.

376 *Coyle did not discuss the argument*: According to Sections 14462 and 14463 of the California Business and Professional Code, concerning farm name as trademark for farm products, "Any person selling or marketing the products grown on a farm may use the name of the farm as a trade-mark on the products of the farm, in the same manner as provided for other trademarks, and subject to the same rights and duties. . . . Registration under this article shall have the same effect as the registration of a trade-mark."

377 *"Do you realize what he's saying?"*: According to interview with Whiting.

377 *"I guess it's true"*: Joe's remark recalled by Mike Gallo.

378 *turned the July 31 hearing*: Descriptions and quotations from "Motion for New Trial/Vacate Judgment, Motion for Stay Pending Appeal, Motion to Amend Pretrial Statement, Motion to Disqualify Judge Robert E. Coyle," and Transcript of Proceedings, July 31, 1989 (filed in record, August 3, 1989) and from personal observation and notes.

379 *an unsigned declaration from Denis Rice*: The Defendants' Reply Brief to Plaintiff's Opposition to Motion for New Trial, filed July 24, 1989, had indicated an attached declaration from Denis Rice. It was not included in the filing, however, and Herzig's then associate Joseph Yanny informed the court that it was forthcoming. On July 27, a courier delivered declarations to the court, but they were unsigned; Howard, Rice partner Alan Sparer then informed the court that the declaration in Rice's name "would not be signed by Mr. Rice and should not have been filed." (The court was then also notified that Howard, Rice no longer represented Joe and Mike.)

380 *On August 3, Judge Coyle denied*: "Order re Motion for New Trial or to Alter, Amend or Vacate Judgment," prepared August 3 and filed on August 4, 1989.

381 *He made no mention of his property holdings*: Yanny's remarks about Coyle's property investments and his vineyard holdings had only been made during oral argument and weren't included in written motions. According to the *Fresno Bee*, July 3, 1989, in a 1987 lawsuit, Coyle had ruled against a man claiming that the idea of the famous "dancing raisins" was his and had

been stolen by the California Raisin Advisory Board for its advertising campaign. Coyle was a coinvestor (his share worth $15,000 to $50,000, according to his financial disclosures) in a Kerman vineyard that produced raisins (and whose profits presumably might be affected by a successful advertising campaign). As the *Bee* reported, when Coyle was later asked about the possible conflict in deciding this case, he asserted through a spokeman that "so far as he knows, 'the parties involved in the Kerman vineyard' had no interest in the dancing raisin lawsuit. He declined to elaborate further on his agricultural holdings or discuss his financial disclosure statement." The article also noted his half-interest in a 240-acre vineyard near Davis (sold in 1985) and his recent ruling in favor of the winery. However, Coyle refused to discuss his involvement in vineyards over the years, despite the fact that in these two cases it did raise questions.

381   *to prepare an amicus curiae brief*: Brief of Linda Ann Gallo Jelacich on Behalf of Her Minor Daughter, Ann Marie Jelacich, as Amicus Curiae in Support of Appellants, prepared by Stanley Fleishman, submitted to the United States Court of Appeals for the Ninth Circuit, January 18, 1990. Winery's Opposition to the Motion to File Brief as Amicus Curiae, filed January 22, 1990. Ironically, according to the Senate Judiciary Committee hearings, Judge Coyle had coauthored a *Hastings Law Journal* article on "The Rights of an Adopted Child to Inherit Under the California Probate Code." But in his injunction he seemed to have overlooked the rights of any future adopted child since none would be "born with the name Gallo."

381   *Pat Lynch wrote Whiting to complain* and *"There's going to be"*: According to John Whiting. Whiting's response of January 9, 1990, to Lynch's January 2 letter of complaint included as Exhibit D-3, in the Appeals Brief.

382   *Whiting filed Joe's appeal with*: Defendants' Appeals of Summary Judgment and Trademark Infringement decision, filed with the United States District Court of Appeals for the Ninth Circuit, in San Francisco, January 18, 1990. Winery's Opposition Brief (Appellees' Brief) filed March 3, 1990. Defendants' Reply Brief (Appellants' Brief) filed April 24, 1990.

382   *his cheese sales reached $35 million*: Confirmed by Mike Gallo, who also reported Phil Bava's satisfaction with the 1990 grapes.

383   *On January 2, 1990, Aileen and Julio*: Their automobile accident reported by the *San Jose Mercury-News*, January 3, 1990, January 4, 1990, and January 13, 1990.

383   *"I'm sure Aileen must have"*: Interview with Sherrie Gallo. The *Modesto Bee*, January 12, reported Frank Damrell Jr.'s announcement of "new witnesses" who claimed Aileen was not at fault.

383   *"Funny thing how Ernest"*: According to Mike Gallo.

383   *The CHP, however, was not convinced*: According to investigating officers. The *San Francisco Chronicle*, February 17, 1990, reported the wrongful death suit filed by Kauk, and on February 28, 1990, reported Aileen's no contest plea to vehicular misdemeanor manslaughter.

384   *In 1989, the winery bought the 600-acre*: According to the *Los Angeles Times*, September 19, 1990, and the *San Francisco Chronicle*, November 28, 1991.

385   *"I never know what's going on"*: Julio's comment related by Jack Shinn. According to Shinn, his conversation with Julio ensued when, in 1989, Bob Gallo informed Shinn's Woodbridge Winery, the cooperative established after Prohibition by the Woodbridge Vineyard Association (and different

from the Winery co-owned by Uncle Mike Gallo in 1928), that Gallo would no longer buy its bulk wine. They had done so for many years, and Shinn had complained to Julio about the decision, but to no avail. Julio said he was unaware of the cancellation and implied he could do nothing about it. Because nearly 100 percent of Woodbridge's wine had always been sold to Gallo, Shinn said Gallo's cancellation had forced the board of directors to sell the winery to Sebastiani.

387 *he gave an interview: The Wine Spectator* interview with Ernest, September 15, 1991.

387 *they would market an estate-bottled:* Announced by Ernest in *The Wine Spectator* interview as well as in the *Los Angeles Times*, August 20, 1991.

387 *an estimated 4.3 million cases sold* and *marketing a Hearty Burgundy Limited Release:* According to the *San Jose Mercury-News*, December 4, 1991.

387 *"Golden Turkey Awards":* Announced in the *San Francisco Examiner*, November 30, 1991.

387 *the winery had proclaimed an experiment:* Reported in the *San Francisco Chronicle*, July 12, 1990. On January 25, 1991, the *Chronicle* reported that "after a voluntary seven-month ban," Thunderbird and Night Train Express were returned to shelves, and quoted Nancy Russell, director of the North of Market Planning Coalition, which organized the anti–street wine campaign: "I don't know how they're getting it, but I've seen truckloads of Night Train being delivered to the stores."

388 People, *as well as several tabloid:* The Jeffrey Dahmer photograph appeared in *People*, September 16, 1991, and in tabloids, such as the *Globe*, September 17, 1991.

388 *Angelo (Buff) Bufalino led the winery's:* Confirmed by Bufalino, who also denied wine industry rumors that he was upset that he'd been forced to leave the winery earlier than he had planned.

388 *lobbying the Bureau of Alcohol, Tobacco:* According to the *Modesto Bee*, February 21, 1992, which also reported lobbying efforts by Senators Dole and Seymour and the contributions they had received from Gallo.

389 *In February 1991, after his:* Oliver Wanger confirmed by full Senate as federal judge (U.S. District Court, Eastern District of California) on March 21, 1991, according to press officer of the Senate Judiciary Committee.

389 *he launched his campaign:* Reported by the *San Francisco Chronicle*, November 12, 1991.

389 *Ernest and Julio made another move:* According to Mike and Joe Gallo, who also confirmed the previous verbal and written promises from Julio and the possible consequences of the winery's latest action. Whiting confirmed Ernest's earlier threat to force Joe to accept the license and Joe's proposed legal action.

390 *"because generic wines aren't selling":* Bava's remarks quoted by Mike Gallo.

390 *Joe's impression was reinforced when he read:* According to Joe and Patricia Gallo; Ernest's remark quoted from *The Wine Spectator* interview (cited above).

391 *Three years earlier:* According to *The New York Times*, May 2, 1988, Riney resigned because he expected to be fired from several Gallo brand accounts, which Ernest felt he was not giving enough attention to, such as E & J Brandy. Riney was said to be the originator of the Frank Bartles and Ed Jaymes commercials, and even after his resignation the winery continued to use their characters in their advertising. (In 1992, however, they were dropped from Bartles & Jaymes ads, and the actors went on to promote a golf magazine.)

EPILOGUE

PAGE

392 *United States Court of Appeals for the Ninth Circuit:* Issued for publication February 7, 1992; Judge Fletcher's rulings quoted directly from text.

393 *Joe's attorneys filed a Petition:* Quotations from text of the petition.

394 *From the beginning, Herzig said:* According to Herzig.

394 *On April 28, he filed:* Quotations from text of Herzig's declaration.

395 *On June 22, 1992, Judge:* Order to amend February 7 opinion quoted from text of decision.

395 *he and Patricia decided:* According to Patricia Gallo.

INDEX

Adweek, 297
AFL-CIO, 262, 263
Agricultural Labor Relations Board
 (ALRB), 273, 274
Alcohol Tax Unit, 127, 137, 139, 140, 151
Alicante Bouschet, 40, 51, 60
Alleruzzo, Paul, 60–64, 66–69, 95, 96, 339
Almaden Winery, 247, 267
Amador Dispatch, 29–31
American Airlines, 240
American Society of Enologists, 225, 280
American Vineyard, 158, 159
Amerine, Maynard A., 281
Anderson, A. E. "Bud," 183
Anderson, E. R., 146, 183
André Champagne, 18, 217, 252, 257, 271,
 349
Angelica, 75, 79, 145
Angelo, Petri, 186
Arata, David, 160
Arata, Mabel Coffee, 160
Arlington National Cemetery, 237
Armanino, W. J., 53, 54
Army, U.S., 157–58, 228, 236–37, 344
 Air Corps, 179
 Sixty-third Infantry Regiment, 161
 Twenty-first Technical School
  Squadron, 158

BancItaly Corporation, 73, 87
Bank of America, 52, 105, 116, 118, 122
Bank of Italy, The, 118
Barbera, Charlie, 63, 66, 128, 166, 209
Barberone, 242
Barstow, James H., 287

Bartles & Jaymes, 18, 242, 298, 356
Basciglia family, 187
Bava, Phil, 382, 389, 390
Bennett, Joan, 344
Bertola, Fred, 29
Bertsch, Ken, 178–80, 183–85, 203, 204,
 211, 219, 222, 235, 240, 241, 252–54,
 259, 270, 276–79
Bewley, R. Stuart, 298
Bianco, Aloysius (Ali), 40, 218
Bianco, Assunta, *see* Gallo, Susie Bianco
Bianco, Battista (grandfather), 25–30, 36,
 231
Bianco, Celestina (aunt), *see* Gallo, Celia
 Bianco
Bianco, Lydia (aunt), 36
Bianco, Stella (cousin), *see* Dorais, Stella
 Bianco
Bianco, Tillie (aunt), 25, 27, 28, 92
Bianco, Virginia Campadelli
 (grandmother), 25–29, 73, 80, 231
Bianco, Walter (uncle), 25, 26, 30, 36, 116–
 117
Big Red Book, 240
Blacks, wines marketed to, 189–92, 198–201
"Black Thursday," 82
Bleiweiss, Harry, 188
Blue Heron Ranch, 236
Blue Label Malt Shop, 97
Bolles, John, 226
Bomse, Stephen, 287, 289–90
Bonded Winery No. 60, 80
Boone's Farm wines, 18, 242, 252, 271, 298
Boxer, Barbara, 389
Bregman, Walter, 269, 278

Brengetto, Gino, 115
Brengetto, Peter, 100, 103, 115–16
Brennan, Frank, 264–65, 282, 287
Brennan, William, 265
Bronco Winery, 347
Brown, Jerry, 273, 345
Brown-Forman, 298
Bufalino, Angelo (Buff), 268–69, 388
Bufalino, Russell, 269
Bufalino, William (Bill), 269
Bureau of Alcohol, 118, 120–24, 126, 127,
    129, 135, 138, 183, 196, 340
Bureau of Alcohol, Tobacco, and Firearms
    (BATF), 129, 137, 139, 143, 182, 339,
    340, 347, 388
Bureau of Industrial Alcohol, 119
Burgess Winery, 74
Burgundy, 94
    See also Hearty Burgundy
Burgundy Pastosos, 242

C. Gallo Wines, 171
Cabernet, 79
Cabernet Franc, 384
Cabernet Sauvignon, 17, 242, 245, 384,
    387
Cadlolo, Charles, 52
Cadlolo family, 55
California, University of
    Berkeley, 128, 136, 243, 246, 267
    Davis, 133, 136, 138, 156, 164, 185, 243,
        245, 337
    Hospital, 334
    Law School, 344
    Medical School, 299
California Canners and Growers, 269
California Cooler, 298
California Highway Patrol, 383
California Polytechnic, 225
California State Department of
    Agriculture, 59, 280–81
California State Department of Labor
    Relations, 263
California Vineyardists Association (CVA),
    84, 93
California Wine Advisory Board, 200
California Wine Association, 78–80
California Wine Commission, 201
Campagna, Louis, 210
Campbell's Soup, 183
Canandaigua Wine Company, 188
Canyon Creek Ranch, 384
Capone, Al, 45, 58, 61, 64, 65, 67, 94, 210,
    212, 239
Carignane, 51, 89
Carlo Rossi Vineyards, 18, 244, 271, 280,
    387
Carnegie Tech, 177

Carnelian grapes, 51
Carrasquilla, Ofelia, see Gallo, Ofelia
    Carrasquilla
Carson, Johnny, 359
Carter, Jimmy, 282, 283
Castagnasso, Enrico, 78, 80, 81
Cella Brothers, 52
Chablis Blanc, 18, 243, 387
Champagne, 252
Chardonnay, 17, 242, 387
Chariots of Fire (movie), 298
Charmat, Eugene, 388
Chavez, César, 262–75, 279, 280
Chenin Blanc, 222, 243, 245, 390
Cherokee wine, 200
Chianti, 75, 79
    of California, 214
Chicago Crime Commission, 210, 212
Ciccarelli, Anthony, 83
Ciocca, Art, 248
Cisi, Pete, 90–91, 125, 148
Citizen Action, 283
Claret, 94
Cleary and Zeff, 344
Coast Guard, U.S., 157, 217
Coca-Cola Bottling Company, 248, 299
Coffee, "Bud," 160
Cold Duck, 243
Coleman, James, 194, 195, 199
Coleman, Susan Aileen Gallo, 137, 194,
    218, 222, 249, 320
College of Holy Names, 194
Colson, Charles, 264
Concannon, 43
Congress, U.S., 38, 102, 281, 282
Conn, Donald, 84, 93, 94
Consolidated Foods Corporation, 285, 287,
    289, 291, 308, 353
Constitution, U.S.
    First Amendment, 305, 308, 341, 342,
        354, 374, 375, 377–79
    Fourteenth Amendment, 354, 377
Conway, Peter, 278
Cornell University, 156
Costa, Mary, see Gallo, Mary Costa
Cote D'Oro (restaurant), 203, 345
Cottonwood Ranch, 250, 295
Coyle, Robert, 343, 346, 351, 353–55, 357–
    361, 363–65, 368, 369, 371–81, 389,
    392–95
Cranston, Alan, 281–83, 345, 350
Cranston, Kim, 283
Crawford, Charles, 156, 157, 162, 163, 169,
    185, 211, 222, 229, 231, 242, 333, 341
Creager, William, 111–12
Cream of California Wine, 146
Cresta Blanca, 44, 75, 79, 145, 167, 178
Crete, Michael, 298

Cribari Winery, 187
Crocker, Myron D., 287, 288, 290, 291, 343, 352, 353, 389, 394–95
Culkin, Macaulay, 387
Cummings, Nathan, 285–89
Curzi, Sal, 53

Dahmer, Jeffrey, 388
Damrell, Damrell & Nelson, 344
Damrell, Frank, Jr., 344–45, 350, 383
Damrell, Frank, Sr., 194
Davis, Bruce L., 287
Delfino, Andrew, 227
DeLoca, John, 201
DelRey Cooperative Winery, 187
Del Rio Golf and Country Club, 204, 345
Democratic party, 194, 283, 389
Depression, the, 85, 92, 113, 329
DeRosi, Pete, 79, 82
Dibiaso, Nicholas, 287
DiLucca, Don, 62, 68–69
Di Pietro, Linda, 349–50
Distillers Outlet, 146
Dole, Robert, 283, 388
Donahue, Jack, 240
Dorais, Bill, 205
Dorais, Stella Bianco, 36, 40, 117, 205–6, 218
Dow Chemical, 268
Dry Creek Corporation, 282, 284, 285

E. & J. Brandy, 18
Eden Roc, 18, 215, 217, 252
Empire Traction Company, 120
Emporium, 96
Epstein, Leon, 334, 337, 338, 340
Ernest Gallo Foundation, 281
Escalon Tribune, 50
Escola Ranch, 174, 221, 236
Esola, Frank, 33–35
Ewell, Ben, 354
Ewell, Roland D., 354

Federal Bureau of Investigation (FBI), 94, 210
Federal Communications Commission (FCC), 271
Federal Election Commission, 388
Federal Land Bank, 105, 116
Federal Trade Commission (FTC), 240, 271, 272, 276–79, 284, 287, 299, 360
Fenderson, Albion "Al," 177–79, 187–91, 203, 210–11, 214, 216, 217, 243, 262, 265, 272, 278
Fiala, Marie, 287
Field, Mervin, 362, 372, 379
Fine, Richard, 320
Fiscalini, I. W., 149–51, 153, 154

Fitzsimmons, Frank, 264, 267, 274
"Flavor-Guard" bottle, 199
Fleishman, Stanley, 381
Fletcher, Betty, 385–86, 392–95
Folda, Charles, 33
Folsom Prison, 35
Forbes magazine, 18
Forresti, Dante, 52, 118, 186
Fortune magazine, 18
Foster Farms restaurant, 319, 365, 367, 369, 390
Fowler, Robert, 150, 152, 153, 322–25
Foxx, Redd, 244
Franek (distributor), 146
Frank, George, 215, 241, 279
Franzia, Amelia, see Gallo, Amelia Franzia
Franzia, Carlyse, 248
Franzia, Giuseppe, 55, 96, 135
Franzia, Teresa, 124
Franzia Winery, 62, 66, 95, 215–17, 248, 258–59, 347
Franzinelli, Benjamin, 197–98, 255–57
Frei Brothers Ranch and Winery, 297, 384
French Colombard grapes, 146, 222, 243, 245, 300, 319, 390
Fresno Bank of America, 113
Fresno Bee, 112, 344
Fresno State College, 250, 281
Frieburg, John, 168–70, 172, 177
"Friend Decision," 341, 342, 373, 392
Fruit Industries, 84, 94
Fruitvale Ranch, 99
Fusco, Joseph, 94, 211–12, 214, 239

Gabiatti family, 286, 287
Gallo, Adelaide (Mario's wife), 87
Gallo, Aileen Lowe (Julio's wife), 132, 134, 163, 175, 203, 228, 233, 286, 296, 340, 359, 371
  in car accident, 383–84
  children of, 137, 194
  and deaths of Joe, Sr., and Susie, 105–7, 111, 114, 115
  grandchildren of, 249
  at holiday celebrations, 195
  marries Julio, 101–4
  Mary Ann and, 160–62, 222, 320
  political contributions by, 283
  and son's suicide, 206–9
  and Uncle Mike, 123, 196
Gallo, Amelia Franzia (Ernest's wife), 89–90, 98, 99, 101, 102, 132, 134, 135, 138, 278, 371
  children of, 148, 192–93
  and deaths of Joe, Sr., and Susie, 115
  grandchildren of, 250
  at holiday celebrations, 195

Gallo, Amelia Franzia
  (Ernest's wife) (cont.)
  and launching of cheese company, 295–
    296
  marries Ernest, 96–97
  Mary Ann and, 161, 320
  political contributions by, 283
  on rafting trip, 228
  shopping sprees of, 248–49
  sixtieth wedding anniversary of, 391
  wealth of, 202–3
Gallo, Celia Bianco (aunt; Uncle Mike's
  wife), 25, 27–29, 33–35, 42, 48, 54, 73,
  75, 85–88, 92, 105, 117, 124, 196, 233
Gallo, Charles (no relation), 171–74, 285,
  289, 321, 349
Gallo, Christopher (David's son), 250
Gallo, "Crazy" Joey (no relation), 250
Gallo, David Ernest (Ernest's son), 148,
  192–96, 201, 203–6, 216–19, 228, 231,
  248–50, 254, 256–61, 278, 296, 320,
  366, 371
Gallo, Edward (cousin), 33
Gallo, Ernest, 17–19, 52, 54, 56, 74, 75, 77
  adolescence of, 51, 53–55, 58–60, 63, 66–
    72
  and Alcohol Tax Unit problems, 137,
    139–44
  birth of, 29
  charity work of, 281, 299
  childhood of, 31, 32, 36–42, 44–48
  Charles Gallo sued by, 171–74
  conflicts between father and, 88–93, 98–
    100
  conflicts between Julio and, 161–64, 192,
    220–21
  Cribari Winery acquired by, 187
  development and promotion of Gallo
    label by, 145–46, 155
  and dissolution of partnership, 174–76
  and distributorship, 145–48
  domination of Joe by, 230–35, 251
  estate taxes and, 281–85
  family background of, 19
  Federal Bureau of Investigation and, 94
  Federal Trade Commission and, 276–79,
    299
  Gallo Salame Company sued by, 285–
    291
  and Glass Company, 199
  and grape growers, 244–47
  as guardian of Joe, 131–34, 149–54
  headquarters built by, 225–28
  Hispanics and, 249
  and Joe's divorce, 223–24
  and Joe's livestock business, 222
  Joe's relationship with, 138–39
  and "juice" business, 95–97

and launching of cheese company, 295,
  296, 300
and Livingston vineyards, 164–65
marriage of, 89–90, 96–97
marriages of sons of, 249–50
organizational strategy of, 170–71
and parents' deaths, 111–18
personnel recruitment by, 251–54
on rafting trip, 228–30
sales and marketing practices of, 167–71,
  177–81, 183–85, 188–92, 199–200, 209–
  216, 238–44, 247–48, 297–98
and shipping business, 58–60, 6?, 66–70,
  81
sons and, 148, 192–93, 195–96, 204–7,
  216–20, 256–61
Time magazine cover story on, 247
and trademark infringement lawsuit
  against Joe, 13–16, 19–20, 173–74,
  300–341, 344, 345, 347–50, 353–69,
  371, 374, 376, 377, 382–87, 389–96
and Uncle Mike, 196–98, 254–57
and underground tanks, 82–85
United Farm Workers boycott of, 262–
  276, 280, 281
wealth of, 198, 201–4
and Wine Institute, 200–201
winemaking methods of, 166–67
winery started by, 102–3, 105, 118–31,
  134–37
during World War II, 156–61, 165
Gallo, Ernesto (Joey's son), 250
Gallo, Gloria (cousin), 42, 87, 88, 196
Gallo, Joseph, Sr. (Giuseppe; father), 19,
  74, 88, 138, 155, 160, 171, 186, 196,
  254, 320, 329
Antioch ranch of, 39–42
arrival in California of, 24–25
birth of children of, 29, 32, 41
death of, 105–8, 111–18, 148, 207, 255,
  321, 333
Escalon vineyard of, 49–54
estate of, 119–23, 125–31, 149, 154, 175,
  321, 322, 324–26, 328, 330–31, 347,
  348, 392
Federal Bureau of Investigation and, 94
financial problems of, 103–5
immigration of, 23–24
inlaws and, 29–31, 36–37
and "juice" business, 95–96
marriage of, 27–29
separations from Susie, 31–33
shipping business of, 55–70, 81, 82, 339
sons' conflict with, 88–93, 98–100
strictness as father, 54–55, 71–72, 76–77
underground tanks of, 82–86
winery founded by, 25
and Woodbridge Winery, 75–77, 81

Gallo, Joseph, Jr. (Joe; called Pete as a child), 17–19, 56
  adolescence of, 96, 99, 100, 131–34
  and Alcohol Tax Unit problems, 141–144
  in army, 157–62
  birth of, 41
  brothers' domination of, 230–35, 251
  childhood of, 41, 47, 48, 53–55, 71–72, 76, 77, 81–83, 88, 92–93
  children of, 195–96
  and dissolution of partnership, 174–76
  divorce of, 223–25
  family background of, 19
  first marriage of, 160–61
  and Gallo Salame Company suit, 288
  and Glass Company, 199
  goes to work for winery, 138–39
  guardianship estate of, 149–54
  launching of cheese business by, 295–97, 300
  livestock business of, 221–22, 225, 236, 250
  at Livingston vineyards, 162–65, 170–71, 245
  and parents' deaths, 105–7, 111, 113–15, 117–18
  relationship of Julio and, 148
  second marriage of, 228–31
  and son's death, 237
  and start-up of winery, 120, 121, 126, 127, 129–30, 136
  trademark infringement lawsuit against, 13–16, 19–20, 173–74, 300–344, 347–386, 389–96
  and United Farm Workers boycott, 266, 274
  wealth of, 204
Gallo, Joseph Ernest (Joey; Ernest's son), 148, 192–93, 196, 201, 206, 216–20, 248–50, 258–61, 272, 278–79, 319, 320, 361, 366, 371
Gallo, Joseph Ernest, Jr. (Joey's son), 250, 319, 361
Gallo, Julie (Bob's daughter), 345, 350
Gallo, Julio, 17–19, 56, 74, 75, 228
  adolescence of, 51, 53–55, 58–60, 63, 69–72, 76–77
  and Alcohol Tax Unit problems, 142, 144
  birth of, 32
  charity work of, 281
  childhood of, 32, 36–47
  children of, 134, 137, 193–95, 205–9, 218
  conflicts between Ernest and, 161–64, 192, 220–21
  conflicts between father and, 88–93, 98–100
  Cribari Winery acquired by, 187

development of new wines by, 179, 185, 188, 242, 243, 297–98
  and dissolution of partnership, 175, 176
  and distributorship, 146
  domination of Joe by, 231–35, 251
  estate taxes and, 281–84
  family background of, 19
  and Gallo Salame Company suit, 285–90
  and Glass Company, 199
  and grape growers, 244–47
  as guardian of Joe, 131–34, 150, 151, 154
  and headquarters building, 225, 227
  Hispanics and, 249
  hospitalization of, 148–49, 154, 156
  and Joe's livestock business, 222
  and "juice" business, 96
  and launching of cheese company, 295, 296
  and Livingston vineyards, 164–65
  management of winery by, 147–48
  and marketing practices, 168–70
  marriage of, 101–4
  and parents' deaths, 105–7, 111, 114–18, 148
  and promotion of Gallo brand, 155
  and shipping business, 58–60, 63, 69–70, 81
  and start-up of winery, 120–31, 134–38
  Time magazine cover story on, 247
  and trademark infringement lawsuit against Joe, 13–16, 19–20, 302–5, 307, 309–13, 315–17, 319–27, 329, 330, 332–341, 344, 345, 347–50, 353, 355–57, 359, 361, 364–66, 368, 369, 382–84, 386–87, 389–96
  and Uncle Mike, 196–98, 254–56
  and underground tanks, 83, 85
  United Farm Workers boycott of, 264–268, 272, 274, 280
  wealth of, 198, 201, 203–4
  winemaking methods of, 166–67
  during World War II, 157–61, 165
Gallo, Linda (Joe's daughter), *see* Jelacich, Linda Gallo
Gallo, Maria (cousin), 33, 42, 86, 87, 97, 197
Gallo, Marie Therese Damrell (Bob's wife), 194, 203, 249, 284, 320, 345
Gallo, Mark (Bob's son), 284
Gallo, Mary (Charles's wife), 172–74, 285, 289, 320, 321, 349, 357
Gallo, Mary Ann Arata (Joe's first wife), 160–62, 164, 195, 220, 222–25, 233, 234, 320
Gallo, Mary Costa (David's wife), 249–50
Gallo, Matt (Bob's son), 384
Gallo, Micah (Mike's son), 371, 396

Gallo, Mike (Joe's son), 19, 117–18, 195–196, 217, 223–25, 231, 233, 235, 237, 249–51, 266, 295, 296, 388
and trademark infringement lawsuit, 16, 301–5, 307, 310–13, 316, 318, 319, 324, 332, 340, 341, 351, 358, 361, 364–66, 369, 371, 374, 377, 378, 381, 383, 389–391, 395, 396
Gallo, Mike (Michelo; uncle), 24–25, 27–29, 31, 55–57, 76, 83, 95–96, 104–5, 116, 122–23, 196–98, 254–55
as bootlegger, 41, 44–46, 48, 53–54, 97–98
bunko schemes of, 33–36
children of, 33
death of, 255–57
divorce of, 85–88
immigration of, 23–24
and Woodbridge Winery, 72–75, 77–82
Gallo, Ofelia Carrasquilla (Joey's wife), 249, 250
Gallo, Patricia (Joe's second wife), 133, 228–31, 235, 250, 295, 296, 333, 371, 382, 390, 395, 396
Gallo, Peter (Joe's son), 195–96, 223–25, 228, 233, 236–37, 245, 250
Gallo, Phillip (Julio's son), 194–95, 205–9, 220
Gallo, Robert Julio (Julio's son), 134, 193–195, 203, 209, 249, 284, 297, 319, 320, 334–37, 345, 365, 366, 371, 383, 384
Gallo, Rocco (Charles's son), 172, 173
Gallo, Sherrie Spendlove (Mike's wife), 251, 366, 382, 383, 385, 396
Gallo, Stefanie Amelia (Joey's daughter), 250
Gallo, Susann Aileen (Julio's daughter), see Coleman, Susann Aileen Gallo
Gallo, Susie Bianco (Asunta; mother), 25, 42, 46, 49, 53, 54, 88, 90–93, 99, 100, 133, 196, 326
Aileen and, 103–4
Amelia and, 96
beaten by Joe, 28–29, 31, 32
births of children of, 29, 32, 41
death of, 106–8, 111–18, 123, 148, 207, 255, 321, 333
estate of, 118, 154, 322, 324, 330–31
marriage of, 27–28
separations from Joe, 31–33
and underground tanks, 82, 85
Gallo, Theresa (David's daughter), 250
Gallo, Vivian (Uncle Mike's wife), 197
Gallo Bay Sales, 183
Gallo Bros. Ranches, 152, 153, 156, 158, 159, 174–76, 327, 328
Gallo Cattle Company, 221, 377

Gallo Glass Company, 175, 199, 229, 231–233, 302, 319, 345, 384
Gallo Salame Company, 236, 285–91, 301–304, 306–10, 313–15, 317, 320, 321, 334, 337, 349, 352–56, 373, 375, 376, 379, 393–95
Gallo Tank Lines Company, 156, 159
Gallo Wine amendment, 281–84
Gallo Wine Company of Louisiana, 146
Garatti brothers, 43
Gardali, Kay, 382
Gardali, Sam, 229
Gardali, Sam, Jr., 228, 229, 250, 382
Genna, Sam, 64
Genna gang, 64, 65, 67
Genolio, Pietro, 30–31
George Washington University, 177
Giovannoni, Samuele, 53, 54
Giovannoni, Vincente, 53, 54
Glass Containers, 198
Goetsch, Gene, 295
Golden Wine Cooler, 298
Gold Seal distributorship, 212
Gourmet Trio, 244, 275
Great Valley Wine, 146
Greenaway, Roy, 345
Grenache Rosé, 186, 214, 243
Guild Winery, 145, 167, 177–80, 185, 192, 209
Gypsy Rose, 199, 215

Hai Tori, 200
Haight, Brown & Bonesteel, 385
Hall Ranch, 133, 160
Hammer, Armand, 177–78
Handford Weekly Sentinel, 28
Haslett Warehouse Company, 142, 143
Hawkins, B. C., 150, 153
Hearty Burgundy, 18, 242–43
Limited Release, 387
Heller, Ehrman, White & McAuliffe, 287
Henderson, William D., 287
Herd, Charles, 139–41, 143
Herzig, Al, 308, 309, 320, 341–43, 354, 355, 374–75, 377, 378, 379, 381, 382, 385, 394–95
Herzig, Thelma, 308, 320, 378, 381, 382, 385
Heublein Distillery, 299
Heuer, Bill, 234
Hiram Walker Distillery, 166
Hispanics, 249
Holmboe, Larry, 367–70, 376
Hoover, Herbert, 84, 102
Hoover, J. Edgar, 94, 177, 180
Hopis, 200
House of Representatives, U.S., 389
Ways and Means Committee, 282

Howard, Donald, 354
Howard, Rice, Nemerovski, Canady, Robertson & Falk, 332–34, 338, 339, 341, 342, 343, 350–52, 358, 362, 374– 375, 378–81
Huntington, Robert, 215, 240, 241

Illinois State Liquor Control Commission, 212
Inglenook Winery, 247
Internal Revenue Service (IRS), 284, 285
Italian Swiss Colony, 70, 127, 135, 145, 167, 177, 179, 185, 200, 209, 211, 215, 241, 244, 384
  Silver Satin, 188, 191
  Vin Rosé, 185–87

J. W. Dant whiskey, 177
Jackson, Jess, 332, 333
Jalisco Cheese Company, 318
Jelacich, Ann Marie, 381
Jelacich, Kenny, 250, 319, 361, 369, 381, 382
Jelacich, Linda Gallo, 195, 222–25, 228, 233, 250, 313, 320, 345, 351, 365, 377, 381, 382, 385
Jenkins, Jack, 125
Johnson, Justine, 344
Joseph Farms Cheese, 381–82
Joseph Gallo Cattle Company, 18
Joseph Gallo Cheese Company, 15, 19, 295–97, 300, 308–9, 317, 359, 361, 362, 367, 370–73, 376
Joseph Gallo Cottonwood Dairy, 18, 19, 221
Joseph Gallo Farms, 377
Joseph Gallo Feed Lot, 221
Joseph Gallo Vineyards, 18, 221, 236
Justice Department, U.S., 84, 94, 97, 98, 196

Kane, Max, 104, 107, 108, 112, 113, 115, 125, 139–43, 157
Kaplan, Elliot S., 276, 287
Kauk family, 383–84
Kearny auction yards, 69
Keating, Charles, Jr., 283
Kefauver, Estes, 212
Kellogg, Ann Franzia, 170
Kellogg, Charles, 170
Kendall-Jackson, 332
Kennedy, John F., 362
Kennedy, Joseph P., Sr., 228
Kent, Don, 214
Klor, Sam, 225
Knowles, Legh, 240
Kraft Foods, 361

Lancers, 243
Lang, Jennings, 344
Las Palmas Winery, 187
Life magazine, 169, 228
Lincoln Savings & Loan, 283
Livermore Herald, 45
Local Rule 123, 343, 352, 394
Louis Martini Winery, 78, 80
Lowe, Aileen, see Gallo, Aileen
Lowe, Anna, 101
Lowe, Nilus, 101, 134
Lynch, Patrick, 317–18, 332, 334, 342, 343, 349, 351, 358–62, 364, 365, 367, 369– 372, 374, 379–82, 385–86

McCarthy, Joseph, 177
McClatchy News Service, 337–38
McCormick, Barstow, Sheppard, Coyle & Wayte, 287
McCormick, Barstow, Sheppard, Wayte & Curruth, 317, 344, 346, 352–54, 360, 379, 380, 393
McCullough, Ouida, 255
McGowan, Bert, 257
McHenry, Pat, 298
McHenry Mansion (Modesto), 281
MacKay, William, 171, 174
McKee, William, 287, 297
McLaughlin, "Skip," 244
Madria, 252
Madria Sangria, 252
Madrigal, Frank, 107, 112, 113
Malaga, 146
Manischewitz Wine Company, 242
Martini and Rossi, 244
Massachusetts Consumer Protection Act, 346
Matkovich, Jacob "Jake," 63–67
Matkovich, Guy, 64, 67
Mattel Toy Company, 308
Maze, Claude, 56
Memorial Hospital North (Modesto), 281
Merced Junior College, 237
Merit Liquor Company, 212
Merlot, 384
Merrigan, Paul, 247–48, 251–60, 267–71, 277, 279
Midcal Aluminum, 218, 276
Milani Winery, 74
Mitchell, Edward A., 45
Modesto Bee, 111, 114, 265, 343, 345, 350, 388
Modesto Chamber of Commerce, 160
Modesto Cooperative Winery, 187
Modesto High School, 58, 67–68, 192, 194, 281
Modesto Italian-American Club, 57

Modesto Junior College, 71, 138
Modesto Planning Commission, 152
Mogen David Wine Company, 209, 211, 242
  Little Brown Jug, 252
Mondavi, Cesare, 62, 63, 66, 70, 74, 121, 209
Mondavi, Helen, 62
Mondavi, Mary, 62
Mondavi, Peter, 62, 63
Mondavi, Robert, 62, 63, 83, 121, 201
Mondavi, Rosa, 62
Mondavi Winery, 95
Mooney, John, 33–34
Moore, Wallace, 113
Morand Brothers Beverage Company, 210
Mountain Red wines, 216, 244
Muscatel, 94, 243

Napa Valley Cooperative, 187
National Guard, 217
National Labor Relations Board, 347
Native Americans, 200
Navahos, 200
Navy, U.S., 194
NBC, 269
Needham, Harper & Steers, Inc., 297
Nevins, David, 274
New York Times Company, 337–38
Night Train Express, 18, 252, 299, 305, 358, 387
Nixon, Richard M., 264
Norman B. Craig Agency, 269
Notre Dame University, 204–5, 216, 281
Nuzzo, Mario, 210

Oakland Tribune, 98
Ogilvy & Mather, 297
Old Fishermen's Club, 57
O'Melveny & Myers, 317, 332, 339, 341, 360, 364, 366, 385
Oregon State University, 193–94
Orrick, Herrington & Sutcliffe, 287
Osteraas, Paul, 164, 234
Owen, Jack, 287, 291, 304–8, 310, 318, 360, 365, 371
Owen, Wickersham & Erickson, 287
Ozella, Pete, 80

Pacific Agriculture, 354
Pacific Wine Company, 63, 128, 209
Paisano wine, see Vino Paisano di Gallo
Palombo, Arthur (Art), 212, 216, 239, 240
Panteleo, 62
Pappas, John, 286
Pappas Company, 299, 345–46, 353, 395
Paterno, Tony, 63, 66, 128, 209
Pattishall, Beverly, 287, 291

Pattishall, McAuliffe & Hofstetter, 287
Paul, Herbert, 207
Paul Masson Winery, 247, 395
Pearl Harbor, 156
People magazine, 388
Petite Bouschet, 51
Petite Sirah, 243, 245
Petri, Angelo, 51–52
Petri, Louis, 52, 186
Petri Winery, 145, 167, 241
Pink Chablis, 18, 243–44
Port, 94
Portuguese-Americans, 250
Premier Wine and Spirits, 299, 346
Price, Edward Dean, 334, 337, 338, 342, 356, 357, 377, 379, 382, 383, 389, 392, 394
Price, Martin and Crabtree, 344
Procter & Gamble, 183, 242
Prohibition, 17, 38–102, 119, 120, 122, 125, 127–29, 173, 197, 201, 212, 228, 254, 289, 322, 328, 329, 348, 385
Proposition 134, 388
Publiker, 177

Q-V Liquors, 189

Raboli Brothers, 43
Reinhardt, Stephen, 385
Republican party, 388
Rhine, 145
Rhine Garten, 214
Rhodes, Leonard, 121–24
Riboni family, 74
Rice, Denis, 332–34, 342–54, 349, 350, 352, 354–63, 368–70, 372–75, 378–80, 389
Richards Wild Irish Rose, 188, 199
Riesling, 94
Riney, Hal, 297, 298, 391
Riorda, Jack, 70
Ripple, 18, 214, 241, 242, 244, 271, 298
Robins, Davis & Lyons, 276
Robins, Zelle, Larson & Kaplan, 287
Robinson, C. Ray, 224
Robson, John, 388
Romano, Donald J. (Buddy), 210, 213–14, 219, 239, 240
Romano, Michael J., Sr., 210–11, 213
Romano, Michael J., Jr., 210, 213, 219, 239, 240
Romano, Tony, 94
Roma Winery, 52, 145
Romero, Cesar, 191
Roos-Atkins, 96
Roosevelt, Franklin Delano, 102, 177
Rosentiel, Lewis, 178
Ross, Fred, 272

Rossi, Charlie, 95, 128, 217, 244, 254, 256
Rossi, Pietro Carlo, 244
Rotary Club, 160, 161, 203–4, 345
Ruocco, Vincent, 384
Rutman Distributing Company, 299

Safeway Supermarkets, 170
St. Stanislaus Catholic Church, 57
St. Stanislaus Cemetery, 207
Sanford and Son (TV show), 244
San Francisco Bulletin, 45
San Francisco Chronicle, 80, 87, 98, 113, 285, 358
San Francisco Examiner Golden Turkey Awards, 387
San Francisco International Exposition (1915), 38
San Joaquin County Fair, 51
San Luis Obispo State College, 245
San Pablo Bottle, Malt, and Supply Company, 41, 73, 86–87, 97
San Quentin Prison, 34, 35, 41
Santa Fe Grape Distributors, 60, 62
Santa Rosa Press-Democrat, 338
Sara Lee, 285
Sauterne, 94, 145
Sauvignon Blanc, 245, 384
Scheer, Arnold, 245
Schenley Industries, 178, 212, 214, 239
Schraiberg, Manny, 94
Sciaroni, Louis, 52
Sciaroni, Joe, 54–55, 125
Scott, John, 140, 141
Seagram Distillery, 166, 298, 299
Sebastiani, August, 74
Sebastiani, Don, 75
Sebastiani, Lorenzo, 74, 78, 81
Sebastiani, Samuele, 74–75, 78, 80, 81, 85, 87
Sebastiani, Sylvia, 75
Sebastiani Winery, 74, 82, 201
Selecky, John, 243
Senate, U.S., 212, 282, 388
Severino, John, 73, 75, 78–80, 82
Seymour, John, 388
Shanken, Marvin, 386
Shannon Funeral Chapel, 122
Shastid, Jon, 221, 229, 282, 296–97, 316, 327, 328, 330, 336
Silva, Joe, 79, 80
Sioux, 200
60 Minutes (TV show), 268
Solomon, Dan, 269, 349, 362, 383
Sorensen, Ted, 362
Sorensen, Robert C., 362, 373
Spanada, 18
Sparer, Alan, 350, 351, 361, 367–69, 375, 379

Spendlove, Sherrie, *see* Gallo, Sherrie Spendlove
Sportsmen of Stanislaus, 345
Stanford University Business School, 167, 215–17, 281
Hospital, 284
Law School, 224
Medical School, 281
Stanislaus State College, 250
Stock market crash, 82
Stockton Vineyards, 52
Strauss, Robert, 282
Supreme Court, U.S., 341, 395
Sweeney, Neil, 193, 240–41, 262, 264

Tang, Thomas, 385
Tartar, Incorporated, 157
Taub, Marty, 191
Taylor, Edward, Sr., 93, 118, 122, 123, 126, 131, 146, 148–54, 157, 175, 324, 327, 328, 345, 348
Taylor California Winery, 247, 395
Teamsters Union, 262–71, 273, 274
Tegnor Ranch, 158, 160, 326
Tet offensive, 236
Thayer, Patty Johnston, 358
Thomas, Snell, Jamison, Russell, Williamson & Asperger, 287
Thompson, Bud, 53
Thompson, J. H., 73
Thompson seedless grapes, 39, 104, 146, 147, 158, 214, 245
Thornton, Lloyd, 240
Thunderbird, 18, 189–92, 198–201, 211, 214, 226, 241, 244, 247, 271, 288, 299, 305, 356–58, 387, 388
Tickled Pink, 200
Tokay, 94, 145, 245
Tonight show, 359
Tott's, 18
Transamerica Corporation, 81, 82, 149
Treasury Department, U.S., 282
Triolo, P., 53, 54
Triple Jack, 215
Tupin, Joe, 337, 338
Turano, 62
Twister, 199, 271
Tyrolia, 271

United Distilleries of America, 177
United Farm Workers (UFW), 262–69, 271–74, 276, 280, 284
U.S. Patent Office, 155, 172, 174, 320
United Vintners, 186, 241, 297
Ursini, 62

Valley Agricultural Company, 158–59
Valley Vintners, 218, 252, 276

Vangelis, 298
Vander Wall, Davis Grant, 345
Van Merit Beer, 212
Vietnam War, 200, 236–37
Vine Glo, 94
Vino di Tavola, 178, 179
Vino Paisano di Gallo, 96, 179, 214, 242,
    254, 271
Vin Rosé, 186–87, 214, 241
Vintners International, 395
Virginia Dare wines, 94, 178
Volstead Act, 45, 84

Wacey, Irwin, 215
Waggoner, Joe D., 282
Wagner, Albert, 44, 125, 138
Wagner, Rudy, 44, 90, 136, 138–40, 143,
    147–48, 156, 157
Wallace, Mike, 268
Walsh, John, 119
Wanger, Oliver, 287, 288, 291, 317, 318,
    342–44, 346, 351–57, 359, 361, 364,
    367, 370, 380, 388–89, 394, 395
Wanger, Walter, 344
Warner Lambert, 251
War Production Board, 177
Warren, Earl, 98
Watergate scandal, 264
Watt, Sam, 146, 168
Watt, Mrs. Sam, 146
Weatherup, Roy, 385
Weiner, Bernie, 260, 261, 278
Wente Brothers, 43
West magazine, 201
Western Union, 86
Wetlands Commission, 227

White Crane Ranch, 236
White Port, 146, 168
Whiting, Carol, 381
Whiting, John, 138, 224, 230, 237, 266–67,
    296, 301, 303–14, 316–18, 320–33, 335–
    336, 341–43, 351–52, 354, 355, 360,
    362, 370, 374, 375, 377, 378, 380–82
Wiley Local Option Law (1911), 37
Williams, Howard, 178, 179, 185, 189, 191,
    211, 214
Williams, J. M., 122
Willis, Bruce, 298
Wilson, Pete, 389
Wine Institute, 200–201, 242
Wine Spectator, The, 333, 387, 388,
    390
Winery, Distillery & Allied Workers Union,
    347
Witter, Bonnie, 278
Witter, Richard (Dick), 215–16, 243,
    251, 252, 253, 260, 262, 275, 277–79,
    298
Woodbridge Winery, 72–73, 75, 77–82, 85,
    87
Woods, William, 119
World War II, 155–61, 340, 344
Wright, H. B., 122
Writers' Project, 205
Wycliff, William, 18

Yanny, Joe, 379–81, 393
Young & Rubicam, 297

Zavell, Frank, 279
Zinfandel, 40, 51, 60, 62, 68, 89, 242, 243,
    245

PHOTO CREDITS

The State of California: 4; Eddie Adams/Sygma: 8; Linda Gallo Jelacich: 9, 20, 26, 33; The
Modesto Bee: 10; Fred Mertz: 16, 18; Forrest Jackson/The Modesto Bee: 17; Tom Van Dyke/
The San Jose Mercury-News: 19; Mike Gallo: 29; James D. Wilson/Woodfin Camp: 30;
Nancy Whiting Bramell: 34; Meryl Schenker: 35; Daily Journal Corporation: 36; The Fresno
Bee: 37, 38, 39